THE PURCHASING HANDBOOK

A Guide for the Purchasing and Supply Professional

SIXTH EDITION

JOSEPH L. CAVINATO, Ph.D., C.P.M.

RALPH G. KAUFFMAN, Ph.D., C.P.M.

EDITORS IN CHIEF

Sponsored by the National Association of Purchasing Management

Contact NAPM at P.O. Box 22160, Tempe, Arizona 85285-2160
800/888-6276, fax: 480/752-7890, Web site: www.napm.org

Library of Congress Cataloging-in-Publication Data

The purchasing handbook : a guide for the purchasing and supply
  professional / editors in chief, Joseph L. Cavinato and Ralph G.
  Kauffman.—6th ed.
      p. cm.
    "Sponsored by the National Association of Purchasing Management."
    ISBN 0-07-134526-4
    1. Industrial procurement. 2. Purchasing departments—Management.
  I. Cavinato, Joseph L. II. Kauffman, Ralph G. III. National
  Association of Purchasing Management.
  HD39.5.P873 1999
  658.7'2—dc21   99-28707
                                                                      CIP

McGraw-Hill

*A Division of The **McGraw·Hill** Companies*

1 2 3 4 5 6 7 8 9 0   DOC/DOC   9 0 9 8 7 6 5 4 3 2 1 0 9

ISBN 0-07-134526-4

*The sponsoring editor for this book was Catherine Schwent and the production supervisor was
Tina Cameron. It was set in Palatino by Pro-Image Corporation.*

Printed and bound by R.R. Donnelley & Sons Company.

This publication is designed to provide accurate and authoritative information in regard
to the subject matter covered. It is sold with the understanding that neither the author or
the publisher is engaged in rendering legal, accounting, or other professional service. If
legal advice or other expert assistance is required, the services of a competent
professional person should be sought.

> *—From a Declaration of Principles jointly adopted by a Committee of the American Bar
> Association and a Committee of Publishers.*

McGraw-Hill books are available at special quantity discounts to use as premiums and
sales promotions, or for use in corporate training programs. For more information, please
write to the Director of Special Sales, McGraw-Hill, 11 West 19th Street, New York, NY
10011. Or contact your local bookstore.

 This book is printed on recycled, acid-free paper containing a
minimum of 50% recycled de-inked fiber.

CONTENTS

CONTRIBUTORS

Mir F. Ali, MBA, Ph.D. Managing Director, AIM/AMC Corporation, Las Vegas, Nevada (CHAP. 23)

Richard Antus, CMIR Manager, Investment Recovery, GTE Supply, Irving, Texas (CHAP. 28)

William Atkinson Freelance Writer, Carterville, Illinois (CHAP. 3)

Jack Barry President, E-time, Inc., Fairfield, Connecticut (CHAPS. 10 and 33)

William Boan, CMIR Clinton, Missouri (CHAP. 28)

Ron Brooks, CMIR Central Zone Manager, Weyerhaeuser Company, Hot Springs, Arkansas (CHAP. 28)

Martin J. Carrara, J.D., C.P.M. Attorney, Staten Island, New York (CHAP. 27)

Joseph R. Carter, D.B.A., C.P.M. NAPM Professor and Chair of the Supply Chain Management Department, Arizona State University, Tempe, Arizona (CHAP. 4)

Lawrence J. Clark, C.P.M. Purchasing Manager, Burleigh Instruments, Fishers, New York (CHAP. 24)

Gary Colgrove Manager of Resource Recovery, 3M Company, St. Paul, Minnesota (CHAP. 28)

Thomas A. Crimi Supply Chain Team Coordinator, Texaco, Inc., Houston, Texas (CHAP. 40)

Richard Cuniberti, C.P.M., CMIR Supply Manager, Resource Recovery and Ecology Services, BASF Corporation, Mount Olive, New Jersey (CHAP. 28)

Constance Cushman, J.D., C.P.M. Attorney, New York, New York (CHAP. 27)

Ed Dauginas Director of Purchasing, Raw Materials, Unilever Home and Personal Care USA, Trumbull, Connecticut (CHAP. 9)

Thomas M. De Paoli, Ph.D., C.P.M., SPHR   Principal, Apollo Solutions Consulting, Apollo Solutions, Sheboygan, Wisconsin (CHAP. 14)

Lisa M. Ellram, Ph.D., C.P.M., A.P.P., CPA, C.M.A.   Associate Professor of Supply Chain Management, College of Business, Arizona State University, Tempe, Arizona (CHAP. 20)

M. Theodore Farris II, Ph.D., C.T.L.   Faculty, University of North Texas, Denton, Texas (CHAP. 38)

Donavon J. Favre   Associate Partner, Global Supply Chain Management Practice, Andersen Consulting, Cleveland, Ohio (CHAP. 1)

Henry F. Garcia, C.P.M.   Director of Administration, Center for Nuclear Waste Regulatory Analyses, San Antonio, Texas (CHAPS. 29 and 36)

Larry C. Giunipero, Ph.D., C.P.M.   NAPM Professor of Purchasing and Supply Management, Florida State University, Tallahassee, Florida (CHAP. 11)

Frank Haluch, C.P.M.   President, Haluch & Associates Ltd., Trumbull, Connecticut (CHAPS. 19 and 32)

Mary Lu Harding, C.P.M., CPIM, CIRM   Consultant, Harding & Associates, Bristol, Vermont (CHAP. 31)

Michael Harding, C.P.M., CPIM   Consultant, Harding & Associates, Bristol, Vermont (CHAP. 31)

Carolyn Jackson, CMIR   ARCO Western Energy Company, Taft, California (CHAP. 28)

Steve Kesinger, C.P.M., A.P.P.   President, The Kesinger Group, Katy, Texas (CHAP. 6)

Dennis Knutz, CMIR, ASA   Director, Investment Recovery, Weyerhaeuser Company, Tacoma, Washington (CHAP. 28)

Roland Kotcamp, C.P.M., CMIR   Director, Niagara Mohawk Power Corporation, Liverpool, New York (CHAP. 28)

Brian G. Long, Ph.D., C.P.M.   President, Marketing and Management Institute, Inc., Kalamazoo, Michigan (CHAP. 21)

Arnold J. Lovering, J.D., C.P.M.   Director, Supply Chain Management, Raytheon Company, Lexington, Massachusetts (CHAP. 17)

Jane Male, CAE   Executive Director, The Investment Recovery Association, Mission, Kansas (CHAP. 28)

Leslie S. Marell   Attorney at Law, Law Offices of Leslie S. Marell, Hermosa Beach, California (CHAP. 34)

William J. Markham   Principal, Global Strategic Sourcing Practice, A.T. Kearney, Inc., Chicago, Illinois (CHAP. 2)

Deverl Maserang   Corporate Director, Routing and Logistics, Pepsi Bottling Group, Somers, New York (CHAP. 38)

Paul A. Matthews   Managing Partner, Global Supply Chain Management Practice, Andersen Consulting, Wellesley, Massachusetts (CHAP. 1)

Mark S. Miller, C.P.M., CIRM   Manager, Materials Control, Case Corporation, Racine, Wisconsin (CHAP. 26)

José T. Morales   Vice President, A.T. Kearney, Inc., Chicago, Illinois (CHAP. 2)

Michael P. Niemira   Vice President and Senior Economist, Bank of Tokyo-Mitsubishi, Ltd. Research Department and Adjunct Professor of Economics, Stern School of Business, New York University, New York, New York (CHAP. 25)

Robert A. Novack, Ph.D.   Associate Professor of Business Logistics, The Pennsylvania State University, State College, Pennsylvania (CHAP. 7)

James T. Parker, C.P.M.   Director of Purchasing, University of Utah, Salt Lake City, Utah (CHAP. 18)

Terrance L. Pohlen, Ph.D.   Assistant Professor of Business Logistics, College of Business Administration, University of North Florida, Jacksonville, Florida (CHAP. 38)

Michael Rhodes, CMIR   Corporate Investment Recovery, Virginia Electric & Power Company, Richmond, Virginia (CHAP. 28)

Thomas H. Slaight   Vice President, A.T. Kearney, Inc., Chicago, Illinois (CHAP. 2)

Linda L. Stanley, Ph.D.   Associate Professor, School of Business, Our Lady of the Lake University, San Antonio, Texas (CHAP. 16)

James Tognazzini   Facility and Operations Manager, UPS Worldwide Logistics, Irving, Texas (CHAP. 38)

Richard J. Toole   Associate Partner, Global Supply Chain Management Practice, Andersen Consulting, Atlanta, Georgia (CHAP. 1)

Robert J. Trent, Ph.D.   Associate Professor of Management, Lehigh University, Bethlehem, Pennsylvania (CHAP. 8)

Virginia M. Tucker, Ph.D.   Associate Dean for Executive Education and Associate Professor of Business Administration, The Pennsylvania State University, State College, Pennsylvania (CHAP. 12)

Roland R. Tunez   Director–Supply Chain Management, Network Purchasing Team, BellSouth Telecommunications, Inc., Atlanta, Georgia (CHAP. 13)

Elaine N. Whittington, C.P.M., A.P.P., CPCM   Educator, G & E Enterprises, Sunland, California (CHAP. 22)

Alvin J. Williams, Ph.D.   Chair and Professor, Department of Management and Marketing, University of Southern Mississippi, Hattiesburg, Mississippi (CHAP. 30)

Donald L. Woods, J.D., C.P.M.   State and Local Government Consultant, Las Vegas, Nevada (CHAP. 41)

Bruce J. Wright   President, B. Wright & Associates and Total Systems, Inc., Midvale, Utah (CHAPS. 35 and 37)

Joseph A. Yacura   Senior Vice President, Worldwide Procurement, American Express, New York, New York (CHAP. 39)

Rene A. Yates, C.P.M.   Director of Materials, B.A. Ballou & Company, Inc., East Providence, Rhode Island (CHAP. 15)

William Yerkey   General Manager, Investment Recovery, Union Carbide Corporation, South Charleston, West Virginia (CHAP. 28)

Richard R. Young, Ph.D., C.P.M.   Assistant Professor of Business Administration, Academic Program Director for Purchasing Continuing Education, The Pennsylvania State University, State College, Pennsylvania (CHAP. 5)

PREFACE

The *Purchasing Handbook—A Guide for the Purchasing and Supply Professional* reflects the field at a milestone in its evolution and sets the tone for its contributions to organizations for the first five years of the next millennium. The book builds upon the tradition of the field as reflected by its long history from its first publication in the 1920s. But unlike previous editions, which captured the field's state of the art at a moment in time, this edition has a future orientation that assists the reader in preparing for newly demanded processes, skills, and systems. This edition contains contributions from field leaders that point to a new direction of "supply" that is in addition to the traditional buying role in the firm. This edition parallels the National Association of Purchasing Management's (NAPM) change and shift forward as it continues to identify how the world of purchasing and supply is changing and prepares its membership to attain the levels of contributions now demanded of it.

Many new topics and much new material are included in this edition. Purchasing as a strategic activity blended with that of the firm or organization is contained within Part 1. This is followed by chapters devoted to marketplace intelligence, purchasing as relationship management, electronic systems and e-business opportunities, outsourcing/insourcing, supply, and the need to market purchasing and supply within the firm.

Several chapters are updates of concepts that have been evolving during the 1990s. Re-engineering, outsourcing, total cost of ownership, and others are now accepted parts of the field. Each chapter on these evolving topics contributes new material for the benefit of readers in their careers and in their roles in their organizations.

The book also provides a solid base of updated material of the field's core concepts. These include, but are not limited to, such topics as MRO, contracting, forecasting, inventory management, legal aspects, and budgeting. Together, these build a showcase of the field's state of practice.

We would like to give hearty thanks to each of the authors for their contributions to this edition and the field; to their employers, countless co-workers, family members, and friends who no doubt served as readers, proofreaders, and sounding boards; and lastly, to those persons in the lives of the authors who no doubt endured weekends and evenings without the benefit of their company while they toiled to develop and write their chapters. Thank you, all.

Joseph L. Cavinato, Ph.D., C.P.M.
Ralph G. Kauffman, Ph.D., C.P.M.

ABOUT THE EDITORS IN CHIEF

JOSEPH L. CAVINATO, PH.D., C.P.M., in January 2000 joined the National Association of Purchasing Management (NAPM) as a NAPM Distinguished Professor of Supply Chain Management and Senior Vice President. Prior to joining NAPM, he was an Associate Professor of Business Logistics at The Pennsylvania State University, and a frequent consultant to organizations worldwide. Dr. Cavinato is co-editor of *Supply Chain Casebook–1999*, author of *Supply Chain Logistics Dictionary*, and co-author of *Supply Chain Enterprise Benchmarks* as well as numerous other books. He has published extensively in professional journals and presented papers internationally at academic and professional conferences.

RALPH G. KAUFFMAN, PH.D., C.P.M., is Assistant Professor of Management and Coordinator of the Purchasing and Supply Management Program at the University of Houston-Downtown. Prior to entering academia, he gained more than 27 years of purchasing and supply management experience with Oryx Energy Company as manager, procurement and materials management. Dr. Kauffman is chair of the National Association of Purchasing Management's (NAPM) Non-Manufacturing *NAPM Report on Business®* and the prior chair of the Manufacturing *NAPM Report on Business®*. He has published articles in management journals and presented papers at national and international academic and professional conferences.

PART ONE

The Strategic Contributions of Purchasing and Supply

Purchasing and supply affects the strategic capabilities of the organization in many ways. Where in the past many viewed it as a standalone function, it is now seen as a set of value-adding processes that link directly to the market and the organization's ability to innovate and deliver value in the marketplace.

The new presence of major consulting firms is one of the hallmarks of the growth and evolution of the field. This stems from senior managements who now recognize the importance of each expenditure and related impacts and opportunities of purchasing and supply upon their organizations. The major consulting firms have the scale and breadth of scope to develop insights on strategic and macro levels. The three chapters in this section set the stage for the field from the top of the organization.

Chapter 1 presents concepts and viewpoints on the evolution of the economy, firms and organizations generally, and how purchasing and supply fits in them specifically. Chapter 2 takes a closer look at how purchasing can be a contributor within the organization. Chapter 3 bridges the conceptual future to the practicing present. It is the overview of an extensive scan of the business environment and the senior levels of purchasing with a reporting of how the field is expected to change within the next five years.

CHAPTER 1

The Future of Purchasing and Supply

Editor
Paul A. Matthews
Managing Partner
Global Supply Chain Management Practice
Andersen Consulting

Associate Editors
Richard J. Toole
Associate Partner
Global Supply Chain Management Practice
Andersen Consulting

Donavon J. Favre
Associate Partner
Global Supply Chain Management Practice
Andersen Consulting

Trying to predict the future of procurement? Take a number.

Between eProcurement, global sourcing, electronic catalogs, strategic alliances, and supply chain integration, today's procurement professional, just to survive, had better be part Internet guru, part strategy consultant, and part world geography professor. But amid the buzzwords, the articles, and the "experts'" prognostications, one fact is clear: the procurement function continues to grow in importance and complexity. As world markets open to new sourcing networks and companies learn to link critical business functions across enterprises, the procurement process will become a primary element of any successful company's competitive strategy.

This chapter addresses several of the most important changes that practitioners struggle with, including developing a coherent procurement strategy, understanding and using new technology, structuring a procurement organization for maximum impact, and more tightly integrating suppliers. Relevant to each of these four topics, however, are the underlying trends causing these changes.

INDUSTRY TRENDS—HOW WILL THEY IMPACT PROCUREMENT?

While the possible combinations and permutations of procurement's future path are endless, four key trends appear most likely to fundamentally shape tomorrow's procurement practices: Globalization, Industry Consolidation, Technology Advancements, and Supply Chain Synchronization.

Globalization

Globalization is revolutionizing the scope of the procurement function. Initially, sourcing across borders was a defensive tactic to maintain competitiveness by reducing cost in response to foreign entrants who were penetrating domestic markets. However, forward-looking companies now recognize international supply management as a key driver of financial performance and overall competitiveness. Companies with global sourcing capabilities seek to reduce costs, improve quality and flexibility, and enter markets faster.

Political, social, economic, and technological factors have all contributed to the development of an open, global marketplace. Multinational firms are no longer riveted on local operations, but are synchronizing disparate divisions and geographies to create formidable leverage. Smaller companies that lack significant influence alone are joining ranks to form purchasing consortiums and buying clubs. The impact of globalization on the United States is evident in the rise in imports from $40 billion in 1970 to an astounding $1,048 billion in 1997.[1]

As companies turn from domestic to global sources of supply, procurement professionals must be cognizant of both the opportunities and the threats when constructing an international sourcing strategy. Companies that fail to pay attention to the risks associated with global sourcing will lose the anticipated benefits, while more astute organizations will execute procurement strategies that mitigate risk and enhance value. Just as an investor purchases a diversified portfolio of financial instruments, a global sourcing strategist can insulate a firm from adverse conditions by leveraging the global supply market.

Understanding world markets can be difficult, since each country is both unique and complex. In order to develop and manage the optimal

---

1. U.S. Census Bureau, on-line balance of trade statistics

portfolio, procurement professionals must understand the key drivers shaping the global purchasing industry: politics, infrastructure, currency, climate, and culture.

Politics

A country's government can have dire and dramatic influence on global sourcing. It controls the movement of goods through tariffs and trade agreements, and political unrest or imposed trade embargoes can cause sudden interruptions in supply. Ocean Spray Cranberries, a leading beverage manufacturer, realized the impact of political chaos when Bosnia erupted in civil war and OSC's main supply of raspberry concentrate dried up virtually overnight. As prices skyrocketed, OSC quickly sought out alternative sources in Latin and South America.

Procurement professionals should monitor the political climate to avoid disastrous situations. Enron's Dabhol Power Project in Maharashtra, India, is a well-documented example of a company that failed to consider the political environment before entering an emerging market. In the early 1990s, Enron attempted to enter the power market in India, an industry that was in the process of being privatized. When the government suddenly changed hands, the project was cancelled. Enron is still recovering from this mishap.[2]

Governments' regulating bodies also exert tremendous influence over offshore purchasing relationships. Labor laws, health and safety standards, and environmental compliance are just some of the factors to weigh in devising an international sourcing strategy. Not only can regulations have a tremendous impact on the cost of doing business, but failure to comply can have dire public relations and legal consequences. For instance, environmental legislation in Western Europe requires companies to manage waste generation and disposal throughout the entire product lifespan.

Infrastructure

Closely linked to a country's political system is its financial, physical, and technological infrastructure. The global economy is presently experiencing its worst crisis since World War II. The world's second-largest economy, Japan, is in financial turmoil, nearly crippled by a severe credit

---

2. "Enron Development Corp: The Dabhol Power Project in Maharashtra, India," *Harvard Business School Publications*, July 6, 1998.

crunch and recession. The Japanese banking system has lost almost all its true capital and cannot lend,[3] while emerging economies such as Russia, Malaysia, and South Korea are on the verge of dropping out of the global economy. These unstable financial systems increase the risk of offshore sourcing. As the economy becomes increasingly global, the linkages and interdependencies across countries will continue to rise.

Other aspects of a country's infrastructure also matter. From the quality of the road systems to access to ports, physical attributes will dictate the feasibility of tapping a particular source. Beyond the transportation system, another key infrastructure issue is the country's communications network. Quality of telephone systems, speed of modem connections, and access to both digital and analog lines should be evaluated. Additionally, the information technology capabilities of individual suppliers may be generations behind the information systems infrastructure that supports corporate headquarters, further complicating the ability to interface and communicate. While these shortcomings may not represent significant barriers, the increased cost, time, and complexity of working with inferior infrastructures must be assessed and managed accordingly.

Currency

Managing a global supply network exposes companies to fluctuations in foreign currency exchange rates. The futures market for foreign currencies enables companies to hedge themselves and mitigate exchange rate risk by locking in exchange rates. These fluctuations can also represent opportunities for companies that have flexible sourcing strategies. For example, multinational electronics and computer firms in Korea are renewing purchasing contracts with Korean manufacturers, primarily due to the steep depreciation of the Korean won. Also, the weak Canadian dollar in conjunction with NAFTA has spurred a tremendous increase in cross-border purchases. See Figure 1–1.

Perhaps one of the biggest changes in global procurement has been the creation of the common currency of most of the European Union, the Euro. Comprised of the currencies from many countries, prices are now leveling throughout the "Eurozone," now that they must be stated in the new Euro as well as the original currency. Buyers can now compare prices across several countries, and sellers find it difficult to maintain

---

3. "Easing the Crisis of the World Economy," *The News and Observer* (Raleigh, NC), September 20, 1998.

F I G U R E   1–1

Examples of Currency Fluctuations in the Late 90's

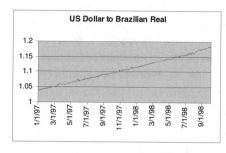

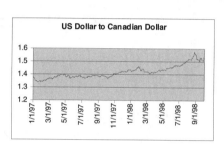

different margins for various country markets. In 2002 the local currencies within the Eurozone will disappear and be completely replaced by the Euro. At the time of this writing the U.K. has elected to remain outside the Euro, but this might change in a few years.

Climate

Agricultural products are exposed to the uncontrollable factors of weather and climate. To minimize the risk of depending solely on one geography, procurement managers purchasing agriculture products should adopt a strategy of selective global sourcing. For instance, several leading beverage manufacturers source apple concentrate from three continents to smooth supply disparities driven by uncontrollable events. This strategy mitigates supply risk and provides increased flexibility to manage demand fluctuations and cost.

Culture

One of the biggest challenges and risks in terms of global sourcing is learning to work within cultures that have different languages, customs, and ethics. Yet it is critical to develop an understanding of a foreign supplier's culture prior to establishing a relationship, whether through cultural coaches, immersion in the new environment, and/or strong relationships with locals who will help avoid the pitfalls. Indeed, language barriers and improper business etiquette can be a major obstacle to establishing a successful sourcing relationship. Seemingly innocent behavior, such as showing the sole of your shoe to an Arab or rushing into business conversations in Latin America, have caused countless business deals to collapse. Cultural mishaps can undermine the ability to conduct business and develop any trusting relationship.

Industry Consolidation

The corporate motto for the 1990s seemed to be "bigger is better." Consider the following:

- Merger and acquisition activity across all sectors worldwide totaled more than $1.8 trillion through the first nine months of 1998.[4]
- 51 of the largest 100 economies in the world were corporations.[5]
- The 300 largest corporations accounted for one quarter of the world's productive assets.[6]

Both "buyers" and "sellers" in nearly every major sector have felt the impact of consolidation. The banking industry alone has experienced nearly $400 billion worth of consolidation (see Figure 1–2).[7] Traditional supply sectors such as oil and gas, chemicals, and utilities have been strongly affected. On the "buyer" side, sectors such as telecommunications, insurance, and transportation equipment have experienced significant merger and acquisition activity.

Furthermore, the pace of consolidation is not expected to slow. Charles Roussel, a partner and director of Andersen Consulting's Mergers, Acquisitions and Alliances Center of Excellence, expects to see consolidation continue in many sectors. "Despite almost a decade of reengineering, there is still considerable excess capacity in many markets—

---

4. A. Lindgren, and T. Tedesco "Mega-Merger Mania: The Long-Term Implications," *The Vancouver Sun*, May 14, 1998.
5. Ibid.
6. Ibid.
7. Ibid.

F I G U R E   1–2

Value Consolidations by Industry Sector

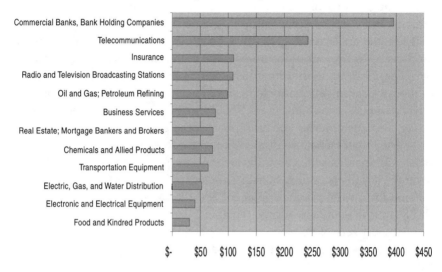

pharmaceuticals, paper and pulp, and automotive to name a few. Those companies with operational savvy and already streamlined cost structures will reap significant competitive advantage by decreasing industry capacity through selectively acquiring and rationalizing assets in their target markets."[8] In fact, some sectors will see the pace of consolidation increase—particularly industries such as utilities where deregulation will lead to dramatic competitive change.

Given this frenzy of consolidation activity, and the predictions that there is no end in sight, how will the procurement function be impacted?

Industry consolidation will lead to greater overall procurement efficiencies as newly formed companies leverage their size and influence to push suppliers for more services and lower costs. Suppliers will respond through consolidations and strategic alliances of their own. Through consolidation and/or alliances, tomorrow's suppliers will offer a greater breadth of products, cost-cutting technologies, value-added services, and international networks. In return for these new efficiencies and capabilities, successful suppliers will demand long-term, sole-sourcing agreements from their customers.

8. *Mergers & Acquisition Activity by SIC Code in Rank US$,* Securities Data Company, Inc., September 22, 1998.

Strategic Alliances

Two fundamental types of strategic alliances will play a role in the procurement strategy of tomorrow: the traditional long-term buyer–seller alliance and cross-company supplier partnering. Although not new, each will become an increasingly critical component of the new procurement landscape. As organizations operate more and more virtually (e.g., Nike, Sara Lee, Chiron), with numerous alliances in their orbit, the complexity of their procurement relationships will intensify; at various times, in various relationship configurations. The different parties may all be supplier, buyer, and customer to one another at some point in the relationship.

The buyer–seller alliance will continue to expand in both scope and scale. Companies will continue to look for procurement alliances that leverage suppliers' skills. Martin Krueger of Blommer Chocolate noted, "It's no longer the purchasing agent and the salesperson interacting. It's the technical people working together."[9] Alliances shaped by the improved skill sets of consolidated suppliers—particularly R&D/product development—will continue to supplant relationships focused strictly on price.

The airline and aerospace sectors represent an excellent example of two highly consolidated industries taking strategic buyer/seller alliances to the next level. The number of worldwide suppliers of large jetliners has been reduced to a handful—most notably Boeing and Airbus. These two companies can provide one-stop shopping for jetliners and all associated services and can pursue long-term, sole-sourcing relationships with their customers. Boeing demonstrated this through their agreements with several major airlines. Delta, Continental, and American Airlines have all signed long-term (e.g., 20 years) agreements to purchase all aircraft larger than regional jets from Boeing. The first orders from Continental and Delta represent $10.7 billion worth of business to Boeing.[10,11] These long-term alliances illustrate how both buyers and suppliers in a consolidated industry can derive significant procurement-related benefits.

The second type of alliance will involve the partnering between suppliers of complementary products. As buyers continue to consolidate

---

9. Interview by Charles Roussel, Andersen Consulting, Mergers & Acquisition Center of Excellence, September 29, 1998.
10. "Supplier Roundtable Pieces Together the Industry," *Candy Industry*, May 1998, A2–A11.
11. Note that Airbus and the EU have challenged the legality of these exclusive contracts. As such, the commitment to a single provider may not be legally binding.

F I G U R E   1-3

Foreign Revenue and Assets for Top 100 U.S. Multinationals

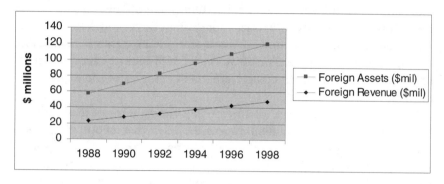

	1988	1990	1992	1994	1996	1998
Foreign Assets ($mil)	57.5	70	82.5	95	107.5	120
Foreign Revenue ($mil)	23	28	33	38	43	48

their supplier bases and look for procurement efficiencies, it will be the large-scale, *full-service* suppliers that get their business. To deliver this "one-stop shopping" capability, suppliers are merging and/or developing go-to-market alliances with suppliers from other industries. American Express uses this concept to develop alliances and joint ventures to become the financier of choice to small business. To supplement its financial service offerings, American Express developed relationships with AT&T Capital for equipment financing, Wells Fargo and Banc One for loan underwriting, and MCI and AT&T for calling card services.

The Global Provider

As industry consolidation and global expansion continue, the number of giant multinational corporations will grow. Recognizing the advantages of purchasing multiple products from a single provider, these corporate giants will look to distributors and wholesalers capable of providing services on a national or international level (see Figure 1–3).[12]

This trend is particularly strong in the indirect purchasing segment. Local and regional office supply dealers have been acquired by national

---

12. C. Boisseau. "Continental's Considering Lone-Supplier Deal with Boeing," *Houston Chronicle*, April 15, 1997.

super-chains at an unprecedented rate. In 1986, 19.9% of manufacturers' shipments went to small and mid-size dealers; by 1995, this number had dropped to 4%. Through consolidation, super-chains like Staples, Office Max, and BT Office Products, Inc. (BT OPI) have the purchasing power and supply chain tools to extract more competitive prices from manufacturers. These national powerhouses are now aggressively extending their presence in Europe. For instance, BT OPI recently acquired three companies in Germany and the Netherlands as part of their global expansion efforts.

The consolidation of industries will ultimately result in significant improvements in procurement processes, but what about good, old-fashioned competition? Won't prices rise as the number of suppliers drops? Probably not. The competitive marketplace and government regulation will ensure that some level of competition always exists. Just as there are still at least two jet airline manufacturers, there will continue to be at least two of everything else, although weaker players will be eliminated.

Technology

Technology innovation is radically redefining all aspects of businesses' operations, from sales and marketing to process control, manufacturing, and delivery. The Internet has vastly expanded direct access to consumers and, with computer database systems, has dramatically reduced business transaction costs through system automation. Current customer interaction costs range from $40 to $400 (via a sales representative) to $2 to $5 (telephone) to $0.10 to $0.40 (Internet) per transaction.

The technologies used range from multimillion-dollar enterprise resource planning systems (ERP) to thousand-dollar, hand-held order/delivery systems. While using these technologies to sell and supply can broadly be defined as electronic commerce (eCommerce), electronic procurement (eProcurement) refers specifically to supply chain, business-to-business purchasing. ERP applications can fully integrate a supply chain's request, order, receipt, and inventory processes to facilitate direct business-to-business transactions. Transactions can be made via the Internet or electronic data interchange (EDI) systems that automate high-frequency, high-value communications between suppliers. As the benefits of technology are realized, the business-to-business eCommerce market was projected to grow from $17 billion in 1998 to $105 billion in 2000[13] and capture 16% of purchases by the year 2000.[14]

Advantages

Many new procurement technologies are creating value for organizations in three significant ways:

1. *Reduced costs of goods and services:* eProcurement solutions make the purchasing process easy for and visible to unsophisticated business customers, leading to increased compliance with negotiated purchase agreements. Recognizing this, Pepsi-Cola streamlined its purchasing process with an automated purchasing system (APS). This system reduced transaction times from days to 15 minutes and reduced purchase errors from 10% to less than 1%.

2. *Higher productivity and reduced processing costs:* eProcurement automates paper-intensive tasks, reducing cycle times and purchase order processing costs, allowing purchasing professionals to spend time on higher-value activities. One Fortune 500 company found that processing costs for 60% of their purchases fell from $80–$125 to $10 per transaction using eProcurement and on-line catalogs. General Electric's Trading Post Network (TPN) reduced average purchase order processing costs from $50 to $5.

3. *Better information and better planning:* Purchase data collected from integrated systems can be used to evaluate and improve sourcing policies and process flows and prepare for supplier negotiations. Integrating business process information with suppliers reduces working capital requirements and inventory levels. For example, the software developer Descartes Systems Group will be releasing a website to help computer manufacturers and distributors with inventory levels and assembly time by tracking inventory purchases real time via a Web-based tracking system.

There are also risks in using new technology in the procurement process. The first is cost. ERP systems can exceed $10 million, making

---

13. *Forbes* and Andersen Consulting Analysis, September 30, 1998.
14. B. Erwin et al., *Sizing Intercompany Commerce*, Forrester Research, July 1997.

them risky for many small businesses. Obsolescence is always a concern, and companies must carefully evaluate the "shelf life" of technologies they select. Also, new technology means that additional training will be required in order to prevent improper use. Finally, organizational structures must be properly aligned with the new technologies. When Pepsi-Cola streamlined and centralized its procurement process with an automated purchasing system and a central data warehouse, the company's structure and corporate culture had to change as well.[15]

The benefits of new technology in procurement do justify the risks, but organizations must manage these risks during the implementation process.

Application

The number of supplier-designed applications continue to evolve for eCommerce. There are companies designing Internet procurement, ERP, and EDI applications. No one eCommerce application is optimal for every company, nor can one solution meet all of a company's procurement needs. For example, technologies to support mission-critical/strategic resource procurement and non-mission-critical resource procurement differ greatly.

Technologies for noncritical resource procurement allow buyers to find the lowest price and to streamline the procurement process through automation. Buyers' ability to access suppliers over the Internet creates negotiating leverage. For instance, Grainger's on-line catalog lists over 100,000 products from various suppliers. GE's TPN system was designed for noncritical resource procurement and has reduced automated electronic bidding from 21 to 10 days by allowing buyers to search and place orders from private on-line catalogs. Additionally, procurement cards offered by American Express, Visa, and MasterCard allow companies to outsource procurement for small MRO orders.

In contrast, mission-critical products require closer supplier relationships. ERP and EDI systems allow companies to integrate process data with suppliers to improve overall supply chain efficiency. Computer-automated design (CAD) systems and data exchange systems have played a key role in managing the supply relationship and forming buying consortiums. The Big 3 auto manufacturers developed an Automotive Network Exchange (ANX), a secure network system that links auto

---

15. *Electronic Commerce Weekly*, Killen & Associates, Inc., 1995.

suppliers. This network creates a standard buying protocol and allows manufacturers to integrate purchasing and capture economies of scale.

Technology will play a greater role in the procurement process for all companies as adoption increases beyond pioneering companies. In fact, The Gartner Group estimates that over 80%[16] of large U.S. enterprises will use the Internet for procurement by the year 2000, and Forrester Research estimates that by 2002, Internet commerce will reach $327 billion.[17] With this type of growth in Internet use, companies that are able to quickly integrate the Internet and other technologies into the procurement process will gain a competitive advantage.

Supply Chain Synchronization

To compete successfully in the future, companies will integrate beyond their own organization and align their core processes and business functions with an extended enterprise consisting of suppliers, customers, and third-party providers. This "supply chain synchronization" entails managing the flow of materials and information from suppliers' suppliers to customers' customers to optimize service at the lowest possible cost.[18] While many purchasing organizations have made tremendous headway in improving their company's operations, these functionally driven efforts were largely internal. Supply chain synchronization transcends company boundaries to establish the end-to-end supply chain.

Benefits

Supply chain synchronization begins with understanding the underlying business rationale for customers' initial demand and moves through suppliers' planning and operations to respond. The benefits of this holistic supply chain view include:

- Enhancing revenue by bringing new products to market first or faster than the competition and penetrating segments more broadly through mass customization
- Reducing cost through operational improvements in sourcing, manufacturing, distributing, and retailing

---

16. "Champions of Change at Pepsi," *CFO: The Magazine for Senior Financial Executives,* vol. 13, no. 12, December 1997, pp. 49–52.
17. "eCommerce Continues to Gain Importance," *Electronic Commerce, Multimedia Business Analyst,* May 21, 1997, no. 15, p. 10.
18. Erwin, op. cit.

♦ Improving asset utilization and capital deployment by rationalizing capacity and reducing inventory

♦ Heightening customer service through shortening lead times, improving fill rates, and offering an expanded portfolio of services

Execution

To achieve these benefits, purchasing organizations must successfully link suppliers into the extended enterprise. The sophistication of the linkage usually depends on the maturity and magnitude of the supplier relationship. For critical inputs, synchronization requires shifting from transactional to interactive and interdependent relationships, all of which involve sharing of information, aligning and leveraging of each party's technology, joint planning and development, and selective shared decision-making. Some purchasing organizations have integrated suppliers' employees into the manufacturing process by having on-site help to manage the quality and availability of component supply. Others have established gain-sharing initiatives, where the benefits of efforts to reduce costs and improve service and quality are shared.

Procurement can also help manufacturing standardize materials and change product designs to reduce complexity. For example, procurement integration early in the design phase of a product will impact cost, cycle time, inventory, and serviceability and, most importantly, can often be a major element in the overall marketing decisions about product viability.

3M's supply chain initiative helped reengineer procurement and intra- and intercompany supply processes. Procurement is now a critical component of the company's innovation process, a focal point of 3M's mission and strategy.[19] 3M's new product initiative will be launched at its state-of-the-art flexible circuit product line facility in Singapore. The facility will integrate 3M's customers (most notably Hewlett-Packard, located down the street) and suppliers. Suppliers will deliver components and materials two to three times a week to achieve high inventory turn rates and maximize working capital efficiency. This example of supply chain synchronization is expected to improve 3M's new product conceptualization and execution dramatically while lowering development cycle cost.[20]

19. Hintlian, Keech, and Moore, *Supply Chain Synchronization,* a working paper under consideration in an upcoming Prentice Hall book.
20. 3M Annual Report, 1996.

As supplier relationships become more sophisticated, procurement professionals will be taxed with managing the synchronization of these suppliers. One way to minimize supplier complexity is to use a tiered system of synchronization such as the one used in the automotive industry. Suppliers are regrouped into a hierarchy, and the automotive companies interact only with the first tier of suppliers. Tier one suppliers then manage the remaining supply base.

PROCUREMENT STRATEGY

The trends shaping the procurement landscape signal challenges and necessary changes to procurement strategy for many companies. Chief among these strategic challenges are:

- Tightly linking procurement strategy to corporate and business unit strategy
- Developing strategic, but flexible, relationships with critical suppliers
- Evolving the procurement focus from cost to revenue enhancement

Building Strategic Links

Without question, top-level executives now realize that procurement can be a source of untapped value in the corporation. After years of underutilizing procurement as a source of competitive advantage, executives are trying to develop and capture the benefits of world-class procurement organizations. One essential element of capturing that value is ensuring a more strategic approach to procurement, one that marries procurement strategy to overall business strategy.

Ensuring that the links are in place may seem obvious, yet many companies fail to do so. In part, this is a result of the traditional approach to strategic planning. In many organizations, corporate strategy is set at the highest levels and defines the overall vision and direction of the corporation. Once that vision is set, business unit strategies are developed to identify objectives to support the corporate strategy. Traditionally, large companies have established independent functional strategies to pursue those business unit objectives. Many times, these functional strategies optimize the functional area (i.e., low-cost procurement without regard to quality; long manufacturing runs without regard to inventory) rather than advance the business unit or overall corporate strategy.

F I G U R E   1-4

Traditional Strategic Planning Hierarchy

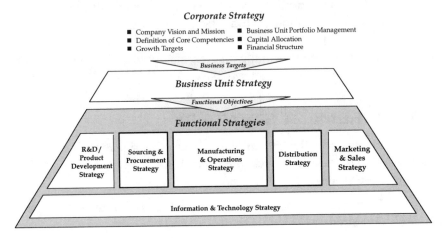

Corporate Strategy

- Company Vision and Mission   ■ Business Unit Portfolio Management
- Definition of Core Competencies   ■ Capital Allocation
- Growth Targets   ■ Financial Structure

Business Targets

Business Unit Strategy

Functional Objectives

Functional Strategies

| R&D/ Product Development Strategy | Sourcing & Procurement Strategy | Manufacturing & Operations Strategy | Distribution Strategy | Marketing & Sales Strategy |

Information & Technology Strategy

See Figure 1–4. This kind of disconnect is a recipe for frustration, both inside and outside the procurement function. In the future, firms will need to institute coherent, linked functional strategies that not only support the supply chain objectives but also directly contribute to meeting the business unit strategic objectives. See Figure 1–5.

As core capabilities are built around procurement and sourcing, these capabilities will be able to impact and influence the overall corporate strategy. For example, both Chrysler and Ford have successful cost-reduction programs with their suppliers that give them a cost advantage over General Motors. The impact on corporate strategy is a newfound ability to grow market share in key business segments.

Developing Strategic Yet Flexible
Supplier Relationships

The movement to closer, more strategic partnerships with a relatively small number of suppliers is commonly accepted in theory as a best practice, yet implementation is certainly not universal. As these strategic partnerships to reduce supply chain costs become more widespread, we will begin to see *competition between supply chains, in addition to competition between companies.* In this type of competition, cost is one factor to consider in assessing supplier relationships, but value enhancement potential is just as important.

F I G U R E   1–5

New Role of Functional Strategies

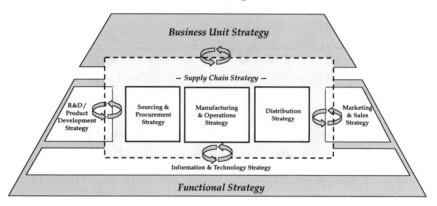

Strategic partnerships with suppliers will become much more value-based, rather than cost-based. Compensation along the supply chain will become more closely linked to the value added by each of the partners. This may cause some conflict in the chain as companies gravitate to areas in which they can capture the most value, turning suppliers into competitors.

An emerging example exists within the energy industry in oil exploration and production. Oil field service companies such as Halliburton and Schlumberger are suppliers to major oil companies in all aspects of developing oil wells. Domestically, they have not taken equity positions in fields or wells, but in overseas exploration they *are* bidding against the same major oil companies they supply. Frequently these suppliers/owners partner with foreign governments to explore and produce oil. The supplier has become the competitor because it has correctly identified a position in the supply chain where it can capture value.

Consequently, relationships with suppliers will become substantially more complex as would-be partners examine the value along the supply chain and assess each other's capabilities to capture that value. From the standpoint of identifying opportunities, procurement and sourcing professionals are uniquely positioned to understand which segments or pools within the supply chain are the most valuable and to exploit those opportunities. On the flip side, they can assess competitive threats, not only from traditional direct competitors, but from supply chain partners seeking to expand their involvement.

The ability of some suppliers to expand their roles and compete directly for customers raises significant strategic issues for procurement professionals. Some of the more pressing are whether joint development is possible and how much information is exchanged about general business strategies. Ultimately, procurement executives will need to weigh the risks and rewards of having relationships with suppliers who have the potential to compete with them, and determine if those risks are too high.

Moving from Cost Containment to Revenue Enhancement

Traditionally, procurement has focused on reducing costs. However, the evolution from focusing on item cost to analyzing total cost of ownership and supply chain optimization indicates that the next logical step is to identify ways in which procurement can enhance revenue. Procurement does have the potential to impact revenue in-flows by affecting both the price and the volume of finished goods.

From a price standpoint, carefully cultivating supplier partnerships can improve revenue streams from the finished goods if the partnerships result in securing enhanced raw materials. Typical enhancements include improving the quality and performance of the finished good, enhancing the attractiveness or features of the finished good, and increasing the level of customer service support. From the volume-improvement side, suppliers can be prime drivers of improvements in fill rate (availability), capacity, and manufacturing yield, for example. See Figure 1–6.

Although revenue enhancement is possible, it will require operational changes: specifically, more extensive supply chain interaction with functional areas such as new product development and manufacturing operations. The level of interaction required extends beyond periodic meetings to actual collaboration on the processes themselves over an extended period of time. In addition, traditional cost-modeling equations will probably need refining to reflect the new emphasis on revenue enhancement.

THE FUTURE OF "PROCUREMENT–TECHNOLOGY"

Nothing will shape, energize, and direct the future of procurement more than the pervasive and profound impact of technology. As a primary

Procurement Improvement

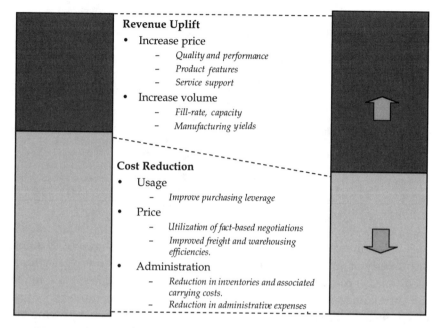

Revenue Uplift
- Increase price
  - Quality and performance
  - Product features
  - Service support
- Increase volume
  - Fill-rate, capacity
  - Manufacturing yields

Cost Reduction
- Usage
  - Improve purchasing leverage
- Price
  - Utilization of fact-based negotiations
  - Improved freight and warehousing efficiencies.
- Administration
  - Reduction in inventories and associated carrying costs.
  - Reduction in administrative expenses

Present   Future

enabler of business strategy, technology opens doors to new markets, products, services, business processes, and enterprises that are competitively and collaboratively superior.

Three emerging technology trends will have a revolutionary impact on procurement:

- eCommerce and the Internet
- Virtual value networks
- Open markets

eCommerce and the Internet

At the leading edge of this technological transformation, eCommerce and the Internet's role in reducing costs and improving customer service will shape procurement's capacity and provide the most of the momentum going forward.

F I G U R E   1-7

Factors Affecting eCommerce Adoption

Forces Reaching Across Industry Boundaries

- Increased *customer* sophistication, demands and expectations
- An increasing pace and intensity of *competition* characterized by consolidations, *alliances* and *partnering* and the proliferation of *new entrants*
- Aggressive *globalization* lowering trade barriers for access to broader markets and international supply chains
- Technology-enabled *virtualization* supporting globalization through the elimination of barriers of time, space and form

Barrier to Adoption

- *Technological Readiness*—lagging enterprise IT assimilation/adoption rates, IT project prioritization, industry infrastructure standardization, and the integration of eCommerce with legacy systems.
- *Organizational Readiness* — changing traditional cultures, building skilled resources and augmenting business capabilities through deliberate and dynamic business strategies.
- *Market Readiness* — the ability to quantify and convey the value of eCommerce, unclear customer & business partner demand, and issues of privacy and trust.

ECommerce, simply defined, is "an interchange of goods, services, or property of any kind . . . through a universal and ubiquitous electronic medium."[21] From a minimal start in the early 1990s, by 1998 it accounted for approximately $17 billion in business-to-business commerce.[22] Various industry estimates show this transaction medium to be growing between 100% per year to that of a doubling every three or four months.

Rates of adoption and magnitudes of change do vary across industries, with pioneering efforts in Financial Services, Electronics/High-Technology, Media and Entertainment, and Travel Services. However, the attention on eCommerce will focus on *how* it will continue to manifest itself industry-wide. The battle between the forces for and the barriers to convergence will intensify, charting the economically viable progress of eCommerce across industries, as shown in Figure 1–7.[23] Conquest is nonetheless imminent—only the rate of convergence and the precise operating model remain unknown.

Clearly, the Internet and EDI play key roles in enabling the full realization of eCommerce benefits, although in different ways. With both a low usage cost (variable) and a low entry (fixed) cost, the Internet will continue to be adopted rapidly and ubiquitously by businesses whatever

21. T. Kawalec, F. Schneider, and S. Johnson. "Industry eCommerce Assessment," Andersen Consulting Internal Presentation, September 1997.
22. Kawalec et al., op cit.
23. Erwin, op. cit.

their scale. In the next three to five years, Internet tools requiring only minimal training will become even more robust and transparent.[24] Freed from scale limitations, any mom-and-pop shop will have the ability and motive to dive into eCommerce through its own virtual storefront.

However, scale economies will not evaporate. Coupled with the speed and standardization benefits of EDI, the Internet will make direct links between suppliers and consumers easier, eliminating cost-laden middlemen, brokers, and agents.[25] Transaction processing via an EDI backbone will be fast, cheap, and extensive and will leverage prior investment in Internet infrastructure.[26] Cheap distribution capabilities of large providers will undercut many mom-and-pop shops that cannot deliver service/value commensurate with the prices charged. Over time, the virtual Internet world will resemble the real world: large, ubiquitous providers with low-cost positions and niche providers with service-oriented positions.

Similarities aside, electronic procurement will embody a different operating model and shift in bargaining power. Electronic procurement specifically and eCommerce generally will knit supplier and buyer business processes together to deliver seamless transactions.[27] Although electronic procurement will facilitate business-to-business processes between suppliers and buyers, buyers will be the primary beneficiaries. Buyers will come together and leverage their cross-industry purchasing power to establish more efficient and effective business processes linkages with suppliers. This will be displayed through the emergence of *virtual value networks* and *open markets*.

Virtual Value Networks

Even as eCommerce takes hold, giving merchants a direct link to buyers, suppliers from various industries will be collaborating behind the scenes to form unique networks that restructure traditional supply chains. This developing electronic marketplace will be characterized by multiple relationships operating in real time to fulfill demand and exhaust supply.

24. Kawalec et al., op cit.
25. C. Nebolsky, and L. Silverman, *The "Top 50" Key Technologies*, Center for Strategic Technology (*CSTaR*), June 1998.
26. Kawalec et al., op cit.
27. *Internet EDI: Analysis & Market Survey*, Andersen Consulting Technology Library Database, May 1998.

In a marketplace dominated by these virtual procurement networks, the current dominance of supplier-centric, push-based supply chains is being eroded by pull-based demand chains. Through its Trading Post Network, GE bought more than $1 billion worth of goods and supplies via the Internet in 1997.[28] By 2000, GE aims to have all 12 of its business units use TPN and expects to save $500–$700 million (on $5 billion of purchases) over the next three years.

However, as the need to satisfy global demand through a complex array of information, product, service, and resource flows intensifies, such demand *chains* alone will prove inadequate. As an intermediate solution, demand *networks* will be created to manage these more frequent and complex flows. One example is Dun & Bradstreet's (D&B) D-U-N-S number, created to help companies link suppliers with common goals.

Nonetheless, these solutions will give way to virtual value networks, otherwise referred to in academic circles as "ecosystems" or "cyberspace communities." In replacing the demand networks, these virtual value networks will serve to redirect competition away from product–versus–product or enterprise–versus–enterprise toward competing value networks endowed with the ability to fully and effectively address the needs of targeted community members.

Virtual value networks will dynamically organize, or integrate, around "moments of value", where cross-industries partners bring together a full set of products, services, and experiences to satisfy the procurement needs of each participating community.[29] The market will consequently evolve toward a more collaborative structure with value—derived from products, services, information, and resources—embedded in exchanges between network members. Disintermediation—the bypassing of networks of middlemen and brokers—will occur as enterprises satisfy procurement needs through combinations of network members. Global economic and industry restructuring will follow in the wake of virtual value networks, yielding a new assemblage of opportunities and threats.

Open Markets

A second major derivative of eCommerce will be open markets for procurement. These open markets will be typified by capital market exchanges where mechanisms to link buyers' needs with suppliers' solutions are provided. eCommerce will impact such an exchange's market

---

28. V. Niven, "eProcurement White Paper," Andersen Consulting Internal Presentation, July 1998.
29. Ibid.

efficiency through new economics that flow from standardization, global reach, and real-time interaction. Present-day eCommerce exchanges, as models for future open procurement markets, function as electronic auctions in satisfying a range of needs impacting procurement:

+ Matching or aggregating supply and demand
+ Creating secondary markets
+ Transacting business and corresponding financial payments and settlements
+ Auctioning off excess capacity or off-loading assets[30]

These open markets will have the inherent advantages—simplification, speed, and security—afforded by eCommerce and the Internet/EDI infrastructure. Specifications, part numbering, and procurement categories will all be simplified through standardization and consolidation. Speed will be furnished by the transaction-processing capabilities of an EDI backbone coupled with the capabilities of the Internet. Lastly, security will be achieved through sophisticated firewalls and encryption technology.

As with virtual value networks, open markets will also assume a buyer-centric viewpoint in the short to mid-term. This "pull" strategy will use a bidding mechanism that requires buyers to identify and post requirements for commodities and/or specialty items on a Web site, evaluate any bids received from preapproved or registered suppliers within an agreed time frame, and award contracts to the lowest-cost suppliers.[31] The immediacy of transmitting bids via the Internet will compress the process significantly. More importantly, analysis of the bids, such as the rapid determination of the bid's impact on total supply chain cost, will be possible.[32] This on-line market channel will facilitate real-time market making, both in MRO supplies and in critical direct material components.

In the long term, ownership and governance of market mechanisms and information will migrate to neutral third parties. Buyer-centric open markets will promote real-time bid visibility and information asymmetry, driving prices down. Suppliers will inevitably consolidate to recover lost margins, leveraging any and all opportunities for scale economies.

30. Kawalec et al., op cit.
31. K. Downer, "Paradigm Shift: Value Creation through Procurement," Andersen Consulting White Paper, December 1996.
32. S. Maddila, "Internet Enabled Supply-Demand Chain Planning," Andersen Consulting White Paper, August 1997.

Through consolidation and cost rationalization, suppliers will realize increased bargaining power and the corresponding ability to improve information and elevate bid prices. As enterprising third parties recognize such discontinuity, neutral, secure, expansive marketplaces will arise where these larger procurement "players" will meet to "make the market." In the future, such virtual value networks of buyers and sellers across industries will meet in open markets to consummate limitless procurement initiatives.

THE PROCUREMENT ORGANIZATION OF THE FUTURE

The expansion of procurement's focus from buying to more strategic sourcing, and its transformation from an internally focused function to an externally "networked" one, imply several changes for the procurement function in most companies. Among the most important are changes to the structure of a procurement organization, the roles procurement professionals will be expected to assume in the future, and the skills needed to perform the expanded roles.

Matching Procurement Organizational Structure to Strategy

Although many companies acknowledge the increasing importance of procurement, few have made the necessary organizational changes to position procurement within the highest strategic levels of the corporation. Indeed, as recently as 1995, respondents to a Center for Advanced Purchasing Studies (CAPS) study indicated that

> purchasing had a low level of involvement in major corporate activities, despite previous research that demonstrated the value of the supply function as a competitive weapon. It is found that a surprisingly large number of firms appointed individuals lacking prior purchasing experience to the position of CPO.[33]

---

33. H. E. Fearon and M. R. Leender, "Purchasing Organizational Relationships," expands the CAPS' earlier study (1988), to include data/information on the centralization/decentralization issue; head count; changing responsibilities; reengineering/downsizing; teaming; reporting; and how purchasing fits into organizational strategy. University of Western Ontario, November 1995.

However, there is an increased willingness to elevate procurement to higher levels in organizations. In fact, many companies in a variety of industries—IBM, Weyerhaeuser, Stanley Works, and Bristol-Myers Squibb—have already appointed Chief Procurement Officers (CPOs) or equivalent positions. Not every company will have a CPO. Rather, it will depend on the industry and the criticality of procurement to the business. In industries where procurement constitutes a large percentage of the overall cost structure (e.g., automotive), procurement will continue to gain in prominence. However, in industries with low or nonstrategic procurement (e.g., financial services), procurement will be used only to drive cost reduction, without a development of the CPO position.

Another scenario is also possible. Some companies may opt to develop an executive-level position that encompasses more than procurement, something akin to a Chief Supply Chain Officer. This type of executive would oversee procurement as well as other functional areas such as manufacturing, new product development, and distribution. As companies increasingly view the supply chain as a web of interdependent functions, having one individual charged with maintaining an integrated view would make more sense than having only a series of functional heads.

The organization structure of the future will likely be split along strategic versus tactical procurement, given the vastly different skill sets and business impacts of the two segments. For the tactical procurement, the organization will be small as technology further facilitates end-user ordering of the high-volume, low-value items. In many cases, such tactical procurement may be outsourced, with low levels of effort and concentration on the part of the company to develop skills in this area. For the more strategic commodities, the organizational structure will link sourcing decisions with the corporate and business unit strategic objectives through the CPO or equivalent position.

Organizational structures will vary depending upon the strategic prominence of procurement and the skills available. However, despite this variance, there will be common trends. For example, there is a general consensus that a "matrix kind of organizational approach and an increasing use of cross-functional teams and cross-location teams"[34] will become the standard. If so, these organizational forms and processes will require integrated information systems "whereby people can know what

---

34. R. Monczka, and J. Morgan, "Supply Chain Strategies," *Purchasing Magazine*, 1997.

is being bought around the world, what is being paid, and who are the suppliers we're trying to leverage up."[35]

Changing and Expanding Roles, Responsibilities, and Skills

Many industry veterans and academics are speculating on the future roles and responsibilities of procurement. A theme common to almost all predictions is that procurement will be responsible for more strategic aspects of the business and that the job will be broader and more complex. Unfortunately, it is clear that the skills and capabilities of the ultimate procurement professional of the future are rare in today's market.

Executives quoted in a recent article in *Purchasing Magazine* acknowledged just how much the job has changed. Terry Carlson (Corporate Vice President—Purchasing, Maytag Corp.) believes that "[t]oday's procurement pro is expected to wear a coat of many colors, that of strategist, analyst, company ambassador, team leader, team participant, and salesperson." To play these roles, buyers must possess a wide range of skills, including international buying experience, strong analytical ability, and computer training. George R. Milne, C.P.M. (Vice President—Purchasing, Delta Faucet) agrees, and suggests that "applicants must have a cross-pollination in other disciplines such as computer science, production control, inventory management, economics, and accounting." Indeed, Thomas Hogue (Vice President—Materials and Services, Intel Corp.) describes the prime purchasing candidate as having an MBA with a technical undergraduate degree, arguing that companies "can teach commercial skills, but not technical ability."[36]

Furthermore, it is very likely that procurement professionals will not be lifelong members of the procurement function, or even start their career there. Rather, for many, playing a procurement role will be seen as a necessary step in progressing through the management ranks. Procurement will be an area in which a "high flyer" can have a large and immediate impact on a corporation's performance and gain visibility at higher levels.

---

35. Ibid.
36. C. Koumantzelis, "Purchasing in the Future Will Require Higher Skill Levels," *Purchasing Magazine*, December 11, 1997, p. 44.

A recent example of this is Thomas Stallkamp, promoted in January 1998 from Executive Vice President—Supply and Sourcing at Chrysler to President of Chrysler Corp. In Tom's 27 years at Chrysler, he moved between procurement-specific and general operational roles, serving as general manager for several operations. His promotion recognized his success with procurement programs such as SCORE, which removed billions of dollars from Chrysler's cost base.

Procurement professionals in the future will have much greater visibility but will also shoulder greater demands and more responsibilities. With both will come higher expectations. As procurement moves from a tactical function to its strategic position, procurement professionals will need to be business managers first and foremost. They will be the focal point pulling together the supply chain for internal and external improvements. With the new focus on procurement, the level of competition will certainly go up substantially. The good news for the procurement professional is that the opportunities will go up commensurately.

SUPPLIER INTEGRATION

The next evolution of the supplier and customer relationship will dramatically change the way companies compete in the future. To compete successfully in the 21st century, companies will need to view and operate their supply chains as extended enterprises with long-term, trusting supplier partnerships and well-integrated linkages. In the future, suppliers and customers will form teams that will compete against other supplier-customer teams. Their goal, of course, will be to provide the right products or services to the end consumer as cost-efficiently and as quickly as possible. This collaborative effort will allow the teams to achieve exponentially better results than individual organizations could accomplish on their own.

As more organizations view the supply chain this way, activities within one organization or its supply chain partners upstream or downstream from it will become part of a larger enterprise-wide picture. This will require suppliers and their customers to resolve their traditionally adversarial relationships fostered by the old business–to–business paradigm. Because of the tight integration that the extended enterprise concept creates, organizations will necessarily share people, common values, and processes as well as costs and other information. These extended enterprises will be software driven business–to–business linkages in which suppliers, manufacturers, retailers, and customers are tied together in a free flow of goods, money, information, and processes.[37] However, effectively linking suppliers and customers will be difficult, requiring linking internal workflow management systems, external supply chain management tools, and the Web.

Recent initiatives between suppliers and customers in new product development and collaborative planning and execution demonstrate how these extended enterprises are being developed.

New Product Development

Many companies are looking to new product development as a place to begin creating a more extended enterprise. One reason is the need for lower costs. A majority of product development costs are locked in very early in the product development cycle. In fact, for many companies, over 70% of costs for new product development have been committed to by the end of the concept and specification/planning phases. By comparison, only 30% of cost commitments occur during the latter prototype development and testing/launch phases. Unfortunately, the costs committed to in the earlier phases are not expended until the latter development phases, when it is too expensive to significantly alter product designs.

In addition to lowered costs, successful supplier integration during new product development can yield other benefits, including reduced development time, improved quality of purchased materials, and better access to and application of new technology. These integrated partnerships also benefit suppliers by helping them make the right investment in people and technology to better support their customers. Accordingly, it is imperative to have cross-functional teams, including suppliers, involved in the NPD process as early as possible. A recent study by the Michigan State University Global Procurement and Supply Chain Electronic Benchmarking Network identified supplier membership on the new product development project team as the greatest difference between most and least successful integration efforts.[38] Companies like

37. J. M. Greenbaum, "The Extended Supply Chain: Coming to a Millennium Near You," *Software Magazine*, vol. 17, no. 7, July 1997, pp. 31.
38. G. L. Ragatz, "Success Factors for Integrating Suppliers Into New Product Development," *Journal of Product Innovation Management*, vol. 14, no. 3, May 1997, pp. 190–202.

Chrysler are leading the way in getting suppliers involved in the new product development process early.

> Chrysler uses a Platform Team concept that closely aligns cross-functional teams, including suppliers, with specific vehicles. These Platform teams are intended to be fluid organizations, expanding and contracting as products are defined and developed. As members of the team, suppliers play a crucial role in the vehicle development process.[39]

In addition to suppliers becoming more integrated on new product development teams, companies will begin to outsource more of the design and development work to key suppliers. For example, Chrysler may give a supplier primary responsibility for designing a component or assembly, such as a seating system. In such instances, the system or first-tier supplier is asked to determine the target cost of the individual subcomponents that are to be sourced from a second- or third-tier supplier.[40]

While the integration of suppliers in the new product development process can yield significant and positive results, many customers may be apprehensive about starting this process. Some helpful tips to start the integration process are as follows:

- Design for early supplier involvement.
- Solicit supplier's suggestions for substituting alternative materials or obtaining information about as-yet unannounced components or processes.
- Establish close relationship with a few suppliers by negotiating purchases and meeting regularly with their key players and executives.
- Manage the relationship to maintain trust and find ways to share risks and cost with suppliers.
- Draft formal agreements with suppliers that include a description of the joint relationship, expected results, ownership, patent rights, and nondisclosure provisions.

Pressure to compress design cycles will continue to increase, together with the need to reduce product development costs and use new technologies. Accordingly, the transformation of new product design will continue to evolve from an activity handled primarily by engineering to

---

39. Ragatz, op cit.
40. Ragatz, op cit.

an expanded process involving multiple functions across the organization and key suppliers. Companies that find ways to integrate talented suppliers into their NPD process successfully will have exposure to expertise and technology that can position them to capture significant competitive advantages in the marketplace.

Collaboration and Planning

Increasingly, customer demands are requiring organizations to find new ways to improve supply chain responsiveness while trying to lower total costs. Across industries, enterprises are quickly realizing that to accomplish this challenging task they must closely align with their best supply chain partners. Collaborative Planning and Execution (CPE) is another way that supply chain partners are banding together for mutual benefit. To create the most accurate demand forecasts, supply chain partners merge and reconcile forecasts, set order fulfillment strategies, and participate in joint capacity planning.

With CPE, each organization reviews its partners' evolving demand forecasts to create a more accurate, integrated forecast. Frequently data is shared and integrated using the Internet.

Companies are using this method of collaborative forecasting in a variety of industries, including Heineken Brewery, Bay Networks, Eastman Chemical, and a few automotive companies. For example, Subaru recently announced that it will implement a collaborative solution to help create more bottom-up forecasts. More than 50 Subaru managers access the corporate intranet to compare production numbers against sales data and forecasts. Instead of sending paper projections from the corporate offices, Subaru will depend on district sales managers to provide up-to-date feedback on the forecasts for their regions. It will be the managers' responsibility to alert corporate headquarters if changes are required based on market conditions. All this allows Subaru to be more responsive to marketplace changes

While collaborative planning software applications are still in the early stages, fast technological advances are expected. A few examples are Logility's Resource Chain Voyager, RedPepper, Manugistics, and i2. Other initiatives, like Collaborative Planning Forecasting and Replenishment, are massive joint projects involving such big-time buyers as Kmart, Procter & Gamble, Hewlett Packard, Warner Lambert, Sara Lee, and a score of others. Their aim is to help supply chain partners better collaborate and coordinate activities.

Today, enterprise-wide collaboration is limited by technology. While EDI has helped business-to-business communication, companies and their suppliers will require that supply chain planning software, workflow systems, and the Web be linked and integrated to facilitate timely, accurate responses to business partners' request for commitments and information. Attempts to meet this need are currently being undertaken by several supply chain software companies. Complete synchronization of each enterprise within the supply chain via business process and technology will allow partners to benefit from increased asset utilization, reduced inventory across the supply chain, and decreased lead times.

Joint Financial Analysis

The tighter integration of suppliers and customers will lead to more aligned performance metrics and data tracking for better decision-making. In the future, performance goals will focus on *managing for joint profitability* of suppliers and customers. Supply chain partners will track historical and forecasted profitability and share it with supply chain links. In addition, the need to optimize product mix will lead to increased use of activity-base costing to determine account, brand, and product profitability. Overall account performance will be measured against cost targets by customer segment, including the total cost of getting products to the shelf and providing service to customers. All of these calculations will become product performance metrics for suppliers. Accordingly, collaboration will lead to extensive use of performance measures linked to shared risks and rewards among partners.

In the future, demand forecasts will be developed by consensus and negotiation among partners, and there will be extensive sharing of actual demand information. Companies that design products with both the customer needs and enterprise-wide performance in mind will shorten the time required for developing new products and filling the pipeline. These companies should, consequently expect to benefit from increased revenues and operating margins.

CHAPTER 2

Creating Supply Advantage by Leveraging the Strategic Nature of Procurement

Editor
William J. Markham
Principal
Global Strategic Sourcing Practice
A. T. Kearney, Inc.

Associate Editors
José T. Morales
Vice President
A. T. Kearney, Inc.

Thomas H. Slaight
Vice President
A. T. Kearney, Inc.

Leading companies around the world have transformed procurement management from an underexploited administrative activity to a board-room-level competitive weapon. This chapter examines the management practices that leading firms use to create supply advantage.

INTRODUCTION

The traditional role of procurement management is to ensure that there is a supply of services and materials to support a business's operations and save money in the process. Buyers deep within the organization accomplish this every day. Common tactics include reducing the number of suppliers to obtain volume discounts and maintain stronger control and using competitive bidding to ensure that suppliers provide their

---

goods and services at a "competitive" price. From these actions, the typical company is usually able to keep pace with underlying market price changes for purchased goods and services.

Leading companies, however, cut these costs by 12% on average by using more sophisticated approaches focused on reducing total costs, not just price paid. Because companies typically spend half or more of their revenues on external purchases of goods and services, these leaders enjoy a cost advantage of more than US$60 million for every US$1 billion in revenue.

But cost advantage is only part of the procurement mission for leading firms. They best use their procurement prowess to maximize the value added by their suppliers. For example, they have chopped 62% off their new product development cycle times, and 41% from their raw materials inventory—improvements two to three times those of typical companies. The percent figures and savings are even higher when project and maintenance purchases are included in this analysis

Leaders don't stop there. For them, excellence in procurement means finding strategic supply market opportunities that can shape and advance corporate goals. For some, this means maintaining cost leadership, or developing local sources of supply to enable expansion into emerging markets. For others, it means finding or developing highly capable first-tier "systems suppliers," thus allowing the company to focus its resources and assets on its own core capabilities. For others still, excellence in procurement means identifying and securing control of "choke points" in supply sources several levels back in the value chain, or continually scanning the supply market for new technologies that will make tomorrow's products possible.

PROCUREMENT: A BOARDROOM-LEVEL CONCERN

In 1997, A. T. Kearney released the results of a research study of senior executives of 463 of the world's largest companies (sales volume of $1 billion or greater). The study identified the most pressing concerns facing these executives and probed their strategies to respond. The survey participants were based in Europe, Asia/Pacific Rim, North America, and South America, and industries included consumer products, retail, communications, healthcare, finance, oil and gas, automotive, transportation, and utilities.

For the surveyed executives, "critically important" concerns were:

- Managing relationships with customers
- Increasing their company's cost competitiveness
- Using information technology effectively
- Managing change
- Increasing shareholder value
- Achieving revenue growth
- Adapting to industry restructuring
- Globalizing the business
- Developing and managing value-added relationships with suppliers

Insights from strategies that these companies are pursuing indicate an increasing role for suppliers and an increasing emphasis on procurement excellence:

Value-based customer relationships are becoming the business focus. CEOs have heard the message from their marketplaces. Companies seeking long-term customer relationships must provide higher value: more innovation, better quality, greater responsiveness and agility, all at lower cost. Competing on a single dimension is not enough. The entire organization, indeed the entire value chain, must be focused on this goal.

Suppliers will play an expanded role in delivering value to the end customer. At a minimum, companies must work with suppliers to ensure that they provide products and services efficiently and reliably. After all, the suppliers control upwards of 70% of the final cost of many products. More importantly, however, companies must encourage the creativity and harness the resources of their suppliers to support the new product innovation and geographic market coverage that *their* customers demand.

Companies will need to manage a portfolio of relationships. Companies should be wary of the hyperbole surrounding the pervasiveness of customer–supplier "partnerships." Even a vague commitment to "work together" qualifies as a partnership relationship for some companies, but few such relationships will become truly rich partnerships. For that to occur, customer and supplier must agree and set joint business goals. Then managing the relationship for results is key. Fundamental to this is trusting that each party can and will perform as agreed, whether it be in terms of willingness to share information, of open communication, or of product quality. This trust comes from demonstrated performance and in turn fosters continued growth of the relationship.

Senior management must lead and drive changes. Implementing this broader extended enterprise (customer–company–supplier) value chain approach will require even greater senior executive leadership and involvement. It touches too many parts of the business; individual departments and functions will be limited in what they can accomplish. For many companies, it may mean a consolidation or reprioritization of initiatives to focus resources where the payback is greatest. And it will require a critical look at the decisions made, attention paid, and resources applied to the supply side of the value chain. This also includes challenging the assumptions that have led to "comfortable" relationships with existing suppliers. Executives must ask whether these are the best suppliers to help accomplish the corporation's goals going forward.

ACHIEVING PROCUREMENT EXCELLENCE: UNDERSTANDING AND APPLYING LEADERSHIP PRACTICES

Since the mid-1980s, A. T. Kearney, Inc. has conducted continuing in-depth research into how companies create supply advantage. In 1996 and 1997 (see Appendix: Leadership Practices in Procurement Research), we examined how 77 European and North American companies have brought their procurement capabilities to the forefront in their organizations and in 1999 expanded the research into a global "Assessment on Excellence in Procurement," covering 162 companies in 28 countries. Based on our research, we believe that supply advantage comes from excellence in procurement management. And procurement excellence requires a company to understand and apply leadership practices across eight dimensions, as portrayed in A. T. Kearney's *House of Purchasing and Supply*[SM] framework (see Figure 2–1):

- ◆ Purchasing and supply strategy
- ◆ Organization
- ◆ Sourcing
- ◆ Supplier management and development
- ◆ Day-to-day purchasing
- ◆ Performance management
- ◆ Information management
- ◆ Human resource management

FIGURE   2–1

House of Purchasing and Supply^SM Framework

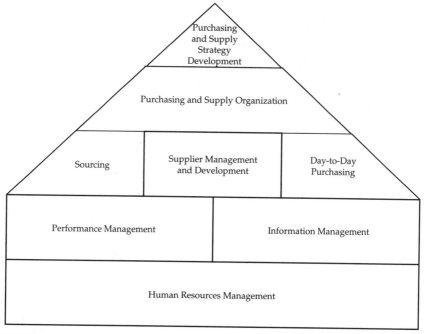

© A. T. Kearney, Inc.

In the remainder of this chapter, we examine each of the eight dimensions of leadership practices in procurement, relating examples of companies that have used these techniques to advantage. We highlight a company in which procurement executives work with corporate planning to develop a strategy that is tied to market realities and supports the firm's broader strategic goals. We describe how companies use procurement expertise to strategically manage supply markets, identifying and developing unique relationships with the best suppliers. Finally, we suggest a technique any company can use for self-assessment and for setting a course of action.

PURCHASING AND SUPPLY STRATEGY: FINDING AND CAPTURING THE VALUE IN SUPPLY MARKETS

A deep understanding of supply markets can help shape corporate strategy, allowing a company to capitalize on opportunities afforded by a supplier's products, unique skills, and capabilities. Such knowledge can guide the evolution of the company's future goals and objectives.

Procurement leaders:

+ Seek opportunities to shape corporate strategy by exploiting supply market opportunities
+ Establish policy and allocate resources based on opportunities and risks across their entire portfolio of purchases
+ Proactively define how procurement activities will be organized, conducted, and managed to capitalize on opportunities

By exploiting supply market opportunities, companies can redesign the value chain. They do it by continuously evaluating insource/outsource opportunities, gaining control of critical resources, achieving cost leadership, driving technological innovation, and enabling entry or expansion into new product areas or markets.

One of the world's leading global technology firms uses many of these approaches. Its network of 40 procurement teams gathers industry intelligence on a range of key supply market issues. It uses the network to know where it can capture an edge; for example, by understanding where critical capabilities are in short supply and from what direction the next technological breakthrough is coming.

Using this strategic information, senior management can adapt the company's value chain to take advantage of market developments. In one case, the manufacturer discovered and created advantage in a supply market three levels back in its supply chain that provided critical production equipment for suppliers to the manufacturer. At the time, it was unusually concentrated and capacity-constrained. By locking up a long-term contract for the output of one of these equipment suppliers, the global technology firm was able to block its competition. Suppliers to the manufacturer got priority when demand boosted production equipment orders; suppliers to its competitors waited in line. This allowed the firm to ramp-up its own production and get to market faster than its competition.

Senior executives at this firm consistently involve the procurement organization in all strategic decisions that affect customers, competitors, and suppliers. One executive characterizes the procurement organization as "the eyes and ears to the supply market." It participates in strategic business decisions including marketing alliances, production joint ventures, and other business partnerships. Procurement executives provide input to the process and create contingency plans to enable the company to react to the repercussions some strategic decisions may have on the supply base.

A leader in the services industry uses procurement excellence as a platform for growth. Faced with fierce competition, the company forged a plan to improve market share by becoming the low-cost provider. It targeted purchased goods and services as a prime area for improvement, since outside expenditures made up a large part of its cost base. Looking across its entire expenditure base, the company established a plan of attack for each category. For some, straightforward cost cutting was the answer. For others, expenditures were great enough and the impact on customer satisfaction high enough to warrant special attention.

The company addressed these special categories in a number of ways. In one approach, for example, it tracked and analyzed a category's total life cycle costs: acquisition, installation, warranty, and the operating costs customers incur in using the product. This analysis provided unique insights into major cost savings opportunities and the risks to customer satisfaction the company faced in changing suppliers or specifications. Although the company acknowledges that the system was a challenge to set up and an even greater one to maintain, the system is considered a critical tool because the company can now base future purchasing decisions on the "real" cost of each item. By simultaneously lowering its cost base and improving customer satisfaction ratings, the company has made its sales soar.

Once a company knows how it can use procurement excellence to gain strategic advantage and has determined how it will allocate resources across its portfolio of purchases, it then must make decisions about the best ways to organize, conduct, and manage procurement. It must decide, for example, how the procurement organization will fit within the corporate organization structure. Who will have responsibility for sourcing, supplier development, and day-to-day purchasing? What processes will the company use for these activities? How will the company track results and drive performance? And what role should information technology play in procurement processes? Making and executing these decisions proactively is the bridge between procurement strategy and the other seven dimensions.

PURCHASING AND SUPPLY ORGANIZATION: ADAPTING FORM TO FIT FUNCTION

Most leading companies have made major changes in their procurement organizations in the past decade, and many are not done yet (see Figure

2–2). A common theme is movement away from strict centralized approaches to procurement, and toward a center-led approach. A centrally managed procurement unit acts as a mechanism to share best practices, ensures that the company uses consistent approaches to supplier management, and capitalizes on opportunities to leverage purchases and employ economies of scale. It also allows people with distinct expertise—for example, specialists for particular commodities or experts in supplier development—to reside organizationally wherever it makes the most sense.

Procurement leaders:

- ◆ Employ a center-led approach to direct, set policy, and coordinate procurement activities throughout the organization
- ◆ Adapt the organizational structure for procurement to fit the overall organization structure
- ◆ Use teaming approaches to embed procurement expertise into the company's key processes
- ◆ Elevate procurement organizationally to management board-level decision-making

A global chemical manufacturer is among the best examples of this center-led approach. Under pressure to push profit accountability down

FIGURE   2–2

Organizational Change is Significant in Procurement

Significant Change in the Past 10 Years...

Past 10 Years   Past 5 Years

Percentage of Participants Experiencing
Organizational Change in Procurement

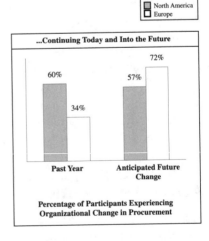

...Continuing Today and Into the Future

North America
Europe

Past Year   Anticipated Future Change

Percentage of Participants Experiencing
Organizational Change in Procurement

Source: A. T. Kearney, Inc.

to its business units without diluting the benefits of its central procurement, the company created a hybrid organization. In the hybrid, purchasing is centrally planned and coordinated yet geographically dispersed. Each geographic region, or division, focuses on the needs of its core businesses while also purchasing key commodities for other divisions. Chief purchasing officers (CPOs) in each of the most important divisions report, in turn, directly to the corporate CPO.

The hybrid structure allows business units to combine the expertise of purchasing professionals with the benefits of centralization. The business units develop common processes and procedures, coordinate purchases, standardize training, and leverage commodity expertise. The purchasing process also benefits from being close to customers' needs. Business units share best practices, and the company takes a single, consistent approach to managing its suppliers.

Similarly, the CPO of a global manufacturing company has a small team of procurement professionals that coordinates procurement activities across the company. The team works with business units to develop a strategic plan for procurement, leverage cross-unit buying opportunities, and maintain common policies and procedures, training, and performance measurements. The company leverages its purchases and instills best procurement practices while accommodating the unique needs of each business unit. Information garnered from the company's worldwide procurement staff helps the company position itself more effectively in the market and respond more quickly to changes.

With the use of teaming approaches, procurement expertise can be integrated into key processes of the business; for instance, in capital planning, production and operations, market entry and expansion, advanced technology acquisition, new product development, acquisitions, and divestitures. The main idea is to merge the best of procurement with the best of the company.

Procurement strategy and organization set the direction for a company's procurement success. Excellence, however, also requires strong capabilities in each of three core processes: sourcing, supplier development, and day-to-day purchasing.

SOURCING: GETTING BREAKTHROUGH RESULTS BY CHALLENGING THE STATUS QUO

With 50, 60, and even 70% of a company's total cost coming from external purchases of goods and services, it only makes sense for companies to maximize the value they get from this expenditure. Leaders have learned to challenge decades-old assumptions about which are the best suppliers and to overcome internal inertia that restricts their options.

Procurement leaders:

♦ Develop sourcing strategies differentiated by expenditure category and based on market dynamics

♦ Deeply involve end users in the sourcing process for knowledge and buy-in

♦ Apply a rigorous sourcing approach that examines internal needs against supply market options to find the lowest total cost solution

♦ Challenge specifications and usage patterns to ensure that each expenditure is providing the best value for the company

♦ Identify, select, and negotiate with strategically advantaged suppliers, not just the ones with the lowest price today

A "one-size-fits-all" sourcing strategy makes little sense across a portfolio of purchases. In some categories, suppliers may be plentiful and eager to compete, while in other categories, supply options may be limited. Some categories may have a larger impact on the business in terms of total expenditures or on the competitiveness of end products, while the impact of other categories may be relatively small. Leaders take into account these and other factors in tailoring a sourcing strategy for each category.

Procurement leaders also deeply involve end users in the sourcing process. A case in point is a global computer manufacturer. The company has nearly 50 cross-functional commodity councils made up of end users to manage the lion's share of its external purchases. Council members help develop and standardize rigorous methodologies, across all expenditures, that support the company's strategic goals. They share their expertise and operate across borders to make decisions about different purchase categories, and they are instrumental in formulating purchasing strategies that cement relationships with suppliers—relationships that help keep the company on the cutting edge of supplier performance. The council also convenes supplier forums to formulate improvement plans for specific areas, particularly where appropriate to leverage new technologies.

Furthermore, leaders examine internal needs against supply market options to find the lowest total cost solution. A good illustration is a consumer products leader that was grappling with two separate issues: It was trying to remove the bottleneck in its production process to sustain growth in a highly profitable product line, and it was reviewing its strategy for sourcing a key raw material.

In a traditional approach, the company would address each issue separately. For instance, the solution to the bottleneck might require a major capital investment in equipment, and the raw material solution might entail searching for lower cost sources of supply. Instead, this company looked at both issues simultaneously, determining that in-house processing of the raw material was a major contributor to the production bottleneck. The company identified suppliers to provide preprocessed materials that entered the production process after the bottleneck. By taking an innovative look at the situation, the company avoided the capital investment, and through sophisticated sourcing techniques it even lowered the cost of the materials purchased, despite the higher value-added.

Another leader slashed 30% off the cost of its printed materials in the first year by challenging specifications and usage patterns. Of these savings, 20% came from better management of its specifications—for instance, simplifying the range of options and specifying items that were easier to produce—and 10% came from improved pricing through supplier negotiations. The company brought suppliers into the process early and had a well-thought-out plan in which prices were based on total purchase volumes. Additional incentives were built into the pricing structure. For example, if specifications changed, suppliers could cut costs. Several large suppliers also agreed to staff on-site order and help desks to improve service.

Procurement leaders identify, select, and negotiate with strategically advantaged suppliers, not just suppliers with the best price today. In fact, one highly publicized breakup of a 25-year relationship between a consumer products company and its supplier went a long way in challenging longstanding, "comfortable" supplier relationships. The bond ended when the company took a fresh look at the supply market. It discovered alternative suppliers with both a technological and a cost advantage. The new supplier now provides the quality that the company wants in a product with improved features and benefits for 20% less cost.

SUPPLIER MANAGEMENT AND DEVELOPMENT: CREATING POWERFUL EXTENDED ENTERPRISES

Leading companies seek to develop strong relationships with their suppliers to increase innovation, raise quality, improve cycle times, increase customer value, and boost profitability. This frequently results from a structured program that is designed to deepen the ties between the company and its suppliers.

Procurement leaders:

- Manage supplier relations to ensure continuous improvement and two-way learning
- Integrate with suppliers to wring out excess cost and increase value from the relationship
- Develop suppliers where needed capabilities do not exist in a current supply market

While many companies have begun various programs to manage and develop their supplier relationships, one company, a global automotive manufacturer, has systematically elevated supplier management to the highest level of organizational concern, setting the standard for world-class.

This manufacturer's entire corporate organization is involved with developing and maintaining some of the deepest supply relationships in the industry. Nearly 900 people are dedicated to full-time support of suppliers. The company teaches a complete program of productivity improvement and enhancement to all levels at the supplier plants. Suppliers have been so pleased with the results—including average productivity increases of 50% and quality improvements of 66%—that they asked the manufacturer to "drill down" the process further into other parts of the suppliers' organizations as well as at their subsidiaries. On average, supplier support teams visit each supplier's installation 15 times during the year. Productivity and technical standards are reevaluated and communicated monthly. Suppliers are routinely graded and their efforts critiqued. The company maintains a hierarchy of suppliers, with those at the top involved in product development and further technological innovation.

The result of such intense supplier management? The automaker has almost no supplier turnover, it calculates that the program has returned five times its investment, quality of the end product has improved 97% in six years, and productivity has doubled.

Another facet of supplier management and development is involvement of suppliers in business operations. In fact, deep supplier integration was a key goal of a multinational food manufacturer. The company typically paid its bottle supplier (which consistently ranked at 99.9% in quality checks) for delivering product at the beginning of the filling line. Yet production complained of breakage farther down the line. Management brought the glass supplier into the plant to collaborate on ways to reduce breakage. The joint effort resulted in a change in how line employees filled the bottles and hence a 20% reduction in total cost—including the costs of glass, product wastage, and machine repair.

Supplier development is often the key to pulling together all of the elements of an organization's value chain. A leading manufacturer, for example, uses a combination of people—internal procurement people, former procurement employees, suppliers, end users, and engineers—to challenge specifications for new products, consider design alternatives, and determine the effectiveness of potential new production processes and materials. Divisions meet quarterly with suppliers and senior executives to review their quality programs and objectives and set joint goals. The discussions zero in on strategically critical product development opportunities. As a result, suppliers now participate in the design stage of new products. Even basic commodity suppliers have become involved in order to push through quality improvements, and weight and cost reductions as early in the process as possible.

A U.S. consumer products company has set the standard for developing suppliers where needed capabilities do not exist. When the company entered the European market, it found that local suppliers of a key ingredient were priced much higher than in the United States. Because the ingredient made up a substantial part of the cost of goods sold, the company, to retain growth, had to reduce the cost of this item or cut its margins. Looking at alternatives to buying the ingredient as a finished product, the company examined the supplier's raw material prices and processing costs. It decided to reduce raw material prices by developing its own supply market, purchasing raw materials directly from low-cost suppliers in Europe and thereby moving one level back in the supply chain. To address processing costs, the company worked with converters to implement U.S. manufacturing technologies that dramatically improved efficiencies and cut processing costs. Ultimately, the company was able to enter the market, meeting both its growth and profit targets.

DAY-TO-DAY PURCHASING: RUTHLESSLY ATTACKING UNNECESSARY AND WASTEFUL ACTIVITIES

As companies enter the 21st century, A. T. Kearney estimates that 90% of normal procurement transactions will be eliminated and 99% of the remaining transactions will be completely automated. Non-value-adding transactional activities will disappear, while necessary transactional activities will be transparently integrated into other processes of the business.

Procurement leaders:

♦ Automate or elimate day-to-day activities or delegate them to users or suppliers

♦ Cut waste from routine transactions

♦ Redeploy procurement people onto high-value-added activities

Leading companies began long ago to whittle down their supply bases to just a few key suppliers. Today they are going a step further, arranging for their suppliers to take on many of their day-to-day transactions. Many have initiated programs such as continuous replenishment and supplier-managed inventory. One multi-billion-dollar consumer products leader has developed such close ties with its key suppliers that it has provided them with electronic access to the corporation's sales-order system. The company's suppliers follow all sales orders placed and determine what to deliver, where, and when. No orders are placed at the supplier, and invoices are paid on all failure-free deliveries.

Leaders also employ every potential method to cut waste from their routine purchasing processes, from electronic commerce technologies to procurement cards. Gradually they have also been zeroing in on the most technologically advanced methods—on-line catalogs, Internet buying, and direct materials purchasing—to make the most significant transaction cost reductions possible. Already many companies use on-line parts catalogs to standardize the selection process and cut down the time it takes to find parts from potential suppliers. One leading company has developed a host of techniques to control costs. Today only 5% of the company's orders are processed through purchase orders; the rest are processed through its end-user acquisition system. Instead of paying $75 per transaction, the company pays just 37 cents.

Attacking and eliminating such wasteful activities frees up procurement resources. Leading companies look for ways to redeploy these resources to value-adding work, rather than simply taking the cost savings. Where skills allow, procurement people are reassigned to activities such as supply market analysis, supplier evaluation and supplier-company improvement projects. Where skills are lacking, leaders provide training and development. This shift from clerical to high-value-added activities is apparent in our research findings. In the three years prior to our study, companies cut procurement staff by 12% per $100 million purchased while increasing their procurement budgets by 25% per employee (see Figure 2–3).

PERFORMANCE MANAGEMENT: USING FORMAL APPROACHES TO DRIVE IMPROVEMENTS AND RESULTS

The best companies are moving to formal programs to track and improve the performance of the procurement process. Common goals and metrics for performance tend to provide the glue to keep the procurement organization working together. A performance management scheme often includes nontraditional measures of performance that focus on the actual contribution to profit from procurement activities.

F I G U R E   2–3

Companies are Moving Toward Smaller, More Highly Skilled Procurement Organizations

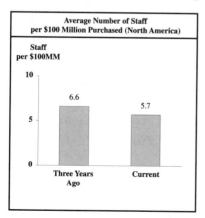

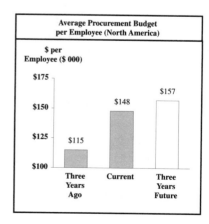

Source: A. T. Kearney, Inc.

Procurement leaders:

- Demonstrate senior management commitment and leadership to improve procurement process performance
- Implement and operate formal improvement programs with suppliers
- Carry out ongoing formal improvement processes internally

Leading companies consider senior executives' commitment and leadership essential to improving their process performance. Indeed, senior managers at a computer industry leader designate supplier measurement as a key part of their goal to rationalize the supplier base and make the system one of the world's most effective. The entire system is designed to enable comparisons with the company's chief competitors—evaluating performance relative to competition and adjusting for influences such as relative market shares. Different indices for different suppliers are compared against one another so that improvements can be quantified and then used to set new benchmarks for improvement. All divisions use the same performance measures. These measures are also used for performance incentives throughout the procurement process.

Many of the companies studied point to improvement programs with suppliers as a key to their success. These can include formal measurement systems, incentives, risk and reward sharing, and two-way feedback. A computer manufacturer, for example, put in place comprehensive metrics so the impact of procurement on its business could be precisely understood. The system helps ensure that the company is aligned with the most strategic suppliers and gets the maximum advantage from each relationship. Every month, the company's suppliers meet with the company and receive a report on their overall performance and their performance relative to their peers. The basic report includes:

1. Market information (suppliers, locations, capacities, trends, price history, and cost drivers)
2. The company's needs (volumes, current and past sourcing strategy, consuming locations, quality requirements, and storage capacities)
3. Current supplier information (pricing, lead times, service and technical support)

Reports are customized for each purchasing category according to the product and its impact on the business. A typical report, for example, takes into account the strategic nature of the product, its perceived value to the company, and, most importantly, input from the commodity team. These are also the criteria for how often the company meets with the supplier.

A European manufacturer launched incentive and risk-sharing programs to better manage quality performance of the company's suppliers. To this end, all of the company's suppliers must meet three basic requirements. First, they must take part in a failure-method-evaluation analysis to identify preventive measures against failure of its products. Next, suppliers must agree to a bonus/penalty pact, based on failure rates of deliveries. For instance, a supplier whose product has less than a specific number of rejections receives a bonus; suppliers who have more than a certain number of rejections are penalized and required to set up an action plan to improve their success rates. Finally, suppliers with high rejection rates are required to pay for repairs performed by the company. The company attributes a 5–10% improvement in product quality to these programs.

In addition to measuring supplier performance and offering incentives, which are relatively common among the leaders, some companies also offer incentives to their own procurement departments. The incentives are designed to improve user and/or customer satisfaction with the process as well as transaction efficiency. One consumer products company offers incentives to all departments involved in procurement to work as one team. Marketing and sales, research and development, production and purchasing work together to meet targets set by top management. The targets are measurable; focusing on improving the procurement process by reducing costs and adding value. Either all departments get the incentive or none do. The results have been so successful that the company has broadened the program to include its suppliers.

Many leading companies use a relatively common performance improvement tactic known as compliance management. They track and take corrective action to eliminate noncompliance with authorization procedures, use of nonstandard specifications, use of nonapproved suppliers, and unnecessary use of expedited or premium service. A leading company in the services industry, however, is reversing this traditional one-way measurement by reporting its own performance in contract compliance to its suppliers. In periodic report cards, the company gives its suppliers access to information to help them plan their businesses. Such reports help the company understand where cost-saving opportunities lie and where behavior must change so that the benefits offered by the supply relationship can be realized. It also demonstrates the company's commitment to its agreements. In fact, by providing firm commitments and delivering on its promises, the company is realizing more than 40% savings in five critical commodities, and the company's key suppliers are getting additional volume as the company acquires new businesses and introduces its formal compliance conversion program.

INFORMATION MANAGEMENT: EXPLOITING THE POWER OF INFORMATION TECHNOLOGY

One of the areas in which many companies lag is information management to support procurement activities. Most companies, for example, are not yet able to make procurement data widely accessible to other functions or to exchange it easily with major suppliers (see Figure 2–4).

F I G U R E   2–4

Information Exchange is Limited Outside the Procurement Organization

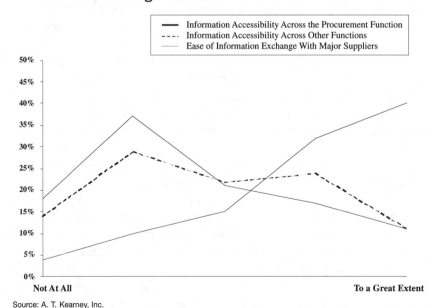

Source: A. T. Kearney, Inc.

Yet leading companies have overcome many of the barriers, and effective management of information has been their hallmark.

Procurement leaders:

- Share information extensively, internally, and with suppliers
- Employ powerful analytical tools that enable management of performance
- Exploit the emerging generation of information technology

Extensive information sharing among companies is rapidly becoming a necessity in determining a firm's competitive advantage. Internally and externally, leaders are establishing computer ties—from common platforms and protocols to common coding systems and data warehousing—that make it possible to capture previously unavailable data and make it accessible instantly.

Superior procurement performance depends on access to quality data on all external purchases, including formal and "informal" transactions. Such data can be particularly difficult to organizations. Yet the leaders are masters of information management. One consumer products company, for example, developed a process for capturing all external purchase information from all divisions and businesses through its accounts payable system. Using data warehousing, the company has created a purchasing database to compare suppliers and components, which helps it spot buying patterns and opportunities. The information is helping the company strengthen its relationships with suppliers, standardize specifications, and gain volume discounts. In much the same way, a global manufacturing firm is making information integration with suppliers a key strategy. It is already using electronic commerce technologies for 95% of purchases and is now going on-line with its largest suppliers in an effort to become fully linked worldwide. The capabilities necessary to implement such a link-up—from common commodity and supplier codes to real-time information flow—are already in place.

Many of the companies employ powerful analytical tools to manage performance in a variety of areas, including goal tracking and exception and compliance reporting. They are also identifying new opportunities through data mining. A leading chemical company, for example, has implemented a sophisticated information system to ensure that performance tracking mechanisms are in place and well understood. End users rely on these mechanisms to evaluate purchases on a daily basis, to make certain they conform (and don't conflict) with purchasing in other areas of the company. Over 90% of the company's external spending is subject to corporate purchasing methodologies communicated across the company's intranet and monitored by a standardized system of automated purchase orders.

Finally, leaders are exploiting the emerging generation of information technology. They are using the Internet to find and screen new sources of supply around the globe in minutes rather than days and are pioneers in electronic forums where buyers and sellers meet on-line to negotiate and execute transactions. They are connecting their companies with suppliers through web-based technologies such as extranets, thereby bypassing the high costs and difficulties in implementing traditional electronic data interchange. And these companies are not just performing buying functions using this new technology. They are also linking their product design and engineering processes with their suppliers and giving their suppliers electronic access to replenishment planning information.

HUMAN RESOURCE MANAGEMENT: BUILDING SUPERIOR PEOPLE

The foundation for achieving procurement excellence is a highly capable, highly motivated workforce. Leaders have erased the stereotypical view of the old-line purchasing agent by acquiring, developing, and nurturing a new breed of procurement professionals with educational backgrounds, skill sets, and broad perspectives that equal those of peers in other organizational units.

Procurement leaders:

- Recruit and attract talented people for the procurement organization from a variety of sources, both internal and external
- Invest heavily in developing procurement capabilities and skills both inside the "formal" procurement organization and throughout the network

Several of the companies surveyed recruit directly for undergraduate and graduate degree positions in procurement management. They seek superior educational credentials and work experience both in procurement and in related areas such as manufacturing and supply chain management, financial analysis, and information technology. They also recruit rising stars internally, either through formal career development and job rotation programs or by targeting specific fast-track individuals.

Part of the reason that they are able to recruit so successfully is that they have demonstrated that gaining procurement experience is a plus in their organizations. It provides challenging work, broad exposure via cross-functional teams, and enhanced career opportunities within procurement and elsewhere in the organization.

After the talent is on board, leaders in procurement continue to invest heavily in developing capabilities and the skills. Training, incentives, and career development are the norm for people both inside the formal procurement organization and throughout the team network. They make large investments in training to upgrade the skills of their procurement teams: identifying current skill requirements, determining the skills needed to compete effectively in the future, evaluating skill gaps, designing individual development plans for staff members, and investing to develop comprehensive training programs.

APPLYING LEADERSHIP PRACTICES

Companies can use lessons learned from the leaders to revolutionize their own approach to procurement. Using the following self-assessment, a company can examine its current capabilities and set a course for future action.

1. *Compare against the leadership practices in procurement using the practices and examples in this chapter as a guide.* Begin by defining the strategic role of procurement for your organization. Then determine what each leadership practice means in the context of achieving the procurement strategy. Then consider how widely and how well the practice is applied and assess whether the practice is delivering clearly measurable results. To get a broader perspective, ask people from various departments in the organization for their independent assessment. Finally, look for differences of opinion; they often point toward opportunities.

2. *Identify poor practices.* Look for evidence that the company is treating procurement as a backwater activity:
   - Limited tools available to monitor the cost of purchased goods and services
   - Fragmented activities and responsibilities within and across business units

   ♦ Buyers who focus on the risks, not the rewards, of change
   ♦ Personal relationships that influence business relationships
   ♦ Incremental buying without challenging previous decisions
   ♦ Too little investment in developing procurement skills
   ♦ Full range of supply options not understood
   ♦ Goods and services bought informally

3. *Size the opportunity.* Use the benchmarks in Table 2–1 as a broad guide. Has the company achieved leadership levels of cost reductions, inventory reductions, and new product development cycle time improvements? If not, how big is the gap? What would closing the gap mean for the business?

4. *Map a plan of attack.* Do not tackle all fronts at once. Rather, choose the areas with the most immediate need or the biggest potential payback and expand from there. A good beginning is to answer the following questions:
   ♦ Are there additional strategic moves the company needs to make in the supply market to support market entry or product development, lock up capacity at choke points in the supply chain, or outsource low-value-added activities?
   ♦ Are there major organizational barriers to improvement?
   ♦ Has the company fully exploited sourcing opportunities across its purchase portfolio?
   ♦ Are there untapped opportunities to work more closely with key suppliers?

T A B L E   2–1

Implementing Leadership Practices Drives Performance

Evaluation Categories	Three-Year Savings on Total Purchasing Expenditure Base	Five-Year Raw Material Inventory Reduction	Five-Year Reduction in New Product Development Cycle Time
Leaders	12%	41%	62%
Strong Performers	10%	33%	38%
Industry Standard	2%	< 20%	< 20%

Source: A. T. Kearney, Inc.

> ◆ Can process improvements for ordering and replenishment of low-value purchases save more than the cost of these items?
> ◆ Are information systems limiting the ability to achieve results?

CONCLUSION

The leading companies profiled in this chapter have a singular understanding of the business potential from creating supply advantage. Procurement excellence helps capture these business opportunities by enabling their executives to shape the supply market and focus resources on strategic suppliers in key commodities.

These leaders have learned to extract maximum strategic value from procurement activities by establishing objectives based on supply market opportunities, capacity issues, technology changes, and competitor activities.

As leaders enter the next millennium, they will begin to push their procurement models further. Many will extend the use of joint investments to deepen their relationships with key suppliers, and some will make supplier innovation (in terms of product and technical advances) not only a prerequisite for the relationship but the key method of determining who will be a preferred supplier.

Effective use of procurement is squarely positioned as a 21st century boardroom issue. Applied strategically, procurement is a competitive weapon to secure market advantage, increase product value, drive faster time-to-market, and enable successful market expansion.

Appendix

Leadership Practices in Procurement Research

Background and objectives: Over the past 10 years, A. T. Kearney has helped more than 200 corporations strengthen their procurement capabilities. To support our work, we have conducted ongoing research into the practices employed by leading companies. In our 1996/1997 research study, A. T. Kearney set out to investigate the degree to which leading edge companies had a strategy for procurement and what practices they used to turn that strategy into reality. Key objectives included the identification of current cross-industry leadership practices; the discovery of relative benchmarks and models for other companies; an in-depth understanding of the impact of leadership practices on performance; and the identification of significant trends in, as well as a vision for, the future of procurement.

Selecting the participants: We came up with a preliminary list of participants by first examining the records of the participants in our previous Leadership Practices in Procurement study (1992) along the dimensions of profitability and use of the leadership practices. We then compared the resulting list of names against the recognized procurement leaders identified in the literature. Finally, we questioned current clients about their first-hand knowledge in the industry, filtering the list through their insights as well as those of A. T. Kearney senior executives.

Compiling the questionnaire, beginning the research: The research was conducted in three phases:

1. Preparation, in which we formulated and tested the questionnaire and researched the participants
2. Data gathering, in which participants filled out the questionnaire and took part in comprehensive personal interviews
3. Data analysis, in which we evaluated and cross-checked input from questionnaires and the interviews to determine common themes. We then came up with a new set of leadership practices, benchmarked those against the screen of the 1992 results, and evaluated them in concert with the participants. A practice won a leadership designation if it could be applied across industries and across geographies and would result in significant value when implemented.

Participants: 77 companies participated from Europe and North America, representing the agriculture and construction equipment, automotive, high-tech, appliances process, pharmaceutical, consumer products, telecommunications, transportation, and health services industries.

Participant profile: The global average purchases ranged from US$50 million to US$25 billion, with an average of US$2.8 billion. The average procurement budget was US$20 million, and the average head-count was 160. The maximum budget was as high as US$300 million, and the maximum head-count was 2,600.

Scoring: We evaluated the participants' current practices against the leadership practices for each of the eight dimensions: Did the company recognize the practice as critical to the implementation of its procurement strategy? Had the practice been developed and operationalized? Was the practice delivering tangible benefits (e.g., cost, time, service, and quality)? Depending on the extent to which the leadership practice was in use, we then ranked the company using a scoring system from zero to three: A zero meant the company hadn't done anything with the practice; a three meant the company had implemented the practice on all categories across the organization. Finally, we calculated an overall score for each company, classifying it as a leader, strong performer, or industry standard. No one company followed every leadership practice across each of the eight dimensions. Even among the leaders, we found gaps in identifying and implementing some key practices, which means there is still plenty of room for even the best to add significant value through procurement.

CHAPTER 3

Purchasing in the New Firm of the Future

Editor
William Atkinson
Freelance Writer based in
Carterville, Illinois

INTRODUCTION

What is the job of "purchasing management" turning into in today's organizations? Procurement from a 30,000-foot airplane view was presented in the previous two chapters by major consultants discussing what they see evolving from the economic landscape and senior management emphases. The current chapter comes down to the level of landing patterns and runways to discuss what practitioners see and are doing to prepare for their purchasing activities for the future.

The report *The Future of Purchasing and Supply: A Five- and Ten-Year Forecast* cites 18 key trends that are already evolving for what can be expected in the field in the near and intermediate term.[1] Purchasing is changing from simply buying according to "rights": the right product, right price, right time, right quality, and right supplier. It is turning into building strong components and capabilities in the organization so that purchasing can position itself in the market to acquire products and services efficiently and effectively.

---

1. *The Future of Purchasing and Supply: A Five- and Ten-Year Forecast,* a joint research initiative of the Center for Advanced Purchasing Studies, Nat'l Assn. of Purchasing Management, and A. T. Kearney, Inc., May 1998.

TREND #1: ELECTRONIC COMMERCE

While electronic commerce is already well entrenched in many organizations, it will become even more prevalent in the future, accelerating at a rapid rate over the next ten years.[2]

"We see two benefits to electronic commerce," states Sam Farney, Manager of Development in Supply Management for United Technologies Corp. (Hartford, Connecticut). "First is timeliness—the ability to capture and track information in real time." The second is the value of data capture itself. "In the past, we were well into the following year before we were able to compile information on where we had spent our money the previous year," he continues. "With electronic commerce, we can capture and analyze this information immediately."

The primary tool for this growth is and will be the Internet (Internet, intranet and extranet technology). While many firms are already using the Internet for information sharing and accessing electronic catalogs, these applications only scratch the surface. Other potential uses for the future include order tracking, funds transfer, production planning and scheduling, and receipt acknowledgement.

"When I entered the procurement profession in 1961, I was told that the best way to get orders typed and processed quickly was to buy boxes of candy for the women in the typing pool," reflects Gene Richter, Vice President and Chief Procurement Officer for IBM (Somers, New York). "Since that time, we have benefited immensely from EDI, but the most significant tool I have ever seen in my 39 years in purchasing is the Internet. We are going to do in two years with the Internet what it took us 20 years to do with EDI."

Currently, everyone in IBM's procurement function is in the process of converting transactions to the Internet, which IBM calls "E-Procurement." "It is our Number One priority for 1999, and probably also for 2000," adds Richter. In fact, the company has a publicly stated goal of signing up 12,000 suppliers and $10 billion of purchases (when annualized, this amounts to $22 billion or about one-half of our total buy) by the end of 1999.

Before organizations can fully utilize the benefits of the Internet in the procurement process, however, they will need to address two important challenges:

---

2. *Ibid.*, p. 26.

1. Security. Once this is appropriately addressed, purchasing transactions will likely "explode" on the Internet.

2. Being sure organizations that utilize the Internet in line with their strategic needs, rather than just their tactical needs.

One of the most exciting benefits foreseen in the expansion of electronic commerce is the ability to more fully utilize "pull systems" (see Trend #7 below.) That is, electronic commerce will facilitate the concept of allowing activities at the end of the supply chain (e.g., sales to an end-use customer) to prompt action further down the chain (e.g., production, delivery, etc.).

TREND #2: STRATEGIC COST MANAGEMENT

Cost reduction has always been a key focus in procurement, and this goal is not expected to change. If anything, it will become even more important as organizations continue to seek ways to reduce costs so as to maintain a competitive advantage in the marketplace.[3]

What *will* change is how organizations go about cost reduction strategies. Through the 1980s, price reduction ("win–lose") was the most popular method of choice. In the 1990s, this was gradually replaced by cooperative cost reduction ("win–win") between the customer and supplier. "The emphasis really *does* need to be on cost, not on price," agrees IBM's Richter. "The goal is to get cost out of the system, which provides advantages that we can pass on to our customers." In years past, many companies beat suppliers down on price. "They either went out of business and you didn't have to deal with them anymore, or they found ways to cut costs on their own," he adds. "In either case, the customer didn't have to participate. Now, the customer does."

In the future, the cost reduction strategy will expand to include many more players in the supply chain: the company, its customer, its suppliers, the suppliers' suppliers, and so on down the chain. All of these entities will work together to identify cost reduction opportunities that provide "multi-win" rather than win–win or win–lose results.

Strategies will include:

---

3. *Ibid.*, p. 27.

- Multi-organizational process improvements that target the identification and elimination of non-value-added costs and activities
- Formula pricing approaches for engineered and specified products and services (to ensure equitable profits and ROI)
- Cost models and cost-saving sharing in noncommodity markets

The primary challenge that supply chain participants will have to face to succeed with strategic cost management is willingness to cooperate and open their doors to their trading partners.

"We are in the early stages of understanding and utilizing the full benefits of strategic cost management," states UTC's Farney. "We look at the total cost equation, identify where costs exist in the system, and then identify what it will take to remove or reduce those costs." As the company progresses in this area, Farney hopes to be able to reach second- and third-tier suppliers.

TREND #3: STRATEGIC SOURCING

The crux of strategic sourcing is close working relationships with suppliers. Strategic sourcing, in fact, will drive supply chain management initiatives. There seem to be two trends in this area:

1. Supplier assessment metrics will become more detailed and precise as purchasing and supply spends more and more time examining finer and finer levels of detail in performance.
2. The metrics that measure supplier performance will become more individualized as companies create specific metrics for individual supplier performance.[4]

That is, there is no strong trend toward reducing complexity in order to standardize and apply one metric throughout a supply chain. Complexity will be increased.

The challenge over the coming years will be to walk the fine line between designing appropriate metrics that are specific for particular chains that utilize them and at the same time not making them so complex that they are difficult to manage on the corporate level.

---

4. *Ibid.*, p. 28.

TREND #4: SUPPLY CHAIN PARTNER SELECTION AND CONTRIBUTION

This trend is a logical outgrowth of organizational efficiency. Organizations begin by improving efficiencies within their own departments, then between departments, then with suppliers, and finally throughout the entire supply chain.

- *Selection.* Supply chain partner selection will be critical in the role that supply partners play as reciprocal business functions expands. Lean supply chains will become a competitive advantage. "Supplier selection is the most important thing that we do," emphasizes IBM's Richter. "Our emphasis is not necessarily on who is the best today, but who will be the best two to four years from now. This may mean that we occasionally compromise on some needs with suppliers who are currently struggling but who we believe will be world leaders in the future. Fortunately, though, this trade-off is rare."

- *Contribution.* Supply chain participants will continue to rely on each other more and share more and more resources with each other to maximize value-added contributions and reduce duplication of resources. For example, partners will participate in joint planning, and dominant supply partners will increasingly influence projects at the design and development stages. "In terms of supply chain partner selection and contribution, the first thing we do is decide whom we should be working with and why," states UTC's Farney. "The next step is to develop relationships with those suppliers. Here, we begin to set mutual goals and track each other's commitments and performance against those commitments, the result of which is trust. It is really important to work together and prove our worth to each other." The third step is partnership and true supplier integration.

To accomplish supply partner chain goals, many organizations will create strategic purchasing competency centers with highly trained personnel who study their supply chains and identify opportunities to achieve competitive advantage via their:

- Choices of supply chain partners
- Determination of core competencies

  ♦ Influence of design, manufacturing, operations, and sourcing[5]

TREND #5: TACTICAL PURCHASING

The future holds significant changes for tactical procurement activities and how they are handled. "There will, however, always be a place for tactical purchasing," states IBM's Richter. "It will always be a part of the job."

Strategic purchasing will continue to focus on supplier evaluation, selection and development. While structural purchasing departments will not be eliminated.

  ♦ Many of the tactical purchasing activities (ordering, quoting, expediting, etc.) will be automated.
  ♦ Others will be outsourced to third parties and/or purchasing consortia. Examples include low-value, non-critical standard commodity items that can be outsourced to full-service providers. These trends are likely to result in headcount reduction in purchasing and supply departments.[6]

"With electronic commerce being used on the high-transaction side and supplier partnerships on the product side, I believe that tactical purchasing will become an operational function," states UTC's Farney. "An important step in this evolution, however, is to separate the roles. You can't ask tactical purchasing people to help you move toward strategic purchasing, because they have day-to-day buying responsibilities. They simply won't have time for strategic work. You need to assign that to other people."

TREND #6: PURCHASING STRATEGY DEVELOPMENT

It is expected that there will be increased linkages between supply chain strategies and company/business unit strategies, partly as the result of:

  ♦ Supply chain strategies becoming more focused and formalized and

---

5. *Ibid.*, p. 28.
6. *Ibid.*, p. 29.

◆ Organizations seeking more innovative sources of competitive advantage[7]

"There are tremendous upside opportunities in this area," emphasizes UTC's Farney. "We utilize a concept called 'convergent strategies.' Here, buyers look for suppliers whose strategies are leading to the same 'future point' as our organization is. For example, if we want suppliers to be able to do higher order assembly work for us, we need to identify suppliers who aspire to become higher-order assemblers."

Cost, technology, quality, and time drivers throughout the supply chain will become better identified. Two results will be that:

1. Supply chain performance will be measured more effectively.

2. Executive performance will be linked to internal and external supply chain performance.

To facilitate the increasing importance of supply chains, strategic purchasing and supply personnel will be required to develop strategic alliances even more than in the past, both with key suppliers and with key customers. Two results will be:

1. Full pull systems will be deployed, with reduced cycle times featuring models where payments to suppliers are more closely linked to actual work performed or usage.

2. Insourcing/outsourcing decisions will be regularly made by a cross-functional executive group as part of the strategic sourcing process.

TREND #7: DEMAND-PULL PURCHASING

Demand-pull purchasing was seen as a challenge that might not be able to be met prior to the widespread usage of the Internet. "The Internet is becoming a fabulous tool to achieve demand-pull purchasing," agrees IBM's Richter. "It is our belief that if organizations are not working toward demand-pull these days, they are digging their own graves."

By utilizing Internet technology, demand-pull systems will allow purchasing and supply professionals to access information from suppliers and from customers and to track performance of business units.

---

7. *Ibid.*, p. 30.

The Internet will be the primary tool for combining supply chain partner databases that will be accessible by the partners, creating a seamless link.

"Demand-pull will be very automated and transaction-oriented," adds UTC's Farney. "The key to success is identifying the suppliers who have this kind of flexibility. We are currently involved in the concept, and one of my major responsibilities is developing supplier capabilities."

Many organizations already involved with demand-pull purchasing and supply are operating on a part-number-by-part-number basis around the world.[8]

While the Internet will facilitate demand-pull purchasing, the challenge will be getting all of the supply chain partners' systems to work together. UTC's Farney notes that many large OEMs are involved in demand-pull with some of their first-tier suppliers. "However, there are challenges getting second and third tier suppliers involved," he adds. "Getting their involvement may actually make or break the success of the whole process. Organizations that are responsive to demand-pull requirements will survive. Those that do not may fall by the wayside."

TREND #8: RELATIONSHIP MANAGEMENT

There will be an increasing focus on relationship management with supplier chain partners (suppliers and customers), driven by increasing global competitiveness, limited resources, and the need for a global reach while maintaining flexibility. This activity will be managed at the senior level of organizations, which strive to leverage knowledge from the supply chain partners.[9]

"Procurement people will need to learn to manage relationships, rather than transactions," suggests UTC's Farney. "The transactions will take care of themselves."

"Relationship management is a critical component of strategic sourcing," adds IBM's Richter. "We work hard to build relationships with our suppliers, and we measure ourselves in many ways to make sure that we have good supplier relationships."

Many organizations may actually combine relationship management of suppliers and customers into a single office. This group will

---

8. *Ibid.*, p. 30.
9. *Ibid.*, p. 31.

develop strategy, coordinate internal activities and processes, and further establish multiple-enterprise communication methods. Success here will depend on participants building trust, improving communication, and fostering interdependence.

Throughout all of this, strategic purchasing and tactical purchasing functions will remain intact. The strategic purchasing group will continue to be integral, although much of the tactical purchasing activity may be outsourced.

TREND #9: PERFORMANCE MEASUREMENT

In the future, supply chains will operate with a common set of performance measures that are directly tied to individual companies' strategic and business unit performance and measures.[10] However:

- Some type of common performance metrics will need to be established in particular for supply chains in specific industries.
- As supply chains are developed, new benchmarks will need to be developed and then tied to specific corporate goals.
- The core measures will be augmented by measures that are specific to buyer–supplier situations.

Cost will remain the most important aspect, given that costs are carried throughout the supply chain. Performance metrics other than cost, however, will remain difficult to define.

"We measure on-time delivery performance and quality in a number of ways, but the most important component is price against the market. For example, if the market prices decrease 30% on a commodity, we expect our suppliers to come down more. If market prices increase 20%, we expect our suppliers to increase less. We use this measure to assess supplier performance and our own performance," states IBM's Richter.

"We see a shift taking place in performance measurement," adds UTC's Farney. "Rather than measuring individual suppliers or our own performance, we see a future where organizations will measure the performance of the total supply chain, then look for areas of opportunity to improve the chain in ways that will benefit all of the players."

---

10. *Ibid.*, p. 32.

TREND #10: PROCESS UNCOUPLING

Organizations will continue to evaluate their insourcing and outsourcing decisions via a systematic process. The assessments will require determinations of core competencies in all states of:

- Technology development
- Product/process/service design and development
- Manufacturing/operations, logistics, and service

Organizations will likely elect to outsource (uncouple) when:

- It is demonstrated that competing firms possess superior capabilities that leave no chance of catching up, and/or
- Competitors are achieving superior performance.[11]

"We see this as a slower trend, because a lot of companies tend to be slow to be self-critical," suggests UTC's Farney. "That is, it can be difficult for an organization to discover and admit that its suppliers can do some things better than it can."

In some cases, process uncoupling may require that organizations increase the number of participants in their supply chains.

"We outsource everything that is not a core competency," states IBM's Richter. "Each year, a little bit more goes out the door." Ten years ago, about 27% of IBM's total revenue was spent with outside suppliers. Today, it is close to 54%.

TREND #11: GLOBAL SUPPLIER DEVELOPMENT

As organizations increase the amount of business they conduct on a global level, they will recruit suppliers to expand with them. The development of world-class suppliers in emerging markets is already happening and will intensify in the future. The Internet will facilitate much of this growth.[12]

"First, we identify the part family which we want to source," states UTC's Farney. Then, we identify the best place in the world to acquire it. These steps are very much tied to our overall strategy."

---

11. *Ibid.*, p. 32.
12. *Ibid.*, p. 33.

"Global supplier development is routine at IBM," adds Richter. "We have a group called the Global Procurement Support Group, which identifies and proposes sources in the farthest reaches of the world market." These include India and Eastern Europe for software development and Israel and the Far East for electro-mechanical suppliers.

Firms will continue to source goods and services from existing suppliers in foreign countries, but the new trend is to develop sources in foreign countries where they did not exist before. Procurement organizations will accomplish this by asking their current world-class suppliers to grow with them—to penetrate existing markets or provide resources in those markets where they previously did not exist by developing manufacturing capabilities in foreign markets.

TREND #12: THIRD-PARTY PURCHASING

Organizations will continue the trend toward purchasing more and more non-tactical products and services via:

- Master contracts,
- Consortia, and/or
- Third-party companies.

The latter two can often offer more leverage and buying expertise than the organizations doing the outsourcing. All three strategies can help organizations get out from under the mundane administrative duties and costs associated with these kinds of purchases.[13]

"We don't see the wholesale turning over of purchasing to third parties," observes UTC's Farney. "Most of what is turned over will be tactical, non-strategic items, where the transaction count is high, and where what you really need is a record of what's taking place, not necessarily tight controls over each transaction." The benefit of third-party involvement, according to Farney, is the opportunity to achieve the highest transaction efficiency possible.

While IBM's Richter also sees an evolution toward some third-party purchasing, he is a bit more cautious about the potential benefits. "I think it would be folly for giant companies to participate in a consortium," he

---

13. *Ibid.*, p. 33.

states. "Doing so would only be lending your buying leverage and expertise to companies that don't have it. You would be trying to get suppliers to sell to everyone at the same price they sell to you, which would harm your competitive advantage."

He also questions the wisdom of outsourcing production procurement. "This involves a lot of forward design work, and you don't want to be revealing your design secrets to a third party that could share them with other companies," he cautions.

The place where third-party procurement has the best opportunity, he believes, is in non-production procurement. "This can include office equipment, travel, temporary services, MRO supplies, and so on," he states.

Regardless of how much an organization becomes involved in third-party purchasing, however, purchasing and supply departments will still continue to oversee and manage these activities, primarily because of the high dollar volumes involved, which need to be verified and tracked.

Again, as is true of a number of other trends, the Internet will be a primary facilitating tool. Secured Internet networks will electronically handle order-placing, releasing, receiving, and accounting. Users will select products, materials, and services directly from on-line databases maintained by suppliers or consortia. Account settling will be handled automatically.

TREND #13: VIRTUAL SUPPLY CHAIN

In the future, companies will begin to create "virtual legal organizations" that focus on specific customers and markets. These companies will join together and commit resources to exploit these temporal opportunities. These short-term alliances will exist without the legal entanglements of mergers or long-term contracts.[14]

There is no reason to believe that this will be a strong and immediate trend, though. Other trends are more pressing and obvious. However, organizations will begin to see benefit in the concept as:

• Mergers become increasingly more difficult
• Corporate resources are stretched thinner as organizations continue to invest in opportunities in developing global economies

14. *Ibid.*, p. 34.

UTC's Farney is one who sees the virtual supply chain as representing a trend that will evolve slowly, but will still come about. "The more we understand the chain and what the process looks like, the more we will see opportunities for the virtual supply chain," he explains. "The first step, however, is to simplify the chain and remove waste and redundancy."

Prior to beginning work together on a virtual supply chain, the participants will establish risk sharing, reward appointment, resource contribution, and the basis for ending the relationships.

Groupings of "systems suppliers" will join together to coordinate the completion of the final product/service bundle under a joint risk/ reward sharing agreement. Resources and assets will be contributed jointly under the direction of a supply chain captain and a coordinating team.

TREND #14: SOURCE DEVELOPMENT

A few observers believe that competition among suppliers is the ideal approach. Implicit in this belief is the idea that it may be counterproductive to expend time, effort, and resources on developing the capabilities and responsiveness of existing suppliers.

Others believe that supplier development is critical to supply chain development and long-term strategic goals. They believe that it makes more sense to develop existing key suppliers than to continue to seek new suppliers.[15] Those in this category envision buying and supplying firms joining together not only in joint ventures, but in other noncontractual arrangements to develop needed resources.

"Supplier development is a fundamental and absolute responsibility of a good procurement department," emphasizes IBM's Richter. "We do this all over the world." The assistance occurs at many levels. With well-developed suppliers, IBM explains what its needs will be two to four years down the road and then offers research and other high-level assistance to the suppliers. With less-developed suppliers, it may begin by simply emphasizing the importance of basic quality and helping them achieve this.

"We view source development as offering two benefits," states UTC's Farney. The first is a strategic sourcing tool. "We expect some suppliers to excel while others will not. As we work with them, we will

---

15. *Ibid.*, p. 34.

see how they begin to differentiate themselves and will focus more business with those who excel." The other benefit is the opportunity to remove cost from the supply chain.

TREND #15: COMPETITIVE BIDDING/NEGOTIATIONS

Despite the trend toward supply chain relationships, competitive bidding will continue to hold a place in procurement practices, since it is instrumental in ascertaining market prices. In some sectors, such as government, competitive bidding will continue to be the dominant source of interaction between buyer and supplier.[16]

"There will always be a role for competitive bidding," states IBM's Richter. "That is, in spite of the trend toward supplier relationships, people tend to perform better when there is the threat of competition lurking out there." However, IBM's strategy is not to shift suppliers quickly and cavalierly. "We may add or reduce the amount of business we do with suppliers by certain percentage points, but few suppliers would be at risk of losing all of our business."

The competitive nature of bidding keeps the company fresh. "For example, we may get three bids in at four dollars and one at two dollars," continues Richter. "We may find that the two-dollar supplier doesn't know what he's doing, but we may also find that he has an innovative way of making the part that no one else has thought of."

What may be a more significant change in competitive bidding and negotiating is in who conducts the bidding negotiations processes. Given the growing trend toward outsourcing tactical procurement buys (to consortia and third parties), professional negotiators may become more prevalent and instrumental in conducting negotiations instead of the purchasing departments.

TREND #16: STRATEGIC SUPPLIER ALLIANCES

The success of many organizations will depend on their ability to clearly establish external resources and competency needs and develop two-way

---

16. *Ibid.*, p. 35.

business and technical exchanges that benefit both parties. "We focus on how to help each other and identify core competencies," states UTC's Farney.

Organizations will need to establish strategic supplier alliances in order to:

- Maximize leverage and synergy of resources,
- Meet their continuing needs for flexibility and asset management
- Meet the challenges of global competition and higher performance expectations[17]

Strategic alliances may take the form of co-locating employees at buyer or supplier locations, working together on new product development, sharing confidential information, and/or engaging in concurrent engineering.

The overriding goal is for both organizations to work together for continual improvements designed to benefit both organizations. This will require unprecedented two-way communication that allows the participants significant access to each other's product and process technologies. "The Internet will be a big help in communications," states IBM's Richter. "However, there will still be a need for a lot of face-to-face communication, visiting each other and getting to know each other personally."

TREND #17: NEGOTIATION STRATEGY

While the purpose and the approach may continue to change, negotiations will still be a critical element of success in supplier–customer relationships.

The purpose will continue to evolve from win–lose to win–win. "We really don't see this as a wave of the future," observes IBM's Richter. "Most of us have figured this out ten to fifteen years ago."

What will change is the approach—shifting from a "heated, emotional debate" to looking objectively at cost saving potentials. Negotiations will therefore become more complex as more factual information is made available and introduced into the process.[18] "We expect that one

---

17. *Ibid.*, p. 35.
18. *Ibid.*, p. 35.

role of purchasing will be to bring senior executives from the two companies together, and they will provide leadership to the joint effort," adds UTC's Farney.

Again, the ultimate result will be establishing mutual-win situations that result in overall lower total cost for both parties.

TREND #18: COMPLEXITY MANAGEMENT

In sum, procurement professionals will have three challenges:

1. Managing the new tools and processes (e.g., supply chain management, Internet technology, strategic alliances)
2. Keeping up with change as it occurs and identifying its implications and opportunities
3. Dealing with all of the complexity that the first two challenges bring to bear

That is, there are really three issues of complexity: the complexity of the new tools and processes, the complexity of change itself, and the complexity of managing the interactions between the tools/processes and change.[19]

Dominant companies in supply chains (e.g., the largest and most instrumental suppliers and customers) will be required to manage the complexity issues and provide leadership to the other members of the supply chain. "We see increased needs for both technical skills and business skills in supply management," reports UTC's Farney. "For example, procurement professionals will need to understand business issues in a substantive way." These will include analytical skills, financial drivers, what affects performance of an organization, new product development, marketing, engineering, technology, manufacturing, recognition of where costs are and where opportunities exist to remove costs, knowledge of how to achieve consistent quality and customer satisfaction. "The complexity is in bringing all of these together," he states.

However, one of the best ways to succeed with complexity management is to seek the assistance of supply chain partners and even people in your own organization—asking for relevant resources.

"The issue of complexity never seems to get any easier," explains IBM's Richter. While he sees the Internet as offering a lot of assistance

---

19. *Ibid.*, p. 36.

in this area, he also believes procurement professionals need to solicit and utilize the services of colleagues in other departments. These include engineering to help evaluate suppliers' current technologies and long-term technology roadmaps; quality for incoming quality, defects, warranty concerns, etc.; logistics for the most efficient modes of transportation; and finance for the best piece prices and best long-term deals.

"The one thing we want to make sure of is that our buyers utilize these resources," he emphasizes. "We don't want them to think that they know it all themselves and can do it all themselves."

This, in fact, may best sum up the theme of all the 18 trends: The future of purchasing resides in interdepartmental and interorganizational cooperation. The days of isolation simply do not exist anymore.

CONCLUSIONS

The 18 trends presented in this chapter are expanded upon throughout the book. They do not change what purchasing's key role is: price management, assurance of supply, and optimal quality acquisition of products and services. What does change is how individual buyers, purchasing and supply managers, and organizations go about attaining these goals today. In the past, it started with receiving a requisition or working off an annual plan. Today it requires building an infrastructure of systems, capabilities, and relationships in order to accomplish these ends efffectively.

The Strategic Approaches of Purchasing and Supply

This section of the book presents many of the new concepts being applied in the field. It begins with an overview of supply strategy development in the organization. The "Knowledge of Supply Markets" chapter presents insights into what is possible in the new realm of capturing marketplace intelligence for both long- and short-term advantage. "Purchasing as Relationship Management" is reflective of how purchasing can obtain advantage with suppliers through new dimensions of relationships as well as the need to focus upon internal linkages in ways that are stronger than ever before.

Supply chain management presents insights into how organizations are building and managing component linkages to seek cost and service advantage. This is followed by "Strategic Alliances and Partnerships" as a means of developing benefits from closer relationships with suppliers.

Global supply management is a requisite for the purchasing and supply professional and their organization today. The chapter, "Global Procurement Synergies", takes a unique approach to how to integrate the buying power advantage of a large organization that spans many countries. This topic is on a higher plane than the traditional nuts and bolts of overseas buying and importing. In a book of this size, justice cannot be done to that subject, which is adequately covered in many other books and sources in the field.

Organizations are outsourcing at rates never before seen in the economy. The chapter devoted to that subject explores where, when, and how this is best done. It also presents the reverse mode of bringing activities back into the organization—insourcing.

Lastly, these chapters set the stage for how the organization then goes to market to select the most appropriate supplier. This includes the range of how to identify suppliers and how to evaluate them for potential and eventual use.

Development of Supply Strategies

Editor
Joseph R. Carter, D.B.A., C.P.M.
NAPM Professor at Arizona State University and
Chair of the Supply Chain Management Department

INTRODUCTION

Competitive firms entering the 21st century cannot afford a purchasing process that treats all items, products, commodities, and services in the same way. The traditional purchasing paradigm is changing, and that bodes well for the profession and the economy. Blind reliance on numerical benchmarks such as purchase price variance and landed cost threatens to keep firms from acquiring distinctive competitive advantage in today's supply constrained marketplace. As more and more firms are discovering, positioning the purchasing process into a segmenting of different supply strategies, supply tactics, and supply management approaches is the only way to effectively link supply strategies with overall firm goals, product marketing strategies, and competitive efforts. This differentiation process is often referred to as "supply segmentation."

The supply segmentation technique provides a mechanism for discriminating between the various items and services that are purchased by a firm with the goal of developing specific strategies to meet the needs of the organization with respect to separate and logical categories of items. Supply segmentation is an excellent marketing tool for convincing senior management of the critical role that purchasing can and does play in the support of corporate level strategies and firm profitability.

pter will begin with a discussion of "ABC" analysis as ap-
_____ purchase of goods and services and its limitations. A dis-
cussion of the supply segmentation approach to supply strategy development will follow, including development of a spend analysis and
categorization of purchases. The chapter will end with a discussion of
supply management goals and the supply management strategy development process.

ABC ANALYSIS

A variety of segmenting systems is available to help in purchasing planning and item control systems. A popular classification system is based
on the dollar volume of purchases per item. Such a scheme is often referred to as "ABC" or "Pareto" analysis. ABC or Pareto analysis shows
that a small percentage of the items purchased can be linked to a large
percentage of the dollars spent by the firm. ABC analysis then classifies
these purchased items/services in order of importance as either "A,"
"B," or "C" items. It has been empirically demonstrated that ABC or
Pareto analysis holds in a wide range of situations.

As an example, in purchasing, ABC analysis usually holds for items
purchased, number of suppliers, inventories, and other measures. ABC
analysis is often referred to as the 80–20 rule, where approximately 20%
of the items/services purchased account for about 80% of the purchasing
dollars spent. An example of ABC analysis that results in three classifications of items, A, B, and C, is presented in Table 4–1.

Naturally, these percentages can vary from organization to organization. Some companies even use more than three classification levels.
Nonetheless, the concept of categorizing purchases is a very powerful

T A B L E   4–1

Example of ABC Analysis

Classification	Percent of Total Items Purchased	Percent of Total Purchase Dollars
A Items	10–20	70–80
B Items	30–50	10–20
C Items	40–70	10–20

and useful purchasing concept. It allows a prioritization of supply strategies and efforts in the areas of potentially highest returns. For example, a manufacturer, XYZ Company, with total annual purchases of $254,725,000 had the breakdown provided in Table 4–2.

The data presented in Table 4–2 can be categorized and prioritized as demonstrated in Table 4–3. A similar analysis of the firm's suppliers or inventories would be expected to show a similarly high portion of total value from a relatively small number of suppliers or items.

There are several ways in which a purchasing manager can use such a categorization scheme. For example, it is only sensible to expend

T A B L E   4–2

XYZ Company Purchases

Item Dollars	Annual Usage in Units	Unit Cost	Purchase Dollars (000)	Percentage of Tot. Purchase
1	5,000	$ 1.50	$ 7,500	2.9
2	1,500	8.00	12,000	4.7
3	10,000	10.50	105,000	41.2
4	6,000	2.00	12,000	4.7
5	7,500	0.50	3,750	1.5
6	6,000	13.60	81,600	32.0
7	5,000	0.75	3,750	1.5
8	4,500	1.25	5,625	2.2
9	7,000	2.50	17,500	6.9
10	3,000	2.00	6,000	2.4
			$254,725	100

T A B L E   4–3

XYZ Company ABC Segmentation

Class	Item Numbers	Percentage of Total Items	Percentage of Purchases Total Dollars
A	3, 6	20	73.2
B	2, 4, 9	30	16.3
C	1, 5, 7, 8, 10	50	10.5

more managerial resources and efforts on A and B items than on C items, as presented graphically in Figure 4–1.

LIMITATIONS OF ABC ANALYSIS

ABC analysis provides a tool for identifying those items that will make the largest impact on the firm's overall inventory cost performance when improved inventory control procedures are implemented. A perpetual inventory system, improvements in forecasting procedures, and a careful analysis of the order quantity and timing decisions for A items will provide a larger improvement in inventory cost performance than will similar efforts on the B and C items. But the ABC analysis primarily focuses on aspects of cost only. Therefore, ABC analysis is only a first step in improving inventory and thereby supply management performance.

ABC analysis helps focus management attentions on only one aspect of what is really important, that is, inventory costs. Unfortunately, to classify items into A, B, and C categories based on just one criterion

F I G U R E 4–1

XYZ Company ABC Analysis Resource Allocation

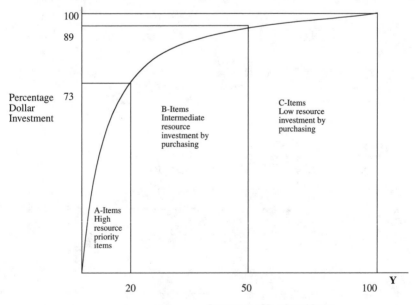

Percentage of Purchased Items

is clearly to overlook other important criteria. Also, the guidance provided by ABC analysis relates only to the relative direct financial importance of certain items/services and does not extend to developing supply management tactics and strategies in dealing with complex markets and competitive suppliers.

It is because of these limitations and others that another technique, called "supply segmentation," was developed. This tool has won wide acceptance and application in the development and implementation of supply strategies.

THE SPEND ANALYSIS

To begin constructing a supply segmentation portfolio, the firm must develop a "spend" analysis of all the goods and services that are purchased by the firm. Total purchases must be aggregated across divisions and/or strategic business units (SBUs) both for individual items/services and by individual suppliers. The spend analysis can be a laborious and tedious undertaking, but it is critical nonetheless. There are outside suppliers, such as Dun & Bradstreet, that will assist a firm in developing the spend analysis.

The concluding step is to graph each of these stock-keeping units (SKUs) and service categories on a chart in which the horizontal (X) axis represents the relative cost/value of the item or service and the vertical (Y) axis represents supply market risk or exposure, as pictured in Figure 4–2.

F I G U R E   4–2

Spend Analysis Matrix

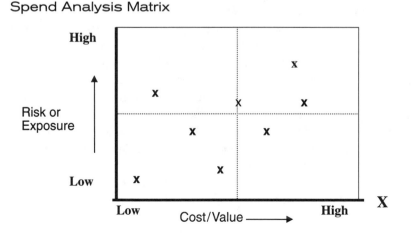

In many cases, individual items and/or services can be grouped into commodity categories and then plotted, where such a grouping is relevant.

The cost/value axis represents the importance of the item, service, or commodity in terms of its annual dollar spend within the firm. Cost/value is usually measured as the total annual dollar amount purchased for each item/service. For example, a million items at $20 each totals to a $20 million annual spend and is plotted as such. The total annual purchase amount can be adjusted higher or lower if there are any factors of cost that are not captured by the spend analysis; for example, import duties and some transportation and warehouse costs.

Each firm must define the risk/exposure axis according to its own situation and needs. For most it will be a mixture of technological factors, supply availability, technical requirements, and environmental issues.

The initial spend analysis can be the subject of heated debate, as individual managers from various business units may have different views as to the relative importance and exposure of some items, commodities, or services.

For example, one business unit could view application-specific integrated circuits (ASICS) as a commodity purchase, while another business unit could view ASICS as a critical technology. In such cases, it may be wise to split the item's purchases into two distinct commodity groups.

Supply Segmentation Analysis

With the initial spend analysis complete, the next step is to segment the purchases by dividing the chart into four or more categories, as depicted in Figure 4–3. Each category has been assigned a name that describes the supply imperative of the items/services classified within it.

The items/services represented in quadrant I, low risk/exposure and low cost/value, are referred to as *tactical*. These are the routine items, commodities, or services that do not enter into the direct value-added price of the finished products of the firm. Their cost/value is low and the potential harm through disruption to the firm due to supply availability issues is low. These are commonly standardized items in plentiful supply from a wide number of suppliers. Many MRO (maintenance, repair, and operating) items/services, office supplies, and administrative items are examples of tactical items/services.

The items/services categorized in quadrant II, low risk/exposure and high relative cost/value, are referred to as *leverage*. These items/

F I G U R E   4–3

Supply Segmentation Matrix

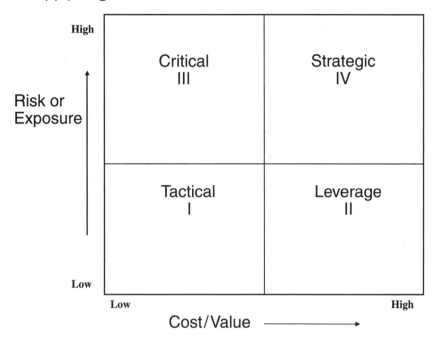

services are true generic, basic purchases that represent high dollar expenditures but a low risk to the firm. Corrugated packaging, basic production goods, fasteners, and some coatings are examples of items that
would fall into this quadrant of items/services. Because there can be little
difference between competing brands of these items/services, suppliers
often attempt to differentiate themselves to the purchaser through ser-
vice-related attributes.

The items/services categorized in quadrant III, high risk/exposure
and low cost/value, are referred to as *critical*. These are low relative cost/
value items/services that provide a potential market difficulty and resulting high risk/exposure to the firm. Examples may be spare parts that
are available from a very few suppliers with long lead times or backlogs,
critical services such as specialty heat treatment, and specialty chemicals.
The risk/exposure to the firm is high, yet the final customer either does
not care for the special purchase nature of the item/service or is not
aware of it.

The items/services categorized in quadrant IV, high risk/exposure and high cost/value, are referred to as *strategic*. Strategic items and services provide a firm's products with competitive or distinctive advantage in the marketplace. Such items provide the firm with both a high risk/exposure and high relative cost/value environment. Examples of these items may be any unique custom-designed item, a component that permits a lower total cost, higher reliability, a more environmentally friendly operation for the final customer, or a unique advertising campaign tied to the final product. The value of these items/services is measured in terms of customer satisfaction and value-added for them, and not purchase price.

Segmenting purchased items and services in this way makes it easier to delineate the required strategies and tactics to apply in various supply markets and environments. Each of these quadrants has a uniquely different competitive and operating impact upon the firm. In contrast to ABC analysis, which focuses upon dollar volume and high-unit-cost items, the supply segmentation approach captures the interaction between supply market risk or exposure and the cost/value impact to the firm. Using the supply segmentation approach, purchasing can see clearly how various items/services actually impact the competitiveness and profitability of the firm.

Supply Management Targets

The items/services segmented into the four quadrants have considerably different supply market characteristics. Not surprisingly, the purchasing goals associated with these items/services will be quite different, as shown in Figure 4–4.

The greatest number of parts and services will end up being classified as *tactical*. These items, being of low cost/value and having low risk/exposure, are those on which resources expended should be minimized. The supply management target is to dramatically increase the efficiency of the purchasing process, thereby significantly reducing transaction costs.

Individual item or service purchase price is of little importance in this category. A large improvement in the purchase cost of the *tactical* items will result in a relatively small saving in total spend, whereas a small improvement in the total purchase cost of the high cost/value items will result in a larger proportional savings.

F I G U R E   4–4

Supply Segmentation Purchasing Goals

	Critical	Strategic
High	REDUCE RISK	SUPPLIER PARTNERS
Risk or Exposure	Tactical	Leverage
Low	STREAMLINE PROCESS	MAXIMIZE LEVERAGE
	Low	High

Cost/Value ⟶

Critical items/services, while of low value, are nonetheless very important to the effective operation of the firm. Here the major goal will be to reduce the risk or exposure to the firm of any supply disruptions, even at a premium price. In general, the business is relatively insensitive to the price of these items. Nevertheless, these items should be kept under frequent review to ensure that they do not become a major cost item and thus move into quadrant IV. Also, every effort should be made to find ways of moving these items/services down into quadrant I, that is, reclassifying them as tactical. Purchasing managers should constantly assess the supply market, watching out for changes in the supply base and the global economy.

Leverage items/services are of high cost/value but have no major complications that would increase the resulting level of risk or exposure. Frequently there will be an acceptable number of competitive suppliers. It is in this area that buyers can seek out opportunities to reduce total landed cost and improve the profit contribution of these items/services. With a secure supply market, purchasing managers can afford to leverage their buy with a single source, that is, to reasonably increase the level of risk in order to gain volume efficiencies.

The situation in quadrant IV, *strategic*, is very different. These items/services are of high cost/value, and every effort must made to prevent any potential negative financial impact upon the firm. But the use of volume leveraging as a weapon may not be wise. These items/services also exhibit a high level of supply market risk or exposure for the firm, which suggests that volume leveraging in a single source of supply might not be logical. These items/services lend themselves to a longer-term planning horizon and "partnering" mentality. These items/services should be managed for their value-adding impact on the firm's products and market share.

PRICE VERSUS COST IN THE SEGMENTATION ARENA

Price is only a small part of the total acquisition cost of an item/service. This fact vividly applies to the supply segmentation approach to supply strategy development. The following paragraphs will address this concept in more detail.

Leverage items/services are frequently benchmarked on the basis of price, but today price should include several other aspects of costs. For example, freight costs, payment terms, delivery expenses, warehouse charges, and inventory carrying costs are frequently used as a direct addition to the supplier's quoted price. Freight costs are being factored into the purchase cost, and many suppliers are asked to quote a "landed cost," which adds most movement and inbound storage costs to the purchase price. Payment terms, including the currency of payment, can significantly impact cash flow, cost-of-capital, and product cost integrity. Inventory costs, arising from lot sizing and timing of purchase decisions, are increasingly being added into the overall cost equation for these types of items and services.

Tactical items/services are significantly impacted by the transactional nature of the buying process. In addition to the supplier's quoted price, the cost of managing the acquisition process is of concern. For example, in many firms the cost of managing and generating a purchase order can exceed $200 per transaction. Given the low dollar volumes purchased in this category, the acquisition cost can exceed the supplier's quoted price per order. It is imperative that the acquisition cost of tactical items/services be measured accurately and compared to the purchase price of the commodity.

The segmentation costs of *critical* items/services are made up of the cost of plant or equipment downtime and utilization costs when the critical items/services are unavailable. Should a custom-designed item/service be purchased in this category? In some cases, the benefit of using a custom-designed item/service diminishes in comparison to the risk or exposure of not having that critical item/service available when needed.

The costs of *strategic* items/services are often measured as part of customer value-added or in terms of their impact on ultimate customer service and satisfaction. These items/services often provide the key decision point that determines why the customer purchases from your firm instead of a competitor. Key metrics applied to these items/services are maintainability and reliability costs or even avoidance costs.

THE SUPPLY STRATEGY DEVELOPMENT PROCESS

The supply segmentation approach highlights the need for different supply strategies for each quadrant of the matrix. Figures 4–5 and 4–6 present examples of certain strategic approaches to managing the cost of items/services purchased based in Figure 4–5 on the technical complexity and value of the item purchased and in Figure 4–6 based on the level of risk/exposure and value of the items/services purchased.

The supply strategies applied to *tactical* items/services should involve streamlining the acquisition process. For example, this can be measured in terms of the buyers' time expended in the entire order process cycle. These are low-value activities that contribute very little to the strategic directions of the firm. The acquisition process should be minimized, eliminated, or outsourced. Many integrated supplier relationships, such as electronic data interchange, supplier bar coding, electronic funds transfer, and supplier-managed inventory systems, are available. A key purchasing goal is to reduce the time spent by personnel in the firm on the acquisition, delivery, stock-keeping, and payment of these items/services.

FIGURE   4–5

Material Cost-Reduction Strategies Based on Level of
Technical Complexity and Value

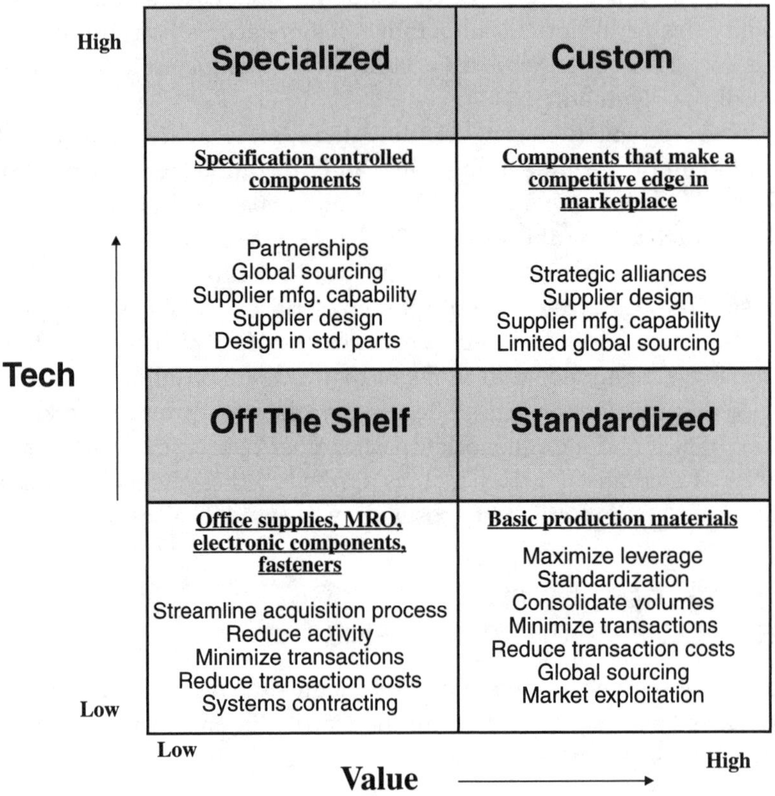

	High	**Specialized**	**Custom**
		Specification controlled components	Components that make a competitive edge in marketplace
Tech		Partnerships Global sourcing Supplier mfg. capability Supplier design Design in std. parts	Strategic alliances Supplier design Supplier mfg. capability Limited global sourcing
		Off The Shelf	**Standardized**
		Office supplies, MRO, electronic components, fasteners	Basic production materials Maximize leverage Standardization Consolidate volumes Minimize transactions Reduce transaction costs Global sourcing Market exploitation
	Low	Streamline acquisition process Reduce activity Minimize transactions Reduce transaction costs Systems contracting	

Low   **Value** ⟶ High

The supply strategies applied to *leverage* items/services are mainly traditional. The appropriate supply strategies within the *leverage* quadrant should focus upon short-term contracts to enable the buyer to constantly seek out and change to lower-cost sources. Buyers should pursue a proactive supply strategy to find new suppliers and/or substitute products globally. Buyers should be driven by the need to make a significant contribution to corporate profit by reducing costs in this high-volume quadrant.

Overall, the supply management emphasis placed on *leverage* items/services will be to increase profit margin, that is, to use competitive purchasing practices to increase corporate profitability. As a result,

F I G U R E   4–6

Material Cost Reduction Strategies Based on Level of
Risk and Value

High	**Critical**	**Strategic**
	Very unique and "over specified" MRO items and capital equipment	Components that make a competitive edge in marketplace
Risk or Exposure	Reduce or eliminate	Strategic alliances Partnerships Limited global sourcing Supplier development
	Tactical	**Leverage**
	Office supplies, MRO, Administrative	Basic production materials, Packaging
Low	Streamline acquisition process Reduce activity Minimize transactions Supplier managed inventory	Maximize leverage Standardization Consolidate volumes Reduce transaction costs Global sourcing Active sourcing/mkt knowledge
	Low	High

Value ⟶

the firm should expect to see decreases in unit costs, increased market security, and detailed supplier knowledge. Purchasing should expect to see an increase in supply market knowledge and the number of orders, better timing and sensitivity of order placement, and possible supplier change. The supply base will range from local to national to global sources of supply.

Critical items and services should be analyzed for elimination. Early supplier design involvement, where needed, early purchasing design involvement, and close communication with engineering and users during the design phase for the product or service can help reduce the custom-designed nature of these items and services before they are "locked in." For existing items/services, value analysis and value engineering techniques can be effectively used to eliminate, or at least reduce, the need for these items/services. The supply strategy is to make changes that will "shift" these items/services to either tactical (lower risk/exposure) or leverage (lower risk/exposure and increase value) or turn them into strategic items/services (increase value) that have market impact or lend competitive advantage (see Figure 4–7).

Items and services in the *strategic* quadrant require the highest level of purchasing competence. In some instances, long-term contracts may be very suitable, but in other circumstances, medium-term contract lengths are preferred. Purchasing teams need to obtain detailed information on individual suppliers and work to develop them for mutual advantage. It is in this quadrant that the "supplier strategic alliance" concept can most effectively be implemented. The total cost of acquisition (TCA) of each item/service must be closely monitored and controlled using competitive benchmarking techniques and price and cost auditing.

FIGURE 4–7

Supply Segmentation Movement Goals for Critical Items/Services

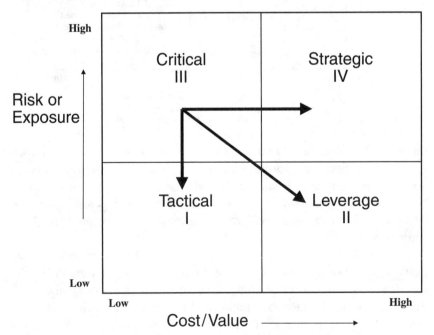

All of the items/services categorized in this quadrant need to be kept under continuous review to ensure that suppliers continue to supply at high levels of customer service and that costs are kept within targeted limits (target costs).

The supply management emphasis applied to items/service found in the *strategic* quadrant is to maximize competitive advantage. This is broader than just price advantage and includes rapid innovations, earlier time to market, and superior product quality. The value-added nature of strategic items/services should be enhanced in any way possible.

Segmentation Quadrant Strategies

The supply segmentation approach assists in the development of realistic functional-level, namely supply management, strategies. Once again, Figures 4–5 and 4–6 provide examples of a few specific supply strategies. A further discussion of the supply management strategy development process follows.

Many of the specific supply management strategies for *tactical* items/services call for increased involvement of suppliers both onsite and offsite. While these items/services account for a small percentage of purchasing dollar expenditures, these items/services frequently account for the vast majority of purchasing transactions and the resulting administrative costs of managing the acquisition process. The issue that drives all supply management strategies in this quadrant is minimizing the number of transactions and thereby lowering the resulting administrative cost of acquisition. With acquisition cost per transaction approaching $200 for the typical order, acquisition cost can be 50% or more of the total order cost. The main supply management strategy is to minimize the number of separate transactions through the consolidation of large numbers of orders with fewer suppliers through the use of blanket orders and other supply base rationalization and order reduction strategies. The use of procurement cards (P-Cards) is a frequently implemented and rewarding strategy. With P-Cards, users can order directly from suppliers by telephone to a certain dollar authorization level specific to each firm. This dramatically reduces transaction levels since orders are summarized on the card's monthly statement and a single monthly payment is made to a financial institution instead of directly to numerous suppliers. For more commonly and frequently ordered items/services, the use of integrated suppliers and outsourcing strategies may be appropriate. The use of EDI linkages with suppliers, although not common with items/services within this quadrant, is certainly an option to consider for higher volume purchases. Supplier-managed inventories and consignment inventories are two other supply strategies applied to items and services categorized within this quadrant.

Leverage quadrant items/services supply strategies stress the minimization to purchased item/service total landed costs. This entails volume leveraging where appropriate, with additional spot buys to meet unplanned capacity need variations. Supplier partnering strategies are of less importance with these suppliers, since traditional purchasing techniques seem effective. The items/services in this quadrant should be viewed as generic in nature. This reflects the nature of the supply market environment and the characteristics of the items/services. For example, the supply market for these items/services is characterized by low barriers to entry, resulting in several sources of supply for each item/service. The buying firm has low switching costs to move volumes across suppliers, resulting in a low loyalty to any one source of supply. The total landed cost is the major supplier selection determinant. Supply strategies should all involve some sort of volume leveraging, such as concentrating purchases across diverse business units and adding potential volume to the supplier equation by suggesting longer-term contracts.

This quadrant is where many of the purchase dollars are expended. Therefore, cost reductions, cash flow management through dollar cost averaging, and volume timing supply strategies are of critical importance. Just-in-Time purchasing strategies were developed for items located in this *leverage* quadrant. Also, supplier quality assurance strategies are in frequent use.

The supply strategies pertaining to *critical* items/services pertain to decreasing product/service variety. In a retail environment this means reducing the number and variety of stock-keeping units. In a manufacturing environment the supply strategies involve developing item/service standardization, using value analysis or value engineering techniques, and using cross-functional teams to improve and develop efficient processes to manage assets over their useful life. Custom-designed tools, capital equipment, and support items/services form the majority of items/services in this quadrant. While these items/services represent a small portion of the total annual spend by purchasing, they represent items/services that require frequent interaction between purchasing personnel and other user functions. Even though the cost savings potential is limited, the potential for bad publicity for purchasing should something go wrong is great. These items therefore command more purchasing time and attention than they are worth. What can purchasing managers do?

In order to add value to items/services found in the *critical* quadrant, purchasing involvement in the order cycle must begin as early as possible, preferably even in the design stage. The supply management strategies must reflect this need through implementing early supplier design involvement and supplier R&D. Purchasing can proactively support the user by reducing the number of sources through exclusivity of design and simultaneous engineering concepts. Non-item costs, such as inventory carrying, training, transport, and maintenance costs, become a critical issue in the supplier selection and evaluation process. The cost of acquisition, in contrast to quadrant I items/services, is a very small proportion of the total item cost. Technical expertise and teaming skills are critical for purchasing personnel involved with these items/services.

Developing supply strategies for *strategic* items/services involves gaining competitive advantage through new technology access and development and fostering a high level of unique services from suppliers. This quadrant is full of critical items and services that the firm needs to maintain operations and market share. These are commonly unique items, services, and technologies without easy substitution. Many of these items are sole sourced. The costs of materials, acquisition, inventory, and transport are frequently a secondary consideration. Supply strategies must be to deepen the buyer–supplier relationship through sole sourcing, alliance partnering, and joint ventures, especially with foreign suppliers.

Total landed cost is not the driver of relationship development for items/services in this quadrant. Much of the negotiations revolves around cost-sharing discussions between the buyer and supplier to determine which firm is better situated to perform which activity within the supply chain. The managerial focus of purchasing is placed upon customer service innovation and product/service enhancement.

SUMMARY

Within each quadrant not all suppliers have the same impact or require the same supply strategy. Experience has shown that within each quadrant a limited number of suppliers account for the majority of purchasing resource expenditure activity. Key account suppliers must be actively managed. One individual or team—for example, a commodity team—

should have the responsibility across strategic business units for the key supplier(s) of that commodity group. This will mean the use of all supply management strategies across the plethora of commodity groups sourced globally.

No single strategic approach is appropriate throughout the range of products and services used by the typical company in today's competitive environment. Unlike the historical purchasing paradigm that treated the purchasing process for most goods and services the same, the supply segmentation approach toward supply strategy development delineates them into differing efficient and effective strategies.

The extent of usage of this technique depends upon the dollar purchase volume, the criticality of the items/services purchased, and the resources available within purchasing. The usage of the supply segmentation approach for supply strategy development can shift purchasing activity from a tactical orientation into a strategic role within the firm, contributing significantly to profit, value-added, and market penetration.

The advantage of using the supply segmentation approach is that supply strategies can be aligned with corporate strategy, thereby exploiting purchasing expertise for company advantage.

BIBLIOGRAPHY

Elliott Shircore, T. I., and P. T. Steele. (1985) "Procurement Positioning Overview." *Purchasing and Supply Management, Official Journal of the Institute of Purchasing and Supply.* December 1985.

Steele, P., and B. Court. *Profitable Purchasing Strategies: A Manager's Guide for Improving Organizational Competitiveness Through the Skills of Purchasing.* London: McGraw-Hill, 1996.

Vollmann, T. E., W. L. Berry, and D. C. Whybark. *Manufacturing Planning and Control Systems,* 4th ed. New York: Irwin/McGraw-Hill, 1997.

CHAPTER 5

Knowledge of Supply Markets

Editor
Richard R. Young, Ph.D., C.P.M.
Assistant Professor of Business Administration
Academic Program Director for Purchasing Continuing Education
The Pennsylvania State University

What should purchasers know about the markets from which they purchase? For many years, organizations around the world have invested considerable energies and resources to better understand the markets in which they operate. Specifically, businesses have sought to know the potential aggregate demand in the marketplace for the goods and services they offer, recognize those events that are occurring that affect their market segment vis-à-vis new or lost competitors as well as products, and understand who their customers are and the nature of those customers. While there are many opinions regarding what constitutes "the best" kind of knowledge that purchasers should possess, it is certainly most advantageous to view these requirements in a holistic manner, drawing specific parallels with the knowledge that marketers have traditionally sought, whether they are dealing with a tangible product or some form of service such as those found in health care, information technology or finance.[1] That is, by understanding both the customer market and the supply market. By appreciating how these two markets interanimate one another, purchasers can begin to map for themselves what they need to know about their markets.

---

1. Any reference to *product* should be construed to imply *service* as well as tangible items as the intention is to use the former in its broadest economic sense: something created and offered to the market.

F I G U R E   5-1

Supply versus Customer Market Perspective

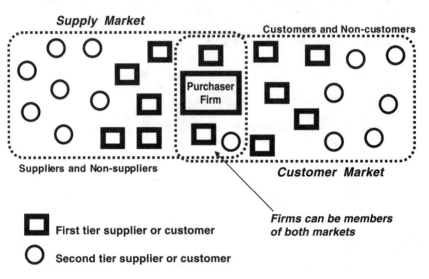

In considering this issue of supply market knowledge, a panel of top purchasing executives provided the following quote and visualization: "[It is] the systematic detection of changes occurring in the supply market and their subsequent interpretation as potential opportunities and threats to [the] customer market position."[2]

DATA VERSUS KNOWLEDGE[3]

Today purchasers are literally inundated with bits of data concerning their suppliers, the markets in which those suppliers participate, and the functioning of the economy as a whole. Turning such data into meaningful, useful information—supply market knowledge—is one part of the purchaser's tasks, but so is leveraging that information into knowledge that increases the competitive advantage of the purchaser's firm.

2. Developed by the Acquisition Research and Development Center, The Pennsylvania State University, Senior Executive Panel Meeting, December 1996.
3. Adapted from an earlier model developed at the Acquisition Research and Development Center, The Pennsylvania State University, August 1996.

F I G U R E   5–2

From Data to Knowledge

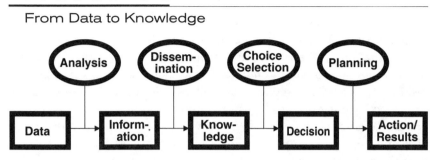

For the sake of clarity, we prefer to use these several terms within the context of the model in Figure 5–2.

Before attempting to understand the supply market, purchasers must first possess a clear understanding of what is meaningful to their own organizations. Collecting data without a clear purpose only serves to consume scarce and/or valuable resources. Therefore, before collecting data, purchasers should look into their own organizations to understand the products or services those organizations sell, the processes and technologies necessary for the creation of those products and services, the materials and services required as inputs, and the multiple tiers of suppliers necessary for providing them.

A detailed understanding of the fundamental processes of one's organization and of the uses of supply market knowledge is the filter through which data is collected, analyzed, interpreted, and subsequently disseminated within that organization. As this last point suggests, such knowledge is useful to many functions within the organization, not just purchasing.

THE USES FOR SUPPLY MARKET KNOWLEDGE

Purchasing must acquire knowledge about its firm's supply markets for a wide range of reasons. For example, knowledge of the supply market provides opportunities for increasing purchasing's efficiency and effectiveness in making purchases. Supply market knowledge is principally useful for eight categories of purchasing applications:

Cost Modeling

Increasingly, purchasers are looking to build models with which to understand better the logic behind a supplier's pricing, especially as it pertains to materials, direct labor, and overhead expenses. This requires an extensive amount of supply market knowledge, including, but not limited to, prices paid to suppliers, wage rates paid to employees, extent of employee benefit packages, ages of equipment utilized, methods of depreciation, efficiency of equipment, costs of owning and operating facilities, and impact of indirect employees. Typically, cost modeling is used to support contract negotiations, provide quantitative mechanisms for adjusting pricing, and lead to a better understanding of the process that culminates in make-or-buy decisions.

Negotiation

The better prepared the negotiator, the higher the probability of success in any negotiation. Negotiation preparation may well be one of the most fundamental justifications for understanding supply markets because the well-prepared negotiator understands the seller's situation on three levels: macroeconomic, industry, and company-specific. Negotiation preparation means understanding the relative strengths and weakness of both the buyer and the supplier, not only in the present but in the future, since buyers and suppliers inevitably change as certain opportunities and threats arise. For example, a supplier could be facing the loss of a major customer because of a shift in technology, an investigation of its environmental policies and practices, an announced takeover by another firm, or favorable import tariff treatment for a critical raw material. Any such change in circumstance could affect the buyer's position in various kinds of negotiations.

But one should also consider that supply market knowledge can reveal much about the supplier's organization, specifically who is in what position of authority and what their relative responsibilities are as they may relate to the purchaser's firm. In other words, it can provide important insights into who the purchaser will be negotiating with.

Ensuring Continuity of Supply

Knowing the dynamics of the market vis-à-vis supply and demand can be critical to maintaining supply flows. Moreover, many purchasers fail to anticipate or recognize situations where a supplier may be vulnerable to capacity constraints as a result of problems with its suppliers.

Vulnerability can affect a supplier who is a manufacturer as well as suppliers who are distributors, the dynamics of which bear both similarities and differences. In the case of a distributor, consider the following questions:

1. What other lines do they carry and is there a possible substitution?
2. What is their relative position with the manufacturer and can they use this position as leverage to resolve the purchaser's problems?
3. Has the purchaser concentrated enough leverage with the distributor to warrant effective problem-solving, or has it spread its business around so thinly as to have lost all conceivable leverage?
4. Have sufficient accurate demand projections been shared with the supplier to allow planning in their supply chain?

Manufacturers pose somewhat similar issues, but that of leverage never seems to diminish. Consider the following:

1. In addition to planning for quantity of material, has consideration been given to time concerns for scheduling capacity and supplier deliveries?
2. Are we concerned with materials that add significant value to our own products but are only available from one or a very limited number of sources, thereby increasing our risks as purchasers?
3. If the question above does not apply to our supplier, does it apply to our supplier's supplier and thereby become one of our vulnerabilities?

Service providers pose some issues which, while perhaps having some commonality with manufacturing, provide some unique paradigmatic twists:

1. Since a supplier cannot inventory services, have they made the necessary investment in capacity to meet peak demand?
2. Single suppliers may frequently be single sourced. What options may exist to supplement their capacity from other suppliers or internally?

3. Is the service so specialized that the supply chain becomes even more esoteric as we investigate the supplier's suppliers?[4]

Sourcing Alternatives

It is axiomatic that the more a purchaser knows about the participants in any given market, the better that purchaser is at identifying sources of supply. Frequently, additional sourcing can be accomplished with an existing supplier if the purchaser properly understands the full capabilities of that firm. Using existing suppliers—particularly those with whom the purchaser has had a satisfactory relationship—can be beneficial for two reasons: (1) suppliers come with a tacit recommendation, and (2) doing so constrains the number of supplier relationships that the purchaser needs to manage. There does remain the need to understand in sufficient detail the supplier's capacity, whether they are providing goods or services, the degree to which it is utilized, their supply chain, the technology employed, and the amount of capital that they may have available to support the business that the purchaser may wish to place.

Strategic Planning

While not essential to purchasing *per se*, the dissemination of information about the supply market is often critical to the formulation of corporate strategy. There have been many instances where top management has formulated plans for major service offerings or product line expansions only to be stymied at a later date by constraints on the availability of additional quantities of materials, products or services. Similarly, purchasing should alert senior management to potential future constraints, reductions, or interruptions in supply because such constraints can pose a threat to the entire firm. However, as purchasing typically bears much of the blame when this occurs, purchasers should notify senior management of *any* significant constraints in order to reduce this (often unfairly apportioned) blame. (These can be difficult calls to make—see the section—Disseminating Knowledge, for the analysis, interpretation, and dissemination of such information.)

---

4. For a complete discussion on serivce industries, the reader may want to also see *Logistics in the Service Industries*, Oak Brook, IL (Council of Logistics Management), 1991.

Accessing Supplier Innovation

One frequently overlooked benefit of mastering knowledge of the supply markets is to gain an understanding of technologies and processes that could further one's own products, services and processes. Firms can no longer exist solely on their own, developing all of their own technology and inventing their own manufacturing and business processes. Even famous innovators like AT&T and IBM now often rely on the innovations of others, as the latter clearly did for both components, such as disk drives from Seagate and its operating system from Microsoft for its PCs. Knowing who has what innovations is the first part of the challenge. The second is to convince innovative suppliers that the purchaser's firm is a logical choice for them to introduce of their innovations.

Procurement Process Improvement

Understanding the business processes employed within the supply market may yield significantly larger savings than price negotiations. Some industries are better at doing this than others, especially when it comes to identifying individual suppliers who are open to improvements in business processes. As most purchasers are aware, *integrated supply* is now a common practice for many suppliers of MRO items, however, engaging in this emerging practice requires not only improved information technology, perhaps including electronic commerce, but a different mindset by supplier and purchaser alike.

Less well known is the fact that some leading firms are using similar practices for other items. For example, Honda of America Manufacturing has an arrangement for metal body component stamping that essentially uses no purchase orders and no separate invoices for individual shipments, and a single, precisely timed payment each month to the supplier. Moreover, Honda now uses just one supplier, with whom it has the most intimately detailed relationship. While other benefits accrue from such an arrangement, one must also appreciate the amount of supply market knowledge—both at the supplier level and at the industry level—necessary to achieve this level of efficiency.

Reducing Cost/Adding Value

All of the applications listed above can ultimately be categorized as cost saving or value adding. In some cases, cost saving can be achieved through price reduction, but note how many of these applications address other non-price issues that result in increased competitiveness for the purchaser's firm. When it comes to supply market knowledge, purchasing adds value when it acts as a knowledgeable disseminator of supply market information to all parts of the company. By doing so, purchasing can often shed its traditionally limited role and become recognized for the strategic effort that it can play in leveraging the supply market to the best advantage of the firm.

DETERMINING WHAT TYPE OF KNOWLEDGE TO COLLECT

Although there is a huge amount of data to be collected, analyzed, interpreted, and disseminated, the collection task need not be onerous provided it can be broken down into four distinct groupings which can be discussed. To go from the general to the specific: (1) macroeconomic, (2) industry-specific, (3) supplier-specific, and (4) internal, or the purchaser's own firm.

Macroeconomic

Begin by determining as completely and as accurately as possible the overall performance of both the world economy as well as the domestic economy, remembering that these do not always work perfectly in synch with one another. Of course, the fact that they do not can actually be a benefit: events affecting one geographic region may actually be a leading indicator for what will affect another. In this era where many, if not most purchasers have reached a comfort level with globalization, nations and regions are considered to be economically interdependent. That is, today's supply is affected not only by immediate and obvious opportunities and threats, but opportunities and threats to its suppliers as well as customers throughout the entire supply chain.

Domestic performance can be evaluated on four criteria, but before doing so, one should consider the events of the present relative to what represents typical ranges. Note that these are the basics; there are many others available, most of which can get quite industry-specific:

1. Level of unemployment
2. Prices at producer and consumer levels
3. NAPM Purchasing Manager's Index
4. Interest rates

Despite what is reported by the popular media, the following benchmarks may prove useful when deciphering where we are domestically vis-à-vis the business cycle:

1. Unemployment in recent years has fluctuated typically between 4% and 10%. Most economists believe that anything below 4% for an extended period tends to be inflationary. Be aware that different countries as well as different regions of the U.S. will each have their own rate due to regional industrial specialization and other demographic factors.

2. Price changes, usually referred to as inflation when discussing the consumer price level, have been in the range of 0% to 10%. As an early warning indicator, watch the producer index, as increases will occur there before being passed on to consumers. Recent years have seen this fluctuating in the 2–4% range; however, it is not impossible for a phenomenon known as *disinflation* to occur, in which case the percentages are negative.[5]

3. The National Association of Purchasing Management's (NAPM's) Manufacturing *NAPM Report on Business*® reports on nine indicators through a diffusion index. The Purchasing Manager's Index or PMI is a composite index based on the seasonally adjusted diffusion indexes for five of the indicators reported on. A PMI reading above 50% indicates that the manufacturing economy is generally expanding; below 50%, that it is generally declining. Widely reported in the financial press, check NAPM's magazine, *Purchasing Today*,® for a graphical summary report or the NAPM web site at *www.napm.org* for the full report and history. NAPM's Non-Manufacturing *Report on Business*® debuted in June 1998 and provides an economic report for nonmanufacturing industries across the country.

4. Interest rates—especially the prime rate, which is that charged by major commercial banks to their best creditworthy business customers—suggests how willing firms will be to take on investments. This number has fluctuated between 5% and 12% in recent years. Do not confuse prime rate, which is

---

5. For additional current information, the reader is referred to current issues of *Economist* as well as to R. Eisner, *The Misunderstood Economy: What Counts and How to Count It*, Harvard Business School Press, Boston, Massachusetts, 1994.

determined by the largest commercial banks, with the discount rate, or that rate which these banks charge one another for the use of reserves. This latter rate is established by the Federal Reserve, a semiautonomous unit of the U.S. government. Changes to either rate, when they occur, are highly publicized.[6]

5. Exchange rates—the value of one currency expressed in terms of another. Because of their trading status with the U.S., the significant ones to watch are the Canadian dollar, Japanese yen, British pound sterling, German mark, and French franc. The stronger the U.S. dollar, the less expensive for foreign purchases, but the greater the adverse impact on export sales.[7] Recent developments with the European Union have seen efforts begun to implement a common currency, the Euro. Ultimately this will simplify the purchaser's role in monitoring currency fluctuations with a large number of developed nations.

Another concern is the changes being made to public policy. Some of these can affect supply, while others will affect suppliers' cost structures. Within this group, consider past initiatives. (This is not to comment on their relative merits, but rather to suggest that there are cost and availability issues involved.) These include:

1. Environmental restrictions on emissions from certain industries, limits on mining and forestry, increased costs due to more comprehensive recordkeeping.

2. Changes in import tariffs and non-duty barriers to imports, including new standards or prohibitions of certain goods from certain countries. Prior attempts to place quotas on steel is but one example, with the result being to curtail foreign purchases in favor of potentially more costly domestic ones. More far-reaching initiatives may derive from the increasing trend of nations joining trading blocs. Both the European Union (EU) and the North American Free Trade Agreement (NAFTA) suggest that simplified trade and lower barriers may be

---

6. See J. DeRooy, *Economic Literacy: What Everyone Needs to Know about Money and Markets*, Crown Publishers, New York, 1995.

7. For extensive coverage of global business including exchange rates, refer to current issues of the *Economist* as well as *The Economist Guide to Economic Indicators*, John Wiley and Sons, New York, 1992.

achieved with the consequence that other nations have begun to either lobby for inclusion to create their own, as is the case with the Association of Southeast Asian Nations (ASEAN).

3. Changes to taxing regimes may have dramatic impacts, however, the major issues are currently sales and excise taxes plus certain user fees, usually on utilities or for the use of facilities. Purchasers should be aware of potential changes, including a value-added tax. Recent years have also seen other taxes considered, including a carbon tax on fuels.

4. Increases in minimum wage rates, legislated increases for certain insurance coverage, and various licensing initiatives.

Finally, do not overlook the interaction among the economic, technological, cultural, and political elements of a society. What affects one, will undoubtedly affect each of the others at some point. This is especially true when trying to understand events in other societies. See Figure 5–3.

Industry-Specific

There are two markets in any given industry: customer and supplier. Because the purchaser's firm represents but one firm in that market, there has to be a concern for the other purchases. Who are they? What are their specific uses for the item or service? Do they have the same price tolerances as the purchaser who is performing the analysis. Is their end product deriving greater value from this material or item than is yours?

F I G U R E   5–3

Seeking Cause from Effect

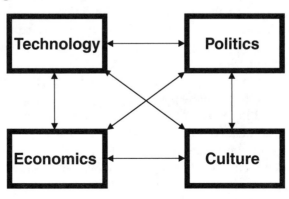

Never fall into the trap of believing that a particular purchaser should pay less because its volume is higher. There are plenty of examples of lower-volume purchasers who are paying lower prices because of a range of other factors, including (1) very consistent demand over time, hence the supplier can use them for base loading capacity; (2) that there are other non-price elements in their relationship beyond the obvious single product or service requirements; or (3) that there is an improved business process between buyer and seller that has reduced the costs for both. Of this last issue, too many purchasers fail to realize that their way of doing business may needlessly impose additional costs on suppliers and ultimately themselves.

Getting Caught by the Unknown Competition

In the late 1960s and early 1970s, the electronic components industry purchased significant quantities of conductive inks and related solutions for the manufacture of capacitors. The principal component in these materials was platinum and a related element, palladium. While there was some value added by the suppliers, Engelhard being one, it was minimal.

In the early 1970s, the U.S. Environmental Protection Agency began to require lower tailpipe emissions from motor vehicles. Among the various acceptable means to accomplish this in a relatively short period of time was the use of a catalytic converter, a device now found on literally all gasoline-powered automobiles, which consists of a ceramic honeycomb structure, coated with platinum or palladium. Almost overnight, supplies of platinum and palladium were depleted as massive quantities were diverted to the automotive industry.

Although many electronics firms made many visits to the metals suppliers (some even threatening lawsuits), relief from the supply problem was slow to arrive. The problem, of course, was that the metals producers realized far better margins by adding value to manufacture the complete catalytic converter than by compounding precious metal inks and solutions. Moreover, the electronics purchasers did not see other industries as competitors for the material, and actually considered each other as competitors, despite the coverage that catalytic converters had been receiving in the business press at the time, both in the general business journals and in metals industries trade publications.

Purchasers must consider what drives success as well as failure in their industry. In computers, for example, the ability to develop and bring to market a continuous stream of innovative products is a critical success factor. Conversely, while innovative products are not usually a concern for suppliers of commodities such as bulk soda ash, for example, the ability to provide the necessary tonnage at the time it is required would remain a principal concern.

The wholesale distribution business serving MRO buyers is quickly moving away from a unit pricing-driven situation to one where information technology can be used to leverage lower inventories required by the purchaser as well as drive the cost out of the transaction systems. Selling firms that recognize this fact are more likely to survive than those that do not, principally because they understand what is driving success in their industry. For far too many MRO items, the cost of procurement incurred jointly between purchasers and suppliers exceeds the value of the goods transacted. Under these circumstances, the greatest savings will not come from lower selling prices but from reduced overhead costs enjoyed by both parties.

Purchasers should also know all that is to be known about a supplier's supply chain. Does the purchaser recognize the names of the supplier's suppliers, understand their relative capacities, who their competitors are, and what their vulnerabilities are? In both the early and late 1970s, many purchasers were unpleasantly surprised to learn that some of the items they were buying were substantially dependent upon petroleum feedstocks: the two Arab Oil Crises precipitated a curtailment, if not total loss of supply.

Supplier-Specific

Of all the tiers of market knowledge, purchasers are expected to know the most about suppliers. However, there remain many purchasers who have never visited a supplier facility, nor even actually seen the materials or services that are provided to their own firms. Nevertheless, every purchaser should be expected to have eight basic pieces of knowledge when building a profile of any particular supplier:

1. Capacity
2. Product range (including capabilities)
3. Pricing and profit
4. Capital sources, costs, and criteria for use
5. Benchmarking partners
6. Technologies
7. Processes employed
8. Management and ownership

Capacity

Purchasers should know how much total capacity the supplier has, how much of it is being utilized, and what percentage the purchaser represents. Purchasers should be able to answer one simple question: How much leverage do I, the purchaser, have at current levels of output and how much vulnerability do I have should my demand increase? Note that the use of the word "leverage" in this instance goes far beyond price, as the preferred meaning should infer relative importance or influence over what the purchaser needs, whether it be delivery, additional capacity, innovation, technical assistance, or inventories, to name just a few. Note again that the capacity issue can affect nearly like consequences, for example, the supply of:

1. Printed materials required by financial services firms
2. Laundry services needed by hospitality and healthcare providers
3. Raw materials in manufacturing

Product Range

Although closely linked with innovation, knowledge of the supplier's *potential* capabilities can prove useful for future requirements as well as enhance existing ones. Specific capabilities of obvious importance include manufacturing technologies employed, analytical processes related to quality assurance and control as well as research, access to the research strengths of the suppliers with whom your supplier has a close relationship (supply chain), and financial capabilities (including access to capital and favorable borrowing rates). Obviously, purchasers should determine what resources of the suppliers are (a) unique and possess value and (b) can be efficiently and economically accessed. The above only suggests some of the areas possible. The list is endless, but what is possible must be known before it can be accessed.

Pricing and Profit

Here, the purchaser must determine whether a supplier is making a profit on the purchaser's business and, if so, whether the supplier is making a lower margin on the purchaser's business than it happens to have with others. Supplier profitability has the potential to impact the viability of long-term supply continuity, as well as the purchaser's access to other capabilities, including innovation.

Capital Sources

Although this is discussed in the section on capabilities, purchasers need to understand not only what sources of capital their suppliers have, but what the relative costs (interest rates) for these funds happen to be, as well as the criteria for their use. These issues are important because they affect suppliers' decisions whether to acquire new manufacturing technology, support extensive research and development efforts, keep current with information technology, or invest in inventories to support the purchaser's ongoing business needs. Moreover, does the supplier have the wherewithal to add capacity and grow as the purchaser's business grows?

Benchmarking Partners

The purchaser should discover the firm to which the supplier most consistently compares itself. This is a double-edged topic because it is important to understand who the supplier considers to be its competition, but should it engage in noncompetitive benchmarking, it may have a greater opportunity to seek out the best practices irrespective of the industry. Consider, for example, whether the best customer service processes are to be found in the auto industry. One could select a firm and say it was the best among automakers, which might be true, but it would not likely utilize the overall best customer service practices. Why would anyone want to emulate the best firm in that group instead of finding the best processes utilized by anyone—say, L. L. Bean, Xerox, or Dell Computer?[8]

Technologies

Purchasers should determine what technologies are employed for those goods being furnished. This applies not only to manufacturing, but to the analytical aspects of quality control and information systems. However, purchasing should be aware that the supplier using the latest technology is not necessarily the best supplier in the particular situation. It is, rather, a question of whether the appropriate technology is being employed given the product, quantity, and intended use by the final customer.

---

8. For a thorough understanding of benchmarking concepts including noncompetitive benchmarking, see R. C. Camp, *Benchmarking: The Search for Industry Best Practices That Lead to Superior Performance*, American Society for Quality Control, Quality Press, Milwaukee, 1989.

Processes Employed

While in many ways the technologies discussion above also applies here, purchasers are advised to consider the business processes employed by their suppliers. Many of these may be archaic, costing both buyer and seller considerable amounts due to one or more of the following circumstances:

1. Rigid order processing procedures cause delays or other lack of responsiveness.
2. Lack of responsiveness may require the purchaser to maintain otherwise unnecessary high levels of inventory.
3. Ineffective sample and product information delays slow research and development.
4. Requiring all customer communication to flow through sales creates a bottleneck equivalent to all purchaser communication flowing through purchasing.

Management and Ownership

Public firms, or those whose stock is traded on some stock exchange, tend to provide easier access to information. These are the largest firms, and ownership is typically widely dispersed, at least in the case of North American firms, with the management employed being professional.[9] The degree to which management owns the firm's stock can vary a great deal, however. Private firms are those whose stock is held by an individual, a group of individuals, a trust or estate, or another corporation that holds it as a nonconsolidated subsidiary. In the case of smaller firms, there are many aspects of ownership that may be of concern to purchasers, including:

1. Family ownership and operation, where the motivation may be to employ family members regardless of their capabilities. In the short term, these will not usually be found in critical functions that could potentially spell failure of the firm. In the longer term, however, management and ownership succession may prove to be the vulnerability as these family members become heirs to the company stock.

---

9. Note that there are some very large privately held corporations in North America: United Parcel Service and M&M/Mars in the United States and a number of Canadian firms, including Irving Petroleum.

2. Family-run businesses where profitability is not a primary objective and disclosure of financial statements are not routine. Traditional measures such as return on sales or return on capital employed, if obtainable, are not usually comparable to those of public firms. This is not to imply that such firms are less successful or viable, only that since they have different objectives, their visible results may differ.

3. Professional management of a firm owned by a financial institution, such as a merchant bank or venture capital firm. Viability may be dependent only on the firm's ability to provide satisfactory returns on a quarter-by-quarter basis. While much of the stock of many European corporations is owned by banks rather than by individuals or mutual funds, there has historically been more tolerance for low returns over a longer period of time, provided the end result was significant market position.

Purchaser's Firm

Collecting all these external data is important; however, it must also be linked to the internal situation in order to provide context. Purchasers must understand not only what they are purchasing, but how it is used to manufacture their firm's goods and/or services, which requires that they understand what their own firms manufacture and how they do so.

Understanding one's own firm must occur in an even broader context: knowing what the growth prospects are for one's own products or services and where they are sold. Understanding how these products are sold requires developing an understanding of one's own customers and their particular requirements. Moreover, one must understand what kinds of financial resources are available and what the cost of their use is. In other words, purchasers must learn all the things about their own firms that they must know about their suppliers. Consider, for example, how one could go about answering the following:

1. What three issues would senior management say face the business in the next three to five years?

2. Do we know the true value needs or potential of our existing customers?

3. Can we cite the cost or value needs of each of our internal customers?

4. What new technologies will redefine the needs of our internal customers within the next three to five years?

5. What are the current and/or future opportunities and threats to our internal customers?

6. What will drive change to our overall business?

7. What are the cost drivers in our business?

8. Other than price, how can costs be forced from our business?

9. How do our internal customers measure themselves? Are purchasing's efforts enhancing or detracting from them?

10. What information do our internal customers need? What does purchasing now know or can it potentially obtain, that can be shared, thereby enhancing the performance of the internal customers?

COLLECTING DATA[10]

A number of resources are commonly employed for collecting the data described above. Some of these are formal processes, others less so.

Formal Processes

An overabundance of data probably crosses every purchaser's desk in the form of daily newspapers and trade journals. Some of these have specific industry focus, such as the *Chemical Marketing Reporter, Electronic News, Board Markets,* and *American Metals Markets,* as well as those focusing on banking, healthcare and transportation industries specifically. Others including *The Wall Street Journal* and *Journal of Commerce,* are much broader in coverage and thereby have a much greater appeal. These may be characterized as public sources, since they are widely distributed and have a modest subscription price.

There are also free sources of information, such as a firm's annual report or the Form 10-K required by the U.S. Securities and Exchange Commission. Government sources such as the Bureau of Labor Statistics, the Federal Reserve Bank, and the Commerce Department can provide

---

10. Some additional methods for collecting and analyzing market information can be found in Larry Kahaner, *Competitive Intelligence,* New York (Simon and Schuster), 1996.

a wealth of information about the economy in general. Similarly, securities dealers can provide investment prospecti, secondary reports (like those published by Standard & Poor's or Value Line Investment Survey), and individual firm and industry analyses. Alex Brown & Sons is well known for its analysis of transportation firms, while Prudential Bache has previously published a concise weekly newsletter on commodity metals, with a particular strength in precious metals, gold, silver, platinum, palladium, rhodium, and iridium. There have also been instances of firms going to the U.S. Central Intelligence Agency to learn more about a particular mineral source located in other countries.

The private category of formal information collection is also purchased information, but it is usually much more focused. For example, much can be gleaned from Dun & Bradstreet Reports, especially whether a firm has: (1) pledged particular assets and has Form UCC-1's in place, (2) been slow in paying its suppliers, which raises various questions about their finances, and (3) in place adequate management talent, as revealed by their short biographical statements. Private sources can be expected to be very expensive, meaning that purchasers should have a clear understanding of what information they are seeking. For example, Kline & Co. is particularly knowledgeable about the supply markets for raw materials from the chemical industry. Their public information can cost thousands of dollars per report, while their privately commissioned research is often priced in the tens of thousands of dollars.

Another way to obtain information is the supplier visit. This can be invaluable for obtaining a very detailed understanding of individual firms. Unfortunately, this visit is not sufficiently understood and supported by top management and is often limited by travel budget constraints. But corporate travel policy may not be the only reason that purchasers do not visit their suppliers; lack of discipline for conducting effective visits is also a widespread phenomenon. Despite the expense, one may wish to visit critical suppliers with a cross-functional team consisting of purchasing, engineering, quality control or assurance, and financial representatives, since the approach offers multifaceted expertise and an opportunity for collaboration. While preplanning is essential to a successful visit, most teams seek to learn about capacities, technologies utilized, cost structure, and whether the firm is financially sound. The key is to tour everything that the supplier will show you: production is mandatory, but also try to look at warehousing, research and development, and the quality control labs. Exceptionally well-executed supplier visits essentially include observing everything:

1. Who are their other customers? Look at the quality awards hanging in the lobby, names on job orders in manufacturing, labels on finished goods in the warehouse, and logos on trucks at the shipping dock. Note, too, the common elements whether the supplier is engaged in manufacturing, warehousing or transportation services, or is the outsourced information technology services provider.

2. Extent of housekeeping?

3. Equipment used? Observe manufacturer's nameplates, but also model numbers. If on tour, assess capacity by doing a rough count for a few minutes. This also applies to any equipment needed to provide your firm with services.

4. Employees, again, make a rough count during a tour. Counting cars in the parking lot has also given some sound results. Get a sense for labor relations by closely observing even the shortest of discussions. A quick "hello" may provide a clue.

5. Financials, what is the extent of materials in the warehouse? Will someone give an idea as to backlog?

While visits are very useful, a less expensive approach that is frequently overlooked is the supplier questionnaire, where all of these questions and more are asked on an annual basis, with the results kept in a supplier profile folder. The North American subsidiary of a large European firm regularly assesses whatever suppliers they can by viewing their homepages on the Internet, enabling them to get a flavor of the financials and product line offerings. Additionally, many firms maintain a "what's new" section that discusses everything from expansion plans to labor negotiations to locations of facilities.

Informal Sources

Perhaps the most ubiquitous of the informal sources of market information comes from sales representatives routinely calling upon purchasers. While much of the information may be suspect because it contains a certain bias, it remains highly useful for corroborating information from other sources. Normally, one can get a sense for issues such as capacity utilization, source of supply, process changes, capital expansion plans, and project status, to name just a few. Needless to say, the better the relationship with the supplier representative, the better the information, both qualitatively and quantitatively.

Supplier sales representatives are not the only source of supplier contact. Supplier personnel, whether from engineering, customer service, manufacturing, purchasing, or general management, can all contribute to the body of knowledge about the industry in general, and the particular supplier in particular.

A final category is nonsuppliers, including competitors as well as seemingly independent firms. While engaging competitors in supply market knowledge conversations is relatively difficult, opportunities frequently present themselves at industry association gatherings as well as through ad hoc contacts. For example, it may not be unusual for two or three transportation managers of large chemical manufacturers to informally discuss developments in the ocean shipping industry. While they were careful never to engage in any practices that might even suggest antitrust problems, this was a legitimate and highly reliable source of information.

Combining Sources

After a while it becomes apparent that there are many sources of data, some of which is redundant. After reviewing clippings from trade journals, supplier questionnaires, reports of visits to suppliers, reports of supplier representative visits, supplier literature including annual reports, Dun & Bradstreet reports, other specialized reports, government sources, and other bits and pieces, a purchaser can establish two important categories: (1) that for which there appears to be corroboration from multiple sources, and (2) that where there appear to be conflicts. In the case of the former, the purchaser can feel comfortable with the knowledge. For the latter, additional data, assuming they are about a potentially critical issue, need to be collected.

Knowledge Selectivity

Not every item or service purchased requires the same level of scrutiny or the same diligence in collecting information. For example, purchasers employed by computer manufacturers need to be keenly interested in the supply markets for integrated circuits, passive electronic components, hard drives, and video displays because they represent a high value-added portion of the final product. Conversely, they should care relatively little about the supply markets for office supplies and other low value-adding and less risk-containing items. Because some forms of knowledge-gathering can be both time-consuming and expensive, purchasing management needs to address what is important and what is not. In other words, where does supply market knowledge add value to the purchasing process and where does it not?

FROM DATA TO KNOWLEDGE

Collecting data is a continuous process because markets are always changing. For the same reason, purchasers must forever be analyzing market information. If there is a trend towards displacing lower-level purchasing activity with systems applications, there is also a rationale for hiring highly skilled professionals—many with technical training—for managing more complex purchases.

As one begins to collect market information, the various bits and pieces should start to fit into an overall scheme or model suggesting various supply market scenarios that will affect the purchaser's firm over a range of time frames: some immediately, others in the future. In a more mechanical approach, certain information can be input into cost models, but an admittedly messier undertaking is the issue of scenario building that attempts to take small pieces of data, which some academics have labeled "factoids," and assemble them into a story suggesting potential future events. Once such a scenario is created, developing recommended courses of action becomes an imperative, but the problem is in seeing far enough into the future that (1) one has time to act on the situation, and (2) there is sufficient confidence that the indicators are pointing to potential opportunities or threats. Too short a time horizon means that one will only be reactive.

An intermediate step that some leading companies employ is development of key supplier and market profiles. Typically, the information contained in one of these periodic documents attempts to summarize the following:

- *Ownership and equity interests.* Essentially, this is a "who owns whom" situation. Purchasers should be interested not only in who is a wholly-owned unit of whom, but in who has any level of equity interest. On one hand, a partial interest may lead to a future takeover. On the other, it may result in board of directors' representation, technical exchange (including patent licensing and engineering assistance), or favorable buying and selling relationships.

♦ *Supply relationships.* Who appears to be buying from whom? Long-term contracts frequently appear as news items in such publications as the *The Wall Street Journal*, while other situations are a bit more obvious, such as the chemical plant fed by a pipeline from its key supplier or the steel mill having a coke battery as its neighbor. There are many other ways in which supply relationships can be discovered, including observing the names on trucks at plant sites and packages in warehouses.

♦ *Other alliances.* There are numerous other opportunities for firms to cooperate that may be stronger than a pure buyer–seller relationship, but weaker than equity ownership. These include joint research, shared manufacturing capacity, and cooperative marketing arrangements, to name a few.

♦ *The "in-betweens."* There are relationships that may be very short-term, but in any event are extremely difficult to detect. These include which firms:
  ♦ Occasionally cooperate
  ♦ Finance one another
  ♦ Co-pack or toll for one another
  ♦ Share technical expertise.

One of the most frequently-heard criticisms of such analyses is that they are unwieldy because of the large quantities of qualitative and quantitative data involved. While such criticism is well founded, it cannot be used to excuse away the need. One way frequently employed is the SWOT analysis. SWOT, standing for strength, weakness, opportunity, and threat, attempts to take all of the information extant and categorize it between internal and external factors by asking three basic questions:

1. Where do we stand relative to our own strengths and weaknesses?
2. Externally, what are the opportunities and threats confronting us?
3. What is our position, options, or other decision-making biases vis-à-vis the external conditions, past history, or traditional responses (inertia)?

Because of the magnitude of the analysis undertaking, many organizations are also employing cross-functional teams as an effective method for building additional perspectives into the analysis process, accessing the expertise found in other disciplines, speeding the process through the sharing of tasks, and improving the dissemination of results to interested parties within the organization. If time is an important currency for product development, the cash-to-cash cycle, and customer response, then detecting, analyzing, and disseminating supply market knowledge should not be an exception.

DISSEMINATING KNOWLEDGE

In order to be effective, the results of supply market knowledge efforts need to be reported throughout the organization. Unfortunately, many purchasers see such information as proprietary, intended only for their own internal consumption. Improved supply market knowledge certainly bolsters negotiating effectiveness and fosters the development of more comprehensive supplier strategies. However, every firm has a widely-scattered and varied audience that would not only value purchasing-developed supply market knowledge, but would be able to use it to increase the competitive advantage of the entire firm. Further, by sharing its knowledge, purchasing raises awareness throughout the company of its own strategic importance.

Other groups typically interested in such knowledge include:

- *Senior management:* With its need to remain constantly aware of the opportunities and threats facing the firm, senior management is interested in achieving improved understanding of their firm's four markets: customer, labor, finance, and supply. Purchasing is responsible for being the window on the supply market. For similar reasons, each of the functional areas has a need to understand the dynamics of those markets which others have primary responsibility for watching.
- *Marketing and sales:* Threats to customer markets can come from several directions. While threats from competitors and changes in customer behavior normally come to mind, issues affecting continuity of supply as well as changes in materials costs are also critical to marketing plans.
- *Research and development:* As new products are developed, it obviously does little good to devise a new product for which

there is a limited supply of material or a supply that will be channeled to more remunerative end uses. Innovation and opportunities to share technologies should not only be welcomed, but aggressively sought.

+ *Operations:* Fluctuations in quality, limitations on quantity, and changes in suppliers all tend to represent variations that are unsatisfactory to manufacturing managers whether they are manufacturing a product or producing a service. While advance information will not always be able to preclude such eventuality, it does tend to assuage the suddenness of such events. Manufacturing managers, despite the current environment, still largely focus on minimal interruptions to throughput and maximized capacity utilization.

+ *Finance and accounting:* Changes in cost structures through either prices paid to suppliers or increased inventory levels may wreak havoc with cash flows as well as overall profitability. Advance warning will often permit the ability to plan alternative measures as well as affect the timing of bond or equity issues, securing lines of credit, and that information periodically provided to securities analysts.

+ *Legal:* Sometimes, supply situations are affected by laws and other governmental regulations. Action to lobby for changes to such laws and regulations, or independent action may be warranted, but they cannot be undertaken with sufficient lead time unless they are detected by some early warning mechanism.

How Often Should Supply Market Knowledge Be Reported?

This is probably the most difficult question of all because one has to find the right mix between too much information and too little. The following are some approaches for segmenting the information into bits and pieces that are manageable not only for purchasers to analyze and disseminate, but for interested parties to use:

+ *Annually:* A "white paper" providing an overall summary of the industry, including estimates of overall capacity, its utilization, the types of technology employed, the suppliers and their various relationships with other firms, and pricing dynamics. Such an analysis should be performed only for those materials and services that have strategic importance.

- *Quarterly:* Update on pricing dynamics, capacity utilization, and important changes in relationships, such as (a) competitor W just signed a long-term agreement for 100% of their requirements with supplier X, or (b) supplier Y just purchased three plants from possible supplier Z.

- *Monthly:* Changes to our own situation vis-à-vis commitments. This could include such issues as, our demand has decreased, or an abnormal increase in demand forced us to supplement supplies purchased on contract with some spot business.

- *Ad hoc:* Clearly, major and unusual circumstances need to be communicated. These could include: supplier Y suffered an explosion and fire, idling their plant for six months, supplier Z decided to leave the market and convert their plant to make another product, or Congress is considering a bill that will either prohibit the importation of this product or impose new taxes on its manufacture and sale.

Form of Reporting

Since credibility is paramount, any dissemination of marketplace knowledge needs to abide by four basic rules:

1. It must be important. Not every item or service purchased has a sufficiently high priority. Nor is every fact about even the most major items worth taking the time to report. Knowledge must have a significant financial impact, possess sufficiently important consequences, or strategically affect outcomes relative to the firm's overall objectives.

2. The information must be accurate: *corroborate what gets reported.* Hearsay from a single source that is reported and found to be wrong damages purchasing's credibility significantly, not only for this item, but for everything else that may be reported in the future.

3. Keep it short and concise. Provide enough information to tell the story, but not so much that management will not read it. A couple of pages should be sufficient. Tables and graphs are an especially effective means of conveying lots of information quickly.

4. Give your interpretation. Provide an explanation as to how current and/or future events will directly impact your firm. Be specific. It also helps to use others internally as sounding boards, but if you do, be sure to name them as collaborators if you hope to engage their assistance in the future.

Caveats

Collecting, analyzing, and disseminating supply information, while not frequently cited as a primary function of purchasing, is critical to the manner in which the function is perceived by senior management—indeed, by everyone else in the organization. The supplier information collection and distribution process demonstrates to the organization that purchasing plays a strategic role in the organization. By making this clear, purchasing increases awareness of the fact that purchasing is no longer simply a transactionally-driven function.

Because this knowledge role is resource-intensive, we repeat that it must not be universally employed, but reserved for only the most important items and services purchased. Moreover, because quality information is better derived from suppliers with whom the purchaser has the best relationships, this suggests that fewer, close relationships are far more manageable than many, more superficial ones.

Knowledgeable purchasers must also develop an intuitive sense. This comes not from reading reports, although that is an important dimension, but rather from collecting—often first-hand—many small pieces of information (remember, think "factoids") and inferring conclusions from them. Often these facts will come from observations, and hence opportunities to see operations first-hand can be an invaluable tool.

Finally, data needs to be corroborated. Reports, articles, and pieces of information must be measured against first-hand observation. This process might be called performing the sanity check, for it asks if the numbers on the page can possibly represent reality.

SUMMARY

Market knowledge does not represent an optional "extra" in modern purchasing. Rather, it is necessary and vital for the efficient and effective management of the flow of the goods and services that is so vital to the ongoing conduct of business. To undertake any aspect of the purchasing activities or attempt to employ any of the recently developed supplier-dependent initiatives—be it manufacturing resource planning, Just-in-Time, integrated supply, or value analysis—without detailed supply market knowledge only serves to increase the probability of failure.

CHAPTER 6

Purchasing as Relationship Management

Editor
Steve Kesinger, C.P.M., A.P.P.
President of The Kesinger Group

It is critical to understand where we have traditionally been in the past to appreciate where we are headed and need to be into the future. Relationship management in many organizations has been functional, with some communication between other functional staff, some communication with internal customers, and a "filter" role with primary suppliers.

Purchasing staff were expected to have competency in the "hard skill" areas, such as negotiating, understanding terms and conditions, conducting bid analysis, developing requests for proposal, and the like. These individuals were not evaluated based upon their management of the key relationships in the supply chain, nor were they provided incentive for that. In fact, by "hoarding" information and playing the communication linkage role between internal users and suppliers, they were justifying their existence. In reality, these practices caused miscommunication, delayed communication, and frustration between all parties. While everyone's intentions were sound, in many cases they lacked the expertise to speak for engineering, maintenance, and operations. In addition, most lacked strong communication skills because these competencies were not developed in many cases.

What started out in organizations as "segmentation of responsibilities" for control purposes had become functional silos and bottlenecked communication. It was time for a change.

UNDERSTANDING RELATIONSHIPS RELATIVE TO TODAY'S SUPPLY CHAIN MANAGEMENT

Opportunities

Consider Figure 6–1 below. It is important to recognize that multiple organizations exist across most supply chains.

F I G U R E   6–1

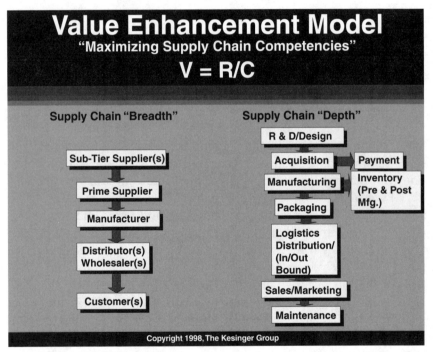

Each organization must:

$$\text{Plan} \Rightarrow \text{Buy} \Rightarrow \text{Make} \Rightarrow \text{Deliver}$$

in order to provide a product or service, and each organization presumably adds value to the overall process. In addition, each organization has its own corporate culture (more on this later), its own mission and objectives, its own processes and reward systems, its own management systems, etc. Once we take a supply chain view, we can easily see how communication and relationship management become so critical to success.

As we become more strategic in our focus, the use of cross-functional teams becomes essential to success. Someone must possess excellent communication, facilitation, and change management skills to achieve the goals of these teams. The procurement/purchasing profession is in the best position to lead these efforts in strategic sourcing. Purchasing staff are the closest to the supplier relationships, have the understanding of their organization's own objectives, and are ultimately responsible for supplier performance in most progressive companies.

Complexities

As with all things, opportunities also bring about risks and complexities. Stepping into a leadership role in the relationship management across supply chains can be intimidating and somewhat risky, but the rewards and satisfaction are great. This chapter will provide insight into becoming more effective in this role and increase your chances of success. Some complexities might include:

- *Differing internal and external priorities:* You may not have agreement on direction, role of suppliers, or which suppliers to utilize within your own organization. In addition, your company's priorities and those of your key suppliers may differ.

- *Company cultures:* Culture is defined as "the way we do things around here to ensure success." Each company has a primary corporate culture, and these do not always align across the supply chain. Understanding these differences is the first step, and pursuing a relationship strategy that maximizes each company's strengths is next. We will discuss this in detail later in the chapter.

- *Individual styles:* Complexities arise from differing individual styles as well. A variety of instruments exist that assess individual personality styles, including (but not limited to) the Meyers-Briggs assessment and the "D.I.S.C." instrument. Most instruments categorize style into one of four categories, with one category typically being dominant in each individual. Each of these styles possesses strengths and weaknesses, just as does each corporate culture noted above. The key in both cases is to understand them and leverage the strengths while minimizing the weaknesses.

Impacts of Integrated Supply

Over the past few years, many companies have begun to compete through integrated supply offerings. These firms "bundle" materials or services in order to simplify the entire acquisition process for the buying firm. They provide one source for buying and invoicing and typically simplify the transaction costs through some form of electronic commerce.

It is critical to look at relationship management skills prior to choosing an integrated supplier. After all, they are in essence managing the supplier relationships on the buyer's behalf, and they need to be very skilled in this area. Prior to entering such a relationship, the buying firm should understand how these integrated suppliers manage their relationships with *their* key suppliers. If they cannot do so effectively, it will reflect negatively on their offering to the buyer.

PURCHASING'S ROLE IN 21ST CENTURY RELATIONSHIP MANAGEMENT
Overall role

Purchasing should be positioned to be the lead in terms of supply chain relationship management. That does not mean they should be the communication conduit for every discussion held internally and externally within the supply chain. It does mean they should lead cross-functional supply chain teams and should be a focal point for ensuring that effective relationship management takes place internally and externally. This includes facilitating communication wherever appropriate, resolving conflict, and dealing with resistance across the supply chain where it exists.

Role with Senior Management

It is critical for purchasing not only to have a strong relationship with senior management, but to obtain respect for what they can do to add value to the organization. Effective management of the relationships with senior management consists of:

- *Understanding the organization's and senior management's key business objectives:* Alignment between supply chain efforts and overall business objectives is critical. If your firm competes in high-technology industries, innovation and cycle time reductions are critical to success. If your firm is in a more mature market, low cost leadership may be the critical component. In managing your relationship with senior management, demonstrate how your efforts achieve these critical items.

♦ *Identifying uniqueness from the purchasing perspective:* Senior management needs to understand what is unique about their supply chain efforts. What unique skills offer them a competitive advantage in the marketplace? Purchasing, in their role as a senior management interface and relationship builder, must possess and articulate their uniqueness to the supply chain effort. These unique skills may be in areas such as leadership of cross-functional teams, alliance building and renewal, measurement, value analysis/engineering, marketplace knowledge, electronic commerce, and the like.

♦ *Involving senior management in a sponsor role to assist in achieving these objectives:* Senior management must play a critical role in the enhancement of purchasing's supply chain improvement efforts. A senior manager should sponsor each major supply chain effort by providing support, overall guidance, assistance when resistance is encountered, and alignment and focus with senior management of other supply chain firms.

♦ *Reporting successes:* An important element of relationship management is communication. Share issues and successes with the sponsors and other interested stakeholders. Advise them of obstacles and obtain their assistance in removing these where appropriate. Provide examples of how your unique skills have added value to the organization.

Role with Internal Team Members and Customers

Purchasing should play a key role in relationship management at a peer level as well as with senior management. This role more frequently in- volves providing leadership to cross-functional supply chain strategy teams. The ability to manage the change process and communicate with all stakeholders becomes critical, as well as the ability to determine which decisions need to be made by consensus and which need to be made by senior management.

Role with Suppliers

Purchasing plays *the* key relationship management role with the suppliers. This does not imply that purchasing manages all the communication. However, it does imply that purchasing is responsible for the overall buyer–supplier relationship management and should play a lead role in the development of mutual goals, measurement systems and metrics, and contract alignment.

CONDUCTING YOUR RELATIONSHIP MANAGEMENT "GAP ANALYSIS"

We have discussed the relevance of relationship management in the supply chain effort and why it is so critical to success. We have also discussed some of the complexities involved. It is time to look at the skills necessary to be successful in this key area of purchasing and supply chain management.

Identifying Critical Relationships

We all must prioritize our daily activities due to time constraints, and prioritizing relationships is no different. We can identify those relationships that are most critical to our business success and focus the majority of our time on improving these relationships. We must consider management, peers, subordinates, customers, and suppliers in this assessment. Things to consider might include:

- How key is this relationship to the major objectives and goals we have?
- Will this be a longer-term relationship or for a short-term project?
- How strong is our relationship today?

Assessing Personal Strengths and Improvement Areas

Each individual should assess his or her own performance in key relationship management areas. By looking at key skill areas and assessing effectiveness and importance, one can develop a proactive plan to address deficiencies (Table 6–1).

We will briefly describe and discuss each key skill area noted above.

+ *Listening/testing for comprehension:* How well do we really understand what the other party is trying to tell us? Do we test for understanding by restating what the other individual has said to us?

+ *Facilitation:* How well can we facilitate cross-functional teams in the accomplishment of their goals and objectives? Have we learned and applied key facilitation skills to make our meetings efficient and effective?

+ *Change management leadership:* Do we understand how to identify and engage key stakeholders in our supply chain efforts? Are we effective in establishing a communication plan for our efforts that considers the "who," "what," "when," and "how"? Do we adequately assess what others are thinking or feeling about our efforts?

+ *Assessing individual styles:* Are we effective in determining individual styles of our key peers, managers, subordinates,

T A B L E   6–1

Key Skill Assessment

Key Skill Area	Importance (High–Medium–Low)	Current Effectiveness (High–Medium–Low)
Listening/testing for comprehension		
Facilitation		
Change management leadership		
Assessing individual styles		
Negotiation with multiple parties		
Conflict resolution		
Establishing alignment of supply chain stakeholders		
Company culture assessment		

customers, and suppliers? Do we work to meet their individual styles instead of just doing what we think is best?

+ *Negotiation with multiple parties:* How well do we negotiate with various internal customer groups and external suppliers when each group has a different position? Are we effective at moving individuals off their positions and back to the overall team objectives?

+ *Conflict resolution:* How well do we manage daily conflict? Do we recognize that conflict can be either negative (revolving around attacking people and their ideas) or positive (revolving around attacking problems and issues, not people)? When conflict arises, are we able to separate individuals' positions from objectives? It is important to note that most conflict arises when two or more parties take a position and staunchly defend it while spending minimal time listening to the other party. If clear objectives have been established for solving the problem, an effective facilitator can move the individuals from their positions back to the objectives. This will remove the emotion and get everyone back to attacking problems, not people.

+ *Establishing alignment of supply chain stakeholders:* Have we adequately assessed the motivations of the various individuals? Once we understand their motivations, do we have a plan to address them, or to deal with issues in a different way? If individuals working in a team are not aligned, what is the cause? Is it conflicting priorities from their management, lack of interest in the problems the team is addressing, personal issues, disconnects in the reward and recognition system, or something else? It is important to recognize these issues early on and address them to ensure adequate alignment.

+ *Corporate culture assessment:* Have we identified which corporate culture we tend to favor? How about the corporate culture of our key suppliers? Have we met to discuss our collective strengths, weaknesses, and opportunities for synergy?

Steps to Close the Gap in Key Areas

Once you have identified those key areas needing the most attention, a plan to "close the gap" needs to be established. Some ways to accomplish this include:

- Finding and spending time with a mentor who possesses excellent skills in these areas
- Attending formal training on areas like effective listening and communication
- Reading books and magazines on these topics
- Searching the Internet for helpful information and tools
- Making a concerted effort to practice on the job every chance you have

Selling Yourself as a Change Agent

To become an effective change agent, an individual needs to possess skills in each of the key skill areas noted above. When one is working with cross-functional teams, it is helpful to address strategic issues by looking at three distinct segments.

The first segment involves the up-front preparation. This includes determining team members, developing a charter, and understanding sponsor roles. A charter is a key document in managing expectations and relationships. A well-defined charter will include the following:

- Team goals and objectives
- Team members with roles defined
- Team sponsor(s) with roles defined
- Time commitment of each team member
- Identification of team leader and sponsor
- Timeline for completion
- Budget
- Reporting requirements
- Deliverables at end of the project or at specific timeframes
- Sacred cows: those items, suppliers, etc. that are "off limits" to the team

As part of the initial team effort, develop a communication plan. This will improve buy-in to future recommendations and will likely generate useful input as well. Box 6–1 provides a template for your communication plan.

The second segment involves assessing your "current state" by conducting process mapping/analysis and looking at outside influences such as regulatory activities, impacts of technology, state of the economy, competition, etc.

B O X   6–1

Communicate what? (summaries, meeting notes, etc.)

To whom? (consider managers, peers, internal and external customers, suppliers)

When? (weekly, monthly, as needed, etc.)

How? (e-mail, newsletter, focus groups, etc.)

Why? (What is purpose of sharing information: obtain input, information, approval/support, etc.)

The third segment involves developing your "future state" or "preferred future." Relationship management skills are critical in this segment as well. On occasion, a cross-functional team will look to benchmark other firms to generate creative solutions. Key relationship management skills for benchmarking include:

- Clearly defining needs and objectives
- Ensuring that there is alignment; benefit for both parties
- Using time wisely
- Ensuring that all parties know what will be covered in advance of the benchmarking visit
- Adhering to confidentiality

Providing leadership and managing relationships through these three segments will improve supply chain performance. It is now time to further discuss ways to improve supply chain performance through effective relationship management.

DRIVING SUPPLY CHAIN PERFORMANCE THROUGH EFFECTIVE RELATIONSHIP MANAGEMENT

Understanding the Role of Corporate Culture

A significant area for improvement is in the management of relationships between buyer and seller. As we focus on improving our alliance-type relationships, understanding the differences between our corporate cultures can drive our relationships to the next level of performance.

Many firms have become effective in the key "technical" elements of alliance management, including:

♦ Establishing mutual goals and objectives

♦ Ensuring alignment within both firms

♦ Establishing a measurement system for both parties

♦ Receiving senior management's active support

♦ Holding regular review meetings

♦ Developing an "alliance/relationship manager" role that has accountability for success (one from each company)

♦ Developing a process for escalating and dealing with problems as they arise

While these are all critical to success, corporate culture is one area that is still largely untapped in managing these alliance relationships. Developing a better understanding of this key area will further improve communication between and understanding of one another. It will allow each company to understand their own and the other side's strengths, weaknesses, and opportunities for synergy.

Corporate culture is defined as "The way we do things around here to ensure success." Every company tends to favor one of four cultures, although large companies may have differing cultures in differing business units. Box 6–2 shows what the four cultures look like.

Let's describe each culture in more detail.

Collaborative Culture

The collaborative culture works effectively in teams. Collaborative culture companies like to obtain input from all relevant parties when making decisions. Teams can be formal or informal, have a tendency to gather on a moment's notice to work on issues and resolve problems, and are characterized as:

B O X   6–2

Personal	Actuality		Impersonal
	Collaborative	Control	
	Cultivational	Competency	
	Possibilities		

- People-driven
- Participative
- Democratic
- Synergistic

The negative side of this culture is a tendency to work on issues and look for consensus when a quick decision by one leader would be more appropriate under the circumstances. It also tends to clash with the competency culture, which is described below.

Control Culture

The control culture works well with clearly established guidelines, policies, and procedures. The control culture companies tend to have detailed specifications and standards for conducting business and are characterized by consistency across locations. This culture works well in cases where consistency is critical, such as in fast food restaurants. Customers expects the same standard at any restaurant they visit across the globe, and a control culture allows this to be a reality (or close to a reality!). These companies are characterized by terms such as:

- Dominance
- Directive
- Policy and procedure driven
- Conservative

The negative side of this culture is its tendency to reduce or discourage creativity.

Competency Culture

The competency culture values individual excellence and intelligence. Competency culture companies compete by providing innovative products that are first to market. They value individual excellence and decision-making because it is core to their competitiveness. These companies are often firms in the high-tech fields. They are characterized by terms such as:

- Superiority
- One of a kind
- Visionary
- Intense

These firms think about possibilities in the future and bring us new products and innovations of existing products. The negative side of this culture is its lack of focus on the people side of issues. It is the opposite of a collaborative culture, and these two cultures tend to have many disagreements when they work together.

As an example, one collaborative culture company was involved in the installation and start-up of a new human resources system. The software company providing the installation was a competency culture company. While this was a very appropriate culture for the software company, the buying and selling firms had difficulty dealing with one another throughout the process. The collaborative culture (buying firm) wanted to meet often to provide input into the planning and resource decisions for the installation. The competency culture (selling firm) felt they were the experts and wanted the buyer to stay "hands off" so they could get their work completed.

If these two companies had recognized their cultures and learned to work with the differences while leveraging their strengths, the results could have been different. Possibly these companies could have met once at the beginning of the project to develop a performance specification with an incentive contract for excellent performance. This would have met the need of the collaborative culture company to provide input into the process, and it would have allowed the competency culture company to show their excellence with minimal involvement from the buying firm.

Cultivation Culture

The cultivation culture is the direct opposite of the control culture. This culture is typically found in nonprofit organizations. Cultivation culture companies believe that having a common value system is important, and they strive to allow their employees to maximize their contributions to the things they value. They have minimal controls in place, instead relying on people to "do the right thing." This culture is characterized by terms such as:

- Realize potential
- People-driven
- Empower
- Appeal to common vision

The negative side of this culture is lack of control. These companies will have difficulty dealing with a control culture unless they address their differences up front in the relationship.

What does all this mean in terms of relationship management? As purchasing professionals, we should work to understand our culture and the culture of our key suppliers. We should strive to:

- ◆ Define our respective cultures
- ◆ Understand what makes these cultures strong
- ◆ Understand the weaknesses of these cultures
- ◆ Develop a plan to leverage the synergies and deal with the differences

Understanding How to Work with Individual Styles

One way to look at personality styles is by considering the four categories in Box 6–3:

- ◆ *Doers:* These are Type "A" individuals, who are very task oriented and excel at "getting things done." They are strong at completing an assignment or task but have a tendency to accomplish this without thinking about relationship management.
- ◆ *Talkers:* These are the relationship builders. They tend to know everyone and are good natured and positive. They have a tendency to "get off track" and have difficulty staying focused, so strong facilitation and team leadership is necessary to keep the team moving forward and working at the right things.
- ◆ *Thinkers:* These are the visionaries in the organization. They tend to think about "what could be," but have difficulty focusing on the details and specific tasks.

B O X   6–3

Doers	Talkers
Guardians	Thinkers

◆ *Guardians:* These take comfort in the "way things have been done in the past." They are comfortable with policies, procedures, and guidelines in conducting their work. They help a team by keeping it somewhat grounded but can be a hindrance to significant change management efforts.

In addition to understanding and managing corporate culture differences, the effective manager of relationships will do the same for individual styles.

Dealing with Conflict

A critical part of relationship management involves dealing with conflict. We need to recognize that conflict must exist, and it can either be negative or positive. Positive conflict deals with attacking problems, while negative conflict comes from attacking people and their ideas and positions. Channeling individuals back to the overall objectives will help them focus their energies on attacking problems, not people. Do not shy away from conflict, and do not attempt to just "brush it under the carpet." If you do, it will surface in some other way and may be more intense when it does.

Understanding Types of Resistance

Typically, resistance comes from one of three sources, or possibly a combination of them:

◆ *Vulnerability: The fear that someone might find out I have not been as effective in my role as I would like people to believe; the fear that someone might be able to do it better than I have.* Encourage the vulnerable person. Find the positive contributions that person has made in the past and let him or her know you value those contributions.

◆ *Loss of Control: The fear that I may not have the power, influence, independence, etc. that I have had in the past.* When coming across fear of loss of control, move slowly! Don't assume control quickly; do it in a slow, measured fashion. You can always make more progress, but if you move too quickly, the door may be closed for good.

> ♦ *Lack of importance: I am resisting this effort because I do not see the value for my time or the time of my staff.* When you run into resistance because others do not see the importance of your project/efforts, it is important to develop a value proposition. The value proposition must clarify how value is added *as the customer defines value.* It should define what value will be gained, what costs and resources will be involved, and what the timeline will be for results.

Learning to Ensure Alignment Between Buyer and Seller to Improve Strategic Relationships

Relationships between key individuals and companies can be improved by ensuring alignment. Questions to consider include:

- ♦ Do we understand how each firm in the supply chain competes (product leadership, low cost leadership, integrated supply or services)?
- ♦ Do we understand what the key cost and value drivers and competencies are that will ensure success?
- ♦ How can we help one another improve our competitiveness?
- ♦ What is most important to the end customer?
- ♦ Do our reward systems/contracting strategies encourage accomplishment of these things?
- ♦ Do we measure those key items that will help us compete?
- ♦ Do we share risks and rewards?
- ♦ What do we each do today that prevents improvement in our competitiveness?

Relationship Management in Supplier Selection and Measurement

Recognizing the corporate culture of each firm in the supply chain will provide insight into the relative strengths of each company. Firms from the collaborative culture tend to be excellent at relationship management and often compete by offering integrated supply and services. Customer satisfaction is a key component of their competitiveness, and this will likely be a significant measurement criterion in the relationship.

Firms from the control culture tend to be very efficient in acquisition and distribution, and this allows them to be the low cost producer. Leveraging their spend capabilities is also crucial to their competitiveness. Total cost and/or labor rates will likely be significant measurement criteria in the relationship.

Firms from the competency culture tend to be innovators and continue to reduce cycle time. Bringing innovative products and services to market quickly is what provides their competitive advantage. Cycle time and value improvements from innovation will likely be significant measurement criteria in this relationship.

Supply chains must learn to leverage their relative strengths and compensate for their individual weaknesses. Strong relationship management is needed to bring this into focus and deal with it in an effective manner.

Tying It All Together: Taking Relationship Management to the Next Level

The following checklist provides things to consider in moving purchasing's relationship management to the next level. It can be used to conduct a "gap analysis" individually and within your department.

- √ Have we identified major opportunities by considering key cost and value drivers?
- √ Have we identified our key stakeholders (suppliers, peers, internal and external customers, management)?
- √ In our strategic supply chain efforts, have we developed a clear communication plan that addresses the "who," "what," "when," and "how"?
- √ In our cross-functional supply chain teams, have we developed a charter that defines the key elements noted previously?
- √ Have we assessed the key skill areas, rated importance and effectiveness, and developed a plan to "close the gap" where appropriate?
- √ As we work to improve our supply chain relationships, have we considered corporate culture and the effects it has on our relationships?
- √ Once we define corporate cultures, have we worked with the key supply chain organizations to maximize our collective strengths while compensating for weaknesses?

√ Have we assessed individual styles and preferences of our key stakeholders? Do we effectively "speak their language"?

√ When coming across resistance, do we effectively identify the type of resistance and deal with it in an appropriate manner?

Relationship management is critical to success today in all aspects of life. With the expanded roles and expectations of purchasing professionals, the time is right to focus intensely on a relationship management effort. While the results are more intangible and hard to measure, the consequences of not doing so are significant. As we continue to work on our key skill areas, developing communication plans and assessing corporate culture and individual styles, it will become a normal part of the way we operate. Our effectiveness will then be truly enhanced.

CHAPTER 7

Introduction to Supply Chain Management

Editor
Robert A. Novack, Ph.D.
Associate Professor of Business Logistics
The Pennsylvania State University

INTRODUCTION TO SUPPLY CHAIN MANAGEMENT

Supply chain management (SCM) is the newest management concept to engulf the business world. Some firms have created positions with the title of Vice-President of Supply Chain Management. Other firms, like Becton-Dickinson, have formed divisions dedicated to SCM.[1] The question arises, however, of the definition of SCM. Some believe the term to mean the same as *logistics management.* Some believe that manufacturing practices are at the heart of SCM. The reality is that SCM is not the responsibility of any single department or function within a firm. Rather, SCM is an enterprise model. It not only goes beyond the control of a single department but also spans the responsibility of a single organization. Many definitions of SCM have been offered. For the purposes of this chapter, however, SCM is defined as:

> An integrated collection of organizations that manage information, cash, and product flows from a point of origin to a point of consumption with

1. For a further discussion of Becton-Dickinson's Supply Chain Services Division, see R. A. Novack, C. J. Langley, Jr., and L. M. Rinehart, *Creating Logistics Value: Themes for the Future,* Council of Logistics Management, Oak Brook, Ill., 1995, pp. 88–91.

the goals of maximizing consumption satisfaction and minimizing the total costs of the organizations involved.[2]

Three key elements comprise this definition. First is the notion of information, cash, and product flows between organizations. Traditional business practice has been to manage these flows separately. In an SCM environment, they are managed in parallel. Second is the maximization of consumption satisfaction. This recognizes the importance of the point of ultimate consumption for a supply chain's output rather than the importance of just the next member in the channel. Third is the goal of minimizing total costs for all organizations involved in the supply chain. Historically, many firms have focused on minimizing their costs at the expense of their suppliers and/or customers. SCM requires that total costs for all members be minimized. SCM is a new way of doing business in any market, requiring significant changes in many organizations.

The purpose of this chapter is to briefly introduce the concept of supply chain management and focus on the strategies being used in business today in its implementation. The remainder of this chapter is divided into four parts: SCM Background, SCM Goals, SCM Strategies, and The Future of SCM.

SCM BACKGROUND

Many of the premises underlying SCM are not new to business or academics. One key premise is that of integration. Figure 7–1 is an attempt to show the evolution of integration to Total SCM integration.[3] The introduction to this chapter mentioned that some authors use the concepts of SCM and logistics management interchangeably. Although this is not correct, there is a logic to their beliefs. One of the basic processes that must be managed in SCM is the logistics process. As seen in Figure 7–1, during the 1960s and before, the various activities associated with the logistics process were managed independently within most organizations.[4] There was little or no integration among the activities. The economic pressures of the 1970s forced many organizations to look for areas

---

2. A. W. Kiefer, and R. A. Novack, "An Empirical Analysis of Warehouse Measurement Systems in the Context of Supply Chain Implementation," manuscript submitted for review to the *Transportation Journal*, Vol. 38, No. 3 (Spring 1999), pp. 18–27.

3. J. J. Coyle, E. J. Bardi, and R. A. Novack, *Transportation*, 5th ed. Southwestern, Cincinnati, Ohio, forthcoming, ch. 1.

4. For a more thorough discussion of this evolution to total integration, see J. J. Coyle, E. J. Bardi, and C. J. Langley, Jr., *The Management of Business Logistics*, 6th ed, West, Minneapolis, Minn., 1996, ch. 1.

F I G U R E   7–1

Logistics Evolution to Supply Chain Management

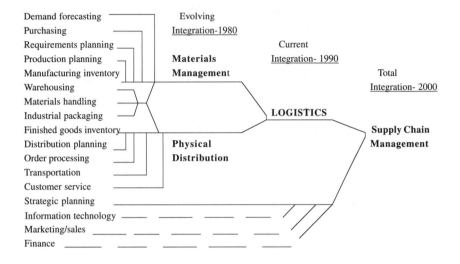

Fragmentation 1960

of cost reductions. One of these areas was in the integration of various logistics activities. By the late 1970s to early 1980s, these logistics activities developed into what can be called *materials management and physical distribution*, or *inbound and outbound logistics.* These were attempts to integrate these activities within a single organization, normally with manufacturing being the focal point of inbound and outbound movements. The successes achieved with this integration gave many organizations the insight to further integrate these two areas into what today can be called logistics. The initial efforts here were to coordinate these activities within a single organization, i.e., to help minimize a single firm's logistics cost. More progressive organizations, however, saw the opportunity to coordinate their logistics efforts with those of their suppliers and/or customers. This integration across the boundaries of a single firm provided the basis of SCM, since traditional logistics is responsible for product flow. Thus, many SCM efforts among organizations begin with the integration of their logistics activities. Logistics, then, is a part of SCM. This is evident in the concept of Total Integration in Figure 7–1. Since SCM involves the management of product, information, and cash flows, other areas besides logistics need to be involved equally. Information technology, marketing/sales, finance, and logistics all influence these three critical flows among members of a supply chain. As such, their processes must be coordinated with those of their customers and their suppliers. A good example of this is how Procter & Gamble embraced the concept of Efficient Consumer Response.[5] This model relied on logistics opportunities, promotion and product introduction opportunities, and pricing opportunities to offer the consumer the lowest possible prices on P&G products at the store shelf. Today's environment, then, is one of integrating all critical processes across businesses in the supply chain. This requires a new way of organizing and doing business for many firms.

Someone once said that the only thing constant in business today is change. As previously mentioned, SCM requires businesses to change the way they interact with other firms. Several of these changes necessary to evolve to SCM can be seen in Table 7–1.[6]

Traditional inventory management practices focused on minimizing inventories at a single firm level. In doing this, inventories were many times pushed back to suppliers. This negatively influenced the costs of these suppliers. An SCM orientation manages the total inventory in the

T A B L E   7–1

Comparison of Key Characteristics of Traditional Systems with Supply Chain

Factor	Traditional	Supply chain
Inventory management	Firm focused	Pipeline coordination
Inventory flows	Interrupted	Seamless/visible
Cost	Firm minimization	Landed cost
Information	Firm control	Shared
Risk	Firm focus	Shared
Planning	Firm orientation	Supply chain Team approach
Interorganizational relationships	Firm focus On low cost	Partnerships Focusing on landed cost

5. Novack et. al., op. cit., pp. 176–180.
6. Adapted from L. Ellram and M. Cooper, "Characteristics of Supply Chain Management and the Implications for Purchasing and Logistics Strategy," *International Journal of Logistics Management*, vol. 4, no. 2, 1993, as cited in Coyle and Langley, op. cit., p. 11.

pipeline, from initial suppliers through intermediaries to the final point of consumption. This view of inventories also allows firms in a supply chain to measure landed cost versus individual cost. Landed cost is the cost of delivering a product to the final point of consumption. This radical change in viewing cost requires a tremendous amount of sharing among firms in a supply chain. Firms must be willing to share information, risk, and planning to achieve true supply chain excellence. An example of this is Collaborative Planning, Forecasting, and Replenishment (CPFR). This initiative, begun with a trial between Wal-Mart and Warner-Lambert, includes the sharing of product demand forecast between a firm and its supplier. In the Wal-Mart example, it supplied Warner-Lambert with its projected sales of Listerine at its Wal-Mart stores. Over time, these projections were so effective that Warner-Lambert achieved significant improvements in shelf availability as well as reduced finished goods inventory. These improvements increased the profitability of both firms. These types of initiatives require more than traditional interorganizational relationships. True supply chain relationships have grown from a transaction to a partnership focus. In a partnership environment, all firms share in each other's successes and failures. Because of this interorganizational reliance, communication and cooperation are required for the success of SCM.

Supply chains will differ depending on the industry. Some are more focused on outbound moves (e.g., to customer), some on inbound (e.g., to manufacturing), and others on a balance flow (e.g., wholesaler). Figure 7–2 is an example of a supply chain for automotive parts.[7] This supply chain is predominantly focused on inbound moves to both the automobile manufacturing plant (original parts) and the replacement parts distribution center. Four levels of suppliers are included, from raw material extraction to part production. This exhibit represents what can be called the logistics network because it shows the links between physical nodes in the supply chain. Figure 7–3 shows the accompanying product, information, and cash flows that link these firms in the supply chain.[8] This diagram focuses on only a part of the logistics network shown in Figure 7–2. Product flows are shown as parts movements; information flows are shown as purchase orders, invoices, bills of lading, and freight bills; and

---

7. This diagram is taken from a case study written on the automotive parts supply chain written by the Center for Logistics Research, Penn State University, copyright 1996.
8. Ibid.

F I G U R E   7–2

The Automotive Steel Supply Chain

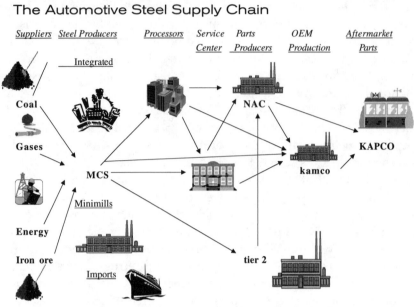

Source: Becton Dickinson Co.

F I G U R E   7–3

Core Process Review. Ordering/Invoice Process: Major Flows

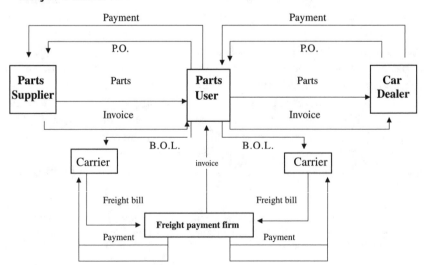

cash flows are shown as payment. Many firms understand these flows but still manage them independently of one another. An SCM orientation manages these flows in harmony with one another.

The concept of SCM has had a long evolution to its status today. This was necessary because of the radical changes required in the traditional ways firms managed their businesses and their relationships with one another. An SCM strategy will not succeed in all firms. It is not a panacea, nor is it a passing fad. SCM is a strategy for communication, coordination, and sharing among firms, with the intent of maximizing consumption satisfaction. The next section discusses some of the specific goals that SCM uses to achieve this satisfaction.

GOALS OF SCM

The implementation of any strategy relies on the achievement of certain goals. SCM is no different. This section will offer four goals that should be included, at a minimum, in SCM implementation.[9]

Reduce Channel Cost Through Logistics Operations

Cost control is a major driving force behind the decisions made by many organizations. The problem occurs when a firm wants to reduce its costs at the expense of one of its partners in the channel. A firm's costs have a direct influence on its pricing strategy. Increasing a supplier's costs, for example, by forcing it to hold more inventory results in one of two scenarios: (1) the supplier will raise its prices or (2) the supplier's profit margin will be reduced. In either case, the relationship between the supplier and its customer will be strained. A true supply chain orientation will attempt to eliminate costs, not transfer them to another partner in the channel. Opportunities to eliminate costs can be found in transportation, facilities, inventories, and information systems. Decisions in any one of these areas influence costs in the others. Only when these four areas are managed in concert will supply chain costs be eliminated. For example, the Collaborative Planning, Forecasting, and Replenishment initiative, although focused on inventory reductions, has implications for the other three areas. The mechanics of this initiative could influence how

---

9. This section is based on the research results presented in Novack et al., op. cit., ch. 2.

a firm processes orders (information systems), schedules production (facilities), and routes its private fleet for finished goods delivery (transportation). Controlling costs within the supply chain means managing these four elements within a single firm as well as among firms.

Increase Channel Service

Customers are constantly demanding better service from their suppliers. Again, this requires cooperation among all firms involved in the supply chain, for better service many times requires more cost. Probably the most important service elements in the supply chain are cycle time and its reliability. This is true whether it is cycle time through a warehouse, manufacturing cycle time, transportation cycle time, or order processing cycle. Some firms try to manage certain aspects of cycle times at the expense of others. For example, a customer requires delivery of a product in seven days from order placement. The supplier needs one day each for order processing, raw material acquisition, inbound transportation, manufacturing, transportation to a warehouse, storage/processing in the warehouse, and transportation to the customer. If manufacturing decides to increase its cycle time to two days, either the customer will receive the shipment late or another area of the supplier's total process will need to decrease its cycle time, presumably at a higher cost. Cycle time service, as was the case for costs, is influenced by decisions in transportation, facilities, inventories, and information systems. For example, the use of the Internet for catalog ordering has changed the shape of some supply chains, but has improved cycle times for delivery to some customers. These smaller orders require changes in transportation modes, manufacturing scheduling, and warehouse location. The decision by many firms to use the Internet, however, was made in order to to improve cycle time service to their customers.

Improve Firm and Channel Partner Revenue

Many firms make decisions to influence their own revenue growth without concern for the growth of their channel partners. Controlling costs during revenue growth will also result in increased profits. Although this strategy can be very productive, it might not result in the maximum possible revenue/profit growth for an individual firm. Some firms, such as Procter & Gamble, initiate programs to help their customers grow their business.[10] Their rationale is that as a customer's revenue/profit grows, it will increase its purchases of P&G products. This strategy has been very successful for P&G. Once again, revenue enhancement can be generated by decisions made in transportation, facilities, inventories, and information systems. For example, assume a manufacturer is willing to build store specific pallets for a customer at its manufacturing site (a facilities decision). This pallet now bypasses the manufacturer's warehouse and goes directly to the retailer's warehouse. The retailer is able to avoid storage at its warehouse by cross-docking the pallet to the store delivery vehicle. The pallet is delivered to the store and wheeled to a particular aisle, where the shelves are restocked. The manufacturer has eliminated more costs in the process than it has added at its plant. These cost savings are passed to the retailer in the form of a lower product price. The retailer can keep the improved margins, making the manufacturer's product more profitable to the retailer, or the retailer can reduce the price of the manufacturer's product at the shelf level. The first option will probably cause the retailer to buy more of the manufacturer's products at the expense of competition, since they bring in higher margins. The second option should result in more consumer purchases of the manufacturer's product at the expense of competition. In either case, both the retailer and the manufacturer enjoy an improvement in revenue/profit. One firm's success is dependent on the success of the other.

Improve Channel Satisfaction and Loyalty

The relationship between satisfaction and loyalty has been developed at length in the academic literature.[11] Satisfying a customer, or any channel partner, consistently over time results in a high level of loyalty from that customer. This loyalty is a long-term condition and results in long-term revenue growth. Channel partner satisfaction is influenced by decisions in transportation, facilities, inventories, and information systems. Loyalty is influenced when a firm performs these four processes for a customer consistently over time. For example, L. L. Bean made a conscious decision to utilize the services of FedEx for all catalogue customer orders.[12] Before this decision was made, L. L. Bean had used the services of several

---

10. Ibid., pp. 148–152.
11. Ibid., see discussion on pp. 36–38.
12. Ibid., p. 197.

carriers. Although L. L. Bean excelled at accurate order fill, customers were experiencing variability in order cycle times because of variable delivery times. FedEx guaranteed next-day delivery on 99.7% of all L. L. Bean orders. Performing this consistently has allowed L. L. Bean to improve its customer satisfaction. In turn, L. L. Bean has developed a loyalty to FedEx because of its consistent service over time. FedEx also allows on-line tracing through its Web page. This consistent service can also have an influence on inventories at both L. L. Bean and its customers. Thus, a decision in transportation influenced inventories, facilities, and information systems. These decisions, in concert, have resulted in channel partner satisfaction and loyalty for FedEx, L. L. Bean, and its customers.

These four goals of SCM are not mutually exclusive. In fact, they are very much interdependent. This relationship can be seen in Figure 7–4. Cost eliminations and service improvements result in profit and revenue growth for channel partners. This growth has a direct influence on channel partner satisfaction and loyalty. Continuously achieving these goals in the supply chain, or channel, serves to strengthen the relationships among channel partners, resulting in even more cost eliminations and service improvements.

FIGURE   7–4

Goals of Supply Chain Management

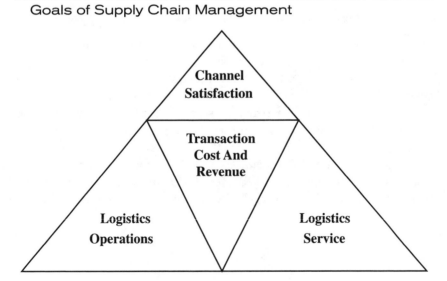

Although the nature of these SCM goals is rather easy to grasp, the tools and techniques to achieve them are not. However, many firms have implemented and perfected many processes and concepts that have allowed them to progress on the road to goal achievement. The next section discusses some of these processes and concepts.

SCM PROCESSES AND CONCEPTS

Firms have used various methods to achieve the goals of SCM. This section will briefly discuss some of the more common practices used among firms today in achieving these goals.

Relationship Management

Traditionally, many business relationships were managed on a transactual basis. Loyalty and a guarantee of business were not common in these relationships. These types of relationships still exist today. However, firms are beginning to understand that different types of relationships are necessary in a supply chain environment.[13] Such relationships are longer in nature and require more investments by the firms involved, but have been found to be extremely successful in achieving the goals of SCM. The popular term for these relationships is *partnership.* Although technically many of them are not true partnerships, they are more complex and longer in nature and seem to satisfy the requirements of SCM. A good example of this type of relationship can be found in the automobile industry with the concepts of Lead Supplier and Lead Logistics Provider (LLP). A Lead Supplier is responsible for delivering an entire subassembly of a car to the assembly line for installation. This is different from traditional relationships in the size and complexity of the subassembly. For example, a Lead Supplier might be responsible for delivering an entire dashboard to the assembly line. This would require the Lead Supplier to subcontract with all dashboard parts suppliers, manage those relationships, ensure the quality of all parts, and oversee the assembly

---

13. For a detailed discussion of these various types of relationships, see D. M. Lambert, M. A. Emmelhainz, and J. T. Gardner, "Developing and Implementing Supply Chain Partnerships," *The International Journal of Logistics Management,* vol. 7, no. 2, 1996, pp. 1–17.

of the final unit. This provides the car manufacturer with less transactions with suppliers to acquire a dashboard and places more importance on the relationship between the Lead Supplier and the car manufacturer. The Lead Logistics Provider concept applies to logistics services as the Lead Supplier applies to parts. For example, GM uses LLPs at its plants to coordinate all inbound movements to the assembly line. This single LLP coordinates and subcontracts with all other inbound logistics suppliers to ensure that parts and subassemblies are delivered to the assembly on time and in the proper sequence.

Such relationships place a tremendous amount of responsibility on the parties involved to make them successful. Many times relationships fail. However, successful partnerships have several characteristics in common:[14] Trust, shared vision, win–win attitudes, open communications, long-range focus, ability to endure, enabling technology, emphasis on measurement, organizational commitment, realistic expectations, emphasis on innovation, sharing of risks and rewards, and joint teams. As this list shows, these relationships require substantial investments by the firms involved in people, time, and technology. The relationships take a long time to develop and must be accompanied by relevant measurements to indicate whether success is being attained. They rely heavily on trust; each firm must believe that the other is acting in the best interest of the relationship. The end result of these types of relationships is a true sharing of risks and rewards among the firms involved.

Cash Management

One of the critical flows in SCM is that of cash. Many businesses survive or fail based on cash flow. Cash flows can be influenced by many factors, one of which is cycle time. For example, the typical firm will invoice its customers based on the time a shipment is made. Most customers will begin to process this invoice when proof of delivery is provided. During the time between order receipt and customer payment, the supplier has an investment in the inventory as well as all the value-added activities associated with it. The shorter the cycle time, the faster the cash flow for the supplier. One method to facilitate this process is the electronic transmission of the proof of delivery (POD) document by the delivering transportation carrier to the customer. This document is relevant because

---

14. This discussion is based on the results of a workshop on partnerships, sponsored by the Penn State Center for Logistics Research, University Park, Pennsylvania, 1997.

many firms need it to match with the original purchase order as well as with the packing slip before they begin to generate a check to the supplier.

Another method to facilitate the cash flow process is called the *evaluated receipts process.* Instead of the lengthy process described above for payment, the evaluated receipt process allows the customer to remit payment to a supplier based on what was received. This initiative can begin at the customer's receiving location when the original P.O. is checked against the proof of delivery receipt or the packing list. If these documents match, the payment of an agreed-upon price is sent to the supplier. This process eliminates the time used for the matching process in accounts payable and the time needed to manually generate a check. In this case, manual check generation is replaced by EDI transmissions. This process can also eliminate human error associated with manual document preparation. Most of all, the evaluated receipt process reduces time and variability in the cash flow process for the supplier. This can result in lower costs for the supplier, which will ultimately influence the supplier's pricing strategy.

Information Management

The importance of information management has increased dramatically over the last five years. Not only are more data available, but also more technology to utilize and manage the data. This section will not attempt to offer a comprehensive view of information management, but will discuss a few of the more common applications in information management.[15]

One of the more important applications of information management in the supply chain is Electronic Data Interchange (EDI). EDI allows for the automatic transfer of data from application to application without human intervention. Some typical types of EDI transmissions include purchase orders, bills of lading, advance shipment notices, shipment status, invoices, and payments. The degree of EDI penetration in firms varies widely from industry to industry. For example, the automotive industry maintains a high degree of EDI integration with its Tier 1, Tier 2, and Tier 3 suppliers. The types of transmissions in these relationships include not only those mentioned above but also production forecasts.

---

15. For a more comprehensive discussion of information management, see Coyle, Bardi, and Novack, op. cit., ch 13.

F I G U R E   7–5

Levels of EDI Relationship

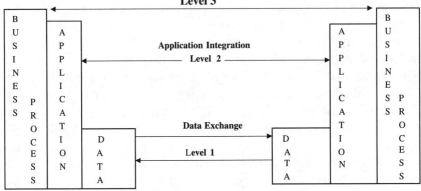

Source: Becton Dickinson Co.

Another industry embracing EDI is healthcare. Even before the Efficient Healthcare Consumer response initiative, some firms in this industry developed a wide array of EDI applications. One of these firms is Becton-Dickinson (BD), which manufactures products such as catheters, hypodermic needles, and other types of hardware used in healthcare. A main customer group for BD is healthcare distributors. Figure 7–5 shows the three types of EDI integration BD implements with its distributor customers.[16] Table 7–2 is a detailed explanation of the different characteristics of the three levels of integration.[17] As this exhibit shows, Level 3 integration is more process oriented and is more likely to be used with distributors in partnership with BD. BD uses Level 3 integration as a sustainable competitive advantage in a very cost-conscious, service-sensitive industry. In some industries, however, EDI is underutilized or not utilized at all. Although the technology needed for EDI is relatively inexpensive, some firms do not see the justification for the investment.

---

16. Novack et al., op. cit., p. 186.
17. Ibid., p. 187.

T A B L E   7-2

Levels of EDI Relationship

	Level I	Level II	Level III
1. Focus	Data exchange	Application	Process integration
2. Scope	Process step	Process application	Total process cycle
3. Driver	Channel efficiency	Cost reduction/service improvement	Sustainable competitive advantage
4. Enabler	Affordable/easy-to-use technology	Cooperation/I.T. infrastructure	Partnership/advanced I.T. capability
			Functional expertise
5. Cost/time to implement	Low/quick	Low to high/quick to long	Low to high/ongoing
6. Barrier	Critical mass	Cost/technical risk	Cultural change/business risk
7. Measure of success	# of T/Ps	Cost/service	Market share
8. Example	850 P.O.	Order processing:	CRP
		◆ 850 P.O.	◆ 867 sales tracing
		◆ 855 P.O. Ack.	◆ 856 ASN
		◆ 856 ASN	◆ 861 receiving

Source: Becton Dickinson

Inventory Management

A critical area of focus for all firms, whether in SCM or not, is inventory. Inventories comprise a significant expense for many firms. Traditional inventory management techniques utilized a "push" technique from one stocking location to another. This produced a significant demand uncertainty among channel partners, requiring each to produce to stock and maintain redundant safety stocks. Today's inventory management style focuses on the "pull" method, where the firm is literally producing to order. Probably the most famous application of this inventory technique is by Dell Computers. Dell offers customers the opportunity to configure their personal computers to their specifications, given a certain limited number of options. Dell then assembles the PCs and ships them to the customers. This method has significantly reduced finished goods inventories for Dell and has made them extremely competitive in the PC market.

Many different types of inventory management techniques have evolved over the past few years. One of the most innovative is called Vendor Managed Inventory (VMI) or Vendor Managed Replenishment (VMR). Popularized by Wal-Mart, this technique gives a supplier visibility of its inventories at either a store level or a customer's distribution center level. With this visibility, a supplier can see existing inventory levels by product and generate replenishment orders to arrive just in time at the customer's location. This has served to take significant uncertainty out of demand and has allowed inventories to be eliminated from the channel.

The most recent innovation in inventory management is called Collaborative, Planning, Forecasting, and Replenishment (CPFR). Again initiated by Wal-Mart, this technique shares forecast data by product between a customer and its suppliers. A customer will share its forecast of what it thinks it will sell of a supplier's products through Web-based technology. If the forecast is within certain parameters set by both the supplier and the customer, no changes are made. The supplier then either readies inventory or produces the product. The first application of CPFR was between Wal-Mart and Warner-Lambert on its Listerine product line. Shelf availability on Listerine increased substantially, producing an additional amount of profits, equivalent to what a new product introduction would bring. Because Warner-Lambert has this forecast, it is able to schedule production to meet the demand, eliminating the need to produce Listerine to stock.

The CPFR process begins with both the retailer and brand manufacturer developing a joint detailed line item forecast of product demand. This is detailed by each stockkeeping unit and to the point of weekly sales, deliveries, and the timings of special promotions. This forecast is then agreed to and shared between them on a web-based Internet linkage. The manufacturer then builds its internal Materials Requirements Planning (MRP) schedules of production and related timed deliveries to the retailer. The manufacturer is also responsible for monitoring the shelf inventories at the retailer and replenishing when needed.

CPFR provides for an exception analysis process to monitor that retailer inventory levels do not go above or below acceptable levels. This is a basic upper limit and lower limit measure that is connected to the supplier's MRP system as well as the retailer's inventory management system. All exceptions are checked against the forecast and event calendar of promotions. This takes into consideration build up of inventory for special events and promotions. Thus, CPFR is a detailed hands-on planning, monitoring and daily operating system that reduces costs for the supplier and retailer as well as leading to increased unit sales for both.

Inventory management provides significant opportunities to eliminate channel inventories, not shift them among channel partners. When inventory is eliminated, all channel partners will see profits and, in the case of Listerine, service increase. This is consistent with the four goals of SCM.

Performance Measurement

Probably the most frustrating and complex issue in SCM is performance measurement. Traditional measurements focused on the operations of a single firm in the channel, minimizing the impact these measurements had on other channel members. The issue today is to identify measurements that can be shared by partner firms and agree on their definition. Very little work was done in this area until 1996, when two firms, PRTM and Advanced Manufacturing Research (AMR), formed the Supply Chain Council (SCC) with 73 firms as members. Today the SCC has over 400 members and is a nonprofit trade organization. This organization developed a model called Supply Chain Operations Reference (SCOR), which has four parts: plan, source, make, and deliver. Each of these parts is considered a primary process in the supply chain with performance

T A B L E   7–3

Nabisco Case Fill and Revenue Lost

	Case Fill %	Cases Shipped (k)	Cases Canc. (K)	Sales Canc. (Sm)
Family A	96.2	2,886	114.0	2.280
Family B	99.1	991	9.0	.630
Family C	95.3	3,812	188.0	4.700
Family D	98.2	4.419	81.0	2.187
Subtotal	96.9	12,108	392.0	9.797
Other	98.2	2,160.4	39.6	.911
Grand total	97.1	14,268.4	431.6	10,708

All numbers are disguised.

attributes, metrics, and best practices. For example: Plan has four sub-processes, Source has three subprocesses, Make has five subprocesses, and Deliver has three subprocesses. The three subprocesses in Deliver are: (1) deliver stocked product; (2) deliver make to order product; and (3) deliver engineered to order product. Subprocess 1 has four performance attributes: (1) cycle time; (2) cost; (3) service/quality; and (4) assets. For each of these performance attributes, standard metrics are offered. For example, the two metrics offered for cycle time are published lead time and order fulfillment cycle time.[18] The point of this model is to offer agreement on the processes in the supply chain and provide agreed-upon measures that cut across supply chain partners.

The SCOR model provides an excellent framework for quantifying the operations in the supply chain. What is necessary are models to translate these operations metrics into financial results. This is not traditionally how supply chain, and especially logistics, performance has been measured. Part of the problem in relating supply chain operations to financial performance has been the lack of data and methodologies to relate service changes to revenue changes for a firm. One firm that has been able to develop this relationship is the Nabisco Foods Group. Table 7–3 shows how the supply chain organization at Nabisco reports the effect of its case fill to upper management.[19] This methodology assumes

---

18. This information was taken from *Supply Chain Operations Reference Model: Level 1 and 2 Reference Guide*, Supply Chain Council, August 1, 1997.

19. Novack et al., op. cit., p. 144.

T A B L E   7–4

Nabisco Logistics Costs and Service and Business
Unit Contribution

	Latest Forecast		Proposed P&L		
	$M	% of Net Income	$m	% of Net Income	Change $m
Net sales	500.0	1292	512.9	1292	12.92
BUC*	166.7	431	171.9	431	4.40
Income before taxes	66.7	172	68.3	172	1.60
Net income	38.7	100	39.7	100	1.00

[1]A $1 reduction in inventory results in a direct $1 increase to business unit cash flow.
[2]It takes $12.92 more sales, or $4.40 more BUC, to generate the same $1 increase to cash flow.
[3]Assuming an average case selling price of $25, a BUC margin of 33.34%, and a YTD case fill average of 97.1% (Exhibit 21), each 0.1% in business unit case fill contributes $166,800 to BUC.
*BUC = business unit contribution
All numbers are disguised

that if a case of product is not shipped to a customer, the sale of that case is lost. The bottom line of the report is that an overall case fill of 97.1% results in lost sales of over $10 million per month. This information is used to rationalize investments in supply chain initiatives to avoid lost sales.

Supply chain operations have traditionally been viewed as cost centers within most organizations. In this view, cost increases are viewed negatively by upper management even if the increased cost resulted in an overall financial improvement for the firm. What is needed is the ability to relate supply chain costs to the financial health of the firm. Nabisco has made advances in this area also. Table 7–4 shows a financial analysis performed by this group on the implications of inventory reductions on cash flow, revenue, and BUC (Business Unit Contribution).[20] As this exhibit shows, a $1 reduction in inventory has direct cash flow and profitability implications for brand managers and the firm as a whole. The ability to translate supply chain cost changes to a firm's profitability changes upper management's view of the supply chain from a cost center to a profit or investment center.

Finally, one of the objectives of SCM is to make all channel partners profitable. If a supplier's customers are profitable, they will invest more

20. Ibid., p. 149.

T A B L E   7–5

Procter & Gamble Continuous Replenishment Services, Analysis Summary: Sample Customer

	Per Case			
	Base	**Option**	**Change**	**Per Year**
Acquisition price	$50.00	$50.00	$0.00	$0
Warehouse/dc				
Handling	$ .270	$ .270	$0.00	$0
Occupancy and equipment	$ .300	$ .260	$0.04	$10,000
Interest on inventory	$ .060	$ .006	$0.054	$13,500
Total warehouse	$ .630	$ .536	$0.094	$23,500
Transportation to store	$ .240	$ .240	$0.00	$0
Store				
Handling	$ .463	$ .463	$0.00	$0
Occupancy and equipment	$ .379	$ .379	$0.00	$0
Interest on inventory	$ .046	$ .046	$0.00	$0
Total store	$ .888	$ .888	$0.00	$0
Before tax profit increase (cost)			$0.97	$23,500
One-time cash flow increase				$250,000

Inventory reduction	BASE	OPTION	CHANGE
Whse cases	20,000	15,000	5,000
Whse days	20	15	5

5,000 cases × $50 acquisition price + $250.00

All numbers are disguised.

in the relationship with that supplier. This conclusion is well recognized by Procter & Gamble. Supply chain initiatives, like that shown in Table 7–5, are undertaken to help reduce the cost of P&G's products to retail customers.[21] If a retailer makes more margin on P&G products than it does on the competitors', the customer would be prudent to invest more in the relationship with P&G. Table 7–5 is an example of an analysis done by P&G on the impacts of continuous replenishment service on cash flow. This particular initiative by P&G would provide the customer with a one-time cash flow increase of $250,000. The point of this type of

21. Ibid., p. 151.

analysis is to show that making customers profitable improves the financial status of the supplier in the long run.

Although performance measurement in the supply chain has proven elusive over the years, firms are beginning to develop methodologies to capture the operating and financial impacts of supply chain initiatives. These methodologies address both firm issues and supply chain issues. Although more development is needed, these methodologies provide a strong base from which to advance in showing the true strategic nature of SCM.

CONCLUSION

The underlying premises of SCM are not new to the business world. What is new is how and where they are being implemented. This chapter was intended to offer some insights on where SCM came from and where it is going. It was also intended to discuss what SCM is and what it isn't. The flows of product, information, and cash have always existed among firms. Unfortunately, they were managed separately if they were managed at all. Improvements in cost, service, revenue, and satisfaction have always been important in business. In SCM, however, the focus of these improvements is not necessarily for a single firm but for the supply chain as a whole.

SCM found its roots in the development of the logistics concept. This concept focused on the integration of activities within a firm to produce the lowest total cost. The SCM concept focuses on integrating these activities among firms so that cash, product, and information flows are coordinated so that all firms can achieve the lowest total cost.

What does the future hold? The next stage evolution of SCM might see the inclusion of more firms into a single supply chain. Many supply chains today include only one supplier level and one customer level. Future supply chains might include multiple suppliers and customers as well as transportation carriers and other third-party firms. Competition among supply chains within a given industry will increase, changing the nature of the relationship firms have with one another in a single supply chain. Organizational boundaries between firms within a supply chain will become even more blurred as each firm becomes more specialized in its contribution to the supply chain and its investment in the success of the supply chain increases. These changes will offer significant opportunities for the purchasing profession to become a key integrator in the management of supply chains. The ability to establish relationships with other firms and manage their contributions to the success of the supply chain will allow for a high level of visibility in the organization for the purchasing professional.

Regardless of what transpires in the future, it is safe to say that firms that practice traditional management styles will not be able to compete. The new way of doing business is SCM. As more firms see the benefits of SCM, they will invest even more heavily in its implementation and development. Change will continue to be inevitable. Firms must constantly assess the competitive environment and technological/relationship opportunities. However, firms embracing the concepts of SCM will benefit from the change and will be in a position to survive and grow in a dynamic environment.

CHAPTER 8

Strategic Alliances and Partnerships

Editor
Robert J. Trent, Ph.D.
Associate Professor of Management
Lehigh University

INTRODUCTION

A recent gathering of purchasing managers featured a presentation by a well-respected supply management executive. During his presentation the executive enthusiastically discussed his firm's effort in creating supply chain alliances and partnerships. The talk addressed the usual array of alliance/partnership topics—managing confidentiality, creating support structures, developing trust, measuring success, and sharing information. Soon after the presentation began, an attendee asked how many strategic alliances and partnerships this company had with suppliers. The group, expecting to hear that this progressive purchaser had dozens of alliances and partnerships in place, was surprised when he replied that his firm had two but planned to add a third. Three strategic alliances and partnerships? This approach to sourcing, which many believe is critical for creating competitive market advantages, surely warrants more than three! When asked why his firm did not have more of these agreements planned or in place, the executive responded with a question of his own—"Do you *really* know what it takes to establish and manage these relationships? We don't think we can handle any more than three." Strategic alliances and partnerships are like best friends—an individual can have many friends, but how many are truly best friends? Alliances and partnerships, like best friends, should be special and unique.

Strategic purchasing alliances and partnerships require time, a commitment of resources, and extensive information sharing before they yield the benefits envisioned by their use. As a result, few truly strategic alliances and partnerships exist today. When an organization says it has 50 or 60 strategic alliances or partnerships in place, it is likely referring to longer-term agreements or partner-like relationships that focus on single sourcing or cost reduction, rather than true alliances or partnerships that require extensive collaboration. In fact, an unhealthy perception of supplier partnerships still exists among many purchasing and marketing professionals. The purchaser views the partnership as an opportunity to get a lower price from the supplier (with no cooperative focus on cost drivers), while the supplier views the partnership as an opportunity to "lock up" the purchaser's entire purchase requirement.

Many organizations could benefit from the *selective* use of well-designed strategic alliances and partnerships. The two primary groups within the supply chain, buyers and sellers, must increasingly collaborate to identify market and improvement opportunities. However, just as boundaries within an organization can be dysfunctional, so too can boundaries between interdependent supply chain members. Cooperative advantage requires the crossing of interorganizational boundaries in new and nontraditional ways.[1] Nontraditional strategic alliances and partnerships feature extensive crossing of organizational boundaries.

This chapter explores the important topic of strategic alliances and partnerships, particularly between purchasers and suppliers. The chapter includes (1) an overview of strategic alliances and partnerships, (2) a framework for developing collaborative agreements, (3) the characteristics of basic and higher-level alliances and partnerships, (4) the factors critical to alliance or partnership success, and (5) three best practice cases that highlight the ideas presented throughout the chapter.

OVERVIEW OF STRATEGIC ALLIANCES AND PARTNERSHIPS

What are strategic supply chain alliances and partnerships? Unfortunately, no standard definition of these concepts is available.[2] The terms

1. T. D. Jick, "Customer–Supplier Partnerships: Human Resources as Bridge Builders," *Human Resource Management*, vol. 29, no. 4, Winter 1990, pp. 435–454.

2. Purchasing professionals should discuss with their firm's legal counsel the use of the word "partnership." In a legal sense, a partnership entails certain obligations and responsibilities. Purchasers are using the term in a much more general sense than the legal community. One leading firm has prohibited its purchasers from referring to relationships with suppliers as *partnerships*. Instead, this firm prefers the term *alliance*.

partnering, joint venture, alliance, cooperative agreement, collaborative relationship, and *interorganizational partnership* are often used interchangeably to describe contemporary efforts at cooperation among organizations.[3] One perspective defines a supplier partner as a firm with whom another firm has an ongoing relationship, involving a commitment over an extended period, and a mutual sharing of the risks and rewards of the relationship.[4] Another view is that a strategic alliance is a relationship between firms in which the parties cooperate to produce more value (or a lower cost) than is possible in a market transaction.[5] Finally, the definition endorsed in this chapter views strategic alliances or partnerships as

> A long-term, mutually beneficial business relationship containing specific elements unique to the relationship: an agreement detailing performance requirements and conditions, structures to promote successful interaction between parties, organizational alignment, clear measures of success, and a high level of mutual commitment."[6]

Why is there such interest surrounding collaborative purchaser–supplier agreements?[7] Most perspectives or definitions recognize that alliances and partnerships, when executed properly, can be effective ways for developing new technologies and products, obtaining critical resources, investigating new market opportunities, and complementing core competencies and incompetencies.[8] Alliances or partnerships may also satisfy a basic need or requirement to improve supplier relations or promote supply chain cooperation and effectiveness. Others rely on alliances or partnerships to gain access to critical technology, often before the technology is available to the marketplace.

Whatever the reasons for pursuing collaborative agreements, the parties to an alliance or partnership should have one primary objective when crafting an agreement: to beat the market. Alliance partners

---

3. J. Maes, and M. Slagel, "Partnering: A Strategic Management Tool for Change," *Organization Development Journal,* vol. 12, no. 3, Fall 1994, pp. 75–83.

4. D. Blancero, and L. Ellram, "Strategic Supplier Partnering: A Psychological Contract Perspective," *International Journal of Physical Distribution and Logistics Management,* vol. 27, no. 9/10, 1997, pp. 616–629.

5. J. D. Lewis, *The Connected Corporation,* The Free Press, New York, 1995.

6. R. M. Monczka, "The Global Procurement and Supply Chain Benchmarking Initiative—Strategic Supplier Alliances and Partnership," *GEBN Pilot Module Report,* Michigan State University, East Lansing, Michigan, 1995.

7. Throughout this chapter *collaborative agreements* or *collaborative relationships* are general references to strategic alliance or partnership agreements or relationships.

8. L. M. Meade, D. H. Liles, and J. Sarkis, "Justifying Strategic Alliances and Partnering: A Prerequisite for Virtual Enterprising," *Omega,* vol. 25, no. 1, 1997, pp. 29–42.

achieve this by pursuing two possible paths. The first path focuses on creating more *value* for the purchaser's end customers than would be available if the purchaser did not enter the alliance or partnership. The second path emphasizes achieving lower total costs. Efficiency or cost-reduction opportunities are possible when suppliers and customers collaborate. Such savings help firms offer market-beating prices without damaging supplier margins.[9]

Although well-executed alliance and partnership agreements can lead to competitive advantage, the shift toward collaborative relationships has challenged many firms, particularly in the United States. Developing longer-term, tightly integrated relationships with fewer suppliers conflicts with conventional wisdom and traditional U.S. supply practices.[10] Multiple sourcing, competitive bidding, and short-term commitments have been typical supply base management approaches. Operating for so long in a traditional mode means that many firms have never developed the knowledge, skill, or experience to propose, negotiate, and execute collaborative agreements.

Organizations must address a range of issues when pursuing alliances and partnerships that are usually not a concern with traditional contracting. These include, for example, confidentiality of information, the risk of providing early insight into product and technology development plans, risk sharing, merging of organizational cultures, and the ownership of intellectual property developed jointly. The idea of making a substantial investment in a relationship with a single source raises concerns about dependence and vulnerability.[11] One firm found that its access to innovation within the supply community decreased after developing a high-profile alliance. Nonalliance suppliers presumed the alliance supplier was guaranteed all future business and decided that technology presentations to the purchaser were a waste of time and resources.

Some purchasers believe that a single-source alliance or partnership relationship exposes them to opportunistic behavior by the supplier.[12] To counter this, a purchaser may use fewer suppliers to make the volume

9. Lewis, op. cit.
10. J. Richardson, "Restructuring Supplier Relationships in U.S. Manufacturing for Improved Quality," *Management International Review*, vol. 33, no. 1, 1993.
11. Richardson, op. cit.
12. O. E. Williamson, "The Logic of Economic Organization," *Journal of Law, Economics & Organization*, vol. 4, Spring 1988, pp. 65–94.

F I G U R E   8–1

Strategic Alliance and Partnership Implementation Process

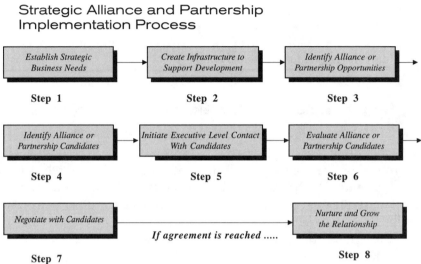

of business important, but still make suppliers compete with one another by relying on more than one source. This may reduce supplier bargaining power, improve quality, and lower total costs.[13] Without question, the alliance/partnership model conflicts with the practices and objectives of some sourcing organizations.

Pursuing collaborative agreements or relationships is not without risk. However, with effective risk management comes the opportunity for reward. Since competition now occurs between supply chains rather than individual firms, those organizations that have configured the most efficient and effective supply chains will be best positioned to assume market leadership. Executive managers that believe this to be true must consider the selective development and use of strategic alliances and partnerships.

STRATEGIC ALLIANCE AND PARTNERSHIP IMPLEMENTATION PROCESS

Figure 8–1 presents an eight-step framework for pursuing strategic alliances and partnerships with suppliers. This process is consistent with

---

13. M. Porter, *Competitive Strategy*, The Free Press, New York, 1980.

Spekman's four sequential steps in the alliance-building process: strategy development, partner assessment, contract negotiation, and control/implementation.[14] Most organizations have few strategic alliances and partnerships in place simply because the process of executing and managing these agreements is quite extensive.

Step 1: Establish Strategic Business Needs

It makes little sense to establish an alliance or partnership before determining if this approach satisfies business needs. The purpose of strategic alliances and partnerships is to create competitive advantages where less is available from traditional sourcing approaches. Alliances and partnerships must align directly with business needs, whether these are corporate or business-level needs.

Lower-level or basic alliances and partnerships often emphasize cost reduction as their primary focus. Alliances and partnerships, however, can also emphasize quality improvement, cycle time reduction, technology development, and product and process development support. The key point is that many alliances and partnerships should be higher-level agreements that link directly to what the business, rather than purchasing, must do to be successful.

Step 2: Create the Infrastructure to Support Alliance and Partnership Development

While it is possible to develop lower-level alliances and partnerships on an as-needed or ad hoc basis, strategic agreements require a support structure to oversee the process. Leading-edge firms often use cross-functional teams to carry out the detailed planning and execution of collaborative agreements. The logic of using cross-functional teams during alliance or partnership development is straightforward. Since strategic alliances and partnerships have an organizational rather than functional scope, it makes sense to have members from throughout the organization be part of the process. Not only does this bring together greater knowledge and skill, it also helps promote buy-in to the process. Of course, using a cross-functional team is no guarantee of success.

---

14. Meade et al., op. cit.

F I G U R E   8–2

Identifying Alliance/Partnership Opportunities—Portfolio
Analysis Approach

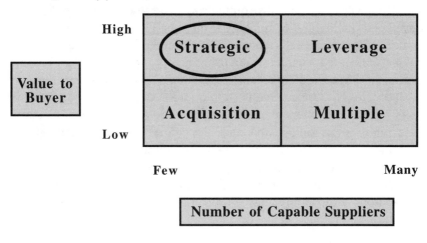

Teams with responsibility for developing alliance or partnership agreements are subject to the same risks that affect all teams (noncommitted
members, poor leadership, lack of data, lack of resources, etc.). Please
see Monczka and Trent[15] for a detailed discussion of effective cross-
functional teaming.

Step 3: Identify Alliance and Partnership Opportunities

Figure 8–2 highlights a segmentation tool for identifying alliance and
partnership opportunities. This model, based on work initially by Kraljic
and later adapted by Haluch, requires users to identify those items, materials, or services that would benefit most from an alliance or partnership. Organizations must identify the families of items and services used
within a business, and then place those items and services in the appropriate quadrant. The strategic quadrant will include the most likely candidates for alliances and partnerships. These items have a disproportionate affect on the business needs identified in Step 1.

---

15. R. M. Monczka, and R. J. Trent, *Cross-Functional Sourcing Team Effectiveness*, published
    by the Center for Advanced Purchasing Studies (CAPS), Tempe, Arizona, 1993.

Acquisition Quadrant

Items and services belonging in this quadrant are lower-value goods and services that receive relatively fewer total purchase dollars. Supplier switching costs are usually quite low, with the items having well-developed quality and technology standards. However, these items consume a disproportionate amount of time and effort to acquire. A purchaser's primary focus in this quadrant involves removing the effort and transactions required to obtain these items—*standardize and streamline wherever possible*. Organizations should stress lower dollar purchase systems, such as procurement cards, automated releasing systems, electronic data interchange, on-site managed inventory, and negotiated blanket agreements purchases over the Internet or intranets, to remove transaction-related costs. Strategic alliances or partnerships are not a logical approach for procuring these items, although longer-term agreements with distributors, for example, may offer some cost-reduction benefit.

Multiple Quadrant

Lower-value items with many possible suppliers characterize the items and services in this quadrant. As in the acquisition quadrant, these items usually feature well-developed quality and technology standards with low supplier switching costs. Purchasers should focus on price analysis while allowing the market to identify the most efficient producers. Applying pressure and offering shorter-term commitments is a logical sourcing approach. Pursuing alliances and partnerships for items within the multiple quadrants is also not an effective use of time or resources.

Leverage Quadrant

Items and services in this quadrant receive medium to high total purchase dollars with different suppliers able to satisfy the purchaser's requirements. A logical sourcing approach involves combining purchase volumes across locations, possibly with longer-term agreements. A purchaser's focus should expand to include not only price analysis, but also cost analysis. Because these items usually have established quality and technology standards, alliances and partnerships may be of limited value. Alliances and partnerships, if used for items and services in this quadrant, are usually less advanced agreements that focus on reducing cost or guaranteeing material availability.

Strategic Quadrant

Items or services belonging in the strategic quadrant are critical, higher-value goods and services with fewer suppliers capable of satisfying the purchaser's requirements. Value may represent a large commitment of dollars, the item or service may have a major impact on product or process performance, or the item or service may affect a purchaser's ability to satisfy its customers. Items or services belonging in this quadrant are often highly customized or unique to the purchaser's requirement with unproven or undeveloped technology. Because supplier-switching costs are high, a logical sourcing approach *features the development of longer-term collaborative relationships and agreements.*

The strategic quadrant contains the most likely opportunities for developing collaborative agreements with suppliers. Because these items are so important, collaborative agreements should feature aggressive cost, quality, and cycle time improvement targets. They may also focus on product and process technology development. Effectively using alliances and partnerships requires careful identification of those items and services benefiting the most from a collaborative (versus merely a cooperative) approach to sourcing.

Step 4: Identify Alliance or Partnership Candidates

The ability to identify alliance or partnership candidates requires reliable information. Many firms rely on their performance evaluation systems to identify current higher-performing suppliers. If these suppliers also provide items and services that are strategic to the purchaser, then opportunities may exist for pursuing a collaborative relationship. At times a firm may want to search outside its current supply base. Forming an alliance or partnership provides an ideal occasion to search for the best supply sources wherever they exist.

Identifying an alliance or partnership candidate may be relatively straightforward. A purchaser may have a longstanding relationship with a supplier, and it may become evident that elevating the relationship to one that formally endorses collaborative efforts makes sense. This may reduce the time required to plan and execute the agreement, since the participants likely have a working knowledge of each other. The potential partners may also have developed a level of trust. Experience indicates that the parties to a higher-level alliance or partnership often have some history or experience between them before initiating a strategic agreement.

Step 5: Initiate Executive Level Contact between Companies

While lower-level alliances and partnerships typically feature manager-to-manager contact, strategic alliances and partnerships capture the attention of executive management. Indeed, an executive manager of one company may discuss with an executive manager of another company the possibility of pursuing a collaborative relationship. If executive management feels comfortable with this idea, then the process may proceed to the next level of development. At this point executive managers usually assign ownership and responsibility for further discussion to an individual or group elsewhere in the organization. Detailed planning and negotiation between the parties rarely happens at the highest organizational levels (see Step 7). However, executive managers often demonstrate their commitment to the process by signing the documents governing the alliance or partnership.

Step 6: Evaluate Alliance or Partnership Candidates

Once a candidate (or candidates) has signaled an initial willingness to proceed, the process of detailed assessment begins. Evaluating possible partners is an intensive task requiring time and resources. Simply stated, selecting a strategic partner has longer-term consequences if not performed properly. Often, cross-functional teams visit a supplier (and at times a supplier team may visit a purchaser) to assess the candidate's fit and capabilities. The cross-functional team, while still focusing on traditional assessment areas related to any critical supplier selection decision, should pose questions targeted directly to the development of collaborative agreements:[16]

+ Has the supplier signaled a willingness or commitment to a partnership-type arrangement?

16. R. E. Spekman, "Strategic Supplier Selection: Understanding Long-Term Buyer Relationships," *Business Horizons*, July–August 1988, pp. 80–81.

♦ What is the supplier's motivation for entering into a collaborative agreement?

♦ Is the supplier willing to commit resources that it does not commit to other customers?

♦ What does the supplier offer that is unique or valued?

♦ Does the supplier have a genuine interest in joint problem-solving and a win–win agreement?

♦ Will there be free and open exchange of information and personnel across functional areas between the companies?

♦ Does the supplier have the infrastructure or trust to support such cross-functional interdependence?

♦ Is the supplier's senior management committed to the strategic alliance or partnership?

♦ Will the supplier share cost data?

♦ What will be the supplier's commitment to understanding our problems and concerns?

♦ Is the need for confidential treatment of information taken seriously?

♦ How much future planning is the supplier willing to share?

♦ How well does the supplier know our business?

♦ Are the corporate cultures compatible? (This is an important issue with foreign candidates.)

♦ How does the supplier view us as a possible partner?

While not exhaustive, this list provides insight into the issues that are important to the alliance or partnership process. It is relatively straightforward to assess these items using objective scales during the supplier evaluation process.

Step 7: Negotiate with Candidates

Strategic alliances and partnerships almost always require negotiation. These agreements usually involve large dollars, feature complex or changing technical requirements, or have the supplier perform value-added activities or services that are not part of a traditional purchase agreement. The need to negotiate many non-price issues highlights the additional effort required to properly execute collaborative agreements. Negotiation does not mean that the parties must arrive at a detailed longer-term contract. The process requires, however, discussing key issues and requirements before elevating a relationship to an alliance or partnership status.

Alliance and partnership agreements can address many non-price issues, which adds to their complexity and scope. Examples of issues often subject to negotiation include:

- Agreement on a supplier's allowable costs
- Volume requirements

- Relationship-specific asset investment
- Performance expectations and requirements
- Risk and reward sharing

- Agreement exit clauses

- Continuous improvement targets
- Performance incentives

- Capacity committed to the purchaser
- Agreement length and renewal
- Problem resolution mechanisms
- Ownership of intellectual property
- Joint resource commitments
- Technology support and assistance
- Resource support commitments
- Nonperformance penalties

The primary goal of negotiation is to reach an agreement that satisfies each party. Negotiation offers no guarantee that a purchaser and supplier will reach agreement. An irreconcilable difference on any major issue could create a deadlock, which means that the parties have failed to agree. Deadlock, however, may be a better alternative than reaching an agreement that is not in the best interests of each party.

Step 8: Nurture and Grow the Alliance or Partnership

The real challenge with collaborative relationships is ensuring that performance matches or exceeds the expectations surrounding their use. How can the parties ensure this happens? First, the alliance or partnership should feature shared objectives and goals that the parties can achieve only by working together. Each party can also assign a relationship "owner," who is a manager or team assigned the responsibility for addressing the relationship's specific needs. Performance-measurement systems also allow the continuous assessment of progress with feedback that helps drive improvement. Formal meetings should also occur between alliance or partnership participants. These meetings promote strategy alignment, encourage trust, and demonstrate a mutual commitment to the relationship. Exiting the relationship can also be part of this step. The relationship should continue only if it satisfies each party's needs or continues to provide competitive market advantages.

The process of establishing collaborative agreements with suppliers is more complex than traditional or longer-term contracting. Making alliances and partnerships a continuous part of an organization's sourcing effort requires a structured rather than an ad hoc approach.

STRATEGIC ALLIANCE AND PARTNERSHIP CHARACTERISTICS

Alliances and partnerships differ widely in their scope and effectiveness. Having collaborative agreements is not a yes or no proposition—yes, these agreements are in place, or no, they are not. One agreement or relationship may be basic, while another is strategic or advanced. Furthermore, an alliance may start as basic or general in its focus but evolve over time to create new and exciting opportunities for the participants. Whatever the reason for the alliance or partnership, certain features differentiate more advanced (i.e., strategic) agreements from less advanced agreements.[17] Box 8–1 summarizes these differentiating characteristics.

Basic supply chain alliances and partnerships usually focus on cost- and risk-reduction opportunities. Risk reduction refers to assurance of material or service supply. Development is less structured or formal than with moderately or advanced agreements. By definition, basic alliances and partnerships have low organizational visibility, with the agreement targeted to a specific item(s) or service. These agreements also do not feature strong linkages to functional or business goals. While a reduced purchase price is often a key measure of success, basic agreements may also focus on transaction cost reduction. For example, MRO partnership agreements, which are normally basic-level agreements, focus pri-

17. Monczka, op. cit.

B O X   8-1

Alliance and Partnership Characteristics

BASIC

- Minimal use of cross-functional/cross-locational teams
- Less structured development process
- Focus on risk and cost reduction
- Limited to functional executive involvement
- Measure success by purchase price reduction
- Minimal linkage to business or functional goals
- Low organizational visibility

MODERATELY ADVANCED

- General reasons for entering alliance or partnership
- Direct linkage to functional goals
- Development follows a structured process
- Cross-functional/cross-locational teams manage the process
- Strives for performance gains in cost, quality, delivery, and cycle time

ADVANCED

- Alliance or partnership supports strategic business needs
- Features exchange of key personnel
- Relationship has high executive visibility and contact
- Often focuses on technology development
- Strategic performance measures used to evaluate success—new markets entered, new technology developed
- Extensive use of cross-functional/cross-locational teams

marily on reduced transaction costs and availability of supply. It would be difficult to argue that these agreements provide a strategic market advantage.

Moderately advanced alliances and partnerships begin to align directly with functional goals. Furthermore, development follows a more structured approach rather than the ad hoc approach that characterizes basic agreements. Cross-functional or cross-locational teams are active in the development and execution of these agreements. Besides cost and risk reduction, moderately advanced agreements may target quality, delivery, and cycle time improvements. These performance areas, while important from a functional purchasing perspective, often do not link directly to specific customer needs or strategic business requirements.

A smaller percentage of alliances and partnerships qualify as strategic or advanced. Advanced agreements support corporate or business unit needs directly—they are organizational rather than functional in scope. They align directly with business needs or support end products or services. A key characteristic of an advanced agreement is the exchange of key personnel with performance results receiving scrutiny at the highest organizational levels. While less advanced agreements stress cost reduction or quality improvement, advanced alliances and partnerships often feature the development of new technology that becomes an integral part of a finished product or process.

Viewing alliances and partnerships as basic, moderate, or advanced does not imply that one type of agreement is better than another. For certain applications, a basic-level agreement will satisfy each partner's performance expectations. To transform a basic agreement, when that is what the situation requires, into an advanced or strategic agreement is likely a waste of resources. However, developing a basic or moderately advanced agreement for an opportunity that requires an advanced agreement may leave value "on the table." This happens when organizations lack the expertise, experience, or confidence to initiate strategic agreements. Not only must organizations identify alliance and partnership opportunities, they must also consider whether to pursue a basic, moderately advanced, or advanced agreement.

STRATEGIC ALLIANCE AND PARTNERSHIP CRITICAL SUCCESS FACTORS

Research and experience with strategic alliances and partnerships reveal a set of factors that are critical to the success of collaborative relationships. These factors are of such importance that the absence of any one of them can inhibit a strategic alliance or partnership or even cause it to fail.

Executive Commitment

Executive commitment is, without question, central to the successful development of collaborative relationships. But why is commitment so important? As mentioned, executive managers from one organization often initiate alliances by contacting executives at a potential partner. This contact conveys a message that the alliance or partnership is strategically important and warrants executive's management's attention.

Executive management also has the authority to commit the resources required to support the development of strategic agreements. Personnel, information, and budget are critical to the development process. Without resource support, collaborative relationships have a drastically reduced chance of succeeding. Finally, executive commitment sends a message throughout each organization that collaborative agreements are important and deserve support. Alliances and partnerships cannot succeed without organizational buy-in.

Rigorous Supplier Selection Process

Selecting an alliance partner is perhaps the most important sourcing decision a purchaser makes. Because the effort required to develop and manage alliances or partnerships is extensive, supplier-switching costs are extremely high. If a purchaser has not already identified a partner, then it must go through a rigorous and often time-consuming process to identify candidates. Performance-measurement systems often help a purchaser "screen out" lower-performing candidates from the existing supply base. Intensive site visits, for new suppliers or to gain further understanding of current suppliers, are also a key part of the selection process.

Joint Strategy Development, Problem Solving, and Continuous Improvement Efforts

For many reasons, joint activities are perhaps the most critical and sought-after benefit of alliances and partnerships. Joint efforts offer the opportunity to align strategies and coordinate activities between firms. These efforts also promote a co-destiny or dependency between the parties, which supports greater communication. This in turn creates greater understanding and trust between partners.

Organizations pursue joint strategy development, problem solving, and continuous improvement in a variety of ways:

- Regular joint strategy review and development meetings. Ideally, these meetings should shift between purchaser and supplier locations. The meetings should focus on discussing progress toward specific targets established jointly and identifying future opportunities
- Establishment of executive-level supplier councils
- Sharing of technology roadmaps and future product plans
- Establishment of continuous improvement teams
- Development of cross-organizational teams to manage and improve the alliance or partnership
- Co-location of alliance/partnership personnel

Goal Congruency

Goal congruency is important for several reasons. First, it implies that the partners have taken the time and effort to establish goals. The probability of a successful outcome increases with the presence of actionable goals. Second, it means that attempts are being made to satisfy the requirements and needs of each party. Without congruence, it is unlikely the parties will reach agreement concerning the value of an alliance or partnership. One alliance under study failed simply because incongruent goals created irreconcilable differences.

Alliance or Partnership Support Mechanisms and Documents

Cross-functional teams are often used to develop alliance or partnership agreements. However, using teams to structure alliances or partnerships is no guarantee of a successful outcome. One alliance featured sourcing teams that were not empowered to act on behalf of business unit management. This resulted in lengthy approval and buy-in that delayed the agreement. Another alliance had cross-locational team members with allegiances to their own facilities rather than the company as a whole. As with any team, cross-functional alliance teams must demonstrate they are capable of effective team interaction.

Many, but certainly not all, alliances and partnerships have one or more negotiated documents governing the relationship. This document may be a longer-term purchase agreement. As mentioned in Step 7 of the implementation process, these agreements address an assortment of non-price issues, including performance-improvement requirements, conflict-resolution mechanisms, commitment of relationship specific assets, and supplier incentives to further invest in the relationship.

A misconception exists that all alliances and partnerships are formalized through longer-term agreements. Experience at one company suggested that an inverse relationship existed between the length of an alliance or partnership agreement and the probability of a successful relationship. In many respects alliance and partnership agreements are different than longer-term purchase contracts. The underlying foundation of an alliance or partnership is trust, which is not something the parties can negotiate into a lengthy agreement. Detailed agreements and control mechanisms (such as document control logs) may be necessary in the early stages of an alliance or partnership, but their necessity often diminishes as the relationship evolves and trust develops.

While longer-term agreements often precede the formation of alliances and partnerships, other types of documents also support collaborative relationships. Rather than a formal contract, some firms develop a *memorandum of understanding* outlining the partners' expectations, commitment, and longer- term goals in broader rather than specific terms. One firm refers to the document that underlies its most important alliance as a *covenant*, which implies a deeper commitment to alliance goals. Box 8–2 provides an example of a partnership memorandum of understanding.

Regardless of the governance document used, the documentation process is ideal for communicating the relationship's expectations, requirements, and objectives. Signing the document also indicates a commitment to the partnership.

A Continuous Focus on Win-Win Opportunities

Collaborative relationships must continuously focus on *win–win opportunities*, particularly during joint strategy development sessions. The central theme of a win–win relationship is recognizing the needs and wants of each party. Furthermore, by collaborating, the parties can increase value rather than competing over how to divide a fixed payoff. Competition between alliance partners is not healthy to the relationship's longer-term performance potential.

Collaborative relationships demand a win–win attitude. When disagreements arise, a win–win approach requires the parties to work together to resolve their differences. These relationships must feature mutual cooperation rather than the competitive outcomes typified by

B O X   8–2

PARTNERSHIP MEMORANDUM OF UNDERSTANDING

The parties to this partnership have a mutual desire to be financially successful, maintain and expand their market leadership, and establish and maintain a win–win relationship that creates value for both parties. The foundation of this relationship is trust and mutual cooperation, and each partner will work to foster a trusting relationship and challenge the other to improve continuously.

To these ends, the partners agree to:

- Meet at least twice per year to establish goals, prioritize activities, and measure results
- Create a mutually beneficial purchasing agreement
- Work together toward improving product quality, improving process yields, and reducing process costs
- Maintain a nondisclosure agreement and document control procedures to protect individual interests

We also agree to share:

- Information about internal strategies and future plans
- Resources and expertise in a manner that creates the greatest value

For this partnership to be successful, each partner must adhere to certain commitments.

Purchaser's Commitments

- Purchaser will rely upon the supplier to provide engineered materials.
- Purchaser will provide design, technical, and marketing knowledge about industry requirements and how the supplier partner's products add value in this market. The purchaser will work with the supplier to create solutions to industry specific problems.

Supplier's Commitments

- Supplier will provide purchaser with access to new technologies.

Supplier's Commitments Continued

- ♦ Supplier commits to solve completely any material and processing problems.
- ♦ Supplier will provide purchaser with design, technical, and marketing knowledge about the use of engineered materials throughout the world, when ethical.
- ♦ Supplier will strive to provide material systems and technology for use in the purchaser's processes.
- ♦ Supplier will benchmark materials and services worldwide, with assistance from the purchaser, and to share the results.

_____   _____
Purchaser Representative   Supplier Representative

Date _____   Date _____

---

adversarial win–lose relationships. The partners within a successful alliance or partnership routinely scan their environment for new opportunities.

Extensive Communication and Information Sharing

A major difference between traditional contracting and collaborative agreements concerns the amount of information that moves between organizations. Because alliances and partnerships address a wider range of topics than traditional agreements, extensive communication and information sharing are essential. For example, a purchaser may share future product development plans and determine how these align with the supplier's technology development plans.

Communication and information sharing within a collaborative relationship occur in many ways, including regular meetings between alliance or partnership managers, perhaps to draft alliance strategies or report on progress or performance; co-location of personnel from one organization to another; point-to-point or parallel communication between functional groups; electronic mail; video or teleconferencing; and newsletters. Frequent communication should be a major secondary benefit—frequent, open, and accurate communication correlate directly with the development of trust.

Development of Trust

Various research has concluded that trust is a major predictor of alliance or partnership success.[18] While seemingly intangible, trust refers to the *belief in the character, ability, strength, or truth of the alliance partner.* Fortunately, the parties to an alliance or partnership can promote interorganizational trust, thereby increasing the likelihood of success. Various ways to promote trust include developing open communication across the organizations; co-locating personnel; following through on promises and commitments made; acting ethically and honestly; acting on the alliance's behalf rather than self interest; publicizing alliance success stories and personal narratives, especially those that enhance the partner's standing internally; treating information and data gathered within the relationship as confidential; and conducting regular meetings between the organizations.

Resource Commitments

Resources required to support an alliance or partnership take many forms: budgeting for travel and meetings; creating teams to develop and execute the agreement; providing relevant information; providing qualified personnel; providing the team to educate internal customers about the relationship; designating liaisons between the partners; and providing the time to support alliance or partnership activities. As mentioned, executive management plays a key role in making sure the resources required to support an alliance or partnership are available. Purchasers (and suppliers) that believe collaborative relationships require only marginally more resources than traditional contracts are making a serious error.

Clear Indicators or Measures of Success

A number of sourcing executives have complained about a lack of measurement systems to evaluate alliance or partnership progress. Others

---

18. Ibid.

complain about their inability to quantify the hard or tangible benefits resulting from the relationship, which makes justifying these agreements difficult. While establishing performance targets or goals is essential, measuring progress toward those goals is equally important. In fact, a recent study involving *MRO distributor partnerships* and *distributor–customer alliances* found that over 56% of respondents said their organization could not quantify the savings realized from these types of agreements.[19] For example, many alliances feature a shift from price (which is easily measured) to total cost of ownership (which is a difficult measure to capture accurately). Failing to capture the right data creates the risks of an erroneous conclusion about the success or failure of a collaborative relationship.

Internal Education Regarding Alliance or Partnership Goals and Expected Benefits

The development of collaborative agreements represents a change process at most organizations. As with any change, resistance is possible, particularly if participants do not understand or appreciate the expected goals and benefits sought from the relationship. For example, an alliance partner may receive a company-wide purchase contract. To avoid resistance at the business unit or plant level, progressive organizations educate users concerning the benefit of using the partner. Internal education is vital for overcoming resistance to an alliance or partnership.

Ability to Maintain the Alliance or Partnership When Personnel Change

Perhaps the greatest challenge faced by alliances or partnerships arises when the original participants no longer have direct involvement with the relationship. Indeed, one alliance under study failed when executive instability at the supplier caused a re-evaluation, and eventual termination, of the agreement. Because trust is often *between people representing organizations*, a shift in personnel can alter the relationship's dynamics.

---

19. R. J. Trent, and M. G. Kolchin, *Reducing the Effort and Transactions Costs of Purchasing Low Value Goods and Services*, published by the Center for Advanced Purchasing Studies (CAPS), Tempe, Arizona, 1999.

Successful alliances are those that maintain their continuity when personnel change. This requires making the alliance or partnership an accepted part of each organization's structure.

Research with supply chain alliances and partnerships reveals that *higher levels of trust*, along with greater *communication and information sharing*, correlate strongly with alliance and partnership satisfaction. *Joint strategy development* and *continuous improvement efforts* that create dependency also correlate highly with alliance/partnership success and satisfaction.[20] Organizations must pay close attention to those factors that will impact the success of a collaborative relationship.

MAKING STRATEGIC ALLIANCES AND PARTNERSHIPS A REALITY–BEST PRACTICE EXAMPLES

The following cases offer insight into how firms use collaborative agreements to create competitive market advantages. The first case summarizes an alliance focused on obtaining *strategic production materials*, the second highlights a leading-edge partnership committed to *advanced technology development*, and the third reports on an alliance emphasizing *early process design involvement*.

Best-Practice Discussion:[21] Strategic Material Alliance

Faced with intense competition, increasing customer expectations, and reduced product life cycles, Whitlin Corporation, a Fortune 500 appliance manufacturer, realized that the need to achieve a competitive advantage from its sourcing efforts was greater than ever. Executive management decided that a key part of its sourcing strategy should involve an alliance with a steel supplier, since steel is a major component used in all appliance products. Sourcing executives at Whitlin confronted serious questions regarding their future steel sourcing strategy:

---

20. Monczka, op. cit.
21. This example is adapted from Monczka, Trent, and Handfield, "Purchasing and Supply Chain Management," *International Thomson Publishing*, 1998. The company names are changed per the request of the firms involved in this alliance.

+ What do we need to do to be competitive?

+ Who is best suited to be the primary steel supplier?

+ What do we need to know to form an alliance, and how do we get the information required to answer questions regarding our organizational cultures, technological roadmaps, and longer-term directions of both organizations?

+ How do we implement a strategic alliance?

+ How do we establish a strategic alliance in terms of confidentiality agreements, termination agreements, and negotiation strategies?

+ How do we evaluate the supplier and provide feedback to ensure the alliance continues with regard to continuous performance, goal achievement, and commitment?

+ What do we do if we do not meet our objectives—change the situation or simply terminate the agreement?

Whitlin determined that it had to reduce its supply base and con-solidate volume with a single steel supplier who would target invest-ment specifically to the appliance industry. Most integrated steel pro-ducers in Whitlin's region stressed the needs of automobile producers during their marketing strategy development. Whitlin's expectations in-cluded *leveraging of the selected supplier's technical capabilities through early supplier involvement, day-to-day supplier redesign support,* and *continuous process improvement.* At the same time, executive management realized that in order to obtain these benefits, the supplier had to receive value from the relationship. The alliance had to create a win–win business environment, or else it was unlikely the supplier could justify the nec-essary investment in steelmaking technology for the appliance industry.

While these deliberations were occurring at Whitlin, executive mar-keting managers at Quality Steel, an integrated steel producer located in the same geographic region as Whitlin, were considering their own set of questions. Four higher level marketing managers had made the de-cision to reduce their customer base and were in the process of forming a new marketing plan to execute that decision. This decision resulted from Quality Steel's total quality management program, which dictated that to delight the customer, one must identify and make investments that satisfied each customer's unique needs.

A critical part of Quality Steel's strategy involved approaching key customers with the idea of entering into longer-term purchase agree-ments. In doing so, the company recognized that the best opportunity for reducing supply chain costs would be through early involvement with customers during new product development. This would require major investment in state-of-the-art steel processing technology tailored to the specific needs of each customer's industry. Quality Steel's marketing strategy became one of *reducing costs through early involvement in customer new product design while making capital investments in product design capabilities and new production facilities.*

While Whitlin had used Quality Steel as a supplier for several years, the idea of forming a formal buyer–supplier partnership was relatively new. As higher-level managers explored the idea, it became clear that a *complementary* strategic vision existed that could make an alliance between Whitlin and Quality Steel a reality. This vision had as its basis Whitlin's need to sustain a competitive advantage by supporting its own customer's requirements and Quality Steel's need to transition to a strategy that required collaboration with fewer customers. Thus, Whitlin sought to work with Quality Steel to reduce costs vis-à-vis the competition, and Quality Steel sought to obtain a major share of Whitlin's total steel volume. While this seemed straightforward, almost seven years were required before the alliance delivered benefits at the level envisioned early on by the partners.

Roadmap to Trust

The vision underlying this alliance slowly became a reality once each party understood that reducing cost did not simply mean lowering the price paid per ton of steel. Rather, reducing cost required *taking cost out of business processes*, which requires time, collaboration, and information sharing. The two companies established point-to-point communication linkages throughout the value chain, not just between purchasing and sales, to support the cost-reduction effort. The end goal became maximizing profitability at both companies while minimizing the use of explicit formulas and equations formalized in contract form.

As expected, the companies encountered a number of hurdles as the alliance progressed. However, as the vice-president of purchasing at Whitlin stated, "Neither of us let these problems get in the way of cost-reduction efforts, which in the long run far exceeded the changes in market steel prices." Overcoming hurdles in the relationship required a seamless organization and the elimination of bureaucracy. Functional personnel from each firm communicated directly with their counterparts, up to and including the chief executive officer. "The reason why this relationship works," said the vice-president of marketing at Quality

Steel, "is that Whitlin created an environment that allowed questions to be laid out on the table every time a new issue came up."

Alliance Timeline

The following illustrates the commitment of time and effort required to execute this strategic alliance. It also points out how alliances evolve as success is demonstrated and trust develops:

- In 1984, Quality Steel began to share its market strategy and management vision with Whitlin. This alliance is somewhat unique in that Quality Steel took the initiative when pursuing the alliance.

- By 1986, Whitlin had reduced its supply base from eleven steel suppliers to seven, and Quality Steel had invested over $1 billion in new capital equipment and technology. This investment was specifically targeted for Whitlin's industry requirements rather than Quality Steel's other major market, the automobile industry. The supplier required access to Whitlin's engineers to identify the various ways the purchaser used steel, which Quality Steel had to translate into process specifications. At this point, Whitlin provided assurances that Quality Steel would progressively receive a larger share of its orders. This required faith by the supplier, since the parties did not enter into the mechanics of accounting or contractual negotiations. An important action by Whitlin, and one that helped further develop trust within the relationship, was that the purchaser placed the orders it said it would.

- In 1988 and 1989, Whitlin conducted a higher-level alliance review. This evaluation resulted in an increase in orders to Quality Steel by 30%. Simultaneously, the two parties began their first joint cost-reduction project, which sought to eliminate costs from business processes.

- By 1990, Whitlin had reduced its steel suppliers to four. The companies held a joint leadership meeting to bring the alliance to the attention of each company's highest corporate officers and to formally develop a supplier council. The companies also developed a joint long-range vision, which was deemed critical to alliance success.

- The alliance solidified in 1993. By this time, Quality Steel had established resources at its technical center dedicated to the needs of Whitlin.

♦ In 1994, Whitlin increased its orders to Quality Steel by another 15%, bringing the total to approximately 80% of the purchaser's total steel requirements. At this point, the two companies were developing joint strategies. Purchasing management at Whitlin and Quality Steel were now actively involved in top-level strategic planning. To date, the strategic alliance between Whitlin and Quality Steel is still in place and providing strategic market benefits that a traditional relationship simply cannot provide.

Issues and Concerns

Throughout the process of moving the alliance forward, the companies had to address a number of issues. First, differing employee practices and cultures between the two companies sometimes led to conflict. The partners alleviated this conflict by promoting greater cross-organizational communication and interaction. Whitlin assigned a buyer, for example, to work at the supplier's facility. The sharing of cost data was also problematic, but this happened at staggered times as the partners targeted specific cost drivers. A recognition that success required the open sharing of seemingly confidential information helped resolve this issue.

Quality Steel became concerned that a single sourcing policy might result in losing touch with the marketplace. The supplier was also concerned about confidentiality of information, including proprietary process technology. At the same time, Whitlin was concerned about the risks of relying on a single supplier. What if process technology changed and Quality Steel failed to endorse the new technology? These concerns were ultimately overshadowed by the belief that the alliance, and the value the alliance created, was allowing both companies to become low-cost–high-quality producers.

Lessons Learned

Managers at Whitlin and Quality Steel recommend that organizations who are considering supplier alliances think early on about how they will deal with issues such as risk sharing, strategy alignment, communication, confidentiality, and growth. Although no single or right answer exists, alliance partners must tailor their response to these issues according to the specific situation. For example, Whitlin and Quality Steel had to undergo a significant organizational realignment before personnel could work cross-organizationally.

The supplier council was instrumental in the success and growth of this relationship. It supported the sharing and alignment of higher-level strategies and tactics so that each party became aware of the other's needs and activities. Even though the CEO at Whitlin changed several times during this period, the level of trust that had developed ensured that the relationship continued. The supplier council played a key role in promoting trust. Eventually, the relationship was no longer between people but between organizations. Senior management discussions, through formal meetings and informal "pick up the phone" conversations, also helped promote trust.

Representatives from Quality Steel also worked directly at Whitlin's development center, which created daily opportunities for informal communication and trust building. Quarterly performance reviews by Whitlin allowed Quality Steel to understand how well it was meeting its customers' performance expectations.

Both parties continue to view the relationship as a *covenant*, which implies a greater commitment than a formalized longer-term contract. Moreover, a covenant implies an enduring promise that provides a way to manage expectations. The relationship's most important belief has been the need to satisfy the consumer who purchases the finished appliance. This alliance, which highlights the value of a collaborative approach to supply chain management, also highlights the intensity and commitment required to make true strategic alliances or partnerships successful.

Best-Case Discussion: Advanced Technology Development Partnership

This case reports on a formal partnership created to *develop advanced technology* at a unit of a $5 billion global electronics company. The competitive environment facing this purchaser required faster development of products with greater functionality, less electronic packaging, and a lower price. A strategic partnership featuring early involvement seemed a logical approach for gaining supplier commitment to specific industry needs. The agreement featured here focuses on the technical development of advanced materials, often before the existence of a specific product requirement. Early supplier involvement occurs at the earliest stages of an advanced technology development process.

Partnership Development

During the late 1980s, a Chief Engineer at the purchaser put forth the idea of developing a supplier partnership covering engineered materials, a strategically important family of items. At this time executives from the purchaser and a selected supplier began to discuss what each expected from a formal partnership. An important point concerns how the purchaser selected its partner. The two companies had a long history of working together (dating back to 1964). This provided each company with a degree of familiarity. In fact, for many years this supplier was the purchaser's primary source of engineered materials. While not the highest-performing supplier across every product line (smaller high-quality niche producers existed), it was the most consistent performer batch to batch or lot to lot. Furthermore, this supplier had an excellent record of on-time delivery and responsiveness to customer needs.

The purchaser sought certain benefits from a collaborative relationship, including reduced product price; competitive benchmarking support where the supplier helped identify the approaches, processes, content, and materials used by competitors; and new material research and development support that would shorten product development cycle times. The supplier partner also had to satisfy or agree to certain requirements. It had to have available capacity and consistent quality; the purchaser reserved the right to approve each supplier manufacturing site with no switching of production from site to site without permission; the supplier had to be willing to sign letters of understanding and nondisclosure agreements; and the supplier had to provide a period of exclusivity for new materials developed jointly.

The consensus after a joint executive meeting was to explore the partnership further. The two companies formed a subcommittee with four to five people from each company participating. The subcommittee met four times within a one-year period to develop the partnership agreement (nondisclosure, expectations of each party, etc.). Subcommittee members committed themselves to this task because they knew executive management wanted this partnership to become a reality. The two firms entered a formal partnership agreement in 1991. After signing the agreement, each party trained and educated employees extensively about the partnership. The parties reviewed the partnership in 1994, at which time they agreed to renew the agreement.

Controlling the transfer of documents and information between companies was an important concern early in the partnership, particularly within the purchaser's legal department. A single manager at each company controlled confidential or proprietary documents moving across organizational boundaries. This manager maintained a logbook that listed transferred documents and information. As the partnership evolved, the exchange of information became more open, making reliance on the logbook less of a requirement. While the document control process is technically still in effect, the parties no longer adhere to this procedure.

Early efforts between the partners focused on technical projects *with minimal chance of failure*. The first project, which was highly feasible, involved replacing a metallic conductor the purchaser developed with one developed by the supplier. The next two projects were also short-term projects designed to deliver quick returns. The fourth project involved a longer-range vision in a technology area about which the purchaser wanted to know more.

Initially, the partnership did not create new business opportunities. However, a joint project showed the commercial value of collaboration. Within this project, the partners developed cost, quality, and delivery targets for a specific new product. This project represented a major technological advancement in engineered materials. Through collaboration, the parties estimate they reduced product development time by a year. The project's success allowed the company to enter a new line of business eventually worth several hundred million dollars in new sales.

Collaboration now occurs in *anticipation* of future product requirements. All engineered material needs that require external support involve this supplier. New materials developed jointly have helped generate new revenue. In fact, a major competitor now purchases items developed through this partnership.

Partnership Support

Underlying this relationship is a *declaration of partnership* and an accompanying partnership *memorandum of understanding*, both of which are supported at the highest executive of each company. The documents formalizing this partnership specify what the companies agree to and their commitment to the partnership. The formal memorandum governing this partnership has as its foundation a spirit of trust and expectation rather than legal stipulation.

Perhaps the most important feature of this relationship is how the parties identify opportunities for joint development. Formal partnership meetings occur three times a year, with the location switching between the purchaser and the supplier. Each party commits six to eight people to these meetings, which focus primarily on reporting the progress of joint projects and identifying future opportunities. While the parties still engage in negotiations, they discuss project descriptions, rationale for the project, and timing, rather than pricing issues. The supplier must still compete for purchase requirements that are not part of co-developed projects.

The partners have agreed to work on four key projects simultaneously. Some projects are vague and uncertain as far as timing. Others projects involve technology "tweaks" that progress at a steady rate. One project usually supports a specific product application. After completing a project, the partners replace it with a new project. Managing the top four projects is where the real involvement between the partners occurs. The supplier budgets approximately $1 million annually to support project development, although no special charges accrue to the purchaser. Development costs become part of material costs.

Cross-functional teams, with representatives from each company, work jointly on approved projects. Each partner provides a team leader, who is responsible for making periodic presentations to management concerning project status. If a joint meeting takes place at the purchaser's headquarters, then the purchaser leads the presentation. If the meeting occurs at the supplier's facility, then the supplier's team leader leads the presentation. Membership from the purchaser includes representatives from design/product engineering, research and development, manufacturing engineering, and sometimes a factory representative. Supplier membership includes technical marketing, materials science, and an applications representative.

A major benefit of this relationship has been the ability to work together to help achieve the purchaser's commercial objectives. For example, the partners once spent several days discussing how to meet future competitive challenges. The parties concurred on general marketplace trends and generated and ranked over a hundred new project ideas. The supplier has even agreed to represent the purchaser's interest and take ownership of certain ideas. In another example, the partners conducted a technology roadmap meeting where they identified a competitor's technology, which they leapfrogged during the next development project. Again, this highlights the value of strategic supply chain collaboration.

Key Experience and Insights Gained

The purchaser offers valuable insights from this partnership—a partnership that sourcing experts agree represents the highest level of purchaser–supplier collaboration:

- Create the structure to support partnership development and growth, including:
  - a joint committee to craft the agreement;
  - a declaration of partnership with signatures evidencing each party's commitment;
  - incoming and outgoing proprietary document control forms, at least for initial control;
  - a memorandum of understanding concerning confidential and proprietary information;
  - regularly scheduled joint meetings to identify joint opportunities.
- A formal agreement (although not necessarily a contract) is critical for formalizing supplier involvement.
- Expect early resistance to information sharing from both sides. As technical experts share information, the purchaser learns about the supplier (which exposes the supplier). On the other hand, the supplier begins to learn about the purchaser's technical and product plans. The situation is compounded when the supplier has units that sell to the purchaser's competitors.
- Development of trust is complicated when the parties to the partnership have units that compete. An early perception held by some at the supplier was that the purchaser simply wanted access to proprietary chemical formulations. Others at the purchaser thought the supplier would give product designs and plans to competitors. Here, the joint subcommittee responsible for crafting the initial agreement worked to overcome early misperceptions.
- Overcoming resistance to information sharing takes time. Once the relationship continued for a few years, the companies elevated the partnership to the next level of technical challenge. This involved developing highly engineered materials that can withstand extreme conditions. Managers now say that telling the staffs apart on a joint project is difficult.
- Start with early wins—success begets success. An early technical success created confidence in each party's ability to work together as partners.
- Transferring learning about the partnership throughout each company is critical. Having support systems rather than

individuals in place to guide the partnership helps "institutionalize" the relationship. Each change in personnel can result in a time-consuming relearning and reforming of the partnership.

♦ Joint intellectual activities can strengthen the relationship. The parties to this relationship have jointly published technical papers and received patents.

♦ An understanding of expected outcomes must exist before beginning a project. A lack of understanding created early strains within this relationship. For example, an early project featured the supplier helping the purchaser develop a chemical formulation. It mistakenly thought future business required the formulation, which was not the case.

♦ Both sides must get something of value from the partnership for it to continue.

♦ After completing a project, celebrate jointly. This brings the parties within the partnership even closer.

♦ To benefit fully from a *technology partnership*, the purchaser must team with a supplier who has access to technology worldwide or, ideally, has its own worldwide research centers.

♦ Benefits of this partnership and early supplier technical involvement include:
  ♦ reduced new product development time due to early technology development;
  ♦ new market opportunities resulting from new technology development;
  ♦ periods of technology exclusivity from the supplier partner;
  ♦ greater awareness of cost drivers;
  ♦ improved ability to prove the viability of new materials in a production environment.

♦ Maintaining a sense of competition is still important. Within this partnership, competition comes from knowing the partner's cost drivers and performing target costing.

A consensus exists among those involved with the partnership that it represents the ideal collaborative relationship. The two companies continue to develop leading-edge technology, often for direct product application. A consensus also exists that a formal partnership was vital for obtaining the level of joint collaboration attained within this partnership.

Best-Practice Discussion: Early Supplier Involvement Process Technology Alliance

Several years ago, sourcing executives at a major chemical company asked themselves a question most sourcing executives should ask: how can their company create cost- and time-based advantages through strategic sourcing? A major area of concern at this company involved the time and cost required to retrofit or build new production facilities. This firm had to reduce time and cost if it expected to stay competitive in world markets. Executive management began to ask whether aligning with key suppliers could help reduce the time and cost associated with retrofitting or building new facilities.

A major cost within process-focused facilities involves the designing, installing, and maintaining of process-control systems. These systems monitor and control the operation of an entire facility—they are the facility's nerve center. Historically, the choice of control systems was a business unit rather than corporate decision (this firm has over 20 business units). With up to fifteen suppliers providing different control system technology, moving operators between facilities and maintaining each system was difficult. Each system also required intensive training tailored to that system's technology. Furthermore, since each system was custom designed, higher investment costs and longer development cycle times resulted. The inevitable result was a reactive design process that offered no opportunity for early supplier involvement. Competitive bidding also extended the time required for completing a facility. Was there a better way to design and source control systems?

While this company relied extensively on longer-term agreements to support material and equipment requirements, it had never entered into a strategic alliance or partnership-type arrangement. Executive management made the decision to pursue an alliance featuring early supplier design involvement with carefully selected suppliers. These suppliers would have responsibility for designing control systems for all new and retrofitted facilities. After an exhaustive evaluation and selection process, the purchaser identified and negotiated a longer-term alliance agreement with two control system suppliers. For reasons that are not important to this discussion, the purchaser assigned each supplier to support separate business units.

The control system alliance was the first alliance agreement pursued by this company. This agreement has had the greatest positive impact of all nontraditional (i.e., longer-term) supplier agreements established to date. Even within this alliance, one supplier is proving to be more valuable than the other in terms of participating early in the design of retrofitted and new facilities.

Integrating with the Purchaser

The two control system suppliers attend corporate-level executive management meetings with the purchaser to discuss control systems technology. The alliance partners educate the purchaser concerning the direction of system control technology, which may then become part of the purchaser's process development plans. This involvement occurs well before the formal retrofitting or construction of new facilities begins.

The purchaser has assigned a manager with responsibility for managing and growing the relationship with each alliance supplier. Furthermore, each supplier is a formal member of design teams working at the corporate level. Both suppliers have also co-located a full-time manager at the purchaser. The costs for early supplier design support, including personnel costs, become part of a project's total cost. The purchaser requests a period of exclusive use for developments arrived at jointly.

While the suppliers do not know each process or application for every business unit, neither does the purchaser fully understand systems control equipment and technology. By working together at higher-level technology meetings and through design teams, the parties begin to understand each other's requirements and capabilities. The purchaser, through its longer-term *asset requirements plan*, influences how the alliance suppliers direct their R&D investment. On the other hand, the suppliers now influence the purchaser's retrofit and new facility designs. Design teams incorporate supplier-provided control system technology, rather than custom designing each system. This supports the company's primary goal of developing the lowest total cost system with the supplier earning a fair return on investment.

Besides providing technology support, this alliance has streamlined the time and effort required to retrofit or build a new facility. Previously, the purchaser would have worked with a design contractor on each project. The primary contractor had responsibility for subcontracting with a control system supplier. Now the purchaser works early on with its alliance partners and bypasses the design contractor altogether (along with the time and costs associated with that step). Furthermore, the purchaser can express its requirements directly to the control system supplier rather than through a design contractor.

Because the control system suppliers support multiple business units, visibility to each unit's requirements is critical. The purchaser has created a corporate-wide *process-planning network* to further its integration goals. Membership in this network includes business unit personnel skilled in control system technology. This network attempts to reach a consensus about what technology the business units require. As with any agreement crafted at the corporate level, user buy-in is critical. The corporate process-planning network helps create buy-in from business unit personnel by providing a forum to address business unit needs.

The two alliance suppliers are active participants in this network. The network provides a forum for expressing corporate and business unit desires to the suppliers. It also helps business unit personnel become familiar with the systems control suppliers, which is important because many had no previous experience with these suppliers. Because the alliance suppliers are competitors and serve separate business units, they meet separately with user groups. In fact, the two alliance suppliers have little, if any, contact with each other through their alliance with the purchaser.

Besides early design support, alliance suppliers have committed to help control facility operating costs through the efficient use of control system technology. One of the partners, for example, has placed a full-time engineer at a business unit to help control investment and operating costs. While difficulties have surfaced over information sharing, the business unit realizes its investment costs are too high compared with foreign competitors and is willing to continue with this approach. The business unit is analyzing carefully the benefit of in-plant supplier support.

This case provides key insights and lessons learned about alliances featuring early supplier involvement:

♦ A company should pursue relatively few alliances that focus on early design involvement. Firms must target early involvement opportunities carefully due to the resource requirements associated with design integration and supplier partnering.

♦ Successful early supplier involvement requires extensive and open information sharing. A company must manage the issues associated with providing early insight into product and process plans.

♦ Two-way communication is vital for understanding the needs and requirements of each party. Here, formal design team membership, executive level technology meetings, point-to-point communication, and involvement with a corporate process-planning group are formal mechanisms supporting alliance goals.

- Early design involvement relationships should shift from marketing to technical participation. Each party must be willing to commit the technical resources required to support alliance objectives.

- Early design involvement often evolves from the formation of longer-term agreements, which makes longer-term agreements vital prerequisites to early supplier involvement. They provide the foundation upon which to pursue early involvement opportunities.

- Design integration between companies usually requires new work processes and systems. Joint design activities create a new set of challenges that existing processes and systems cannot handle.

- Alliances and early involvement opportunities should evolve as relationships mature. Three to five years are often required before a purchaser can initiate early involvement fully with a supplier. Purchasers should continuously grow existing relationships and develop new relationships as required. Agreements and relationships require careful management (by managers) and continuous review and/or modification to be successful.

Perhaps the best indication of the value of this alliance is that early involvement has reduced by half the total time (including engineering time) required to retrofit or build a new facility. This alliance has directly supported this company's objective of becoming more competitive in world markets.

CONCLUSION

Even though advanced alliances and partnerships require a major commitment of resources and time, intense competition is driving firms in every industry toward integration and collaboration. Since individual firms can no longer meet the demands placed on them by acting in isolation, alliances and partnerships become a realistic, perhaps even necessary, response to competitive threats. For a company to provide maximum value to its customers, it must receive maximum value from its suppliers.[22] Strategic alliances and partnerships represent an effort, with the collaborative support of key suppliers, to create competitive market advantages by exceeding the value expectations of end customers.

---

22. Lewis, op. cit.

CHAPTER 9

Global Procurement Synergies

Editor
Ed Dauginas
Director of Purchasing, Raw Materials
Unilever Home and Personal Care USA

THE "GLOBAL" PROCUREMENT ENVIRONMENT

Global Scope and Scale

Today the term *global* is used to indicate both scale and scope in describing procurement activities. This term is appropriate in referring to the scope of procurement activities, but usually falls short upon examination of the scale of these "global" activities. There is a general preconception that once the scope of effort has been defined, the scale of the activity will automatically follow. There are several reasons for this:

1. The scope of procurement activities is defined and authorized by senior management and is formally commissioned by the organization itself. Organizational structures and reporting relationships are defined and objectives are agreed upon. This is usually done according to geographic subdivisions and usually follows the hierarchy of global, regional, and country.

2. The scale of procurement activities is more aspirational than definitive and stems from the belief that as purchasing volume of any given material or service increases, costs will automatically become lower. Theoretically, this is valid, but there are many factors that inhibit the realization of these anticipated economies of scale.

3. Supplier organizations are usually not completely global in scope and at best function in only several regions. Obviously, large-scale global agreements can only be made with suppliers who are themselves global in scope and organization. In reality, there are few truly global suppliers who can offer such arrangements.

4. Knowledge and experience of procurement personnel has been aquired in a local business environment and is centered on traditional procurement processes such as quotations, analysis of tenders, and negotiation of supply agreements. These practices, which have been optimized at a local level, are inadequate for obtaining the benefits of true global scope and scale.

Global Business Environment

The trend since the end of the Second World War has been in the direction of new, larger companies operating in more geographical areas. This evolution has been punctuated by the cost escalations associated with the "oil shocks" of the 1970s and the period of corporate mergers and acquisitions in the 1980s. In the 1990s, technology and governmental regulatory philosophy simplified the complexity of conducting business on an expanded geographical basis. Quality and productivity improvement initiatives inspired by Japanese industry have been adopted by most companies. The effect has been to reduce overall costs and improve profits.

Larger companies have begun to compete for markets and materials in new geographical areas. All of these factors have changed the characteristics of the global procurement environment.

Global Procurement Environment Characteristics

These changes in the global business environment have resulted in a global procurement environment with these characteristics:

Quality: Quality has increased and uniformity of specification has improved with the adoption of 1S0 9000 standards. Productivity gains have continued to reduce the cost of quality. Mergers and acquisitions by companies have facilitated standardization of sales specifications.

Communications: Recent technological advances have reduced the costs of telecommunications, and availability of these systems is now worldwide. The use of cellular phone systems and the Internet continues to spread.

Data transmission and management: The cost and availability of data processing hardware and software continue to decline. Combined with the improvements in telecommunications, this means that rapid, low-cost transmission of data is now the norm.

Regulatory climate: Tariffs continue to be reduced and removed. Larger-scale regional trading blocks such as NAFTA and the European Common Market have permitted reduction in costs and complexity associated with governmental regulation.

Labor: In general, labor costs continue to escalate, but this is somewhat ameliorated by productivity gains and the ability to source materials from areas with lower labor costs.

Transportation: The costs associated with all modes of transport (ocean, air, land) continue to decline as a result of governmental deregulation.

Currency values: Currency fluctuations continue, and the frequency of shifts and the magnitude of differentials is increasing.

Competition: Companies now face competition for markets and for low-cost sources of materials and services. Equally if not more important is the competition for providers of technology, leading to the creation of new products.

These characteristics, when considered in total, indicate a global procurement environment where the historic cost drivers continue to decline (quality, communications, data management, transportation, and labor) with diminishing governmental regulation of trade. These cost-favorable characteristics are balanced by the risks associated with major currency valuation shifts and the competition for low-cost materials and services coupled with the competition for access to new technology. Both local and global procurement organizations must now operate in this new and constantly changing procurement environment.

GLOBAL PROCUREMENT ORGANIZATIONS

Procurement organizations must complement the manufacturing or non-manufacturing organizations that they support. In general, procurement organizations can be centralized, decentralized/coordinated, or totally decentralized. The characteristics of these organizations are profiled below.

Type of Organization	Centralized	Decentralized/ Coordinated	Totally Decentralized
Management structure	Classical hierarchy	Coordinators/ committees/ teams	Classical hierarchy
Procurement responsibility	Geography/ Material or Material/ Geography	Geography/ Material or Material/ Geography	Local organization
Decision-making	By authority level	By group consensus	By authority level
Procurement strategy	Global/ Regional	Regional/Global	Local only

It is obvious that both the centralized and decentralized/coordinated procurement organizations possess the characteristics to operate on a global basis. Because we are interested in global synergies, we will consider only these two types and omit the totally decentralized procurement organization from this discussion.

Organizational Synergies

In both the centralized and decentralized/coordinated organizations, the procurement responsibilities are assigned either by geography/material or by material/geography. For most companies the majority of procurement personnel are located in a central office with regional procurement offices in locations capable of efficiently supporting manufacturing operations. Whenever the responsibilities are assigned with primary emphasis on geography or materials procurement, synergies will be obtained by coordination of the activities of the secondary area of emphasis.

For example, a company that has several regional procurement offices reporting to the central procurement office can be said to be organized with primary emphasis on geography. In each of these offices there will be personnel with specific material expertise. Synergies can be obtained by linking the personnel with material expertise into committees or teams focused on these materials. Similarly, a procurement organization with primary emphasis on specific materials can achieve synergies by forming committees or teams from personnel with material procurement responsibility for different geographical areas.

It is important to understand the purchasing authorities that exist in each type of procurement organization. There essentially are three types of purchasing authorities: *fully executive, coordinating,* and *collaborative.*

Fully executive purchasing authority means that an individual has been assigned the purchasing responsibility for specific geography or materials as well as the authority to carry out this responsibility.

Coordinating purchasing authority is the authority given to an individual (coordinator) to coordinate the individual authorities of purchasing personnel in different locations who are responsible for procurement in their respective geographies. This coordinator will decide procurement strategies for the concern and set the limits for variance from these strategies. This individual is responsible for conflict resolution and ensuring that corporate goals and objectives are met. Essentially the coordinator is a statesman who will set strategy and define policy, but who will exert authority only when necessary.

Collaborative authority is the authority given to a group of individuals (team or committee) to achieve objectives in line with corporate procurement objectives. This team will have a leader who is responsible for facilitating the working of the team toward its objectives. In short, he or she will ensure that the collective output of the team is greater than merely the sum of its members' efforts. The team leader will facilitate collaboration and cooperation of the team members towards the attainment of the objectives. This is much more difficult than the coordinator's role because progress towards attainment of objective and conflict resolution must be achieved by group consensus and adroit use of tie-breaking techniques. Team leaders must possess strong leadership and teamworking skills.

Attainment of objectives and progress of strategy are most difficult for organizations that confer coordinating and collaborative authorities on managers. Individuals are more comfortable with their old strategies and independent decision-making. They need to be convinced that synergies will be developed by group action and motivated by the attainment of positive results.

In summary, global procurement synergies can be obtained by adoption of organization structures that will coordinate procurement activities on two levels: the primary and secondary points of emphasis (either geography/materials or materials/geography).

GLOBAL PROCUREMENT PROCESS

The process by which procurement synergies are developed can be divided into four distinct stages:

Stage 1: Data collection

Stage 2: Determining material valuation

Stage 3: Procurement strategy formulation and execution

Stage 4: Nontraditional step changes

Stage 1: Data Collection

To achieve procurement synergies, relevant data must be collected.

The following data should be collected from each procurement office or location where procurement activities are conducted:

1. Current demand
2. Forecasted demand
3. Current suppliers
4. Potential suppliers
5. Specifications
6. Transaction currency
7. Length of current agreements
8. Total delivered cost

Items 1 through 7 are self-explanatory. Item 8, total cost, should be expressed as follows:

- Ex works or origin price (the price at supplier's shipping point)
- Transport and insurance
- Local receipt and handling charges
- Time value of money

Many companies ask their procurement organizations to negotiate delivered prices so that the allocation of procurement costs and the maintenance of material cost standards is facilitated. This tends to mask the ex works price and makes analysis via cost models extremely difficult.

Stage 2: Material Valuation

Traditional procurement activities were focused on a detailed comparison of quotations received from suppliers. This is an acceptable method when one is operating in a single geographical supply market, but when one is analyzing two or more geographical supply markets, these traditional methods do not always provide an optimal approach. It is often more useful to value materials as to what they are worth in the global market. This causes a shift in procurement philosophy to considering what is the minimum price that an organization is willing to pay for a specific material. The following sections describe data and cost analysis techniques that are focused on material valuation.

Data Analysis

The collected data should be analyzed in order to establish the current value of materials and benchmark pricing. This is accomplished as follows:

Refine raw data so that it is on a consistent basis for comparison. Examine specifications and identify differentials for premiums or discounts based upon quality.

- ◆ Create a "snapshot" of current pricing converted to the currency applicable to the majority of transactions using current exchange rates.
- ◆ Scan for apparent pricing inequalities. (Note: it is not uncommon to find pricing differentials of greater than 100% at this stage.)
- ◆ Perform detailed cost analysis on "high-potential" materials.
- ◆ Establish benchmarks and targets.

Cost Analysis

Two analytical methods can be used to establish benchmarks:

1. Least Ex Works price (L.E.W.) analysis
2. Markup Over cost Model or (M.O.M.) analysis

L.E.W. Analysis This method utilizes comparison of ex works pricing and recomputes delivered cost for each location from the supplying location with the L.E.W. price. A table is then constructed showing each ex works price and the delivery costs for each location using the L.E.W. price (Table 9–1).

From this L.E.W. analysis the L.E.W. price would yield a benefit when computed for L1, L3, and L5. A benchmark based on this analysis would then be established for each receiving location.

T A B L E   9–1

L.E.W.

		L1	L2	L3	L4	L5
A	Receiving location	L1	L2	L3	L4	L5
B	Current delivered cost from data	1.05	1.02	1.03	1.01	1.10
C	L.E.W. price from data	1.00	1.00	1.00	1.00	1.00
D	Delivery cost (from L.E.W. location to receiving location) from data	.02	.04	.01	.01	.06
E	L.E.W. delivered cost (C + D)	1.02	1.04	1.01	1.01	1.06
F	Differential (B – E)	.03	(.02)	.02	0	.04
G	Benchmark delivered price (lesser of B, E)	1.02	1.02	1.01	1.01	1.06

M.O.M. Analysis   This method involves the construction of a "cost model." Ex work's prices are then compared to the cost model and the markups over model (M.O.M.) are expressed as a percentage of the ex works price.

Cost Models

Cost models should be constructed based upon the actual costs incurred by the supplier in the country where his manufacturing operations are located. Cost models should be chosen so as to represent the highest percentage cost element in the suppliers cost structure. For example:

- If the cost structure for the item indicates that material(s) make up the largest element of cost, then a model based on this material(s) should be used.
- If the cost structure for the item indicates that labor or energy is the largest cost element, then a labor- or energy-based cost model is warranted.
- Similarly, if the major cost elements are roughly equal, then a model incorporating both should be constructed.

While it is desirable to have very robust cost models containing all cost elements, this is not always necessary. These techniques are effective with simple cost models addressing only the major cost elements.

Once the model has been chosen, it should be uniformly applied to the ex works price of each supplier being analyzed as shown in Table 9–2. The basic equation is:

T A B L E   9–2

M.O.M. Analysis

	Supplier	S1	S2	S3	S4	S5
A	Ex work price/unit (from data)	1.03	1.01	1.02	1.00	1.04
B	Material cost/unit from model	.54	.53	.55	.54	.55
C	M.O.M./unit (A − B)	.49	.48	.47	.46	.49
D	M.O.M./price (C ÷ A)	.49/1.03	.48/1.01	.47/1.02	.46/1.00	.49/1.04
E	% M.O.M. (C ÷ A) × 100	47.5	47.5	46.1	46.0	47.1

$$\text{M.O.M.} = \frac{\text{Ex Works price} - \text{Material cost from model}}{\text{Ex Works price}}$$

In this example the least M.O.M. is 46.0 for S4, which was computed by the M.O.M. equation.

Similarly, the benchmark price for S1, S2, S3, and S5 can be computed as follows:

$$\text{Benchmark price} = \frac{\text{Material cost from model}}{1 - \text{Benchmark M.O.M.}}$$

From the M.O.M. analysis in Table 9–3 the benchmark price on an ex works basis suggests a positive differential for S1, S2, and S5.

T A B L E   9–3

Calculation of Benchmarks from M.O.M. Analysis

	Supplier	S1	S2	S3	S4	S5
A	Ex works price/unit	1.03	1.01	1.02	1.00	1.04
B	Material cost/unit from model	.54	.53	.55	.54	.55
E	Benchmark M.O.M. %	46.0	46.0	46.0	46.0	46.0
F	Material cost/unit from model ÷ 1 − Benchmark M.O.M.	.54 ÷ (1 − .46)	.53 ÷ (1 − .46)	.55 ÷ (1 − .46)	.54 ÷ (1 − .46)	.55 ÷ (1 − .46)
G	Benchmark price (ex works)	1.00	.98	1.02	1.00	1.02
H	Differential (A − G)	.03	.03	0	0	.02

Target Setting

From Table 9–1 the benchmarks (G) are as follows:

Receiving location	L1	L2	L3	L4	L5
Benchmark delivered price (G)	1.02	1.02	1.01	1.01	1.06

From Table 9–3:

Supplier	S1	S2	S3	S4	S5
Benchmark ex work price (G)	1.00	0.98	1.02	1.00	1.02

Pending successful negotiations to reduce the supplier's ex works price, an additional benefit might be realized from a new L.E.W. analysis, since the ex works price for S2 is clearly lower than any of the original ex works prices.

Clearly, both analyses should be performed and targets should be selected that will optimize cost to the procuring organization.

Stage 3: Procurement Strategy Formulation and Execution

Strategy Formulation

With benchmarks and targets identified, a strategy to achieve these targets should be formulated. The strategy should encompass the following steps:

- Eliminating price differences identified in the L.E.W. and M.O.M. analysis
- Maximizing the impact of scale by reallocating volumes among existing suppliers
- Reducing the number of suppliers and reallocating volumes

Conventional procurement approaches are aimed primarily at maximizing the benefits associated with volume reallocation and the creation of one or a few large "deals." The strategy outlined above, however, provides for a more rigorous and time-phased approach that will ensure that maximum benefit is obtained from each step. This prevents the opportunity for suppliers to offer preliminary volume incentives as part of addressing pricing differentials.

Elimination of Pricing Differentials   Experience shows that mixed targets from L.E.W. and M.O.M. pricing analysis will yield optimum results. Leveling prices on an L.E.W. basis will reduce prices such that domestic manufacturers will engage in "shadow pricing," i.e., establishing prices just below or "in the shadow" of full delivered prices from L.E.W. suppliers. Leveling prices on an M.O.M. basis will yield results reflecting each supplier's feedstock position or process efficiency. The adroit use of targets derived from both methods will yield maximum benefit as targets are recalculated with each iteration.

Reallocation of Volume among Existing Suppliers   With the first step of price leveling accomplished, it is opportune to assess and obtain the benefit of reallocating or dislocating volume from existing suppliers. Analysis of volume pricing offered from suppliers using M.O.M. methodology will generally indicate the effect of amortization of fixed cost over volume. This will be indicated by a reduced M.O.M. for additional volume increments. The change in M.O.M. percentage indicates the volume sensitivity associated with suppliers' pricing strategy.

This volume sensitivity information, coupled with a corresponding L.E.W. analysis, permits targets to be established and negotiated on an iterative basis, similar to that employed to eliminate pricing differentials.

Reducing the Number of Suppliers and Reallocating Volume   This step is similar to that previously discussed in that it maximizes volume sensitivity. Obviously, if one or more suppliers are removed from consideration, increased volume will be allocated to the remaining suppliers. Available capacity should be ascertained for each supplier, and the reduced number of suppliers *must* be able to supply the required volumes. A cushion or reserve capacity provision should be included in the plan. The analysis performed for volume sensitivity using M.O.M. methodology can be used to predict fixed cost amortization effects. Negotiation targets can then be established for each supplier. As in the preceding steps, M.O.M. and L.E.W. analysis can be performed for each iteration.

Strategy Execution and Negotiations

With targets identified and a strategy formulated, negotiations to achieve targets may commence. Care must be taken in order to organize, structure, and sequence negotiations so that the maximum benefits are obtained.

Organizing the Negotiations   In any global negotiation, it must be made perfectly clear who is accountable for the conduct of the negotiations and who ultimately will decide to make the final agreements. The individual who has been empowered to make the final decision should also name the negotiation team and formulate the structure and sequence of the negotiations.

Negotiation Structure   Negotiation should be structured so as to provide the maximum benefit for the organization, and consideration should be given to the objectives, timing, candidate suppliers, term of agreements, and volume sensitivity.

- *Objectives:* The objectives of the negotiation should be based on the ability of the organization to accomplish the following:
  - Simple leveling of prices to L.E.W. or M.O.M. targets
  - Reallocation of volumes to existing or new suppliers
  - Concentration of volumes with a reduced number of suppliers

The ability of the organization to implement each approach will determine the ultimate structure of the negotiations.

A detailed analysis of data and refining targets is all that is required in order to accomplish simple leveling of prices.

Reallocation of volumes amongst existing or new suppliers requires that all using locations have approved the suppliers for use in these locations. This may be a mere formality or may require several months and the employment of appropriate technical resources. Data analysis and target refining are also required.

The prerequisites for concentration of volumes to a reduced number of suppliers are target refining, supplier approvals, and a thorough analysis of candidate suppliers available capacity. Contingency plans for the suppliers that are the most logistically challenging should be developed as well.

Obviously the timing of the negotiations is dependent on when the organization will have accomplished the prerequisites. The term of agreements should also be consistent with this timing. For example, the objective to level pricing differentials should exclude agreements for a term longer than the time to obtain supplier approvals, as this will delay/inhibit progressing to the next objective.

Negotiation Sequencing   Proper sequencing of negotiations can often lead to additional favorable results. The choice of how negotiations will be conducted is left to the negotiation team leader and team members. The sequencing of negotiations, however, should be carefully calculated to allow for adequate response time and the evaluation of preliminary results from negotiating sessions.

When "level pricing" is attempted, the first supplier with whom to begin negotiations should be the one that is most likely to reconsider pricing based upon resolution of previous competitive pricing situations. Should negotiations result in meeting or exceeding pricing targets, provisions to reevaluate L.E.W. and M.O.M. analysis with this new pricing may result in setting lower targets. This reevaluation of targets should be built into the overall negotiation timetable.

Similarly, in the reallocation of volumes, the initial sessions should be conducted with suppliers who have historically responded favorably to increased volumes, or perhaps those with the largest amount of annual uncommitted capacity. Reevaluation of L.E.W. and M.O.M. targets should then be conducted based upon these preliminary results. In the reallocation of volumes among a reduced number of suppliers, the analysis of volume sensitivity using M.O.M. methodology will suggest the first candidate with whom to negotiate.

Stage 4: Nontraditional Step Changes

Stages 1, 2, and 3, as previously discussed, represent the traditional methods of obtaining the benefits of increased volume and maximizing procurement leverage with suppliers. While this will yield reduced costs over time, some additional approaches offer additional cost-reduction potential: specification rationalization and supplier process analysis.

Specification Rationalization

Specifications are usually developed and adopted when a new material first enters the organization's manufacturing system. The specification describes all of the necessary and pertinent attributes that define the material. In general, the initial specification is often derived from the supplier's sales specification, modified to express any special requirements needed by the procuring company. Once established, these specifications remain in force unless modified for manufacturing, cost, or availability issues. Few organizations conduct formal routine reviews of their historic specifications.

Over time, manufacturing process technology changes (for both suppliers and procuring organizations) offer frequently overlooked opportunities to modify specifications. Global procurement organizations often find themselves having to accept less than optimal supply arrangements due to the dissimilarities of specifications and the "checkerboard" of approved sources for the same or similar material. A source of continued cost improvement can be found through the formal review of existing specifications. This review can be conducted by a group or committee, which can identify the specifications to be reviewed and organized to conduct value analysis for each specification parameter.

This review committee should be composed of procurement, technical, and manufacturing personnel. Their objective should be to identify which parameters of the specification can be modified, define the cost to modify the parameters, prioritize the cost improvement opportunities, and prepare the implementation plan to achieve the cost benefits.

Supplier Process Analysis

Another source of cost improvement available to global procurement organizations is supplier process analysis. This technique focuses on all aspects of the supplier's manufacturing process, including the raw materials and manufacturing technology utilized to produce the material. General raw materials specifications and the supplier's probable sources are identified from technical data about the manufacturing process and from the information used to construct cost models for the M.O.M. analysis.

The next step is to look for commonality in the supplier's raw materials and probable sources with the procuring organization's own raw materials and suppliers. If common raw materials and or suppliers exist, then areas of synergy should be investigated.

Once areas of potential synergy are identified, the "ideal process" should be constructed. The feasibility and potential cost benefits associated with this ideal process should be studied by a team of procurement, technical, and manufacturing personnel, and a project plan should be developed similar to that described for specification rationalization.

Oftentimes cost improvements are generated by the commissioning of material conversion arrangements in place of purchase agreements, and in some cases self-manufacture of certain materials or components is adopted.

CONCLUSION

In this section we have examined the global business and procurement environments, global procurement organizations, and a global procurement process.

In order to operate effectively in this global environment, an organization must compete not only for cost-effective materials but also for sources of new technology for innovative products. Additionally, there is increased competition in "home markets" as foreign companies market their products and source materials and technology for their own operations.

Global procurement organizations must consider the geography/material matrix in order to organize their sourcing activities efficiently. Multidisciplinary teams or committees should be commissioned to effectively obtain synergies from this matrix.

Global procurement processes must be optimized to achieve the benefits of traditional leverage associated with materials valuation and reallocation of procurement volumes. L.E.W. and M.O.M. analysis should be utilized to determine negotiation targets. Negotiations should be carefully organized and sequenced to achieve minimum benefit. Every opportunity for continuous cost improvement should be identified, and nontraditional approaches should be initiated. Sustained cost improvement is possible through specification rationalization and supplier process analysis techniques.

Global procurement synergies can be obtained by companies that have sensitized their procurement organizations to the dynamics of the global business environment, authorized them to operate with global scope, and employed techniques that will achieve the benefits of global scale.

CHAPTER 10

Challenges of Outsourcing in Supply Chain Procurement: How Best to Cope with the Changing Opportunities

Editor
Jack Barry
President
E-time, Inc.

Increasingly, companies are making the decision to outsource portions of internal business processes—from information technology to janitorial services. In the past, the supply chain procurement professional played a minor, if any, role in the decision or the implementation and contract management. While the basic premise of outsourcing is valid, that is, to leverage the volume and skills advantages of dedicated external expertise, the execution can often be flawed. Examples are contractural relationships that are vaguely delineated and contract management that can become a costly and legal mess. The key to success is not outsourcing itself but the ability to manage the outsource relationships. The Roman poet Seneca said it best: "If you do not know your home port, steering any course will do"!

Most companies now realize the role of the external outsourcer is not dissimilar to the role of external supplier. Thus the supply chain procurement professional is now viewed as an integral part of the decision process and the key part of the contract performance management.

The timing of that increased responsibility could not be more critical. While outsourcing has traditionally been focused in the overhead functions and information systems and technology areas, many companies are now evaluating the supply chain procurement and logistics activities as ideal candidates to be outsourced to third party firms as well. While applicable to all outsourcing relationships this chapter will focus on the challenges of outsourcing the supply chain procurement and logistics functions. The lessons learned from IT outsourcing can and should be benchmarks for the new and more dynamic outsourcing of the supply chain. The supply chain professional must be prepared to lead this effort.

In the increasing drive to reduce costs, innovative companies have long outsourced processes and services that are either not cost-efficient if done in-house or not core to the business and therefore diluting management focus. Most companies already outsource the major parts of their supply chain logistics functions: for example, warehousing, customs clearance, and freight auditing. In fact, the $400 billion U.S. freight transportation industry is a prime example of companies outsourcing an internal capability, i.e., the ability to ship and receive materials via external third party commercial rail, air, and trucking companies as a substitute for using in-house private carriage fleets. The growing third party logistics (3PL) service is an extension of that logic. Where in the past companies elected not to invest in the physical assets of vehicles and warehouses but kept the investment in the management personnel to run the processes, now innovative companies are even outsourcing the entire processes and assets to 3PL providers like Ryder, FedEx, and others.

If any company has not actively investigated and pursued outsourcing segments of its supply chain procurement and logistics activities, it will. It is in the best interest of the supply chain procurement professional to understand the value of outsourcing and be prepared for the inevitable challenge of outsourcing.

Outsourcing is not new. It even exists in the animal kingdom. There may even be an Aesop's fable on outsourcing—a fable that should be a lesson to all who intend to outsource seemingly noncritical, noncore processes or who do not understand the value and risks of outsourcing.

A particular species of African ant is a fierce competitor in its environment—which could be seen as its "marketplace." The ants' vision and strategic market positioning quickly established them as the market leader. Once the ants conquer the lead position in their marketplace, they settle back to a richly rewarded life of ease. But the ant seeks to pursue efficiency in its core activities. As the dominant insect, they then capture termites, who, not having the technological knowhow or financial resources of the ants, become slaves or subservient suppliers who must provide a full range of services to their client, the ant. In an effort to outsource noncritical functions to the termites, the ants have discovered that there is a cheaper, better, and faster way to get nourishment. The ants have their outsourcing provider, the termites, who actually acquire and chew the ants' food and then regurgitate the partially digested, semifinished work-in-process pulp, which the ants then eat. There is no messy, time-consuming chewing for these smart ants. Better to let lower-valued termites perform those functions so as to allow the ants to concentrate all their efforts on more strategic value-added endeavors like building more anthills. Unfortunately, if the termites should die, so do the ants because they have lost their ability to independently chew and digest food.

Most outsourcing advocates could learn a lesson from these ants and a better lesson from the termites. It may not be a core function and it may be noncritical, but can you survive without it?

On the business side, outsourcing has reached such a level of acceptance within businesses that it has become *conventional wisdom*. Recently several heads of major high tech firms declared that they were outsourcing their information technology because IT was not a core competency! Similarly, today major companies are placing an increased emphasis on achieving excellence in supply chain management and concurrently looking to 3PL to outsource major segments of supply chain management. These two visions are not in conflict.

A word of caution is appropriate here in that there is a wide difference between outsourcing and abdication. For example, *Reader's Digest* does not have printing capabilities, Xerox has outsourced its IT department, and most companies do not have interstate trucking and rail capabilities. These are examples of outsourcing, not abdication, and those capabilities certainly would not be considered noncritical, noncore processes.

On the other side of risk, or abdication, are the examples from the 1960s and 1970s where many companies "exported" the manufacturing of electronic components to the Far East, particularly Japan. They started with piecework, then expanded to subassemblies, and finally they completely outsourced with finished goods and private brands. In the race to lower the cost of manufacturing, many of these firms gave away their labor skill base and technologies to their suppliers who later became their competitors and finally the market owners. The American based television industry is a prime example of this phenomenon.

Today many companies export their information technology piecework to India. A serious question is, how long will it take before IT piecework becomes programs, programs become systems and later core technology, and outsourcing firms abdicate their real core strengths?

If a business does not know the difference and does not know what, how, and why it is doing critical or noncritical processes, outsourcing will only complicate the problems. We need ways to distinguish between the critical and non critical.

Much of this chapter is based upon extensive survey and interviewing research conducted by the author in 1994, 1995, and subsequently in 1998–99. This work was directed toward MRO acquisition and use within the firm. The points that follow present elements of the MRO outsource decision as well as general points for consideration in any outsourcing decision.

OUTSOURCING OF PROCUREMENT, ESPECIALLY MRO

The outsourcing of MRO procurement is rapidly gaining favor as a new "best practice." Many companies have found that 50% to 80% of supply chain procurement activities involve MRO and these must be managed differently than production materials. Where MRO fits in the overall scheme of supply chain procurement can be noted in Fig. 10–1. This quadrant model is based upon a distinction between value to the firm

F I G U R E   10–1

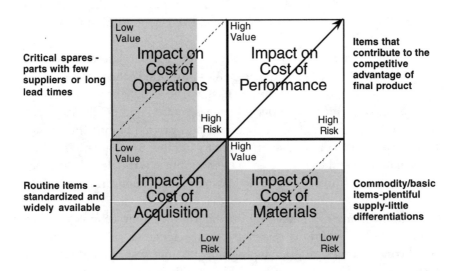

versus risk in procurement and product/service use. General MRO is generally seen as a low value/low risk product and service activity. Very unique and specialty MRO (overly or too-tightly specified) items are generally positioned in the upper left quadrant.

Typically, the material and services included in the general definition of MRO are:

1. Electrical and mechanical (includes repair parts, apparatus and equipment, plus those materials to support capital projects)
2. Electronic (parts and equipment and computers and peripherals)
3. Professional equipment (includes laboratory equipment and supplies)
4. Industrial supplies (includes general maintenance supplies)
5. Safety and health care equipment, parts, and supplies
6. Machine shop supplies (industrial machinery, equipment, and tools)
7. Office supplies and equipment
8. Chemical supplies and equipment
9. Automotive and fleet parts, equipment, and supplies

The MRO market is less than 25% of purchased costs but over 75% of all shipments, inventoried items, accounts receivable and payable, and the transactions processing cost. The transaction "cost to acquire" these low-value, low-risk, high-transaction items can often exceed the cost of the materials.

MRO is a non-differentiated marketplace with thousands of sellers and buyers—accounting for over 75% of purchases, transport, storage, inventory SKUs, and accounts payable transactions. It is often characterized as having substantial long, non-value time delays, and many hidden costs. Sellers are concerned with high and long outstanding receivables—high cost of order management, and high logistics costs and financial risks. Buyers are concerned with high material's costs, high costs of administration, and lower levels of quality and standardization.

Table 10–1 summarizes some major differences between Direct Production Materials and Indirect Materials MRO.

MRO procurement and logistics is a significant target area for cost reductions, quality improvements, innovation, and lead/process time reductions. Our research reveals that over half of all MRO transactions

T A B L E   10–1

Major Differences Between Direct Production Materials and Indirect Materials MRO

	Direct Production Materials	Indirect Materials MRO
Source	MRP	Catalogs
Forecasted	Yes	Rarely/difficult
Order format	Digital	Voice/fax/paper
Order frequency	Scheduled	Unscheduled
Average value	> $5,000	< $2500
Transit Mode	TL, Rail, LTL	LTL, Parcel, Air Express
No. of suppliers	< 250	> 5000
% of expenditures	> 80%	< 20%
% of transactions	> 20%	> 80%
Admin. cost as % mat'l cost	< 1/2 of 1%	> 25%

account for less than 2% of total procurement of firms and organizations at an average expenditure per transaction of less than $50, with an average cost to acquire and administer of over $65.

MRO OUTSOURCING

Most MRO items can be and are effectively outsourced. Initially, many companies treated most MRO items as location-specific so that any efforts to consolidate, standardize, or outsource were difficult at best. The reality is that almost 80% of MRO items are independent of local operations and can be consolidated, standardized, and outsourced at both lower cost and higher service quality to those local sites.

Businesses that have consolidated, standardized, and outsourced their MRO items have realized cost savings in material, inventory, and personnel ranging from 10% to 35% (as a percent of material cost). Interest in outsourcing the procurement and logistics services for MRO has grown considerably for several reasons which are as follows:

+ Many managements have accepted the idea that, in many cases, third parties can provide procurement and logistics services more efficiently.

- Some have have used third-party procurement and logistics as a way of reducing staffing levels.
- The acceleration of new technologies, particularly in procurement and logistics information systems, has made procurement and logistics management more specialized, providing opportunities for third-party services, and
- The ability of MRO suppliers to consolidate activities and spread some of their procurement and logistics costs across the volumes of multiple customers has contributed to the higher efficiency of their core businesses.

In a 1995 survey of both chief financial and chief logistics officers from the top 1,000 U.S. companies, the functions they identified as being currently outsourced were the known traditional highly competitive, low-margin functions. Starting with the outsourcing of supply chain logistics services, the replies as to the percent of firms currently outsourcing were as follows: customs clearance 45%; freight audit 41%; transportation 37%; warehousing 31%, and freight payments 30%. When asked about MRO products and services, 15% relied that their firms were currently outsourcing it, but 74% replied that MRO should be outsourced. Senior finance and operational management increasingly recognize MRO procurement and logistics as a prime candidate for outsourcing.

THE ROAD TO OUTSOURCING: SOME CRITICAL CONSIDERATIONS

Overall perception of the outsourcing of noncritical procurement functions as a major opportunity is growing as illustrated by the following examples.

- GE and IBM have substantially outsourced the MRO procurement of some plants to external third-party providers.
- Petrochemical companies like Sun Oil, Exxon Chemical, W. R. Grace, Pennzoil, and Chevron are currently evaluating outsourcing the MRO functional activities of purchasing, storage, warehouse and toolroom operations, payables, and delivery that support maintenance operations with a third party provider.

♦ Ford, Pacific Bell, and Ameritech are reassessing the accounts payable aspects of MRO procurement as a candidate for outsourcing.

♦ Others such as Bechtel and Conoco, are actively looking to enter the market as third party providers—using their skills and volume advantages to buy MRO materials and services— to outsource the MRO procurement function of utility companies.

In today's business environment, when companies are aggressively downsizing and rationalizing the total investment base in the supply chain to gain cost advantage, MRO is a prime target for reduction in staff, investment, assets, facilities, and "control."

Should a company build processes and capabilities to rival its competitors or rely on outsourcing to provide these functions without a major investment? The issues of mission, wisdom, risk, dependence, budget, and future positioning are often ignored in that decision process. The answer is different for each business, but some of the key factors weighing on the decision are in the following sections.

The Market for the Product/Service

Often, in a stable market, outsourcing is an effective alternative, when all other factors are equal. In a stable market, there are always ample capacity and enough providers to ensure competition, and, if all else fails, the company can revert back to providing that service directly. Of course, the twin fallacies are that markets are never stable for long and that the effort to restart discontinued outsourced operations involves long delay times and is painful. Our research reveals that most companies do not have realistic re-insource contingency options developed, or even disengagement plans from the initial outsource relationship. Further, missing from most outsourcing relationships are the specific plans addressing critical issues such as training, quality, responsiveness, emerging technology, and the ability to control the loyalty of the anticipated outsourcing partners. In their place are bland, nonquantifiable contract terms in the forms of beatitudes regarding goodness and virtue. Bottom line: an objective scope of the market situation of both outsources and the needs of the business are essential as a critical first step in this decision.

Dynamic Cost Benefit Analysis

Most original assumptions are not static. The cost benefit analysis for outsourcing must be able to requantify the risk and cost to outsource and "un-outsource" under different assumptions and situations. What is important here is to identify and improve the underlying business process needs and the required contributions even before considering outsourcing. It is critical to understand and quantify the primary stakeholder's requirements that are the underlying business processes. This avoids the following problem that has arisen in many firms along this path: applying a "burning" outsourcing solution without knowing the "burning" need.

Critical analysis should include the development of user requirements, process mapping, and effective benchmarks. We've noted often that experienced senior managers assume they can "wing it" in determining what is required, what is actually happening, and what the realistic benchmarks are. Outside help can be invaluable in the objectivity of validating the business requirements and clarifying the perceptions versus reality. Of upmost importance: the processes must be user driven.

Streamline the Pipeline

It is especially important to reduce the individual transaction volume and complexity of processes, otherwise unnecessary transaction "sludge" will clot and slow down the entire system. "ABC" analysis, or Pareto Law, is very helpful here.

The essence of this "ABC" analysis is a business cannot manage all items—therefore only manage the "A" items.

The powers of computers have led some to believe that all transactions can and should be managed. Loading a system with every commodity coder, variable and transaction (for example, MRO purchases and freight payable transactions) simply ensures a costly automated replica of the former manual system with little or no financial payback.

The key, therefore, is to reduce the volume and level of transactions to greatly increase the chances for a viable system—whether or not outsourcing is the ultimate solution.

Some key specific questions that are useful here are as follows.

- ♦ What are the strategic values that outsourcing will allow as sustainable competitive advantage in the rest of the firm?

- Can a competitive advantage be accessed from the outsource firm?
- What is the baseline measurement of current operations, and how will improvements in cost, speed, and quality of services be measured?
  - What are the processes in place today?
  - Who are the customers of these processes?
  - What are their goals and critical success factors?
  - Are these goals appropriate and are they consistently met?
- How are the processes measured to add value?
- What are the significant opportunities to improve these processes?
- What will it take to realize these improvements?
- How do processes stack up to "best practices"?
- Is the company organized, staffed, and trained appropriately for the present and the future?
- Can current processes and information systems adequately support the world-class organization you aspire to become?
- What level of benefits can be expected from improvements?
- What action plan is required to get moving?
- How integral is the process to key business strategies?
- What benefits does outsourcing offer and how important are they?
- What is the likelihood of a successful partnership?

Outsourcing decisions should be driven by the strategic factors of alignment, performance, and future requirements along with a base traditional business case analysis. Many outsourcings are non-strategic such as building maintenance, cafeteria services, and copying/printing. On the other hand, some are quite strategic such as joint research and development with a supplier. Businesses need a firm set of criteria, which determine when an outsourcing partnership relationship is appropriate in strategic settings. Some of the criteria must be in place at companies; some are provider-specific, and others require joint capability.

Outsourcing could and should be considered only when:

- An outsourcing relationship contributes directly to a business strategy.

+ The outsourcing technology—products and services—provided will involve the advancement of technology, concepts, and methods.

+ Both the company and its outsourcing partner are willing to commit to future investment and assume and share both benefits and risks of the relationship.

+ Both the company and its outsourcing partner are willing to openly share critical and confidential business information to improve performance and productivity.

+ The outsourcing partner will be able to provide service to the total operating and service network.

Understand the Realities of Technology

Technology is an enabler and not a solution—and often proven technology is more valuable than relying upon leading-edge but unproved technology.

Computers add speed and accuracy and thus visibility to problems and the development of solutions. If a business cannot solve or visualize the solution manually, does not understand the critical processes to be improved, or cannot quantify the desired outcome, then the chances are that an operating system will not only not help, it will hinder attaining desired goals.

Users Must be Involved in All Phases of the Outsourcing Solution, Creation, and Implementation

It is essential that operational users dominate the outsourcing project team and that they are empowered in the process. Our experience is that this avoids getting a technologically superior and operationally or financially unsound solution that later fails to deliver. In spite of good intentions and formalized user committees, most outsourcing solution developments are dominated by information and finance managers. Users are viewed as a necessary evil to be ignored or placated. On the other hand, it is better to have an unsophisticated solution that users will use than a showcase state-of-the-art outsourcing solution that does not meet user's needs—and is ignored and overridden.

That is why most users end up manually modifying the solutions. They often try to make it real and in doing so create a different system and results than expected. A tried and true tip here is to check your user's CRT if there are more than three "post-its" stuck to the screen—that's proof that there is an informal system being used, not the one you thought you installed. Only the stakeholders or users can understand what the problem is. They must take a most active role in the development or implementation of the solution. Otherwise you will fail.

Try to Avoid Speed

Senior managers often push for early positive indications that the outsourcing is a success, and herein lies a caution. This often brings pressure to slice some time here, cut some corners there. Most times this is harmless and merely reduces the "fat" that should be in the outsourcing installation plan (but call it contingency, not fat). A common problem we've noted is that a contingency is not then available to fall back upon. Make a plan and stick to it!

CONCLUSION

In truth, all the major operating outsourcing relationships can work well when they are based upon a sound strategic base, solid analysis, and the discipline to continuously ensure the integrity of the relationship and the accuracy of the value. Unfortunately, few companies are able to maintain that discipline past the short run. That results in two final states: (1) the formal outsourcing relationship is replaced by the informal outsourcing relationship, whose level of operating discipline cannot be maintained; and (2) the outsourcing solution never addresses the problems, and therefore the formal outsourcing relationship continues to run and is ignored in all practical applications because no one cares if it is right, since it is not part of the business. In all cases, the businesses incurred a high level of cost and made a large investment of time for a minimal long-term benefit.

It is necessary to assess and validate the assumptions about the ability of the environment to accept the demands of the new outsourcing relationships; in particular, companies must identify and anticipate organizational, communicational, and infrastructure barriers and gaps that will hinder introduction and implementation of the outsourcing relationship. The assumption that technical and functional managers really know or understand the *actual unwritten* or perceived rules of business is dangerous and mostly false. Without a disciplined stage-setting phase, your outsourcing relationships will try to replicate the business rules as imperfectly understood by technicians and functional managers, not actual users. Otherwise the result is not reality but a perception of reality. Unfortunately, the critical preplanning or stage-setting issues are usually not identified or anticipated until they stop the show.

The outsource arrangement is a living relationship and will change—be flexible. It needs to be a continuous and seamless evolution that will allow your outsourcing relationship to grow with the environment. The "Big Bang" approach to installations of major outsourcing relationships are generally costly and difficult; and once installed, painful memories and inertia often prevent continuous subsequent improvements.

Effective outsourcing relationships require processes for training, feedback measurement, and user training. If discipline can be assured, most outsourcing relationships will achieve extraordinary results and will probably require smaller, less unique, simpler outsourcing relationships to achieve desired results.

A final point: outsourcing relationships are not autopilot arrangements. They require oversight, management, and even leadership. High level professional supply chain procurement skills and competencies are necessary in managing these unique outside suppliers.

CHAPTER 11

Identification and Evaluation of Sources

Editor
Larry C. Giunipero, Ph.D., C.P.M.
Florida State University and
NAPM Professor of Purchasing and Supply Management

INTRODUCTION

Effective purchasing has been defined as doing the five "rights" correctly—that is, obtaining products, goods, and services at the right price, quality, quantity, time, and source. Of these five rights, the selection of the right source most impacts the other four "rights," and is the one which purchasing has a great deal of ability to add value to the procurement process. The identification, evaluation, and motivation of the proper sources ensures that the firm will receive the proper quality, quantity, time, and price. Thus, selecting the right supplier is key to the purchasing process. Perhaps more importantly, right selection is an important ingredient in producing products and services of high quality. Collectively, individual source decisions forge the total supply base of the corporation. This supply base and its overall effectiveness impact profitability, competitiveness, time to market, new product success, and overall business performance.

An important part of the selection process is evaluating suppliers. *Supplier evaluation* has two different meanings in the purchasing process. The first, termed *supplier qualification,* refers to prepurchase activities and involves prescreening or prequalifying potential suppliers with whom the purchaser may enter into a business relationship. The second refers to a set of systematic records, kept to evaluate suppliers' actual performance on a continual basis, and is most often termed *supplier performance evaluation.*

Drivers of the Source Selection Process

Purchasing should be continually refining and evaluating (with other members of the sourcing team and top management) which specific goods and services should be purchased as opposed to being produced or performed within the organization. One decision rule could be that a firm make only those parts that are critical to the firm retaining a high-quality product or that give the firm a competitive advantage. In another case, when suppliers have a cost or market advantage, purchasers should source these items. Often a new product or service will generate a unique set of purchasing requirements. Changes in specifications may render a part that was previously made internally a candidate for sourcing. Poorly performing suppliers may warrant increased assistance or elimination and subsequent development of new sources. Services that are viewed as core competencies will be performed internally, while those that are not viewed as value-adding will be candidates for outsourcing. In summary, it is important for the purchaser to be aware of what factors determine which items are candidates for sourcing. Sourcing more externally often comes at a price, such as during the General Motors strike during the summer of 1998, which was mostly the result of disagreements between the United Autoworkers Union and the company over the increased amount of external sourcing versus in-plant manufacture.

SOURCE SELECTION MODEL

The source selection model used in this chapter (see Figure 11–1) is adapted from the four-stage model developed by Heinritz, Farrell, Giunipero, and Kolchin.[1] This model consists of:

1. The identification/survey stage, in which all possible sources for a product or service are explored

2. The inquiry stage, in which the relative qualifications and advantages of potential sources are analyzed

3. The negotiation and selection stage, in which the appropriate supplier(s) is selected and the appropriate contract arrangement and expected type of relationship are set in place

---

1. Heinritz, S. F. and Farrell, P. V., Giunipero, L. and Kolchin, M. *Purchasing Principles and Applications*, Prentice Hall, Englewood Cliffs, New Jersey, 1991, p. 151.

F I G U R E   11–1

Source Identification and Evaluation Model

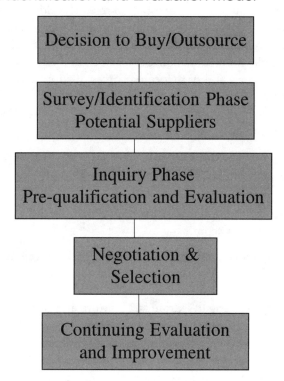

4. The experience stage, in which the continuing supplier relationship develops and evaluations of performance are measured.

The major focus in this chapter is on stages 1, 2, and 4 as they relate to the identification and evaluation of sources.

Identification/Survey Stage

Once it is determined that the requirement will be purchased externally, the purchaser begins the identification process. The exact specifications may or may not be fixed, but the general nature and purpose of the product are usually known. What is available on the market? Who makes such a product, or who can make it? Who can supply it most satisfactorily and most economically?

The original survey of potential sources should overlook no possibilities, provided they are reasonably accessible and there is some assurance that they meet required standards of quality, service, and price. The advent of electronic data sources located on the Internet has greatly enhanced the buyer's ability to locate sources of supply. Most major suppliers now have homepages on the Internet that allow the purchaser to quickly scan the product offerings and list prices of the suppliers' goods. Examples of some of these supplier sites are:

1. AMP Inc., the connector supplier at, www.amp.com
2. Marshall Industries an electronic parts distributor at www.marshall.com
3. Roadway Express a transportation firm (trucking) at www.roadway.com.

The growth of information and subsequent order placement electronically is projected to increase at phenomenal rates in the incoming years. Stephen Bell of Forrester Research highlights this trend: "Businesses will move conventional trade to extranets. . . . More and more businesses and regular suppliers will start to exchange information." Business on the Internet reached $43 billion in 1998, and was expected to grow to $109 billion by the end of 1999 and a whopping $1.3 trillion by 2003, according to Forrester Research.[2] This exchange of business information electronically is being adapted by business of all sizes from large to small. For those who work in large multidivisional companies there is a wealth of information about suppliers used by other business units or recommended by corporate purchasing on the company's intranet. Whether the search is conducted electronically or manually, the major sources of information about suppliers are listed in Box 11–1 and briefly discussed.

Many sourcing directories are now in electronic form as well as the conventional printed format. Trade directories provide comprehensive and well-organized listings of the whole range of manufactured products and manufacturers on a nationwide basis, usually with at least a general indication of size and commercial rating. The *Thomas Register of American Manufacturers* is a national trade directory used by many buyers. There

---

2. Stephen Bell, *1998 Forrester Report*, "Resizing On Line Business Trade," Forrester Research Cambridge, Massachusetts, 1998.

B O X   11-1

RESOURCES TO IDENTIFY SOURCES OF SUPPLY

- World Wide Web
- Company intranets
- Supplier home pages
- National and regional trade directories
- Suppliers salespersons
- Yellow Pages
- Professional associations and meetings
- Supplier catalogues and mailings
- Trade shows and trade fairs
- Professional purchasing publications
- Technical trade journals
- Chamber of Commerce
- Internal users
- Purchasers at other locations in the buyers company
- Historical purchase records

is an electronic version on CD-ROM and one available on-line at www.thomasregister.com. Supplementing these are regional directories such as those issued by state chambers of commerce and, on a still more local scale, the classified section of telephone directories. An excellent regional directory is the *Chicago Buyers' Guide,* which lists manufacturers and distributors in the Chicago area. Other state and regional directories are *Directory of Florida Businesses* and the *Directory of Southeastern Businesses.*

Specialized trade directories list concerns that do not have product lines of their own but provide industrial services, such as machine shops, heat treaters, and custom fabricators of plastic parts. With the continued expansion of world markets, more and more directories of suppliers in foreign countries are becoming available. These include publications such as Dun & Bradstreet's *World Marketing Directory* and *Predicast's F & S Index* by Predicast's Inc.

The buyer's collection of manufacturers' and distributors' catalogs is another reference source of prime importance. Many of these are now provided in CD-ROM formats that permit reduced space and easy access through their indexing systems.

Several purchasing managers also maintain a commodity information file in which they have collected suppliers' mailing pieces and data sheets, advertisements, and new-product announcements from business magazines. Some of this information is so new that it has not yet found its way into the standard catalogs, but the alert buyer can have it on hand when needed.

Salespersons are an important source of information, both on their companies' products and capabilities and on their application to customers' processes. Experience has shown that the most successful salespersons do not limit their services to buyers merely to selling their products and services. They strive to meet the buyer's needs, not only with their products but with whatever information, services, and technical advice are available from their companies.

Telephone directories, particularly in large cities, can provide a quick review of sources in a local area. Chambers of Commerce are also excellent sources for local area suppliers. There are many sources of published information, including advertisements and articles in purchasing publications such as *Purchasing Today®*, *Purchasing*, and *Electronic Buyers' News*. For specific commodities, technical trade journals will prove a useful source of information.

The buyer can build a workable list of likely sources using information from the publications and persons mentioned above. Those that appear to be reliable and stable, have the needed capability and experience, and are conveniently located should be put initially at the head of the list. Conversely, those firms that have low capitalization or credit ratings or whose products are not in the required quality range should be excluded.

Of course, the extent of the identification efforts and the time expended on these efforts depend on the purchase dollar amount, the criticalness of the purchase, and whether it is a new purchase or routine repurchase. If the product required is of a routine nature, the buyer may issue the order to a continuing source or send out a request for bids from a list of preferred suppliers. If the product is more important or more complex or one for which there is likely to be a continuing need, there will be a much more extensive inquiry and research into suppliers and their capabilities.

Inquiry Stage

The inquiry stage involves prequalification of potential sources, narrowing the field from possible sources to acceptable sources. More importantly, depending on the nature, size, and importance of the purchase, it is during the inquiry stage that decisions are formed concerning future projections on the potential for extended relationships, given the increased importance of relationships in the context of managing an entire supply chain. On particularly large purchases, the review scope during the Inquiry phase can extend to the supplier's supplier. For good supply chain management requires involvement with not only the direct supplier but the supplier's supplier. Regardless of the relationship sought, a critical analysis by the buyer is needed to gather more specific *information on critical areas* such as:

- Production facilities and capacity—age, type of equipment, and personnel
- Financial stability—through analysis of financial statements
- Product quality and quality philosophy—quality reputation and TQM
- Technological expertise—meeting both current and future requirements
- Manufacturing efficiency—producing the item economically
- Cost and overhead structure—direct, indirect, overhead, and profits
- General business policies—in emergencies and shortage conditions
- Handling rush, weekend, and nighttime requests
- Position in the industry—market share and leader or follower
- Major customers and suppliers—obtain names and contacts
- Management skills and performance—motivation, empowerment, and results
- Environmental compliance and attitude—lip service or commitment

The aim at this point is to find those suppliers who are capable of producing the item in the required quality and quantity, who can be relied on as a continuous source of supply under all conditions, will keep their delivery promises and other service obligations, and are competitive on price.

Cross Functional Teams

When the projected purchase will result in a continuing relationship or involve substantial expenditure or when the quality of the part to be bought is critical, inspection and evaluation of potential suppliers are generally made a team effort. Although the specific makeup of the group may vary, a typical team might include representatives from the purchasing, quality control, engineering, and operations departments. It is good to involve a team qualification process since the synergy gained by having multiple parties interact will improve the supplier. A multifunctional sourcing team approach offers purchasers several advantages over an individual approach, including:

1. Input from parties ultimately involved in the procurement
2. Consideration of a wider range of buying criteria
3. Responsiveness to user needs
4. Increased acceptance by users of the products
5. Understanding by other functions of the range of tradeoffs considered in making the final purchase

While much of this information can be obtained through logging on to the supplier's website, discussions with supplier personnel, and reading published material, in the final analysis commitments for critical high-dollar purchases require a visit to the supplier's facilities. However, it is a good idea to evaluate the financial strength of the supplier prior to incurring the expense of a visit.

Credit Rating

Financial failure can cause serious disruptions in the supply chain and subsequent loss of profits and marketshare. Dun & Bradstreet's (D&B) or other credit rating agencies can provide important information. Dun & Bradstreet, Inc. is available through the company (1-800-234-3867) or can be obtained at the NAPM Web site at www.napm.org.

Figure 11–2 illustrates such a typical D&B report. This report covers nine basic areas of information, each with its special use to the buyer.

1. *Business summary.* This provides an overview summary of the important facts about the company. These include: name, address, Chief Officer, annual sales, net worth, number of employees, and primary business.

F I G U R E   1 1 – 2

Credit report showing payments, highlights, and current information regarding a fictitious supplier.

BUSINESS SUMMARY

GORMAN MANUFACTURING COMPANY, INC	DUNS: 80-473-5132

	CONTROL	1965
	SALES F	$17,685,297
492 KOLLER STREET	NET WORTH F	$2,838,982
SAN FRANCISCO CA 94110-0000	EMPLOYS	105 TOTAL
TEL: (650) 555-0000		100 HERE

CHIEF EXECUTIVE: LESLIE SMITH, PRES	PRIMARY SIC NO. 2752
	COMMERCIAL PRINTING

SPECIAL EVENTS

10/12/98	On Mar 26, 1998 the subject experienced a fire due to an earthquake. According to Leslie Smith, president, damages amounted to $35,000 which were fully covered by their insurance company. The business was closed for two days while employees settled personal matters.

RISK SUMMARY

```
              SUPPLIER RISK SCORE FOR THIS FIRM = 8

  ▪▪▪▪▪▪▪▪▪▪▪▪▪▪▪▪▪▪▪▪▪▪▪▪▪▪▪▪▪▪▪▪▪▪▪▪▪▪▪▪▪▪▪▪▪▪▪▪▪▪▪▪▪▪▪▪▪

     Lowest Risk                         Highest Risk


          1    2    3    4    5    6    7  < 8 >  9


  ▪▪▪▪▪▪▪▪▪▪▪▪▪▪▪▪▪▪▪▪▪▪▪▪▪▪▪▪▪▪▪▪▪▪▪▪▪▪▪▪▪▪▪▪▪▪▪▪▪▪▪▪▪▪▪▪▪
```

The Supplier Risk Score Models predict the likelihood of a firm ceasing business without paying all creditors in full, or reorganizing, or obtaining relief from creditors under state/federal law over the next 18 months. The score was calculated using statistically valid models derived from D&B's extensive data files.

                    INCIDENCE OF FINANCIAL STRESS
The Incidence of Financial Stress is the proportion of firms with scores

(Courtesy of the Dun & Bradstreet Corporation.)

2. *Special events.* This section lists any major events which have occurred in the recent past and the impact these may have on the company and its future performance. This could include lawsuits, fires, loss of a major customer, new product developments, and so on.

F I G U R E   11–2

(Continued)

RISK SUMMARY (continued)

in this range that discontinued operations with loss to creditors.
Based on historical data in Dun & Bradstreet's files, the incidence of
financial stress over the past year:

INCIDENCE OF FINANCIAL STRESS: 3.28% (328 PER 10,000)
- Supplier Risk Score 8

INCIDENCE OF FINANCIAL STRESS: .65% (65 PER 10,000)
- National average

INCIDENCE OF FINANCIAL STRESS: .87% (87 PER 10,000)
- Manufacturing Industry Segment

SUPPLIER RISK SCORE ANALYSIS

KEY FINANCIAL COMMENTARY:
- Accounts payable to sales ratio is in the lower quartile for this
  industry.
- Quick ratio is in the lower quartile for this industry.
- Positive net worth is present for this firm indicating lower risk of
  financial stress.
- Return on assets is between the median and upper quartiles for this
  industry.
- Total liabilities to net worth ratio is between the median and lower
  quartiles for this industry.

RISK COMMENTARY
- Suits, Liens, and/or Judgments are present - see PUBLIC FILINGS section.
- Sales for the Fiscal year ending DEC, 1997 are Up by 36.0%.
- Net worth for the Fiscal year ending DEC, 1997 is Up by 33.6%.
- Average Payments are 12 day(s) beyond terms.
- Average Industry Payments are   8 day(s) beyond terms.
- Firm's debts on 20 occasion(s) have been placed for collection as
  reported to Dun & Bradstreet.
- Fire or other disaster reported - see SPECIAL EVENTS and HISTORY sections.
- Special events have been reported.
- UCC Filings present - See PUBLIC FILINGS section.
- Financing secured - See BANK/PUBLIC FILINGS sections.
- Operations reported profitable.
- Financial Appraisal Ranking is 3 based on a scale of 1 (Highest)
  to 4 (Lowest) compared to the industry. The appraisal is a calculated
  average based on the firm's quartile ranking.
- Statement prepared by Johnson, Jordan and Jones, CPA's.
- Under present management control 34 years.

3. *Risk summary.* This is a rating from 1 to 9, lowest to highest
    risk, which indicates the likelihood of a firm discontinuing
    operations and still owing outstanding debts. The firm, in this
    condition, may seek protection from creditors through
    bankruptcy proceedings. The risk summary also indicates the
    degree of financial stress; providing a percentage of firms
    which are likely to cease operations, given this overall risk

F I G U R E   11–2

(Continued)

FINANCIAL PROFILE

(Based On A Fiscal Statement Dated Dec. 31, 1997.)

The Financial Appraisal Ranking of the Supplier = 3
(Calculated average based upon the supplier's quartile ranking in the
available ratios.   1 = highest through 4 = lowest)

	PROFITABILITY	SOLVENCY	SHORT TERM	EFFICIENCY	DEBT UTILIZATION
	(Return on Net Worth)%	(Current Ratio)	(Quick Ratio)	(Assets/ Sales)%	(Total Liab/ Net Worth)%
This Supplier	20.6	1.3	0.6	47.3	194.4
Industry Median	16.0	1.6	1.4	51.9	156.8
Quartile Rank (Supplier)	2	3	4	2	3

Key to Quartile Rank: 1 = top quartile through 4 = bottom quartile.
Industry norms based upon 28 establishments.

rating. The stress level is compared to industry and national
averages. Comments concerning quartile rankings for key
financial indicators are provided, as well as trends in key areas
such as sales, debt, and net worth.

4. *Financial Profile.* This part of the report, including sections
   identified as Highlights, Current, and Supplemental data,
   usually showing recent financial rates, return on net worth,
   quick ratios, current ratio, percent assets to sales and total
   liabilities to net worth. From this section of the report, a buyer
   can tell which suppliers have enough capital to handle the
   buyer's requirements, information which can be just as
   important as whether the current capital equipment can
   effectively handle the necessary volume. This section is an
   important factor in assigning the credit rating.

5. *Operation.* This section of a Dun & Bradstreet report is the one
   a buyer probably scrutinizes most closely. It lists the physical
   facilities of the business, including size and location of plants
   and warehouses; proximity to transportation facilities such as
   rail sidings and docks; machinery and equipment in instances
   when considerable volume is under contract or made to
   individual specifications; number of employees; active seasons;

F I G U R E 11-2

(Continued)

OPERATION

10/12/98   Commercial printing specializing in advertising posters,
catalogs, circulars and coupons.
    ADDITIONAL TELEPHONE NUMBER(S): Facsimile (Fax) 415 555-1000;
Toll-Free (800) 555-5555.
Has 175 account(s).   Net 30 days.   Sells to commercial concerns.
Territory : United States.
Nonseasonal.
    EMPLOYEES: 105 which includes officer(s).   100 employed here.
    FACILITIES: Rents 55,000 sq. ft. in a one story cinder block
building.
    LOCATION: Central business section on well traveled street.
    BRANCHES: Subject maintains a branch at 1073 Boyden Road, Los
Angeles, CA.

Standard Industrial Classification (SIC) Summary:
2752 00 00 Commercial printing, lithographic

HISTORY

10/12/98
    LESLIE SMITH, PRES   KEVIN J HUNT, SEC-TREAS
    DIRECTOR(S): THE OFFICER(S)

    Incorporated California May 21 1965.   Authorized capital consists
of 200 shares common stock, no par value.
    Business started May 21 1965 by Leslie Smith and Kevin J Hunt.
100% of capital stock is owned by the officers.

    LESLIE SMITH born 1926.   Graduated from the University of
California, Los Angeles, in June 1947 with a BS degree in Business
Management.   1947-65 general manager for Raymor Printing Co, San
Francisco, CA.   1965 formed subject with Kevin J Hunt.
    KEVIN J HUNT born 1925.   Graduated from Northwestern University,
Evanston, IL in June 1946.   1946-1965 was general manager for Raymor
Printing Co, San Francisco, CA.   1965 formed subject with Leslie
Smith.
    AFFILIATE: The following is related through common principals,
management and/or ownership.   Gorman Affiliate Ltd, San Francisco, CA,
started 1965.   DUNS #80-480-0217.   Operates as commercial printer.
Intercompany relations: None reported by managemen

and usual selling terms. In addition, other aspects of the
business needed for a complete understanding of the
company's operations are described.

6. *History.* This section of the report describes the background of
the business. It covers issues such as when it was started, by
whom, what the starting capital was, what the authorized and
paid-in capital was, when present management assumed
control, and a number of other pertinent facts. This section
also describes the previous experience of the owner, partners,
officers, and directors. The section also lists outside business

F I G U R E   11–2

(Continued)

PUBLIC FILINGS

```
        The following data is for information purposes only and is not the
        official record.  Certified copies can only be obtained from the
        official source.


                        * * * JUDGMENT(S) * * *

DOCKET NO.: 94CV321
JDGMT AWARD: $5,003                         STATUS: Unsatisfied
JDGMT TYPE:  Default judgment               DATE STATUS ATTAINED:    08/13/1996
AGAINST:     GORMAN MANUFACTURING COMPANY,  DATE ENTERED:            08/13/1996
             INC                            LATEST INFO COLLECTED: 10/02/1996
IN FAVOR OF: JOHN SMITH
WHERE FILED: CONTRA COSTA COUNTY SUPERIOR
             COURT/MARTINEZ, MARTINEZ, CA

                        * * * SUIT(S) * * *

DOCKET NO.: 96CV123
SUIT AMOUNT: $1,000                         STATUS: Pending
PLAINTIFF:   JOHN SMITH                     DATE STATUS ATTAINED:    08/13/1996
DEFENDANT:   GORMAN MANUFACTURING COMPANY,  DATE FILED:              08/13/1996
             INC                            LATEST INFO COLLECTED: 10/02/1996
CAUSE:       Civil Rights
WHERE FILED: CONTRA COSTA COUNTY SUPERIOR
             COURT/MARTINEZ, MARTINEZ, CA

DOCKET NO.: SC19951218
SUIT AMOUNT: $20,000                         STATUS: Pending
PLAINTIFF:   DUN & BRADSTREET, BETHLEHEM, PA DATE STATUS ATTAINED:   12/18/1995
DEFENDANT:   GORMAN MANUFACTURING COMPANY,   DATE FILED:             12/18/1995
             INC                             LATEST INFO COLLECTED: 12/19/1995
CAUSE:       Breach of contract
WHERE FILED: KERN COUNTY MUNICIPAL COURT /
             WEST DISTRICT, BAKERSFIELD, CA
```

interests of partners or officers and the subsidiary and affiliated companies of a corporation. It also provides the buyer with the background education possessed by the seller. For example, a technical firm may have several engineers in top management, which could be a factor in why the firm invests heavily in R&D but is not well known for its marketing efforts.

7. *Public filings.* This contains legal proceedings filed against the firm and the case status, award settlement, and plantiff's name. These are useful to the purchaser to determine any large litigation, outstanding, which would directly affect the continued health of the business.

F I G U R E 11–2

(Continued)

PUBLIC FILINGS (continued)

---

* * * LIEN(S) * * *

A lienholder can file the same lien in more than one filing location. The appearance of multiple liens filed by the same lienholder against a debtor may be indicative of such an occurrence.

BOOK/PAGE: 23/506
AMOUNT: $230 Sales and use   STATUS: Open
TYPE: State Tax   DATE STATUS ATTAINED: 08/13/1996
FILED BY: STATE OF CALIFORNIA   DATE FILED: 08/13/1996
AGAINST: GORMAN MANUFACTURING COMPANY, INC   LATEST INFO COLLECTED: 10/02/1996
WHERE FILED: CONTRA COSTA COUNTY RECORDERS
             OFFICE, MARTINEZ, CA

BOOK/PAGE: 32/506
AMOUNT: $50,000 Corporate income tax   STATUS: Open
TYPE: Federal Tax   DATE STATUS ATTAINED: 08/13/1996
FILED BY: INTERNAL REVENUE SERVICE   DATE FILED: 08/13/1996
AGAINST: GORMAN MANUFACTURING COMPANY, INC   LATEST INFO COLLECTED: 10/02/1996
WHERE FILED: CONTRA COSTA COUNTY RECORDERS
             OFFICE, MARTINEZ, CA

There are 2 Open and/or closed UCC's in Dun & Bradstreet's file that Dun & Bradstreet has matched to this supplier at this address. Details are available by calling 1-800-DNB-DIAL.

The public record items contained in this report may have been paid, terminated vacated or released prior to the date this report was printed.

FEDERAL GOVERNMENT

(As reported to Dun & Bradstreet by the Federal Government and other sources.)

Congressional District: 08

Activity Summary:

Possible Candidate for Socio-Economic Program Consideration:

Borrower (Dir/Guar):	- NO	
Administrative Debt:	- NO	
Contractor:	- NO	
Grantee:	- NO	
Debarred, Suspended or		
Ineligible Contractor:	- NO	

Labor Surplus Area:	- N/A	
Small Business:	- YES (1997)	
Women-Owned:	- N/A	
8(A) Firm:	- N/A	
Minority Owned:	- N/A	

---

8. *Federal government.* This provides an update concerning the firm's status as a supplier to the federal government. Of special importance is the potential supplier's qualification for any special category programs, such as small business, women-owned, or minority-owned enterprise.

F I G U R E   11–2

(Continued)

PAYMENT TRENDS

```
SUPPLIER VERSUS INDUSTRY PAYDEX
-------------------------------

              PRIOR 4 QTRS                      CURRENT 12 MONTH TREND
           '97 --- --- ---     '98 --- --- --- --- --- --- --- --- --- '99
Supplier   MAR JUN SEP DEC     FEB MAR APR MAY JUN JUL AUG SEP OCT NOV DEC JAN
PAYDEX     74  70  70  70      UN  73  73  73  75  72  72  72  72  72  72  72

Industry (Based on 1,275 establishments in SIC 2752)
PAYDEX

  UP QRT  80  80  80  80       79          80          80          79
  MEDIAN  75  75  75  75       75          75          76          75
  LO QRT  66  67  67  66       66          66          67          67
```

PAYDEX scores are updated daily and are based on up to 13 months of trade
experiences from the Dun & Bradstreet trade file.

```
PAYMENT SUMMARY                          KEY TO PAYDEX
---------------                          -------------

Average High Credit:        $40,372     PAYDEX      PAYMENT
Highest Credit:            $500,000     ------      -------
Placed for Collection:           20     100         ANTICIPATE
Cash Experience(s):               8     90          DISCOUNT
No. of Trade Experience(s):     186     80          PROMPT
                                        70          SLOW TO 15
                                        50          SLOW TO 30
                                        40          SLOW TO 60
                                        30          SLOW TO 90
                                        20          SLOW TO 120
                                        UN          UNAVAILABLE
```

Accounts are sometimes placed for collection even though the existence or
amount of debt may be disputed.

SUPPLIER EVALUATION COMPLETE

9. *Payment Trends.* This section of the credit report shows how the
   supplier pays its bills. If a supplier is soundly financed and
   pays its bills according to terms, it is reasonable to assume
   that the organization can get the required materials when it
   needs them. On the other hand, often the first sign of
   approaching difficulty is the inability to meet bills as they fall
   due. If the trend is toward tardiness, the possibility arises that

F I G U R E   11–2

(Continued)

A HOTLINE TO D&B PERFORMANCE AND QUALITY INFORMATION

IMPROVEMENTS MADE TO SUPPLIER EVALUATION
■■■

Recent improvements have been made to the Supplier Evaluation Report
you have received. Here are the highlights:

1) By utilizing statistically valid models, more firms can now be
   scored on their risk level, including those where a financial
   statement is unavailable.

2) Incidence of Financial Stress is presented for the company being
   scored, its industry, and for all companies. This report shows the
   number of times (expressed as a percentage) this firm is more likely
   to fail than the national average, and the number of companies per
   10,000 that do fail. The national average failure rate and then the
   industry segment failure rate follow, together with the number of
   companies per 10,000 that fail.

3) The Supplier Risk Analysis section has been improved with additional
   key commentaries that support the 1-9 risk score calculation.

SUPPLIER PERFORMANCE REVIEW HELPS PURCHASERS FIND THE BEST SUPPLIERS
■■

Knowing what other customers have experienced is an important part
of your supplier qualification process. D&B will survey four (or
more) customers of your potential supplier in eight key performance
areas:

     - Delivery timeliness   - Total cost
     - Technical support   - Problem responsiveness
     - Quantities delivered   - Product quality
     - Personnel attitude   - Overall satisfaction

To minimize subjectivity, the customers surveyed are selected
randomly from our files. Industry averages are provided, together
with your potential supplier's ratings, for benchmarking purposes.

FOR MORE INFORMATION OR TO PLACE AN ORDER, CALL: 1-800-476-2446

the supplier will be unable to get prompt shipment of the
materials needed to meet delivery schedules.[3]

Supplier Visits

Supplier visits involve collecting first-hand the information about a particular supplier. The buyer needs to be alert and gather all necessary

---

3. H. E. Fearon, D. W. Dobler, and K. H. Killen, eds., *The Purchasing Handbook*, 5th ed.,
   McGraw-Hill, New York, 1993, ch. 6, pp. 149–153.

information while being sensitive to the supplier's limitations. Many of the items inspected and analyzed are similar to those mentioned above (see page 241 discussion on information about Critical Areas). The major difference is that the plant visit allows for collection of primary data through actual observation. During its visit, the supplier qualifications team should look at several areas of the supplier and their operations, including:

1. Management capability
2. Total Quality Management
3. Technical capability
4. Operations and scheduling capability
5. Financial strength
6. Personnel relations
7. Information systems
8. Environmental and ethical issues

Management Capability   Management is ultimately responsible for the performance of any business. Management policies also affect the way employees are treated and rewarded, the emphasis placed on quality, and the investment made in research and technology. However, the execution of these policies is carried out at the middle and lower levels of management. Thus, the management analysis needs to take a critical look at the tenure and background of the management team and key lower-level managers who are responsible for more of the daily work routines. Good managers have a vision of where their organization will be in the future. This vision is ultimately expressed in the form of three- and five-year plans. The purchaser should ask about these plans in order to gain insight into the future relationship potential. Management's overall ability to control the organization in a suitable manner clearly can influence a supplier's performance. This influence is very evident when there is a major change in management.

Total Quality Management   Total Quality Management (TQM) is not a program but a philosophy and method of doing business. It requires that the firm be committed to continuous improvement in all areas. Selected areas which the buyer can evaluate to determine a quality philosophy are:

1. Level of management commitment to TQM through policies and actions

2. Programs of education and training for employees
3. Use of statistical methods in operations such as statistical process control and Pareto diagrams
4. Employee involvement and empowerment on projects
5. Seeking and using customer feedback
6. Continual analysis of product designs
7. Lean manufacturing practices

General Quality Certification or Audits   In determining a quality emphasis, buyer's may not require an in-depth quality audit if the firm holds a general quality certification. While most purchasers acknowledge the need for a comprehensive on-site team the cost and loss of productivity in the supplier's operation are an issue. If a supplier must continually face audit teams from many different customers in the same industry, all looking for different data from these multiple audits. Another issue is the exactness of the specifications communicated. ISO 9000 certification is more of an outcome process. It states that if one follows the proper quality steps, the result will be a quality product.

Most buyers prefer build specifications, which describe the requirements, in detail, as opposed to generic specifications, which allow the supplier greater latitude. Those using build specifications then encourage the supplier to improve the processes necessary to make a specific item. Regardless of the specification used, an audit is necessary to ensure that the documented processes of ISO 9000 are followed. ISO is an assessment of the accuracy of the documentation involved in the quality system, but not of the maturity.[4]

Those who favor third-party certification have often internalized the ISO 9000 or Baldridge standards internally. They feel that it also saves the supplier time and allows their personnel to concentrate on helping the supplier in other areas. Those who favor their own audits feel that the independent quality standards are only a starting point for more intensive efforts, such as use of statistical process controls, continuous improvement gained by total quality methods, and focus on the need to understand the buying company's quality requirements and expectations.

---

4. A. Porter, "Audits Under Fire," *Purchasing*, November 5, 1992, pp. 50–55.

Technical Capability   Clearly, technical capability is a factor when expertise in a particular field is the prime objective of the purchase. This may be as specific as the demonstrated scientific knowledge of a few individuals in a supplier's company or as broad as the general expertise of a specialty producer. Contributions to the design of the buyer's product may be sought, or application engineering for utilization of the supplier's product may be the goal. Tool design or value engineering of components may be desirable. A legitimate objective for the buying organization is the extension of the buyer's engineering resources to include the technical capability of the supplier. Good suppliers are now either directly involved with their customers' engineers or asked to assume more of the engineering responsibility for their customers.

Operations and Scheduling Capability   Even more obvious is the need to consider the operations capability of prospective suppliers. For a manufactured product a supplier should have suitable, reasonably modern equipment, and enough of it to meet quantity requirements in the time available. Such equipment should be available for the production of the buyer's needs, and not already scheduled for other work. The supplier should be capable of controlling its production and providing a realistic schedule. Efficient shop operations should have a well-defined process flow that allows costs to be controlled and prevent unpleasant surprises regarding delivery. The supplier should have sufficient staff with the right skills and should be capable of producing material of the required quality with a quality assurance system that can ensure consistency. Service providers should also have modern efficient facilities. A distributor should have efficient stores and warehouse operations, and there should be evidence of efficiency in material movements in picking, packing, and shipping of orders.

In addition to physical flows through a facility, there also should be an evidence of efficiency in information flows via formal scheduling and control systems. These systems establish schedule priorities, track production lead times, and monitor inventories and shipments. Most firms today use some form of a computerized inventory system, such as Material Requirements Planning (MRP) systems. Larger firms may have this MRP system incorporated into an MRP II system or an Enterprise Resource Planning (ERP) system that controls the entire organization's operations. Whatever system is used, it is important to see and understand how this system translates into providing the purchaser with the necessary items. A key question to ask is what the actual production lead time is. This can then be compared with the salesperson's quoted lead time to reveal the extra time in administration and backlog. Once this is established, the buyer can work with the supplier on ways to reduce lead time.

Personnel Relations A buyer needs to assess the impact of human resources efforts on company morale. If the facility is unionized, how are labor–management relations at suppliers' plants? Poor relations can result in erratic delivery performance and inconsistent product quality. Good relations, on the other hand, may provide a buyer with lower-priced components in addition to good quality and delivery. It is important to determine the expiration of union agreements and be prepared to consider supply alternatives at contract termination time. An assessment of the general attitude of staff and support personnel is necessary. Is management willing to invest in training to maintain employee skills? Is there a high degree of turnover in nonmanagerial ranks?

Financial Strength A supplier's financial strength can be of crucial importance in preventing a supply interruption. It is a routine matter to obtain the financial background of an unknown source. It is also prudent to review the financial strength of current suppliers from time to time to avoid unpleasant surprises. Short-term financial problems can ruin the buyer's production schedule and also may cause temporary production stoppages and loss of tooling. Numerous texts and publications give the ratios that are good indicators of financial health. Fortunately, good data are available on most suppliers. For publicly held firms, annual reports contain financial information. The Securities and Exchange Commission requires that publicly held firms file quarterly (10Q) and annual (10K) reports. This information is also available on the Internet at www.sec.gov/edgarhp.htm. For privately held companies, the purchaser should ask for audited financial statements or obtain a report from a credit agency such as Dun & Bradstreet. (See D&B report earlier in this chapter.)

Once the data is obtained, key ratios for analysis can be determined. A few of the more important ones are listed below in Box 11–2. Having determined these key ratios, the buyer should compare them to those of other comparable firms in the industry to get an idea of the relative position of the supplier. With small suppliers it is important to check these numbers frequently, since major changes in debt or sales can create

B O X   1 1–2

KEY FINANCIAL INDICATORS

Profitability:
  Net profit margin = Profit/Sales
  Return on equity = Profits/Owner's equity
Liquidity:
  Current ratio = Current assets/Current liabilities
  Quick ratio = Cash + Receivables/Current liabilities
Asset Utilization:
  Inventory turnover = Sales or Cost of goods sold/Inventory
  Fixed asset turnover = Fixed assets/Inventory
Ownership of Assets:
  Debt ratio = Long-term debt/Assets
  Times interest earned = Profits/Interest payments

---

major problems for the supplier. Also, small suppliers are more subject to liquidity problems, with cash receipts not arriving soon enough to pay the bills. The buyer must monitor these events to see if they are short-term issues or symptoms of longer-term problems.

On a large one-time order, the buyer can evaluate a supplier's ability to finance a large work-in-process inventory to avoid having to fund the firm through progress payments. Additionally, it may be wise to estimate a supplier's ability to grow in financial capability along with the long-term growth of the buyer's requirements. In a long-term supply relationship the buyer is asking that the supplier keep him or her posted on the supplier's financial changes. The converse is also true; where long term relations exist, the buyer must be willing to be equally open with data and share any changes in his/her firm's financial conditions with the supplier.

General Questions

Information Systems   Information systems capabilities are becoming the backbone of modern organizations. In the not too distant future, the lack of sufficient technology may render a supplier uncompetitive regardless of product quality. Electronic communications are becoming the norm among businesses. E-mail has become as necessary as a telephone, and more ordering and forecasting information is being transferred electronically. Electronic systems are evident in other functions beside buying and selling. For example, design engineers utilize computer-assisted design (CAD) systems, receiving and shipping, use bar coding. Networked systems (often called Intranets) allow all functions within an organization to share common data to assist in making quick, accurate decisions. While it is important to talk with the chief information officer (CIO) of the supplier firm, it is just as important to look at the use of technology throughout the organization.

Environment and Ethics   Environmental concerns have been an important issue in the conduct of a firm's business since the passage of the Hazardous Transportation Act in 1974 and the Resource Conservation and Recovery Act in 1976. Both these bills brought increased awareness and responsibilities to firms that create or ship hazardous materials. Some firms are actively engaged in promoting their efforts through "green buying" and ISO 14000 certification. Such efforts show environmental concern on the supplier's part and also assure the purchaser that he or she will be more likely to receive products which will not create disposition or handling problems.

It is unwise to deal with suppliers that are known to have questionable ethics. Buyers who knowingly associate with such firms expose themselves to the probability of being "known by the company they keep." Such a reputation, however unjustified, can drive away reliable, competitive sources. In addition, such buyers may expose their firms to a number of serious business risks. An unethical supplier may reveal proprietary information to competitors or use it itself. The firm may knowingly bid low to buy-in, only to raise its price later. The firm may knowingly promise a delivery that cannot be made in order to get an order, or it may claim the ability to produce a product that is beyond the capability of the firm, fully intending to "subcontract" the order to other firms. Unscrupulous firms may even resort to commercial bribery in an attempt to achieve a supply position that was not warranted. Even though there may appear to be short-term advantages to making special deals with unethical sources, long-term objectives will often be jeopardized and seldom do the short-term advantages actually materialize. This is particularly true when dealing with suppliers who are in the hazardous transportation or disposal business. The buyer's firm is usually liable for "cradle-to-grave" responsibility, and using a cut-rate carrier or disposal facility could result in significant costs and liability to the buyer's firm.

Sourcing Practices   It is also necessary to review the supplier's sourcing practices. The team would consider:

1. Materials and services purchased and the relationships with key suppliers, including any evidence of outreach to help them improve

2. Whether the materials procured are compatible with the production methods

3. Whether redesign and standardization are practiced on key materials

4. Whether supplier lead times are documented and well managed

5. Whether the purchasing department is actively searching for new materials. Finally, in a supply chain management environment, it is helpful to examine how frequently the supplier audits and works with its suppliers. Box 11–3 contains a checklist of the specific information that should be collected during the visitation. This ties into general categories covered earlier in this chapter and can also be used with the supplier's supplier.

Figure 11–3 shows a sample supplier capability form used in collecting these data. Personal contacts with key people in management and production are a very helpful asset in the event that emergency or special requirements need to be discussed later.

Approved Supplier Lists

The result of the supplier qualification efforts at this point should result in a list of several acceptable supply sources, all capable of furnishing the requirements, with whom the buyer would be willing to place an order. In most organizations this is termed the *approved supplier list*. Overtime suppliers on the approved list may grow into much more valuable partners through superior performance. Depending on their performance, suppliers on the approved list can be classified into categories such as conditional, approved, certified, or partnered. These are discussed further in the experience stage.

The move toward closer relations with key suppliers to support an over all supply chain management program requires more intense and detailed prepurchase evaluations. In these more proactive systems, much more time is spent in prequalification activities. This is shown in the

B O X   1 1 – 3

INFORMATION OBSERVED AND COLLECTED DURING FACILITY VISIT

✓ Age of the facility and key equipment

✓ General employee morale and experience

✓ Research and development facilities

✓ Technical processes and controls

✓ General process flow of customer orders

✓ Meeting key personnel responsible for order handling, processing, and scheduling

✓ Information systems and compatibility for electronic ordering and invoicing

✓ Environmental practices procedures and facilities

✓ Presence of Total Quality Management philosophy

✓ ISO 9000 or ISO 14000 Certification

✓ Baldridge Award application

✓ Caliber of supervision and inspection personnel

✓ Degree of automation in scheduling and priority systems

✓ Preventative maintenance procedures

✓ Evidences of good management and good housekeeping in plant operations

✓ Calibration and inspection of testing equipment

✓ List of larger customers

✓ Major systems affecting scheduling ERP, MRP, DRP

✓ Labor history and contract expiration dates

✓ Engineering and design capabilities

✓ Practice as to the maintenance of raw material stocks

✓ Continuous process and cost-improvement programs

✓ Facility size

✓ Health and safety compliance

✓ Competence to engage in early supplier involvement

✓ Ability to deliver frequently in small quantities

✓ Technology to handle electronic transactions

✓ Purchasing expertise and practices

F I G U R E   11–3

Front Side of a Capability Survey Form. To This Basic Form can be Added Special Survey Forms Covering Quality Control, Manufacturing, and Other Functions of Special Interest.

Beckman• INSTRUMENTS, INC.	BECKMAN USE ONLY
	APPROVED
	APPROVAL WITHHELD

CAPABILITIES SURVEY

NOTE: Please return this form with equipment brochure to
Purchasing Manager, Beckman Instruments, Inc. _____ Division
Address _____

TO BE FILLED IN BY SUBCONTRACTOR: Date _____

Full name of company _____

Office-Street address _____   Telephone _____

    City _____   State _____

    Person to be contacted _____   Position _____

Plant-Street Address _____   Telephone _____

    City _____   State _____

    Person to be contacted _____   Position _____

Type of business: (check one)   Proprietorship ☐   Partnership ☐   Corporation ☐

Subsidiary of _____

PRINCIPAL OFFICERS: (OF FACILTY TO BE SURVEYED)

NAME	TITLE
NAME	TITLE
NAME	TITLE
NAME	TITLE
NAME	TITLE
NAME	TITLE

Please, attach total organization chart   TYPICAL CUSTOMERS

NAME	ADDRESS	BUYER
NAME	ADDRESS	BUYER
NAME	ADDRESS	BUYER

Financial Information:
Name and Address of Bank _____
NAMES AND ADDRESSES OT THREE CREDIT REFERENCES: (Concerns from whom you have purchased materials)

NAME	ADDRESS
NAME	ADDRESS
NAME	ADDRESS

Financial Statement attached for year ending _____

Lenght of time company has been in continuous operation _____

PAGE 1 OF 2

(*Courtesy of Beckman Instruments, Inc., Fullerton, Calif.*)

F I G U R E 11–3

Reverse Side of Capability Survey Form

FOR INFORMATION (A survey team will call on you to discuss some of the following in more detail)

Type of work company is best prepared and well equipped to do (specify capabilities and reference)

Survey Team
Use Only

1 _____

_____

_____

_____

2 _____

_____

_____

_____

Other work company can do:

_____

_____

_____

_____

Special skills possessed by company personnel:

_____

_____

_____

TOTAL NUMBER OF EMPLOYEES	COVERED AREA	UNCOVERED AREA
	SQ FT	SQ FT
NUMBER OF QUALITY CONTROL EMPLOYEES		NUMBER OF SHOP EMPLOYEES
NUMBER OF SHIFTS* BEING WORKED		AVAILABLE PLANT CAPACITY
PERCENTAGE OF WORK FOR PROPRIETARY ITEMS		
TYPE OF PRODUCT UNDER CONSIDERATION		
OTHER TYPES OF PRODUCTS AVAILABLE		

SIGNATURE _____ TITLE _____

FORM PA 19 12   FEBRUARY 1968   187-200   PRINTED IN THE U.S.A.

example of Honda of America Manufacturing Inc.'s efforts (see Box 11–4).

Negotiation and Selection Stage

Once the qualification phase is completed, a third stage leads to issuance of the contract or initial order with the selected supplier(s). The various

B O X   1 1 – 4

EXAMPLE OF A
PRE-QUALIFICATION EFFORT[5]

Honda of America describe their approach to prequalification as being very front-end loaded. After initial prescreening of a very detailed part estimate and thorough understanding of Honda's specifications, a team is sent to the supplier's plant to perform a Quality Assessment Valuation. This team is comprised of purchasing and engineering representatives. While the assessment covers quality, it also looks at worker attitudes, management systems/ background, safety compliance, potential environmental problems, cleanliness, cycle time, etc. The sourcing team then rates each supplier visited. Further discussions are held with selected firms and suggestions are made for improvements in areas as noted by the sourcing team. During the suggestion phase, the supplier's management team visits with Honda's top executives to ensure an understanding of what is expected in terms of quality, cost control, and sourcing arrangements. Specific evaluation is then made of the particular part. Discussions center on the failure mode, effects analysis model. The model asks the supplier to isolate a critical dimension which is most likely to create a failure, then determine the effects and analyze how to analyze the failure mode. The supplier and Honda agree on the terms, price arrangements, and expected quality requirements. It is agreed that sourcing will be awarded for the life of the part (usually four years). Suppliers are given anticipated quantities every 6 months.

issues involved in the selection of the type of source and contract have strategic impact on the firm's supply base structure and size as well as subsequent relationships. A supply base is usually measured by the number of active suppliers a firm does business with. Three major factors will impact the size of the supply base. First, the supply base structure relates to the different categories of suppliers, such as distributors or manufacturers, large or small firms, etc. A distributor will provide certain advantages that a manufacturer cannot match, but at what differential in cost/price? Secondly, placing 100% of the requirements with a single

5. L. Giunipero, "Supplier Evaluation Methods," *NAPM Insights,* June 1990, pp. 21–23.

source provides leverage and keeps the supply base small and manageable. However, maintaining multiple sources improves assurance of supply. Thirdly, the supplier's field service capability, its warehouse network, or its access to scarce raw materials will influence supply base size.

In many cases the buyer will have to send out a Request for Quote (RFQ). While price, delivery, and terms are the key factors in evaluating a quotation, other very specific questions can be broached. Examples of such useful questions are:

+ What is your backlog of orders for this product?
+ How many customers do you have for this product?
+ Will you need additional capital to fulfill this order?
+ What percentage of your annual production of this item does this order constitute?
+ What percentage of your total production does this product line represent?

These are somewhat nontraditional questions and in some cases may encounter supplier resistance. However, candidates for long-term relationships (buyers and sellers alike) must be able to understand the implications of joining forces with each other. Buyers must be willing to be just as open as they are asking suppliers to be.[6] For a fuller discussion of these issues, see the earlier chapters of this section.

The ultimate selection decision requires analysis of a number of complex issues. Selection factors may range from 2 or 3 (e.g., price and delivery) on basic purchase to a list of 12 to 15 factors on a complex strategic long-term supply contract that will involve a close working relationship across several levels of the supply chain.

It is good, when analyzing proposals from multiple suppliers that require the evaluation of many factors, to develop a multi-attribute model. These models are not intended to be substitutes for certification and process improvement programs, but they do allow evaluation of competing suppliers in a number of dimensions. An example of a multi-attribute model for supplier analysis is shown in Table 11–1. In this model a weighting or points are assigned to each factor or criterion. Each supplier is scored on a 1 to 10 scale, with 10 being considered excellent for each of these criteria. Thus, base bid is given 10 points and Supplier

6. Fearon et al., op. cit., pp. 145–146.

T A B L E   11–1

Multi-attribute Evaluation Point Weighting Example[7]

Factors	Weight	Supplier A	Supplier B	Supplier C
Base bid	10	6/60	8/80	9/90
Unit Prices for additions or subtractions	10	8/80	7/70	9/90
Supervision	7	6/42	5/35	8/56
Location	4	8/32	10/40	7/28
Supplier presentation	3	7/21	7/21	8/24
Compatability with present systems	4	8/32	4/16	10/40
Management team	8	9/72	7/56	8/64
Quality system	8	8/64	6/48	9/72
References	5	7/35	6/30	8/40
Prior experience	9	8/72	8/72	9/81
Totals	68/680	510	488	585
Rank		3	6	1
Percent of maximum score		75.0	68.8	86.0

C is given 9 points on "price," indicating that Supplier C bid the lowest price, but perhaps not as low as the buyer's target price. Multiplying the weight 10 times the 9 rating results in Supplier C receiving 90 points for this category. "Quality System" was given a weighting of 8, and again Supplier C was rated with a 9. This gave Supplier C 8 × 9, or 72 points for their quality system. Adding up the points for Supplier C gave the supplier a total of 585 points out of a possible maximum number of points of 680. The 680 is equal to 68 total points multiplied by a maximum of 10 points per category.

Regardless of the method used for selecting the supplier or type of arrangement, some negotiation will take place requiring additional discussions with the selected supplier. The negotiations occur over the details and terms to determine where the best ultimate value lies. This will basically be in terms of quality, service, and price. Beyond that, it will

7. Heinritz, S. F., Farrell, P. V., Giunipero, L., Kolchin, M., and Kiernan, J. "Purchasing Principles and Applications," *Purchasing World*, p. 393.

be influenced by the intangibles of interest, cooperation, and skills that enhance the value of all these factors, and beyond that, the decision may hinge on special circumstances. An example is a minority-owned business or woman-owned company that has all the intangibles to succeed and merely needs some technical help to improve a few processes. Conversely, a larger firm may be desirable, with its superior engineering or technical capabilities and the ability to serve the buying company at multiple locations worldwide.

Experience Stage

The final stage of supplier selection is experience, which involves following up to ensure that the supplier meets the terms and conditions of the contract—conformance to specifications, on-time delivery, and keeping the buyer aware of any major changes at the supplier's facility. When performed for one contract, this is often referred to as *contract management*. Where continuing relationship for requirements are purchased, contract management takes the form of *supplier evaluation*. The real test of supplier selection is satisfactory performance by the supplier after order placement. This becomes the deciding factor in whether the selected supplier will continue to receive the buyer's business or be replaced by another source.

Categorizing Suppliers

Sources who perform well and have the ability to meet or exceed the buyer's requirement become valuable members of the supply base. Unfortunately, not all suppliers have the capabilities or performance to merit higher status, and thus a categorization of suppliers is developed in many organizations. For example, Droesser, Frels, and Swartz[8] describe Deere & Company, Inc.'s supplier categorization as consisting of:

- *Conditional:* An existing supplier whose performance does not meet minimum standards or a new supplier who has not yet established a performance history
- *Approved:* Meets minimum standards and can supply components for existing products but not new ones

---

8. W. Droesser, S. Frels, and G. Swartz, "Finding the Perfect Fit," *NAPM Insights*, October, 1995, pp. 4–5.

♦ *Preferred/key:* Has proven ability to meet sourcing objectives and a mutual commitment to a continuing long-term relationship

♦ *Strategic alliance:* Characterized by integrated management planning and scheduling; shared technology and plans; access to each other's financial information; and a commitment of resources by the supplier

Objective evaluation and rating of supplier performance has gained considerable acceptance in purchasing departments of all types in recent years. But even when sophisticated on-line computerized systems are used to compile comparative statistics on vendor performance, interpretation of those statistics and other qualitative factors is left to the buyer's and cross-functional team's judgment.

Supplier Performance Dimensions

Rating systems generally involve the three basic considerations in a good purchase: quality, service (delivery), and price. Any one of these may be given more weight than the others. Quality is most important, for example, for a manufacturer of complex components for integrated circuits. Price might be given equal weight in an evaluation system used by the manufacturer of highly competitive "throw-away" items like paper plates. Subcategories can be defined under each major area. For example, the delivery/service category could include on-time delivery, order processing cycle time, technical support availability, and lead time stability.

Formulas for rating suppliers vary in complexity, again depending on the nature of the item bought, the quality required, and the competition within the supplying industry. One company that buys its requirements under blanket orders uses a relatively simple system to measure supplier performance on two counts: quality and delivery. Price performance has been determined when the contract was originally awarded. Each shipment against the order is rated as follows: by date requested, 100%; one day late, 98%; two days late, 95%, and so on, down to 73% for six days late. The formula is calculated subtracting 100 from the number of days late plus one, plus the previous penalty. For example, one day late equals $100 - [1 + 1 + 0] = 98$; two days late equals $100 - [2 + 1 + 2] = 95$, etc. If quality is to specifications, the supplier is rated 100%. If using departments complain about quality of shipment, the rating drops to 95%. For each complaint thereafter, the supplier loses 5% more. Suppliers are notified periodically of their performance records. Those falling below the standards of quality and delivery are warned that they are in danger of losing the business and placed on probation for a period of time with no new business.

Individual Evaluation Measures

Some firms wish to isolate quality and delivery and analyze them separately. A few of these quality and delivery measures are listed below:

1. $\text{Quality} = 100\% - \dfrac{\text{number of lots rejected}}{\text{number of lots received}}$

2. $\text{Quality} = 100\% - \dfrac{\text{dollar value of rejected items}}{\text{total dollar value of shipments}}$

3. $\text{Quality} = 100\% - \dfrac{\text{number of parts received}}{\text{number of parts rejected}}$

4. $\text{Quality} = 100\% - \dfrac{\text{parts per million defective}}{\text{parts per million defective}}$

5. $\text{Delivery} = 100\% - \dfrac{\text{number of late or early shipments}}{\text{number of shipments received}}$

Measures concerning on-time delivery raise questions of how best to define it. Firms need to decide if they measure:

- Purchasing's request date versus actual ship date
- Supplier promise date versus actual ship date
- Supplier promise date versus actual receipt date

The third alternative, supplier promise date versus buyer receipt date, is quite popular. However, this requires factoring in a transit time. After *on time* has been defined, most firms then establish a "window" (i.e., if the shipment is three days early to two days late, it is considered on time).[9]

A study by Hewlett-Packard Corporation found that the greatest hindrance to on-time performance was in the buyer–seller communication process. Buyers and suppliers were clear about what they had agreed on in only 40% of deliveries. Many times suppliers were unsure whether the date on the purchase order was a shipment date or delivery

---

9. Heinritz, Farrell et al., op. cit., p. 183.

date. In contrast, in 90% of cases the actual transit times were on schedule. Changes made to clarify the communication process resulted in an increase in on-time deliveries from 21% to 51%.[10]

Categorical Rating Plan

The categorical plan involves rating a supplier under a three-point ranking system: satisfactory (+), unsatisfactory (−), or neutral (0). Purchasers keep notes on supplier performance and then rate each supplier periodically (monthly or quarterly) by placing suppliers in one of these three categories. Additional input for this type of evaluation can be obtained from each member of the cross-functional sourcing team's other users, quality, and receiving personnel. Suppliers are then informed of their ratings. Most of the ratings given under this system have multiple attributes. For example, the supplier may receive an unsatisfactory (−) for after-hours support but a satisfactory (+) for delivery and a neutral (0) on price/cost. The major advantage of the categorical plan is simplicity of record-keeping and low cost. The disadvantages to broad categories of evaluation is that they do not give the supplier specific data on improvement, and recent events tend to influence these subjective ratings, particularly if the raters take no or poor notes on past activities.

Weighted Point Plan

The weighted point plan is a more comprehensive mathematical supplier-rating formula used by many purchasing departments. It is designed to provide a comparative evaluation of supplier performance, particularly in cases where an item is procured from two or more sources. The formula is based upon the principles that (1) the evaluation of a supplier's performance must embrace all three major purchasing factors—quality, price, and service—and (2) the relative importance of these factors varies in respect to various items. The first step, therefore, is to assign appropriate weights to each, adding up to a total weighting factor of 100 points. For example, in a given case, quality performance might be rated at 40 points, price at 35, and service at 25, and these percentages are subsequently used as multipliers for individual ratings on each of the three purchasing factors. The assignment of these weights

---

10. D. N. Burt, "Managing Suppliers Up to Speed," *Harvard Businesss Review,* July–August 1989, p. 133.

is a matter of judgment. In the company where this system originated, the importance of quality ranges from 35 to 45%, price from 30 to 40%, and service from 20 to 30%.

The quality rating is a direct percentage of the number of acceptable lots received in relation to total lots received. In the rating of price, the lowest net price (gross price minus discounts plus unit transportation cost) obtained from any supplier is taken as 100 points, and net prices from other suppliers are rated in inverse ratio to this figure. The delivery/service rating is a direct percentage of the lots received as promised in relation to total lots received.

These three ratings are multiplied by their respective weighting factors, and the results are added to give a numerical "incoming material rating" for each supplier for a given item. Perfect deliveries, on scheduled time, at the lowest net price earn a rating of 100 points. Any rejections, lapses in delivery, or prices higher than the lowest quotation reduce the rating. At the same time, there is an objective basis for determining the extent to which superior quality and service offset higher prices in overall value and satisfaction (see Box 11–5).

Cost Ratio Plan

This plan attempts to capture costs associated with actual supplier performance in the areas of quality and delivery. It is the most comprehensive in terms of a total cost approach to purchasing. Costs uniquely associated with quality, delivery, and price are determined for each supplier. This total is then totaled to produce an overall cost ratio. Quality costs include rework, rejection processing, and the like. Delivery costs include production downtime, expediting costs, higher price substitutes, and so forth. The adjusted price for each supplier in a particular commodity is then compared. Box 11–6 indicates that it costs a 5% premium to buy from the supplier due to the cost of quality and delivery. Thus a supplier charging $1.04 and having perfect quality and delivery would be a lower-cost source even though the supplier's price is 4% higher. Of course, an alert buyer would work with the supplier in an attempt to improve the quality and delivery.

Currently not many firms use the cost ratio approach to supplier evaluation, since the data-collection requirement is extensive and time-consuming. However, with continuing development of personal and hand-held computer hardware, this evaluation approach will be used more frequently in the future. Monczka and Trecha (1988) extended the cost ratio plan by identifying nonperformance costs for delivery, material

B O X   11-5

WEIGHTED POINT PLAN EVALUATION

Supplier A has delivered 58 lots during the past year, of which two were rejected. The percentage of good lots is 96.5. Multiplied by the weight factor of 40, this gives supplier A a quality rating of 38.6. The lowest net price from any suplier is $0.93 per unit. A's price is $1.07. By inverse ratio, A's price performance is 86.9 percent. Multipied by the weight factor of 35, this gives supplier A a price rating of 30.4.

Of the 58 lots delivered, 55 were received as promised. This is 94.8% performance. Multiplied by the weight factor of 25, it gives supplier A a delivery rating of 23.7.

The sum of these figures gives supplier A a total performance rating of 92.7.

Supplier B, who furnished 34 lots during the same period, was the lowest-price supplier at $0.93 per unit, so has a price rating of the full 35 points. However, four of the lots were defective, giving B a quality rating of 35.3. Also, supplier B was late with five deliveries, so B's service rating is 21.3, for a total performance rating of 91.6. In this instance, therefore, supplier A is judged to be the more satisfactory source, and the buyer is warranted in placing the bulk of the business with A in spite of A's substantially higher price. If supplier B could be induced to cut delinquencies in either quality or service by one half, or if the price factor were deemed relatively more important in respect to this item, B would have the better rating.[11]

quality, and price.[12] The total cost of supplier performance is the unit price plus nonperformance costs.

Performance Based Evaluation Systems

While the ultimate goal of any selection system is to attain perfect quality with 100% on-time delivery and 0% quantity variance at a competitive

---

11. S. F. Heinritz, P. V. Farrell, L. Giunipero, M. Kolchin, *Purchasing Principles and Applications*, Prentice Hall, Englewood Cliffs, New Jersey, 1991, p. 183.
12. Robert Monczka and Steven Trecha, "Cost-Based Supplier Performance Evaluation," *Journal of Purchasing and Materials Management*. Spring, 1988, pp. 2–7.

B O X   11–6

Quality Costs:

Incoming inspection	$500
Costs of sorting	100
Cost of reworking	0
Additional paperwork	100
Total	$700
Purchase expenditures	
With supplier A	$14,000

$$\text{Quality Cost Ratio} = \frac{\text{Purchase (\$) Expenditures + Cost of Poor Quality}}{\text{Purchase (\$) Expenditures}}$$

$$= \frac{\$14,000 + 700}{\$14,000} = 1.05$$

price, the use and application of traditional evaluation systems suffer certain shortcomings. Regarding use, some organizations adopt a cookbook approach to evaluation, using a system borrowed from another company. However, the dimensions or weightings that are appropriate for one firm may not be appropriate for another. For example, a software development firm found that on-time delivery was the key evaluation factor in its rating of suppliers. Secondly, the evaluation numbers need to be easily collected and compiled. One electronics corporation thought it was measuring delivery performance by comparing supplier promise date to actual ship date. However, several of its key suppliers were not providing this data and were evaluated on the request date on the purchase order. Thirdly, since supplier performance is part of the larger supply chain performance, it is important to know what major corporate goals are important to your firm's customers. This helps establish a supplier weighting in line with customer expectations. Previous research supports these issues. Collela states the objective of supplier performance measures should be to support improvement by helping supplier find the root cause of the problems.[13] Harding feels each form must develop valid factors that are easy to use and relatively distinguishes between

---

13. G. Colella, "Performance Measures for Purchasers and Suppliers," *1997 International Purchasing Conference Proceedings,* May 1997, pp. 317–322.

different supplier performances.[14] Buffa found that successful systems focus on:

1. The selection of measurable performance factors such as quality, delivery, cost, and service
2. Setting of reasonable weightings
3. Ease of administration
4. Communication of the results to suppliers
5. Rewarding of outstanding performers[15]

In addition to problems associated with applications, traditional systems suffer the following shortcomings:

1. They are often individual-oriented between buyer and seller.
2. They focus mainly on the buyer–seller interface.
3. They are after the fact and therefore reactive.
4. They have no specific strategies established for performance.
5. They are often based on a bid-buy system, which is still perceived as price-oriented.
6. They are transaction-based.[16]

Given these limitations, and with the increasing acceptance and usage of supply chain management in conjunction with TQM/JIT by U.S. industry, formal evaluation and performance ratings have moved towards broader-based evaluation system. For example, under Ford Motor Company's long running and well-publicized Q-1 program, suppliers are rated on how well they perform in providing defect-free quality parts according to a seven-category rating system.[17] Despite such highly publicized quality programs, problems still exist as many firms still consider quality a static, not a dynamic process. In contrast is the plan–do–check action cycle (PDCA) proposed by Dr. Edward Deming for improving quality.

14. M. L. Harding, "Creating Your Own Supplier Evaluation Formula," *Purchasing Today®*, November 1997, pp. 12–13.
15. J. Buffa, "Vendor Rating Puts Profits in Purchasing," *Purchasing World*, 31:5, May 1987, pp. 40–42.
16. L. C. Giunipero and D. Brewer, "Performance Based Evaluation Systems Under Total Quality Management," *International Journal of Purchasing and Materials Management*, Vol. 29, No. 1, Winter 1993, pp. 37–38.
17. L. C. Giunipero and D. Brewer, "Ford's Q1 Program Drives Suppliers," *Quality*, 24:9, September 1985, pp. 36–38.

The overall intent of truly successful measures is to view the evaluation process as a method towards improvement and not just a ranking system for awarding business. Under long-term relationships fostered by supply chain management environments, the focus is on improving efficiency between firms. Thus firms must consider or at least pursue improvement. Bernard reflects this thinking in proposing that supplier performance management is future oriented and that problems be treated as opportunities to improve the relationship, not as weapons to beat the supplier at negotiation time.[18] Pursuing improvement requires primary focus on suppliers' improvement records.

In essence, the performance-based system takes a much broader view and seeks to involve several members of both firms in an effort to reduce the total cost of business. Results from implementing these programs require a longer-term view of the supplier relationship. Additional characteristics of performance-based rating systems include:

1. Strategic thrust
2. Team approach
3. Broad evaluation parameters
4. Evaluation of factual data
5. Frequent communications
6. Improvement goals[19]

Strategic Thrust   If top management views purchasing as a contributor to corporate effectiveness, performance system is ultimately tied to customer satisfaction. The focus is on continuous performance improvement and operational and cost efficiencies over a period of time.

The Team Approach   While traditional rating systems tend to be oriented toward buyer and seller, performance systems involve a team approach. For example, as previously mentioned, Honda of America Manufacturing, Inc. sends an audit team composed of representatives from purchasing, engineering, and quality out to review supplier performance on a yearly basis. At these meetings, progress toward lowering the overall cost of business is discussed and suppliers are asked how they can reduce their cost of operation.

---

18. P. Bernard, "Managing Vendor Performance," *Production and Inventory Management*. First Quarter, 1989, pp. 1–7.
19. L. C. Giunipero, op. cit., pp. 40–41.

It is important to remember that developing effective teamwork takes time. Periodic meetings should be held with users to discuss their satisfaction with purchasing's efforts concerning their critical requirements. This process can help tear down the functional barriers between purchasing and internal departments and create a unified approach to selection.

Broad Evaluation Parameters   Traditional evaluation criteria focus on price, quality, and delivery. A performance-based systems approach is more encompassing and includes focus on lowest total cost. Costs include quality and delivery, but also issues such as safety and environmental impact. Firms should consider evaluating potential environmental problems that the supplier's present process is creating and proposing an alternative with environmentally safer processes. This work should be conducted during the prescreening/prequalifying stage of the supplier-selection process.

Evaluation of Factual Data   Greater emphasis is placed on collection of factual data that are used to make present and future decisions. Much of the basis for traditional evaluation was subjective. Price was perceived by users and suppliers as the major evaluation criterion since it was easily quantified. Quality and delivery were considered but were less likely to affect selection decisions. Performance-based systems must place a greater emphasis on identifying supplier's key processes and using data to measure the supplier's effectiveness and continuous improvement in lowering the cost of business between both organizations.

Frequent Communication   Communication in traditional systems between buyers and sellers is usually infrequent, with emphasis on the supplier's failures (defectives, nonconformities, etc.). No real effort was made to discuss the underlying reasons for these failures. Communication often involved the transfer of very subjective or incomplete data.

Improvement Goals   Performance-based systems maximize the use of data that are then used to convey specific improvement targets, set goals, monitor performance, and evaluate that performance. Goal-setting works best when a few objectives of top management are supported by the entire company. Such an approach gives the organization and its suppliers a degree of focus in working towards common goals.

Using Performance-Based Systems

Performance-based systems should be particularly focussed on suppliers who provide critical or large-dollar items. They will require much more time than traditional systems, since the quality of the supplier's process is the most important indicator of their performance. If the supplier's upstream processes are measured, in control, and stable and possess high process capability ratings, then the probability of meeting the customer's needs is enhanced. Accomplishing this requires a closer working relationship with suppliers. Goods from quality suppliers can enter the purchaser's facility without inspection. Many firms term this class of suppliers *certified suppliers*; they are eligible for long-term contracts and may receive priority when jobs are competitive.

Performance-Based Systems Case

An illustration of using performance-based evaluation systems is exhibited at a large utility company who implemented such a program. Supplier management was invited into the company for an orientation session describing the performance-based approach. The focus of supplier selection and evaluation would emphasize quality improvement. In this respect, suppliers needed to submit a quality improvement (QI) plan to the company. Once the QI plan was accepted, the supplier in conjunction with the company selected a project for improvement. Upon completion of the project, the supplier evaluated the results of the process. The review team from the company attended the supplier's self-review. Finally, the supplier made a presentation to the purchaser's top management about their company, the improvement efforts, and their ability to solve the company's problems. These "certified" suppliers underwent annual reviews. They were rewarded for their efforts by long-term contracts, potential for increased business, and quicker payment. Supplier performance was reported quarterly and incorporated into the bid system. This made suppliers much more responsive to quality and delivery issues. With the new criteria bid evaluation included three other factors in addition to price: certified status, supplier performance, and product evaluation. Suppliers in the "certified" category could receive up to a 10% credit for their efforts. Supplier performance was based on on-time delivery, overages and underages, packaging, damaged goods, wrong parts, and complete packing lists. Product evaluation included product performance experience (length of life, maintenance costs) and conformance to specifications. Suppliers had to show quality system improvements and solve a problem that improved their process and in most cases benefited both firms. The process was marked by continuous interaction between the buying firm and the supplier.

BIBLIOGRAPHY

Burt, D. N. "Managing Suppliers up to Speed," *Harvard Business Review*, July–August 1989, p. 133.

Colella, G., "Performance Measures for Purchasers and Suppliers," *1997 International Purchasing Conference Proceedings*, May 1997, pp. 84–86.

Erickson, K. C., Whittier, R., and M. S. Oswald. In H. E. Frearon, D. W. Dobler, and K. H. Killen, *The Purchasing Handbook*, 5th ed., McGraw-Hill, New York, 1993, ch. 5, pp. 129–168.

Giunipero, L. C. "A Team Based Approach to Supplier Evaluations," *NAPM Insights*, June 1994, pp. 50–52.

———— "Performance Based Evaluation Systems under Total Quality Management." *International Journal of Purchasing and Materials Management*, vol. 29, no. 1, Winter 1993, pp. 35–41.

Harding M. L., "Creating Your Own Supplier Evaluation Formula," *Purchasing Today*®, November 1997.

McGinnis, M. A. "Building Better Performance Measures," *NAPM Insights*, May 1995, pp. 50–53.

Monczka, R., and S. Trecha. "Cost-Based Supplier Performance Evaluation," *Journal of Purchasing and Materials Management*, Spring 1988, pp. 2–7.

Porter, A., "Audits under Fire," *Purchasing*, November 5, 1992, pp. 50–55.

PART THREE

Organization and Competencies of Purchasing and Supply

An organization is a composite of people, systems, and linkages, all designed to attain certain goals and objectives. This section spans the key facets of these elements.

Competencies and skills are seen by many as the core components of a field. Chapter 12 is written by an individual who has spent her career in identifying and developing them for many fields, not the least of which is purchasing, with her NAPM-awarded doctoral dissertation.

Chapter 13, on developing purchasing and supply organizations, comes from the actual experience of a telecommunications firm as it shifted from a long-standing traditional group to a fast-paced, market-competitive group.

Reengineering is a part of the landscape in every organization in the world today. Following on the previous chapter, chapter 14 covers the basics of how to conduct a reengineering study and follow through for effective purchasing and supply.

Managing personnel is a major part of purchasing management. Chapter 15 presents the unique features of building and sustaining an effective purchasing and supply organization. Alignment of purchasing strategies and actions with organizational strategies is key to establishing a meaningful performance measurement system is emphasized in Chapter 16.

Ethics and responsibility are central to the day-to-day activities of the purchasing professional. Chapter 17 is presented by an individual who has spent much of his career devoted to observing, researching, teaching, and presenting their key parts and overall concepts.

CHAPTER 12

Competencies and Skills in Today's Purchasing

Editor
Virginia M. Tucker, Ph.D.
Associate Dean for Executive Education and
Associate Professor of Business Administration
The Pennsylvania State University

Historically, all support functions of an organization were viewed as just that, support, and not as important contributors to the business. They were viewed by the rest of the company as a necessary evil, units that existed to handle the details of what the real decision-makers wanted to accomplish. Personnel established "people rules" and completed any employee-related forms. Accounting collected and compiled numbers. Transportation determined the cheapest way to get product from Point A to Point B. Purchasing completed the necessary steps and paperwork to acquire what other departments needed in order to operate effectively.

The mode for all of these functions was very reactive. They waited to receive requests from other parts of the firm, went behind closed doors to do "their thing," and then gave the completed project back to the original solicitor.

For many years this method of operating worked sufficiently well. Markets moved slowly and had long product life cycles. Companies faced clearly defined and well-understood, single-dimension competitors. Organizations worked in very functional formats, with thick walls between the silos.

Time to market was not a driving competitive issue, and therefore time to complete tasks within the firm was not a critical factor. People could take the time required to hand off a process to another department, wait for it to be completed, receive it, and then, if perhaps something was wrong, even send it back to repeat the process all over again. Business was competitive but not necessarily complex. For the most part, marketplaces were stable, rational, methodical, predictable, and sanely paced. For those times, the mode of reactive support functions was fine. And so it was for purchasing as well.

Today the business environment has changed greatly, and with it have the demands that organizations place on all "support" functions. The keys to a company's success today are being a creative leader in the marketplace and changing the way your industry operates. Everyone is focusing on time to market, shortened product life cycles, competition from unknown sources, forming alliances with other companies, and facing "coopetition"—competing against the same companies you work cooperatively with, source from, and sell to in other venues.

What does this mean for the way companies function? Simply, they must be able to work in alliances, understanding that no longer can any one firm do everything required to come to the marketplace; they must function proactively and quickly; and they must do it creatively. Bottom line: all portions of the organization must be able to work together in a cross-functional and team-based manner. Each individual employee in the company must be an expert in his or her area but also must understand the overall competitive environment and functionings of the firm. No longer can we afford to have support functions that work in a reactive mode. No longer do we have the time to have support functions receive information, work on it in a black box, and then throw it back over the transom. Today every traditional support function is required to operate in a business-partnership mode, be the expert in its area, fully understand how that area interacts with every other area of the firm, and proactively work together with the rest of the organization to create the best product or service possible.

In the traditional organization, purchasing's focus was on clarifying specifications for what production or some other department wanted to buy, identifying potential sources and qualified suppliers, compiling RFQs, going out for bid, and determining which supplier could best meet the criteria—usually based on lowest cost. The capabilities and skills required to perform these functions were quite straightforward. As the competitiveness of the global environment increased in the late 1980s, senior managements realized that there were great opportunities for competitive advantage in the area of sourcing and began looking to purchasing to become more sophisticated and play a more strategic role in the firm. Cavinato found in 1987 that top management perceived the need for purchasing, as a function and as individual professionals, to possess a broad, general management perspective on the business and to become more proactive in contributing to the strategic operation of the organization. These characteristics had not previously been considered job requisites for the traditional purchasing professional. Additionally, these top managers expressed the need for purchasing to work on promoting this new image throughout the firm, utilizing new forms of performance in order to change existing stereotypes and demonstrate the potential contribution to be made by the function. The interesting factor was that beyond realizing the need for this change to occur in the function, no one could specifically identify what skills would be required to be successful in this role.

In the late 1980s, this author set out to answer this important question by conducting surveys with executives from multiple organizations around the world to determine what skills were important for purchasing personnel to possess. The key to determining these priorities was asking general and line managers, not purchasing professionals, what they perceived to be important—in other words, what skills and capabilities they believed purchasing professionals needed to possess to be able to aid them and to be effective in playing the new strategic role the organization needed them to play in order to compete. This survey has recently been updated to determine the current perception of importance of skills and capabilities for the year 2003.

Based on the stated objectives of senior management to have purchasing become more proactive and strategic in nature, the survey was designed to investigate 41 skills in seven basic business capability categories. The *strategic management perspective* category measured understanding of corporate and business unit strategy, environmental impacts on each, and commitment to organizational success. The *business perspective* category measured understanding of the technologies used by the company, the company's customers and competitors, and the financial status of the business. The *internal consulting skills* category measured the ability to scan the organization to identify issues with purchasing implications, provide creative solutions to problems, and work as a corporate team member. The *purchasing functional* competence category measured the individual's knowledge of the latest developments in the purchasing field. The *procurement planning perspective* category measured the ability to anticipate and address procurement problems, identify key result areas, and develop appropriate procurement programs. The *ability to design and implement plans* category measured the capacity to sell solutions of problems to managers outside of purchasing, perform appropriate cost/benefit analyses, and manage a program within a budget.

The *management and leadership skills* category measured the ability to recruit and develop subordinates, communicate effectively, and exhibit high standards of performance. (See Box 12–1 for a full list of the questions.)

Interestingly, there was not 1 skill among the 41 in these categories that general and line managers deemed to be unimportant to the success of the purchasing professional in the new required role. The perceptions ranged from mildly to strongly important, depending on the item. The organization clearly wanted purchasing professionals to enhance their business capabilities and understanding and to apply this knowledge to create appropriate purchasing solutions. This required, among other things, expanding their expertise to include the ability to perform cost/benefit analyses and purchase for total value to the firm. It was at this time that we started seeing a shift towards requiring purchasing to take a more proactive stance and actively contribute to the strategic objectives and goals of the firm. It also was obvious, however, that many stereotypes of the reactive purchasing function negatively impacted the ability of purchasing to be effective in the new environment. The message was the mixed one that "we believe it is important for you to be this business partner, but we are not sure we trust you to be able to do it."

The results of the updated surveys show that only 5 of the 41 items will be less important for the purchasing professional to possess in the year 2003 than they were in 1988. Another 12 will remain of virtually the same importance, and all of the rest will be significantly more important. In other words, the bar keeps rising.

Anecdotal information gained recently in a doctoral dissertation on measurement and through interviews with purchasing and non-purchasing executives shows that the organization is now defining the job of the purchasing function to be one of building relationships across the firm and with outside firms for the purpose of adding competitive advantage to the organization through strategic sourcing processes. It also has become apparent that the perception of purchasing has risen in companies because the personnel are out in the organization demonstrating the ability to purchase for total cost and total value to the firm. Interestingly, the five items that decreased in importance from 1988 to 2003 all contribute to the ability to purchase for total value and play the role of relationship manager across the organization. They are: "practices purchasing as total value for the firm and not purchasing for price," "analyses costs and benefits of alternative purchasing options and chooses among them accordingly," "can effectively sell solutions

B O X   1 2 – 1

MANAGEMENT SKILLS ASSESSMENT– PURCHASING INSTRUMENT (QUESTIONS ABBREVIATED FOR SPACE)

Key: Right-hand column indicates change in importance from 1988 to 2003 as indicated by non-purchasing managers.
D = Decreases; S = Virtually Stays the Same; I = Increases

IMPORTANCE

STRATEGIC MANAGEMENT PERSPECTIVE
1. Understands overall corporate mission   I
2. Knows key strategies for major lines of business (LOB)   S
3. Understands need to link LOB strategies with corporate   I
4. Monitors business conditions/understands corporate
   performance measures   I
5. Monitors business environment/understands purchasing
   implications   I
6. Is committed to success of organization   I

BUSINESS PERSPECTIVE
7. Can interpret financial statements and performance
   measures   I
8. Develops purchasing programs in terms of financial
   implications   I
9. Understands current/future technologies/materials of firm   I
10. Understands firm's immediate and ultimate customer needs S
11. Understands competitors' strengths and weaknesses   I

INTERNAL CONSULTING SKILLS
12. Scans organization/environment to identify issues with
    purchasing implications   I
13. Develops purchasing programs clearly linked to strategy of
    LOB   I
14. Provides creative solutions to needs identified by
    LOB management.   I
15. Serves as intermediary to focus supplier relationships   I
16. Fosters purchasing reputation by working as team member S
17. Demonstrates high credibility/sound ethical judgment   S

PURCHASING FUNCTIONAL COMPETENCE
18. Practices purchasing as total value for firm, not for price   D
19. Understands global issues facing purchasing for firm   I
20. Is current regarding legal and regulatory issues   S

IMPORTANCE

21. Is informed about new purchasing developments and
    methods   I
22. Informs firm of potential social/political/economic impacts S
23. Sponsors innovative approach to sourcing/negotiation/
    supplier management   S

PROCUREMENT PLANNING PERSPECTIVE
24. Anticipates purchasing problems facing LOBs/actively
    addresses   I
25. Helps LOB managers anticipate changes with purchasing
    implications   I
26. Develops short-term purchasing plans consistent with L-T
    objectives   I
27. Can identify key results areas and set appropriate objectives S

ABILITY TO DESIGN AND IMPLEMENT PLANS
28. Chooses correctly based on cost/benefit analysis of options D
29. Uses appropriate program control and monitoring processes   I
30. Can manage a program within a budget   I
31. Can effectively "sell" solutions throughout organization   D
32. Works effectively with managers outside purchasing   I
33. Can influence others without direct authority   S

MANAGEMENT AND LEADERSHIP SKILLS
34. Exhibits high standards of performance   S
35. Is an effective listener   S
36. Acts consistently/instills trust   S
37. Stretches subordinates to fulfill potential   I
38. Recruits/selects high-quality professionals   I
39. Communicates effectively in writing and orally   D
40. Can manage conflict effectively   D
41. Adequately prepares successors   I

throughout the organization," "communicates effectively both in writing and orally," and "can manage conflict effectively." The only explanation for the decrease in importance of these items can be that line and general managers perceive these capabilities to be a new baseline of skills and therefore have somewhat diminished their value on paper. Even so, they are still rated between important and strongly important and therefore are skills the effective purchasing professional needs to hone.

ANALYSIS

The role that line and general managers want purchasing professionals to play is that of business partner. This means being someone who is adept at general business practices and happens to specialize in purchasing. Over the past ten years, many organizations have taken executives from other functions and put them in charge of purchasing. The purpose was to bring a general business understanding and perspective to the purchasing function. Interestingly, functional expertise has always been the lowest or second-lowest ranked of the seven capability categories. Managers outside of purchasing expect you to possess the purchasing capabilities. What adds value for them is when the purchasing professional understands the business needs and constraints that manager is facing and can help come up with creative solutions to solve those issues.

In order to do this, purchasing professionals must be astute businesspeople. This requires understanding the business and industry in which your company operates. You must constantly be monitoring that industry environment to know current and future trends. To do this effectively requires that you be able to answer the following questions:

1. What is the industry in which your firm competes?
2. What are the pressures facing this industry?
3. Who are the customers in this industry?

This can be a two-level question. First, who are the customers buying products of the nature that you produce? Second, if you are in a firm that sells to other businesses as opposed to the ultimate consumer, you must also know who are the ultimate customers for the end product that your components go into making. The important factor at both levels is identification of current and potential customers. Too often we identify our market by listing current customers. If someone says they have 90% market share, we should examine how finely they are defining the market, for the more finely we define our market and customers, the more we limit our potential to identify new customers and thus increase sales.

4. What are the needs of the primary and ultimate customers in your industry?

The tricky part here is to identify not only existing, well-known needs, but also potential needs that are not being met or may even be unrecognized by the customers—both immediate and ultimate. In the business-to-business environment, companies want to work with suppliers who understand that company's customers' needs as well or even better than they do. This requires looking beyond your immediate customer to the uses and potential uses of the products in the marketplace.

Once you understand the market and customer needs, you must answer the next question.

5. Who are the competitors in this marketplace—who is your company competing against and (sometimes even more important) who are potential competitors?

These could be companies who currently compete only in one related portion of your market. More difficult to identify, but often the ones who change the way an industry operates (and are therefore most important to watch out for), are companies who currently do not compete in your market but have related products or substitute products and therefore could enter your market. Do not forget to look at new technologies that could be possible substitutes for your product in the future.

Once you know the competitive environment, you must understand how your company is positioned to compete.

6. What is your corporate mission and strategy, and what are the line-of-business strategies for each area of the firm?

In other words, how are you segmenting the market and how are you competing in each of those segments? What are the competitive pressures in each of those segments? These are the issues facing your "customers" daily, the people throughout the organization to whom you are providing your services. If you do not understand the demands facing them, you cannot be of assistance in helping them solve their needs.

Once you can answer all of the above questions, you must determine how purchasing can best contribute to the company's success.

Your role is to be the sourcing consultant to your internal customers, to identify for them the purchasing implications of the above information. This means alerting them to potential sourcing issues, both problems and positives (areas where you might be able to gain an advantage). To be effective in this role leads you to another set of questions about how you operate in the organization.

1. Do you have a system in place to gather environmental data and relay it throughout the company?

In leading-edge companies, purchasing has realized that it is the one function of the company that is in a position to gather information on all industries. Think about the fact that no other function that interacts with the outside world is really on the receiving end of information. Marketing and sales both are focussed on pushing your company's products out. Others that are communicating with other firms are focussed on one area, such as engineering or manufacturing. In purchasing you are constantly meeting with representatives from diverse industries, from those providing your critical components to those providing office supplies. You are in the position to listen to all of these representatives and learn from them what is happening in their industry. The power in this is that purchasing is the one function in the company with first-hand information on the economic environment and specific industry environment in which your company is competing. The challenge for your purchasing department is to develop a systematic way of gathering this crucial data and relaying it to the rest of the organization. Today information and learning are the most powerful competitive tools that any company can have. Your ability to gain the information, understand its competitive implications (not just purchasing implications), and then pass it along to the rest of the organization in a manner that enables them to use it will elevate your purchasing organization to new heights in the perspective of the company.

2. Is your stance in working with your firm proactive?

If you are waiting for others to come to you with requests, you are doing something wrong. You need to be actively involved in the daily activities of your internal customers. The pace they are working under today is too frenetic for them to have to come searching for you—so frenetic, in fact, that they do not have the time to think of all of the purchasing implications of what they are doing. Your job is to understand their strategy, their objectives and goals, and the daily operations they are undergoing. This means participating actively in their business, attending meetings, being present. And, most importantly, constantly thinking about the purchasing implications of what they are doing. Is there a raw material they are relying on that might be at risk in the market? Is there a potential substitute material for something currently being used that might be more effective or cheaper? Could they possibly become more efficient by having a supplier do some of the process they currently do, taking over the manufacturing complexity and cost?

3. Are you helping to create the business strategy with your internal customer?

Firms today that view their businesses from cross-functional perspectives, taking into consideration all factors, are the more successful ones in the marketplace.

4. Do you know what factors are common across the different lines of business in your organization?

If one part of the company is facing an issue, are you telling them that someone in another department has already solved this problem— and thereby saving the company money and time? Again, this is the advantage of being a function that interacts with all facets of the firm. You can carry the knowledge across the silos.

5. Do you know the performance measures and status of each area of your firm, do you develop your suggestions and plans in terms of their financial implications for the firm?

These are the two items in the survey that increased the most in importance between 1988 and 2003. Finance is the language of business. If you cannot speak it fluently, you cannot be a valued contributor to the success of the company.

6. Are you current with developments in sourcing and purchasing that are occurring in the field and in other companies, and are you actively bringing these into your company?

7. Are you serving as the relationship manager between your company and your suppliers?

Are you the interface that knows all of the points of contact between the organizations and manages the success of the interactions? Your company's relationship with its suppliers is key to its ability to compete today. Are you bringing supply chain management to life or simply giving it lip service?

8. Are you bringing talented people into the organization and developing them effectively to serve in this new purchasing role?

Recruiting and developing successors showed the second two greatest survey gains in importance between 1988 and 2003. Purchasing has moved beyond a reactive, clerical function to one that needs high-quality, professional businesspeople who understand what it means to compete in today's global environment. You are expected to make sure your company has the right people capable of delivering.

The bottom line for being successful in the area of purchasing today is to be a good businessperson who happens to work in purchasing. Understand your company's marketplace, its customers (immediate and ultimate), its competitors (current and potential), and how you as an organization are competing in this environment. With this knowledge base as your foundation, proactively bring purchasing's abilities to contribute to the competitive position of the firm to the table.

CHAPTER 13

Developing a Purchasing Organization

Editor
Roland R. Tunez
Director—Supply Chain Management
Network Purchasing Team
BellSouth Telecommunications

INTRODUCTION

Envision a dynamic, fast, and flexible organization with driven, talented people who are energized and productive. There is a sense of urgency without panic. They have the tenacity and creativity of front-line units. An organization that gathers market intelligence, is connected to the customer's needs, works with and as needed, even leads cross-functional teams to set aggressive targets, develop corporate strategies, and execute these to bring sustained value and net income contributions. A team that is well represented and supported throughout the corporation by senior management.

Is this a sales team? No! It is a purchasing organization!

Purchasing is an important and yet often overlooked business function. Whether a firm's core competency is services, sales, or manufacturing, either for-profit or nonprofit, understanding and managing costs and supply streams is essential for growth and competitive advantages. As much as 50% of revenues from sales are consumed by purchases within a firm.[1] The purchasing organization is the first line of defense in releasing these purchasing dollars back into the firm's operations and ultimately untold millions of dollars towards net income contribution. This

---

1. J. D. Lewis, *The Connected Corporation: How Leading Companies Win Through Customer— Supplier Alliances,* New York: The Free Press, 1995, p. 10.

opportunity is not easily realized. Purchasing organizations need to be developed and structured to yield sustained results to a firm's bottom line and be an integral player in creating competitive advantages. Many firms recognize this and include their purchasing organization as a viable contributor to their strategies, with direct linkages to the financial results. These firms invest resources into developing their purchasing organizations and set high expectations for their contribution to the bottom line. In these firms the planning and execution of supply stream strategies are as integrated, aggressive, and targeted as those strategies that are focused on the growth and revenue components of their operations. This chapter addresses the process of developing a purchasing organization for strategic purchasing and a competitive advantage. This process is structured into three sections: The Purchasing Organization, The Organizational Fundamentals, and Developing a Purchasing Organization: The People Part of the Equation.

THE PURCHASING ORGANIZATION

In this section we start with an expanded view of the purchasing organization, recognizing the purchasing function as a powerful competitive advantage to be developed for success. Then, in order to understand current opportunities, we look briefly at the historical evolution of purchasing, and finally finish this section by discussing supply market management, which is being widely accepted as a "best practice.[2]

Purchasing is a Competitive Advantage to be Developed for Success

Purchasing is a business function that has a significant impact on many key components of a firm's operation. At first glance, purchasing functions impact the obvious: acquisition costs and material streams. However, highly evolved strategic purchasing organizations extend their reach beyond the realm of acquisition of products, services, raw materials, invoicing, and logistics. The purchasing organizations shift from a

---

2. J. L. Cavinato, *Developing The Purchasing Organization Workshop: Lecture Material April 20–24, 1998,* Penn State Executive Programs, The Pennsylvania State University, University Park, Pennsylvania.

standalone "buying process" to a cross-functional process that is interwoven throughout operations. To create a competitive advantage, these purchasing organizations develop successful and productive relationships with the suppliers and the internal clients they support. They tap into the expertise within the firm and in the supplier base to help craft optimum solutions.[3] These relationships can improve new product development, speed to market cycle times, and resale of retired assets, and can drive costs out of both the firm and their suppliers' operations that ultimately can be leveraged into competitive advantages and achieving targeted financial results.

Additionally, as the business and economic operating environments continue to increase in their global scope, the ability to secure target pricing, finite and limited resources, and the cost-effective and efficient movement of goods and services across the globe can very well differentiate a firm's market position and financial results.

Sunil Lakhani, Director of Advanced Manufacturing Technology, Motorola's Paging Products Group, states: "The real payback comes from better service and a faithful supplier; you can't buy that."[4] Clearly, the value and competitiveness that a purchasing organization can bring to bear in a firm's operations are beyond the traditional purchase price variance approach of the past. This is often easy to plan but wickedly difficult to achieve. Many factors can interfere, including cultures, organizational structures, behaviors, and past practices, and this can lead to adversarial relationships and mistrust. Dr. J. Cavinato formerly from The Acquisition Research and Development Center, The Pennsylvania State University, advises that over time, some firms end up paying a premium for introducing uncertainty into a supplier's operations.[5]

The Evolution of the Purchasing Function

In order to develop a current and forward-looking purchasing organization, it is important to take a brief view of the historical evolution of purchasing. This evolutionary curve was developed by Dr. J. Cavinato.[6]

Chronology of events (see Fig. 13–1):

---

3. Lewis, op. cit., pp. 95–97.
4. Ibid., p. 130.
5. Cavinato, op. cit.
6. Ibid.

F I G U R E   13–1

The Evolution of the Purchasing Function

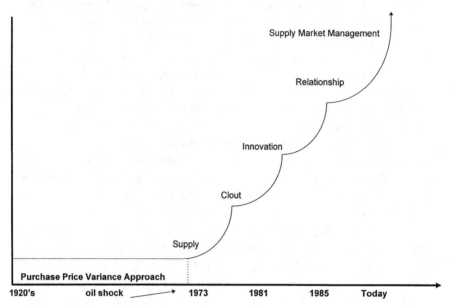

Source: Cavinato, Joseph L., Ph.D., C.P.M., The Pennsylvania State University, 1997.

1. From the 1920s until the global oil shock of 1972–1973, the principal function of purchasing was to "buy it for less." Initial first cost is the primary focus for many firms.

2. The oil shock impacts global business operations, and dramatic changes in supply stream costs, reliability, and availability necessitate the development of supply stream planning and strategies beyond initial first cost reductions. The supply streams shift from being mostly cost drivers to being strategic sources of products and services with significant bottom line impact. "Buying for less" is no longer sufficient. The primary focus shifts from initial first cost to total cost of ownership.

3. The immediate short-term reaction was to exert clout on the suppliers to ensure cost, reliability, and continuity. As with most short-term-focused initiatives, the results were sudden but limited. More cooperation and collaboration was needed to achieve continuous improvements and win–win solutions.

4. In order for the buyers and suppliers to achieve continued total cost of ownership improvements, reliability, and responsiveness to markets, there has been increased development in the levels of integration and collaboration among suppliers, purchasing organizations, and other functional groups in the firms. Currently, many purchasing organizations are accepting as a best practice supply market management, which is a portfolio of all of the functions in the evolutionary curve. This elevates purchasing to the level of "strategic purchasing".

SUPPLY MARKET MANAGEMENT: THE CURRENT BEST PRACTICE

Purchasing is being transformed into an analogue of marketing and sales. Supply streams and suppliers can be managed with a portfolio approach by the purchasing managers to achieve specific objectives from product development and technical solutions to costs, performance, and quality. Leading edge-purchasing organizations have demystified purchasing. They approach purchasing with the same tenacity as, and use managed cross-functional techniques commonly used by, line units such as sales, marketing, and manufacturing. These purchasing organizations have "earned their wings" in their firms. They are able to unlock the power that can be hidden and remain untapped in purchasing.

Dr. J. Cavinato conducts an annual survey of over a thousand firms worldwide to identify current trends, issues, and concerns in the field of supply chain management. The 1998 survey information was based on 1,138 responses from 1,540 targeted firms and their senior managers.[7] The following are the top ten "Best Practices Firms Were Seeking to Accomplish During 1998" identified by the respondents who are currently developing initiatives around these practices:

1. Electronic strategy development
2. Market intelligence tools for the buyer's market
3. Process focus throughout the firm/chain
4. Synergies across divisions/regions of a firm
5. Core competencies and skills analysis

---

7. Ibid.

6. Getting purchasing out of transactions
7. Suppliers in various linkages
8. Learning and applying negotiations in a range of new ways
9. Supply management (P/L responsibility)
10. Cost modeling the chain and supplier economics

This list is indicative of a movement in the purchasing functions towards an integrated approach focused on understanding the supply market dynamics. From these market dynamics supply stream strategies are crafted to include a broad range of value-adding elements, from cost-saving electronic commerce to negotiation with value analysis information to cost modeling jointly developed with the suppliers. The steady stream of development in the field of purchasing continues to position purchasing functions for developing as a front-line operation tied to the bottom line.

Dr. J. Cavinato points out that there is a measurement gap problem:[8] The measurements used by many firms to manage purchasing organizations are often partially or even entirely focused on the "traditional" purchase price variance approach.[9] The implication is that measurements can result in a purchasing organization compromising its ability to optimize value and competitive advantages for the firm. Measurements drive behaviors, set expectations, and ultimately yield certain results. This is true for most organizations, and purchasing organizations are no exception. The key is to achieve alignment across the purchasing organization, from the strategies to the structure to the measurements that help drive it to expected versus actual results. This leads us to the next section.

THE ORGANIZATIONAL FUNDAMENTALS

There are a multitude of sound, proven organizational development principles that can be applied to most organizations and will achieve the expected results. Purchasing organizations are no exception. In this section we explore two principles that are basic building blocks for developing purchasing organizations: the role of senior management in supporting the development of purchasing organizations, and the various

---

8. Ibid.
9. Ibid.

alignments that need to be trued up between the firm and the purchasing organization.

Senior Management Support: The Purchasing Organization Needs to Earn Senior Management Support

The single most critical factor for the successful development of a purchasing organization is senior management support, which serves as a catalyst for development in three ways. Senior management:

1. Can quickly and effectively close the cultural gap between line and staff

2. Provides the resources and changes in the organizational structure and design to support purchasing strategies

3. Is the point of origin for the leadership required to effect the significant and sustainable changes that may be necessary for the development of purchasing organizations?

One proven technique for gaining senior management support is to "speak the language of senior management." The initiative must have a clear and rational purpose and be supportive of the firm's financial and strategic objectives. It is incumbent upon the purchasing organization to identify and help develop integrated strategies and bring them to fruition. This in turn will facilitate senior management support. Jordan D. Lewis states that "firms with the most effective supply alliances enjoy ongoing and visible support from the highest corporate levels."[10]

Senior Management Support: Closing the Cultural Gap

The classic cultural lines of contention in an organization are often drawn between functional groups, such as staff and line operations, or sales and manufacturing. Purchasing organizations can also, as a result of such a cultural rift, be on the opposite side from the firm's core business functions that they support. This rift can be a significant barrier to development if strong cultural values have evolved that recognize and support critical decision-making authority as belonging primarily to one business

---

10. Lewis, op. cit.

unit, often a core unit, and to a lesser degree (except for special circumstances) to another unit, usually a staff, head quarters, or other support unit. The purchasing organization is often embedded into the organizational structure as a support unit for the core business units. Senior management needs to be able to identify and address this ageless cultural gap with policies, procedures, linked measures across functional groups, and open support for the desired state.

Senior Management Support: Providing Resources for Organizational Design

For purchasing strategies to be effective, the entire firm must design and integrate its operations to support purchasing strategies. This level of collaboration and coordination is usually achieved through clear and decisive senior management support and at times even directives. Oftentime decisions to reallocate resources to support the development of a purchasing organization will require senior management approval, as will the redesign of reporting relationships, creation of new positions, and elimination of others. The delegation of authority and the freedom to maneuver will need to be shifted to those in the position to develop and approve such initiatives. These efforts may also require support from the top. Finally, there will need to be a concerted effort to recruit and retain top talent, which may include the redesigning of salaries, rewards, recognition, and the working environment. All of these will successfully challenge the status quo only if supported by senior management.

Senior Management Support: The Point of Origin for Leadership

If the firm or the purchasing organization has not started to move along a development curve from the current state to an identified and desired state, and doing so represents a major change, then this process, like all major changes, can be a large and complex undertaking. Judith M. Bardwick explains the conflicts that arise from the resistance to a need for change: "Leaders evoke emotional connections in followers only to the extent that followers are emotionally needy."[11] It is not sufficient to have

---

11. J. M. Bardwick, "Peacetime Management and Wartime Leadership," in F. Hesselbein, M. Goldsmith, and R. Beckhard, eds., *The Leader of the Future*, Jossey-Bass, San Francisco, 1996, p. 132.

a clear and logical need for change. Those who will have to change and follow must have an emotional connection to the need. As the point of origin for leadership, senior management needs to step up to the plate and lead this effort if the firm is to follow and bring the desired state to reality.

Alignment Between the Firm and the Purchasing Organization

For the purchasing function to be effective and therefore supported, absolute alignment between the firm's objectives and those of the purchasing organization is necessary. This alignment is usually the following:

1. Financial pro forma plans
2. Business plan
3. Sales plan
4. Purchasing plan

Ultimately the purchasing organization, if it is to develop and grow as an integrated contributor to the firm, must be productive and effective in setting and achieving its objectives in unison with the rest of the firm. The following is a list of key organizational items which need to be supported and linked between the firm and the purchasing organization:

- *Vision and mission* should be common and valued. "We are all seeing and maneuvering across the same business landscape, and our commitment to the outcome is equally important to all of us!"

- *Objectives and metrics* are set so that they are linked measurements between functional groups and the purchasing teams. They need to be targeted toward driving behaviors and performance results so that when they are achieved, the purchasing and business objectives are mutually met.

- *Roles and responsibilities* should be clearly identified and communicated to ensure peak performance in the face of the inevitable stress and confusion that all organizations encounter from time to time. This also increases the efficiency and effectiveness of the players.

- *Strategic and tactical plans* should be developed in unison and be supportive of each other to achieve one common outcome.

- *Culture,* meaning values, behaviors, symbols, performance expectations, and management, and the many other drivers that form and reinforce a business culture, should be focused and targeted to support collaborative planning and decision-making. Policies and procedures also need to support this culture.

Let's take a moment to recap:

- *The Purchasing Organization:*
  - *Purchasing is a competitive advantage to be developed for success:* Purchasing is more than acquisition and logistics. By tapping into the firm's and supplier's expertise through strategic relationships and alliances, purchasing organizations can improve product development, speed to market, and ultimately market positioning and financial results.
  - *The evolution of the purchasing function:* Developments and improvements in the purchasing function have moved this function from price variance to supply market management. The emphasis shifts from initial first cause to total cost of ownership.
  - *Supply market management—the current best practice:* This elevates purchasing to an integrated business approach analogous to sales and marketing. The methodology includes a holistic cross-functional process with market intelligence, objectives, and strategies. The supply streams are managed as portfolios with linkages to the firm's competitive needs and bottom line.
  - *The measurement gap:* A purchasing organization can compromise its ability to deliver optimum value if the measurements and behavioral drivers are not supportive of strategic purchasing.
- *The Organizational Fundamentals:*
  - *Senior management support:* The single most critical factor for the successful development of purchasing organizations. Senior management provides three key elements: through its support, it can close the cultural gaps between line organizations and support organizations; it can effect the allocation of resources for the redesigns and staffing decisions; and as the point of origin for leadership, it can

provide the open support for and leadership in the change
effort that is essential for the firm to follow the lead and
bring the desired state to fruition.

♦ *Alignment between the firm and the purchasing organization:* The
vision and mission, objectives, metrics, roles and
responsibilities, and strategic and tactical plans need to be
aligned and supported by the firm and the purchasing
organization. The cultural values and drivers need to be just
as much aligned.

DEVELOPING A PURCHASING ORGANIZATION: THE PEOPLE PART OF THE EQUATION

In this section we bring to light the central players who ultimately make
a purchasing organization successful. In the end, the triumph of any
undertaking rests squarely on the shoulders of those who are closest to
the action and have to execute the plans. Competitive advantages, senior
management support, best practices, and alignments across the firm will
only be as successful as the people on whom we depend upon to make
it happen. Enough cannot be said of the front-line people in any organization who day in and day out get results through their actions and
attitudes. In purchasing organizations these are the purchasing managers
or supply managers and the managers of these managers. As much rigor
and attention are necessary in selecting and retaining these valuable people as in selecting suppliers.

Each of the following four operational variables within the purchasing organization needs to be incorporated into the development
plan. We will expand upon each one individually in this section.

1. *The structure of the purchasing organization:* Is the structure
   conducive to the required speed and responsiveness?

2. *The supply stream portfolios and appropriate strategies:* Are the
   supply streams properly identified with their relevant
   strategies?

3. *Staffing the supply stream portfolios:* Do we have the people,
   skills, and resources assigned to each portfolio to develop and
   execute supply stream strategies and achieve objectives?

4. *The "engine for continuity":* Are the performance measures,
   rewards, etc. capable of sustaining long-term results?

The Structure of the Purchasing Organization

In the complex matter of structuring a purchasing organization, the focus must be on the operational imperatives, including speed, accuracy, flexibility, and responsiveness. The question to be answered through the organizational structuring effort is whether the structure allows the purchasing organization the ability to perform and exceed the needs of the business. Keep in mind that the life blood of a purchasing organization is its ability to perform as expected with continuous improvement. The structure and the subsequent workflows, roles, and responsibilities should be positioned to improve rather than impede peak performance. The industry, the competitive imperatives, and the firm's culture all help to shape the individual structures. As a help in the development of this crucial element, the following are organizational factors to be considered from a purchasing perspective:

1. *Reporting relationships and layers of control:* Most organizations have at one point or another struggled with the ancient issue of centralized versus decentralized controls. When the purchasing managers and their managers are skilled and effective, it is advisable to push accountability and decision-making authority as low into the organization as possible in accordance with the appropriate degree of risk abatement required, with it kept in mind that optimum speed and responsiveness is generally achieved with fewer rather than more layers of decision-making and controls.

2. *Structuring the purchasing organization around supply stream portfolios:* Here the goal is manageability and level loading of the portfolios for maximum performance. In the assessment of the assignments to the purchasing managers, there can be numerous ways to slice and dice the workload. Purchasing portfolios can be structured by suppliers, by common supply streams, by relevant and related technologies, by end user or internal customer, even by functional group.

3. *Structuring the purchasing organization to meet the internal customer needs:* The objective here is to be able to deliver purchasing functions in such a way as to meet special projects or unique needs, such as emerging technologies or product development. These positions are staffed for the need of the customer, be it speed, accuracy, or project management-type services.

4. *Integrated purchasing teams:* Teams can be set up literally, virtually, and for special needs. The goal is for the team of purchasing managers to be able to bring the specialty of each on task as needed to serve a business need. These teams also allow for multitasking for maximum efficiency.

5. *Purchasing support functions:* Additional consideration must be included in the structure to allow for purchasing support functions, including project management and analytical research. These should be set up to provide the purchasing organization information and ancillary services to boost efficiency and effectiveness.

6. *Additional considerations:* In the structuring of the workloads and portfolios, it is important to include in the assessment the skills, strengths, and weaknesses of the purchasing managers to ensure a good fit with the supplier and the needs of the business, as well as the degree of importance of the role the supply stream and/or the supplier plays in the competitive needs of the firm.

In summation, all purchasing organization structural topologies should be focused on improving the performance of the purchasing personnel as well as the supplier and the internal client.

The Supply Stream Portfolios and Appropriate Strategies

The purchasing organization is positioned between the firm and the suppliers, each of which has objectives to meet and will certainly maneuver accordingly to achieve those objectives. This is a precarious position to be in. Without a structured process that enables the team to segment supply stream portfolios into specific categories, each with unique and relevant strategies targeted to the needs of the business, the purchasing organization can quickly be overwhelmed and its ability to add value be compromised. The Penn State University Acquisition Research and Development Center and Dr. J. Cavinato have developed a "Quadrant Approach to Procurement and Supply."[12] The following sequence of three

---

12. Cavinato, op. cit.

2×2 matrices begins with a supply stream portfolio segmentation rationale (Fig. 13–2), this is followed by the relevant supply stream strategies (Fig. 13–3), which are quadrant specific, and finally by the critical skills required for each quadrant (Fig. 13–4).

Staffing the Supply Stream Portfolios

The purchasing managers need a broad range of competencies in order to perform their purchasing functions. To be effective in the complicated field of purchasing, they must be alert, motivated, focused, and highly skilled. These skills and behaviors have to be assessed, evaluated, developed, and rewarded. Top talent will flow towards and stay longer in

FIGURE 13–2

The Supply Stream Portfolio Segmentation Quadrants. 1. Each supply stream is evaluated for degree of risk or uniqueness to the firm and the value/profit potential. 2. The costs relevant to the business is also identified. 3. This segmentation then allows for quadrant specific strategies to be applied to the supply stream portfolios in each quadrant.

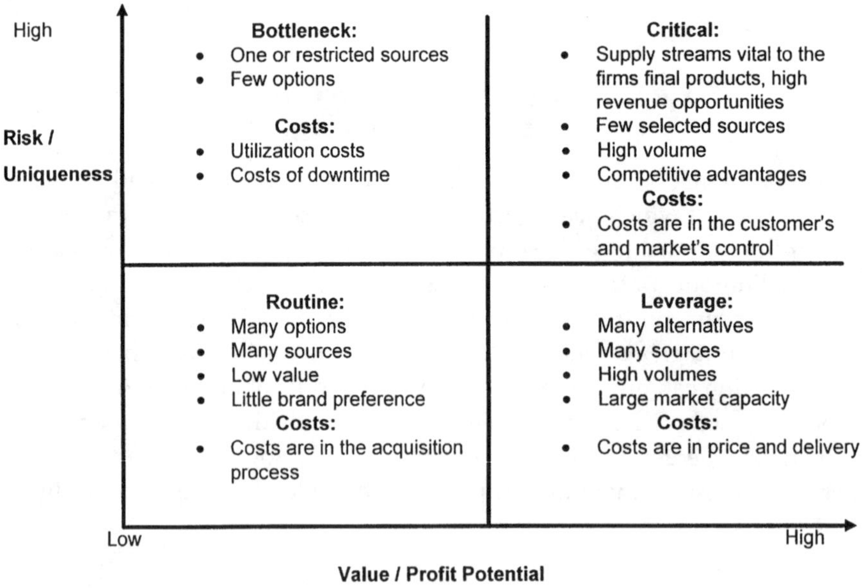

High	**Bottleneck:** • One or restricted sources • Few options **Costs:** • Utilization costs • Costs of downtime	**Critical:** • Supply streams vital to the firms final products, high revenue opportunities • Few selected sources • High volume • Competitive advantages **Costs:** • Costs are in the customer's and market's control
Risk / **Uniqueness**		
	Routine: • Many options • Many sources • Low value • Little brand preference **Costs:** • Costs are in the acquisition process	**Leverage:** • Many alternatives • Many sources • High volumes • Large market capacity **Costs:** • Costs are in price and delivery
Low		**High**

Value / Profit Potential

F I G U R E   13–3

The Quadrant-Specific Supply Stream Strategies. Each quadrant's specific strategies are targeted to address the implications for the firm, given the degree of risk and value of the supply streams.

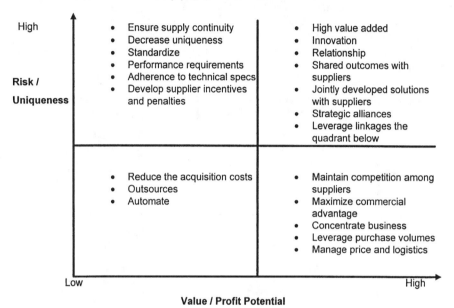

	Value / Profit Potential

energized organizations that reward superior performance and develop their people for success. Many organizations from time to time find themselves having to address the issue of declining performance. Many factors can contribute to declining performance; in response to these, numerous remedies to improve performance have been developed and successfully implemented. The following are some widely practiced techniques that can work well to develop purchasing organization.

Set Clear and Aggressive Performance Expectations

Performance follows expectations. Setting clear and aggressive performance expectations is likely to yield high levels of focused and targeted performance. As can be expected, the reverse is also true. A purchasing organization needs superlative performance results to be able to gain and

F I G U R E 13–4

The Quadrant-Specific Skills to Manage the Supply Streams and Strategies. 1. The skill sets for each quadrant are tied to the strategies and the nature of the supplier relationships unique to each quadrant. 2. Most purchasing managers should have strong business acumen, good interpersonal skills, critical and strategic thinking abilities, and negotiating skills. These are consistent with the core functions performed by purchasing organizations.

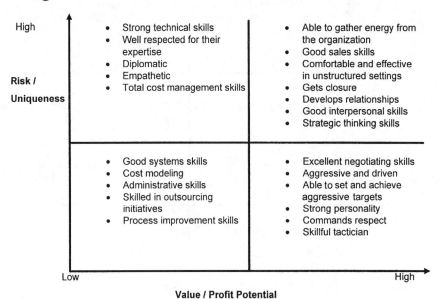

High

Risk / Uniqueness

- Strong technical skills
- Well respected for their expertise
- Diplomatic
- Empathetic
- Total cost management skills

- Able to gather energy from the organization
- Good sales skills
- Comfortable and effective in unstructured settings
- Gets closure
- Develops relationships
- Good interpersonal skills
- Strategic thinking skills

- Good systems skills
- Cost modeling
- Administrative skills
- Skilled in outsourcing initiatives
- Process improvement skills

- Excellent negotiating skills
- Aggressive and driven
- Able to set and achieve aggressive targets
- Strong personality
- Commands respect
- Skillful tactician

Low   High

Value / Profit Potential

leverage the senior management support and the collaboration of the other business units in the firm for continuous improvement. Performance expectations for purchasing managers include the ability to understand the supply/supplier portfolios, gather intelligence, form strategies, set quantifiable objectives, and work cross-functionally with the business units and suppliers to achieve expected results. Also, there should be an expectation of progressive movement along learning and growth curves. Set objectives for the purchasing managers to acquire certifications in critical skills, such as the Accredited Purchasing Practitioner (A.P.P.), Certified Purchasing Manager (C.P.M.), from the National Association of

Purchasing Management (NAPM), or Certified in Production and Inventory Management (CPIM) from APICS, and other certifications such as project management.

Develop a Fair, Objective, and Quantifiable Performance Evaluation Process

Purchasing managers usually perform many and diverse work functions as part of their craft. They develop a thorough understanding of their supply stream portfolios, the client's needs, and the firm's objectives. Armed with information and market intelligence, purchasing managers develop strategies and solutions to meet a multitude of business needs, ranging from supplier performance improvements to negotiating and achieving target pricing, structuring contracts, and supply chain process improvements. These work functions should have a clear purpose and quantifiable results. A useful tool for setting in place a fair, objective, and quantifiable performance evaluation process is Management by Objectives (MBO). The following is an MBO-suggested sequence.

1. In the fourth quarter of the year begin the quantification of the expected results from strategies, solutions, and deliverables that the purchasing managers identify for the upcoming operating year.

2. Develop personal improvement plans with quantifiable outcomes as well for the coming year.

3. Apply the MBO methodology, which may include bottoms-up results and, as necessary, top-down input. These should roll up to the purchasing manager, his or her manager, and all the way up the purchasing organization.

4. Set in place a periodic performance review plan throughout the year.

5. Take performance management and improvement at the people and organization levels seriously. Develop a rigorous plan and stick to it. This is a critical process that can eventually bring great success or failure to the firm and the purchasing organization. A very sobering saying is, "If you don't do it well, someone else will!"

6. Take time to have fun! Good people getting great results can create a very exciting workplace.

Develop Job Descriptions and Job Competencies

Linkage and clarity are the key success factors here. There must be an absolute linkage between the job descriptions of purchasing managers and the firm's needs. The purchasing team should seek expertise in this area, which usually resides in the Human Resources (HR) department. The competencies, which include the knowledge, skills, abilities, and attitudes, also need to be linked to the job description and clearly identified with observable behaviors specific to each competency. This is a critical process that can enable the purchasing organization to evaluate and develop its people for peak performance. The performance implications of skill gaps or will gaps are equally important and need to be accurately assessed for improvement. Once a solid job description has been put in place and the competencies associated with the job description have been clearly communicated, perform a standard competency gap analysis and codevelop with each individual a development plan with timelines, milestones, feedback, and quantifiable improvements.

Provide the Resources Necessary

High performance expectations managed by a well-structured performance evaluation process are not enough. There are likely to be skill gaps to be closed, which requires resources in time, training, and development. A changing business environment requires equally dynamic purchasing managers, who will need a steady stream of resources strategically applied for continued improvement. Develop a resource allocation plan that is both efficient and effective. The purchasing organization needs to lead by example. It should clearly understand and manage its own costs and operating expenses as expertly as those of the firm.

Structure a Recognition and Rewards Plan

Performance is a product of many factors, including expectations, behaviors, attitudes, and values. These in turn are driven and shaped by the working environment. Work into the performance management process a systematic plan to recognize and reward the key performance behaviors and attitudes that will yield expected results. The objective is twofold: to reward and recognize the individual(s) and to openly identify and elevate these behaviors and attitudes to the team. Two additional points: the rewards need to be timely and fair, and the behaviors and attitudes should clearly be identified and above and beyond the expected levels.

Develop Rigorous Selection and Succession Plans

The selections and promotions process is where performance management begins. Gather intelligence from the performance management process and use it to develop rigorous standards and guidelines to ensure that the proper skills sets, attitudes, and observed behaviors are brought in from the start. Build diversity into the purchasing organization. Seek combinations of people from various disciplines such as marketing and sales, field operations, and technical specialties. Develop a rotation plan with other business units and position purchasing as an entry-level department for certain qualified new entrants. Engage senior management to ensure that the purchasing organization has as good a leadership team as other functional groups within the firm. The purchasing functions cut across many functional groups in a firm and offer quality exposure to many levels of management and work groups. This is an exciting proposition that should be marketed to attract talented people.

The "Engine for Continuity"

Maintaining sustained long-term results is a challenge for all organizations. Building simplicity into the working environment, an organizational culture of adaptability, and people with a high tolerance for change are essential. The key is to set in place a change process that makes change simple, fast, and effective. The following are some operational dynamics that can contribute to sustained long-term results in a purchasing organization.

Get the House in Order

- ◆ Set up workflows, policies, and procedures that improve, not impede, peak performance, speed, and flexibility.
- ◆ Build accuracy and simplicity into the organization.
- ◆ Challenge the status quo. Question and eliminate non-value-adding work.
- ◆ Ensure clear roles and responsibilities between suppliers, clients, and purchasing managers.
- ◆ Talented and aggressive people with well-developed marketable and transferable skills can "vote with their feet." To attract and retain top talent in the organization, get a good fix

on the working environment dynamics that these people prefer and incorporate these into the purchasing organization.

Build a Balanced Platform

+ Build business needs, people needs, short term, and long-term variables into the purchasing operations and planning cycles.
+ The leadership team will need to demonstrate these in the conduct of business.
+ Ensure that the lines of communication are open, honest, and two-way.
+ Build 360° feedback mechanisms to keep up with the pulse of the firm, the suppliers, and the purchasing organization.

Develop a Forward-Looking Approach to Purchasing

+ Look for trends, patterns, and forecasts that can preempt coming changes and emerging opportunities.
+ Look to the suppliers and business units in the firm for forward-looking intelligence that they are processing.
+ Become active in trade associations of the firm and of the key suppliers' industries and in purchasing associations such as NAPM.

SUMMARY

Purchasing is an essential business function that can be developed into a powerful competitive advantage. A well-developed purchasing organization can unlock millions of dollars from purchasing and contribute them right to the bottom line. Many firms of all types and sizes have developed their purchasing organizations beyond the traditional buying for less and contracting paradigms to yield exceptional value through integrated strategic purchasing.

Making the people connection is the key to many successful organizational development efforts, and purchasing organizations are no exception. Develop the purchasing organization by creating a working environment that attracts and retains talented people. Achieve results that earn senior management support by working collaboratively with the suppliers and the firm's business units. Learn and apply the best practices in the purchasing field. The purchasing organization is an important and challenging front-line business unit.

CHAPTER 14

Re-engineering Purchasing and Supply

Editor
Thomas M. De Paoli, Ph.D., C.P.M., SPHR
Principal Apollo Solutions Consulting
Apollo Solutions

Anyone who thinks that reengineering purchasing is not the most radical and corporate changing process that a company can undertake is greatly mistaken. Reengineering cannot be done in a piecemeal, half-hearted manner. It requires the total changing of all aspects of purchasing. It is important to change everything about the former traditional purchasing department. Michael Hammer was right when he indicated that your first step is to "blow up" the old system. Dr. Hammer states, "Reengineering means starting over. It doesn't mean tinkering with what already exists and leaving the basic structures intact. It isn't about making patchwork fixes—or jury-rigging existing systems so that they work better. It is about making BIG changes fast." This is a complete remake. What people do, nomenclature, the work atmosphere, and primarily the relationships with suppliers can not just be tweaked. This is radical surgery and a transformation, not just another management program that people hope will go away or that loses momentum over time. Above all, the process requires an intense fervor and commitment that defies explanation unless an individual has actually lived or survived the perilous journey.

Reengineering of purchasing involves a major rethinking and total redesign of company-wide buying practices. The objective is to obtain a tremendous leap in the supply chain elements, such as quality, cost, technology, cycle time, inventory levels, lead time, transactions, and total cost of ownership. The barriers to achieving this major improvement are numerous and intense. There is limited or no top management perception of the role of purchasing and often insufficient license to operate. Out-of-date attitudes among other departments towards purchasing often thwart the process. Management often permits other departments to define what they want purchasing to do which typically is to act as a blind, subservient service department that meets their non-value-adding perceived needs. Purchasing departments are typically bureaucracies rife with disabling policies, procedures, and redundant controls. Purchasing reports to different functions in different companies. This just adds to the confusion about their role. Often, antiquated information systems with little or no value for purchasing are mired in place. Many corporate hierarchies and organizational structures militate against letting purchasing "play in their sandbox." A very high percentage (over 80%) of purchasing departments remain solidly traditional. This inability to change or even progress remains a mystery for the many purchasing professionals. According to Jack Welch CEO of General Electric, "The only two departments in a company that generate revenue are sales and purchasing. Everyone else is overhead." He is dead right. The problem is that the overhead departments rule most organizations.

By far the biggest barrier to reengineering purchasing is the enormous and overwhelming fear of change. Dr. Deming was right when he cited the need to drive out fear. A severe job security issue among purchasing professionals often helps create an atmosphere of fear that is nearly impossible to overcome. Before the journey of reengineering of purchasing can be undertaken, an assessment of where purchasing professionals are on their career path cycle and in their approach is essential. The four career groups along the path are beginners or start-up, adapters or maintenance, risk takers or innovators, and visionary or leading edge (Fig. 14–1). Purchasing professionals can be classified as reactive, mechanical, proactive, and American Keiretsu. The reactive state is the typical firefighting jumping to operating crisis mode of many departments. The mechanical state is the super-bureaucrat who has mastered the inefficient system. The proactive state shows spurts of planning and some significant progress; often it is haphazard. The American Keiretsu is the end state of supply management prowess. The key here is to reskill people and provide the training to lead the reengineering process.

Traditional purchasing rewards exactly the wrong skills and behaviors. It rewards pencil pushers. Requirements are basically dictated to

F I G U R E   14–1

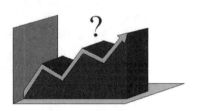

PURCHASING CAREER JOURNEY

➤ 1. Beginners – start up

➤ 2. Adapters – maintenance

➤ 3. Risk takers – innovation

➤ 4. Visionary – leading edge

purchasing, who often select a supplier by a rigid bid process. Unfortunately, most nonpurchasing employees think the bid process protects a company. Purchasing professionals soon realize the opposite is true. It is a process beset with danger and dishonesty. Price is often king. Cheap is regarded as better. The buying department is heavily transaction focused, with multiple and complicated steps required just to purchase an item no matter how small or cheap. Requisitions drive the workload, and the rules inhibit any real relationships with suppliers. Customer needs go out the window and procedures rule.

Progressive purchasing is highly team oriented, especially with cross-functional teams. The examination of the supply chain and total cost of ownership drives the decision-making process. There is a systematic process for supplier selection. Relationship building and management is the key skill for the purchasing professional. Senior management not only supports but understands the process. Purchasing becomes a true business partner and leader.

The supplier relationship is where the traditional and the progressive purchasing differ most. The traditional is short term, adversary based, and mostly commercial. Serious cost cutting is rare. Communication is usually at arm's length. Shopping is continuous, and purchasing is perpetually hunting for a deal. The world is one big strip mall of suppliers. The low bidder often wins the bid. The norm is three quotes and the required blizzard of paperwork for a supplier. The atmosphere is one of low trust and weak commitment, and performance is often not monitored well. Expediting of parts is continuous.

Modern supplier relationships are geared towards the long term—at least three to five years. Close collaboration is open, with mutual sharing of plans, design, goals, and rewards. The lowest total cost of ownership is valued, and value-adding services are the norm. Suppliers are empowered to just get it done. The so-called iceberg of supplier opportunity clearly explains that only 5–10% of efficiency is gained via price, and it is the area of least resistance and work (See Fig. 14–2). The 90–95% of the so-called new frontier of supplier exploration is actual bottom line total cost of ownership savings. This means utilizing a preferred supplier. This is the area of the greatest resistance and opportunity and the realm of relationship building that requires increasing communication and the building of trust.

This new frontier with suppliers has some particular characteristics (Box 14–1). This quantum leap philosophy with suppliers requires the education of purchasing personnel, rapid access to information, and supplier empowerment. Cross-functional business teams and a constant dedication to improve and to reduce time to market are key elements.

An initial reengineering checklist must include a focus on business practices and the dumping of buzzwords. It is necessary to aim high and not to settle for marginal results. Anticipation of strong resistance and

F I G U R E   14–2

THE ICEBERG OF OPPORTUNITY

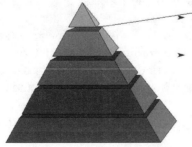

5-10% price buyers area of least resistance

90-95% the new frontier of bottom line contribution or total cost of utilizing given suppliers. Area of greatest resistance and opportunity

B O X 14–1

THE NEW FRONTIER
WHERE THE PURCHASING PROS ARE

- Most-favored customer contracts
- Mutual cost reductions
- Eliminate incoming inspection
- Target nonproduction company costs
- Reduce supply base
- Integrate key suppliers into our business and market it
- Early supplier involvement in design
- Cross-functional teams
- Value engineering

strategies in advance are necessary to respond to the resistance. Performing constant follow-up on tasks, dedicating resources and hours to retraining certain workers, revising job descriptions, changing the cultural norm, changing the nomenclature, changing the work area and the work routine, and using new technology when appropriate are worth considering.

The stages of reengineering are preparation, identification, vision, solution, transformation, follow-up, and leapfrogging. The preparation phase is the most critical. You cannot overprepare for the reengineering of purchasing. Homework isn't fun, but it is essential. Not only must senior management be educated, but a senior vice-president should be designated as a leader or champion of the process. Put in place methods to update senior management on progress and issues. Define the obstacles and potential issues in advance along with setting goals and priorities. Organize a reengineering team and include departments impacted by the change on the team. Of utmost importance, develop a marketing plan for reengineering. You cannot overcommunicate this process. Change creates an atmosphere of inordinate fear. Use of every communication device possible to help alleviate these fears is required. Often, purchasing people, after years of being boring bureaucrats, cannot market the process.

Top management needs to understand one important precept. Suppliers can make or break any business or business plan. According to Dr.

Deming, defective materials or equipment, not human error or the process, causes over 80% of quality variances. Suppliers obviously play the key role in achieving high quality. Suppliers need to be treated as stakeholders, not adversaries. World-class suppliers can become a company's best competitive weapons. They play the quintessential role in reducing time to market.

The major challenges of the next century include maximizing supplier contributions by focusing on supplier partners and continuous improvement. The focus must be on quality, flexibility, and reduction of time to market. Ultimately, company performance is judged by the paying customers or what I call the final end-user customer. Typically purchasing gets totally sidetracked and thinks that internal company customers are their real customers. Nothing could be further from the truth. These internal customers often whipsaw purchasing into doing stupid human tricks. Purchasing is not an unctuous service organization at the beck and whim of internal customers. It is primarily the chief revenue center for the corporation. It should, in conjunction with sales, find out exactly what the paying customers want, not boisterous internal customers, who often just confuse the issue. Purchasing in the reengineering process needs to focus on what specification the ultimate paying customer wants, not the false specifications of engineering, manufacturing, shipping, accounting, etc. This is much easier said than done, which is one reason why companies spend millions on customer research and focus groups.

An initial assessment checklist should include such things as what people's expectations are from purchasing. Don't expect any major insights here. Often their expectations are mired in traditional thinking and self-serving requirements. Purchasing needs to understand what they are evaluated on and how the score is kept. Price reductions are often only 5–10% of the savings potential for a company. New reporting relationships must be discussed. A new organization must be proposed and agreed upon in advance. Purchasing needs to get more involved in the design phase of products and more importantly with sales and get to know the paying customer up front and personal. A resource assessment is required. This is not a process that can be done part-time. Unless people and the team are completely dedicated to the process, it will fail. Resistance to change will be fierce and harsh. One way to overcome the resistance is to ensure that communications of changes are outstanding. It is important to choose a very first project or reengineering task wisely. Initial success in this project is critical for future success. Often it is wise to pick the process that is the most rife with redundancy and will provide a clear victory when streamlining is possible. The reengineering team must be trained in the process, and a facilitator is highly recommended. The team needs to be prepared to be under siege and to be aware of the rule of change. In order to effect a change in most organizations, you must adhere to the "seven times" rule. A change must be presented and driven for at least seven times and explained seven different ways in order for it to start to take hold in an organization.

Flexibility in supplier relationship building is a must. Use the 80–20 rule. Concentrate on building relationships with the suppliers that you spend the most dollars on. Develop strategic relationships only with suppliers who will give you a distinct competitive advantage to your paying or end-user customers. Most corporations can manage only a few of these critical relationships. They must be at the highest level with executive and other personnel exchanges. The other low-value or miscellaneous materials don't really need strong relationship efforts. These relationships can remain strictly commercial. There is no need to waste precious resources on developing relationships with these suppliers. Steer clear of the emotional materials at first. Many people in companies develop personal relationships with suppliers. People love trinkets, dinners, golf, attention, etc. from suppliers. Unfortunately, this doesn't drive money to the company's bottom line. Don't underestimate this personal factor. Identify your key suppliers early. If anyone in your organization has had prior reengineering experience, use him or her as much as possible. Reengineering is often an endurance contest where the last man or woman left standing wins. The problem is, many individuals dig in and hope to wear the reengineering team out. Reengineering is a marathon, not a sprint. Don't be afraid to lose some minor battles initially in order to win the war.

Understanding paying customer needs drives the process. Note internal customer needs only. Concentrate on what counts to the ultimate paying customers. How do we find this out? Ask them! Supplier receptiveness to the relationship's changing needs to be carefully felt out. Top management needs to understand that resistance will be fierce and some individuals will not change and must be dealt with appropriately. Accounting needs to rethink the way it keeps score. Standard cost-based systems are too antiquated to adequately report on progress for this process. Activity-based accounting is much more suited to the reengineering process and correct assessment of progress. Always strive for the highest performance with clear vision and clear objectives. Internal customers or end users that previously were not permitted to perform transactions or even dialogue with suppliers now must be seamlessly connected. Purchasing must get out of the worthless middle-person syndrome. Purchasing needs to forgo its role as rule-throwing obstructionist. The organization must constantly be flexible and look forward to upgrades.

Phase one of the action plan: raise personal knowledge about current purchasing practices and measurements. It is important to spend the time trying to change the mindset of oneself and the purchasing department. Quite frankly, many traditional purchasing professionals don't make the change or the stretch run. Job security is the biggest barrier. At the same time, top management must agree and buy into the reengineering of purchasing. Something this radical needs their undivided support and patience. Start the organization buy-in at the same time. A cross-functional steering team needs to be formed in phase one.

Phase two: work on gaining consensus on objectives and finalizing an overall plan. Top management needs to be informed of progress and different progress indices need to be developed for the now-reengineered purchasing department. Approval of progress to date must be sought and full-scale reskilling of purchasing members must be well underway.

Phase three: implement the actual plan. Select your key supplier partners carefully. Nothing beats supplier prior experience with the reengineering process. Determine your specific materials strategies and assign projects and transformation efforts at this time. Start to hold supplier summits and reeducate purchasing personnel on their new roles.

The three R's of purchasing renewal are found in Box 14–2. Purchasing is faced with overhauling three key areas: drastically reducing or consolidating the number of suppliers, radically reducing the number

B O X   14–2

3 R'S OF PURCHASING RENEWAL

- ◆ Reengineering from a function to a process. Maximize supplier contributions.
- ◆ Retooling of information's systems to rapid response systems so suppliers have direct access.
- ◆ Realignment of roles, or the cross-functional team approach.

of non-value-adding transactions, and reskilling or reeducating purchasing personnel. These are definitely a challenge, for all three must be done simultaneously and at breakneck speed for success to be achieved.

The first R of renewal requires a scientific or process approach to supplier selection. It must be done systematically with known criteria expostulated in advance. At first, supplier reduction may be just a number-elimination game. Later the selecting of the strategic suppliers must be a careful process with cross-functional teams.

The second R is mainly a product of the 1990s. It is not just plunking a personal computer on every desktop, but making rapid instantaneous information available to everyone in the organization in real time and without any censorship. "Without any censorship" is a hard pill to swallow for many traditional corporations, where information is viewed as a weapon to keep employees in line or kowtow to structures. Nothing drives out fear better than open and free communication. Many companies now realize that buying the best software is better and quicker than developing it internally. Internal organizational barriers often preclude homegrown software from being efficient or state of the art.

For the third R, cross-functional teams need to be the norm. Purchasing personnel will spend more and more time outside of their department or area, which is precisely where they belong. Unless the purchasing leader is comfortable with this new arrangement, the new way of doing business with be severely hampered. Intensive coaching of many running teams and tracking of their progress will be necessary. Suppliers can now also assume some of the role of R&D and not think in a vacuum when proposing improvement to materials, parts, or services.

AN EXAMPLE CASE HISTORY OF REENGINEERING OF PURCHASING INTO SUPPLY MANAGEMENT

The case company had lost over $400,000,000 and was ready and willing to try anything radical to fix its financial health. It had over 40,000 suppliers, and purchasing was grossly decentralized or "Balkanized." Pricing was totally out of whack and varied from plant to plant. The company was saddled with a very traditional purchasing organization. Communication between site purchasing was nonexistent. Equipment and capital purchasing was not standardized. Before the process began, benchmarking was conducted. Benchmarking is a continual systematic process for evaluating products, services, and work processes of organizations that are recognized as representing best practices for the purpose of organizational improvement. The pricing was discovered to be off from 10–30% and was different for the very same items at different plants. The benchmark process involved products, services, procedures, and materials. There was a search for best practices, with the initial focus on customers, capability building for purchasing, and market research for suppliers. Empowerment skills were developed for internal end users of materials so that they could purchase materials direct. Purchasing would select the supplier and the transaction process and the end users would follow the course. A huge purchasing computer system had been in the works for ten years at a sunk cost of over $20,000,000. It was unceremoniously scrapped. The performance dial was reset for suppliers, and meetings were held with existing suppliers at which they were asked for lower prices, improved terms, reduced inventory, and cost information. Many sites had over 5,000 suppliers and had to reduce the number quickly. Initially it was just an attrition exercise. Slowly sites started to build relationships with some key suppliers. Some suppliers decided to step up as preferred suppliers and had previous experience with supply management that was found to be invaluable in establishing the relationship. Many of these preferred suppliers that could offer a wide menu of services. The problem was that many of the sites could not decide what they really wanted or valued. Again the nebulous arena of paying attention to customer wants was explored.

One of the initial key concepts for purchasing was to maximize leverage nationally and internationally, if possible, with certain key suppliers. Supplier's costs had to be understood, not just their bids. A clear, systematic supplier selection process was established. Standard contracts and agreements were put in place and commercial terms such as payment terms were standardized. Throughout the process, periodic benchmarking versus competitors was conducted.

Some key discoveries of the process confirmed that pricing was way off base. The bureaucratic cost of maintaining 40,000 suppliers was huge. Purchasing had a transaction audit mentality. Purchasing was clearly transactional, not strategic or a business partner with any other department. Purchasing was not trusted by current suppliers or internal customers. There was a belief that "money was always left on the table." Procurement systems were convoluted and archaic. Meaningful buying data did not exist. Purchasing needed to upgrade manuals and boilerplate contracts.

A procurement or supplier selection process was put in place. Six stages or steps were involved (Box 14–3). The first was defining the customer needs of both the internal and final paying customer. This required examination of what was really needed and a specifications review if necessary. The next step was the gathering of market, supplier, and other intelligence information. Often this is the most neglected area in traditional supplier selection. All potential suppliers were then evaluated on a cost and value analysis according to predetermined criteria. Once the supplier list was narrowed down, the negotiations and conditions were put into place. Implementation and metrics were the final step to be put into place. One of the major goals of this process was to stop the perpetual shopping mentality of most traditional purchasing departments and the constant flurry of bidding activity. The goal is to shop once and be done. The real work is to work constantly on improving the relationship. Shopping constantly for the best deal is a never-ending, quixotic task. Relationship building with suppliers is the core of supply management.

The Porter model is a powerful tool that was used in the supplier selection process. It is a systematic approach to market analysis that is often used by marketing. The goals are industry analysis and enabling purchasing to know as much or more about an industry that a supplier is participating in than the supplier itself knows. This tool reinforced the maxim that the one who has the most information in negotiations has the advantage.

The initial results in this case study were dramatic. Savings of over $50,000,000 were achieved and verified. The viability of reengineering

---

B O X   14–3

PROCUREMENT PROCESS

- ◆ Definition of customer needs—internal and external
- ◆ Market, supplier, intelligence information
- ◆ Supplier cost and value analysis
- ◆ Negotiations and conditions
- ◆ Selection
- ◆ Implementation
- ◆ Do your selection and shopping once

purchasing and supply management was clearly demonstrated to top management. There was a major shift in people capability, the direct result of over 200 hours of procurement capability training. Significant beachheads in transaction reduction were obtained, especially in the small-dollar purchase of fewer than 200 dollars, which made up the vast majority of purchase orders.

Supplier consolidation or reduction results were even more impressive. A typical site, for instance, reduced suppliers from over 5,000 to 200. Some key worldwide materials suppliers dropped from 28 to 4, creating an enormous streamlining impact on the workload of plants. A natural benefit of this was better supplier performance tracking and increased competition among suppliers, especially the 3 or 4 that were competing for a material. In the first stage of consolidation, a significant reduction was carried out in the number of suppliers by category. This did not at first involve a partnership but simply a numbers reduction. In most industries this is achievable, since there are only three or four top-notch suppliers or players in the industry. This effort dethroned the traditional belief that "price is king" and finally permitted purchasing professionals to go for the very best suppliers.

Outcomes of the consolidation efforts included significant volume discounts due to improved leverage and a solid emphasis on total costs and lower transactions costs (fewer suppliers). Set-up costs and operational gains were made due to less complexity and the reduction in material variances. The approach improved confidentiality and focused purchasing efforts on getting the best-in-class suppliers. Quality gains were impressive because often the best materials from the best suppliers were used in product production. Working capital and cycle time also improved because as the relationships with a few strategic suppliers grew, the suppliers could better anticipate wants and needs. Suppliers' roles changed dramatically: they were no longer backslapping salespeople but resources and problem solvers. Value-adding work began and the traditional adversarial posturing days were dead. Suppliers started to discuss and share R&D results. Morale and motivation among purchasing professionals rose appreciably. Expertise was shared across plants, and transaction reduction efforts flourished. Procurement professionals were becoming valued business partners with other departments. Those professionals who didn't grow were transferred or given other options.

The nonmanufacturing or services areas of the company presented the most serious challenge to reengineering efforts. Some companies call this area the MRO (maintenance, repairable, and operating supplies), but in reality, the true definitions of MRO is all the indirect materials (non-manufacturing) or services that a company requires. Often the supplier base in these areas is huge, and the transaction load is heavy. Corporate wide leveraging is usually nonexistent and buying patterns are sporadic. These areas are characterized by a dearth of meaningful data. Fragmented supply chains, and often deep local personal relationships with local suppliers exist, that are very difficult to overcome. Much of the supplies in this area are bought irrationally and for convenience, or for just-in-time delivery to the end-user. The supplies or services themselves are very prone to game playing by suppliers, who will often undercut and deliver rock-bottom prices on a few items in the hopes that they will gain future volume at a higher price.

End-users love to shop—most believe that they are good shoppers. Many believe that they are better shoppers than purchasing professionals. Many do not understand the *total* cost-of-ownership concept, and the fact that they are literally wasting their precious time on nonstrategic, or what I call non-value-adding, buying. This arena gives them the perfect forum to exercise this love. Often emotions, not buying logic, rule their decisions. Procurement professionals must be even more aggressive in this arena in order to successfully achieve reengineering. Broad cross-functional teams are a must here. The teams cannot be disbanded after supplier selection, but must stay in place for the critical implementation phase, or until end-users trust the new supplier. Many studies in the nonmanufacturing arena show that end-users value convenience and on-time delivery more than price. Supplier selection criteria and supplier tracking must revolve around these prerequisites. On-time delivery is paramount, along with what the selected supplier can do to drive out all administrative and logistics cost which include almost totally taking over the supply chain.

Purchasing also must take the initiative to bunch or group supplies and services into supply chains or streams. For example, the cross-functional team may want to group office supplies, fax machines, copiers, desktop computers, and PC support into a category named administrative support. The trick is finding integrated suppliers who can perform in all of these areas with excellence. The fact is that most of the non-manufacturing supplies or services are non-value-adding, yet in many companies they drain too much time and effort from employees. The bottom line is that your paying customers do not really care who you use for office suppliers or services. They want a quality product, competitively priced, and delivered on time. The measure of success in this area is to drive out all non-value-adding costs in the supply chain and to make sure that this area does not distract your internal end-users from more corporate-critical missions or goals. Reengineering efforts must try to combine supplies and services wherever possible, and above all else, simplify!

An after-action report indicated the following keys to success and some essential lessons learned for reengineering. Good market and industry intelligence is critical. Picking the right supplier is a must for the building of trust in the process. It is better to take a long, exhausting time to pick the right supplier than to pick the wrong one. Deselecting a chosen supplier is expensive and greatly undermines the process. The suppliers picked must be world-class. Consolidation or reduction of suppliers must be done as rapidly as possible. The more this process is drawn out, the more local plants and people resist. It is important to get them out of their comfort zone and start to build the new relationship with the new selected suppliers. Leadership support at the top must be informed and supportive. A favorable competitive external environment is helpful but not essential. In industries or markets where there was more demand than supply, or other extenuating circumstances, it was nearly impossible to negotiate strong agreements. Capability improvement for purchasing professionals was an important aspect of the process. Transaction reduction was a key component that gave purchasing personnel more space or free time to work on broader and more value-adding issues.

The reengineering of purchasing leads inexorably into supply management, which is a strategic process that works with the supply community to best select and manage those suppliers that best handle your company's and your customers' needs. As reengineering takes place and consolidation of suppliers becomes a reality, the search for best practices gets into high gear. A best practice is a professionally acknowledged best way or procedure to accomplish a certain task or project. Reengineering leads to some organizational best practices. Purchasing must become a strategic group that drives company strategy. Purchasing strategies must start to become global in scope. Purchasing strategy and suppliers must become linked to business strategy. Suppliers must get to a high level in the corporation and coordinate activities with executives. Purchasing must think of itself as a critical service or staffing, value-adding organization that "sells" its value-added services internally. Cross-functional teams become the norm and many value-adding transactions occur with members of the corporation and suppliers.

Reengineering completely changes the supplier relationship, raising it to a much higher and more strategic level. The supplier selection process is highly disciplined. There are a low number of suppliers, and supplier certification is demanded and valued. Aggressive joint total costs of ownership reduction plans are explored. Key communications and information sharing, with sophisticated electronic connections put into place, evolves. Suppliers are measured on a few key measures and total cost improvement measures. Superior supplier performance is recognized, and formal systems are put into place to measure internal customer satisfaction. Compensation is linked to supplier performance and customer satisfaction. Suppliers are placed under long-term contracts, especially alliances. Some single-sourced materials or services are established, and periodic design reviews are held with strategic suppliers. Endusers are encouraged to purchase directly from approved suppliers. Direct informational links with suppliers become the norm.

Reengineering requires radically different performance measures. Some of the new performance measures to be considered include: System-type purchasing programs that mirror continuous replenishment must be put in place. Purchasing must create a five-year strategic plan. End user-driven transactions like purchase cards must become the norm. The number of professional training hours for purchasing professionals will become an important measure.

High goal targets need to be set, such as a 50% reduction in lead time, a 50% reduction in rejects, a 10–20% reduction in "all-in" costs, a 70–80% reduction in suppliers, and establishment of direct end user-friendly electronic transactions.

During the first stage of reengineering, some initial goals are to standardize prices and to get lower prices via leveraging. The first focus should be on no-inflation clauses, the best standard commercial terms, reduction in inventory, and resetting of the dial of commercial agreements. Stage two results need to focus on fewer suppliers, manage relationships with suppliers, look at supply chain dynamics, achieve some better quality, improve transactions, improve customer service, and greatly reduce non-value-adding steps in transactions. Stage three brings planned material substitutions, design changes and optimal specifications, standardized equipment and processes, improved product life cycle, focus on continuous improvement, and accelerated information sharing.

Some major supply side advantages are: reduced total cost of ownership, improved process consistency, improved supply cycle time, access to more technology and supplier's R&D, reduced risk of supply, improved competitive advantages through strategic alliances, and purchasing taking its rightful place as a true business team partner.

The pace of the change grows to a world-class, almost frenetic pace. Purchasing then concentrates on value-adding work only. Often other departments and people need to be dragged to best practices. Purchasing must summarily reject all requests for non-value-adding work. Goal setting must be very high but achievable. For the next century the information age requires speed and accuracy. Information must be flawless and open to all in the corporation.

Key to enabling purchasing to operate at this hyper-pace is elimination of purchase orders. Purchase orders are often full of steps and totally inefficient, and in the traditional bureaucratic purchasing world, purchase orders take up over 80% of a purchasing professional's time. Often a large percentage of the transactions make up only 10% of the dollars spent. These purchase orders hover around less than $200 and rarely more than $1,000. Benchmarks of purchase order costs can reach $150 per purchase order. Often payment discounts to suppliers are missed due to the sheer volume of transactions and invoices. Purchase order procedures vary between companies, and there is no rhyme or reason for the rules. Buyers spend over 80% of their time being bureaucrats. There is a norm of perpetual crisis and conflict in the wild paper chase. Good buyers are often viewed as "super-clerks" who constantly expedite or rush orders. Purchasing is mired in the transaction bayou, and perpetually treading water with alligators.

Reengineering purchasing requires a take-no-prisoners psyche. Traditional titles must be smashed and all efforts focused on the supply chain. Suppliers are no longer "peddlers" but valued partner suppliers. All traditional nomenclature about traditional purchasing must be destroyed. It only perpetuates traditional behavior and sends exactly the wrong messages to everyone. The focus must be on relationships, not transactions, driving supply management. Best practices such as purchase cards can significantly reduce transaction work and provide superior reporting capability. The use of purchase cards requires trust of end users and some prudence. The rewards, in time, of this best practice for a purchasing department are significant.

Often the simple things help the reengineering process. A clear end users' "how-to" manual that walks them through simple direct purchases will greatly aid the reengineering process. This nuts-and-bolts-type manual should contain preferred supplier lists, contacts for orders, how to advice and illustrations on how-to purchase various materials, details on purchase cards, clear examples, and checklists. Also key is reskilling purchasing professionals. Their new roles require new skills, especially in coaching, team leading, facilitating, process mapping, supply chain analysis, relationship building, and information processing and electronic measures. A key trait for the supply management explorer is the ability to be open to new learning experiences.

Identification of barriers and anticipation of opposition points is also critical for a successful reengineering process. The auditing mentality feeds upon itself. Designing processes for exceptions generates more audits and usually more paperwork. Many traditionalists can't get off the price merry-go-round. To them price is still king. If it were, every American would be driving a Yugo. All end users like to shop, and if they get a better price they automatically condemn the process. In purchasing itself, resistance is often incredibly fierce. There is a real job security issue, and some foot-dragging sabotage can be expected. The built-in adversarial mistrust of suppliers is hard to break, as are old relationships even with inept suppliers. Often deselected suppliers plant sour grapes and badmouth new suppliers, adding doubt to the process. Manufacturing and operations often misunderstand the aims of supply management and just want the materials delivered on time.

Here are some pitfalls to consider before they derail the process. A shoddy, unsystematic supplier selection process will kill reengineering of purchasing instantly. Ethics conflicts cannot be tolerated. Base supplier choices on merits, not trinkets. End users may rebel at being empowered and doing more of the so-called purchasing work. Communication of changes must be thorough and planned to include as many people along the supply chain as possible. Middle management often resists the most fiercely because of the fear of job loss. If process maps are not used to analyze a supply chain, major mistakes can be made. It is often better to save the hard stuff for last and go for some quick supply chain victories first.

Neglecting skills retraining for purchasing will kill the process. An intense skills upgrade is mandatory and needs to become ongoing. Use teams to select suppliers, not hearsay. At times upper management receives valued perks from suppliers and may be very reluctant to change suppliers. Supplier selection requires a lot of unglamorous homework. If this homework is not done, the selection process is bogus. Upper management may be soft in their committment to the process, when they must literally drive the process throughout the company often over screaming bodies. There can be no compromise on this issue. Dispelling fear from the process is essential or people will go underground and resist. A supplier inexperienced in supply management can wreck the change process. Go with experience in supplier selection whenever possible. A weak or incompetent local supplier representative can destroy the relationship building. Insist on the right to accept and approve the supplier representative. Both the information department and accounting fear a loss of control in this process. Involve them in supply change decisions and on selection teams. Make the supplier performance metrics clear from the start. Mistakes will occur. Acknowledge them and share the learnings with naysayers.

Reengineering purchasing is basically a three-step approach:

- ♦ Consolidate suppliers first. If you don't reduce your supplier base, reengineering is not possible. You can't have thousands of relationships.
- ♦ Streamline your transactions and procedures or purchasing will not have time to improve. Transactions are the enemy, and you must give them no quarter. Dumping them gives your people space to work at value-adding projects.
- ♦ Teach new skill sets and get professional help when needed.

Purchasing professionals need to evolve to become agents of change. They must concentrate on relationships and broad-based communication. They must become marketers, especially of the process and the results. Working with suppliers to mutually solve supply change issues is essential. Non-value-adding work must be eschewed. Allies are also essential for the success of this process. Those who don't want to change or won't change must be readily identified and reassigned or transferred.

Agents of change or explorers manifest certain behaviors. They are never satisfied with current accomplishments. They possess an insatiable desire for a better way. They carry out ongoing experiments or seek best practices beachheads. Their standards of excellence are high, and they constantly work to improve relationships. They concentrate on continuous learning and improvement.

When involved in the process, they seek out and exchange information with other purchasing organizations that are also reengineering. This is a "learn as you go" process fraught with some failures that must be treated as lessons learned, not deal-killers. On a personal front, new skills require pushing people out of their comfort zones. Expertise will grow and change. Focus constantly on best practices.

Reengineering purchasing is not a sprint but a harsh ultra-marathon. Losing one's cool or patience only sets the process back. Agents of change will lose some battles, but the war can be won. The purchasing team must get in synch and function as one. Explorers need indomitable spirit to make the reengineering of purchasing successful. Wait for reengineering to just happen and you will be waiting forever. Explorers don't wait for approval. They strike out on the journey. The joy is in the journey.

Reengineer purchasing now!

CHAPTER 15

Human Resource Management

Editor
Rene A. Yates, C.P.M.
Director of Materials
B.A. Ballou & Company Inc.

INTRODUCTION

Recent trends in organizational structure have proven that distinct boundaries are fading and that the future holds a continued blurring of business functions. Whether in the strict sense of Total Quality Management, or through research from such organizations as the Center for Advanced Purchasing Studies, it becomes clear that the success of organizations does not rest upon the establishment of structure. Rather, the ultimate reason for success in any enterprise is people, that asset known as human resources. Effective management of that resource will rely more and more upon a method of acquiring, training, and investing in individuals that marks a break from past practices of developing purchasing specialists.

Trends that have made most of us focus on customers and what they value, combined with the ever-increasing need to control costs, have started a shift toward more general skills. The purchaser today cannot be insulated from the ultimate consumer and what he or she considers important. Today's purchaser must possess an awareness of the enterprise, not simply purchasing. In that context, skills must include not only those specific to the function, but generalized skills such as decision-making ability, problem solving, computer literacy, interpersonal skills, and, above all, the ability to both embrace and manage change.

Customers have become more demanding, and organizations must as well. If supply management is to continue its strategic involvement in a firm, its human elements must have the ability to function and embrace a world of ambiguity. That process certainly begins with the basics, but must rapidly expand to the general and interpersonal skills so necessary in today's world of growing interpersonal relationships and team-based decision-making.

Supply management provides a service and as such, whether in manufacturing, service, or public sectors, must view itself as a consultant. This evolves to the role of an advocate for customers both internal and external and the supply chain that supports it. Ultimately, success depends upon people: their ability to communicate, identify opportunities, and continually add value.

PERSONNEL PLANNING

The Task of Management

Management might best be described as an activity that identifies objectives and then guides resources to the successful attainment of those objectives. The latter cannot be overemphasized. Management is about results. Machines and computers can be guided, but they are limited by their inability to think, reason, and have vision. Leadership, the creation of a vision, and the excitement surrounding it can only be achieved by people. How to inspire, harness, and direct that creativity is the challenge of management. Individuals, by definition, are different. All have varying strengths, weaknesses, and varying levels of interest. How to envision what must be done and best match varying skills to maximize results is the challenge that all managers face.

Planning Elements

The first step in the organization of a department is to determine what must be accomplished. This begins with a vision of what the organization *will* be. From this, a plan must be developed that encompasses what must be done today to achieve that goal. Strengths and skills of departmental personnel must then be matched with the tasks developed. Gaps must then be closed by the provision of training or, in other cases, new or replacement personnel. Once the initial objectives are ascertained, policies, procedures, and finally activities must be identified. These tasks and their costs must be quantified and expressed in a budget. A human resource, like any other resource, is an investment upon which a return must be expected. Value received from proper investment in human resources can easily lead to unbridled results, or even determine the survival of the firm.

Functional Analysis

Determination of what is to be done and how best to allocate that work, and identification of the value-added, are the principal steps in analyzing supply management functions. These activities might include the release of an order, administration of a contract, determination of need, elimination of paper, negotiation strategies for particular commodity teams, organization of material data safety sheets, disposal of hazardous materials, supply base reduction, or supplier mentoring. Whether bordering on strategic or tactical, functions and their value must be understood to ensure proper matching with the appropriate human resource. Tools such as ABC analysis used for management of inventory might have application here as well. In this case, rather than focusing on the smaller number of units that make up the largest dollars in inventory, a manager would assign those tasks with the potential to add the most value to stronger, more skilled individuals.

SUPPLY MANAGEMENT POSITIONS

Staffing requirements in a supply management department include those typical of any staff organization. The positions might be broken down into five categories; management, acquisition function, specialized staff, administration, and training. Titles of positions vary, although "purchasing agent" seems to have at long last disappeared. Typically, the department is headed by a vice-president, director, or manager of purchasing, supply, or supply chain management. Broader organizations might include a supply manager. In sectors other than manufacturing, the titles might include the term "contract," such as a contract manager. Staff might include titles such as buyers, buyer/planners, analysts, administrators, coordinators, engineers, quality, or materials personnel. Nature and scope of responsibilities are not necessarily dependent upon title. The degree of strategic or tactical application of a position is the result of a number of factors, including the breadth of the enterprise, its size, corporate perspective, and policy, the degree to which purchasing expends resources, and the ability to add value to the competitive nature of the firm.

Boxes 15–1 to 15–3 show typical job descriptions for varying levels of personnel in a purchasing/supply department.

B O X   15–1

JOB DESCRIPTION
PURCHASING AND SUPPLY MANAGER

Title	Purchasing and Supply Manager
Reports to	Vice-President Operations
Position Summary	Responsible for all phases of the procurement process from supply, services, and administration of the department. The incumbent must direct the acquisition of goods and services assuring continuity of supply while maximizing the use of assets. This should be done in a team-based environment that can maximize value received from a managed, effective supply base.
Nature and Scope	Oversee annual purchases of $60 million; manage a supply base of 160; direct a staff of 15; responsible for inventories of $12 million.
Principal Accountabilities	Establish procurement policies; develop materials budget and appropriate contracts; direct procurement activities; manage the supply base; provide quarterly forecast on key commodities; implement a supplier rating system based upon value-added; develop a professional procurement group with high quality of service and ethics.
Knowledge/Skills Required	Bachelor's degree; C.P.M. required; five years' experience in the purchasing field with some supervisory experience; knowledgeable of supply chain principals; strong communications skills, analytical skills, and willing to work in an environment that fosters change.

B O X   15–2

JOB DESCRIPTION
PURCHASER

Title	Buyer
Reports to	Purchasing and Supply Manager
Position Summary	Responsible for the preparation and placement of purchase orders for assigned commodities, supplies, and services. Responsibilities include identification and development of qualified suppliers while seeking lowest total cost on purchases while maximizing value. Possible interruptions in supply should be communicated promptly, and the incumbent should take the initiative in developing solutions. Appropriate records should be maintained on activities.
Nature and Scope	This position manages the purchases of $18 million of products and services through a supplier base of 50 to 75. The individual is expected to handle a variety of fluctuating tasks and must ensure that proper negotiations, cost analysis, and professional purchasing practices are followed.
Principal Accountabilities	Manage assigned responsibilities to ensure quality and cost objectives are met; conduct effective negotiations and contract objectives; initiate value-added purchasing through elimination of paper; develop and achieve cost-containment objectives; manage, develop, and reduce the supply base as appropriate; develop procurement strategies to ensure continuity of supply.
Knowledge/ Skills Required	Associate's degree in business and minimum of three years' experience; professional certification of A.P.P. or higher; good oral and communication skills; analytical ability; interpersonal skills that include nondefensive problem solving; computer literacy.

B O X   15–3

JOB DESCRIPTION
PURCHASING ANALYST

Title	Purchasing Analyst
Reports to	Director of Purchasing and Supply
Position Summary	Responsible for the management of projects that identify opportunities for improvement of methods and activities within and related to the purchasing function.
Nature and Scope	This position serves as a strategic extension of the Director of Purchasing. There will be interaction at all levels of the organization, as short- and longer-term initiatives are planned and executed. The facilitation of team-based strategies will be an integral part of fostering and implementing change.
Principal Accountabilities	Attain a level of product and company knowledge; become familiar with supply base and major contributors to organizational strategies; review, sort, and present information leading to identification of value enhancement; identify projects and facilitate team-based improvements; document and report cost savings, value-added, and strategic impact on the organization.
Knowledge/Skills Required	B.S. Engineering or Business; strong problem-solving and analytical skills; experience in team-based improvement; three years' experience in engineering or equivalent problem identification/improvement with root cause analysis.

RECRUITMENT METHODS

The process of seeking out and selecting the proper candidate is a delicate one. Unlike manufactured products, individuals cannot be "made to order." One of the most important tasks of management thus is to identify the "best fit" of skills and personal traits, and then match them to the work to be accomplished. A prime responsibility for a purchasing manager, therefore, is the acquisition and development of competent people who subsequently evolve into a team with customer focus. The result is a group committed to maximizing purchasing's contribution toward increased value, competitiveness, and service to customers.

Internal Recruitment

One of the simplest ways to review a pool of potential candidates is through internal recruitment. Incumbents can come from within the department or from other areas of the organization. This method can provide a good source of candidates who bring an understanding of the organization and also perspective from another viewpoint. This can be of great benefit in a cross-functional team. There are other benefits to internal recruitment as well:

1. Increased morale may result as employees become aware of opportunities for advancement.
2. Reduced training costs can be realized, since the person has a grasp of firm specific knowledge.
3. Known personal traits may allow a level of comfort. Minor issues or concerns can also be addressed up front to the understanding of both parties.
4. A varied perspective may be brought to the department regarding expectations from the viewpoint of the "internal customer."
5. The incumbent can act as a spokesperson to the organization on the value of the purchasing function.
6. Functional or strategic skills possessed may help facilitate the acquisition process.
7. Reduced organizational turnover may result due to continued challenge for the individual and job satisfaction within the firm.

Hiring from within, however, can be a cause for concern as well. If the job is posted, more than one person might apply. How do we not discourage those who were not chosen? If an individual is approached and selected without a job posting, how will others who might have been interested react? Another consideration is that in hindsight, the promotion might have been premature. Environment is a critical factor affecting behavior and motivation, and what appeared to work well in one set of circumstances may not replicate itself in another. Finally, when used as a matter of course, hiring from within can lead to a lack of outward perspective and fresh ideas.

Some have mentioned that promotion from within might be ineffective, since the individual will tend to resist any conflict with their former department. If this is understood, the concern can usually be avoided by arranging key assignments so as not to involve former departments or by addressing the question in the initial interview. Often the effectiveness—or lack of effectiveness—is a function of the individual and not normally a major concern. Most often, involvement with a former department becomes easier because the individual can share purchasing's perspective while still being empathetic to the concerns of the internal customer.

External Recruitment

When there are no suitable internal candidates, or when there is a desire to expand the pool of candidates, a search expands beyond the organization. This can be done in a number of ways, and the type of candidate desired as well as the time available for the search can lead to one of the following types of external recruitment:

1. *Advertising:* Advertising is probably the simplest and most used method for recruitment. It can be done on a local, regional, or national basis, and can even be targeted at industry or professional periodicals. There are normally two types of advertising. The first, called a "blind ad," lists the position but does not identify the organization. This method can be especially useful in identifying candidates who are currently employed but interested in seeking other employment. Since the company is not identified, there tend to be a greater variety of candidates from within and outside the industry. "Open advertising," on the other hand, lists the

company name and hopes to attract candidates who know the firm, its reputation, location, and even culture. This allows for an initial level of screening that at least begins with an individual interested in working for that organization. The main danger of both types of advertising is that they do not allow the firm to control the quantity or quality of the applicants.

2. *College placement offices.* College and university placement offices offer access not only to recent graduates of their institutions, but to alumni. A well-tailored job description listing not only educational requirements but also skills and experience may lead to some viable and actively employed candidates. A disadvantage of using this method is that a large number of candidates may require review. Associations such as the National Association of Purchasing Management (NAPM) can provide lists of academic institutions that offer purchasing curricula and purchasing degree programs.

3. *Placement agencies.* Private employment agencies are popular and can help with the initial screening and matching of personal traits to the organization. In most cases, the employer pays a fee for the candidate hired. These agencies are a good source for finding candidates who are actively employed and interested in making a change, and a number of agencies specialize in the purchasing/supply management field. An example of such a firm is NDI Services, with whom NAPM outsources these requests.

4. *Search firms.* Search firms take a more active role in the process and tend to both develop a database and seek candidates already employed. They are especially effective in conducting searches for management personnel, and although usually more expensive than other methods, tend to produce effective results. Costs for this type of service can easily exceed 20% of the candidate's first year's salary. Qualifications are closely matched, and candidates selected typically have a proven track record.

5. *Professional Associations.* Local purchasing associations are a good source for information on potential candidates. The individuals are known, and if they have been involved in any committees or groups, insight as to the candidate's

performance may be available. The danger in using referrals from organizations is that a person may be recommended because he or she regularly attends meetings or is viewed as "a nice person." Such qualities in and of themselves are not necessarily an indication of an effective professional.

6. *Internet.* A particularly effective method of searching for candidates is the Internet. Without one's ever leaving a workstation, résumés can be scanned and sorted by a number of categories such as title, geographic area, and salary. There are greater than 50,000 job-hunting sites on the World Wide Web, and the Career Center section is the most popular area of NAPM's Web site (www.napm.org). The NAPM Web site also has links to greater than 35 of the better sites.

7. *Miscellaneous sources.* Considering current trends toward temporary and project-oriented workforces, a number of other methods for obtaining personnel might be considered. These include retired executives or managers, former military personnel, and individuals with family commitments. In many cases, the proper "rightsizing" of work can lead to an effective and challenging opportunity for an individual and an effective solution for the firm. In addition, mailed-in resumes and even walk-ins can prove surprisingly timely. Finally, personal referrals or networking can be particularly effective in identifying candidates. Like internal recruitment, this method can give insight into the candidate, but without the threat of offense should the candidate not be selected.

INTERVIEW AND SELECTION

Once a list of candidates has been created from methods such as those described above, the task of selection begins. The candidate list must be reviewed, screened, and prioritized, particularly if it is a lengthy one. The review should focus on the combination of skills, experience, and background that will best serve the organization. The process can be tedious, but it is important, for it is here that information on paper comes to life as decisions are made to select candidates for interview. Care must be taken not to exclude the individual who might have been the ideal candidate.

Conducting an Interview

The process of conducting an interview is a difficult one for most managers, and one in which many are uncomfortable. Unfortunately, it is a very important part of a manager's job, and choosing the best candidate will provide contributions for years to come. Choosing the incorrect individual for a position is costly. Typically the expense can run 30–50% beyond the salary paid, due to training costs, lost productivity, and the additional cost of replacement. With increased importance of cost avoidance in today's environment, the proper selection of personnel can certainly contribute to that effort.

Considering the importance of the selection process, it is surprising that many managers prepare inadequately. Perhaps because conducting an interview is uncomfortable to some, is not done on a regular basis and is not perceived as having the priority of other job-related pressures, often little planning time is allocated for this purpose. Managers will spend many hours on negotiations, computer applications, or cost/price analysis, but relatively little time preparing to select the proper individual who could provide the best results from these tasks. This becomes clear when one considers that over 35% of candidates selected for a job do not remain in that position for one year. Failure is most typically due to improper selection as a result of preparing inadequately, making qualitative rather than objective decisions, and not asking the correct questions during the interview.

Questioning Considerations

Knowing what questions to ask and how to ask them is a skill that few managers hone. The legal professional becomes a master at it, and to a degree so must managers. The goal in asking questions is to learn as much as possible about the candidate. Because of legal implications, the interviewer must be certain to ask questions that are *only* job related. Questions dealing with past salary history, national origin, referrals from friends or relatives, age-related information, conviction records, disabilities, or even the name of a person to notify in the case of emergency could all be grounds for discrimination under equal opportunity regulations. Much of this information may be normal for the employer to have *once the person is employed*, but should not be part of the interview process, since none of these factors are related to the work the person will be asked to perform. Job-related questions, however, when asked correctly, can elicit considerable information about the candidate's skills, abilities, and personal traits.

Skills in asking questions center upon encouraging the person to talk and *listening* to responses. Proper technique results in a conversation as opposed to an interrogation. This is made possible through asking open-ended rather than closed questions. Open-ended questions allow for a greater range of response and ask the candidate to share information. Rather than a yes or no answer or one that states, for example, the college or university attended, open-ended questions will lead to discussions of courses taken and fields of interest. As opposed to merely asking, "Where did you go to school?" one might ask, for example, "I see you graduated from Bryant College. What classes interested you the most?" This will yield considerably more about the individual. As the conversation becomes more focused on the job itself, questions such as the following might be asked:

1. Describe a time when a supplier was late with a critical item. How was the situation handled, and what was the result?

2. Describe the most difficult negotiation you faced. How did you prepare, and what was the outcome?

3. Describe a purchase that required team involvement. What was your role, and did the team reach their objective?

4. Describe an instance where you had to drop a major supplier. How was it approached, and what were the results?

Questions such as these encourage a candidate to enter into a discussion, which provides considerably more insight about the candidate than closed questions. In addition, the dialogue can be continued by exploring topics of choice. This is mainly done through effective listening, followed by questions that will both clarify and ask for more detail.

Selection Criteria

Following the interview process, candidates must be weighed against each other and a choice made. A number of methods are available, both qualitative and quantitative. The latter attempts to remove biases or preferences that may influence the final decision. Ultimately, the correct choice typically lies somewhere between these two extremes, where factual information is considered along with those intangibles that make one individual a better fit with the organization than another.

EQUAL OPPORTUNITY AND DIVERSITY

Although several federal regulations deal with the selection and employment and termination of individuals, there are selected laws that impact the majority of employment activities. These include the Equal Pay Act of 1963, Title VII of the Civil Rights Act of 1964, Executive Order 11246 of 1965, the Age Discrimination Act of 1967, the National Labor Relations Act, the Fair Labor Standards Act, the Occupational Safety and Health Act, the Family and Medical Leave Act, and the Americans with Disabilities Act. A summary of these laws follows:

1. **Equal Pay Act of 1963.** This act requires that individuals with the same skills and responsibility who perform the same work under the same conditions receive equal compensation for that effort.

2. **Title VII of the Civil Rights Act of 1964.** This act prohibits discrimination in employment based upon race, color, national origin, religion, age, or sex by employers of more than 15 in both the public and private sector. Title VII focuses on discrimination in employment conditions, including selection, promotion, transfer, compensation, and training. This act also includes sexual harassment. In this case, unwelcome physical or verbal sexual conduct must not be perceived as a condition of employment, nor must the workplace itself exhibit an environment that has the effect of limiting or interfering with the individual's performance.

3. **Executive Order 11246.** This order requires companies that hold federal contracts or subcontracts that exceed $10,000 not to discriminate in their employment practices. In addition, the order includes affirmative action initiative, in which an employer must attempt to achieve a balance in their workforce that reflects the same proportions of minority groups (including women) that are available in the labor market.

4. **Age Discrimination Act.** This act restricts employers in both the public and private sector of more than 20 from discriminating in employment and termination of individuals who are over the age of 40.

5. **National Labor Relations Act.** Sometimes referred to as the Taft–Hartley Act, this act allows employees to organize and bargain collectively through representatives of their own

choice. Employees also have the right not to participate in these activities unless by previous agreement with the firm and the labor organization it is a condition of employment.

6. **Fair Labor Standards Act.** This act protects employees by requiring employers to pay nonexempt employees a minimum wage and to pay a premium wage for work that exceeded 40 hours in a week.

7. **Occupational Safety and Health Act.** This act requires that work not be performed in unsafe conditions. The purpose of the legislation is to protect employees from working conditions that are considered dangerous or unsanitary. It also defends the employee from retaliation for exercising a right under this statute.

8. **Family Medical Leave Act.** This act requires workers with a minimum of 50 employees to allow a maximum of twelve weeks of unpaid leave to care for a newborn or newly adopted child, or to care for family members or themselves when a serious medical condition exists. Employers are also required to maintain health coverage and job protection during the covered period.

9. **Americans with Disabilities Act.** This legislation prohibits private employers in organizations of 15 or more employees to discriminate in employment because of a disability. Under this act, employers are required to provide candidates with an essential function analysis that lists mental and physical requirements essential to the job. Employers are further required to make "reasonable" accommodations if necessary, including adjustments to work stations or schedules, job restructuring, or modifications to the facility.

The overall intent of these and other laws is to protect individuals and provide equal employment and compensation opportunities in a working environment free of intimidation and dangers in the workplace.

Diversity

Diversity in the workplace goes beyond equal opportunity legislation. It seeks to recognize and take advantage of individual differences, be they in age, gender, or ethnic or geographic background. Diversity also includes physical limitations. Often this topic tends to focus on race, but the scope encompasses most individual differences as well.

Organizations that are committed to promoting diversity have found solid employees who have contributed well to the organization. Circumstances involving family issues, physical limitations, or stereotypes due to geographical region can all be addressed and, in fact, used to advantage in the right situation. In negotiations, a hard line or a softer, more patient approach might be best suited to certain contracts. Those features tend to be part of the culture of certain areas or locations. A "professional" person from the Northeast, for example, might be seen as pretentious in the South.

When dealing with issues of diversity, however, organizations must take care to ensure equity throughout the organization. Flexibility in hours to allow for child or family care for one employee might result in others expecting flextime within the department, or even across the organization! The important issue is that individual differences be recognized and that the organization does not pass by those who could significantly contribute. Each of us has differences, and they should not inhibit what we are willing to contribute. To stereotype a candidate because of group identification only limits the organization's effectiveness. Rather, using effective interviewing techniques and perhaps some flexibility in fitting the job and the individual will allow a manager to realize the greatest results from available human resources.

COMPENSATION

Quality is available only at a price, and this cannot be truer than in the "purchase" of human assets. The single difference that separates one organization from another is its people, and that asset more than any other can return more per dollar invested than any other. People must be committed, and although dollars are not a long-term motivator in and of themselves, the method of compensation can significantly affect the performance of any individual. Purchasing employees, under the Fair Labor Standards Act, are normally classified as exempt. This permits the payment of a time-based salary, as opposed to payment on an hourly basis. With the continued blurring of organizational lines and increasing involvement in teams, compensation for purchasing and supply management personnel increasingly includes a variable component. This is usually based upon the goals set in the performance management process and makes up what has traditionally been viewed as a bonus. Competitive pressures and the need for continuous improvement are resulting in more and more organizations basing a greater degree of emphasis on this variable component that is tied to profitability or value-added.

Benchmarking of total compensation can be done in a number of ways. There are numerous salary surveys from professional associations as well as governmental agencies, or studies can be provided by professional organizations specializing in this service. More and more research is available on this topic through the Internet.

KNOWLEDGE AND SKILLS DEVELOPMENT

Once candidates become employees, they join the team of purchasing professionals who not only contribute to the department and organizational strategy, but begin on the journey of continuous development. That process begins with an assessment of the skills and knowledge base that the individual possesses and a comparison of those elements to the job description and responsibilities. The degree of variation will vary from person to person and organization to organization. It is a function of education level, experience, prior training, degree of motivation, and personal traits, including the ability to learn and apply knowledge. The need may also be a function of the goals and degree of change to be implemented.

Baseline assessment of training needs can be done informally through a supervisory assessment of the individual, which involves observing of how the individual does his or her job. It can be done more formally by assigning and monitoring progress that the individual makes toward goals, or through specialized programs. The choice of methods to address training is a matter of judgment and style. One allows the organization to better control the process, while the other considers the privacy of the individual.

Whether arrived at informally or formally, the identification of gaps in knowledge and skills is essential to effective training and professional development of staff. Classes and seminars in and of themselves will not provide maximum results unless they are matched to the gaps in skills and better prepare the purchaser to contribute effectively through targeted enhancement of personal, professional, and technical requirements as it becomes necessary.

TRAINING AND DEVELOPMENT METHODS

The efficiency of any department is directly influenced by the professional capabilities of its staff. The process of training should not be a casual one. Like any program of importance, it requires planning, identification of goals to be attained, and, above all, involvement from those who will be affected. Training in a profession such as purchasing or supply management should not be viewed as an event, but a continuing process. Hence the term commonly used is *professional development.*

A variety of methods are available to train and develop purchasing and supply management personnel. Some focus on tactical duties, and others are more strategic in nature. For this reason, it is not uncommon for methods such as the following to be used in parallel, particularly as employees grow and gain knowledge of both the organization and the work to be accomplished. Some of the more common methods of training and development include the following:

Written Policies/Procedures

These documents prove effective in orienting a new employee to the organization and the department. They provide a sense of firm-specific information that is a blueprint for how things are currently organized, a sense for the corporate culture, and a general overview of the organization. Policies and procedures are also available for review and reference as questions come up during the training and development process.

Sponsorship

Sponsorship involves a senior employee taking a new person under his or her wing. Sometimes referred to as the "shadow method" or "buddy system," the method works best with new employees or those new to an assignment. Sponsorship allows an individual to be trained by a seasoned employee and then to perform that work under guidance. The main advantage of this method is the opportunity for direct feedback. Its limitations include training being limited to activities performed and, of course, the ability of the trainer. Care must be taken to choose trainers capable of teaching as well as simply knowing the job to be done.

Direct Experience

Training through direct experience can take a number of forms. In each case, the employee actually carries out work with monitoring and feedback occurring regularly. Day-to-day activities are carried out while the individual gains confidence in and familiarity with the process. Working relationships are developed with coworkers, internal customers, and suppliers.

The first method of obtaining direct experience is on-the-job training. Most of this training is conducted on an informal basis, where the employee gains a knowledge of such things as operating practices, the supply base, opportunities for change, and critical issues for the organization. Under this method of "learning by doing", the process itself often becomes the teacher. The employee learns through experience, and is encouraged to ask questions that are not only informational but speculative, that test the process itself and offer opportunity for improvement.

Trial and error, although similar to on-the-job training, tends to rely on the individual to a greater degree. Here the employee receives explanation of an assignment and is allowed to perform. This method is most commonly used in smaller, less formal organizations that do not have the time for or perceive the value of a formal or more planned training program. This method can be effective in that it can evaluate the person's ability to grasp issues and problem-solve corrective action to be taken. It can also test analytical and recuperative skills and the ability to perform under pressure. When using this approach one must be aware of the danger of costly mistakes and damage to the morale of the employee. These risks can then be balanced against the benefits cited, and the learning that occurs through profiting from mistakes and the opportunities that they can afford.

Functional rotation is another method of learning through experience. An employee is rotated among assignments within and outside the department. This might even involve participation on cross-functional teams. The objectives are to provide an expanded base of knowledge, a broadened perspective on the purchasing function and its customers, and a greater level of interrelationships among the individual, others in the organization, and the supply base. Rotation does not necessarily require relocation of the individual as assignments vary. This can be done in a virtual sense by taking advantage of electronic and telecommunication technology. Rotation lends itself well to project assignments and those areas where varying relationships and objectives will present themselves.

Management and Staff Meetings

Attendance at meetings can be a simple, yet very effective method of exposing an individual to participative learning. The exchange of ideas, issues, problems, and opportunities and the resultant discussions offer an excellent environment for training. Learning at meetings will also occur through better understanding of the roles and relationships of attendees and the functions that they perform. Personalities unfold, as does the culture of the organization, in a "live" environment.

Supplier Visits

Visits to suppliers allow for many of the same benefits as do meetings, but with the advantage of the learning occurring at the supplier's place of business. These tours can provide valuable insight into the supplier's culture, management support and commitment to customers, cost-containment strategies, and organizational strategy. The visit should also include a tour of the supplier's purchasing department, which provides an opportunity for comparison and training through informal comparisons and benchmarking. The supplier visit can also provide knowledge about an industry and a better understanding of what is required to satisfy the needs of their customers. Often other supplier capabilities are realized that can provide significant value, either immediately or at some time in the future.

Continuing Education

Training on a more formal basis usually occurs throughout an employee's career. Formal training can occur through classes within the organization or through a seminar or other continuing education program. While on-site training does not allow the opportunity to network with others from different environments, it does allow the program to be tailored to the organization with specific goals and objectives. Also, organizational issues can be readily discussed with the instructor acting as a facilitator and applying principles learned in the class.

The rapid rate of change in today's environment has increased the need for continuing education. The amount of change, although challenging, can be met through a number of different learning environments. Aside from the traditional methods mentioned, distance learning, Internet, and CD-ROM programs offer quality training and instructors at affordable prices. These programs offer exposure to top-level educators and leading-edge topics that would not have been possible only a short time ago. These newer methods of learning are effective and, through interactive features of some, can also provide effective feedback in mastering the topic at hand.

Professional Certification

Another method of development for purchasing and supply management employees is professional certification. Certification can offer purchasing training by providing a cohesive direction within definitive base of knowledge accepted within the profession. Benefits to the individual include a better understanding of the profession and its requirements, a sense of accomplishment and group identification, and a greater sense of confidence. The organization can better benefit from a motivated, more confident employee with a known level of competence and more effective purchasing performance who is a better candidate for promotion. NAPM's certification program (C.P.M.) specifically relates its testing requirements to the tasks performed by a purchasing manager through an extensive job analysis. This process identifies a body of knowledge that reflects specifically the activities performed by a purchasing manager across seven sectors of the economy, including both the public and private sector. Other purchasing organizations also offer certification programs, including the National Contract Management Association, the National Institute of Governmental Purchasing, and the American Society of Transportation and Logistics, Inc.

Professional Purchasing Associations

Membership in professional purchasing associations can provide a number of opportunities for the development and training of purchasing staff. Speakers at association meetings and conferences provide information on a variety of topics. Many organizations also offer trade shows and exhibits. Discussion at these events with other purchasing professionals can lead to a variety of information sources and topics that become part of the individual's repertoire for future reference and consideration. Networking also provides a source for consultation on future topics or problems. This process is not limited to purchasers. Events such as trade exhibits offer opportunities to network with current or potential suppliers as well. This can provide the venue for product, supply base, or industry knowledge that can be used in sourcing, transportation, or supply management decisions. A sourcing or implementation issue that is totally new and foreign to one individual may easily be the area of expertise for another. These discussions are invaluable and often lend more to the development and expertise of an individual than a formalized program.

Professional associations also offer the opportunity for training through volunteer involvement. Serving on or chairing a committee or becoming an officer provides an opportunity to develop and hone such skills as project management, presentation, motivation, problem solving, conflict resolution, and public speaking. The last is probably the most feared by anyone who must face and communicate to a group. Volunteer contribution allows practice in all of these areas, and opportunities exist to learn from others as well. Mistakes can be improved upon—whether made by oneself or others—and a more confident and polished individual returns to the workplace. Volunteering also provides a chance to practice human resource skills, as many of the same problems occurring in the workplace also appear in this environment and are sometimes more difficult to address since there is not a reporting relationship or employment situation in place. Since problems in a volunteer organization may be a bit more difficult to address, the process only makes the skills acquired more effective.

In addition to the National Association of Purchasing Management, professional purchasing associations include:

- American Society of Healthcare Materials Management (ASHMM)
- APICS—The Educational Society for Resource Management
- California Association of Public Purchasing Officers (CAPPO)
- Chinese Association of Purchasing Management (CAPM)
- Food Service Purchasing Group of the National Restaurant Association
- Indian Institute of Materials Management
- National Association of Black Procurement Professionals (NABPP)
- National Association of Educational Buyers (NAEB)
- Newspaper Purchasing Management Association (NPMA)
- Purchasing Management Association of Canada (PMAC)
- Chartered Institute of Purchasing and Supply (CIPS)
- Singapore Institute of Materials Management (SIMM)
- Society of Logistic Engineers

TEAM-BASED SKILLS

In the past decade, managers have discovered that they can accelerate continuous improvement, and the quality of decisions made, by involving those who are affected by the outcome. The principles of this are part of any Total Quality Management process, which accepts diverse points of view that broaden a perspective toward selected objectives. The cliché that two heads are better than one is very often true. For this reason, purchasing and supply managers must develop skills within their staff to deal effectively in an environment involving cross-functional teams that may often include suppliers. Personnel should be exposed to the benefits of team participation and the ultimate improvement in the quality of decision-making.

To work effectively on teams, an individual must possess a skill set that addresses how to function in a team-based environment and relate to team members and a focus on the ultimate customer to be served. Basic principles include how to deal with change, the acceptance of responsibility through ownership, problem-solving and analytical skills, interpersonal skills, management of diversity, conflict resolution, and skills in persuasion. To enhance performance, knowledge of group dynamics and basics of motivational theory should be understood. Theories such as Maslow's needs, Hertzberg's hygiene theory, and McGregor's Theory X and Theory Y styles of management not only continue to be valid today, but have application beyond individuals to the teams in which they serve. Understanding what is important to team members will impact effectiveness, and therefore training should include basics of group dynamics. Elements covered should include how a group functions, group leadership, and an understanding that the main power of a group comes from its members. Human beings have an inherent "need to belong" that groups fill. Leadership in groups is an important consideration, and often the leader is not necessarily the person appointed. For this reason, principles of group involvement are important concepts for exposure and understanding. Training should also include the major benefits of teams: that they are key to the success of diverse or innovative programs and that they provide a higher quality of decision-making, an effective communication network, and a more in-depth understanding of issues and their relation to an objective. Teams also can be instrumental in implementing change by removing resistance. Involvement of members breeds commitment through better understanding and participation, and since they were part of the process development, they have a sense of ownership and confidence in the resultant outcome. Teams, by their enthusiasm and leadership, can also generate pressure toward conformity. A good example of this is the Disney organization and the cleanliness of their theme parks. Walking through, one would feel significant guilt in even tossing a piece of paper on the ground rather than the appropriate receptacle.

PERFORMANCE MANAGEMENT

Managing staff performance is a significant responsibility of any manager. The process may be compared to conducting an orchestra. The conductor must know the functions of individual performers and blend those in the right relationships to yield a cohesive, effective outcome that is pleasing to the audience—in this case, the customer to be served. Typically, this evaluation is referred to as "performance measurement." The difference between measurement and management, however, is an important one. Measurement is a process of reporting results. *Management*, on the other hand, implies taking action to *determine* results. In order to *manage* individual performance, one must know the desired outcomes up front. As discussed in the preceding section, involvement leads not only to commitment, but ownership. For this reason, individuals should be involved in setting goals and their input should be considered. This allows for awareness up front of what is expected and removes ambiguity, interpretation, and perhaps the surprise that later leads to frustration and disappointment. Both the manager and the employee know what is expected and upon which factors evaluation will be based. Whenever possible, measures should be objective rather than subjective. A number of techniques can add clarity and a degree of objectivity to such goals as "improve quality" or "improve supplier awareness."

The management of performance should include constant rather than periodic reviews. When corrective action is required, waiting until a scheduled review date does not promote the intentions of this process. Although formal reviews are important, they should not impede change. In a review of performance, a benefit to both parties is an understanding of variances, whether in the goals themselves or in the perception of them. Communication remains one of the most difficult skills to master, and a simple goal such as lowering the cost of purchases may lead to skyrocketing inventories through forward buying at volume pricing! Following the review, each should have a better understanding of their differences and an action plan for any improvement required. Ongoing feedback through the process of managing performance can avoid wrong paths on the road to continuous improvement. Overall, feedback is most effective when it is specific, fact-based, timely, and fair.

DISCIPLINARY ISSUES

The performance management process invariably highlights variations that must be addressed. For those variances that are within the control of the individual, a change in behavior through corrective action must take place. In such cases, it is imperative that the person be aware of the issue. This perhaps goes without saying, but it is surprising how often this is not the case. Disciplinary issues are not welcomed by many managers, and unfortunately the confrontation required never occurs.

Types of disciplinary issues to be addressed include performance issues, theft, embezzlement, attendance, and attitude. The last can refer to such intangibles as commitment, cooperation, pleasantness, and a willingness by others to approach as needed. Underlying issues may be the root cause of the problem. They can include a perception of inequity, emotional concerns, personality traits, interpersonal relationships, family problems, or substance abuse. Investment in human resources is a significant expense, and recovery or maximization of that investment is critical. When these problems occur, they should be addressed in as careful and confidential a nature as possible. But they must be addressed. The person must be aware of the nature of the issue, and be allowed to express their views. A plan of correction should be followed that includes training, counseling, or reassignment. The manager must be sure to follow legalities or collective bargaining regulations and prepare complete documentation. When it is done correctly, both employees and organizations can benefit from an effective corrective action program.

When these efforts do not produce results, or when there is not a willingness on the part of the individual to change, termination of employment is probably the better alternative for both parties. When this is the case, proper documentation is essential, and the termination interview should deal solely and specifically with the facts. Opinion-based discussions only lend themselves to frustration and unnecessary conflict. When the termination is not based on performance, such as in the case of downsizing, that should be made clear. It is important that the person understand that termination is not the result of performance but rather of the elimination of work, and as a result, the need for the position no longer exists.

SUMMARY

The acquisition and development of human resources is a critical and important element in the success and perception of the purchasing and supply management function. The personal qualifications of a purchaser must include the basics required of any professional: honesty, integrity, commitment, ambition, and a willingness to seek and embrace change in an environment of continuous learning. The purchasing profession adds a greater meaning to these words. Entrusted with the expenditure of a significant portion of the organization's funds, a purchaser is automatically placed in a position of greater exposure. Ethics and a high moral character must be evident within and outside of the firm.

Perhaps the most important characteristic sought in an effective purchaser is the indefinable quality of good judgment—the ability to sift through the enormous quantity of information available, identify an issue and its most important elements, and come to a reasonable conclusion. The need remains the same in any aspect of the purchaser's duties, be they negotiation, supply base management, contract management, inventory management, or investment recovery. The task or strategy remains how best to maximize value received for resources expended.

Routine purchasing can certainly be less than challenging, and transaction-based purchasing can be better served by machines, if not eliminated. But creative purchasing and supply management is a challenge that leads to continued competitiveness and success of the firm. The ingenuity required can only be the result of people: qualified practitioners who are hired and trained and are dedicated to a profession that continues to become an integral part of an organization's strategy to best serve the customers that justify its existence.

CHAPTER 16

Purchasing
Performance Evaluation

Editor
Linda L. Stanley, Ph.D.
Associate Professor
Our Lady of the Lake University
School of Business

INTRODUCTION

There is an old saying, "You can't manage it if you can't measure it." While creating and implementing a good measurement system is important, determining the "best" measures is a complicated task. Purchasing should remember that relevant measures alone will not create results, but they will provide important input to the decision-making process.

A study by the Center for Advanced Purchasing Studies (CAPS)[1] concluded that there are no simple answers to performance evaluation. Business and social environments are constantly changing, and measures are needed that change with the environment. An additional complicating factor is that senior management and purchasing and supply managers do not necessarily agree on which measures are important.

In the past, each functional area developed measures to maximize their individual department's performance. For example, in a service organization, purchasing traditionally focused on supplier cost reductions while marketing measured service quality and finance focused on capital expenditures. However, maximizing functional performance does not necessarily help firms achieve their overall business objectives. A supply

---

1. H. E. Fearon and W. A. Bales, *Measures of Purchasing Effectiveness,* Center for Advanced Purchasing Studies and NAPM, Tempe, Arizona, 1997.

chain management perspective requires organizations to take a process approach and focus on cross-functional and interorganizational issues. As a result, performance measurement also must move from a focus on functional measurement to an integrated approach and improve supply chain performance.[2] Additionally, continuous purchasing performance improvement depends on an organization's ability to treat the measurement system as a dynamic motivational process.

IMPORTANCE OF PERFORMANCE MEASUREMENT

Purchasing and supply performance is generally measured to monitor the health of a business or department or diagnose short-term problems. Good performance measurement systems are a means to review the alignment of purchasing strategies and actions with organizational strategy. They provide for individual and organizational appraisal and feedback systems that shape purchasing strategies and programs.

Individual performance measures serve several purposes, including:

1. Drive strategies and actions
2. Appraise behavior
3. Motivate employees
4. Reinforce behavior
5. Reward behavior

Tracking measures will help organizations in several areas and will be addressed in the next few pages. They include:

1. Determining how well purchasing and supply is meeting business objectives
2. Helping set realistic purchasing and supply objectives
3. Evaluating purchasing and supply management effectiveness
4. Aiding in making self-assessments
5. Gauging movement toward improvement
6. Providing incentives for improvement
7. Spotting operational problems early

---

2. S. A. Elliff, "SCM: Looking at the Whole Picture," *Purchasing Today*®, November 1997.

8. Establishing criteria for success, such as contributions to profitability and customer satisfaction[3]

Business Objectives

The primary goal of any business is making money, or profitability. Contribution to profit is measured by:

1. Return on assets
2. Stockholder equity
3. Earnings per share
4. Stock value
5. After-tax profit

Measures for purchasing departments and individuals should be developed that align with business objectives and are stated in senior management "language." CEOs and presidents from Fortune 500 companies ranked the following as the top five measures of purchasing effectiveness:

1. Quality of purchased items
2. Key supplier problems that could affect supply
3. Supplier delivery performance
4. Internal customer satisfaction
5. Purchase inventory dollars

ESTABLISHING PURCHASING AND SUPPLY OBJECTIVES

Develop a Purchasing and Supply Organization Plan

Purchasing organizations need a plan to set the direction for achieving business goals and objectives. Included in the plan should be the purchasing organization's philosophy to clarify individual and departmental expectations and help all employees understand their role in company performance. Purchasing's goals and objectives that align with company

---

3. Adapted from M. Harding, "Purchasing Performance Measurements on the Leading Edge," *NAPM InfoEdge*, January 1997, p. 2.

goals also should be included to develop individual measures of performance and as a baseline for performance evaluation. Some purchasing goals that align with company goals could include:

1. 100% incoming quality of purchased materials and supplies
2. Maintaining good supplier relations
3. Minimizing inventory investment
4. Achieving 100% on-time delivery of key materials and supplies
5. Maintaining good relationships with internal customers
6. Minimizing the total cost of ownership of materials and equipment

Review Purchasing and Supply Organization

Once an organization plan has been developed, purchasing and supply should analyze their situation by answering some important questions: Where are we today? Where do we want to be in the future? Do we currently have the structure to achieve our objectives?

Some specific questions that should be asked are:

1. Are purchasing and supply policies, programs, and practices aligned with company goals and objectives?
2. What are the specific roles, relationships, responsibilities, and authority of corporate, divisional, and plant/satellite purchasing and supply employees?
3. What is the present relationship between purchasing and supply and senior management?
4. How effective is the purchasing and supply organization's structure?
5. Are adequate purchasing and supply coordination and control mechanisms in place?
6. How well does purchasing and supply interact and communicate with internal customers and internal suppliers?
7. What are current relationships with key suppliers?
8. Is the current purchasing and supply performance measurement system aligned with company goals and objectives?

9. Do purchasing and supply employees have the adequate skills, education, and knowledge to meet company goals and objectives? If not, what will be required to improve the situation?[4]

Once a situational analysis is performed, purchasing managers can implement recommendations to correct any problem areas or processes.

EVALUATION

Guidelines for Measure Development

Based on purchasing and supply's organization plan, existing measures should be reviewed and new measures developed. Performance measures need to be tailored to individual organizations, but should:

1. Be meaningful to the organization
2. Be aligned with business objectives
3. Be representative of trends or progress
4. Be consistent with other groups within the organization
5. Integrate financial and nonfinancial information
6. Measure what is important to customers
7. Adapt to changing customer demands

DEVELOPMENT AND IMPLEMENTATION OF MEASURES

Certain steps that should be taken to develop and implement a useful performance measurement system are addressed in the next three sections.

Database Development

Initially, a database needs to be developed to collect data needed for the measurement system. A database should be set up for each measurement. Some needed information may be available outside the purchasing

---

4. "Evaluating Purchasing Performance," in R. B. Ackerman, ed., *The Purchasing Handbook*, 1992, pp. 315–354.

and supply department. For example, purchasing and supply may need to work with accounting and finance to uncover quality costs, such as quality control and incoming inspection, in the overhead accounts.

Establishment of a database is time-consuming and may take several months. However, accuracy of information is crucial to developing meaningful measures. Therefore analysis and clean-up of available data is particularly important. On-line, real-time information will provide timely trend analysis and the ability to troubleshoot impending and actual problems early. Accurate data also will enable purchasing and supply groups to evaluate progress in an unbiased manner.

Setting Priorities

Secondly, purchasing and supply should set long- and short-term priorities with respect to the purchasing department, its suppliers, and commodities based on organizational goals and objectives. Priorities will shift based on an ongoing review of the measures and as organizational goals and objectives change.

Measurements

Senior managers are measured and rewarded based on their contribution to profit while purchasing and supply is measured on cost reduction through price negotiation. To achieve alignment, purchasing should first work with senior management to change its reward system away from individual-based pay rewards and toward group rewards based on gain sharing, profit sharing, and employee stock ownership plans. These reward systems will be discussed further in later sections. Similar reward systems across an organization will result in the development of effective measurement systems.

In general, performance measures should be stated in terms of contribution toward profit but include measures that are both quantitative and qualitative. Measurement based on profitability requires coordination and agreement among senior management, purchasing, purchasing's internal customers, and external suppliers. Those stakeholders not included will tend to misunderstand or distrust the measures. Evaluation of progress toward customer satisfaction goals and issues regarding cooperation are typically difficult to quantify. For example, measuring the ability to work effectively on teams and responsiveness to internal customers are generally subjective in nature but should be included.

Once a database has been established and priorities are set, purchasing should establish what to measure as well as how to measure it. The current measurements should be evaluated and those that are not interrelated or do not complement and interface with each other should be eliminated. New measures that *are* related and address organizational priorities should be developed. For example, quality of purchased items is related to on-time delivery. A shipment is considered on-time only if 100% defect-free items were shipped. Leadtimes and quality are also related to the effectiveness of the relationship with suppliers.

Once measures are determined, establish the ideal benchmark or baseline for each measure and then monitor the progress toward that goal. The organization's business plan can serve as the baseline for purchasing and supply measures.

Measures can be broken down into the areas discussed below.

Contribution to Profit

Purchasing can contribute to profit by improving prices for a costed bill or materials in for-profit organizations. Any saving in materials purchases goes straight to gross margin. In not-for-profit organizations, purchasing can contribute by underspending allocated funds or sharing surpluses with other functions.

To improve cost savings, purchasing and supply should look at the total cost to buy and install/use an item. Installed/use costs include:

1. Delivery/leadtime (longer leadtimes = higher inventory costs)
2. Incoming inspection
3. Assembly time
4. Rework time

Example

Joe, purchasing and supply manager for Albright Company, is considering switching suppliers for a part. At first, Supplier A appears to be the easy choice based on the price he last paid to Supplier B ($12.00), and the price quoted by Supplier A ($11.25). Based on the traditional practice of estimating cost savings based on a standard price of $12.25, he would save $1.00 per unit or $50,000. However, he decides to do some additional investigation on other costs that could be incurred to use the part. He collects the data shown in Table 16–1 based on a trial production run of the new part.

T A B L E   16–1

	Supplier A	Supplier B
Price/unit	$11.25	$12.00
Delivery time	6 weeks	2 weeks
Assembly time	4 minutes	3 minutes
Production yield	92%	96%
Incoming inspection	$160/lot	$100/lot
Annual use	50,000	50,000

T A B L E   16–2

	Calculation	Net Difference per Part
Cost savings	$12.25 − $11.25	$1.00 savings
Additonal inventory cost	$11.25 × 1.5% × 4 weeks	$0.675 additional cost
Additonal assembly time cost	1 minute × $50/hr factory cost	$0.83 additional cost
Additional yield cost	$11.25 × 4% × 2.5 valued added	$1.125 additional cost
Additoinal inspection cost	($160 − $100)/400 parts per lot	$0.15 additional cost
Net savings/cost per part		$1.78 additional installed cost per part

He then makes some calculations, as shown in Table 16–2.

Based on the data in Tables 16–1 and 16–2, Joe decides to continue buying from Supplier B.

Other important measures to purchasing could include:

1. Throughput: total amount of production that has been sold
2. Inventory turnover
3. Return on assets (net profit/total assets)

4. Distribution of dollars expended on resources, such as capital equipment, direct materials, indirect materials, and services

Supplier Performance

Purchasing and supply managers typically are measured based on the performance of their suppliers. Therefore, effective supplier management programs are important to control quality, delivery, and cost of incoming materials and services. Successful programs help supply managers identify capable suppliers, and then initiate supplier partnership, certification programs, development programs, supplier training programs, and others to ensure delivery of quality parts and services at a reasonable cost in the desired time frame.

Quality Measures

Deming and others argue that organizations can improve productivity, innovation, and profitability by improving quality. Therefore, purchasing and supply's goal should be receipt of defect-free materials, components, supplies, and services from suppliers. Part of purchasing's role is to set standards for their supply base and require suppliers to document their quality processes. Purchasing usually will find quality cost information in marketing, production/operations, and customer service, including:

- Scrap
- Rework
- Repairs
- Premature product failures
- Returns
- Warranty work
- Lost sales
- Loss of reputation
- Changes in inventory levels

Improvements can then be addressed with suppliers as necessary, including setting quality targets by item or commodity, requiring proof of quality shipments, reducing supplier's total cycle times, and receiving notification before changes are made to supplier's process.

Delivery

Delivery performance has direct ties to other important performance measures, including inventory planning, production schedule performance, cash flows, and customer service. On-time delivery compares an organization's actual receipt of items compared to desired or required receipt. For manufacturers, early and late shipments are both costly in terms of additional inventory costs and production disruptions, respectively. For service organizations, late deliveries can result in work slowdowns or lost sales at the retail level.

To allow delivery performance to be accurately measured, predetermined delivery dates must be established for each item. On-time delivery can be measured by:

1. Supplier's leadtime translated to delivery date
2. FOB supplier
3. FOB customer
4. Supplier's acknowledge delivery date

Supplier Management

Supplier management activities should address some key areas. First, determine the purpose of each activity based on current situation. Is the purpose of the activity to gain access to current technological capabilities, sole access to proprietary products or services, or develop just-in-time capabilities? Then determine if the benefits between purchasing and the supplier will be mutually beneficial or strictly one-sided. Are there other suppliers available that will fill that specific need at a higher performance level?

Secondly, set initial evaluation standards and then update those standards as needs change. Develop standards jointly with the supplier (to ensure accurate expectations) based on organizational goals. Measures may be weighted to emphasize greater emphasis on certain criteria. Purchasing can then measure individual criteria using a report card based on the following scale:

5 = excellent
4 = very good
3 = good
2 = fair
1 = poor

Performance ratings are multiplied by their respective weights to obtain weighted scores, which are then summed to derive a total score.

Prepare a cost/benefit analysis before entering into any activity and reevaluate periodically. As times change an activity may no longer be cost effective. Additionally, other suppliers may enter the market with stronger performance at a lower cost. Align an ongoing evaluation system with organizational goals and purchasing's expectations that includes both subjective and objective measures. Objective measures should address delivery times, ability to meet specifications, quality, and accurate complete documentation. Subjective measures could include technical support, effective communication, and responsiveness to changing requirements. Each measure could then be weighted dependent upon its importance to performance. Both measures and weights may change as the relationship changes, so update and modify measures when needed.

Finally, develop an effective reward/recognition system for suppliers. They will be more interested in attaining purchasing's objectives if they know that they will receive something for their efforts. If a formal agreement has been signed, see that potential rewards are written into the agreement. Rewards also should have meaning for the supplier and be linked to performance in specific areas of importance to the organization. Suppliers are motivated to perform through reward programs such as long-term contracts, sharing cost savings discovered through value analysis, and increased volume commitments resulting from supplier certification.

Organizations also recognize suppliers at banquets, in company newsletters, or through actual cost savings.

Other Measures

Measures of service are also important and related to delivery, quality, and profitability. Some measures of service performance are subjective in nature but should be included in the measurement process. Common service measures include:

1. Internal customer satisfaction
2. Accurate recordkeeping
3. Responsiveness to changing situations
4. Administrative cost reduction
5. Participation/success of supplier development programs

6. Participation/success of supplier certification programs
7. Success of cross-functional development activities

TREND ANALYSIS

Good performance measures based on *organizational* goals and objectives include a focus on trends in addition to absolute numbers. In fact, the CAPS's study on purchasing performance[5] found that CEOs wanted trend analysis on all measures with the exception of supplier partner development. Observed trends are reviewed and used to set new goals as needed. All members of the purchasing and supply organization then work toward those organizational goals. Trend analysis also aids in detection of deviations from goals that have a significant impact on other parts of the organization. For example, a small deviation in actual delivery times of incoming materials for manufacturers can result in production stoppages for operations and scheduling disruptions for distribution. As goods move to retailers, similar disruptions create havoc in receiving at their distribution centers and delayed shipment to retail outlets. The results are lost sales and customer dissatisfaction.

Trends can be analyzed by collecting actual performance data and comparing them to desired performance. For example, purchasing's goal for suppliers is to deliver as close to the need date as possible. Early deliveries increase inventory holding costs, while late deliveries can cause operational disruptions. Therefore, it would be important to evaluate delivery trends. Actual to needed delivery dates of an ordered item can be compared using spreadsheet software. Table 16–3 shows some delivery data for a supplier of one item.

Plotting the data results in the graph in Figure 16–1.

Other trends that can be measured and charted include:

1. Time to qualify a new supplier
2. Actual quality compared to target quality
3. Quality improvement compared to targeted goal
4. Cost of quality (prevention, appraisal, internal failures, external failures)
5. Lead time reduction
6. Total cost of acquisition compared to total cost of use

---

5. Fearon and Bales, op. cit.

T A B L E   16–3

Month	Actual Delivery (days)	Required Delivery (days)
Jan	55	40
Feb	51	38
March	48	38
April	47	40
May	40	30
June	50	41
July	40	31
Aug	43	32
Sept	39	30
Oct	35	28
Nov	33	28

F I G U R E   16–1

Delivery Performance Trend Analysis

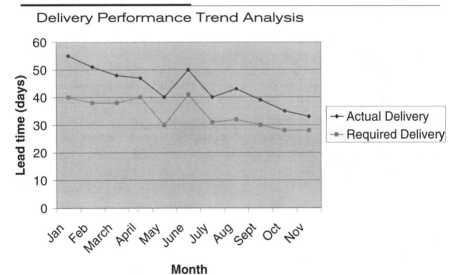

7. Actual cost compared to goal (target, benchmark)
8. Orders delivered directly to factory floor

BENCHMARKING

Performance gaps in certain processes inevitably will be apparent based on trend analysis. To improve these processes, benchmarking other organizations is a popular although time-consuming option. Benchmarking should be saved for those critical processes that have a direct impact on company goals and objectives.

Once a critical process has been identified, purchasing and supply must choose a benchmarking team to understand the current process and be able to recognize best practices in other organizations.[6] A process map or flowchart is a useful tool to document the process. The team must also identify the customers of the process, inputs needed by employees to make the process work, and specific outputs needed by the customer.

Once an internal analysis has been performed, the team chooses a benchmarking partner. Partners may come from other internal departments, other divisions, or competitors. Information about potential partners can be collected from local libraries, online databases, Malcolm Baldridge Award or Deming Prize winners, trade associations, and suppliers or customers. Multiple sources should be contacted to find partners that exhibit excellent practices. Potential partners should then be contacted to find out about their process, their financial status (whether they are profitable), and their willingness to share information.

REWARD SYSTEMS

Appropriately designed reward systems encourage employee development, and well-developed purchasing and supply employees encourage and enhance the development of good sourcing strategies. The individuals who manage suppliers can be motivated through a number of different programs that include personal and group incentives.

Most companies rely on monetary rewards such as salary or a combination of salary and benefits. Benefits come in many forms, from

---

6. J. Maxwell, "Selecting the Right Benchmarking Partner," *NAPM Insights,* May 1995, pp. 55–56.

healthcare and pensions to personal days. The quantification of a pay-check is straightforward, but the value of benefits varies for each individual.

Pay and more general reward systems have been shown to motivate performance.[7] The key issue, then, is how a company designs a compensation system to motivate purchasing professionals to sharpen and develop their skills.

Reward structures remain tied to climbing the corporate ladder. With a job well done, individuals move to the next level, with additional status, salary increase, and benefits.

As organizations move to flatter structures, fewer opportunities exist for new job titles or increased status and incentives are limited to monetary rewards for performing as well as or better than expected. Additionally, many purchasing professionals have similar job titles although they use very different skills. The changing nature of skill sets favors those people with a higher percentage of required skills.

Individual rewards can be separated into base salary and incentive pay. Base salary is the major component of many employees' paychecks and is determined as a function of the job the person holds and the skill sets the person possesses. Because the world in which purchasing professionals work is quick to change and very demanding, the skills required of these individuals are diverse and will become increasingly dynamic in the future. In a salary-only based pay environment people may feel that their skills are not fully recognized or rewarded.

Skill-based pay systems pay people for the skills they possess or acquire. Skill-based pay offers some advantages over salary-based methods, including lower absenteeism and turnover, greater flexibility, and stronger understanding of the organization and importance of their skills, resulting in greater job satisfaction.

In addition to salary- and skill-based pay systems, another motivating tool is incentive pay. Incentive pay is linked strongly to one's performance and can work as a motivator, but focuses on individual performance and in ways that may not be optimal for the organization.

As purchasing and supply professionals work increasingly as members of interdisciplinary teams, group-based incentives often become

---

7. M. Pagell, A. Das, S. Curkovic, and L. Easton, "Motivating the Purchasing Professional," *International Journal of Purchasing and Materials Management*, Summer 1996, pp. 27–34.

more appropriate. Three general types of group-based compensation include:

- ◆ Profit sharing
- ◆ Gain sharing
- ◆ Employee stock ownership plans

In a profit-sharing plan, organizations reward employees with a bonus tied to overall annual performance that may be paid quarterly, semi-annually, once a year, or at some other interval. Administration of a profit-sharing plan is simpler because distribution is not tied to individual contribution. However, profit sharing also is considered a poor motivator because individuals have difficulty visualizing their influence on their organization and factors outside employee control at times affect profitability.

Gain sharing rewards employees based on group performance. A gain sharing plan guarantees a base wage plus an increase (usually less than 1%) for each percent an employee or group produces above a standard. For example, a purchasing group is paid a percent of any cost savings on parts sourced for a new product and each employee shares the bonus. Benefits are distributed more frequently than profit sharing, often soon after the rewarded behavior's occurrence. Gain sharing has been shown to motivate individual performance.

The third type of group reward includes employee stock ownership plans (ESOPs) and stock options. An ESOP plan allows employees to purchase company stock, often at prices below market value. Stock options may be awarded to employees based on performance or simply for service. Stock ownership plans can positively affect employee motivation, particularly in small organizations and when an organization desires a culture change to gain greater employee commitment.

CONCLUSIONS

Purchasing performance measurement and evaluation has become an ongoing process as organizations face the accelerated pace of global competition and technological change. More senior managers today recognize the value of purchasing and supply to organizational success. As a result, a measurement system should be developed with measures that add value and provide information as a basis for continuous improvement.

Measures must be reviewed and changed as organizational goals and priorities change. Individual organizations also must develop a measurement plan tailored to their needs. It is the responsibility of purchasing professionals to speak the language of senior management and include measures that identify financial performance. Additionally, subjective measures are important and should be included in any measurement system.

As stated earlier, measurements in and of themselves will not change performance. However, by combining measurements with action plans for improvement and a good reward system to motivate employees, organizations can remain competitive.

ADDITIONAL READINGS

McGinnis, M. A. "Building Better Performance Measurements." *NAPM Insights,* May 1995, pp. 50–54.

Pilachowski, M. *Purchasing Performance Measurements: A Roadmap for Excellence.* PT Publications, West Palm Beach, FL, 1996.

Stanley, L. L., "Linking Supplier Performance to Purchasing Performance." *NAPM Insights,* May 1995, pp. 67–69.

Ethics and Responsibility

Editor
Arnold J. Lovering, J.D., C.P.M.
Director, Supply Chain Management
Raytheon Company

CONCEPTS OF ETHICS

The noun *ethics* comes from the Greek word *ēthikos*, meaning "moral." The root word in Greek is *ēthos*, meaning "character, disposition, or characteristic spirit." The adjective *ethical* can then easily be seen to mean moral, decent, virtuous, upright, fair, just, proper, straightforward, aboveboard, fitting, and correct.

While the philosophical theory of ethics may be distinguished from the everyday task of making moral decisions, philosophers have usually held that the chief test that can be applied to an ethical system is to ask if it can be harmonized with what often is called "common sense" ethics—that is, with those ethical judgments that at our best we feel constrained to make, apart from philosophical argument, in our ordinary ethical thinking.[1] This begins to sound as though it might apply to a buyer as he or she makes decisions from day to day. Such a conclusion becomes even more likely when one considers one of the main premises in Kant's *Critique of Practical Reason*—namely, that a person should not ask what the particular consequences of a given action will be but what would happen if everybody acted in that way.

From these carefully considered philosophical arguments, one may reasonably conclude that the Golden Rule is a greatly condensed statement of logical ethics. And it may follow that a good philosophy for a

---

1. *Encyclopedia Britannica*, vol. 8, 1971, p. 752.

buyer to pursue would be one that causes him or her to treat sellers in a manner that would be considered just, proper, fitting, and correct if the situation were reversed. What follows, then, is an attempt to articulate the minimum ethical standards that the vast majority of purchasing professionals would consider just, proper, fitting, and correct and to provide some simple insights into the application of these standards.

LEADERSHIP FROM PURCHASING

During the past several decades, purchasing has developed more in a professional and a managerial sense than at any time in its history. Purchasing has emerged from its early clerical status and moved into the management structure. In so doing, it has established itself as a profession. Having achieved this status, purchasing often is looked to for guidance. And one of the areas where purchasing can demonstrate genuine leadership is in the field of ethics. There is little doubt that purchasing is one of the most sensitive areas in an organization, subject to all types of pressures and influence. From experience in this arena, most purchasing managers have much to offer their colleagues. This is especially true as the role of purchasing evolves into procurement material management and supply chain management.

Most top management people are ready to accept guidance from purchasing in the area of total-company ethical concerns. This is not only a challenge to purchasing but also a responsibility—one that should not be ignored. A progressive purchasing manager must meet this challenge in a number of ways.

First, and foremost, ethical conduct in the purchasing department must be exemplary. Next, purchasing managers should assume a leadership role in ensuring that the same high standards adopted by the purchasing group in dealing with suppliers are also in effect throughout the entire company for anyone who deals with supplier organizations. Suppliers, naturally, have contact with many people in the firm not directly subordinate to purchasing. These people or functional activities vary from firm to firm, depending on the organizational structure. Examples might be design engineers, other users or customers, quality-control people, production and operations people, salespersons, public relations and advertising people, and others who use purchased materials and supplies. No company can long afford to have a multiple standard of conduct established by separate departments. The effects of such an approach brand a firm with an unenviable reputation. The top purchasing people in an organization must ensure proper ethical treatment of suppliers by everyone in the organization who deals with them.

A statement of policy often is developed by the purchasing group—and subsequently issued as a management proclamation. This can be very useful in establishing corporate guidelines in the ethics area. Such a statement should not attempt to spell out in detail how to handle all the various situations that might occur, for it obviously would become too lengthy for practical use. Such a policy statement will be far better if it is written in broad terminology but is concise and pointed enough to be readily understood by everyone throughout the organization. It should stress that purchasing is always available for consultation and guidance in coping with any particular problem. Purchasing may further take the initiative and conduct seminars or workshops on the subject. This could be part of the normal employee training program (and should be continually updated), with all employees who deal with suppliers participating in the sessions. Seminars of this sort should be conducted at least once a year and more often if required.

The example set by purchasing in its total approach to the matter of ethics should be an obvious guide to the rest of the company. Proper ethical conduct is as much good judgment as anything else, and certainly purchasing professionals must demonstrate skill in this area. Many organizations have created separate Ethics Offices, and purchasing needs to have a close working relationship with these company professionals.

Elevating the Purchasing Profession

Purchasing professionals dedicated to sound ethical standards can do much to raise the stature of their employers, themselves, and the purchasing profession. Of the many characteristics required for effectiveness in interpersonal relations, several impinge on the ethics area and are particularly important for purchasing people. In all they do, buyers must exhibit honesty, a sense of fairness, dependability, professional capability, and a clear sense of moral responsibility. And finally, buyers must be able to handle their own financial affairs capably. By perseverance and hard work, these objectives are obtainable, and the cumulative result is a real credit to all the people in purchasing. It must always be remembered that one cannot buy an ethical reputation—it must be earned. Once earned, it must be zealously maintained. One bad move can destroy a reputation that took years to build.

APPLYING ETHICAL CONCEPTS IN PURCHASING

The purchasing professional must contend with various aspects of ethical conduct that relate to the buying role from differing viewpoints. Total ethical conduct consists of separate responsibilities to at least four distinct constituencies:

- Employer
- Supplier
- Profession
- Person

Employer

Professional buyers must perform their roles in a manner that protects their employers ethically. A buyer is the agent of the employer. Reputation and fairness are key characteristics that must be established in the buying process. Buyers must avoid all situations where personal gain may result from acts by a supplier that might work in any way to the detriment of the employer. All proprietary information learned in the performance of one's duties must be safeguarded, and buyers must commit their full efforts toward achieving the goals of the employer. Should the goals or practices of the employer ever conflict with the ethical standards of the individual or the profession, a buyer must attempt to manage the situation, usually through change, to eliminate the conflict. Often education and training in sound ethical practices will resolve such differences.

Supplier

A buyer must treat a supplier fairly in all matters. A courteous reception, a complete and open quotation or bidding process, fair competition, well-written specifications and purchase orders, and prompt and equitable administration of open issues are some of the important elements of sound and ethical treatment of suppliers. Effective buyers encourage their best suppliers to bring new ideas and new technology to the relationship and reward these contributions by the awarding of new business. Proprietary ideas must be protected because they are a valuable competitive asset of the supplier and must be treated with proper respect and care. A perceptive buyer searches diligently for those areas of common ground that will allow both the buyer and the seller to maximize their respective benefits from the transaction. The buyer will not knowingly take advantage of an error in a quotation without providing the supplier one last opportunity to reexamine its bid for accuracy and thoroughness. In all the things just discussed, a buyer is expected to strive diligently to develop the very best long-term *value* for his or her employer, discarding any short-term gain in favor of the best long-run position.

Figure 17–1 portrays the Raytheon Company's ethics statement as contained in the firm's booklet entitled *How to Do Business with Raytheon*, which is given directly to suppliers on this topic.

Profession

The purchasing professional is expected to contribute to the development, recognition, and application of the formal ethical standards established by the profession. Perhaps the best-known standard is the *Principles and Standards and of Purchasing Practice with Accompanying Guidelines* issued by the National Association of Purchasing Management (NAPM) (see Box 17–2 at the end of the chapter). Buyers must profess belief in and adherence to these practices before becoming a member of any of the local affiliate associations of the NAPM or being recognized by that organization as a Certified Purchasing Manager (C.P.M.).

Person

Every person brings to a professional buying position his or her own personal values or ethics. It is important that buyers recognize that responsibilities do exist to each of the various constituencies—employer, supplier, profession, and self.

Some Practical Guidelines

There should be no doubt that every act of the purchasing professional is dedicated to the long-term best interest of the employer. Buyers must know the best sources, know the supplier industry, and conduct the purchasing decision-making process in an open and fair manner. Activities

F I G U R E   17–1

Raytheon standards of conduct for buying. (Reprinted with the permission of the Raytheon Company.)

Raytheon Procurement has traditionally made awards to suppliers only on the basis of competitive price, quality and delivery. Sound business judgment as opposed to special favoritism or personal preference should be the basis for the company buying decisions. Sometime ago, the company adopted guidelines and policy requirements to address our business ethics and company Standards of Conduct. These rules were designed to establish and maintain a reputation in the marketplace that meets the very highest standards of ethical conduct. Our suppliers are requested to be aware of our thinking on this important topic, and to adhere to these guidelines at all times, thus making it easier for both buyers and sellers to conduct themselves professionally based upon good business ethical practices.

Supplier Relations

Negotiations with Raytheon should be based on sound business judgment. Buyers must show no favoritism or preference to sellers at the expense of our company. Raytheon expects its procurement personnel to be fair, do no favors, and ACCEPT NO FAVORS. Accepting kickbacks is a crime—both morally and legally. It is the fastest way for procurement personnel to find the way out the door and for sellers to cease doing business with us. The company will prosecute violators wherever appropriate.

Obviously, Raytheon expects its suppliers not to offer such kickbacks. Gifts, free services, discounts on personal purchases are wrong. This is true whether they are for the employee or for anyone else in his or her family or household.

These rules apply not only to procurement professionals but also to any Raytheon functionary who influences the buying process such as engineers, manufacturing, quality, finance, facility and other employees. Trips, entertainment or special considerations of any kind, whether solicited or unsolicited are also wrong. Favors must be declined and gifts must be returned pleasantly, diplomatically, and firmly. We appreciate the supplier community cooperation on these rules. Gifts, services or consideration other than an advertising novelty such as a paperweight, key chain or coffee cup will be returned to the supplier. Novelty items having an apparent value of $10 or more will also be returned. Luncheons with suppliers should not be encouraged. Under some circumstances they are necessary if there is a legitimate business purpose for the get-together. But they should not be a habit. Company facilities should be used whenever possible. We don't encourage outside business lunches. We should use them only when necessary. When they are used as a vehicle for business discussion, Raytheon should take turns paying the bill, particularly when on home ground. Dinners and other forms of evening or weekend entertainment are prohibited. There may be special situations where exceptions are required, and if so, approval of the cognizant Raytheon Department Manager is required in advance. Relations with suppliers should be friendly, objective, and strictly business. Raytheon strongly believes that we are not adversaries, but partners who need to work together to meet the objectives of both the buying and selling organizations.

F I G U R E   17–1

Continued

Conflicts of Interest

Raytheon expects its employees not to allow any conflict of interest between their personal affairs and the business at the company. One may not have a financial interest, position or relationship with any person, firm or corporation that does business with the company that would influence, or could be regarded as influencing, their actions for the company. This applies also to the employee's wife, husband, child, or any other relative who resides in the home. Such family financial interests can become a conflict of the company employee. Any situation which is unclear should be reviewed with management. We expect our suppliers to understand these rules.

Confidential Information

Part of good ethical behavior is to keep confidential business information confidential. This applies both to proprietary Raytheon information and to confidential information offered to Raytheon by our suppliers. Raytheon information that must be kept confidential may include:

Patentable and secret processes.

Production schedules.

Product information.

Prices.

Other proprietary information.

Suppliers often must divulge to the company information that is proprietary to their business. Raytheon will respect these confidences, both for the suppliers' sake and, in the long run, for Raytheon's sake as well.

Laws and Regulations

Raytheon observes all laws and regulations that apply to purchasing—in a locality, in a state, in a country.

Supplier Obligations

Raytheon expects its suppliers to exhibit business behavior that is above reproach or suspicion. We believe that often the perception of a situation can be critical to how it is viewed by others. We want our suppliers to be aware of how actions relating to purchasing can sometimes be perceived. If actions can be perceived by others as wrong, then they may be wrong. The perception often should prohibit the action. If the outside world can perceive behavior as unethical, then it should be avoided. Raytheon Material Management remains committed to open discussions with our suppliers regarding questions about the guidelines we have established. If you are not satisfied with these discussions, Raytheon has also established an Ethics Compliance Office which is available not only to our employees, but to our suppliers also.

Raytheon's goal has been to establish a reputation in the marketplace that meets the highest standards of ethical conduct. We want to protect this reputation for both Raytheon and our suppliers.

and involvement between the buyer and suppliers that in any way diminish, or appear to diminish, this process should be avoided. This precludes any equity or financial dealings between buyer and supplier, and in most cases precludes or discourages the forming of close personal relationships between buyer and supplier personnel if they give the impression of diminishing the chances of fair and vigorous competition. The standards that buyers must maintain are not easy in today's marketplace, and they mandate conduct that is above reproach. The famous American folk humorist and philosopher Will Rogers defined conduct that might be acceptable: "So live that you would not mind selling your parrot to the town gossip."

Renewed attention to ethical compliance has resulted in a recognition of the importance of published written guidelines. These define the expected conduct and behavior of not only purchasing professionals but all those individuals in the organization who may in some fashion influence the buying process informally or indirectly. Written guidelines are needed for all these individuals so that proper standards of conduct are adhered to by all. There are a number of topics that should be addressed in such guidelines—conflicts of interest, reciprocity, sharp practices, bribery, personal purchases, gift giving and receiving, lunches, tickets, dinners, entertainment, kickbacks, personal discounts, legal obligations, and individual responsibilities.

Figure 17–2 is an example of a modern statement on "Standards of Ethical Conduct for Supplier Relationships." This type of booklet is provided to all affected employees by the Raytheon Company. Employers should consider the need for promulgating similar guideline booklets in their own organizations. Many organizations have also adopted the practice of issuing an annual holiday season letter to suppliers to ensure that sound ethical conduct is maintained during this period. Box 17–1 is an example of such a letter issued by M/A-COM, Inc.

Purchasing professionals are in a position to spend and commit company funds or to influence the spending of company funds. The individuals who sell to companies obviously try to influence the buyers favorably to get preference for the selling firms. There are immense pressures on the sales representatives to accomplish their selling objectives. The buyers, who are the tempting targets of this process, are also under immense pressures. It follows that the seller will study the other party carefully in order to determine which of the many things he or she might do would have the greatest probability of success. If the sales representative concludes that a gift or a particular entertainment would greatly

F I G U R E   17–2

Raytheon Company booklet, "Standards of Ethical Conduct for Supplier Relationships." (Reprinted with the permission of the Raytheon Company.)

Standards of
Business Ethics & Conduct

Raytheon

Standards of Ethical Conduct for Supplier Relationships

You re Involved ...

F I G U R E   17–2

Continued

You're a Tempting Target

If you're in a position to spend company money, or to influence spending, you're a tempting target. People who sell to us may try to influence you to give preference to their materials or services.

Raytheon expects you to resist when anyone tries to ply you with gifts or favors. You must always base your buying decisions on competitive price, quality and delivery. The Company expects you to have friendly relations with suppliers. At the same time, you need to be open, honest, businesslike and completely ethical.

The rights of Raytheon customers and shareholders rest on your ethical practice in your relations with suppliers. This brochure points out the main elements of the standards of conduct the Company expects of you. The fine points are spelled out in a series of policies listed at the back of this booklet.

Raytheon has a reputation of integrity to uphold. And so do you.

FIGURE   17-2

Continued

F I G U R E   17–2

Continued

How You Can Be Involved

There are a number of positions within the Company in which you can become involved in purchasing situations. Here are some of them:

- You're a buyer who purchases components from a distributor on a frequent basis. You can decide who gets the business. You're a target for influence. *You're involved.*

- You're a subcontract administrator who selects the names of potential suppliers for Requests for Quotation. These suppliers are given a chance to bid on Raytheon's requirements. *You're involved.*

- You're a quality assurance engineer who surveys potential new suppliers to the Company. Your reports become the basis for approval or disapproval status on qualified supplier lists. *You're involved.*

- You're a manager who knows certain key suppliers bidding for the department's material needs. What you say to the Raytheon buyer will strongly influence the selection of a particular supplier. *You're involved.*

- You're a facilities or manufacturing engineer working on the design of tooling for a highly automated production line. *You're involved.*

When you're involved, you must follow the highest standards of ethical conduct. If you should fail to do so and violate company policy, Raytheon will discipline you appropriately. You can be fired and you can be referred for criminal prosecution.

F I G U R E   17–2

Continued

Your Buying Guidelines

Your Relationship With Suppliers

When you negotiate with suppliers, you must base all prices, terms, conditions and agreements on sound business judgement.

You must show no favoritism or preference to anyone at the expense of the Company.

You must do no one any favors.
> NOR CAN YOU ACCEPT ANY FAVORS.

To accept kickbacks is a crime – both morally and legally. It is the fastest way to find yourself out of Raytheon.

Gifts, free services, discounts on personal purchases – these are also wrong, whether they are for you or for anyone else in your family or household. So are trips, entertainment or special consid-erations of any kind – *no matter whether you solicit these favors or not.*

You must decline favors and return gifts. Do it pleasantly and diplomatically, but firmly.

The Little Kindnesses

Your relations with suppliers should be friendly. Totally objective – but friendly. You and your suppliers are not adversaries. You have to work together to meet the Company's material needs.

It's perfectly okay to exchange the small courtesies, pleasantries and kindnesses that are normal between people working together. They help keep simple humanity in our business dealings. You should apply common sense to your purchasing relationships.

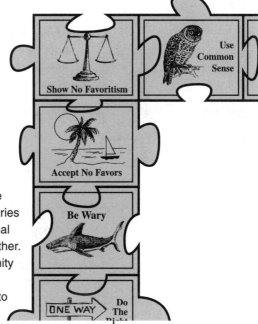

FIGURE 17–2

Continued

Suppose a supplier sitting beside your desk offers you one of his company's pencils. Do you have to turn it down? Of course not. You won't be influenced in your decisions by a pencil.

Then where do you draw the line? Right here:

You must refuse anything – gift, service or consideration – other than an advertising novelty such as a paperweight, key chain or coffee cup. Even then, if it has an apparent value of $10 or more, it is not acceptable. The best rule to follow is, "When in doubt, refuse the gift or send it back."

What about luncheons with suppliers? Maybe. If there's a legitimate business purpose for that get-together. But don't make it a habit. And use company facilities whenever possible. We don't encourage outside business lunches.
Go only when you think it's necessary.
Do you have to fight the supplier for the check? No. But take turns paying for luncheons, particularly when you're on home ground.

What about dinners and other forms of evening or weekend entertainment? These are almost always prohibited. There might be a special situation where you should make an exception. If so, ask your manager for approval in advance.

F I G U R E   17-2

Continued

Conflicts of Interest

You must not allow any conflict of interest between your personal affairs and your business at Raytheon.

This means you may not have a financial interest, position or relationship with any firm or corporation that does business with the Company that would influence, or could be regarded as influencing, your actions for the Company.

This applies also to your wife, husband, child or any relative who resides in your home. Any significant financial interest in their name is a conflict under yours.

If you have a situation which you are not sure is a conflict of interest, talk with your manager about it as soon as you can.

Confidential Information

A part of your ethical behavior is to keep confidential business information confidential. This applies both to proprietary Raytheon information and to confidential information offered to you by suppliers.

Raytheon information that you must keep confidential includes:

- Patentable and secret processes
- Production schedules
- Product information
- Prices
- Any other proprietary information.

Suppliers often must divulge to you information that is proprietary to their business. You must respect these confi- dences, both for the supplier's sake and, in the long run, for Raytheon's sake, too.

F I G U R E   17–2

Continued

Laws and Regulations

Raytheon observes all
laws and regulations that
apply to purchasing – in a
locality, in a state, in a
country. Normally, your
manager will keep you
informed about them. If not, or if you
have any question about the legality or
propriety of a course of action, check
with your manager or the appropriate
Raytheon attorney.

U.S. Government Business Anti Kickback Act

When government business is involved, you are bound by the Anti
Kickback Act. Accepting *anything of alue* for favorable treatment of
a supplier in connection with a buy is a kickback. A kickback is a
federal crime carrying severe penalties for all parties involved.

F I G U R E   17–2

Continued

Your Obligations

If you are a buyer, or if you influence buying, you must recognize your obligation to rise above all the pressures of being a tempting target for suppliers.

If any action relating to purchasing can be perceived by others as wrong, then it really is wrong. The perception itself prohibits the action. If the outside world can perceive your behavior as unethical, then you should avoid it.

Remember, if you have any inkling that one of your actions, or the actions of others around you, might be unethical, do something about it. Take it up with your supervisor. If you still are not satisfied, you may consult with the Ethics Compliance Office.

If you are a supplier, Raytheon wants you to comply with the guidelines in this booklet. If you, as a supplier, know of unethical conduct, consult with the appropriate Procurement Manager, or consult with the Ethics Compliance Office if necessary.

ETHICS Compliance Office
Post Office Box 21
Concord, MA 01742

1-800-334-3091 From Massachusetts
1-800-423-0210 Outside Massachusetts

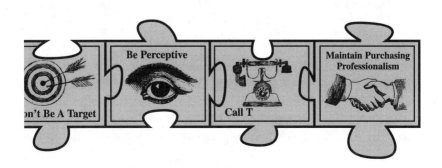

enhance his or her prospects, there is an incentive to offer a gift or entertainment to the buyer, engineer, supervisor, or anyone perceived to have an influence on the buying decision. The intended recipients may send out subtle signals regarding their attitudes toward such gifts and favors. The experienced salesperson can read buyers reasonably well and seldom makes an offer that is received as offensive. Purchasing professionals must resist any unethical attempts to influence the buying process and should conduct the buying process in an open, honest, businesslike, and ethical fashion.

There is a direct correlation between the example set by and actions of management and the frequency with which gifts and favors are involved in an organization. Simply stated, management has a responsibility to set the tone and to cultivate an environment in which sound ethical practices exist.

Purchasing professionals who follow the three simple rules set forth below will not likely fall into trouble over matters of gifts or entertainment.

1. *Keep job and private life totally separated.* The buyer (or any other employee) should never use his or her position of influence over suppliers for personal gain or to enhance his or her standard of living.

2. *Keep relationships with suppliers in balance.* Some employers prohibit their buyers from accepting even the simpler social interchanges, such as lunch at supplier expense. Some, however, recognize that there are social amenities between seller and buyer personnel that are useful, and they insist that the buyer be the host when the occasion warrants it.

3. *When in doubt, ask management.* It is now common to talk openly about ethical questions that arise in business. More and more, firms and institutions are telling their employees to ask their superiors for guidance on ethical matters, exactly as they would ask for guidance on technical, commercial, legal, or other matters.

It is clear that the buyer is subjected to more frequent and probably greater ethical hazards and temptations than are persons in most other occupations. It is equally clear that the means are available for dealing effectively with these hazards. NAPM offers strong guidance in this regard, and its ethical standards committee is available to anyone in the

B O X   17–1

STANDARD HOLIDAY SEASON ETHICS SUPPLIER LETTER[2]
M/A-COM, INC.
SOUTH AVENUE
BURLINGTON, MASSACHUSETTS 01803
(617) 272-3000
TWX-710-332-6789 * -TELEX 94-9464

December,

TO OUR SUPPLIERS:

With the Holiday Season upon us, we want to take this opportunity to acknowledge with gratitude your support and cooperation which have greatly contributed to our success during the past year.

In the course of doing business, it is quite natural that we have developed close relationships with many of our suppliers. This may lead to expressions of friendship in the form of gratuities. However, the integrity of a business relationship could be questioned, regardless of the degree of our relationship, if gratuities are offered.

Our policy at M/A-COM, INC. prohibits our employees from accepting or giving gratuities or hospitality of *any kind*. This includes use of property or facilities, gift certificates, or favors extended to employees or their families.

Your continued cooperation is requested on this matter in the interest of maintaining an ethical relationship essential to both of us. We would greatly appreciate your making certain that our policy is clear to those in your firm who have contact with employees of M/A-COM, INC. We all extend Holiday Greetings to everyone in your organization.

Sincerely,

M/A-COM, INC.
Microwave Associates
Materiel Department

---

2. Reprinted with the permission of M/A Com, Inc.

profession who wants specific counsel or wishes to learn how others have handled similar problems.

RECIPROCITY

Often considered a controversial issue, the topic of reciprocity embodies legal as well as ethical issues that are of paramount importance for the purchasing professional. Through adequate knowledge of the issues and the impacts, he or she can recognize and deal with the sometimes vague characteristics that constitute reciprocal transactions.

Recognizing and Avoiding the Potential for Reciprocity

Simply stated, reciprocity means the mutual giving or receiving of favors. Reciprocity further implies that the transaction is not only *quid pro quo*, but there must be equivalence in value, though not in kind. Stated in terms of purchasing transactions, reciprocity may take three distinct forms:

1. Favoring a specific customer in evaluating or selecting a supplier
2. Influencing a supplier to become a customer
3. Offering a specific commitment to buy, in exchange for a specific commitment to sell

Though some argue that reciprocity makes good business sense, it becomes an ethical issue when the transaction may be formed without proper evaluation of all factors that would ensure that it is the most cost-effective or optimal purchasing decision for the company. This concern should not preclude doing business with suppliers who are customers (or establishing customer relationships with suppliers). Dealing with a supplier who is a customer does not in and of itself constitute a problem if that supplier has been objectively evaluated to be the best source. However, *giving preference* to a supplier who is also a customer should be considered only when all other factors are equal. The professional purchaser must recognize that utilizing a supplier solely due to its customer status constitutes reciprocity. Reciprocity may be in evidence in a transaction regardless of the existence of a formal written commitment to buy or sell, if the intent is based solely on the customer relationship.

Potential to Restrain Trade

Reciprocity becomes a legal issue because of its potential to restrain trade. In the early 1930s, the Federal Trade Commission (FTC) ruled that it was illegal "to abusively use large buying power to restrict competitive market opportunities." In the early 1970s, many major companies entered into settlement agreements with the FTC that forbade reciprocal arrangements and required the elimination of trade relations departments, most of which were originally created to promote sales through purchasing power.

Example of a Letter Prohibiting Reciprocity

Some companies have taken the position that the federal antitrust laws prohibit reciprocal buying and selling and have issued policies prohibiting its practice. Their position has been upheld by the courts. The U.S. Department of Justice and the FTC have been active in searching out and prosecuting violators where restraints of trade are identified. In the late 1960s the Bendix Corporation issued the following letter to all its officers, divisional general managers, sales and marketing managers, purchasing managers, and attorneys. This letter, even today, effectively states the issues involved.[3]

> Attached are notices received from two corporations advising us that they are now under court orders which prohibit reciprocal buying or selling arrangements. By receipt of these notices, Bendix is obliged not to engage in such reciprocal buying or selling arrangements with these particular companies. But we are also under an obligation to refrain from such activities with all of our customers and suppliers in any event. As you know, under the antitrust policy statement promulgated by our Chairman on January 15, 1969, "I will buy from you if you will buy from me," or similar sales arrangements are absolutely prohibited. All purchases and sales by Bendix are to be made solely on the basis of price, quality, service and similar considerations, without regard to the status of the supplier or customer as an actual or potential supplier or customer of Bendix. If these simple principles are applied to your purchase and sales arrangements, we will not become involved in any unlawful reciprocal dealing practice, including any of the arrangements referred to in the attached notices. If you have any questions about any specific sales or purchase agreements or

---

3. Reprinted with permission of the Bendix Corporation.

proposed agreement, you should immediately call the facts to the attention of the Legal Department.

Example of a Reciprocity Position Statement—Service Organization

Service organizations may frequently be confronted with requests or pressure from customers (or in some cases their own employees or management) to develop supplier relationships with their customers.

The position statement below was developed by a financial institution and clarifies for both customers and management the rationale for avoiding reciprocal arrangements. This statement can be adapted to meet the needs of other service organizations, as well as manufacturing firms:

> Our corporation supports a healthy competitive environment for fulfilling our operational needs. Customers are welcome to solicit business, but their customer relationship may become an issue in supplier selection *only* if all other factors are equal.
>
> Potential suppliers who are customers should be reminded, if necessary, that we must make our supplier selections considering optimum price, terms, quality, etc., just as they have selected their banking relationships based on optimum terms and service. The two issues should remain separate.
>
> In order to offer our customers competitive rates and services, it is incumbent upon us to keep our operating costs as low as possible. Effective purchasing practices are one of the many issues which play a role in such costs.
>
> Our corporation believes in courtesy and fair dealing in carrying out our purchasing functions. Every effort is made to perform in both an ethical and a legal manner to support our corporate needs, while supporting the communities we serve.

Clearly, the professional purchaser's role must be one of vigilance in opposing any company commitment that may constitute reciprocity. Legal counsel should be sought if any questions exist regarding the propriety of a potential transaction.

PERSONAL PURCHASES FOR EMPLOYEES

The utilization of personal purchase programs from suppliers, as well as employer-sponsored discount programs, has been discouraged by many purchasing professionals. In some states, laws known as "trade diversion laws" prohibit these practices. Where laws do not prohibit such activities, ethical considerations should prevail.

Trade Diversion Laws

Trade diversion laws make it illegal to sell to employees any materials not manufactured by the employer or handled in the normal course of trade. Exemptions normally include meals, cigarettes, and other items sold through vending machines, as well as articles required for the health and safety of an employee, such as uniforms, safety equipment, and special tools. In these cases where the articles are necessary to operations but not furnished as a condition of employment, purchasing these items and supplying them to the employee (at cost or subsidized by the employer) allows the employer more control over critical elements of the operation.

Illinois, Ohio, Michigan, Minnesota, Pennsylvania, and Wisconsin have stringent trade diversion laws that prohibit a company from selling to its employees any item that it does not usually procure or otherwise handle. It is possible that other states may pass such laws in the future. The Illinois statute typifies this type of law:

> No person, firm, or corporation engaged in any business enterprise in this state shall, by any method or procedure, directly or indirectly, by itself or through a subsidiary agency owned or controlled in whole or in part by such person, firm or corporation, sell or procure for sale or have in its possession or under its control for sale to its employees or any person, any article, material, product or merchandise of whatsoever nature not of his or its own production or not handled in his or its regular course of trade.

Similar prohibitions relating to such sales by state agencies, municipalities, or other local subdivisions are also included in the statute.

Ethical Considerations

The purchasing *function* exists to support the materials requirements of the firm. A purchasing *professional's* primary responsibility is to support the long-term interests of the firm. Utilizing purchasing staff time to develop and administer a personal purchases program detracts from the group's primary responsibility to the employer. Individual personal purchases create perhaps an even greater ethical dilemma, since preferential treatment is involved. Such purchases may also be deceptive if a supplier is expected to provide price and terms for a single purchase comparable with those negotiated on the basis of the employer's volume buying. It is inappropriate to expect such concessions on the part of a supplier that typically cannot recover all costs associated with processing, delivering, and invoicing a single order.

If Management Wants to Establish a Personal Purchases Program

In spite of these issues, management may choose to establish a personal purchases program for its employees. In this case, the responsible purchasing manager has the responsibility to ensure that the program is handled in an ethical manner and that it is legal.

First, legal counsel should be consulted to verify that local laws do in fact allow such programs. Then all suppliers considered for such programs should be made fully aware that the purchases will be for individual employees rather than for the firm's use. Requirements for special invoicing, delivery, and other unique aspects of the purchase should be made clear to the supplier.

If such programs are to exist, they must be equally available to all employees. At the same time, the existence of such special purchasing programs must not interfere with the objective evaluation of each supplier's ability to support the firm's operating requirements for materials and services.

INTERNATIONAL BUYING ETHICS

What Is International Purchasing?

The word "international" means literally "between nations." So it should follow that "international purchasing" is defined as purchasing transactions conducted between parties located in different nations. However, the reality of international purchasing is much more complex. Typically, it involves a seller in one country and a buyer in another. But as the "global village" emerges, more and more often it includes a buyer in one country purchasing from a seller in another, with production in possibly a third and consumption or assembly in possibly a fourth or fifth country. This linkage can be especially complex in high-value, high-technology fields such as electronics, medical equipment, and drugs. Buyers for the end product can face a bewildering array of ethical cultures as they attempt to manage their supply chain all the way back to Mother Earth.

For the purpose of this section, international purchasing is defined as a purchase that may involve ethical considerations from any culture or country other than that of the buyer in question.

What Are International Ethics?

When you are impacted by the ethics of a culture not identical to your own, it is essential to have in mind a process that will minimize the likelihood of the development of ethical problems. For this purpose, "international ethics" are defined as those values or guidelines that, if observed, will be most likely to keep the buyer out of ethical trouble in *any* of the cultures involved in *a* given transaction.

How Do They Differ from U.S. Ethics?

Some American academicians and moral theoreticians have argued that there *should be* no difference. But these people are not required to support complex manufacturing networks or move goods over international boundaries. And it is rather arrogant to argue that all people in the world should abide by U.S. standards before we will deign to trade with them.

So it seems necessary to admit that there *are* differences in ethical standards around the world, without precommiting our countrymen and women to violating our own values when dealing abroad. And it also seems necessary to recognize that the differences arise because not all our trading partners follow business practices shaped by the Judeo-Christian tradition from which U.S. values and standards have evolved. This can lead to direct conflict between these differing values in some circumstances.

Some Guidelines for Staying Out of Trouble

The principal guideline for any buyer from any country dealing outside his or her own culture is to take care to behave in that foreign culture in a way that is acceptable, *for those circumstances,* to home-country management. There is no absolute formula or standard that will apply to the many variations on the theme. Picture, for example, the impossibility of writing a detailed ethical code of conduct for a U.S. purchasing manager responsible for a buyer located in Singapore who is buying components from Japan for subassembly in Kuala Lumpur, final assembly in Hong Kong, and shipment to the world. This scenario is occurring today and will occur more frequently in the future.

The practical guideline for the real world, then, is to bend to the local custom as far as is possible while still being comfortable that the actions to be taken will be seen as proper, upright, fair, fitting, and correct for that situation by home-country management. There is some limit to how far home-country standards (Judeo-Christian or otherwise) should bend when in conflict with foreign standards. There are some deals that *should not* be done, and this process will help a buyer or manager separate them from those that should be done.

To put it in simple terms, it is helpful to start with a clear and visible code of ethical conduct for the home country. This is useful because:

+ Experience shows that visible codes of conduct make a difference in behavior in your own firm. (Chief executive officers (CEOs) generally *do* enforce them when necessary.)
+ They tend to result in reduced temptations put on the firm's employees. (Trading partners and salespeople typically respond to the message.)
+ They produce a more open ethical climate. (The boss is approachable.)
+ They tend to result in lowered internal pressure on the buyer to do unacceptable things. (Sales, manufacturing, engineering, etc. *do* notice.)

With a home-country code of ethics in place, it is then only necessary to:

+ Find out what the local business practices are and how they differ from your own; get local help on this if necessary.
+ Bend to those customs as far as possible without discomfort when necessary to conduct your business.

Seek guidance from your home-country management when you feel discomfort. Combined wisdom is almost always superior to individual judgment in gray areas, and you should expect ethical guidance every bit as much as you expect legal, technical, or business plan guidance.

Talk about it, talk about it, talk about it. Intelligence is in knowing what to do in the ultimate, but wisdom is in knowing what to do *next*. Wisdom comes only from experience, so share that experience and expect others to share theirs, for the common good.

FEDERAL, STATE, AND LOCAL GOVERNMENT ETHICS

Past events in government-related procurement have produced two trends. The first, caused by a series of revelations of possible improper conduct, or at least possible excess payments for purchases, has generated more stringent regulation of purchasing action, thereby constraining government buyers even more. The second, in contrast, is a challenging of the necessity of these stringent requirements. One example is the inquiry concerning whether the concept of sealed bids is fully useful, or whether more negotiated purchasing would lead to better selection of suppliers.

As one well-recognized government purchasing expert has observed:

> [I]mplicit to government procurement practices are three premises. They are specifically addressed by procurement laws, and vigorously enforced through procurement regulations. These premises are:
>
> 1. In awarding government business, every effort must be made to prevent favoritism, collusion, and fraud.
> 2. In soliciting bids for government business, the government must provide the widest opportunity for would-be suppliers to compete.
> 3. In determining sources and prices, the government should employ the workings of "free and open" competition.
>
> Now these are all desirable objectives, and in a democratic society they understandably will be reflected in related legislation. But when the procurement process is employed to pursue these objectives *without judgment or qualification,* primary procurement objectives usually suffer.
>
> Further, when the government imposes these requirements on prime contractors and subcontractors, the results can be disastrous. Sixty to seventy-five percent of every dollar expended by the government with its prime contractors is in turn expended by them with subcontractors. And the principle of survival for all is to play it safe and "buy by the book."

Unfortunately, buying by the book stifles judgment and initiative and inhibits innovation and creativity.[4]

However, until these issues are resolved—and even after the trend is clarified—procurement actions under government-funded contracts should be conducted in a manner above reproach and with complete impartiality. Transactions involving government funds require the highest degree of trust and standards of conduct. In this regard:

- Buyers should avoid any action or circumstances—such as a gratuity (a payment or gift to obtain favorable treatment or influence the award of an order), a kickback (a payment for the award of an order), a family relationship, or a financial interest—that might conflict with the proper performance of their duties or compromise the company's acquisition process.
- Employees should not solicit or accept, directly or indirectly, any gift, favor, entertainment, loan, or anything of monetary value from anyone who is seeking to obtain business from the organization.
- Buyers should, at all times, conduct themselves in a manner that maintains trust and confidence in the integrity of the organization's procurement process.

DEALING WITH EHTICAL PROBLEMS

What Constitutes an Ethical Hazard?

The underlying ethical hazard for all purchasing professionals is the ever-present possibility of a conflict between the personal interest of the purchasing professional and the interest of the employer and its aggregate stockholders. More than in any other discipline, the very responsibilities and decisions inherent in selecting suppliers and negotiating agreements covering investments, specifications, division of effort, division of responsibility, pricing, and terms put a buyer distinctly at risk of entanglement in a conflict-of-interest situation.

In these potentially hazardous circumstances, ethical behavior is generally defined as that which would be seen as proper, straightforward, fair, fitting, and correct by competent, professional peers equally

---

4. Adapted from Louis J. De Rose, "The Problem in Government Procurement," *Purchasing World*, April 1989, pp. 35–38.

informed. Unethical behavior, then, is any behavior that competent and equally informed professional peers would reject as improper, deceptive, unfair, inappropriate, or wrong. Any activity that brings advantage, however slight, to the individual buyer while bringing disadvantage, however slight, to the employer can be seen clearly to be unethical by this definition. It is the occurrence of such behavior that constitutes an ethical problem. An ethical *dilemma* exists whenever management allows conditions to exist that increase the likelihood of such behavior. An ethical *problem* exists when such behavior occurs or is reasonably suspected to have occurred. We deal here with the latter.

Who Must Deal with It?

An ethical purchasing problem must be dealt with quickly by the immediate supervisor of the offending party. He or she may draw on the resources of upper purchasing management, internal auditing, security, and others, but the immediate supervisor is in the best position to interpret whether the behavior ultimately uncovered is proper, straightforward, fair, fitting, and correct within the context in which it occurred. And if the supervisor has any doubts, the judgment should move up the chain of command until it finds a place where the issue can be firmly resolved. It is a derogation of duty and a shirking of responsibility to expect this kind of judgment to be made by anyone outside the direct chain of command of the possible offender—all the way to the CEO, if necessary—for in reality that is where the final ethical tone must be set.

How to Deal with the Problem Itself

During the investigation and judgment, deal with the problem *carefully!* It is first essential to gather sufficient hard facts to establish a conclusion that the behavior in question is either acceptable or unacceptable beyond any reasonable doubt. Like a petit jury, the supervisor is responsible for determining what really happened and whether the action constitutes acceptable or unacceptable behavior. Unlike a petit jury, the supervisor cannot rely on a narrow and specific interpretation of a given statute for separating acceptable from unacceptable. Instead, there probably exists a company code of ethics, or something similar, plus the judgments of line management regarding what is proper, straightforward, fair, fitting, and correct. And there is also the *Principles and Standards of Purchasing*

Practice with Accompanying Guidelines of NAPM, which may well offer additional information if needed.

Getting the facts is not necessarily easier than making the judgment, but there are far more resources available to help in doing it. Internal auditing, and in some cases the organization's own legal counsel, are usually the best first contacts and should be seen always as the purchasing manager's friends. They might suggest the use of outside investigators, IRS agents, postal authorities, and others with the resources and authority to bring facts to bear that could not otherwise be available.

Bear in mind during the investigation that an individual's livelihood hangs in the balance, and care should be taken not to damage any reputations, even by inference, in the process. It is equally important, however, to move vigorously and expeditiously to a judgment one way or the other. When you are satisfied that all the facts that are reasonably discernible have been obtained, a judgment should be made that the behavior as now understood has been either acceptable or unacceptable. This is a "go/no go" condition; do not equivocate.

How to Deal with the Implications of the Problem

If the supervisor's judgment, supported up the management chain as far as necessary, is that the behavior found was totally acceptable, all parties to the investigation should be informed and the case closed. In most situations, it is wise at this point to tell the individual of the investigation and its results, although this is a judgment call for management to make as it closes out the investigation.

If the supervisor's judgment, supported up the management chain of command as far as necessary (including, when appropriate, review by legal counsel), is that the behavior found was not acceptable, the appropriate disciplinary action must be determined and approved by that same management chain. This can range from a reprimand at one extreme to dismissal with prejudice and even civil court action to recover any demonstrated damages to stockholders' interests at the other.

The underlying process for finishing the job does not vary with the severity of the penalty.

1. The individual(s) in question must be told of the investigation, its conclusions, and the disciplinary action decided upon.
2. The individual(s) must be given a chance to see and challenge the evidence on which the judgment was based.

3. Unless the individual presents new evidence or otherwise causes management to review its decision, the disciplinary action should be taken promptly and in a manner that closes the case.

4. It is usually wise to inform all persons in roles similar to that of the individual being disciplined precisely what was found and what is being done about it. Unacceptable behavior occurred, and it is especially important to reinforce the firm's ethical code at this time by making clear the manner in which management interprets and implements that code. To hide the facts at this point is to forego any positive value the incident may hold.

Summary

Any behavior by purchasing personnel that is perceived to be, or is suspected to be, in conflict with the best interests of the organization and its owners presents purchasing management with an ethical problem. The best course is to treat the matter seriously and promptly, using every available service to determine the real facts of the matter. Should the facts lead management to conclude that unacceptable behavior has occurred, the individual(s) should be shown those facts and allowed the due-process opportunity to defend himself or herself. Should the management judgment still be that unacceptable behavior has occurred, appropriate disciplinary action should be taken promptly. And this disciplinary action, along with the facts leading to it, should normally be communicated to everyone in the organization who might be tempted to behave in a similar, unacceptable manner. Only through this therapeutic effort has management sufficiently discharged its fiduciary responsibility to stockholders to do everything within reason to ensure that such unacceptable behavior is not repeated by others in the future.

NAPM STANDARDS AND GUIDELINES

The National Association of Purchasing Management, through its Ethical Standards Committee, has published a document entitled *Principles and Standards of Purchasing Practice with Accompanying Guidelines*. This document is available by contacting NAPM. All purchasing professionals

B O X   17–2

NATIONAL ASSOCIATION OF PURCHASING MANAGEMENT

LOYALTY TO YOUR COMPANY
JUSTICE TO THOSE WITH WHOM YOU DEAL
FAITH IN YOUR PROFESSION

From these principles are derived the NAPM standards of purchasing practice. (Domestic and International)

1. Avoid the intent and appearance of unethical or compromising practice in relationships, actions, and communications.
2. Demonstrate loyalty to the employer by diligently following the lawful instructions of the employer, using reasonable care and only authority granted.
3. Refrain from any private business or professional activity that would create a conflict between personal interests and the interests of the employer.
4. Refrain from soliciting or accepting money, loans, credits, or prejudicial discounts, and the acceptance of gifts, entertainment, favors, or services from present or potential suppliers which might influence, or appear to influence, purchasing decisions.
5. Handle confidential or proprietary information belonging to employers and/or suppliers with due care and proper consideration of ethical and legal ramifications and governmental regulations.
6. Promote positive supplier relationships through courtesy and impartiality in all phases of the purchasing cycle.
7. Refrain from reciprocal agreements that restrain competition.
8. Know and obey the letter and spirit of laws governing the purchasing function and remain alert to the legal ramifications of purchasing decisions.
9. Encourage all segments of society to participate by demonstrating support for small, disadvantaged, and minority-owned businesses.
10. Discourage purchasing's involvement in employer sponsored programs of personal purchases which are not business related.
11. Enhance the proficiency and stature of the purchasing profession by acquiring and maintaining current technical knowledge and the highest standards of ethical behavior.
12. Conduct international purchasing in accordance with the laws, customs, and practices of foreign countries, consistent with United States laws, your organization policies and these Ethical Standards and Guidelines.

Adopted January 1992.

should utilize this document, having carefully read the preamble and the twelve standards with their explanatory guidelines.

ADDITIONAL READINGS

Augustine, N. *Augustine's Travels.* American Management Association.

Crowder, M. A., and D. D. Brown. "Ethical Integrity and the Supply Chain," *Purchasing Today®*, March 1997, pp. 37–40.

DeMente, B. *Japanese Etiquette and Ethics in Business,* 5th ed., NTC Business Books, Lincolnwood, Ill., 1988.

Ethics, Policies and Programs in American Business, Ethics Resource Center, Washington, D.C., 1990.

Harris, G. *Purchasing Policies,* Business Laws, Inc., Chesterland, Ohio, 1990.

Johannesen, R. L. *Ethics in Human Communications,* 3d ed., Waveland Press, Prospect Heights, Ill., 1990.

Killen, K. H., and R. L. Janson. "Ethical Practices in Purchasing." In Killen and Janson, *Purchasing Manager's Guide to Model Letters, Memos, and Forms,* ch. 18, Prentice Hall, Englewood Cliffs, N.J., 1991.

LeClair, D., O. Ferrell, and J. Fraedrich. *Integrity Management,* University of Tampa Press, Tampa, Fla., 1998.

Miller, J. "Written in Stone," *Purchasing Today®*, March 1997, pp. 32–35.

Principles and Standards of Purchasing Practice with Accompanying Guidelines. Ethical Standards Committee, National Association of Purchasing Management, Tempe, Ariz., 1991.

PART FOUR

Components and Capabilities

In this part of the handbook, various tools and techniques useful to purchasing and supply practitioners will be presented. These will encompass a wide variety of subject matter, ranging from total cost of ownership to the marketing of the purchasing and supply function. Purchasing and supply management today has available to it many technical and nontechnical approaches to performing its responsibilities. Some of these are somewhat sophisticated, e.g., supplier price and cost analysis, and have become practical for wide usage only due to the availability of personal computers. Others have been around for many years, e.g., purchasing and supply negotiations, but have become more refined and polished over time. Every professional purchaser who wants to perform his or her job at the top of the profession and with all the power of available tools and techniques needs to be aware of, and have some understanding of, these components and capabilities.

This part of the handbook is intended to introduce a number of these components and capabilities and provide some understanding of when and how they may be useful in purchasing and supply management situations. For those who desire additional information or training on any of the subjects in this part, NAPM and others have available in-depth seminars, books, and other resources.

CHAPTER 18

Electronic Opportunities and Electronic Commerce— New Technologies for Purchasing

Editor
James T. Parker, C.P.M.
Director of Purchasing
University of Utah

INTRODUCTION TO ELECTRONIC COMMERCE AND THE DIGITAL ECONOMY

The technological and electronic revolution of the last few decades has transformed the ways in which purchasers, suppliers, and other participants in the traditional supply chain interact. The terms *electronic revolution* and *information age* have been applied to designate the current era in the same way the *industrial revolution* described the dramatic changes in manufacturing and business processes of the 19th century. This new shift in business processes and the electronic integration of all global supply chain participants has resulted in advances that have essentially eliminated many of the delays and inefficiencies that plagued purchasers in the past. Measurable savings have resulted both within the purchasing arena and throughout the global marketplace. By incorporating the benefits of electronic commerce processes, purchasing and supply managers can spend their time on more strategic functions, such as sourcing new suppliers, developing effective negotiation strategies, doing market research, and performing value analysis.

Developments concerning the Internet and electronic commerce are moving at a rapid pace. While the latest information is provided at the time of this printing, practitioners should make every effort to keep updated concerning these emerging technologies as a matter of professional development.

This new digital economy, tied together by the Internet (the "Net"), also referred to as the World Wide Web (the "Web"), has changed the fundamentals of doing business. Physical location of business becomes of less importance. Speed, flexibility, and innovation have become as important as size and assets. Virtual products, services, and information are as valuable as physical assets. Quality has improved, costs have been reduced, and speed has increased. These changes have required continuous improvement and change of processes, discarding of outdated rules, and elimination outdated assumptions. Business is now capable of operating globally, 24 hours a day, seven days a week.

These changes have also made necessary purchaser–supplier contracts and partnerships that are increasingly complex. Some of even the smallest suppliers must adhere to new electronic methodologies to ensure their long–term viability and competitiveness. Purchasers will continue to demand supplier conformance to developing technological standards and capabilities. With different and sometimes competing needs, suppliers are challenged to both maintain technological competency and keep up with the increasingly divergent needs of their customers. Customers demand individual treatment, competition is keener, change is accelerating, and processes are more fragmented.

Electronic commerce, in whatever form, provides purchasers and supply managers with new and/or improved methodologies for:

+ Internal and external processes for meeting supply needs
+ Obtaining information
+ Sharpening communications
+ Broadening education
+ Finding new ways to identify and qualify sources
+ Adding value through improved strategic planning decisions
+ Providing new opportunities for organizations to remain competitive and innovative

DEFINITION AND DEVELOPMENT OF ELECTRONIC COMMERCE

"Electronic commerce" could be described as the integration of communications, data management, and security capabilities to allow business applications within different organizations to automatically exchange information related to the sale of goods, services, and information. This flow of data between and within organizations is accomplished with minimal human intervention.

The growth of electronic commerce has created challenges for purchasers and supply managers as it has provided opportunities. All industries have been changed by the rapid evolution of this technology. Forecasting and strategic planning are now absolute requirements of both purchasers and suppliers as new electronic commerce capabilities continue to accelerate. Competing standards, high initial costs and costs to constantly upgrade and maintain systems, users' inability to adapt rapidly or lack of technical knowledge, and market forces that drive products into the marketplace before they are ready all combine to create complexity with which it is difficult for supply chain participants to keep up. In spite of these challenges, purchasing and supply management is and will continue to be one of the greatest beneficiaries of improvements in electronic commerce. Box 18–1 describes some of the benefits of electronic commerce.

ELECTRONIC COMMERCE– METHODOLOGIES

Electronic Data Interchange (EDI)

Electronic data interchange, developed in the 1970s, is the exchange of well-defined business transactions in a computer-processable format. EDI

B O X   18–1

BENEFITS OF ELECTRONIC COMMERCE

The main benefits of using electronic commerce include:

♦ Reduced costs
♦ Elimination of paperwork
♦ Time savings and increased efficiencies
♦ Improved supplier management
♦ Enhanced service and quality
♦ Improved access and communication

provides a collection of standard message formats to exchange data between organizations' computers via a compatible electronic service. In 1979, the American National Standards Institute (ANSI) developed a set of uniform national standards for the electronic interchange of certain types of business transactions. These transactions included traditional business processes such as inquiries, purchasing, shipping and receiving, invoices, payments, acknowledgements, scheduling, pricing, reporting, scheduling, and order status. Additional standards cover interchange of data relating to security, administrative data, specifications, contracts, production data, distribution, and sales activities.

EDI allows two or more businesses to exchange information through direct and secure communications links. The term *value added network* (VAN) has been used to describe the private communications conduit for EDI when more than two parties are partnered for electronic transactions. For instance, a buyer and seller may be jointly linked to a financial institution to enable the electronic payment of invoices, eliminating the need for physical invoices and checks. Electronic funds can be exchanged via the standard formats understood by each entity. In a multiple VAN arrangement, suppliers, customers, shippers, warehouses, and other supply chain participants can exchange orders, acknowledgements, status reports, bills of lading, and other documents in a timely and secure manner without generating paper documents. Figure 18–1 depicts the traditional EDI process.

EDI Over the Internet

EDI requires a complex set of standard tools, protocols, and communications conduits to enable businesses to interact electronically. Traditionally, establishing EDI partnerships has required extensive development and high costs to individual businesses. For this reason, most of the organizations that have participated in EDI have been large. Because of sunk investments in infrastructure and other resources, and the known reliability of VANs, many businesses have been slow to abandon traditional EDI technology in favor of emerging electronic commerce technologies on the Net.

Recent improvements in format translation software and Net security and speed have enabled smaller companies to begin using EDI for a fraction of the cost previously required. "WebEDI" is the term that has been used to describe the process used by conversion programs that bridge the traditional EDI data requirements with Internet and World

F I G U R E   18–1

Seller–Buyer Transactions

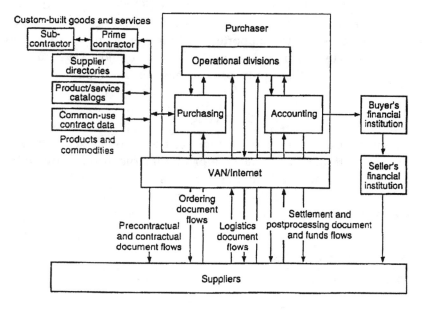

Wide Web solutions. At one time adding an EDI partner cost $50,000; it can now cost as little as $1,000.

In 1998, businesses used EDI transactions to exchange $250 billion in products. This figure is 14 times larger than the value of business-to-business net commerce for the same year. The Gartner Group has estimated that by 2003, the value of Net transactions and EDI transactions will each represent $450 billion annually. By the year 2003, approximately 30% of EDI data will transverse the Net.

Currently, businesses can transmit EDI data over the Net in two ways: by File Transfer Protocol (FTP) and by Simple Mail Transfer Protocol (SMTP) or e-mail. A new standard of Net protocols will replace these two methods and may result in the demise of EDI. Designated eXtensible Markup Language (XML) by the Internet standards committees and consortiums,[1] this language will enable common recognition of

---

1. Industry has a great interest in the development of Internet Standards for EDI groups such as the CommerceNet Consortium. Leading banks, telecommunications companies, VANs, software and equipment companies, and major end users are included in making these decisions.

data (such as prices) on Web pages and enable live documents (such as purchase orders and invoices) to be transmitted between businesses. Figure 18–2 depicts EDI transactions via the Net. Other efforts to develop and implement Internet commerce standards include Open Buying on the Internet. This effort is supported by a number of large corporations with the objective to provide a relatively simple and secure buying/selling environment that can be used by most organizations.

Extranets

An even less expensive alternative for businesses to interact with other businesses is through an extranet, a private Internet-based network between an organization and its close partners, suppliers, and customers. The common interface of a Web browser enables all users to view the same information in a graphical format. These networks allow two or

F I G U R E   18–2

Possible Internet–Business Application

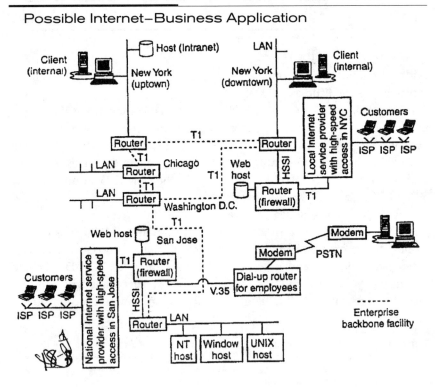

more firms to engage in business processes by utilizing the lower infrastructure costs associated with the Internet and the flexibility of common browser software protocols.

Internal Digital Technologies

The traditional internal computing model in business prior to the mid-1980s involved centralized application programs running on mainframe computers or in some cases "mini"-computers, linked to individual users by dummy terminals. All processing of transactions was done by the mainframe. As the capacity and speed of personal computers increased, it became possible to move routine tasks to smaller desktop computers. Eventually, personal computers were linked and common tasks could be shared between and among these smaller computers. These *local area networks* (LANs) enabled users to exchange messages and information, greatly increasing the productivity of the business unit. LANs enable sharing of common software, printers, and servers and simplify programming requirements.

The term *wide area networks* (WANs) describes the backbone in many businesses that provides connectivity between mainframes, PCs, workstations, LANs, VANs, and other computing and telecommunications devices within an organization. The integration of all these components in a way that enables the secure and logical processing of business information is termed a *rules-based business management system*. The design of processes that manage routine transactions, define limits, and determine exceptions electronically becomes possible when such a rules-based system is established. This automation of workflow processes enables electronic forms processing, remote approval, digital capture of information, high-level reporting, and elimination of redundant and paper-intensive processing.

Intranets

An intranet is "a private or organizational Internet." The intranet revolution began taking off during 1996—the term didn't even exist until the mid-1990s. The development of sophisticated Internet protocols (connectivity tools) enabled an industry of suppliers promoting intranet software and development to evolve over a period of a few months. Intranets efficiently link internal hardware and software in much the same way that these links are enabled on the Internet, providing organizations with common links to legacy systems, data warehouses, LANs, and cross-platform (MACs, PCs, UNIX, etc.) clients at a much lower cost than has ever been possible. The software and related tools manage and filter data from diverse sources, route queries to databases and other servers, and support multiple-client broadcasts throughout the internal system at high speeds. Because intranets are internal to one company or organization, well-designed intranets have more speed, security, and control than the Internet and minimize resultant problems often encountered on the Internet.

Some benefits of intranets include:

1. They are a relatively secure method for organizations to move their business processes on-line by providing a common interface and communications environment.

2. Data can be input without the user having to be concerned about where the information resides.

3. Reports can be generated that are more complete and timely because data is provided from the entire organization, not just the user's department.

4. Information can be made available to employees of the organization at the same time it is made available to the public. This is especially important for organizations that need to make last-minute changes to product designs.

5. Many internal processes can become paperless. Intranets can enable conversion of many paper-intensive purchasing and supply management processes to paperless ones. Material requisitioning, ordering, releasing, receiving, contract storage and retrieval, and contract management are just a few examples. Many of the functions replaced by these technologies required a great deal of paper, storage space, and manual retrieval time. Another area of application has been human resource processes such as providing benefit information, requesting services, recording changes, and providing status reports.

6. Training via an intranet can reduce traditional training costs significantly. Information can be speedily downloaded and distributed for student use, and classroom training time can be minimized.

7. Internal work coordination between departments can be facilitated, including more timely sharing of information and work documents.

8. Installing an intranet has proven to be much less costly and faster than previous connectivity methods and enables many more features, such as browsing and posting information requests. Advanced software and programming tools allow for the development of complex processes without the line-by-line code delays common with legacy systems.

9. Tools that can bring organization newscasts to internal customers on screen savers are available. Termed *push* or *broadcast* technologies, these advancements provide for real-time communications within the organization.

APPROACHES TO SAFE ELECTRONIC COMMERCE

At this time some of the greatest limitations faced by businesses planning to invest in electronic commerce and contemplating moving mission-critical applications to this approach are the issues of security, privacy, and reliability. When the Internet was conceived and developed during the 1970s and 1980s, it was intended as an open conduit for research and military communications purposes. The extent of its growth and use was never contemplated. With the advent of browsers and graphical user interfaces (color, pictures, and graphics) the use of the Internet and the World Wide Web exploded. The Internet is largely unregulated, and standards are continually evolving as new technologies emerge. The burden of security and information integrity lies with the user's system. For companies doing business over the Internet, security is one of the most critical issues. Businesses must be able to prove to suppliers and customers that transactions are safe, secure, and private.

Security Requirements

1. Security of file/information transfers, including secure transactions

2. Security of information stored on Internet-connected hosts

3. Secure enterprise networks, when used to support Web commerce

Security Problems

The problems associated with Internet security are very real, large, and complex and are major factors impeding electronic commerce. The potential for attack on individual sites as well as the entire information infrastructure is recognized as the Achilles heel of cyberspace. For instance, several years ago hackers broke into the Department of Justice home page and changed the name of the page to the "Department of Injustice." The damage was quickly fixed, but the public relations effect was difficult to mitigate. In 1995, 160,000 of 250,000 attacks by hackers on Pentagon unclassified systems were successful. Improvements in security systems since then have made it more difficult for hackers to enter and/or disrupt systems, but security still poses concerns at this time.

Security on the Internet involves a wide range of issues not necessarily related to the data flowing between on-line entities. Areas of concern for purchasers include:

- Security in the electronic marketplace and commerce
- Securing transactions on world-wide networks
- Security on the Internet
- Security on interorganizational and international data flow and privacy
- Encryption standards and application
- External dependencies with outsourcing, suppliers, and consultants
- Virus protection, password authentication, and hardware protection devices
- Displaying and redistributing secure information

Two of the most difficult questions to answer regarding Internet security are:

1. How does an organization protect its internal systems from invasion?
2. Is the Internet safe for commerce?

Neither of these questions can be fully answered at present, despite a great deal of market pressure on software and hardware suppliers to develop standards and provide answers

Security Tools and Programs

Improvements in security tools and programs are announced frequently, so purchasers and supply managers interested in electronic commerce should know the latest in these security developments and track their advancement. A number of internal systems should be considered prior to engaging in electronic commerce over the Internet. "Firewalls" offer protection to data that resides internally by allowing only certain kinds of messages through. This software also can provide reports that monitor the number, types, and profiles of users accessing the system. "Wrappers" run as a layer of software around other software and are a tool against security breaches. Security tools called "proxies" are built into most Internet servers and direct data so that it can be hidden, sometimes routing through other servers. Box 18–2 describes the elements of a secure transaction.

Encryption

Security on the Internet has become primarily dependent on encryption technology, which is based on mathematical algorithms to hide data from

B O X   18–2

ELEMENTS OF A SECURE TRANSACTION

◆ Content security	Information is transmitted free from intrusion
◆ Signature	Identity of parties can be established
◆ Content integrity	Ability to identify any modifications
◆ Origin acknowledgement	Ability to identify origin
◆ Receipt acknowledgement	Ability to establish receipt by final addressee
◆ Delivery acknowledgement	Establishing receipt by intermediary
◆ Key management	Creating, revoking, managing private/public keys

unauthorized users. Secure servers attempt to encrypt data between the browser and the server, but there are almost always methods for hackers or pirates to invade these transmissions. There has been a great deal of improvement in encryption technology in recent years, and standards for many types of transactions have been developed. "Commerce servers," which interface with secure browsers, have provided a level of security for electronic commerce that uses encrypted transactions. Netscape and Microsoft browsers (the two most prominent brands) provide secure transaction identifiers that alert users when a transaction is not secure. Lock and key symbols on Web pages denote whether a connection provides transmission security via encryption.

Cryptography is the science of disguising messages so that only the writer and the intended recipients are able to read them. *Encryption* is the mechanism by which the information in these messages is scrambled—mostly by the use of mathematical algorithms. *Authentication* is the ability of the recipient to determine that the message is from a particular sender, i.e., that it is not a forgery. *Integrity* is the ability of the recipient to know that the message was not altered either intentionally or unintentionally. In addition to algorithms, establishing protocols and sophisticated password communications between two parties on the Net can enhance security of transactions.

Keys

Figures 18–3 and 18–4 describe the use of public and private keys. In order to facilitate the process of secure transactions, an additional piece of input data called a *key* is used in addition to algorithms. A key is used in electronic commerce security as, by analogy, padlocks and combination locks are used in protecting material objects. Two types of keys are used in transactions: public keys and private keys. Encryption can use either of these keys or both. Private-key cryptography (*symmetric cryptography*) entails the encoding and decoding of data with the same key.

F I G U R E   18–3

Symmetric/Secret-Key Cryptography

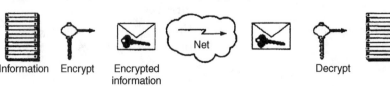

Information   Encrypt   Encrypted   Decrypt
                        information

F I G U R E   18–4

Asymmetric/Public-Key Cryptography

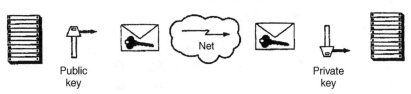

Public   Private
key   key

The key is known by both sender and receiver. The use of this type of security is common between financial institutions, the military, and intelligence operations.

Public-key encryption (*asymmetric cryptography*) uses two keys, a private key and a public key. One key is used to encrypt messages and the other key is used to decrypt messages. The public encryption key is made available to whomever wants to use it, but the private key is kept secret by the key owner. The assurance of security is dependent on the receiver protecting the private key. Because public keys are available to all customers, this approach is much easier to manage than symmetric cryptography. Box 18–3 describes some reasons for security breaches.

Viruses

Electronic commerce often entails the exchange of computer files, which opens up the possibility of downloading an infected file. For example, many public access sites that maintain huge libraries of files do not scan for viruses. A new class of viruses called *macro-viruses* is becoming more common on the Internet and organizational intranets. As individuals trade documents more frequently, the chance of infection is increasing. To protect against viruses:

- Use antivirus software.
- Scan all files downloaded from the Internet and from floppy disks.
- Perform regular data backups.
- Avoid sharing disks as much as possible.
- Purchase software from known sources with wrapping intact.
- Check e-mail with file attachments from unknown parties.

B O X   18–3

REASONS FOR NET SECURITY INTRUSION

- ◆ Theft   Industrial espionage, credit card information, technical specifications, financial information, bids/proposals

- ◆ Malice   Changing, deleting, or corrupting data for nefarious reasons

- ◆ Shutdown   Disabling operations by causing the system not to function

- ◆ Impersonation   Identity theft to conduct fraud or gain unauthorized access

- ◆ Revenge   Vandalism by a disgruntled or former employee

- ◆ Personal gain   Changing data for financial or other advantages

- ◆ Embarrassment   Altering data in a way that is visible to the public

- ◆ Political   Skewing and manipulating information for hostile purposes

Privacy Issues

The explosive growth of the Internet has raised the issue of privacy, which has yet to be adequately addressed by regulation. What many would consider private, or even sensitive, information is being made increasingly available through search tools and services. There is little privacy on the Internet. Cyberspace has thousands of electronic eyes capable of knowing who a user is and tracking a user's every move and length of stay from site to site. Through this information it is possible to construct a very detailed profile of each user's on-line activities.

A purchaser that provides information to an Internet supplier cannot be assured that the information will not be made available to external interests. If a user's name gets on a mailing list for junk e-mail or other unwanted solicitations, it may be difficult to remove.

Private interest groups are beginning to address the privacy issue by providing privacy standards for Internet communication. These organizations are attempting to achieve some level of voluntary compliance and provide ratings for Internet sites based upon the degree of privacy offered to users. Additionally, efforts are underway to provide users with a "privacy assured" label for Internet pages.

Fraud

The unregulated nature, lack of standards, potential for profit, and tremendous growth of the Internet have provided and will continue to provide unscrupulous individuals and groups with opportunities for deception and fraud, such as bogus offers and misleading promotions. The fraud issue is being tackled on several fronts in the United States, most notably by the National Fraud Information Center, a coalition of The National Consumers League, the Federal Trade Commission, and the National Association of Attorneys General, as well as by private enterprises such as major credit card organizations. The Center has created a national electronic fraud database for Internet complaints, assists users in reporting suspicious activity, and provides guidelines and an alert line to warn consumers of scams and the best ways to avoid fraud.

Purchasers and supply managers engaging in electronic commerce should use common sense and established business practice to guard against fraud. Know the other party—a professional-looking Internet site does not guarantee that it is legitimate. Be wary of pages that require disclosure of passwords and credit card account numbers. Whenever possible, research the company through non-Internet methods such as print catalogs and references from existing customers. Test their Web-published phone numbers to be sure they are real. Never disclose checking account numbers, credit card numbers, or other personal or corporate financial data at any Internet site, unless this information will be directed to a known trading partner using secure transactions.

Also be wary of offers where:

+ The item is being sold for much less than normal.
+ The supplier requires decisions to send the money immediately.
+ You have received poor references or indications of problems from other people or organizations.

♦ The supplier does not list an address other than a P.O. box.

♦ Guarantees and testimonials are excessive.

Additionally, many organizations offer free services on the Internet in exchange for personal and other information about potential users. This information is sometimes sold to other organizations that target these users for other sales. Be cautious about providing more information than is necessary.

Note: Suspicious activity on the Internet should be reported to the National Fraud Information Center (www.fraud.org, 1-800-876-7060) and to the state attorney general's office or other consumer fraud agency. The national office of the Better Business Bureau (www.bbb.org) is also in the process of establishing a searchable database on the Net of all member businesses with complaint files.

Establishing Acceptable Use Policies

Each purchasing and supply management employee should understand that access to the Net is mainly for business purposes. However, organizations may vary in the amount of discretion allowed for other uses, with policies ranging from liberal (as long as the work gets done and no unethical, illegal, or immoral activities take place, acceptable use will be left up to employees) to strict. Yet no matter what the tolerance level, boundaries of acceptable use should be well defined and communicated by management to *all* users. Limits not only ensure that business will get done, but protect the organization from potential liability.

ELECTRONIC CONTRACTING

Because it is a relatively new and fast-growing medium, many legal issues concerning electronic commerce are being determined almost daily. In addition to security and privacy, issues for consideration include:[2]

♦ Establishment of working agreements between purchasing and supplying organizations on how electronic contracting will be conducted, what is acceptable and unacceptable, and processes that will be used

---

2. Refer also to Legal Implications of Electronic Commerce, below.

- Application of the Uniform Commercial Code with regard to electronic transactions between purchasers and suppliers
- Potential global disputes where laws differ, since the Net has no national boundaries
- Undefined privacy and copyright protections
- Laws involving taxes, tariffs, and payment standards
- The use of scanned hard copy documents necessary because some organizations and auditors require hard copy documentation

Protections When Using Electronic Contracting

When contracting on-line, follow certain precautions including:

- Establish a working agreement ("trading partner agreement") with the supplier on how on-line technology will be used between the supplying and purchasing organizations in the establishment and use of contracts including security and identification procedures.
- Ask suppliers for confirmation of all transactions, including the specifics of an order and the terms and conditions of the contract.
- Use a special name or code that only the supplier knows.
- Maintain a back-up file of important documentation.
- Keep all electronic communications in files protected from deletion.
- Inspect the order immediately upon receipt and notify the supplier of any problems.
- Request that the supplier confirm in writing any complaints, rejections, or other such communications.

Establishing Guidelines for Contracting

Electronic Data Interchange has historically been the model for electronically driven commercial transactions. But unlike the Net, EDI operates under a closed, secure environment. However, because the business environment for electronic commerce is still being structured, it provides only a quasi-EDI environment, which increases the probability that an on-line contract is enforceable. To ensure such enforceability, purchasers should work with suppliers as part of supplier development programs. For example, as part of the ordering process, the parties can be led through a set of screens containing contracting terms. The parties must respond that they agree to the contract terms before being permitted to progress to the next screen.

Legal Implications of Electronic Commerce

Many changes are underway to resolve the legal issues surrounding electronic commerce, which include:

1. The lack of standards for encryption and digital signatures—a critical issue and goal is to create evidence that transactions actually exist, so they can be authenticated in court if necessary. Digital signatures and certificates of authority can be used to verify authenticity and authorization for a transaction. These methods rely on encryption technology that must also be kept secure and obtained from reliable sources. There must be agreement that digital signatures will have the same effect as a signature on a paper document.

2. Weakness in Section 2 of the Uniform Commercial Code with regard to electronic transactions between purchasers and suppliers. Changes strengthening Section 2 of the Uniform Commercial Code and accommodating electronic commerce will be addressed by the Uniform Computer Information Transaction Act (UCITA). Following ratification of UCITA, individual state legislatures will begin passing the act into law.

3. Uniform laws involving taxes, tariffs, and payment standards.

4. Untested policies of acceptable use with a business.

Also refer to the list of electronic contracting issues previously presented.

HOW TO USE AND APPLY ELECTRONIC COMMERCE

Given the complexities and issues involved in migrating operations to the Internet, purchasing and supply management must determine how it will work with internal staff, customers, external customers, and suppliers to achieve an efficient and effective system of electronic commerce. The scope of migration may be as simple as giving purchasers access to the Internet and creating a Web page or Web site, or as complex as moving major mission-critical functions to the Net, such as order entry, production planning, material requirements planning (MRP), enterprise integration, enterprise resource planning (ERP), or other tying together of organizational functions.

Provide Training

A key area of successful migration to both traditional and emerging electronic commerce technology is ensuring that all users are adequately trained. It is especially important to train individuals who will be updating information, doing searches, making decisions, and defining the boundaries of potential benefit and use.

Provide a training coordinator to establish the curriculum, track employee progress, and determine overall training needs and costs. If organization resources are inadequate to cover basic computer training, outsource this training to local organizations or colleges. The coordinator should determine how best to approach training needs. Determination of group training, computer-based training, Web-based training, or other options must be considered. It is especially important in instances where major systems changes are being made to instill a positive and supportive attitude in employees.

Overall, training should encompass:

- The basics of software and systems being used, and fundamental training on the use and features of the operating system, PCs, and network hardware and software. Also include basic training in the terminology, use, and features of Web browsers and search tools.
- The importance of security, including the implications of breaches, use of passwords, and other security issues. Additional training on acceptable use policies, software licensing, backup procedures, use of e-mail, file transfers, and Net protocol and etiquette is also valuable.
- How to use system and software documentation, access software support lines, and use a help desk.

Joint training with major trading partners and suppliers may be necessary in instances where electronic commerce includes links between financial and supply management systems.

Establish Sources for Data

There are many avenues for collecting and establishing sources of data applicable to electronic commerce. This information should be used to:

1. Establish potential electronic opportunities
2. Amass a database for carrying out purchasing and supply management functions on the Net

Information that is gathered should be shared by posting electronically or a more traditional means of distribution. Note also that the bookmark feature of most browsers is one of the best methods of noting addresses on the Net. Sources of data include:

- ◆ Supplier marketing materials and product advertisements, most of which now include Web addresses. These supplier Web sites, in turn, provide immediate detailed information on the products or services being considered. Using this resource can save time and telephone and mailing costs.
- ◆ Supplier catalogs, many of which allow on-line ordering of products and services.
- ◆ Organizations that make copies of specifications, RFPs (Requests for Proposal), RFQs (Requests for Quotation), and other documents available on their Web sites.
- ◆ All states and the federal government now have Net sites that permit research of laws, regulations, and statutes impacting commerce. The federal General Services Administration (GSA) and many states also provide access to state and federal contracts and bid specifications via the Net. This information can provide valuable pricing information for contract negotiations and benchmarking.
- ◆ Economic and financial sites, which provide the latest information on commodity prices, stocks, exchange rates, industry trends, news, Manufacturing and Non-Manufacturing *NAPM Report on Business*®, Producer Price Index (PPI), Consumer Price Index (CPI), Securities and Exchange

Commission (SEC) filings, and other useful purchasing and supply management data, most of which is free.

♦ Sites that offer virtual shopping and can provide valuable pricing and product information that can be useful to the purchaser.

♦ Subscription services that provide access to searchable databases, some of which include articles and information that may be of particular use to purchasers.

♦ Intelligent search tools that run inquiries on several search engines at the same time.

In addition, on-line financial calculators, direct connections to airlines, searchable international directories of businesses and people, technology, and many other resources are available at no cost to the purchaser.

Set Up a Program to Initiate Electronic Commerce

The decision to migrate purchasing and supply management functions to the Net should not be made without senior management backing. Once this has been obtained, a program to carry out electronic commerce can be initiated. The basic steps include the following:

♦ *Establish formal development teams for each area of consideration.* The teams should consist of individuals with all levels of involvement (both internal and external) in the processes being reviewed, including suppliers and Internet service providers (ISPs). Each member participating must be encouraged to openly communicate and share ideas, issues, and concerns. All options should be discussed, including how much to move and when, who will install the program and oversee it, what functions can be easily converted, and which will involve more risk and cost. A traditional reengineering approach may be used to look at the fundamental processes and how they might change.

♦ *Obtain technical advice.* Individuals with expertise in the technologies involved must provide teams with options for direction. These individuals may be found within the organization, or consultants could be hired. Information gathering using benchmarking and research into what other organizations are doing and what has worked is important, as are considering emerging technologies at this time as well and being open to all ideas. Keep database architecture as flexible and open as possible to accommodate new technologies, applications, and information.

+ *Assess total costs and perform a cost benefit analysis for all options considered.* Total costs should include all elements of the project with both short- and long-term cost implications. These considerations should include: hardware configurations and network topology, software purchase and version control, data conversion migration, communications links to Net service providers, security and firewalls (protection from outside intrusion of internal systems), training, management, and maintenance. Prototyping of the new system, defining business rules, and reengineering processes should be done.

+ *Look at major changes in processes with suppliers.* It is important to identify those suppliers who have the capability and desire to move to new methodologies of electronic commerce and those who are unable or reluctant. The organization may need to formally communicate planned changes and negotiate with suppliers, especially when existing contracts dictate terms of the relationship. Banking relationships could also be affected by these changes and should be examined.

+ *Communicate any potential changes to those affected, including employees, customers, and management.* One of the best methods to communicate this information is via a project Net page.

+ *Test any new methodologies developed and train all participants prior to implementation.*

Review Financial Transaction Options

Purchasers must consider the options with regard to which electronic commerce financial transaction methods provide the most security, comply with supplier requirements, and fit with existing systems. Options currently available on the Net include:

+ *Purchase/credit cards.* Cards are one of the most convenient methods of purchasing on the Net. When using cards, consider how the card information is transmitted, who clears the card, and how validation is handled. Some level of protection against fraudulent use is normally provided by the card issuer. Suppliers may offer services or membership systems that register a user so that the card information only needs to be submitted once.

◆ *Traditional purchase orders and checks.* Ordering via the Net can be accomplished using checks and purchase orders. Typically the order is not released until the check or P.O. is received by the supplier. However, streamlined methods can be developed with primary suppliers, enabling preauthorized P.O. numbers and check numbers to release shipments.

◆ *Electronic cash.* Forms of electronic cash are being developed that will speed the flow of electronic commerce in the future. For example, some organizations are currently selling systems that allow a financial institution to act as an intermediary for a purchaser and supplier. When an order is initiated by a purchaser, the supplier is able to receive immediate funds transfer from the electronic account of the purchaser. Encrypted links and sophisticated software provide the means for this type of transaction. Another system, called E-cash, converts money into true digital form and is being used successfully. Funds are encrypted into electronic form and held by an intermediary institution. Because of the encryption, E-cash can be saved onto a disk, printed onto paper, or sent electronically to a supplier, and because the cash is totally unique, it cannot be overdrawn or spent twice.

The current constraints on the growth of electronic cash include:

◆ The insecurity of some types of electronic payment systems
◆ Governmental regulations
◆ Reluctance of financial institutions to adopt it
◆ User acceptance
◆ Implementation and acceptance of digital signatures

Communicating the Purchasing Function

Purchasers can provide a great deal of information to both suppliers and requestors by developing a Net page for the purchasing and supply organization. HTML (Hypertext Markup Language) is the standard programming language for Net Publishing and has become as simple to use as word processing with the latest commercial Net editors. The ease of use will enable quick updates and enhancements and can eliminate paper documents. These editors are now included in much browser and word processing software. Boxes 18–4 and 18–5 describe the elements and uses of a Web site.

IMPROVEMENTS UNDER DEVELOPMENT

In spite of potential difficulties and negative assessments from some Net pundits and other critics of electronic commerce, a number of significant developments are underway to improve speed, reliability, and use. As information loads on the Internet are doubling every 18 months, major Internet service providers are more than doubling capacity annually. Other areas of improvement underway or continuing include: the technology behind Internet protocol (such as XML), line capacity, bandwidth and connectivity, encryption methodologies and standards leading to better security for electronic transactions and privacy, improved firewall technology that protects internal systems from outside penetration, and automated testing and diagnostic tools. In addition, initiatives such as "open buying on the internet" (OBI) are providing improvements in standards and protocols for business-to-business electronic commerce transactions.

B O X   18–4

ELEMENTS OF A SUCCESSFUL WEB SITE

+ There is a business purpose.
+ The construction is well thought out.
+ The site shows an understanding of how interactive marketing and an alternative delivery channel should be combined.
+ The site has value to the customer.

B O X   18–5

NET HOME PAGE FEATURES

- ◆ Mission statements*
- ◆ Internal policies and procedures
- ◆ Policies toward suppliers and pertaining to relationships with suppliers*
- ◆ "How to's" on working with purchasing*
- ◆ Company or organization locations and directions to them*
- ◆ Supplier information and registration process*
- ◆ Lists of surplus property for sale*
- ◆ Contract pricing, information, and tools such as internal catalogs for internal customers
- ◆ Complete contracts
- ◆ Links to internal inventory and supplier catalogues
- ◆ Standard contract forms and "shell" documents such as RFPs, RFQs, and RFIs*
- ◆ Links to other valuable procurement tools and sites
- ◆ The equivalent of internal and external paper-based documents (this can allow for immediate changes and updates and reduce paper and printing costs)
- ◆ Solicitations for RFQs and RFBs*
- ◆ Contract information and tools to requestors

---

*These items are examples of what would be accessible by suppliers. Remaining items would be accessible only by employees. Additional items for customers, such as product information, catalogs, and ordering information, would also be included in the Web site.

CHAPTER 19

Supplier Price and Cost Analysis

Editor
Frank Haluch, C.P.M.
President
Haluch & Associates Ltd.

PRICE AND SUPPLIER COST OVERVIEW

Prices quoted by suppliers are at best estimates and are therefore subject to analysis and negotiation. The goal of price and cost analysis is to achieve the lowest pricing to which you are entitled. In the long run, selling prices need to cover the cost of direct materials, labor, overhead, and profit to keep suppliers in business. Prices also need to encourage suppliers to accept additional business and motivate them to deliver to the buyer's schedule.

Price analysis compares prices of one supplier with those of another or analyzes quoted prices for their reasonableness. In cost analysis, costs are analyzed either through the sharing of cost information by the supplier or through breaking down their quoted prices into the factors of cost through various methods discussed in this chapter. The goal of both price and cost analysis is to understand how pricing is generated and therefore enable the buyer to question the reasonableness of an element of cost or the entire pricing process.

For the performance of any type of analysis, multiple quantity/ price points are a must. If all you have is one quantity/price point, it is very difficult to perform any analysis. If you have multiple quantity/

price points, there are many valuable types of analyses that can be performed.

PRICE DETERMINATION AND ANALYSIS

Prices are a function of the type of marketplace where the goods or services are offered for sale. The intensity of competition in the marketplace has a significant impact on prices charged by suppliers. In a purely competitive market (commodities or standard items) where there are many buyers and sellers, the market sets the price. Therefore, buyers need to position their material or service requirements in a way that makes them very attractive to sellers and then let the market forces do the work of establishing the price. An "electronic auction" is a new method for establishing pricing for standard items where there are many sellers eager for your business. Electronic auctions use the World Wide Web to solicit bids from the global marketplace (see Chapter 32 of this work for a detailed discussion of electronic auctions).

The opposite of market-driven pricing is monopoly pricing (only one supplier). If, as a buyer, you find yourself in a monopoly situation, the best course of action is to confirm that you are paying the same prices as similar buyers (fear of the U.S. antitrust laws should assist you in getting such certification from a supplier). If the spend is large enough, attempting to break the patent or finding a substitute product may prove to be a cost-effective approach to lowering prices.

There are two other market conditions: monopolistic competition (many sellers of similar goods or services, i.e., plastic injection molding) and oligopolistic competition (a small number of sellers of the same type of products, i.e., machine tool builders). The investment in price and cost analysis will pay significant dividends when applied to items in either of these markets. The choice of whether to perform price or cost analysis is a function of the amount of the spend and resources available to perform the analyses. When the spend is small and resources are limited, the most cost-effective approach is to rely on price analyses.

Competitive Bidding

Obtaining competitive bids is the first step in price analysis. Having sufficient data is key to successfully analyzing a supplier's price structure. Competitive bidding provides you with many different prices for the same item. Requests for proposals need to be structured to obtain multiple quantity/price relationships. Price analyses cannot be performed with only one quantity/price point.

Price Analysis Tools

Quantity Discount Analysis

Quantity discount analysis (QDA) confirms the real "discount" or "increase" in the unit price for the increases in quantity. Buyers never see quotations where unit prices increase as the volume increases. However, many quotations, when examined using QDA, show that the incremental unit price for large quantities is higher than for smaller quantities. QDA displays how incremental unit prices are behaving with regard to increases in quantity. QDA does not provide any insight into why the incremental unit prices are behaving the way they do; it merely provides us with the ability to ask some very interesting questions. By performing this type of analysis, we are able to generate the *actual* unit price for the next quantity versus the supplier's quotation, which shows the *average* price.

There are two different QDA analysis methods: one for specific quantity quotations (1 unit—$3.00 each; 2 units—$2.75 each; 5 units—$2.00 each) and another for range quantity quotations (1–4 units—$3.00 each; 5–9 units—$2.75 each; 10–14 units—$2.50 each).

Specific Quantity QDA Example

You received the following quotation from the Tanner Company for Spacer Bars:

Quantity	50 units	100 units	250 units	500 units	1,000 units
Price/unit	$8.88	$8.38	$8.28	$8.18	$8.13

A QDA specific quotation analysis produced the data found in Table 19–1. Examining the data produced by this QDA analysis, we find:

♦ The price/unit difference: for 50 additional units (50–100) the unit price drops by $1.00 ($8.88–$7.88); for 150 additional units (100–250) the unit price actually increases by $0.33 ($7.88–$8.21); for 250 units (250–500) the unit price decreases by $0.13 ($8.21–$8.08).

T A B L E   19–1

QDA–Specific Quantities Example*

Quantity	50 units	100 units	250 units	500 units	1000 units
Quoted price	$8.88	$8.38	$8.28	$8.18	$8.13
Price/unit differences	$8.88	$7.88	$8.21	$8.08	$8.08
Per unit price differences at breaks	–	$1.00	($0.33)	$0.13	$0.00
Percentage price reduction	–	11.26%	–4.23%	1.62%	0.00%

*See calculation appendix for the calculations and explanation of how to calculate a QDA.

+ The price decrease is very small (250–500 units) even though the volume doubled.
+ There is no decrease in the price/unit difference for 500 additional units (500 to 1,000) even though the volume doubled again.

The buyer might be well advised to ask Tanner Company to explain why the quotation shows that the greater the volume, the lower the price and the QDA analysis shows this not to be true.

Range Quantity QDA Example

You received the following quotation from Jones Electronics Inc. for Relays:

Quantity	1–49	50–99	100–999	1,000–2,999	3,000–5,999	6,000–9,999
Price/unit	$6.25	$2.96	$2.37	$1.69	$1.49	$1.39

A QDA range analysis produced the data found in Table 19–2. Examining the data produced by this QDA analysis, we find:

+ The maximum to order in each quantity range: from 1–49, 23; 50–99, 80; 100–999, 713; 1,000–2,999, 2,644; 3,000–5,999, 5,597. This means that it is cheaper to buy 50 ($148.00) than 24 ($150.00), 100 ($237.00) than 81 ($239.76), etc. So if you purchase more than maximum units to order, you are paying a higher unit price than necessary. If you buy at the minimum of the next price break, it is like you are getting units for free.

T A B L E   19–2

QDA–Range Quantity Example

Quantity	1–49	50–99	100–999	1,000–2,999	3,000–5,999	6,000–9,999
Quoted price	$6.25	$2.96	$2.37	$1.69	$1.49	$1.39
Maximum units to order	23	80	713	2,644	5,597	0*
Per unit price differences at breaks	$6.25	$1.63	$2.30	1.44	1.31	$0.00*
Percentage reduction	—	73.88%	−40.61%	37.31%	8.89%	0.00%*

See calculation appendix for the calculations and explanation of how to calculate a QDA.
*The last column in the QDA range analysis will always be 0 because in order to calculate the various values, data from the next price break are needed.

- The per unit price difference at breaks increases by 40.61% between quantities 50–99 and 100–199 even though the volume is increased by 2×.
- The discount for incremental quantities shrinks as the quantity increases.

Two questions to ask the supplier are:

- Why does the maximum units to order in a price range not equal the highest quantity in the range?
- Why does the discount behave like a roller coaster (moving up and down at varying rates) as the quantity increases?

QDA Patterns

The Lazy L   Graphing data produced by either QDA analysis generate several classic patterns. The first, called the "lazy L" pattern (Figure 19–1), shows an initial steep discount initially and then becomes

F I G U R E   19–1

QDA with Specific Quantity Price Breaks: "Lazy L" Pattern

1. No. units per order	10000	25000	50000	100000	200000	400000
2. Price per unit	$0.0382	$0.0355	$0.0345	$0.034	$0.0338	$0.0336
3. Total price per order	$382.0000	$887.5000	$1,725.0000	$3,400.000	$6,750.0000	$13,439.9960
4. Price diff. between orders	$382.0000	$505.5000	$837.5000	$1,675.000	$3,350.0000	$6,689.9960
5. Quantity diff. between orders	10000	15000	25000	50000	100000	200000
6. Price per unit per order qty diff.	$0.0382	$0.0337	$0.0335	$0.034	$0.0335	$0.0334
7. Per unit price diff at breaks	-	$0.0045	$0.0002	$0.000	$0.0000	$0.0001
8. Percentage price reduction	-	11.78%	0.59%	0.00%	0.00%	0.15%

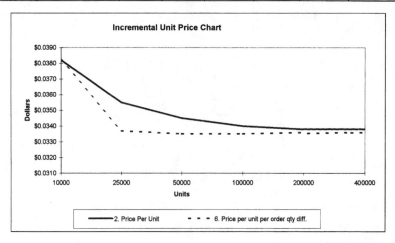

Incremental Unit Price Chart

————— 2. Price Per Unit   - - - - 6. Price per unit per order qty diff.

flat (i.e., no further discount even though the quantity increases). Lazy L patterns may indicate that there are high fixed costs relative to variable costs, which would make pricing very sensitive to volume.

The Roller Coaster   In the "roller coaster" pattern, the price between quantity breaks decreases and then increases, followed by a series of decreases and increases. (Figure 19–2). This pattern may indicate that the item being produced is assigned to production equipment, depending on the volume. High-speed equipment normally carries a high overhead burden, and therefore units produced at the low end of the economic volume for this equipment are more expensive than those at the high end. This phenomenon may repeat itself through the quantity/ price breaks if different processes or equipment are used, depending on volume.

The Ski Slope   The "ski slope" pattern shows a continuously increasing discount (Figure 19–3). This pattern confirms that the more you buy, the lower the price (both average and incremental). When making long-term agreements with volume incentive rebates, one needs to ensure that the ski slope pattern is present.

F I G U R E   19–2

QDA with Specific Quantity Price Breaks: "Roller Coaster" Pattern. This Pattern Represents the Ideal Pricing Discount Schedule.

	1-24	25-49	50-74	75-99	100-149	150-199	200-249	250-499	500-999	1000-1499
1. Unit ranges (i.e., 1-5 6-10 etc)	1-24	25-49	50-74	75-99	100-149	150-199	200-249	250-499	500-999	1000-1499
2. Price per unit	$5.60	$3.68	$2.99	$2.24	$1.90	$1.68	$1.37	$1.31	$0.79	$0.64
3. Total price per order	$5.60	$92.00	$149.50	$168.00	$190.00	$252.00	$274.00	$327.50	$395.00	$640.00
4. Maximum units to order	16	40	56	84	132	163	239	301	810	0
5. Total price per maximum order	$89.60	$147.20	$167.44	$188.16	$250.80	$273.84	$327.43	$394.31	$639.90	$0.00
6. Price diff. between max. order	$89.60	$57.60	$20.24	$20.72	$62.64	$23.04	$53.59	$66.88	$245.59	$0.00
7. Qty diff. between max units to order	16	24	16	28	48	31	76	62	509	0
8. Price per unit per order quantity difference	$5.60	$2.40	$1.27	$0.74	$1.31	$0.74	$0.71	$1.08	$0.48	$0.00
9. Percentage price reduction	-	57.14%	47.29%	41.50%	-76.35%	43.05%	5.13%	-52.98%	55.27%	100.00%

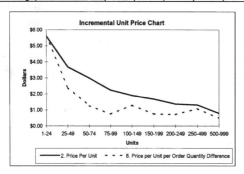

Incremental Unit Price Chart

F I G U R E   19-3

QDA with Specific Quantity Price Breaks: "Ski Slope" Pattern.

	1	10	50	100	150	200	250	300
1. No. units per order	1	10	50	100	150	200	250	300
2. Price per unit	$300.00	$275.00	$250.00	$225.00	$200.00	$175.00	$150.00	$125.00
3. Total price per order	$300.00	$2,750.00	$12,500.00	$22,500.00	$30,000.00	$35,000.00	$37,500.00	$37,500.00
4. Price diff. between orders	$300.00	$2,450.00	$9,750.00	$10,000.00	$7,500.00	$5,000.00	$2,500.00	$0.00
5. Quantity diff. between orders	1	9	40	50	50	50	50	50
6. Price per unit per order qty diff.	$300.00	$272.22	$243.75	$200.00	$150.00	$100.00	$50.00	$0.00
7. Per unit price diff at breaks	-	$27.78	$28.47	$43.75	$50.00	$50.00	$50.00	$50.00
8. Percentage price reduction	-	9.26%	10.46%	17.95%	25.00%	33.33%	50.00%	100.00%

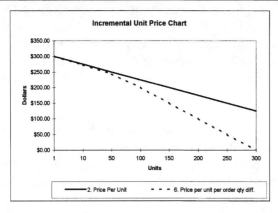

Perform QDA Before Any Other Analysis

Because QDA tells you whether the discount schedule is rational or not, it is the first analysis that needs to be performed. If the QDA analysis shows an irrational discount pattern, then the supplier needs to explain this prior to your investing resources in further analyses.

Fixed and Variable Cost Analysis

The formula Price = Fixed Cost/Quantity + Unit Variable Cost or "$P = F/Q + V$" can be used to express how a supplier generates their pricing. We can use algebra to solve the equation $P = F/Q + V$ for the supplier's "fixed" costs and then use this estimate to determine their "unit variable" costs. The "fixed" and "unit variable" costs determined by this method may not be the supplier's actual "fixed" and "unit variable" costs. The "unit variable" costs that are determined by this method include direct material, direct labor, operating overhead, and *profit*. The more linear the relationship between price and cost, the more accurate the pricing model that can be constructed using this analysis. Note that this analysis method will not yield usable information if the supplier used the "experience effect" or learning curve costing models (these methods generate a different cost pool for each quantity).

Fixed and unit variable cost analysis provides information on whether the item you are buying has high fixed costs or unit variable costs. If an item has high fixed costs relative to its unit variable costs, then any increase in volume will have a significant impact on reducing unit prices. If, on the other hand, the unit variable costs are high relative to fixed costs, then additional volume will little impact on lowering costs. The question to be answered when unit variable costs are high is how the buyer can assist the seller in reducing either direct material or labor costs.

Fixed and Variable Cost Example   You received the following quotation from Cooper Industries for Torque Assemblies:

Quantity	2	5	10
Unit price	$5,000.00	$4,500.00	$4,300.00

From the quotation we can construct the following equations using $P = F/Q + V$:

$$\text{Price}_1 = \$5,000 \qquad \text{Quantity}_1 = 2$$

$$\text{Price}_2 = \$4,300 \qquad \text{Quantity}_2 = 10$$

Solving for fixed costs	Solving for unit variable costs
$P_1 = F/Q_1 + V$	$\$5,000 = \$1,750/2 + V$
$-(P_2 = F/Q_2 + V)$	$\$5,000 = \$875 + V$
$\$5,000 = F/2 + V$	$\$4,125 = V$
$-(\$4,300 = F/10 + V)$	
$\$700 = F/2 - F/10$	
$\$700 = F(0.5 - 0.1)$	
$\$700 = 0.4F$	
$\$1,750 = F$	

We can verify the values for F and V by calculating the price for 5 units.

$$P = F/Q + V$$

$$P = \$1,750/5 + \$4,125$$

$$P = \$350 + \$4,125$$

$$P = \$4,475, \text{ or } 0.56\% \text{ lower than the quoted price}$$
$$\text{of } \$4,500 \text{ (not bad for a few minutes' work!)}$$

Now we can make the assumption that Cooper's "fixed" costs are $1,750 and their "unit variable" costs are $4,125 (remember that unit variable costs calculated using this method include direct material, direct labor, operations overhead, and *profit*). It would seem that working on reducing Cooper's variable costs would be in order, since their variable costs are significantly higher than their fixed costs.

We can use the estimates of fixed and unit variable costs to estimate prices for quantities not quoted, perform break-even analyses, and construct a detailed cost model (by breaking down the variable costs into specific values for direct material, direct labor, overhead, and profit).

Experience Effect

The Boston Consulting Group (BCG) performed studies in the 1960s that found that labor and non-labor-related costs follow a composite learning curve. They labeled this the "experience effect." BCG found that most items declined by 20–30% each time the experience doubled. To convert this decline into an "experience effect factor," you convert the decline into its reciprocal (for the foregoing example, a 20–30% decline converts into a 70–80% experience effect factor). The experience effect is very useful in forecasting prices for items that are purchased on a repetitive basis and where detailed cost data are not available or are too costly to generate.

Experience Effect Example   You are negotiating a contract for the replacement of valves in your building's main flow-control system. The entire job will consist of replacing 160 valves. The contractor you would like to use performed an emergency version of this project consisting of 10 valves a month ago. What would be a reasonable cost per valve for the remaining 150 valves, given that the average cost was

$249.50 per valve for the first 10 valves replaced? The contractor agreed that it took them on average 15% less time each time the number of valves replaced doubled.

Based on the above data, we know that the average cost to replace the first ten valves was $249.50 each and that the experience effect factor was 85%. We can determine the cost to replace the first valve and then calculate the average cost per unit for the total job of replacing 160 valves.

The cumulative average factor for the first 10 valves is 0.583^1 and for 160 valves is 0.0304^2 for 85% experience effect factor. With these factors we can calculate the cost to replace the first valve and then calculate the average cost for 160 valves.

Average cost for the first 10 values = $249.50

Average cost for the first valve = $249.50/0.583 = $427.96

Average cost for replacing 160 valves = $427.96 × 0.304 = $130.09

To estimate the average cost to replace 150 valves, we subtract the cost of the first 10 units from the total cost of replacing 160 valves [(160 × $130.09) − (10 × $249.50) = $20,814.40 − $2,495.00 = $18,319.40]. When we divide the total cost $18,319.40 by 150, we get $122.13 (the average cost per unit to replace the remaining 150 valves).

We could have solved this problem using log–log paper. In fact, using log–log paper is faster than calculating the answer longhand. In Figures 19–4a and b the same problem is solved using log–log paper and by computer.

Experience Effect Potential Applications Sophisticated buyers are using the experience effect to estimate the price for repetitive unique services such as building cleaning services, equipment maintenance services (HVAC, elevators), reconfiguration of modular offices, repetitive low-cost parts manufacturing, repetitive printing, and sales promotional services.

The BCG experience effect has also been used to forecast the cost of new high-tech products such as cell phones, integrated circuits, and

---

1. C. J. Teplitz, *The Learning Curve Deskbook,* Quorum Books, Westport, Connecticut, 1991, Appendix C, p. 190.
2. Ibid., p. 192.

F I G U R E   19—4a

Experience Effect Log–Log Solution

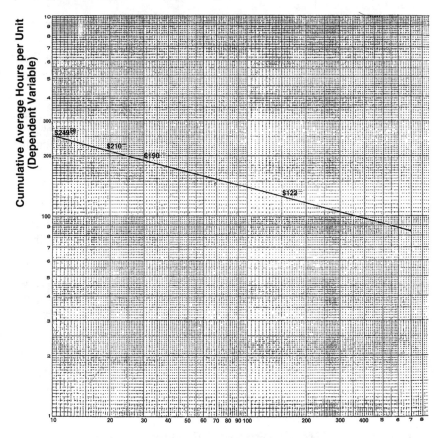

Cumulative Production in Units
(Independent Variable)

laser printers. All that is needed to forecast a future price are data on current volume, price, experience effect factor, and a forecast of future volume.

Price Analysis Case

A detailed analysis of this case using SDS_Notebooks software can be found later in this chapter. Demonstration SDS_Notebooks software can be downloaded from www.sdsnotebooks.com.

F I G U R E   19—4b

Experience Effect Computer Solution

Experience Curve Rate		85%	Unit Price for Additional Quantities Compared to First Order
	FirstOrder	**#1**	
Number of Units	10	150	
Unit Pricing	$249.50	$122.29	
Diff vs FirstOrder	$0.00	$127.21	
		Savings	$19,081.50

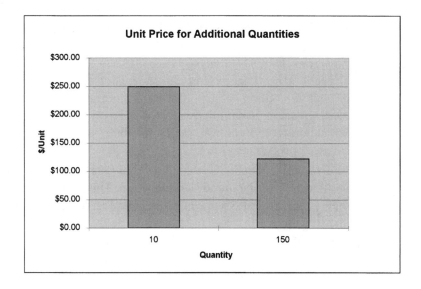

You purchase a "short slide" that is used to connect various filling, packaging, and in-process operations. Because the short slide is designed to fail during jams rather than damage the product, its usage is difficult to predict. Table 19–3 shows information that you have collected on the orders you have placed this year.

All of the requirements in Table 19–3 were purchased from General Fabrications Inc., and you wish to evaluate whether or not you have been receiving reasonable prices.

1. The first analysis that needs to be performed on all pricing is the quantity discount analysis (QDA), for which we would use the cumulative purchases with their respective prices. The underlying quantity discount for incremental volumes shows a

T A B L E   19–3

Short Slides–Purchase History

Date ordered	1/10	4/23	7/12	10/15
Quantity purchased	180	200	172	212
Cumulative quantity	180	380	552	764
Price per unit	$86.00	$79.00	$70.00	$58.00

ski slope pattern (the greater the volume, the greater the percentage discount). (See Table 19–4.)

From this QDA analysis, we could say that General Fabrications has been pricing the short slide on the basis of cumulative volume versus order by order and the discount has been increasing as cumulative quantity has increased. General Fabrication would get high marks for their cumulative volume pricing approach.

2. The fixed and variable cost analysis shows no real pattern for the allocation of fixed and variable costs. This result occurs when either the experience effect or learning curve logic was used to generate prices. This appers to be the case, based on the data in the QDA analysis. (See Table 19–5.)

3. The experience effect analysis leads us to assume that General Fabrications is using an 87% experience effect to generate prices. This figure may be too high, depending on the amount of labor to machine work. A lower experience rate may be

T A B L E   19–4

Short Slides QDA Analysis

Number of Units	180	380	552	764
Purchase price history	$86.00	$79.00	$70.00	$58.00
Price per unit per order qty diff.	$86.00	$72.70	$50.12	$26.72
Reductions from previous break	$0.00	$13.30	$22.58	$23.36
Percentage reduction	—	15.47%	31.06%	46.61%

T A B L E   19–5

Short Slide—Fixed and Unit Variable Costs Analysis: Solving for F and V in the formula $P = F/Q + F$

	1	2	3	4		
Price number						
Price per unit	$86.00	$79.00	$70.00	$58.00		
Cumulative number units	180	380	552	764		
Price pairs	1 & 2	1 & 3	1 & 4	2 & 3	2 & 4	3 & 4
Fixed costs	$2,394.00	$4,273.55	$6,593.43	$10,975.81	$15,876.88	$23,871.40
Variable costs	$72.70	$62.26	$49.37	$50.12	$37.22	$26.75

more accurate. A case could be made that an 80% experience effect is more accurate than the 87%. (See Figures 19–5a and b.)

General Comments

One could use these analyses to probe the supplier for additional information on how the prices where developed. If 80% is used rather than 87%, the price for the last price would be $44.14 versus $57.64, or a potential annual savings of $13,500 (based on 1,000 short sides per year).

COST ANALYSIS

Cost analysis starts with breaking down the quoted price into the elements of cost. Variable costs are those costs that vary directly with the

F I G U R E   19–5a

Experience Effect Computer Solution

Experience Curve Rate	87%	Unit Price for Additional Quantities Compared to First Order		
	FirstOrder	#1	#2	#3
Number of Units	180	200	372	584
Unit Pricing	$86.00	$63.22	$60.27	$57.64
Diff vs FirstOrder	$0.00	$22.78	$25.73	$28.36
	Savings	$4,556.00	$9,571.56	$16,562.24

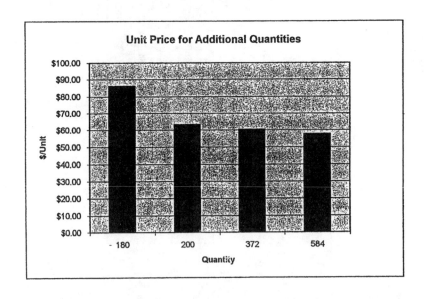

F I G U R E   19-5b

Continued

Experience Curve Rate		80%	Unit Price for Additional Quantities Compared to First Order		
	FirstOrder	#1	#2	#3
Number of Units	180	200	372	584
Unit Pricing	$86.00	$51.06	$47.35	$44.14
Diff vs FirstOrder	$0.00	$34.94	$38.65	$41.86
	Savings	$6,988.00	$14,377.80	$24,446.24

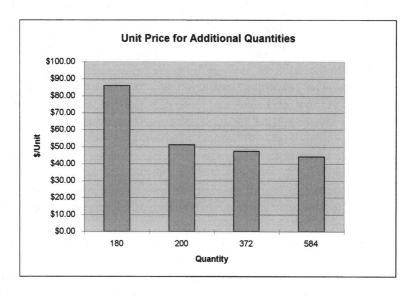

volume of production (direct material, direct labor, overhead). Fixed costs are those costs that are ongoing whether there is any production or not (taxes, depreciation, salaries). Many factors affect costs: the capability of management, labor effectiveness and efficiency, amount and quality of subcontracting, assignment of overhead costs, material prices, and labor categories and rates. These are the areas to examine for potential improvement once you have a complete cost breakdown analysis.

Cost Analysis Tools

The first analysis that is recommended before performing serious cost analysis is a quantity discount analysis, which provides information on whether a rational or irrational discount approach was taken. If the discount approach appears to be irrational (lazy L or "roller coaster"), then prior to investing time in any further analysis, a discussion with the supplier on why their incremental prices are behaving they way they do is a must.

Next, performing a fixed and variable cost analysis will tell you if a learning curve costing method was used to generate the quotation. If a learning curve was not used, then you have generated valuable data for learning curve analysis, break-even analysis, and price productivity analysis.

Learning Curve Analysis

The "learning curve" rule states that whenever the quantity produced doubles, the cumulative average time (labor) is reduced by a constant percentage. The percentage reduction is a function of the relationship between the labor and machine content of the production process. The greater the machine time versus labor time, the closer to 100% the learning rate and the lower the impact of volume on production costs. The greater the labor time versus the machine time, the closer to 70% the learning rate and the higher the impact of volume on production costs. The table shown in Figure 19–6 can be used to approximate the learning rate based on an estimate of the percentage of the total value-added time that is labor paced and machine paced.

For analyzing purchase prices using learning curves, the "Wright curve" or "cumulative average curve" is preferred over the "boeing curve" or "unit theory curve." This is because in a purchasing analysis we are interested in the average labor hours over a number of units produced, not the labor hours required for the next unit of production.

Learning Curve Example   You have bought 100 Ejector Assemblies from Delta Engineering. You have learned during visits to Delta that the ejectors follow an 80% learning curve (75% labor paced and 25% machine paced) and you were able to generate the cost breakdown shown in Table 19–6.

You now have a requirement for an additional 200 ejector assemblies. What would be a reasonable target price, given the information you have accumulated?

The first task is to determine the cumulative average hours required to manufacture a total of 300 units (100 (initial order) + 200 (follow-on

F I G U R E   19-6

Learning Curve Rates

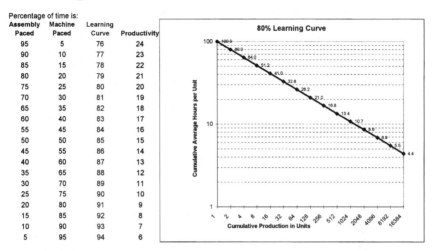

Percentage of time is:

Assembly Paced	Machine Paced	Learning Curve	Productivity
95	5	76	24
90	10	77	23
85	15	78	22
80	20	79	21
75	25	80	20
70	30	81	19
65	35	82	18
60	40	83	17
55	45	84	16
50	50	85	15
45	55	86	14
40	60	87	13
35	65	88	12
30	70	89	11
25	75	90	10
20	80	91	9
15	85	92	8
10	90	93	7
5	95	94	6

T A B L E   19-6

Ejector Assembly Costs Breakdown

	Cost per Unit Initial order 100 units
Material cost	$100.00
Labor (4 hours @ $11.50 hour)	46.00
Overhead (100% of direct labor)	46.00
	$192.00
Profit (25%)	48.00
Total unit price	$240.00

order)). This can be done at least two ways: using Wright tables to calculate the average cumulative hours or using log–log paper to estimate the cumulative average hours.

Solving using Wright tables:

- First 100 units took 4 cumulative average hours to produce.
- The learning curve rate was 80%.
- First we need to calculate the cumulative average hours to produce the first unit.

$$4 \text{ hours}/0.227^3 = 17.62 \text{ hours}$$

Learning curve factor for 300 is 0.159^4

$$17.62 \text{ hours} \times 0.159 = 2.80 \text{ hours}$$

Solving using log–log paper:

- In order to draw a line we need two points.
- We have one point (100 units, 4 cumulative average hours per unit).
- A second point (200 units) can be determined by multiplying 4 (cumulative average hours per unit) × 0.8 (80% learning curve rate) = 3.2 cumulative average hours per unit for 200 units.

Using Figure 19–7 we can now use the learning curve we have drawn to estimate the cumulative average hours for 300 units. The cumulative average hours for 300 units is 2.8 hours per unit. Now all we need to do is the math to estimate the labor cost per unit for the additional 200 units. (See Tables 19–7 and 19–8.)

Price Productivity

Price productivity as used here is a method for determining the amount of cost take-out needed for a supplier to maintain its operating income while reducing the buyer's price to meet a price productivity target. It is a more cooperative/collaborative approach to reducing prices. The price productivity calculator concept came about as a result of a *Harvard Business Review* article in 1992.[5] The article reported on how companies made pricing decisions that negatively impacted their profits. The research produced the following quantitative relationships:

- For each 1% increase in unit price, incremental operating income increased by 11.1%.

---

3. Ibid., p. 191.
4. Ibid., p. 194.
5. M. V. Marn and R. L. Rosiello, "Managing Price, Gaining Profit," *Harvard Business Review*, vol. 70, September–October 1992, pp. 84–94.

F I G U R E   19–7

Ejector Assembly: Log–Log Solution

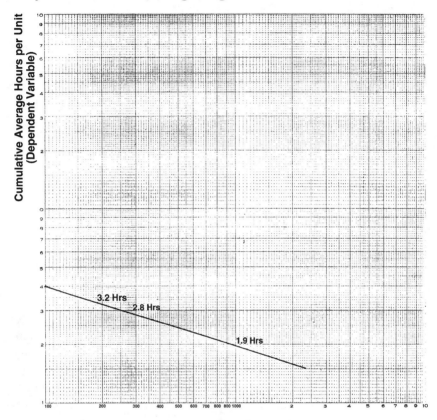

Cumulative Production in Units
(Independent Variable)

T A B L E   19–7

Ejector Assembly: Estimated Labor Cost for the Additional 200 Units

300 units × 2.8 hours =	840 hours
Less 100 units × 4.0 hours =	400 hours
440 hours × 11.50 hour =	$5,060.00
$5,060.00 ÷ 200 units =	$25.30 per unit

T A B L E   19–8

Target Price 200 Additional Ejector Assemblies

	Additional 200 Units
Material cost	$100.00
Labor	25.30
Overhead (100% of direct labor)	25.30
	$150.60
Profit (25%)	37.65
Total unit price	$188.25

♦ For each 1% decease in variable costs, incremental operating income increased by 7.8%.

♦ For each 1% increase in unit volume, incremental operating income increased by 3.3%.

♦ For each 1% reduction in fixed costs, incremental operating income increased by 2.3%.

With these quantitative relationships, we can now begin to measure the impact of changes in volume and fixed and variable costs on operating income (contribution margin (selling price − variable cost) − fixed costs = operating income). Operating income is a better measure of the value of a buyer's business to a supplier than net profit because operating income shows the revenue generated by your business and not the net income. Net income is a function of how the seller is operating its business, which has little to do with the revenue generated by your business.

Price Productivity Calculator

The price productivity calculator is a tool to determine the amount of unit volume increase, variable cost decrease, or fixed cost decrease needed for a seller to decrease its selling price and at the same time maintain its existing operating margin. Calculating the amount of volume increase and variable and fixed cost decrease is a two-step process.

Step 1: Calculating the percent of incremental profit improvement.

Percent incremental
profit improvement* = Operating margin × Operating
profit improvement* × 100

*(per 1% change in unit volume, fixed or variable costs)

Step 2: Calculating the amount of cost take-out (variable or fixed) or volume increase needed to provide the buyer with a price decrease while maintaining its current operating profit margin

$$\text{Percent decrease needed in variable or fixed costs or increase in unit volume} = \frac{\text{Price decrease desired or needed}}{\text{Percent incremental profit improvement}}$$

Price Productivity Calculator Example   Assume that you have a supplier with the following characteristics:

♦ Operating profit improvement per 1% reduction in variable costs = Unknown (use the HBR ratio of 1% = 7.8% from the discussion on page 456–458)
♦ An operating margin of 10%

You wish a 6% price decrease
What is the amount of the reduction in variable costs that is needed to reduce the selling price by 6% and still have the supplier maintain a 10% operating profit margin?

Step 1: Calculating the percent of incremental profit improvement.

$$\text{Percent incremental profit improvement (per 1\% variable cost decrease)} = 0.10 \times 0.78 \times 100 = 0.78\%$$

Step 2: Calculating the amount of variable cost take-out needed to provide the buyer with a 6% price decrease while maintaining the supplier's 10% operating profit margin.

$$\text{Percent variable cost decrease to maintain the seller's operating margin} = \frac{6\%}{0.78\%} = 7.69\%$$

From this calculation, we have determined that if the supplier reduces its variable costs by 7.69%, it is able to reduce the buyer's price by 6% and still maintain a better than 10% operating margin.

You can determine a firm's operating margin or operating income from its annual report or find it listed by industry in the *Quarterly Financial Report for Manufacturing, Mining and Trade Corporations,* published by the U.S. Department of Commerce, Bureau of the Census, at www.census.gov under Business, Economic Surveys. The more homogeneous the firm's product line, the more accurate the relationship between reductions in cost or increases in volume and their impact on operating income. If the company is privately held, you can use the quantitative relationships published in the HBR article.

Price Productivity Macro and Micro Models

Having the fixed and variable cost information (determined from a fixed and variable cost analysis), we can begin to construct both macro and micro price productivity models. (See Tables 19–9 and 19–10.)

Cost Analysis Case

A detailed analysis of this case using SDS_Notebooks software can be found later in this chapter. Demonstration SDS_Notebooks software can be downloaded from www.sdsnotebooks.com.

You received the following quotation from Fab-Tech for High Torque Gearboxes.

T A B L E   19–9

Price Productivity Macro Model: Impact on Operating Income from Decreases in Price and Variable Costs

	Original Quotation	6% Price Decrease and a 7% Variable Costs Decrease
Net sale billed	$43,000.00	$40,420.00
Variable costs	36,950.00	34,363.50
Contribution margin	$6,050.00	$6,056.50
Fixed costs	1,750.00	1,750.00
Operating income	$4,300.00	$4,306.50
Operating margin	10.00%	10.65%

T A B L E   19–10

Price Productivity Micro Model: Impact on Operating
Income of Decreases in Price and Variable Costs

	Original Quotation	Change Generated by a 6% Price Reduction, a 10% Reduction in Direct Mat'l, a 4.05% Reduction in Direct Labor, and an 8.1% Reduction in Variable Overhead
Net sales billed	$43,000.00	$40,420.00
Variable costs:		
Direct material (55%)	20,322.50	18,290.25
Direct labor (15%)	5,542.50	5,318.03
Variable overhead (30%)	11,085.00	10,187.12
	$36,950.00	$33,795.40
Contribution margin	$6,050.00	$6,624.60
Fixed costs	1,750.00	1,750.00
Operating income	$4,300.00	$4,874.60
Operating income change	–	13.36%

Quantity	50	100	150	200
Unit Price*	$800.00	$700.00	$680.00	$670.00

*F.O.B. Shipping Point

The first analysis that needs to be performed on all quotations is the quantity discount analysis. (See Table 19–11.)

The QDA analysis shows a roller coaster pattern. This means that on an incremental basis the supplier is not offering a pricing schedule that reflects that the more you buy, the greater the discount. It would be interesting to hear Fab-Tech explain why, on an incremental basis, the unit prices are increasing as quantity increases.

Fixed and Variable Cost Analysis

Calculating the fixed and variable costs for each price and quantity pair, we generate the information shown in Table 19–12.

T A B L E   19–11

Fab-Tech's QDA Results

Quantity	50 units	100 units	150 units	200 units
Quoted price	$800.00	$700.00	$680.00	$670.00
Price/unit differences	$800.00	$600.00	$640.00	$640.00
Per unit price differences at breaks	0.00	$200.00	($40.00)	$0.00
Percentage price reduction	0.00%	25.00%	−6.67%	0.00%

T A B L E   19–12

Fab-Tech's Fixed and Variable Cost Analysis

Price Pairs	Fixed Costs	Unit Variable Costs
1 & 2	$10,000.00	$600.00
1 & 3	$9,000.00	$620.00
1 & 4	$8,666.67	$640.00
2 & 3	$6,000.00	$640.00
2 & 4	$6,000.00	$640.00
3 & 4	$6,000.00	$640.00

Based on the frequency of $6,000.00 (fixed costs) and $640.00 (unit variable costs), I would select these as a reasonable estimate of this supplier's fixed and variable costs.

Price Productivity Macro

Using the information from the fixed and unit variable cost analysis and from the U.S. Department of Commerce, Bureau of the Census, *1996 Annual Survey of Manufacturers* and the *Quarterly Financial Report*, we can construct an income statement for a quantity of 100 @ $700.00 per unit. Based on an operating income of 9.4%, we can determine unit variable costs less profit to $574.20 ($700.00 × 0.094 = $65.80, $700.00 − ($65.80 − $60.00) = $574.20). (See Table 19–13.)

T A B L E   19–13

Fab-Tech's Price Productivity Macro Model

	Current Quotation	Value of a 1% Price Increase	Change Generated by a 5% Price Reduction and a 7.32% Variable Cost Reduction
Net sales billed	$70,000.00	$70,700.00	$66,500.00
Variable costs	57,420.00	57,420.00	53,216.86
Contribution margin	$12,580.00	$13,280.00	$13,283.14
Fixed costs	6,000.00	$6,000.00	$6,000.00
Operating income	$6,580.00	$7,280.00	$7,283.14
Operating income change	–	10.64%	10.69%

This analysis shows that a 1% price increase is equal to a 10.64% incremental improvement in operating income and that a 5% reduction in price along with a 7.32% reduction in variable costs will generate a 10.69% incremental increase in operating income. Any improvement in variable costs generated by the buyer and seller working together may also apply to other items produced by the supplier so that the impact of buyers and sellers working together to remove waste results in a WIN–WIN, not a WIN–win, outcome.

Price Productivity Micro

Fab-Tech fits into SIC group 34 Fabricated metal products. From the U.S. Department of Commerce, Bureau of the Census *Annual Survey of Manufacturers* (www.census.gov/), and the *Quarterly Financial Report* (www.census.gov/) we can obtain the data shown in Box 19–1.

From these data we can break down variable costs into direct material, direct labor, overhead, and operating profit. (See Box 19–2.)

Using these data we are able to construct the price productivity table shown in Table 19–14. Using price productivity micro, we can demonstrate to a supplier the impact of reductions in direct material and labor (variable overhead assigned to this job is reduced merely by decreasing the amount of direct labor used). Finding a way to decrease the

B O X   19–1

FAB-TECH'S SIC 34 DATA

- Number of employees: 1,483,000
- Payroll: $46,129,800,000

- Production workers: 1,114,400

- Hours: 2,338,800,000

- Wages: $29,722,700,000
- Cost of materials:
  $107,990,400,000
- Value of industry
  shipments:
  $214,006,300,000
- Income from operations:
  9.4% of revenues

B O X   19–2

PRICE PRODUCTIVITY MICRO CALCULATIONS

- Total cost = total revenue /
  cost + profit (if cost = 1 and
  profit = 0.094, then cost +
  profit = 1.094)
- Material cost as % of total
  cost
- Labor cost as % of total cost

- Overhead as % total cost
  (100%–(M.C. + L.C.))
- Labor rate = payroll / hours

- T.C. = $214,006,300,000 /
  1.094
- T.C. = $195,618,200,000

- M.C. = $107,990,400,000 /
  $195,618,200,000 = 55%
- L.C. = $29,722,700,000 /
  $195,618,299,000 = 15%
- O.H. = 1 − (55 + 15) = 30%
  or 200% of L.C.
- L.R. = $46,129,800,000 /
  2,338,800,000 = $12.70 hour

cost of material by 5% and direct labor by 2.4% is not a large task, particularly if this is an initial cost improvement project for an item. The focus needs to be on reducing costs and increasing margins and not on price reductions at the expense of margin.

Learning Curve

Based on the prices quoted, the supplier seems to be using a 95% learning curve rate. (See Figures 19–8a and 19–8b.) That seems high; perhaps

T A B L E   19-14

Fab-Tech's Price Productivity Micro Model

	Current Quotation	Value of a 1% Price Increase	Change Generated by a 5% Price Reduction, a 10% Reduction in Direct Mat'l, a 2.4% Reduction in Direct Labor, and a 4.8% Reduction in Variable Overhead
Net Sales Billed	$70,000.00	$70,700.00	$66,500.00
Variable costs:			
Direct material (55%)	31,581.00	31,581.00	28,422.90
Direct labor (15%)	8,613.00	8,613.00	8,406.29
Variable overhead (30%)	17,226.00	17,226.00	16,399.15
	$57,420.00	$57,420.00	$53,228.34
Contribution margin	$12,580.00	$13,280.00	$13,271.66
Fixed costs	6,000.00	6,000.00	6,000.00
Operating income	$6,580.00	$7,280.00	$7,271.66
Operating income change	—	10.64%	10.51%

a 90% learning is more reasonable. Given a 90% learning curve (see Figures 19–8a and b), the quotation would be as shown in Table 19–15. (Note, in Figures 19–8a and b, "Purchase Price/Unit was calculated using "Ave Cum Hrs.")

Cost-Management Strategies

Costs are the result of decisions, not of price drivers, as many of us have been taught. Therefore, if the cost of an item is too high, one needs to go upstream in the decision process to see if another decision is possible that will reduce the cost of a component. The following questions and principles will assist you in identifying areas to be examined in more detail:

♦ *Bill of material analysis:* What was the source of pricing used to develop the quote?
♦ *Value analysis/value engineering:* Was any item overspecified relative to its function?

F I G U R E   19–8a

Fab-Tech's Learning Curve

Learning Curve Rate	95%	Potential Order Data Entry Table		
Orders	FirstOrder	#1	#2	#3
Number of Units	50	50	100	150
Fixed Costs/Unit	$120.00	$60.00	$40.00	$30.00
Mat'l Cost/Unit	$315.81	$315.81	$315.81	$315.81
Labor Rate	$12.70	$12.70	$12.70	$12.70
Ov'hd % D.L.	200.0	200.0	200.0	200.0
Profit % T.C.	10.4	10.4	10.4	10.4
Ave Cum Hrs	7.60	7.22	7.01	6.86
Ave Hrs this order	7.60	6.84	6.71	6.61

Calculated Learning Curve Results

Units Ordered	50	50	100	150
Fixed Costs/Unit	$120.00	$60.00	$40.00	$30.00
Unit Mat'l Cost	$315.81	$315.81	$315.81	$315.81
Unit Labor Cost	$96.52	$91.69	$88.98	$87.11
Unit Ov'hd Costs	$193.04	$183.39	$177.97	$174.22
Total Unit Costs	$725.37	$650.89	$622.76	$607.14
Profit	$75.44	$67.69	$64.77	$63.14
Purchase Price/Unit*	$800.81	$718.58	$687.53	$670.28

(a)

*Calculated using Ave Cum Hrs.

+ *Variable overhead analysis:* Does it appear to be reasonable?
+ *Labor cost analysis (rate × hours):* Was the correct category (price) of labor used? Does the amount of time to perform the value-added conversion look reasonable?
+ *Scrap allowances:* What scrap allowance was used?
+ *Contingencies:* What contingencies were included in the quote (scrap rework, material escalation)?

Cost-Management Principles

+ Identify the cost elements having significant cost and thus significant opportunities.
+ Analyze those significant cost elements for potential reductions.
+ Isolate non-value-added costs—waste.

F I G U R E   19–8b

Continued

Learning Curve Rate	90%	Potential Order Data Entry Table		
Orders	FirstOrder	#1	#2	#3
Number of Units	50	50	100	150
Fixed Costs/Unit	$120.00	$60.00	$40.00	$30.00
Mat'l Cost/Unit	$315.81	$315.81	$315.81	$315.81
Labor Rate	$12.70	$12.70	$12.70	$12.70
Ov'hd % D.L.	200.0	200.0	200.0	200.0
Profit % T.C.	10.4	10.4	10.4	10.4
Ave Cum Hrs	7.60	6.84	6.43	6.16
Ave Hrs this order	7.60	6.08	5.85	5.67

Calculated Learning Curve Results

Units Ordered	50	50	100	150
Fixed Costs/Unit	$120.00	$60.00	$40.00	$30.00
Unit Mat'l Cost	$315.81	$315.81	$315.81	$315.81
Unit Labor Cost	$96.52	$86.87	$81.68	$78.18
Unit Ov'hd Costs	$193.04	$173.74	$163.35	$156.36
Total Unit Costs	$725.37	$636.41	$600.84	$580.35
Profit	$75.44	$66.19	$62.49	$60.36
Purchase Price/Unit*	$800.81	$702.60	$663.32	$640.71

(b)

*Calculated using Ave Cum Hrs.

T A B L E   19–15

Fab-Techs Revised Quotation

Quantity	50	100	150	200
Cost	$800.00	$702.00	$663.00	$640.00
Savings	–	($200.00)	$2,250.00	$6,000.00

♦ Capture the financial benefit from the reduction or elimination of the non-value-added costs.

♦ Pass on the value improvement to the next member of the value chain (reduced prices).

APPENDIX TO CHAPTER 19

Calculation Appendix

PRICE ANALYSIS TOOLS

Quantity Discount Analysis—
Specific Quantity Calculation

Supplier: Tanner Spring Company
Item: Springs

Quantity	1,000	10,000	100,000	250,000
Price/M	$63.00	$8.50	$3.50	$3.40

See Table 19–16.
Calculation explanation:

Line 1: Number of units are the quantities quoted.

Line 2: Price/unit are the prices quoted by Tanner Spring Company (in $/1,000 units).

Line 3: Price/order is the Line 1 quantities × Line 2 prices.

Line 4: Difference between orders: 4A is the difference between Line 3A and 0, 4B is difference between Line 3B-3A, 4C is the difference between 3C-3B, and 4D is the difference between 3D-3C.

Line 5: Reduction from previous break: 5A is the difference between Line 1A and 0, 5B is the difference between Line 1B-1A,

T A B L E   19–16

QDA Specific Quantity Calculations

	A	B	C	D
1. Number of units	1,000	10,000	100,000	250,000
2. Price/unit	$65.00/M	$8.50/M	$3.50/M	$3.40/M
3. Price/order (minimum)	$65.00	$85.00	$350.00	$850.00
4. Difference between orders	$65.00	$20.00	$265.00	$500.00
5. Differences between breaks	1,000	9,000	90,000	150,000
6. Price/unit differences	$65.00/M	$2.22/M	$2.94/M	$3.33/M
7. Percentage reduction	–	96.58%	–32.43%*	–13.26%*

*Note: a negative price reduction means that the price increased rather decreased.

5C is the difference between 1C-1B, and 5D is the difference between 1D-1C.

Line 6: Reduction from previous break: 6A is 4A divided by 5A, 6B is 4B divided by 5B, 6C is 5C divided by 3C, and 6D is 4D divided by 5D.

Quantity Discount Analysis–Range Quantity Calculation

Supplier: Jones Electronics Inc.
Item: Relay

Quantity	1–9	10–99	100–999	1,000–3,000
Unit price	$6.25	$2.96	$2.37	$1.69

See Table 19–17.

Calculation explanation:

Line 1: Number of units in the range quantities quoted.

Line 2: Price/unit are the prices quoted by Jones Electronics Inc.

Line 3: Price/order (minimum) is the Line 1 minimum quantity $\times$ Line 2 prices.

Line 4: Maximum quantity to order: divide 2A into 3B and place the whole number in 4A, then divide 3C by 2C and place the

T A B L E   19–17

QDA Range Quantity Calculations

	A	B	C	D
1. Number of units	1–9	10–99	100–999	1,000–3,000
2. Price/unit	$6.25	$2.96	$2.37	$1.69
3. Price/order (minimum)	$6.25	$29.66	$237.00	$1,690.00
4. Maximum to order	4	80	713	
5. Price/order (maximum)	$25.00	$236.80	$1,689.81	
6. Difference between orders	$25.00	$211.80	$1,453.01	
7. Differences between breaks	4	76	651	
8. Price/unit differences	$6.25	2.78	$2.29	
9. Percentage reduction	–	55.52%	17.63%	

whole number in 4B, then divide 3D by 2C and place the whole number in 4C.

Line 5: Price/order (maximum): multiply 2A by 4A, and then 2B by 4B, and then 2C by 4C

Line 6: Difference between orders is the difference between Line 5A and 0, then Line 5B-5A, then 5C-5B.

Line 7: Reduction from previous break: 7A is the difference between Line 4A and 0, 7B is the difference between Line 4B-4A, and 7C is the difference between 4C-4B.

Line 8: Reduction from previous break: 8A is 6A divided by 7A, 8B is 6B divided by 7B, and 8C is 6C divided by 7C.

COST ANALYSIS CALCULATIONS

Fixed and Variable Costs Calculations

From the Fab-Tech quotation we can construct the following equation, $P = F/Q + V$.

$$\text{Price}_1 = \$800.00 \qquad \text{Quantity}_1 = 50$$
$$\text{Price}_2 = \$680.00 \qquad \text{Quantity}_2 = 150$$

Solving for Fixed Costs

$P_1 = F/Q_1 + V$

$-(P_2 = F/Q_2 + V)$

$\overline{\$800 = F/50 + V}$

$-(\$680 = F/150 + V)$

$\overline{\$120 = F/50 - F/150}$

$\$120 = F(0.02 - 0.0067)$

$\$120 = 0.0133F$

$\$9,022.55 = F$

Solving for Unit Variable Costs

$\$800 = \$9,022.55/50 + V$

$\$800 = \$180.45 + V$

$\$619.55 = V$

We can verify the values for F and V by calculating the price for 100 units.

$P = F/Q + V$

$P = \$9,022.55/100 + \$619.55$

$P = \$90.23 + \$619.55$

$P = \$709.78$ or 1.28% greater than the quoted price of $700.00

PRICE ANALYSIS CASE

You purchase a short slide that is used to connect various filling, packaging, and in-process operations. The short slide is designed to fail during jams rather than damage the product. Therefore, its usage is difficult to predict. You have collected the following information on the orders you have placed this year:

Date	Quantity	Price per Unit
January 10th	180	$86.00
April 23rd	200	79.00
July 12th	172	70.00
October 15th	212	58.00

All of the above requirements were purchased from General Fabrications.

The 15-Minute SDS_Notebooks Analysis of the General Fabrications Quotation

1. The first analysis that needs to be performed on all pricing is the *quantity discount analysis* (QDA). QDA provides information

on the underlying quantity discount for incremental volumes. From the QDA, I would conclude that General Fabrications has been pricing the short slide on the basis of cumulative volume versus order by order. The resulting curve shows that the more that is bought, the greater the discount (refer to Table 19–4 and Figure 19–9).

2. The *fixed and variable cost analysis* shows no real pattern for the allocation of fixed and variable costs. This result occurs when either the learning/experience curve logic or the dart board method of pricing is used to generate prices. Based on the curve shown in the QDA analysis it appears that learning/

F I G U R E   19–9

General Fabrications Quantity Discount Analysis

1. No. units per order	180	380	552	764
2. Price per unit	$86.00	$79.00	$70.00	$58.00
3. Total price per order	$15,480.00	$30,020.00	$38,640.00	$44,312.00
4. Price diff. between orders	$15,480.00	$14,540.00	$8,620.00	$5,672.00
5. Quantity diff. between orders	180	200	172	212
6. Price per unit per order qty diff.	$86.00	$72.70	$50.12	$26.75
7. Per unit price diff at breaks	–	$13.30	$22.58	$23.36
8. Percentage price reduction	–	15.47%	31.06%	46.61%

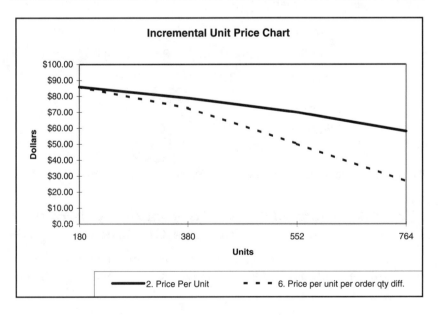

experience curve logic was used (refer to Table 19–5 and Figure 19–10).

3. The *experience curve analysis* leads us to assume that General Fabrications is using an 87% experience effect to generate prices. This figure may be too high, depending on the amount of labor to machine work. A lower experience rate may be more accurate. A case could be made that an 80% experience effect is more accurate than the 87%. If 80% is used rather than 87%, the price for the last would be $44.14 versus $58.00, or a potential annual saving of $13,860 (based on 1,000 short sides per year).

4. Using the economic order quantity calculator (assuming an annual usage of 1,000, order costs (cost to order, receive, and issue payment) of $150.00, unit costs of $58.00 and a 25% cost

F I G U R E   19–10

General Fabrications Fixed and Variable Cost Analysis

Price #	1	2	3	4
Quantity	180	380	552	764
Unit Price	$86.00	$79.00	$70.00	$58.00

		QtyToTest	Prices calculated for quantities in first row			
		1,000	180	380	552	764
Price Pairs	1 & 2	$75.09	$86.00	$79.00	$77.04	$75.83
Fixed Costs	$ 2,394.00					
Vari Unit Costs	$ 72.70					
Price Pairs	1 & 3	$66.53	$86.00	$73.50	$70.00	$67.85
Fixed Costs	$ 4,273.55					
Vari Unit Costs	$ 62.26					
Price Pairs	1 & 4	$55.96	$86.00	$66.72	$61.31	$58.00
Fixed Costs	$ 6,593.43					
Vari Unit Costs	$ 49.37					
Price Pairs	2 & 3	$61.09	$111.09	$79.00	$70.00	$64.48
Fixed Costs	$ 10,975.81					
Vari Unit Costs	$ 50.12					
Price Pairs	2 & 4	$53.10	$125.42	$79.00	$65.98	$58.00
Fixed Costs	$ 15,876.88					
Vari Unit Costs	$ 37.22					
Price Pairs	3 & 4	$50.63	$159.37	$89.57	$70.00	$58.00
Fixed Costs	$ 23,871.40					
Vari Unit Costs	$ 26.75					

F I G U R E   19–11

General Fabrications Economic Order
Quantity Calculator

Trial #	1	2	3	4
Usage in units	1,000	1,000	1,000	1,000
Order costs in dollars	$150.00	$150.00	$150.00	$150.00
Unit costs in dollars	$86.00	$79.00	$70.00	$58.00
Quantity range per unit cost	0	0	0	0
Carrying cost as % of inventory	25	25	25	25
EOQ	**118**	**123**	**131**	**144**
Total annual cost	**$88,619.84**	**$81,567.07**	**$72,345.64**	**$60,092.83**
Minimum order quantity	**118**	**123**	**131**	**144**

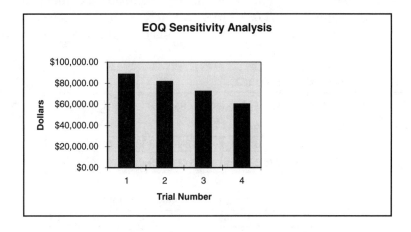

of carrying inventory), the minimum order quantity is 144
(refer to Figure 19–11).

General Comments

One could use this analysis to probe the supplier for additional price
decreases. It would seem likely that a price lower than 44.10 per unit
based could be negotiated for the next 1,000 units. You can generate a
potent negotiating position using SDS_Notebooks, and it takes only a
few minutes to perform each analysis.

COST ANALYSIS CASE
FAB-TECH

700 El Camino Road—San Mateo—California

January 10, 19XX

Mr. Ralph Kilmann
Sourcing Specialist
MBI International
2745 Elk Highway
Redman, OR 97330

Dear Ralph:

Thank you for the opportunity to quote on the High Torque Gerbox. We are confident that we can exceed all your specifications.

We wish to propose the following pricing for the High Torque Gearbox:

Quantity	Unit Cost*
50	$800.00
100	700.00
150	680.00
200	670.00

*F.O.B. San Mateo, California—Terms Net 30

Thank you again for the opportunity to do business with your excellent company.

Sincerely,

Ray Hawks
Vice President Sales

The 30-Minute SDS_Notebooks Analysis of the Fab-Tech Quotation

1. The first analysis that needs to be performed on all pricing is the *quantity discount analysis* (QDA). QDA provides information on the underlying quantity discount for incremental volumes. From analyzing the QDA, I would conclude that Fab-Tech's quotation shows a lower average unit price across all quantities, but the incremental curve shows that the incremental unit prices show an initial decrease followed by an increase. QDA does not expose why the incremental prices are behaving the way the do. It merely presents the data for analysis and formulations of questions (refer to Table 19–11 and Figure 19–12).

2. The *fixed and variable cost calculator* shows a pattern for the allocation of fixed and variable costs when the last three pairs are analyzed. Based on this analysis, I would used $6,000.00 as an estimate of fixed costs and $640.00 as an estimate of the variable costs (note: variable costs include direct material, direct labor, manufacturing overhead, and profit) (refer to Table 19–12 and Figure 19–13).

3. Using the various *price productivity calculators,* I am able to calculate impact on operating income of decreases in fixed and variable costs and increases in unit volume. To determine various financial data to use the Price Productivity Micro and Macro, I utilized two government databases: the *1996 Annual Manufacturers Survey* (www.census.gov/html/#mn) and the *Quarterly Financial Report* (www.census.gov). These analyses showed how decreases in variable costs could generate a decrease in the price for the buyer and an increase in the operating income for the seller (refer to Tables 19–13 and 19–14, Box 19–2, and Figure 19–14).

4. The *learning curve analysis* leads us to assume that Fab-Tech pricing closely fits a 95% learning curve. This reflects a very low learning rate. A more reasonable learning curve rate of 90% would generate a lower price for all quantities quoted (at 150 units the estimated price would be $640.71, or $30.00 per unit less) (refer to Table 19–15, Figure 19–8a and b, and Figure 19–15).

F I G U R E   19–12

Fab-Tech Quantity Discount Analysis

1. No. units per order	50	100	150	200
2. Price per unit	$800.00	$700.00	$680.00	$670.00
3. Total price per order	$40,000.00	$70,000.00	$102,000.00	$134,000.00
4. Price diff. between orders	$40,000.00	$30,000.00	$32,000.00	$32,000.00
5. Quantity diff. between orders	50	50	50	50
6. Price per unit per order qty diff.	$800.00	$600.00	$640.00	$640.00
7. Per unit price diff at breaks	–	**$200.00**	**($40.00)**	**$0.00**
8. Percentage price reduction	–	**25.00%**	**−6.67%**	**0.00%**

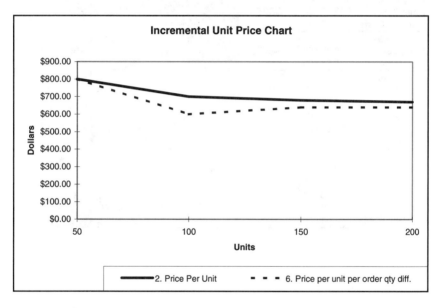

5. The *break-even calculator* shows that the quantity of units needed to reach break-even ranges from 54% to 42%. This would suggest that there is an opportunity for reducing prices (refer to Figure 19–16).

General Comments

These analyses provide the buyer with powerful tools to either force Fab-Tech to reduce their prices or to identify areas were cost may be removed so that the buyer receives lower prices while Fab-Tech maintains or improves their operating income. You can generate a potent negotiating position using SDS_Notebooks, and it only takes a few minutes to perform each analysis.

F I G U R E   19–13

Fab-Tech Fixed and Variable Cost Analysis

Price #	1	2	3	4
Quantity	50	100	150	200
Unit Price	$800.00	$700.00	$680.00	$670.00

		QtyToTest	Prices calculated for quantities in first row			
		400	**50**	**100**	**150**	**200**
Price Pairs	**1 & 2**					
Fixed Costs	**$ 10,000.00**	**$625.00**	$800.00	$700.00	**$666.67**	**$650.00**
Vari Unit Costs	**$ 600.00**					
Price Pairs	**1 & 3**					
Fixed Costs	**$ 9,000.00**	**$642.50**	$800.00	**$710.00**	$680.00	**$665.00**
Vari Unit Costs	**$ 620.00**					
Price Pairs	**1 & 4**					
Fixed Costs	**$ 8,666.67**	**$648.33**	$800.00	**$713.33**	**$684.44**	$670.00
Vari Unit Costs	**$ 626.67**					
Price Pairs	**2 & 3**					
Fixed Costs	**$ 6,000.00**	**$655.00**	**$760.00**	$700.00	$680.00	**$670.00**
Vari Unit Costs	**$ 640.00**					
Price Pairs	**2 & 4**					
Fixed Costs	**$ 6,000.00**	**$655.00**	**$760.00**	$700.00	**$680.00**	$670.00
Vari Unit Costs	**$ 640.00**					
Price Pairs	**3 & 4**					
Fixed Costs	**$ 6,000.00**	**$655.00**	**$760.00**	**$700.00**	$680.00	$670.00
Vari Unit Costs	**$ 640.00**					

F I G U R E   19–14

Fab-Tech Price Productivity Calculations

Price Productivity Calculator Assumptions*

Each 1% Improvement in	Gives an Operating Income Improvement of
Price	**11.10%**
Variable Costs	**7.80%**
Volume	**3.30%**
Fixed costs	**2.30%**

Scenario #1 Variable Cost Impact   Assumptions #1

Calculating the amount of the variable cost take-out needed to provide a buyer with a price decrease while maintaining the seller's current operating profit margin	**7.80%**	Operating profit improvement for each 1% decrease in variable costs
	9%	Operating profit margin
	10%	Price decrease
A variable cost decrease of	**14.25% is required**	

Scenario #2 Fixed Cost Impact   Assumptions #2

Calculating the amount of the fixed cost take-out needed to provide a buyer with a price decrease while maintaining the seller's current operating profit margin	**2.30%**	Operating profit improvement for each 1% decrease in fixed costs
	9%	Operating profit margin
	10%	Price decrease
A fixed cost decrease of	**48.31% is required**	

Scenario #3 Unit Volume Impact   Assumptions #3

Calculating the amount of unit volume increase needed to provide a buyer with a price decrease while maintaining the seller's current operating profit margin	**3.30%**	Operating profit improvement for each 1% decrease in fixed costs
	9%	Operating profit margin
	10%	Price decrease
A unit volume increase of	**33.67% is required**	

*These assumptions are cited in M.V. Morn and R.L. Rosiella, "Managing Price, Gaining Profits," *Harvard Business Review,* vol. 70, September–October 1992, pp 84–94.

Continued

Price Productivity Macro Calculator

Changes In	% Change	% Change	% Change	% Change	% Change
Net Sales Billed	1.00	(5.00)	(10.00)	(15.00)	(20.00)
Variable Costs	0.00	(7.32)	(13.42)	(19.51)	(25.60)
Fixed Costs	0.00	0.00	0.00	0.00	0.00

Results Table

	Current Operations	Results in	Results in	Results in	Results in	Results in
Net Sales Billed	$70,000.00	$70,700.00	$66,500.00	$63,000.00	$59,500.00	$56,000.00
Variable Costs	$57,420.00	$57,420.00	$53,216.86	$49,714.24	$46,217.36	$42,720.48
Contribution Margin	$12,580.00	$13,280.00	$13,283.14	$13,285.76	$13,282.64	$13,279.52
Fixed Costs	$6,000.00	$6,000.00	$6,000.00	$6,000.00	$6,000.00	$6,000.00
Operating Income	$6,580.00	$7,280.00	$7,283.14	$7,285.76	$7,282.64	$7,279.52
Operating Income Changed by		10.64%	10.69%	10.73%	10.68%	10.63%

Price Productivity Micro Calculator

Changes in	% Change	% Change	% Change	% Change	% Change
Net Sales Billed	1.00	(5.00)	(10.00)	(15.00)	(20.00)
Variable Costs					
Direct Material%	0.00	(10.00)	(16.20)	(23.20)	(24.70)
Direct Labor%	0.00	(2.40)	(6.00)	(9.00)	(16.00)
Variable Overhead%	0.00	(4.80)	(12.00)	(18.00)	(32.00)
Fixed Costs	0.00	0.00	0.00	0.00	0.00

F I G U R E   19–14

Continued

Results Table

	Current Operations	Results in	Results in	Results in	Results in	Results in
Net Sales Billed	$70,000.00	$70,700.00	$66,500.00	$63,000.00	$59,500.00	$56,000.00
Variable Costs 100.00 (must total 100%)	$57,420.00	$57,420.00	$53,228.34	$49,719.98	$46,217.36	$42,729.09
Direct Material 55.00	$31,581.00	$31,581.00	$28,422.90	$26,464.88	$24,254.21	$23,780.49
Direct Labor 15.00	$8,613.00	$8,613.00	$8,406.29	$8,096.22	$7,837.83	$7,234.92
Variable Overhead 30.00	$17,226.00	$17,226.00	$16,399.15	$15,158.88	$14,125.32	$11,713.68
Contribution Margin	$12,580.00	$13,280.00	$13,271.66	$13,280.02	$13,282.64	$13,270.91
Fixed Costs	$6,000.00	$6,000.00	$6,000.00	$6,000.00	$6,000.00	$6,000.00
Operating Income as % of sales 9.40	$6,580.00	$7,280.00	$7,271.66	$7,280.02	$7,282.64	$7,270.91
Operating Income Changed by		10.64%	10.51%	10.64%	10.68%	10.50%

F I G U R E   19–15

Fab-Tech Learning Curve Analysis

Learning Curve Rate	95%	Potential Order Data Entry Table		
Orders	First Order	#1	#2	#3
Number of units	50	50	100	150
Fixed costs/unit	$120.00	$60.00	$40.00	$30.00
Mat'l cost/unit	$315.81	$315.81	$315.81	$315.81
Labor rate	$12.70	$12.70	$12.70	$12.70
Ov'hd % D.L.	200.0	200.0	200.0	200.0
Profit % T.C.	10.4	10.4	10.4	10.4
Ave cum hrs	7.60	7.22	7.01	6.86
Ave hrs this order	7.60	6.84	6.71	6.61

F I G U R E   19–15

Continued

Calculated Learning Curve Results

Units ordered	50	50	100	150
Fixed costs/unit	$120.00	$60.00	$40.00	$30.00
Unit mat'l cost	$315.81	$315.81	$315.81	$315.81
Unit labor cost	$96.52	$91.69	$88.98	$87.11
Unit ov'hd costs	$193.04	$183.39	$177.97	$174.22
Total unit costs	$725.37	$650.89	$622.76	$607.14
Profit	$75.44	$67.69	$64.77	$63.14
Purchase price/unit*	$800.81	$718.58	$687.53	$670.28

*Calculated using Ave Cum Hrs from preceding section of Figure 19–15.

Learning Curve Rate	90%	Potential Order Data Entry Table		
Orders	First Order	#1	#2	#3
Number of units	50	50	100	150
Fixed costs/unit	$120.00	$60.00	$40.00	$30.00
Mat'l cost/unit	$315.81	$315.81	$315.81	$315.81
Labor rate	$12.70	$12.70	$12.70	$12.70
Ov'hd % D.L.	200.0	200.0	200.0	200.0
Profit % T.C.	10.4	10.4	10.4	10.4
Ave cum hrs	7.60	6.84	6.43	6.16
Ave hrs this order	7.60	6.08	5.85	5.67

F I G U R E   19–15

Continued

Calculated Learning Curve Results

Units ordered	50	50	100	150
Fixed costs/unit	$120.00	$60.00	$40.00	$30.00
Unit mat'l cost	$315.81	$315.81	$315.81	$315.81
Unit labor cost	$96.52	$86.87	$81.68	$78.18
Unit ov'hd costs	$193.04	$173.74	$163.35	$156.36
Total unit costs	$725.37	$636.41	$600.84	$580.35
Profit	$75.44	$66.19	$62.49	$60.36
Purchase price/unit*	$800.81	$702.60	$663.32	$640.71

*Calculated using Ave Cum Hrs. from preceding section of Figure 19–15.

F I G U R E   19–16

Fab-Tech Break-Even Calculator

Trial #	◉ 1	○ 2	○ 3	○ 4
Unit selling price	$800.00	$700.00	$680.00	$670.00
Unit variable cost	$574.20	$574.20	$574.20	$574.20
Total fixed cost	$6,000.00	$6,000.00	$6,000.00	$6,000.00
Unit sales for break-even	27	48	57	63
Dollars in sales for break-even	$21,600	$33,600	$38,760	$42,210

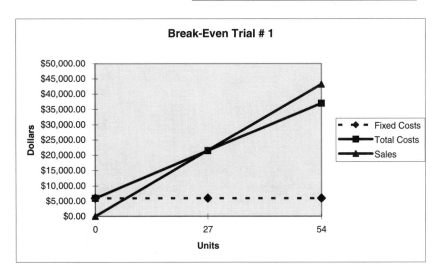

ADDITIONAL READINGS

Allan, G. B., and J. S. Hamond. *Notes on the Use of Experience Curves in Competitive Decision Making.* Harvard Business School, No. 175-174, 1975.

Kuzdrall, P. J., and R. R. Britney. *Price and Discount Schedule Analysis.* Quorum Books, Westport, Conn., 1991.

Total Cost of Ownership

Editor
Lisa M. Ellram, Ph.D., C.P.M., A.P.P., CPA, C.M.A.
Associate Professor of Supply Chain Management
Arizona State University
College of Business

INTRODUCTION

This chapter will explore the concept of total cost of ownership, which is defined here as a philosophy for developing an understanding of all relevant supply chain related costs of a particular transaction or process. In supply chain management, total cost of ownership often focuses on the cost of doing business with a particular supplier for a particular good or service. Total cost of ownership (TCO) considers total cost of acquisition, use/administration, maintenance, and disposal of a given item or service. As will be presented later, TCO modeling does not actually require precise calculation of all costs but looks at major cost issues and at costs that may be relevant to the decision at hand.

HOW DOES TCO COMPARE TO OTHER APPROACHES?

Price is only one element of total cost of ownership, albeit often the largest single one. Viewing *cost from a supplier's perspective* focuses on how much it costs for the supplier to produce and deliver an item or service to its customer. It includes elements such as labor, packaging, raw materials, overhead, and transportation. Understanding such costs may be helpful in performing a sophisticated TCO analysis. It is also relevant if the supplier is willing to work with the organization on reducing TCO. Such cooperation is growing in practice.

Cost from a buyer's perspective is analogous to the TCO concept. Rather than simply buying based on price, the buyer should have a method for determining what a particular purchase really costs the organization, including more obvious issues such as transportation, duties, and on-time delivery, and more difficult to identify issues such as the cost of a supplier field failure and education, training, and administrative support required to work with a supplier. Total cost of ownership is not a new technique by any means, but is receiving increased visibility and concern among organizations for a variety of reasons.

WHY THE INTEREST IN TCO?

Many of the recent changes in the business environment have led to increased interest and improved feasibility for TCO. For example, better computer systems have made it possible for organizations to access data in more flexible ways, to network systems, and to retrieve and organize data in a more usable manner. This was very difficult with most legacy systems. Enterprise systems provide improved data linkages and access. Some such systems even include modules for calculating TCO. The use of PC-based spreadsheet models for TCO, however, is still the most popular approach, due to the flexibility and ready availability of PC spreadsheets. The changing nature of buyer–seller relationships has had a big influence on the desire to better understand total cost of ownership. In a study by the Center for Advanced Purchasing Studies (CAPS) on strategic alliances, reduction in total cost of ownership was cited as the number one reason that buying organizations enter into strategic alliances.[1]

Supply base reduction is another factor driving the importance of total cost of ownership. As an organization reduces its supply base and becomes increasingly dependent on fewer suppliers, retaining the "right" suppliers is important. Similarly, there is a growing realization of the need to go beyond price. As suppliers provide more services and vary their levels of service, it becomes increasingly complex to determine what one is really paying for and whether one is receiving "good value."

---

1. T. Hendrick and L. M. Ellram, *Strategic Supplier Partnerships: An International Study,* Center for Advanced Purchasing Studies, Tempe, Arizona, 1993.

Outsourcing is yet another critical reason to perform TCO analysis. Without an understanding of all the costs of outsourcing versus in-house operations, a fair assessment of the outsourcing proposal cannot be made. This can result in poor decisions that are expensive and time-consuming to reverse.

The development of activity-based cost management (ABCM) has been an important tool to facilitate the use of TCO analysis and automation of TCO. Organizations such as Compumotor[2] and Nortel[3] have used concepts from ABCM to create overhead allocations to allocate activity-based costs to suppliers, providing an automated method for performing TCO analysis on routine purchases.

Related to this is the growing recognition that there are many hidden activities or "cost drivers" within organizations and in dealing with suppliers that render the use of simple accounting data or price alone highly inaccurate for decision purposes. TCO analysis keys in on those cost drivers and hidden costs to support improved analysis and decision-making.

Finally, the concept of supply chain management is really beginning to take hold in organizations throughout the world. Supply chain management recognizes that all the costs of an organization's network, from earliest supplier through final customer, and even disposal, are interdependent. Total cost of ownership analysis supports supply chain management efforts by recognizing and analyzing how an organization's costs and performance have an effect on, and are affected by, the cost and performance of the organizations with which it does business. TCO analysis can be performed at a dyadic level or by incorporating any or all parts of the supply chain.

Table 20–1 illustrates that total cost of ownership may be multiples higher than price, thereby invalidating price as a selection criterion. This example is based on Kodak's TCO analysis of programmable logic controllers (PLCs).[4] PLCs were being purchased by Kodak at the plant level throughout the world, based on price. A group within Kodak whose

---

2. P. Bennett, "ABM and the Procurement Cost Model," *Management Accounting*, March 1996, pp. 28–32.
3. L. M. Ellram, *Total Cost Modeling in Purchasing*, Center for Advanced Purchasing Studies, Tempe, Arizona, 1994.
4. L. M. Ellram and O. R. V. Edis, "A Case Study of Successful Partnering Implementation," *International Journal of Purchasing and Materials Management*, vol. 32, no. 4, Fall 1996, pp. 20–28.

T A B L E   20–1

Price versus Cost: Kodak Example
Purchase of Programmable Logic Controller
The "Iceberg" Model

Cost Element	% of Purchase Price
Purchase costs	100%
Engineering costs	75%
Installation costs	100%
Commissioning costs	12%
Parts & service costs	15%
Maintenance costs	50%
Training costs	5%
Retirement costs	10%
TOTAL	367%

Source: L. M. Ellram and O. R. V. Edis, "A Case Study of Successful Partnering Implementation," *International Journal of Purchasing and Materials management*, vol. 32, no. 4, Fall 1996, pp. 20–28.

mission was to find cost savings/leverage opportunities was convinced that this low price emphasis, which was causing proliferation of models and manufacturers of PLCs, was actually creating higher total costs for the company.

In order to build a business case for creating a global PLC contract, Kodak performed a TCO analysis, as in Table 20–1. Kodak determined that it could cut 25–50% of the 367% TCO of PLCs by using a common PLC worldwide. This analysis was used successfully to demonstrate the benefits of a global contract and to gain cooperation of plants throughout the world.

CHOOSING A PROJECT FOR TCO ANALYSIS

Not every purchase or process analysis is an ideal candidate for TCO analysis. TCO analysis can be complex and time-consuming, so there should be some initial assurance that the potential benefits of the analysis will outweigh the costs. Box 20–1 shows some of the characteristics that make a purchase well suited for TCO analysis. Purchases with these characteristics are ideal for "pilot" TCO projects, where it is very important to show a dramatic difference between TCO and price in order to demonstrate the benefits of TCO.

B O X   20–1

CHARACTERISTICS OF ITEM FOR PILOT TCO PROJECT

- The firm spends a relatively large amount of money on that item.
- The firm purchases the item with some degree of regularity, in order to provide some historical data, but more importantly, to allow opportunities to gather current cost data.
- Purchasing believes the item has significant transaction costs associated with it that are not currently recognized.
- Purchasing believes that one or more of the currently unrecognized transaction costs are individually significant.
- Purchasing has the opportunity to have an impact on transactions costs, via negotiation, changing suppliers, or improving internal operations.
- Those purchasing/using the item will cooperate in data gathering to learn more about the item's cost structure.

Source: L. M. Ellram, "A Framework for Total Cost of Ownership," *International Journal of Logistics Management*, vol. 4, no. 2, 1993, pp. 49–60.

Early success is important in implementing total cost of ownership concepts. An early success, with many dollars involved and a high level of organizational visibility, will create ongoing support for TCO as an approach to doing business. Big successes and high visibility may also help overcome some of the organizational politics and barriers that are part of every change in organizational processes.

TYPES OF TCO ANALYSIS

Firms use two general approaches in performing TCO analysis: a one-time project analysis or a computerized, ongoing system. A one-time project analysis is used primarily to support a specific decision-making situation. Decisions that are well supported by this one-time project analysis include:

- Outsourcing
- Reducing supply base
- Forming alliances
- Looking for areas for improvement/cost drivers
- Selecting of key suppliers

This approach is used more commonly in practice than a computerized system because it is customized to fit the specific situation. The level of detail can be varied significantly, depending on the importance and complexity of the purchase decision. This approach is used by Intel in many of its supplier selection decisions.[5]

The second type of analysis approach, an ongoing computerized system, is much less common. A computerized system is ideal for analyzing recurring purchases, such as raw materials, packaging, MRO, and supplies. The analysis results are often used to:

- Allocate volume among suppliers
- Provide suppliers feedback
- Focus on areas for improvement/cost drivers
- Cost products/services

Again, this approach is rare, and it works best if tied to an ABCM system. With the increase in ABCM, it is expected that automated TCO systems will increase. One organization that uses an automated TCO system tied into an ABCM system is Compumotor. Compumotor, a division of Parker Hannifin, designs and manufactures electro-mechanical positioning equipment for factory automation.[6] It developed a supplier cost model that "measures the cost of an individual supplier throughout the procurement process and serves as a vehicle to identify opportunities for improvement in vendor performance."[7] The costs of materials-related activities such as planning and forecasting, purchasing, inventory management, and supplier management are now allocated as part of materials costs rather than treated as general overhead.

GETTING STARTED

Once a promising project has been identified for TCO analysis, it is essential to identify who to involve in the analysis process. Participants

---

5. Ellram, 1994, op. cit.
6. Bennet, op. cit.
7. Ibid., p. 31.

will vary, depending on the project under consideration. At a minimum, the TCO analysis team should include purchasing, finance/accounting (for credibility as well as expertise), users, key stakeholders, and any functional/technical experts. TCO analysis is most effectively performed in a team setting. Because TCO analysis is time-consuming and complex, it is important to gain the commitment and cooperation of others in advance. Before proceeding, consider: What is in it for others? Why should they cooperate? How will it improve their job environment and company performance? Gaining participation of others in TCO analysis may be a sales job. It is important to consider who will be affected by the outcome of the TCO analysis. Key stakeholders should be invited to provide input so they can be coopted into the process.

It is also important to keep the scope of the TCO analysis reasonable—to make sure benefit exceeds cost. A good way to get started is to view TCO from the perspective of what costs and activities occur prior to the transaction, simultaneously with the transaction, and after the transaction. Pre-transaction costs are those that occur prior to the receiving of good/performance of the service. Transaction costs are incurred at time of purchase, whereas post-transaction costs are incurred after the service is performed or after the item has been received and inspected. The major cost elements that fit into each of these categories are shown in Figure 20–1.

An example from an actual TCO analysis of a potential MRO outsourcing analysis is shown in Table 20–2. After this brainstorming to identify key TCO cost elements, the team needs to determine which costs are really relevant to the decision. Relevant costs are those that are significant, and they will vary among decision alternatives. For example, inspection costs may be a large cost for an organization. However, if the inspection costs will remain unchanged regardless of the supplier chosen or alternative pursued, these costs are not relevant to the decision because they will not affect the decision outcome.

In the case of the MRO decision, not all of the costs initially identified in Table 20–2 were relevant to the decision. Table 20–3 shows the costs that actually turned out to make a difference and explains how those costs were affected.

Determining which costs are relevant is supported by performing a sensitivity analysis, which involves considering the critical assumptions and estimates included in the model. A sensitivity analysis can also be used to answer questions and address concerns about model parameters and assumptions. For the estimated cost and performance elements in the TCO model, the team may have a range of values it believes to be

F I G U R E   20–1

Major Categories for the Components of Total Cost of Ownership

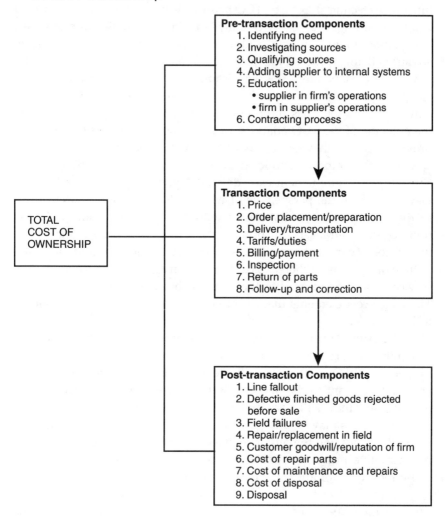

Pre-transaction Components
1. Identifying need
2. Investigating sources
3. Qualifying sources
4. Adding supplier to internal systems
5. Education:
   • supplier in firm's operations
   • firm in supplier's operations
6. Contracting process

Transaction Components
1. Price
2. Order placement/preparation
3. Delivery/transportation
4. Tariffs/duties
5. Billing/payment
6. Inspection
7. Return of parts
8. Follow-up and correction

Post-transaction Components
1. Line fallout
2. Defective finished goods rejected before sale
3. Field failures
4. Repair/replacement in field
5. Customer goodwill/reputation of firm
6. Cost of repair parts
7. Cost of maintenance and repairs
8. Cost of disposal
9. Disposal

TOTAL COST OF OWNERSHIP

Source: L. M. Ellram, "A Framework for Total Cost of Ownership," *International Journal of Logistics Management*, vol. 4, no. 2, 1993, pp. 49–60.

reasonable. For such elements, the team should perform a sensitivity analysis, reanalyzing the total model with different cost and performance estimates to see how sensitive the model is to changes in those costs. Elements should be varied simultaneously to capture the interaction effects among variables. If the decision recommendation changes as the

TABLE   20–2

Key Cost Drivers of Current Operations

Cost	Potential Outsourcing Impact
Pre-transaction	
Order placement	Decreased internal cost—supplier monitors inventory and initiates replenishment rather than internal
Receiving	No change due to union labor commitments
Transportation-related costs	Some increase due to smaller, more frequent shipments
Price	Unclear—larger guaranteed volume offset by smaller individual orders and additional required services
Breaking down orders	Eliminated, as required parts will be delivered to point of use by supplier
Inspection/counting	Same—quantities verified
Post-transaction	
Other administrative activities	Significant decrease because of paperless process, fewer orders, etc.
Obsolescence	Significant decrease due to smaller, more frequent (daily) deliveries

Source: L. M. Ellram and A. Maltz, "The Use of Total Cost of Ownership Concepts to Model the Outsourcing Decision," *International Journal of Logistics Management*, vol. 6, no. 2, 1995, pp. 55–66.

estimates change, the team should investigate those cost elements more carefully, trying to improve its level of confidence. If the decision recommendation is unaffected as the estimate changes, the analysis is robust and thus it is probably not worth the time to gain greater certainty of the value for that variable. When the team is comfortable with the analysis, it is ready to use the data in decision-making and/or present the results to top management.

IMPLEMENTATION ISSUES

Implementing TCO is not without difficulty, even after a successful analysis. The development and implementation of a TCO approach within an organization will likely be a major undertaking, for a variety of reasons. The first critical issue, as mentioned above, is that the firm must move away from a price orientation to a TCO philosophy. Purchasing may have to demonstrate that a TCO philosophy is a superior way to

T A B L E   20–3

Cost Elements Affected in This Outsourcing
Analysis—MRO

Cost Element	How Affected
Price	♦ Renegotiated
Transportation	♦ All FOB destination and more frequent shipments under proposed system
Interest	♦ Reduced cost due to carrying lower inventory levels
Obsolescence	♦ Reduced due to smaller orders under new system

Support	♦ Supplier will provide many more services, such as:
	  ♦ counting inventory
	  ♦ placing orders
	  ♦ breaking down orders once reviewed
	  ♦ providing one monthly invoice
	  ♦ investigating new products/sources of supply
	♦ Reduction of data processing and database management as number of suppliers will be significantly reduced

Source: L. M. Ellram and A. Maltz, "The Use of Total Cost of Ownership Concepts to Model the Outsourcing Decision,"
International Journal of Logistics Management, vol. 6, no. 2, 1995, pp. 55–66.

manage and understand costs. Case studies indicate that the most effective proof of TCO effectiveness may have to come through a successful TCO pilot project.

Second, few firms have accurate cost information for the pre-transaction, transaction, and post-transaction cost components in Figure 20–1. Thus, significant effort may have to be expended to:

1. Develop a process flowchart to highlight the firm's pre-transaction, transaction, and post-transaction cost elements

2. Determine which cost components are significant enough to warrant tracking. This can be done by using Pareto's law and sensitivity analysis. A few key cost components probably make up the majority of TCO expenses for a given item.

3. Determine how those significant cost components will be calculated and monitored

4. Gather and summarize the relevant cost component data

5. Analyze the results

For most firms, data gathering will begin as a significant manual effort.

Third, the firm needs to determine where to begin its TCO efforts. Should it begin with one item, a family of items, items that fit into different buying categories—such as a component, a capital equipment item, and so on? This decision is individual to the firm, depending on the industry and the firm's overall and TCO philosophies.

Fourth, a firm must determine how and where TCO will be used in the organization. Will it be a tool reserved for critical items, or more broadly used? Will TCO be used to select suppliers, manage costs with current suppliers, or allocate purchases among suppliers? Will one TCO model be used to provide the data to support all of those efforts? The proposed scope will have an impact on the way in which a TCO approach is implemented and whether a one-time analysis or an ongoing system would be most effective.

CONTINUOUSLY IMPROVING TCO

TCO analysis should not be treated as a static, one-time analysis (Figure 20–2). Projects that are justified using TCO should be reanalyzed or audited after the project has been implemented for a reasonable time period, perhaps six months to a year. The analysis should consider:

F I G U R E   20–2

Level of TCO Analysis

Goal(s)

Strategic: improve process
- Question fundamental processes
- Re-engineer processes
- Core outsourcing issues

Tactical: work on supplier improvement
- Identify factors driving high costs, both internally and externally

Operational: manage and measure suppliers
- Supplier feedback
- Track performance
- Supplier selection
- Volume allocation
- Allocate costs to products

Source: L. M. Ellram and S. P. Siferd, "Total Cost of Ownership: A Key Concept in Strategic Cost Management Decisions," *Journal of Business Logistics*, vol. 19, no. 1, 1998, pp. 55–84.

- Are results as expected? Why or why not?
- Were any key cost elements or benefits overlooked that should be considered in future analysis?
- Were any key assumptions or sensitivities significantly in error? Could this have been prevented?
- Is there anything else that can be learned for future TCO analysis?

It is also important to monitor and report the actual TCO project results so that TCO gains visibility in the organization and those involved in TCO analysis get proper recognition.

SUMMARY

This chapter provides a brief overview of TCO concepts and methods. While the concept of TCO is relatively simple, its execution may be complex. Internal political issues and rewards systems may hinder TCO progress. Lack of time and data availability can be important issues. Those interested in TCO analysis are urged to investigate TCO processes and have a good understanding of their own organizational reward structures and political issues before proceeding further with TCO development and implementation.

ADDITIONAL READINGS

Carr, L. P., and C. D. Ittner. "Measuring the Cost of Ownership." *Journal of Cost Management*, Fall 1992, pp. 42–51.

Cavinato, J. L., "A Total Cost/Value Model for Supply Chain Competitiveness." *Journal of Business Logistics*, vol. 13, no. 2, 1992, pp. 285–301.

Ellram, L. M. "A Framework for Total Cost of Ownership." *International Journal of Logistics Management*, vol. 4, no. 2, 1993, pp. 49–60.

———. "A Structured Method for Applying Purchasing Cost Management Tools," *International Journal of Purchasing and Materials Management*, vol. 32, no. 1, 1996, pp. 20–28.

———. "Activity Based Costing: An Opportunity for Purchasing Improvement," *In A Changing Environment: 80th Annual International Purchasing Conference Proceedings*, NAPM, Tempe, Ariz., 1995, pp. 1–5.

———. "Activity Based Costing and Total Cost of Ownership: A Critical Linkage." *Journal of Cost Management*, Winter 1995, pp. 22–30.

———. "Total Cost of Ownership." In D. Hahn and L. Kaufmann, ed., Handbuch Industrielles Beschaffungsmanagement, Gabler, Wiesbaden, 1999.

————. "Total Cost of Ownership: An Analysis Approach for Purchasing." *International Journal of Physical Distribution and Logistics Management*, vol. 25, no. 8, 1995, pp. 4–20.

————. "Total Cost of Ownership: Elements and Implementation." *International Journal of Purchasing and Materials Management*, vol. 29, no. 4, 1993, pp. 3–11.

Ellram, L. M., and A. Maltz. "The Use of Total Cost of Ownership Concepts to Model the Outsourcing Decision." *International Journal of Logistics Management*, vol. 6, no. 2, 1995, pp. 55–66.

Ellram, L. M., and S. P. Siferd. "Total Cost of Ownership: A Key Concept in Strategic Cost Management Decisions." *Journal of Business Logistics*, vol. 19, no. 1, 1998, pp. 55–84.

Maltz, A., and Ellram, L. M., "Total Cost of Relationship: An Analytical Framework for the Logistics Outsourcing Decision." *Journal of Business Logistics*, vol. 17, no. 1, 1997.

CHAPTER 21

Purchasing and Supply Negotiations

Editor
Brian G. Long, Ph.D., C.P.M.
President, Marketing and Management Institute, Inc.

Perhaps the most important tool of the purchasing profession is the ability to successfully negotiate agreements of all types. Indeed, for some the ability to negotiate becomes the key factor in their performance as purchasers. A buyer who cannot negotiate effectively is therefore of little value to the purchasing department or the firm. However, negotiation is a tool. Nothing more, nothing less. Its purpose is to secure the best possible long- or short-term agreement for the purchaser's firm or organization, consistent with the concept of lowest TOTAL cost.

PURCHASING NEGOTIATIONS: A BRIEF HISTORY

No one is exactly sure where commercial negotiations began, except that some form of negotiation was probably associated with our very early attempts at commercial enterprises. When ships first sailed to China to buy silk and spices, they certainly found it necessary to perform some kind of bargaining ritual with the sellers. Indeed, early negotiation was most probably influenced by Chinese culture more than anything.

Negotiations in commercial enterprises during the 1,000-year period of the "Dark Ages" were limited by the small scope of "cottage manufacturing" operations. In the era of shop tradesmen, manufacturing skills such as shoemaking, bookbinding, blacksmithing, and coopering were passed on from generation to generation. These small entrepreneurs

had to be skilled in everything from accounting to production to customer service. If raw materials were required, it was essential to become
skilled in purchasing. Because profit margins usually left only enough
money for a meager living, negotiation skills were essential for purchasing raw materials. If poor-quality materials were purchased that resulted
in an unacceptable final product, the customers went elsewhere, and the
entrepreneur starved. If too much was paid for the materials, there was
no profit margin left, and again the entrepreneur starved. Hence, negotiation skills, along with the so-called tricks of the trade, were passed on
from generation to generation.

With the coming of the Industrial Revolution came the factory, and
soon thereafter came the first purchasing agents in the late 19th century.
Unlike today's firms, early industrial sellers customarily set prices at or
near cost plus 10%. Negotiations for purchasing agents were therefore
more apt to focus on quality, delivery, service, and other aspects of the
purchase. It was not really until the 1930s when the lid came off pricing
and salespeople were frequently given the authority to set price at any
level, that the focus of negotiation shifted.

Today's Negotiation Environment

In the new age of JIT, strategic alliances, single sourcing, and supply
chain management, many old methods of purchasing negotiations are no
longer viable. Our purpose is therefore to focus on the new kinds of
negotiation skills necessary to implement the modern purchasing practices that are now mandated by recent evolution in the purchasing profession. More changes may have taken place in the purchasing profession
in the last 10 years than in the previous 50. Management's enlightened
understanding of purchasing's role in the organization has put purchasers under more pressure to show "bottom line" results but at the same
time lower inventories, elevate quality, and improve services by negotiating what seemed like impossible agreements just a few years ago.

Traditional Purchasing

Thirty years ago, the job of purchasing was very different. The typical
purchasing manager was thought to be a gatekeeper, guardian of the
treasury, and funnel through which every expenditure for the purchase
of goods and services should pass. Because of the large dollars they were
often spending, they had the power to demand compliance from suppliers. A sign that hung on the wall in one purchasing office read, "Have
you kicked a supplier yet today?"

In the world of crowded file cabinets, mountains of catalogs, and vaults filled with archived purchase records, the purchasing manager was the person who "knew where to go to buy things," which often resulted in the requisitioner being more than willing to simply file requisitions and wait for fulfillment. Little attention was paid to the fact that the cost of transactions for both buyers and sellers were rising rapidly. It has taken until the 1990s for many firms to realize that these rising costs now mean that purchasing is no longer adding value to well over half the transactions passing through the average purchasing office.

Traditional Negotiation Training

For more than 50 years, purchasers let the sellers set the negotiation agenda. To these traditional sellers, negotiation was a game. The seller would begin by offering to sell for a very high price, and the buyer would counteroffer with a very low price. Then the games began. Both buyers and seller would try to trick each other into an agreement. At least half the discussion was something less than honest. Tricks and lies were thought to just be part of the "game." Furthermore, to these negotiators, "a lie was not a lie when the truth was not expected." Therefore, traditional negotiation training taught both buyers and sellers to (1) use tactics and tricks, (2) creatively lie, and (3) artfully badger the other party. Purchasing negotiation was viewed by both buyers and sellers, as well as by others in the organization, as simply beating down the seller's price—sometimes at the expense of delivery, quality, and goodwill.

Purchasing's New Role

The current purchasing literature is filled with strategies and buzzwords that didn't exist 30 years ago. Such concepts as partnering, strategic alliances, JIT, supplier certification, supplier consolidation, and at least a half dozen other terms demand a new approach to negotiation. The absurd thought of "playing games" with a JIT supplier speaks to the fact that traditional negotiation systems have little or no place in the implementation of modern purchasing practices.

The Supply Management Environment

Many strategists believe that purchasing is evolving into supply chain management, which implies a much broader horizon of responsibility as well as multiple levels of negotiations. Instead of in-baskets filled with seemingly endless stacks of requisitions, the majority of a purchasing professional's work will be administering a series of large contracts for complete commodity groups. In terms of negotiation, the focus will shift from relatively small, day-to-day purchases to large, multi-year contracts. Negotiation skills therefore must focus in two directions: first, the task of negotiating multi-product, long-term supply management agreements; and second, the day-to-day task of bridging the gap between the end users and working with the suppliers to iron out difficulties, revise systems, monitor control systems, and otherwise maintain proper performance.

KEY STRATEGIC APPROACHES

Even though some approaches to negotiation are clearly outdated, at least four primary strategies are prevalent in today's negotiation environment. Although it is also possible to think of these strategies as being on a continuum ranging from "hard" to "soft," there are some key benchmarks of each of these systems.

Power Negotiation

The purchaser always has the age-old power of the almighty dollar. Until the seller has an order, the seller really has nothing. Therefore, the more money a buyer has to spend, the greater the power.

If the buyer (or seller) does not have power, then the power negotiator usually attempts to develop some artificial form of power. Catching the seller in an excess inventory situation or discovering that a salesperson is coming up short for a monthly quota would temporarily shift power to the buyer side. For the sellers, questionable practices like back door selling or stalling the negotiations until no time exists to talk with another seller are just a couple of options for creating an imbalance in the seller's favor. In the past, most large firms did not really negotiate with their sellers. They simply brought their power to bear and demanded better pricing, service, quality, and delivery. Sellers who did not comply were punished with smaller orders or no orders at all.

Positional Bargaining

When buyers and sellers decided to make a "game" out of purchasing negotiations, they established a simple rule: sellers would always start high, and buyers would always counteroffer with some kind of a low and unacceptable number. Both parties would then proceed to defend their respective positions and maneuver the other party with a series of tactics and tricks.

Everyone likes a game, primarily because games are a form of entertainment. However, everyone recognizes that games are not reality. Major difficulties arise when gamesmanship is projected as a way of doing business. The best solutions to business problems seldom emerge from game strategies. For these reasons, some people incorrectly regard negotiation as a game. When a game strategy fails and they fall short of their goals, they don't understand why.

Traditional negotiators also have a win–lose attitude. They believe that in order to gain, someone must lose. Both parties are therefore supposed to sit at the table and bat these offers back and forth until one party or the other, presumably the weaker of the two, gives in and accepts a less than optimum agreement.

Win–Win Negotiation

Negotiation is not a game. Negotiation is business and should be conducted as business. To be transacted effectively, business must be conducted in a win–win manner. The win–win theory of negotiation is based in the growing belief that good suppliers can greatly improve the success of the buyer's firm or organization. It does away with the "zero sum" or fixed pie notion of traditional negotiations and assumes that, if properly negotiated, an agreement can be to the benefit of both parties.

Win–win negotiators look at agreements through the eyes of the parties who are going to perform them. Agreements written on mere pieces of paper do not get up and walk out into the plants and perform. Agreements don't perform, but people do, and these people must be motivated to perform if we expect to receive the greatest value from the contract. If people lack incentives, they will think of numerous reasons why they will not perform or, sometimes even worse, perform poorly.

Win–win negotiators often focus on common ground, for common ground is the basis for all movement in negotiation. The more common ground you have, the closer you are to an agreement. American industry has been severely criticized lately for its short-term, "quarter to quarter" mentality. Win–win negotiation, in answer to these criticisms, is therefore more concerned with the long-run than short-run. A win–win negotiator looks down the road, saying, "Where are we going to be in three years? Let's not sacrifice the present for the future." The other party is then considered to be a partner in success, not an opponent or adversary.

Benevolent Negotiation

In the age of strategic alliances and long-term cooperation between buyer and seller, it is clearly possible to lean too far in the seller's direction. The benevolent negotiator makes the assumption that a seller, if just given the reins, will automatically look out for the buyer's best interest. Proponents will point to isolated examples of success where sellers did, in fact, take over a complete project and provide excellent quality, top-notch service, and reasonable prices. Benevolent negotiation, therefore, is a classic example of too much of a good thing. Even though the seller may make public announcements of cooperation and even perform acts that appear to be in the buyer's best interest, the fact remains that the selling firm is under pressure for profitability just like every other firm. It is still the buyer's responsibility to look out for his or her firm's best interest, and to secure better performance from the seller at each and every negotiation. The core of a purchaser's job is still supplier management and cost reduction.

THE PRAM NEGOTIATION MODEL

As illustrated by Figure 21–1, PRAM stands for Plans, Relationships, Agreements, and Maintenance. These steps constitute the primary steps in any long-term negotiation situation and form the blueprint by which many contemporary purchasers manage their suppliers.

Whereas planning is easily recognized as a step, the modern purchasing negotiator concentrates on building a positive relationship with the supplier. Japanese negotiators seldom even think of doing business before they feel at ease with the other party. They depend on relationships to pave the way for an agreement as well as ensure that it will be properly carried out. On some occasions they will spend years developing a relationship before they conduct business.

With an adequate plan and a good relationship, forming an agreement should be much easier. The goal at this stage is to be in a problem-solving mode so that both parties can reconcile differences and hopefully come up with an agreement.

The last step is maintenance. As the name implies, the goal of maintenance is to maintain the rest of the negotiation process as well as pave the way for the next negotiation. The PRAM model is therefore round, which implies that the process is ongoing. Because of the nature of the industrial market, most purchasing negotiators find themselves facing

F I G U R E   21-1

The PRAM Model: The Win–Win Negotiation Process

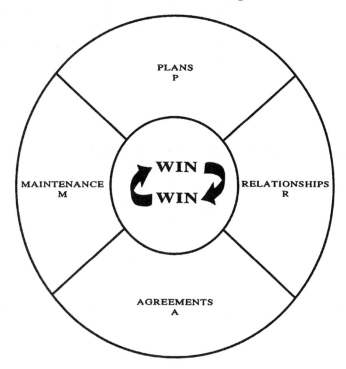

the same sellers and the same markets over and over again. It would therefore be a major mistake in any negotiation to sacrifice the present for the future.

The concept of continuous improvement implies that the negotiation process should get better every time the buyer and seller go around the PRAM model. After many successful negotiations augmented by continuous improvement, the buyer and seller should ultimately attain a nearly perfect business relationship.

NEGOTIATION PLANNING

Although almost everyone concedes the importance of negotiation planning, they almost always simultaneously note that their planning is often inadequate. Some have even characterized their planning as "ready, fire, aim," which really means that whatever planning is done is sometimes done right at the negotiation table itself or in brief recesses or caucuses.

Many people approach negotiation with the idea that "I don't know what I want, but I'll recognize it when I see it." Such an approach makes it fairly easy for the skilled seller to redefine the situation to simply match the seller's objectives—at the buyer's expense.

State of Mind

Perhaps the most important but often overlooked factor determining the outcome of a negotiation is the state of mind of both parties as they embark upon the negotiation. For instance, a seller who has already been told by someone with authority that the decision has already been made in his or her favor will come to the table ready to smugly walk away with an agreement while making no concessions at all. Other factors influencing state of mind include everything from reputations to rumors to how fairly each party felt it was treated last time. Timing is also important. Take the case of a salesperson who has just closed three large contracts for 10%–20% above the going price. Would such a salesperson be in the mood to talk about discounts? Hardly. In fact, until you bring this salesperson back down to earth, it will be difficult to conclude any kind of a reasonable deal.

Another set of factors relates to the tone of the markets that both parties face. A seller's market puts pressure on the salespeople to hold the line on prices and grant practically no concessions that cost money. Conversely, a buyer's market puts pressure on the purchasing person to demand better pricing and more concessions. However, the wise negotiator looks toward the future in an attempt to ensure the long-term profitability and survival of both firms. This does not imply, however, that outside factors such as foreign competition may not be a factor when negotiating a long-term agreement with a domestic seller.

In this same context, it is wise to remember that all the planning in the world cannot totally overcome the forces of supply and demand. When the price of copper rises 10%, and the entire market accepts the price increase, a buyer will be hard pressed to negotiate a price below the current market without providing some kind of additional incentives to the seller, such as purchase guarantees, early payment, or other concessions of equal value.

The Buyer's Key Issues

Negotiation planning must include a system for listing the issues of the negotiation itself, as well as the optimistic and pessimistic outcomes for each of these issues, generally known as settlement ranges. Each of these issues should also be prioritized so that those issues that are most important are considered at all times.

Some issues recur in almost every negotiation, such as price, quality, delivery, service, warranty, and terms of sale. Other issues, such as return policies, restocking charges, engineering charges, rights to technical data, on-site inspections, and various other seller certifications, will be unique to each negotiation.

The Seller's Key Issues

Analyzing the issues for your firm or organization is important, but so is putting yourself in the other party's shoes. Most of the issues that are important to the buyer will also be important to the seller. The task becomes determining targets, settlement ranges, and priorities that constitute their best estimate of what the other party will expect from this negotiation. As illustrated by Box 21–1, the concept of a complete settlement range for both buyer and seller appears like a table of possible outcomes. In the case of "Delivery Time" in Example A, the two parties should be able to reach an agreement somewhere between three weeks and ten weeks. In the case of "Price" in Example B, the settlement range falls between $1,500 and $2,200.

With the goals of each party side by side, planners must now devise a plan or strategy to reconcile the two sets of goals. This step requires creative thinking. It is often much more difficult to come up with a win–win solution than simply to demand the acceptance of your position, offer to split the difference, employ standard negotiation tactics, or put up a good fight in the hope that the other party will give in before you do. A good negotiation planner thinks of opportunities to expand the pie beyond the boundaries of the existing agreement, and considers as many things as possible that both parties can do for each other. Many of these concessions, such as using the buying firm's name in an advertisement, do not necessarily cost large sums of money!

Power. Even in the enlightened era of win–win, power is still reality. The outcome of any negotiation still favors the power party. However, it is also the power party that is able to set the overall tone of the

B O X   21–1

THE SETTLEMENT RANGE

Example A: Delivery Time

Buyer's Perspective		Seller's Perspective
Ideal settlement position	→ 2 Weeks	
	3 Weeks	← Least acceptable position
Target settlement position	→ 4 Weeks	
	5 Weeks	
	6 Weeks	
	7 Weeks	← Target settlement position
	8 Weeks	
	9 Weeks	
Least acceptable position	→ 10 Weeks	
	11 Weeks	
	12 Weeks	
	13 Weeks	
	14 Weeks	
	15 Weeks	← Ideal settlement position

Example B: Price

Buyer's Perspective		Seller's Perspective
Ideal settlement position	→ $1,400	
	1,500	← Least Acceptable position
	1,600	
Target settlement position	→ 1,700	
	1,800	
	1,900	← Target settlement position
	2,000	
	2,100	
Least acceptable position	→ 2,200	
	2,300	
	2,400	
	2,500	
	2,600	← Ideal settlement position

negotiation. As previously noted, the power that a purchaser always has is the power of money. Sellers must sell to survive, and the seller who walks away without an order still has nothing. It has been said that money talks. Therefore, more money equates to more power. When the dollars are large enough, the sellers will listen, even though they might not like what they hear. Modern purchasers therefore consolidate their purchases into a package big enough to attract the attention of the seller. However, the purchaser who goes into the market with only one small order will probably find the seller to be underwhelmed—unless more business is in the offing.

The power that the seller often has is the power to do the job and do it right. A seller with a proven record of on-time delivery, top-notch quality, excellent service, and ease of order placement is clearly in a position of power. A competing seller offering to do the "same job for 10% less" is looked upon by the buyer with a skeptical eye. Letting go of an existing seller that causes practically no trouble for the buyer is not easy, even though economic circumstances may dictate the necessity.

Unscrupulous sellers may try to develop artificial power or take power away from the buyer. The so-called "back door" seller tries to get a product or service "spec-ed in" or committed before the buyer even finds out what is going on. In other instances, the seller may wait until the buyer is in a time bind and is short on inventory or does not even have time to qualify a new supplier.

Cost Analysis

Although a separate topic by itself, cost analysis is sure to grow in importance for purchasing negotiators. As previously noted, one of the major goals of purchasers is, and will continue to be, long-term cost reduction. Therefore, purchasers must come to the table ready to discuss and analyze realistic prices.

One of the key factors that must be researched prior to the negotiation is the seller's major cost drivers. For some firms, it is obvious. In the case of service organizations, it is labor. When plenty of qualified labor is available, costs should remain relatively stable. In the case of a goods-producing firm, the cost drivers are often both labor and materials. If the materials prices are stable, pricing should be stable. If, however, the cost of a key raw material were to rise or fall, so should the end price of the final product.

Questions for the Seller

The final step in negotiation planning is making a list of those questions that the other party must answer. Aside from obvious clarifications, these questions serve a variety of purposes. Some will simply solidify assumptions about the other party, some will provide clarification, some will verify common ground, and others will ensure that the other party is also thinking about a positive agreement for both parties.

DEVELOPING LONG-TERM RELATIONSHIPS

Historically, buyer–seller relationships were frowned upon. It was generally thought that relationships detracted from the "objective" decision-making process and sometimes put purchasers as well as other members of the firms in compromising positions. Some larger firms even developed elaborate rotation patterns to keep the buyers from getting too familiar with the sellers.

Many of these considerations related to the fact that relationship development seemed to be almost synonymous with seller-sponsored entertainment. Typical activities included lunch, dinner, golf, baseball games, and other activities often designed to put the buyer in a positive frame of mind. Although the concept of purchasing ethics can be a separate subject by itself, it is sufficient to say that any form of excessive seller-sponsored entertainment is probably designed to develop a win–lose relationship and therefore obligate the buyer. In response, some firms as well as most governmental units and government contractors simply wrote policies to disallow such activities altogether.

However, the modern purchasing negotiator now faces a need to develop long-term relationships with a limited number of suppliers. A modern relationship is different because:

1. At least part of the time, a positive, well-developed relationship will be the key to resolving problems.

2. Sellers will still say things to buyers outside of the office that they will not feel comfortable saying in the office.

3. Every conversation is a relationship development opportunity. Relationships do not have to be built while money is spent. For instance, a plant tour costs nothing but introduces the purchaser to the firm or organization.

4. Many purchasing departments have developed a policy of reciprocity for activities like lunch and dinner. Under this system, the buyer picks up the check about half the time.

5. Excessive entertainment is not necessary or productive. Going to lunch can be a useful relationship development activity and does not need to cost excessive amounts of money.

Relationship Components

Building "Like"

In days gone by, buyers were trained to put salespeople down. They would not return phone calls. They would leave the seller waiting in the lobby just to make themselves look more important. They would even be downright rude on some occasions.

In today's environment, the opposite is true. Purchasers are accommodating and polite to sellers, but still businesslike. They consider the seller's time to be important and make every effort to keep scheduled appointments. They also return phone calls to legitimate sellers. All of these and other activities are aimed at getting the seller to like the buyer personally.

Other aspects of "like" are psychological. For instance, remembering the seller's name and their company is important. Taking an interest in the seller personally also helps to build a bond.

Building Respect

If the seller likes the buyer, the relationship is one-third complete. But "like" without "respect" is of little or no value for a business relationship.

For the buyer, respect has many dimensions. Being the real decision-making authority is certainly of maximum importance. However, being knowledgeable about the subject matter may be just as important. The buyer is not expected to be a technical expert—just knowledgeable enough about the product, service, or commodity to carry on an intelligent conversation. This allows the seller to communicate effectively. Otherwise, many sellers will say that they have been talking to the wrong person.

Building Trust

Perhaps the most elusive of the three, building trust requires patience and time. Part of trust is conferred by the organization by placing authority in the hands of the buyer. Another part comes from evidence of professional stature, such as the Certified Purchasing Manager (C.P.M.)

certificate hanging on the wall. But the most important part of trust come from working together over a long period of time.

As illustrated by Figure 21–2, all three relationship factors overlap. At the same time, different circumstances may require different proportions of each factor, depending on the marketplace, the dollars involved, the complexity of the issues, and the goals and objectives of both firms.

Modern purchasers form positive relationships everywhere. It has often been said that purchasing people can save their firms more money negotiating inside the firm than they ever will by negotiating with suppliers. In this sense, purchasing negotiators integrate themselves into the firm, form positive relationships with all departments and people with whom they deal, and earn the respect and trust of the entire organization. These relationships open the door of the purchasing function to an excellent opportunity to improve the profitability of the entire organization.

Finally, it is wise to remember that the purpose of a good relationship is to (1) improve communication, (2) increase creativity, (3) enhance problem solving, (4) provide a buffer for human error, and (5) make both parties feel good about the agreement. Otherwise, a relationship that

F I G U R E   21–2

Relationship Components

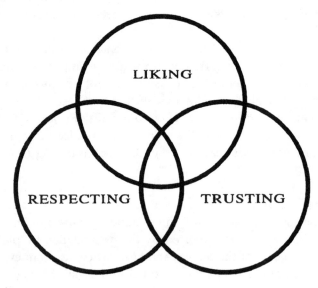

only opens the door for the seller to sell more products or services has little place in modern purchasing and should be avoided.

NEGOTIATING THE AGREEMENT

Good negotiation planning and a positive relationship are essential to laying the groundwork for actually forming a final agreement. However, even this firm foundation still requires skill, patience, and perseverance for an agreement to be reached.

It is essential to get off to a good start. This involves continuing the good relationship that one hopes has already been developed. A good place to begin the discussion is with the common ground that brought you together in the first place. Before you proceed further, this is usually a good time to ask any questions that you may have regarding clarifications of the subject matter of the negotiation.

What you do next will set the tone for the entire negotiation. For instance, it would be tempting to jump in and start negotiating random issues without first looking at the overall picture.

If you expect the seller's help in solving problems, you must first draw him or her into the process. Prior to trying to solve any of the problems, many modern negotiators advocate jointly making a list of those factors where there is agreement and another of those where the parties disagree. The areas of agreement—the common ground—form the foundation of the entire business relationship. The areas of disagreement—the problems—are what stand in the way of forming not only the present agreement but often future agreements as well.

The Myopia of Tactics and Tricks

Traditional tactics often create the poorest possible business agreements. Entering a negotiation session by telling lies or playing tricks encourages the other party to tell lies and play tricks. As the negotiations progress, both parties simply lie to each other until one of the parties convinces the other to accept a lie as truth. The parties commit the agreement to writing, which becomes, of course, a compilation of lies. Both parties sign the agreement with their fingers crossed behind their backs and shake hands as though they had both reached an agreement. Of course, the chances are good that one or the other parties will not perform. When asked why, the defector will probably say, "What do you mean, perform? That agreement was a lie. We thought you knew that."

Some books are primarily a discussion of tactics and tricks, and many seminars are conducted every day that advocate these practices. Box 21–2 describes some of the typical win-lose tactics that are still practiced by some sellers and still advocated by some buyers as well. The fact remains that some people like to read books and attend seminars that make them come back feeling bigger and stronger than they actually

B O X   21–2

TYPICAL WIN–LOSE TACTICS

+ Appeal to profitability
  ("At that price, we're not making any money . . .")
+ Stonewall (hardnose) tactics
  ("That's the best I can do. Take it or leave it.")
+ Stalling
  ("Sorry to put off our meeting, but we need more time to prepare . . .")
+ Flattery
  ("You are my favorite customer . . .")
+ Established policy as a barrier
  ("I'm sorry, my hands are tied . . .")
+ Artificial legal leverage
  ("The law says that we must sell to everyone for the same price.")
+ Moral appeals
  ("If I don't close this sale, we will have to lay people off . . .")
+ Loyalty
  ("But we have been your loyal supplier for all these years . . .")
+ Emotional appeals
  (Crying)
+ Rhetorical answers
  ("Before I answer your question, you must first tell me . . .")
+ Authority variation
  ("I am only authorized to offer . . .")

are, even though many of the ideas they have learned are really fantasies. Business does not exist in a fantasy world.

Modern purchasers also avoid falling into the traps of traditional negotiations. For instance, they avoid defend–attack spirals where one party is badgered into responding with a counterattack, which often results in the other party escalating the attack and may culminate with both parties screaming at each other and breaking off the discussion altogether. In general, a contemporary purchasing negotiator tries to make the other party feel at ease throughout the negotiation.

Recesses and Caucuses

When time is passing but no progress is being made, it is often wise to call a recess or a caucus. The distinction between a recess and a caucus is of degree. In a recess, both parties leave the room with an agreement to resume the discussion at some agreed time, such as an hour or even a week later. In a caucus, just one group leaves the room. In both instances, the purpose is for both buyers and sellers to rethink, redefine, and develop fresh approaches to the problem.

Failure to call a recess or caucus when progress is not being made can be a major mistake. When no progress is being made, the parties may begin to wear on each other's nerves and destroy the positive atmosphere of the negotiations. In team negotiations, a recess will allow both teams to brainstorm as well as redefine and recollect their thoughts.

Frequent Errors at the Table

Another problem is trying to avoid many of the traditional problems of negotiation during the session itself. Some of these reoccurring problems include:

1. *Coming unprepared.* If you do not know what you want or need, then the seller is apt to exert a right of prominence and help you—to the seller's advantage. Furthermore, the sellers may feel that they have wasted their time trying to deal with a person or team that has little or no appreciation for what they have to say.

2. *Committing too soon.* There is nothing that the seller would rather hear than that you or your company has already decided to give the seller the business.

3. *Inappropriate body language.* All good negotiators read body language. What is NOT said is often more important than what is actually said.

4. *Disclosure of competitive terms.* There is nothing the seller would rather know than the exact terms they have to beat. The seller's state of mind then shifts to believing that any offer that is marginally superior should be acceptable.

5. *Team disagreement.* In the right time and place, there is certainly nothing wrong with devil's advocates. However, the negotiation team MUST present a united front at the negotiation table.

6. *Do's and Don'ts.* Finally, as illustrated by Box 21–3, there are some typical do's and don'ts that should be followed in almost every negotiation.

When to Walk Away

It is again important to emphasize that positive agreements cannot always be accomplished. Before walking away, it is wise to ask yourself a few important questions:

B O X   21–3

AT THE NEGOTIATION TABLE: SOME DO'S AND DON'TS

DO Focus on problems, not personalities
DO Identify as much common ground as possible
DO Make the other party feel PHYSICALLY comfortable
DO Make the other party feel MENTALLY comfortable
DO Share information when the seller shares with you
DO Explore additional business opportunities

DON'T Slip into traditional negotiation by making immediate counteroffers
DON'T Talk too much or oversell your ideas
DON'T Make derogatory comments about competitors
DON'T Reject seller's ideas prior to discussion
DON'T Irritate the other party
DON'T Dangle business opportunities that are not yours to offer

1. What is (or are) the key issue or issues that are standing in the way of the agreement? Are they essential to the success of the agreement? Is there any way that they can be resolved at a later time without jeopardizing the essence of the present agreement?

2. Are your goals unreasonable? Have you asked for more than what the seller appears to be able to realistically provide? Are you asking for performance or concessions that exceed the authority of the sellers with whom you are negotiating?

3. Would a recess help? If you gave the seller or sellers a chance to rethink, regroup, brainstorm, call the home office, or otherwise redefine the situation, could the situation change?

4. What is our next best alternative? If there are other sellers to investigate and the prospect of accomplishing our goal still seems feasible, then we may owe it to ourselves and to the alternate seller to take a look. However, getting up and walking away when there is no other viable alternative will put us in a bad negotiation position when we have to come back to beg forgiveness and accept the seller's terms.

If the decision is still to walk away, then one last step is still essential. The explicit nature of the problem or problems that stood in the way of the agreement must be made very clear to the seller so that you, as the negotiator, are not personally blamed for the unfavorable outcome. Furthermore, if the sellers leave the negotiation still focused on the impasse problem, they will probably continue to think of a potential solution.

Finalizing the Agreement

When is a negotiation concluded? To a modern purchasing negotiator, the answer is easy. An agreement is concluded when all of the problems are solved and both parties are happy with the agreement. No more, no less. However, old-school salespeople often bombard the buyer with so-called closing tactics similar to those illustrated in Box 21–4. The purpose of using closing tactics is to hurry up the decision process and force the buyer to make a decision—in short, to get the buyer to quit shopping.

When relationships are positive, is it still necessary to put the agreement in writing? Because of the large number of people who must interface with the agreement on both the buying and selling side, the answer is yes—not because the parties don't trust each other, but simply

B O X   21–4

TYPICAL CLOSING TACTICS

- Artificial time constraint
  ("This offer is only good until 5:00 p.m. today . . . ")
- Rhetorical
  ("Would delivery next Thursday be good, or would you prefer Tuesday . . . ?")
- Physical action
  ("But it is already on the truck and headed this way . . . ")
- Piecemeal
  ("Let's just agree on the basics now and work the details out later . . . ")
- Advance commitment
  ("Your production supervisor has already agreed . . . ")
- Ben Franklin
  ("Let's list why you should buy today rather than another day . . . ")
- Puppy dog close
  ("I left it for the department to try out 30 days ago, and they want to buy it . . . ")
- Time constraint
  ("In order to meet your delivery, I have to call the order in right now . . . ")
- Inducement
  ("If I can have the order now, I can throw in . . . ")
- Closing bomb
  ("I think this is an agreement you can live with . . . ")
- All-inclusive concession
  ("If all it takes to close this deal is to . . . ")
- Fait accompli (fact accomplished)
  ("But it's already installed and running . . . ")

in recognition of the fact that both parties will probably forget the details of the agreement as time passes.

Debriefing

With a signed agreement firmly in hand, the debriefing is one last thing that many negotiators overlook. In purchasing negotiations, this debriefing should not take more than a few minutes. However, ten minutes of immediate debriefing is worth more now than four hours of planning time a year from now. Box 21–5 illustrates a debriefing checklist.

B O X   21–5

THE DEBRIEFING

Take just a few minutes after the sellers have departed and ask yourselves the following questions:

1. Are WE reasonably happy with the negotiated outcome? If not, can we do better next time, or should we begin looking for another supplier?
2. Do THEY appear to be reasonably happy with the outcome? If not, the sellers may drag their feet on performance. The seller may also begin looking for another customer.
3. Did our win–win solution work? If we introduced a plan, did the sellers buy into it? If not, how could it have been improved?
4. What did we do right? What were the key elements of the negotiation that persuaded the seller to accept our terms?
5. What did we do wrong? What were our major mistakes? How could they have been avoided? Is there any permanent damage that we must fix?
6. What information should we have ready for next time? If we need more cost information or a better analysis of the market situation, the time to begin data collection is NOW, not two days before the contract is due.
7. What goals can we realistically accomplish next time we meet? The concept of continuous improvement says that our next agreement should improve.

NEGOTIATION MAINTENANCE

When you negotiate for a vase in an antique store, the performance of the agreement is immediate. Regardless of the wisdom of the purchase, rendering payment gives you the right to immediately leave the shop with your prized merchandise. Future performance is only a marginal consideration because you may never have cause to visit the same store or deal with the same person again.

Purchasing negotiation is quite different. Even the novice purchasing negotiator realizes that closing the agreement is really only the beginning. Indeed, the agreement can only be judged successful if proper performance is forthcoming. For some agreements, the total performance may actually take place over many months or even years. Negotiation maintenance, therefore, is the process of keeping the agreement on track from inception to completion.

Show Commitment

In order for the other party to perform, you must create a feeling of total acceptance. One of the worst things you could do is to create the impression that you are still shopping even after you have reached an agreement. The seller may feel that you are about to renege or that the agreement has no future—even though there has not yet been any performance to be judged.

Courtesy is also an element of commitment. For instance, a new contractor who is introduced to the various departments around the organization feels much more welcome. These introductions not only begin the process of building relationships among the people who must work together, but also create the feeling of commitment.

Keep on Planning

Good negotiation planning is a never-ending process. A good negotiator is always thinking ahead to the next negotiation. In addition to filing all of the planning notes at the conclusion of the negotiation, it is wise to continue to collect and file useful information all year long. A few large firms even go to the expense of hiring a professional clipping service to provide copies of all articles from trade publications that feature their key suppliers. Others simply file whatever information comes along that may pertain to the negotiation of the next contract.

Relationship Maintenance

It only takes a few minutes to regularly touch base with the other party so that both parties are at ease with one another. Holiday greeting cards also help, but they are not effective if they are not personally signed by the buyer.

Agreement Maintenance

Monitoring the agreement as it is performed is also essential. It isn't always the supplier who drops the ball. It is often someone on the buyer's staff who fails to provide certain paperwork or someone in engineering who fails to provide engineering drawings in a timely manner.

ENHANCING NEGOTIATION SKILLS

Finally, questions must be raised about what purchasers can do better to prepare for the future, as well as what areas the purchasing manager should emphasize when hiring and training new personnel. There are ten key areas that should be the focus of these efforts:

1. People Skills

In the old school, purchasers were taught that being overly friendly could be regarded as a sign of weakness. Being a little mean and nasty on occasion would therefore let the seller know who was boss and command respect. As the old school gives way, people skills now appears to be one of those areas where purchasers may be highly undertrained— or even mistrained.

In today's environment, there is often more money to be saved negotiating inside the organization than outside. Building relationships inside the firm is just as important to the purchasing profession of the future as building external relationships. Altogether too many purchasers and their jobs are protected by company procedures demanding that all requisitions of a certain size must go through the purchasing department. In the age of "empowered" department managers, this may not be the case in the future.

Finally, the nature of the buyer–seller relationship is being redefined. All the buyer needed in the past was to have a good relationship with the salesperson. In today's environment, as well as the supply management environment of the future, the buyer's relationship will be with the supplier's entire organization.

2. Team Skills

Too many people in all phases and at all levels of many firms went through team-building seminars in the late 1980s and early 1990s with their fingers crossed behind their backs. In private, they said, "Teams are a great idea, but they won't work at our company." Needless to say, many firms will find it necessary to revisit the concept of team building in order to create the intraorganizational effort necessary to make supply management agreements work as they should.

In other instances, team building is necessary to get purchasing back on the team. Some firms that were successful in team building created teams that did not include the purchasing function. At least some purchasers have lamented in retrospect that they did not adequately assert themselves regarding the importance of including purchasing on the team.

3. Cost Analysis

Old-school purchasers were often taught to badger for a lower price with little or no knowledge of what the actual price ought to be. Old-school sellers dreamed of opportunities to close particular sales at outlandishly high prices and earn large commissions.

In the supply management environment, most pricing will be based on some form of cost-plus pricing. Pricing according to market demand, regardless of whether the current market favors the buyer or seller, will be obsolete for most commodities. Sellers of the future will be asked to submit cost data for scrutinization, will guarantee certain margins, and will be rewarded for cost reductions. Purchasers will work with sellers to take unnecessary costs out of the system, resulting in price reductions.

However, altogether too many purchasers of today are not cost accounting-literate. When asked to define the basic differences between job order and process cost accounting, they come up short. This level of illiteracy must be bridged for the purchaser of the future.

Finally, there is the elusive concept of calculating total cost. It appears easy, but actually negotiating on the basis of total cost requires a whole new perspective and set of skills.

4. Target Pricing

One purchaser proudly declared, "Target pricing? I've been using it for years. I pick a price and tell the seller to meet it or forget it." Sadly, many people today think that target pricing is really just some form of take-it-or-leave it negotiations. In actuality, target pricing involves a detailed analysis of all factors that contribute to price, including materials, services, expertise, inventory, and almost every other imaginable business expense. For obvious reasons, it has worked well for firms who attempt to outsource products they are already manufacturing. In the future, this tool will be used for other procurements as well, especially in the service arena.

5. Computer Literacy

No serious observer disputes the notion that the computer will be the purchaser's most important hardware tool of the future. Almost every purchaser praises the importance of the computer and points to the efficiencies of computerized purchasing over manual systems. However, only a fraction of the professional purchasers of today can run even one of the standard spreadsheet programs. With management's focus on bottom line results, purchasers too often show up at staff meetings without the necessary data to support their positions.

Even many large firms of today admit that they are far behind in computer training for their purchasing staffs. Many purchasers will find themselves to be at a definite disadvantage in many negotiations if they cannot assemble and organize the charts, spreadsheets, and other information necessary to conduct a detailed negotiation.

6. Master of Commodity Information

In the past, purchasers gained clout from being "the" person who knew where to go to find things. Especially with MRO supply management agreements in place for many commodities, the task of sourcing odd items is shifting to the seller. In the supply management environment for production materials, purchasers of the future will have to become the people with the latest and best information about their respective commodities. An old-school solution to the problem of adequate market information was to rely on sellers to provide updates on the market. Is this the fox watching the chicken coop? Not necessarily. But the fact remains that the seller is not always the best source for this kind of information.

Where will purchasers look for commodity information? Several places. First, most news organizations, periodicals, newspapers, 10-Ks, press releases, opinions, rumors, and every other form of human communication will probably be available on the Internet within the next ten years. To the non-purchasing professional, this information overload will be overwhelming. However, a new breed of skilled purchasers will sort out, classify, and clarify this information into a powerful managerial tool. Like other phases of the purchasing process, this process sounds easy, but it is not.

A second source of purchasing information comes from trade periodicals that are often on the purchaser's desk but unread. In the age when everyone is being asked to do more with less, altogether too many purchasers go from month to month without adequately digesting the latest information at their fingertips.

Not all of this new-found information will come from either the printed or electronic media. For instance, the purchaser of the future should attend about three trade shows per year for the purpose of updating the firm's information on leading-edge technologies and potential new sources.

7. Commodity Training

The salesperson for an automotive door latch manufacturer lamented a recent sales call. A new buyer had just been reassigned to purchasing door latches without even a moment's training in the technical aspects, DOT regulations, or quality issues associated with automotive door latches. Five minutes into the conversation, the salesperson concluded that the buyer didn't really know "a door latch from a throttle plate." He further noted that it was probably going to take him several months to teach the purchaser everything that he needed to know about door latches. In the meantime, the purchasers had already concluded their first meeting by badgering for a lower price.

In the supply management environment of the future, commodity training will be essential. Sellers will simply not put up with purchasers with whom they cannot carry on an intelligent conversation about the commodity. Conversely, technically trained requisitioners may become just as frustrated. Months of training are often required before sellers are even allowed to make their first sales call. In the future, similar requirements will be demanded of the purchasing professional. In the absence of this training, both requisitioners and sellers may conclude that the purchaser is not adding value to the transaction and may elect to exclude him or her from the entire process, except perhaps for processing some of the necessary paperwork.

8. Contract Writing

In today's environment, hundreds of transactions are processed daily utilizing the standard purchase order form supported by the standard terms and conditions preprinted on the back. Many of today's purchasers are not even aware of the meaning of all of these T's and C's, let alone their impact.

In the supply management environment of the future, the purchase order will be utilized for spot purchases only. The majority of the supply management agreements will utilize individually negotiated terms and conditions to fit the nature of the commodity and the individual needs of both the buyer and seller. An effective negotiator will therefore need to be trained in the skills necessary to write the contract terms necessary for each major contract. Altogether too many of today's supply management agreements contain terms that were actually prepared by the sellers themselves.

9. Macro-Supplier Cost Management

Many of the top retail firms of today owe their success to a few fairly simple purchasing philosophies. First, they don't listen to sob stories about how costs have gone up and price increases are necessary. They simply ignore these price requests and, if necessary, buy elsewhere. Second, they believe the world is the marketplace, and insist on world-competitive pricing, recognizing that "MADE IN U.S.A." or "MADE IN CANADA" doesn't count for much in the marketplace, whether any of us like it or not. Third, they expect the seller to stand unconditionally behind the product in terms of service and 100% refunds. Finally, they expect the sellers to work with them on cost reduction, marketing, inventory reduction, and a whole host of other things. Although this sounds relatively harsh for an environment of cooperation and strategic alliances, it is a reality that the purpose of supply management is not just to shift costs around but also to reduce them based on a total cost environment. This will be a key challenge to negotiations of the future. In short, future purchasing will continue to focus on cost reduction.

10. Management of Suppliers

Old-school purchasers registered disgust with a seller by simply placing the business elsewhere. Future purchasers will become management consultants to the supplier base and help them with any phase of their business operation. When negotiating large contracts and demanding better pricing, quality, and services based on large volume, purchasers will also earn the right to criticize and manage certain aspects of the seller's business. During the life of the agreement, the focus of the negotiations will then shift to individual negotiations with the seller's personnel in order to bring them up to speed. This by itself will require a whole new set of skills on the part of the purchaser.

CHAPTER 22

Contract and Subcontract Administration and Management

Editor
Elaine N. Whittington, C.P.M., A.P.P., CPCM
Educator, G & E Enterprises

DEFINITIONS

This chapter will use the terms *contract* and *subcontract* interchangeably. Although, in a strict sense, subcontracts constitute a subset of a broader contract classification, in practice the activities involved in administering and managing the two are essentially the same. Also, while the processes described in this chapter are presented without particular comment on the administrative environment, i.e., paper documents or electronic technology, all processes described can be, and in many cases are, conducted in an electronic technology environment using computers, communications technology, and the Internet. Also, while this type of process is often associated with manufacturing or assembly situations, the approaches described are equally applicable to nonmanufacturing situations such as procurement of services, or situations that require a combination of manufacturing and nonmanufacturing activities.

In a medium-sized private sector manufacturing company, for example, most purchases of materials and parts to support the production operation ultimately may be handled by means of a series of purchase orders. The purchase order, along with the appended specifications, becomes the heart of the contractual agreement with a supplier. In such companies, this mutually accepted agreement typically is referred to as a "contract." However, consider a situation in which a large aerospace company has been awarded a contract from one of its customers for a complete functional airplane. Such firms commonly make some of the parts and systems required for the airplane and buy others from outside suppliers. Hence, the firm often subcontracts items such as wings, landing gears, and complex avionic systems. These contractual agreements with suppliers usually are referred to as "subcontracts." A subcontract might be described as a contract that covers the purchase of a complex item for which very detailed administration is required to accomplish successful delivery. Often the item ordered is expensive, and delivery might be in excess of twelve months. A nonmanufacturing example would be a major software developer who has received a contract to develop a major business management system for a large corporation or government agency. The development firm may not have expertise in all required areas and may therefore subcontract the development of certain portions of the overall system.

The major facets of the contracting and subcontracting task involve contract administration and contract management As discussed here, *administration* covers all the actions necessary for the preparation, consummation, and completion of a major procurement. In other words, *contract administration* encompasses the tasks to be accomplished, However, *contract management* deals with how these are accomplished and how they are controlled. Contract management involves the activities covered below:

1. Determination of the extent to which schedule and cost are tracked and reported
2. Reporting and control of hazards—cost, schedule, quality, etc.
3. Management of configuration for the program
4. Management of product support in the after market, if applicable
5. Reliability aspects of the program, if applicable

The following sections cover contract administration and the contract management activities, from the pre-award to the post-award phase, and finally the important task of contract closure.

BIDDER SELECTION

In most cases, excluding partnering arrangements, competitive bidding is preferable in selecting a major subcontractor. In compiling the bidders list, first ensure that all suppliers under consideration are capable financially as well as technically. (To determine technical capability, conduct a "supplier survey" of potentially capable suppliers, using a team of the buying firm's functional specialists to assess manufacturing or other required capabilities. Quality control and various product support capabilities should be incorporated as well as design abilities.) The results of these supplier surveys should be given substantial consideration in the evaluation and selection of bidders. If current suppliers are included in the list of bidders, review your supplier evaluation records to ensure that those suppliers are meeting current requirements in all measured areas.

THE REQUEST FOR PROPOSAL (RFP)

Development of a complete, clear, and concise request for proposal (RFP) is essential in order to get an accurate and complete price from the potential suppliers. An RFP log can be kept to enable tracking of RFPs issued and response dates necessary (see Table 22–1).

RFP Inclusions

Include the following items where applicable:

* *Specification:* Describe completely the required technical performance of the hardware/item to be purchased.

T A B L E   22–1

RFP Log

ABC Widget Program; RFP Log				
RFP No. & Date	**Program**	**Bidders Due Date**	**Comments**	**Date Action Completed**
7022 050199	Chassis Enclosure	Chassis Machine Co Y Chassis Company VC Enclosure Company 060599		060299
7023 050199	Wire Harnesses	Wirewrap Co. PMC Electric Co. XYZ Wires, Inc. RIP Electronics 061599	Requested reply extension	

- *Drawing:* Depict the required physical dimensions and interfaces in detail.
- *Statement of work:* Describe the work required of the supplier during the subcontract period. What is to be delivered and when?
- *Data requirements:* List data that are required and provide the schedule and the format necessary for submittal.
- *Schedule:* Show the milestones that must be achieved and the schedule for them, making sure that final delivery requirements are clearly stated.
- *Instructions to offerors:* Describe the information that is required and how it is to be organized.
- *Terms and conditions:* Attach the terms and conditions necessary for communications and legal purposes (that you intend to make part of the contract).
- *Other considerations:* Any other specific requirements, such as use of electronic commerce processes in the development and management of the contract.

Once the items noted above are established, it may be worthwhile to hold a "bidders conference." During this prebid conference, all potential suppliers can discuss the specifications and requirements with representatives from the various disciplines (i.e., engineering, reliability, quality assurance) to ensure that all bidders have the same information and understand exactly what they are to submit. Questions from bidders during the entire process should be forwarded to all bidders along with the appropriate answers. This allows all participants to compete equally for the order. Note also that a bidders conference can be conducted via a conference call or "on-line" using communications technology. In-person conferences may be necessary where a job site visit, for example, could be important to the bidders.

Outline of RFP Sections

The RFP should include a section dedicated to outlining all the necessary instructions for completion of the proposal. An example of the table of contents for a typical RFP for a large, complex procurement is shown in Box 25–1.

B O X   25-1

INSTRUCTIONS TO OFFERORS

+ **Section 1—Enclosures**
  + A full list of all documents applicable to the RFP.
  + Order of precedence: cover letter, instructions to offerors, listed enclosures.
+ **Section 2—General Requirements**
  + General information regarding the proposal: number of copies, where the proposal is to be sent and when, its expiration date, order of precedence of RFP documents, subcontract terms and conditions and special provisions that are applicable.
+ **Section 3—Technical Proposal Organization and Content**
  + This is a table of contents for the technical volume.
+ **Section 4—Schedule Proposal**
  + Instructions on what is to be included in the schedule volume.
+ **Section 5—Cost Proposal Requirements**
  + Costing instructions, including proposed contract type.
+ **Section 6—Management Proposal Requirements**
  + A section concerning the management requirements for the proposal. This section might reasonably include requests for names and bios on the personnel which the supplier will use, as well as a request for information on all major suppliers to assist in assessing "supply chain management" information.
+ **Section 7—Quality Requirements**
  + A request for a copy of the bidder's quality manual and information concerning whether the supplier is ISO 9000 approved. This section should also note what, if any, "on-site" inspection would be required.
+ **Section 8—Certifications and Acknowledgments**
  + This section includes prime contract flowdown requirements, if applicable. (These are requirements that the buying organization's customer imposes, requirements that "flow down" to all subcontractors.)

CONSIDERATION OF THE APPROPRIATE CONTRACT TYPE

Choose the type of contract carefully. The objective is to provide a strong incentive for the supplier to make the most advantageous price and value offer to the buyer, considering all the contract variables. Choice of an inappropriate contract type often eliminates bidders or results in prices that are much higher than necessary.

The following discussion covers some of the more common types of contracts and explores their advantages and disadvantages. The most common contract types in use today include:

1. Firm fixed price (FFP)
2. Fixed price incentive (FPI)
3. Cost-plus incentive fee (CPIF)
4. Cost-plus fixed fee (CPFF)
5. Cost-plus award fee (CPAF)

There are a number of variations of these basic contract types, which are covered in depth in the Federal Acquisition Regulations (FAR). The FAR includes a description of the contract type, its application, its limitations, and applicable contract clauses. Note that these contract types have universal application potential and are not restricted to government-related procurement.

Firm Fixed Price Contract (FFP)

A firm fixed price contract is one that minimizes the risk for the buyer and maximizes the risk for the seller. For this reason, often the seller will attempt to realize a higher percentage of profit in the price quoted when operating under such a contract. This type of contract requires a minimum amount of administration by both the seller and the buyer, and is quite suitable when the task can be well defined and pricing can be established accurately from available cost or prior sales data.

A major weakness of the FFP is the incentive it gives the seller to inflate profit as a hedge against risk. In addition, a standard firm fixed price contract gives the buyer little, if any, knowledge about a supplier's cost structure. A provision that requires the supplier to make selected cost data available can be included, but such a clause is seldom used because this objective can be achieved more practically by using several other types of contracts. The net result of this situation is that changes in the scope of a job can easily become extremely costly under an FFP. This situation can be compounded when the contract is subject to several changes in scope after the initial placement.

A fixed price contract with economic price adjustment is a common variation of the firm fixed price type contract. It allows for either upward or downward adjustment of the price due to changes in actual costs of labor and/or material, cost indexes of labor and/or material, or published or otherwise established prices of specific items or the contract end item. This type of contract is often employed when the contract period of performance extends beyond a period where prices or labor rates can be accurately estimated. An order that requires deliveries of material over several years may include an economic price adjustment clause. It is imperative that the exact parameters regarding the terms to be used in calculating the price adjustment be included in the contract.

Fixed Price Incentive Contract (FPI)

When this type of contract is used, a target cost, a target fee, and a ceiling price must be established. The target cost and the target fee are a cost and fee that both the seller and the buyer agree are achievable. If the seller overruns the target cost, the fee is reduced accordingly. This type of contract requires that the buyer monitor costs closely, though, because up to the point that the seller reaches the ceiling price, escalated costs can increase the fee if it is expressed as a percentage of actual costs (this is not allowed for government contracts). Therefore this contract may encourage costs to grow as long as they do not reach the ceiling. Close monitoring of all costs by the buyer can curtail this tendency.

An FPI contract is suitable when most of the cost responsibility lies with the seller. FPI contracts contain a higher risk element than firm fixed price contracts, though, as do any of the alternative contracting types. An advantage of the FPI is that it allows a buyer greater visibility into a seller's cost and schedule position.

Cost-Plus Incentive Fee Contract (CPIF)

This type of contract, like all cost-type contracts, ensures that the seller will recover all its legitimate costs. In using a CPIF arrangement, the buyer must negotiate a target cost and a target fee with a minimum and maximum fee adjustment formula based on actual cost, schedule, and performance. On U.S. government jobs, federal regulations place a maximum percentage on the target cost fee allowed for various types of work accomplished. It is important to agree at the onset which costs are allowable.

A CPIF contract is popular for research and engineering development contracts because of the uncertainties associated with such work. Additionally, a CPIF contract allows a shared risk by both the buyer and seller. Finally, its greatest advantage, based on its track record, is that the CPIF is considered to be one of the contract types that affords the highest probability of achieving the desired level of performance.

Cost-Plus Fixed Fee Contract (CPFF)

As in the case of CPIF contracting, a CPFF contract must establish allowable "costs" at the beginning. This is another type of contract for which fee percentages are controlled on subcontracts for government procurements. However, in a CPFF contract, the fee is set at the outset and does not vary as costs increase or decrease. Like the CPIF contract, a CPFF is normally employed in research and development type efforts that involve a number of significant unknowns.

Normally the buyer and the seller agree before the contract is consummated on what the estimated costs of the work are likely to be. The fee is established as a fixed percent *of the agreed upon total cost estimate.* This can be a risky type of contract for a buyer to develop and manage when, for various reasons, it is difficult to estimate what a reasonable total cost level should be. Obviously, the seller will be inclined to reduce the risk by tending to overestimate expected costs. It is much wiser to use more controllable types of contracts for follow-on procurements.

Cost-Plus Award Fee Contract (CPAF)

Use of a cost-plus award fee contract requires that the buyer negotiate a target cost and minimum and maximum target fee. As is the case for all types of cost contracts, using a CPAF requires that allowable costs be negotiated before the contract is finalized.

In this case, the actual fee awarded is based on a relatively subjective assessment by the buyer of the seller's performance, as compared with the specific agreed upon criteria. In most contracts of this type the fee actually awarded to the supplier must fall within the minimum–

maximum range and is not subject to arbitration—the buyer's decision is final.

A CPAF contract should provide incentives to the seller to satisfy the buyer's needs. This type of contract, however, requires a great deal of administrative effort by the buyer to monitor both costs and performance. Detailed information in these areas is required for intelligent and fair decisions to be made concerning the fee to be awarded at the conclusion of the agreed upon performance periods. On the one hand, if the amount of the fee is too low, the supplier may find that other existing jobs produce a better profit level, and the job in question may be considered lower-priority. On the other hand, an overly generous fee may create some complacency and attendant performance problems.

In summary, the following factors should all be considered carefully in determining the appropriate contract to use in a given situation:

1. Is the technology new?
2. Is the item being purchased extremely complex?
3. Is the design complete and stable?
4. Will the contracting period cover a prolonged period?
5. Has the supplier had much experience with this specific type of product?
6. How accurate are the supplier's estimating system and accounting systems?
7. How urgent is the requirement?

Exploring the items noted above will give the buyer a good idea of the degree of risk involved in the purchase and will prove invaluable in determining the proper type of contract to use.

SOURCE-SELECTION PLAN

A good source-selection plan allows a buyer to manage and control the source-selection process to ensure that all sources are treated equally and fairly. Such a plan, properly implemented, will keep award protests and nonresponsive bids to a minimum.

A source-selection plan should contain the following elements:

♦ List of deliverables
♦ List of approved bidders (include ratings for those suppliers currently being used)

- Contract type, details of incentives, if any
- Selection schedule
- List of review groups (i.e., engineering, quality, etc.)
- Evaluation of criteria, scoring forms, etc.
- Reminder statement concerning the evaluator's conduct during evaluation

All members of the evaluation team must treat supplier information in a completely confidential manner. Normally, this activity is performed to determine which suppliers will be asked to submit proposals for the work required. If the supplier for the product being procured is a major supplier, a supply chain management plan or a teaming/certification plan might already be in place. However, if the procurement is very costly and critical, other suppliers may be sought in order to ensure competitive pricing is being submitted.

PROPOSAL EVALUATION

General Considerations

Once received, a proposal must be evaluated for completeness; keep in mind that the technical data must be evaluated by selected individuals qualified for each of the specific tasks. As a general rule, these individuals come from the original supplier survey team. If a bidder's proposal is considered to be "nonresponsive," the proposal should be returned along with a letter of explanation.

Developing "Should Cost" Data

A "should cost" analysis is a valuable tool in assessing a proposal for a follow-on purchase or one that is similar to a prior purchase. Such an analysis provides an idea of what costs are likely to be providing a yardstick by which to measure the proposals received. A proposal that varies greatly from the "should cost" figures should be investigated thoroughly to ensure that neither the supplier's analysis nor the buying firm's analysis has neglected any important element of the specifications.

Each segment of the proposal must be carefully evaluated and rated in order to make an intelligent and a fair judgment of the entire proposal. Some guidelines are noted below that typically are helpful in reviewing and evaluating the various sections of a proposal.

- *Technical material and/or services.* Look for areas evidencing inadequate planning, high risk, overly optimistic yields, and overlooked or misinterpreted elements.

- *Management and schedule of material and/or services.* When evaluating the personnel proposed for the major tasks of the program, look carefully at experience as well as the lines of authority assigned. Be sure that the proposed organizational arrangement provides for necessary authority as well as the corresponding responsibility. Prior to making a final decision, interview the personnel proposed for the various major jobs. Capability and experience are musts for proper administration of a large or a complex contract. Evaluate proposed schedules to be sure that the supplier is using realistic criteria for each facet of the program. Ensure that all tasks include sufficient time to solve all potential problem areas.

- *Cost of material and/or services.* In the preliminary analysis, look for any possible items that may have been omitted. Also cross-check selected important costs to detect possible discrepancies and errors. Compare the costs shown against the "should cost" estimate, if one has been developed. Remember, a very low submitted cost figure may indicate omissions or a lack of understanding of the specifications. Ensure that cost data are presented in the same format for all proposals to facilitate accurate comparisons.

Once all evaluations are completed, the evaluation team may wish to conduct a brief preliminary fact-finding investigation to determine which supplier has the best understanding of the job. This investigation, while thorough, is preliminary; an in-depth investigation will be conducted once the source selection has been made. The activity described at this point allows the evaluation team to question the supplier's proposal team to determine how the tasks were priced, and to assess the level of understanding and completeness represented in the proposal.

The announcement of the successful supplier should be made with the full understanding that cost and contract negotiations must be successfully completed prior to the issuance of a valid contract. However, after the initial announcement, debriefing conversations should be held with all suppliers who participated and were not chosen. This meeting or conversation should reveal to the unsuccessful bidders the areas of their proposals that were considered to be weak. Obviously, to preserve confidentiality and propriety, direct comparisons with the successful bid-der's proposal should never be made.

FACT-FINDING AND NEGOTIATION

This section discusses the key areas of fact-finding and negotiating work involved in the development of a large, complex contract. Fact-finding and negotiation are not a great deal different here than in other pro-curements, except that more thorough organization and in-depth inves-tigation and analysis are required.

Fact-Finding

This fact-finding activity, unlike the preliminary one that might have been done during source selection, is designed to determine the major issues for the ensuing negotiation. During this investigation, the charge is to distinguish between what is factual and what is based on judgment and to identify errors, duplications, and omissions.

The major objectives of the fact-finding exploration are:

- To do the price–cost analysis for the proposal
- If this is part of a government contract, to check the inconsistencies with the government audit
- To resolve any discrepancies found between the technical and the cost segments of the proposal
- To identify the data that are factual and the information that is based on judgment
- To meet the supplier's management team to become better acquainted with the facility and the supplier's capabilities
- To prepare for the upcoming negotiation

For a successful fact-finding exploration, several things must be done. First, a leader must be designated. Next, the team should be ap-pointed and a meeting held to determine each person's responsibility in the activity. The leader should gather as many questions from the team members as possible and submit them in advance to the supplier, along with a list of the team members and their responsibilities. This person is also responsible for obtaining any records necessary to conduct the in-vestigation (e.g., purchase orders, invoices, price history records). The team leader is responsible for arranging the date for the visit as well as all necessary travel and lodging arrangements.

The fact-finding investigation is not a negotiation—it is simply an information-gathering visit. When the investigation is complete, share the preliminary findings to ensure that the supplier is aware of the documents and additional data needed prior to the inception of negotiations. This information should be confirmed in writing once the team has returned from the visit.

Negotiation

Negotiation activities for a large major contract usually are more lengthy and formal than most other negotiations; the process, however, is the same. Thus, although a team is utilized, a strong team leader must be identified and his or her instructions for all team members must be followed closely. Successful negotiations result from a carefully planned team effort.

The buyer's team should prepare and get approval for a negotiation plan based on the results of the fact-finding investigation. A target price range is prepared by listing all items that should be reduced as well as the reasons for the recommended reductions. Anything overlooked in the proposal should be included in the preparation of the negotiation range target. It is customary to determine an opening position, an optimum position, and a maximum position. The maximum position represents the highest price at which the team may settle the negotiation without obtaining additional management approvals. The range document should include supporting evidence to justify all positions.

An important point that must become part of the negotiating strategy stems from the following philosophical concept: making a supplier feel that it has "lost" the negotiation may impair relations throughout the contract. A win–win philosophy is essential.

No negotiations should leave open issues (e.g., the price is established but terms and conditions are left open). Be sure that both parties sign a memorandum of agreement outlining the key elements of the agreement. A note that this agreement is "subject to management approval" can be added. The important thing is to be sure that all settlements are immediately documented and not left to memory or notes. In an ideal situation, a negotiation is completed and approved by the team doing the work. However, if this is not possible, good documentation is a must.

DOCUMENTATION OF THE NEGOTIATION

A written negotiation summary should be prepared documenting the pricing agreements and providing a permanent record of the process. The summary should be written so that anyone who did not attend the negotiation can follow the series of events and understand the rationale of the settlement. The document should note the names and titles of all participants, where the negotiation took place, and what data were submitted. Included should be each issue discussed and details about the positions of each party as well as the final agreement for that particular point in the negotiation.

The document should be organized so the reader can see a summary, a description of the negotiation cycle, a discussion of the series of events that led to the final settlement, and finally a review of the results, including key statements supporting the reasonableness of the final settlement.

The Contract

Once negotiations are complete, a contract must be drawn up and signed by both parties. A number of sections and clauses will define the relationship of the supplier and the buying organization. The objectives of this document are:

- To outline with the supplier its responsibilities and obligations
- To ensure that all areas are defined so that future potential disputes can be avoided

Major contracts vary considerably according to need; however, the following list details the minimum requirements that typically should be addressed:

- *Recitals:* Who the parties are and what type of contract is to be used (e.g., firm fixed price)
- *Effectivity and content:* Date of agreement and list of documents included in the contract
- *Precedence of documents:* Defines the order of document hierarchy
- *Deliverables:* Defines work to be performed
- *Data:* Defines the data that will be delivered

- *Terms and conditions:* Defines changes to the normal purchase order terms and conditions and any special requirements if a government contract is involved
- *Pricing:* Outlines the pricing agreement
- *Schedule:* Outlines the deliveries required for all contract items
- *Inspection:* Defines any special inspection requirements (e.g., first article, source inspection)
- *Packaging and shipment:* Directions for packaging, shipping, and delivery of contractual materials; also includes FOB point or any other shipping agreements
- *Notices and amendments:* Provides a single point of contact for these documents
- *Execution of document:* Provides for authorizing signatures for both parties

Government contracts may also include sections covering necessary reports to the contracting officer and a section concerning government owned property and the use of such property.

A well-written contract is essential to the execution of a smooth relationship with the supplier. Nothing should be left to chance or a handshake—this includes necessary performance, the baseline for measuring performance, reviews, and reporting requirements. Both parties must understand both their rights and their obligations in the relationship.

Purchase Orders

Some major procurements have a number of separate elements that are most efficiently administered by using several purchase orders with individual funding. Some examples are:

Nonrecurring Costs

1. Tooling or special test equipment
2. Engineering or other types of design
3. Qualification testing
4. Units for destructive testing
5. Data
6. Licenses or permits

Recurring Costs

1. Production hardware
2. Production or service support
3. Spare and replacement hardware
4. Packaging and shipping costs
5. Warranty

Letter Contracts

On occasion, projects must be started before fact-finding and negotiation are completed. This requires the use of a letter contract (sometimes called a letter subcontract), which allows the supplier to begin work immediately. When the letter contract is released to the supplier, the following items should be clearly defined:

1. *Funding limitation:* A "not to exceed" amount of money that the supplier may expend
2. *Negotiation schedule:* Dates for the fact-finding activity and negotiations to start and complete, including the date on which the order will be made a firm commitment
3. *Contract requirements defined:* Statement of work and, at a minimum, schedule and quality requirements

Updating the negotiation schedule or increasing funding may be necessary if the original dates are not met. Such changes require use of a formal change order to the supplier. A commonly used rule of thumb is that a firm price and firm contract terms should be agreed upon prior to the completion of 40% of the proposed price. If work is allowed to continue beyond that point, the negotiation may be conducted on the basis of actual costs, placing the buyer in a less advantageous position in the negotiation process.

Acknowledgment and Changes

Formal acknowledgment of the purchase order is sometimes neglected in the heat of pressing operating issues, or at times a supplier may take exception to certain contract provisions and include its own terms, which may conflict with the original requirements of the purchase order. Hence, follow-up should ensure that the buyer and the supplier are in fact in agreement and that written evidence of the agreement is in place. *Any exceptions taken by a supplier require timely action by the buyer to reach mutual agreement on the item in question.*

Large, complex procurements usually involve numerous changes. It is this essential that the contract contain a formal procedure to handle changes fairly and in a timely manner. All changes should be controlled by the contract administrator (also referred to as the subcontract administrator) to ensure that both schedule and cost concerns are incorporated properly into the contract. The procedure should require that the supplier take direction only from designated procurement personnel. Changes should be submitted formally to the supplier, and cost and schedule impact must be transmitted back to the buyer. The contract can allow the buyer to designate preliminary funding and require the supplier to submit firm cost and schedule information within a reasonable period. Some contracts are written to allow minor changes to be incorporated at no cost. Once change costs are negotiated, they should be incorporated into a formal purchase order change. This type of procedure ensures that unauthorized changes do not occur and that casual conversations do not result in changes in direction or in the scope of the contract.

MANAGING THE CONTRACT
The Management Team

The task of establishing the structure for support of the program schedule, budget, and technical performance is a major management function that should begin with a post-award meeting. At this time both the supplier's team and the buyer's team meet to establish comfortable working relationships. Although the practice varies depending on the industry and the nature and size of the procurement, an interdisciplinary team is almost always utilized by the buyer. Typical members of the team and their functions are described briefly below:

- *Contract administrator (subcontract administrator):* Provides the business management skills for the team. The administrator is responsible for all matters which affect cost or schedule. Contractual matters are controlled by the contract administrator as is all correspondence to the supplier.
- *Designer or design engineer:* Provides technical guidance to the supplier through the contract administrator. This individual

turns requirements into specifications and drawings, assists in the preparation and maintenance of the statement of work, chairs design reviews, and monitors all *technical* interfaces with the supplier.

+ *Quality assurance specialist:* Ensures that the supplier has an acceptable quality plan, provides on-site inspection and acceptance of goods and/or services, and coordinates quality problems and waivers with the designer or design engineer.

+ *Reliability engineer:* Ensures that reliability requirements are suitable for the procurement at hand and that the supplier complies with the requirements. This person establishes the level of reliability for the hardware being purchased, generates reliability documents, and approves supplier-generated documents.

+ *Material and services price and cost analyst:* Assists the contract administrator in preparing the cost proposal, analyzes and evaluates supplier submittals, and assists the contract administrator in the negotiation.

In the case of extremely large procurement projects, the following representatives may also be included on the buyer's team:

+ *Program office representative (if applicable):* Provides direction and assistance to the supplier concerning schedule preparation, reporting, and control through the contract administrator; maintains internal schedule and cost control for the program; in coordination with appropriate sales personnel, may be the customer contact between the purchasing organization and the ultimate customer.

+ *On-site representative:* Attends supplier status meetings and provides on-site assistance for quality, engineering, shortage, and cost problems.

Good management requires clear communication of all operating activities by means of reports, charts, and status meetings. However, the supplier must have some freedom to manage its position without undue interference. Problem areas must be brought to management's attention in a timely manner, and solutions or "work arounds" (i.e., plans to complete other tasks until the required material arrives or activities are complete) should be activated. The contract administrator must be willing to offer help and suggestions and share the consequences if necessary.

AREAS TO BE CONTROLLED

The following areas should be defined and controlled:

1. Schedules
2. Budget allocation
3. Contract changes
4. Data management system (if applicable)
5. Data or hardware changes in configuration
6. Quality

At this point in the process, *all schedules* must be detailed and finalized, including important milestones that are critical for successful completion of the project. For instance, a buyer who contracts for the construction of a building must establish dates by which all activities must be complete. Walls cannot be constructed until the foundation is poured, and the framing must be complete before the electrical work can be started. The same is true for any large project. Therefore, planning and control charts should be constructed and agreed upon dates for each milestone established at this time.

The next task is to establish *budgets* for each activity, being sure to hold some reserve for the inevitable changes and unanticipated development problems. Budgets should be established and reviewed quarterly for any necessary adjustments. In addition, budgets must be reallocated if work is modified or changed from one area or department to another. Budgets should be closely tracked, using written reports, to ensure that problem areas are given timely attention. If problems are neglected, overruns may be noticed much too late for effective corrective action to be taken.

It is essential for the administrator to develop a comprehensive system to control contract changes. This system must require appropriate justification and timing for each change. Specific instructions should be in place that control the level of the change, who can approve it, costs involved, and appropriate feedback to all team members that need it.

If the contract being managed includes *data,* delivery dates and configuration must be tracked. Managing a great deal of data requires the use of milestones and a good reporting system.

Quality assurance is another important aspect of the contract that must be managed. Appropriate reporting from the quality assurance department and representation by its personnel at status meetings are mandatory. An undue number of problems in the area of quality tends to cause both schedule slippage and cost deterioration. This area must be managed carefully to prevent an adverse impact on the other operating areas.

CONTRACT CONTROL

Making It Happen

Contract control is the process of "making it happen." The process involves the development of a performance plan coupled with a subsequent understanding and monitoring of performance to date. Contract control also involves the ability to anticipate the actions required to make things happen. Too often a buyer waits until it is too late to effectively take corrective action. That is why milestone monitoring is so important. With this information, a manager can monitor a task or schedule and begin to work on a recovery plan before the entire project is late. Important matters must be controlled in writing. Copies of correspondence to the proper individuals prove very helpful in effecting overall contract control.

Monitoring is only part of the job of contract control. Once the contract administrator receives the reports, they must be reviewed for necessary actions. All contract management team members should receive copies of specific reports that deal with issues in their areas of responsibility so they can be of assistance in controlling and directing necessary "work arounds" or solutions to problems that have arisen.

One of the items often neglected is the simple matter of correspondence. Sometimes when letters are sent to the contract administrator, an appropriate response requires input from other team members. To stay on top of these matters, some contract administrators maintain a log of open correspondence and require status reports at weekly or biweekly program reviews. A program correspondence log can take many forms; a simple document like the one shown in Table 22–2 is used by some organizations.

Supplier Performance Reviews

A word about supplier performance reviews is appropriate. Most programs of any size require that both formal and informal reviews be done at both the supplier's facility and the buyer's facility. Obviously, if there is hardware to review, the team will meet at the supplier's facility. At a

T A B L E 22-2

Correspondence Log

ABC Widget Program; Open Correspondence

Ltr. No. & Date	Subject	Responsibility Due Date	Comments	Date Action Completed
Y010076 051999	Design change	ABC Company 060599	Request signed approval	060299
ABC 03001 061099	Request material substitution	Y Chassis Company 063099	Need change order	062299
ABC 030039 062599	Invoice discrepancies	Y Chassis Company 070699	Unpaid invoice problem	070699
Y010110 071599	Deviation for parts not to specification	ABC Company 082499	Request signed approval	082099

minimum, the following basic guidelines are important when conducting performance reviews:

+ The review should provide a status report of the supplier's performance in the areas of budget, schedule, and technical activities. Examples of schedule and budget control charts are shown in Figures 22–1 and 22–2.

+ Normally reviews are conducted by the contract program manager, with support from the contract team as necessary.

+ All reviews should be scheduled in advance, and all participants should be provided with an agenda.

+ Action items should be gathered and assigned with required completion dates. Follow-up for closure should not wait until the next review but should be assigned to a member of the team for regular status. Action item status should be reviewed by the contract administrator regularly and at the next meeting. If an item falls behind between meetings, the contract administrator must work with the appropriate personnel to obtain closure.

+ Hazards can be included in the review. The contract administrator should attempt to alert all affected personnel of new hazards before the review so that they can provide an appropriate recovery plan at the meeting.

A program management review agenda is shown in Table 22-3. The agenda shown is typical for a major program review held at the supplier's facility. The presenters shown are members of the supplier's team. Reviews held at the buyer's facility might be chaired by the contract program manager or the program manager. This person is designated by the buyer's firm to direct all disciplines represented on the team (engineering, product support, material, etc.).

In addition to "action item" lists being made, minutes should be recorded and published for all meetings. Details discussed at these meetings should never be left to memory; each participant will remember them somewhat differently. Minutes should be distributed to all attendees as well as other interested individuals.

One approach to monitoring costs is to allow the supplier to use estimates at completion (EAC). This approach can help predict costs, but can be less than effective in controlling this area. Clearly EAC should

FIGURE 22-1

Program Tracking Schedule: ABC Widget Program. Electronic Widget Scanner

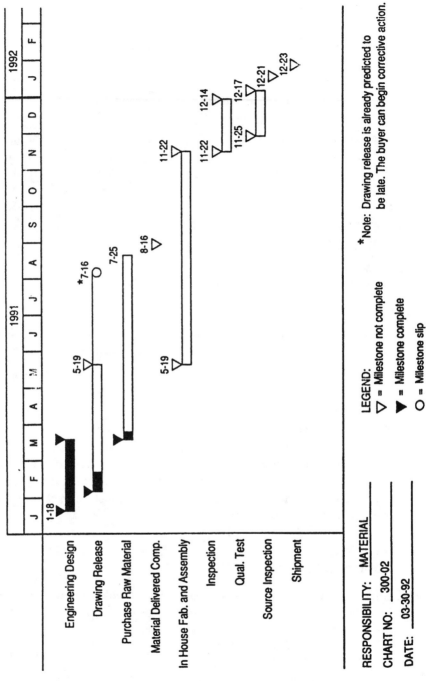

RESPONSIBILITY: __MATERIAL__

CHART NO: __300-02__

DATE: __03-30-92__

LEGEND:

▽ = Milestone not complete

▼ = Milestone complete

○ = Milestone slip

*Note: Drawing release is already predicted to be late. The buyer can begin corrective action.

Source: The Purchasing Handbook, H. E. Fearon, D. W. Dobler, and K. H. Killen (eds.); 5th edition, McGraw-Hill (1992).

F I G U R E   22–2

Budget Tracking Chart

ABC Widget Program: Budget (thousands of dollars)				
Activity	Budget	Current Costs	EAC*	Variance
Engineering	150	120	170	(20)
Material	200	10	200	0
Support	50	5	40	10
Mfg.	300	0	300	0
Inspection	10	0	10	0
Management	50	7	40	10
Total	760	142	760	0

*Estimate at completion.

Responsibility: Finance   Date: 033092.

Source: *The Purchasing Handbook*, H. E. Fearon, D. W. Dobler, and K. H. Killen (eds.); 5th edition, McGraw-Hill (1992).

not become a vehicle to excuse a cost overrun. Once a potential cost overrun has been revealed, recovery is very difficult to effect.

The specific method chosen to manage a contract is not as important as implementation of sufficient controls to achieve the desired results. Trained and competent personnel are the most important ingredient in successful contract management.

CONTRACT CLOSURE

Contract closure involves several activities. Unlike a purchase order, where receipt of the items ordered and subsequent payment constitute closure, a major contract requires the following:

1. All contractual issues must be settled.
2. All changes must be negotiated and incorporated into the final document.

T A B L E   22-3

A Sample Agenda

Widget Project Management Review Agenda Date: _____	
Schedule Status	Program manager
Milestone review	
Activities behind schedule (recovery plan)	
Activities ahead of schedule	
Hazards	
Technical Status	Chief Engineer
Status of current engineering changes	
Special technical areas of concern	
Cost Status	Program Manager
Review of cost overrun or underrun status, shown by program area (manufacturing, material, etc.)	
Review of Action Items	Program Manager
Update status of all open action items	
Current Activity Status	
Material status	Material Rep.
Product support status	Product Support Rep.
Production status	Manufacturing Rep.
Quality assurance status	Quality Rep.
Special Topics	Program Manager
Action Item Review	Program Manager

Source: *The Purchasing Handbook*, H. E. Fearon, D. W. Dobler, and K. H. Killen (eds.); 5th edition, McGraw-Hill (1992).

3. All deliverable items (hardware, data, and reports) must have been received.

4. All bailed (borrowed) equipment must have been returned.

5. All tooling must be returned or assigned to the supplier to maintain to facilitate the manufacture of replacement parts.

6. All classified documents must have been returned.

7. Final payment must have been made

Once the contract administrator ensures that all these items are complete, it is a good idea to convene a meeting of the contract management team. At this meeting each member should submit a written report that (1) shows that all actions are complete and (2) contains a description and analysis of the supplier's performance.

Finally, the contract administrator should write a formal closure document that contains a narrative identifying and discussing the supplier's strengths and weaknesses in the performance of the contract and noting both major difficulties encountered and areas executed in an acceptable manner. Such a file is invaluable if disputes subsequently arise; this file is also useful later when new jobs develop and potential suppliers are being considered.

Quality Assurance

Editor
Mir F. Ali, MBA, Ph.D.
Managing Director
AIM/AMC Corporation

INTRODUCTION

Objective

This chapter explores quality assurance tools and techniques available to suppliers and purchasers. While the principle focus of this chapter is on quality assurance in purchasing, it also recognizes that suppliers need to use the same tools and techniques to produce and deliver goods and services faster, more cheaply, and with quality exceeding minimum requirements. It is easier to accomplish the goal of quality in any organization if the purchasers and suppliers work together as partners with the same focus.

Background

The process-oriented concept of quality assurance originated and was perfected in Japan.[1] It gave birth to Just-in-Time (JIT) manufacturing and Total Quality Management (TQM) tools and techniques before Japanese manufacturers targeted the West for their products. The introduction of Japanese products to the American market was a wake-up call. It revolutionized the marketplace and left American businesses with no choice

---

1. M. F. Ali, "Business Process Reengineering: Cure or Curse," *Electronic Commerce World*, January 1998.

but to use the Japanese tools and techniques to beat them at their own game. It was a matter of survival for American businesses.

It took Toyota (Motor Co.) 20 years to finalize the design of its production system, which packaged the principles of what we now call JIT. After the first oil embargo in 1973, companies throughout Japan began to emulate Toyota's lean production, fanaticism in eliminating waste in manufacturing processes, and constant drive to increase quality. Toyota's continual improvements were achieved through successive process refinements and increased integration of workers and suppliers into the production system.

David A. Garvin notes that external threats played an equally important role in sparking Xerox's interest in quality.[2] In the mid-1970s a number of Japanese manufacturers took aim at the low-priced copier market. Several Japanese companies introduced models that were inexpensive, reliable, and easy to use. Xerox had historically ignored this segment of the market and at first paid little attention to the new entrants. The Japanese machines, however, soon forced the company to take notice. Between 1970 and 1980, Xerox's share of U.S. copier revenues fell from 90% to 46%, largely because of Japanese competition.

Hewlett-Packard has long been known for the quality of its computers, test instruments, and other electronic devices. But in the early 1980s it began to face increased pressure from customers for higher-quality products. Japanese competitors also provided a strong challenge. A detailed study of quality was soon initiated; the company found, to its surprise, that as much as 25% of manufacturing assets were tied up in reacting to quality problems. Management recognized that continuing quality improvement was necessary if Hewlett-Packard was to retain a position of market leadership.

Initially the concept of quality assurance was not readily accepted in the United States, but it gradually became a critical part of the process to produce and deliver goods and services.

What Is Quality

Quality is many things to many people.[3] The answer to the question "What is quality?" can be as vague and general as the answer to the question "What is art?" Quality is becoming part of the business lexicon,

2. D. A. Garvin, *Managing Quality: The Strategic and Competitive Edge*, Free Press, New York, 1988.
3. R. M. McNealy, *Making Quality Happen*, Chapman & Hall, London, New York, 1993.

which favors auspicious-sounding yet vague words, such as "excellence," that can mean many things to many people. A quality product or service is simply one that meets or exceeds the customer's needs or expectations.

The meaning of quality differs from person to person, depending on their position in the supply chain. For example, for the customer, a good-quality product is one that meets his or her needs in terms of performance, appearance, and price. For the product designer, quality is related to a product satisfying functional requirements. For the manufacturer, the definition of quality is based on conformance to specifications at a minimum cost.

Other definitions include:

+ The totality of features and characteristics of a product or service that bear on its ability to satisfy given needs
+ Fitness for use
+ Conformance to requirements
+ The degree to which product characteristics conform to the requirements placed upon that product, including reliability, maintainability, and safety

If we define quality as meeting or exceeding customer's needs or expectations, then we can measure when and how often we are not meeting those needs. By clarifying the definition of quality, we also clarify how we measure it.

Quality Assurance Systems

Duc Truong Pham and Ercan Oztemel note that the purpose of a quality system is to provide a measure of how a product, process, or machine meets customer needs.[4] The concept of quality relates to the functioning of an industrial organization where all departments are required to work closely together to achieve and maintain the desired standards of quality. In a manufacturing environment, typically the functions are divided as follows:

+ Marketing determines customer requirements that provide the basis of product design

---

4. D. T. Pham and E. Oztemel, *Intelligent Quality Systems,* Springer, London, New York, 1996.

+ Product engineering develops specifications from the customer requirements and designs the product
+ Purchasing obtains materials and parts based on the specifications and design
+ Manufacturing develops and operates a process that will transform the materials and parts into finished product that meets the specifications
+ Inspection and testing develops and implements processes to ensure that only good products of the desired quality leave the production line
+ Packaging contains the product, preserves and protects it against damage during storage and handling, and aids in identifying it
+ Storage and shipping stores the product and ships to customers as they require

The success of a manufacturing concern depends on the deployment of a reliable quality assurance system and the establishment of effective communication links between various functions as illustrated in Figure 23–1.

A quality assurance function is established in each organization with responsibilities that may include some or all of the following:

+ Product quality assurance
+ Product reliability assurance
+ Quality planning
+ Supplier quality control
+ Product specification conformance
+ Quality testing equipment control
+ Personnel training
+ Feedback to management on quality concerns
+ Overall quality assurance system management
+ Quality assurance system evaluation
+ Quality system maintenance and improvement

A traditional way of achieving and ensuring the set quality standards in manufacturing concerns is to implement statistical process control (SPC) techniques. SPC is the observation of the quality of a semi-finished or finished product and correlating it with the time histories of

F I G U R E   23-1

Central Role of Quality Assurance

Source: D. T. Pham and E. Oztemel, *Intelligent Quality Systems*, Springer, London, New York, 1996.

the manufacturing process involved and taking appropriate measures to maintain the desired quality level. As manufacturing complexity and uncertainty increase, SPC procedures become more demanding and require implementation skills that must be developed over time using accumulated knowledge of the process involved. Attention has been focused on the use of artificial intelligence (AI) to deal with difficult manufacturing problems because of its ability to "learn" from experience and to handle uncertain imprecise (fuzzy) and complex information in a competitive and quality-demanding environment.

QA TOOLS AND TECHNIQUES FOR SUPPLIERS

ISO 9000

The term "ISO 9000" refers to a series of quality system standards that have been developed by the International Organization for Standardization (ISO). ISO is a worldwide federation of national standards bodies that was founded in 1946 to promote the development of international standards and related activities (such as conformity assessment) to facilitate the exchange of goods and services worldwide. ISO member bodies represent nearly 100 countries, the U.S. member body being the American National Standards Institute (ANSI).

In 1979, ISO formed Technical Committee (TC) 176 on Quality Management and Quality Assurance to address the worldwide trend toward increasingly stringent customer demands with regard to quality combined with growing confusion in international trade resulting from differing national quality system requirements.

In 1987, based on the work of TC 176, ISO published the ISO 9000 Standard Series on quality management and assurance. These standards were based on considerable input from a number of countries, especially the United States, Canada, and the United Kingdom. In particular, the ISO 9000 standards were based in large part on the British Standards Institution's BS 5750 Series, Quality Systems. The focus of the ISO 9000 standards is on imposing a requirement on suppliers of goods and services to establish and maintain an effective, economical, and demonstrable system that ensures that what they supply conforms to specified quality requirements.

ISO 9000 is a quality system standard. It applies not to products or services, but to the process that creates them. ISO 9000 is designed with the objective of applying these standards to any product or service produced by any process anywhere in the world. To achieve this objective, ISO 9000 refrains, to the greatest extent possible, from mandating specific methods, practices, and techniques. It emphasizes principles, goals, and objectives, all of which focus on one objective, the same objective that derives every business: meeting customer expectations and requirements.

The ISO 9000 standards are a set of five documents, ISO 9000, ISO 9001, ISO 9002, ISO 9003, and ISO 9004 known as the *ISO 9000 family standards.*

The individual standards themselves, which are sometimes referred to as the children of the ISO 9000 family, define the quality systems or models applicable to design, development, production, installation and servicing, and final inspection and test of products and services. Since not all endeavors include all of these aspects, three standards were developed to cover different combinations of these activities, and a set of guidelines was issued to assist in choosing the correct standard for application. These guidelines and standards are:

- ISO 9000: *Quality Management and Quality Assurance Standards: Guidelines for Selection and Use.* As indicated by its title, this standard provides information on the selection and use of the ISO 9000 standards.

- ISO 9001: *Quality Systems—Models for Quality Assurance in Design, Development, Production, Installation and Servicing.* ISO 9001 contains 20 sections, each of which specifies requirements for a component of the quality system. ISO 9001 is the *superset* standard of the models for quality systems contained in the ISO 9000 family and ISO 9002 and ISO 9003 are progressively smaller subsets of that standard. ISO 9001 requires the development of a quality manual (model) and documented procedures that define the organization and operation of the quality system. Companies are responsible for creating and maintaining these documents so that they are current and appropriate to the specific business operation.

- *ISO 9002 Quality Systems—Models for Quality Assurance in Production, Installation and Servicing.* ISO 9002 is the model for quality systems that include production but do not include design. ISO 9002 is almost word-for-word equivalent to ISO 9001, except that it does not include requirements for design control. It contains 19 sections of requirements. ISO 9002 requires the development of a quality manual and documented procedures that define the organization and operation of the quality system. Companies are responsible for creating and maintaining these documents to remain current and appropriate to the specific business operation.

- *ISO 9003: Quality Systems—Models for Quality Assurance in Final Inspection and Test.* ISO 9003 is the model for quality systems that do not include design or production. ISO 9003 contains about half of the requirements from ISO 9001 and modifies some of the requirements to suit the inspection and final test application. As required by ISO 9001 and ISO 9002, ISO 9003 also requires the development and maintenance of a quality manual and documented procedures that define the organization and operation of the quality system.

It is critical to understand the difference between these standards before attempting to apply them. As indicated by the difference in title, the standards apply to the extent of activity in which an organization engages:

- Those organizations involved with the last stages of product completion, final assembly, and testing would choose ISO 9003.
- Those organizations that include a stage of manufacture prior to final assembly and test would choose ISO 9002.
- Finally, those organizations that undertake design and development activities, manufacture those designs, and complete final inspection and testing would choose ISO 9001.

ISO 9001 and ISO 9002 are nearly identical. How do you decide which to use? Choose ISO 9001 if your organization carries out the innovative design of products or services; otherwise, choose ISO 9002. The only difference in the standards' requirements is in section 4.4 "Design Control." This section is required in ISO 9001 and is "not applicable" in ISO 9002. Any description or interpretation of ISO 9001 pertains equally to ISO 9002, ignoring section 4.4.

- ISO 9001 applies in situations where:
  - Design is required and the product requirements are stated principally in performance terms, or they need to be established
  - Confidence in product conformance can be attained by adequate demonstration of a supplier's capabilities in design, development, production, installation, and servicing.
- ISO 9002 applies in situations where:
  - The specified requirements for product and stated in terms of an established design or specification
  - Confidence in product conformance can be attained by adequate demonstration of a supplier's capabilities in production, installation, and servicing.

The bottomline is that the ISO 9000 standards establish a standard framework for a quality system. A quality system is a series of checks and balances that, when introduced and followed, will ensure quality of output or product. The framework, as embodied by ISO 9000, identifies specific requirements, each of which affects quality.

Baldridge Award Criteria Framework

In the public as well as the private sector, an increasing number of quality programs are using the U.S. government's Baldridge Award Criteria

Framework (Figure 23–2). In some states, applications for state awards are required to submit applications that show that their organization is familiar with the Baldridge criteria and can prove that the enterprise is adhering to each of the critical areas of the criteria.

The Baldridge Framework has four basic elements:

- *Driver:* The senior executives who create the values, goals, and systems and guide the ongoing pursuit of customer value and organization performance improvement. Management has to lead the quality movement.

- *Goal:* The delivery of ever-improving value to customers. This means continual striving to reduce error rates while working to increase customer satisfaction.

- *System:* A set of well-defined and well-designed processes for meeting customer needs. This calls for designing and implementing the necessary structure, procedures, and guidelines for achieving the desired quality goals.

FIGURE   23–2

Baldridge Award Criteria Framework

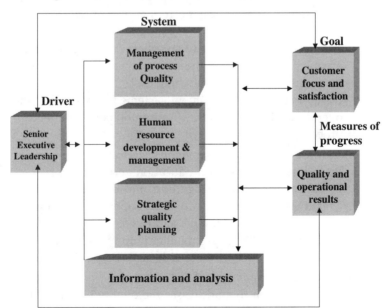

Source: Based on Material in Malcolm Baldridge National Quality Award Criteria, U.S. National Institute of Standards and Technology.

♦ *Measures of progress:* Measures that provide feedback and help the organization identify changes that need to be made. In this way, the enterprise is able to provide ever-better products and services to its customers.

As can be seen from Figure 23–2, senior-level management drives the quality effort. This effort will be successful only if the managers have a well-designed system in place. The customer of this system—customer satisfaction and operational results—lets management know how well it is doing. In turn, this feedback is useful in modifying both the leadership efforts and the system.

The following list highlights activities under each major area:

♦ *Senior executive leadership:*
  ♦ Becoming personally involved in the quality process
  ♦ Clearly communicating the importance of quality to employees
  ♦ Constantly reviewing performance to ensure that the quality focus is maintained
  ♦ Recognizing and rewarding contributions
  ♦ Continually urging everyone to keep improving
♦ *Management of process quality:*
  ♦ Designing and introducing new production and delivery processes that cut product errors and improve service quality
  ♦ Developing programs with suppliers that help link the organization and the supplier in a synergistic way, thus increasing quality and reducing cost
  ♦ Designing quality-assessment systems for evaluating the overall results and ensuring continuous improvement in the process
♦ *Human resources development and management:*
  ♦ Providing everyone with education and training
  ♦ Developing effective recognition and reward systems
  ♦ Creating initiatives that promote cooperation among management, labor, unions, and outside suppliers
  ♦ Designing feedback systems that help measure employee satisfaction and chart these changes along a time continuum
♦ *Strategic quality planning:*
  ♦ Creating a plan that addresses the quality objectives that are most important to the customer

- Focusing on the objectives that will create defect-free products
- Developing a rapid response to customer needs
- Determining how to reduce the time needed to provide goods and services
- Increasing productivity and holding prices at competitive levels

- *Information and analysis:*
  - Describing the types of information to gather
  - Determining how to use this information to measure progress
  - Deciding how this information will be used to still improve internal operations further

- *Customer focus and satisfaction:*
  - Identifying specific customer groups or market niches
  - Soliciting feedback regarding what each group or niche would like, both now and over the next three to five years
  - Identifying the steps that will have to be taken to meet these current and future needs
  - Evaluating customer complaints and developing a response system for handling these issues
  - Identifying the current level and trend of customer satisfaction as measured by surveys and other forms of feedback
  - Comparing customer satisfaction results and trends with those of similar organizations

The Balanced Scorecard

As Kaplan and Norton observe, "If you can't measure it, you can't manage it."[5] An organization's measurement system strongly affects the behavior of people both inside and outside the organization. For companies to survive and prosper in the information age, they must use measurement and management systems derived from their strategies and capabilities.

---

5. R. S. Kaplan and D. P. Norton, "Using the Balanced Scorecard As a Strategic Management System," *Harvard Business Review,* vol. 74, January–February 1996, pp. 76–85.

Kaplan and Norton additionally note that unfortunately, many organizations espouse strategies about customer relationships, core competencies, and organizational capabilities while motivating and measuring performance only through the use of financial measures. They use the concept of a "balanced scorecard" which retains financial measurements as a critical summary of managerial and business performance, but also includes a more general and integrated set of measurements that links current performance along customer, internal process, employee, and system dimensions to long-term financial success.

Kaplan and Norton explain that the balanced scorecard translates mission and strategy into objectives and measures organized according to four different perspectives: financial, customer, internal business process, and innovation.

- ◆ Financial Perspective
  Financial performance measures such as profitability or sales growth are used to indicate whether the company's strategy and implementation are contributing to profitability improvement.

- ◆ Customer Perspective
  Customer-related performance measures such as satisfaction, retention, and market share are used to indicate performance in targeted market segments. Also included in this perspective are specific measures of value delivered to customers such as lead times, on-time delivery, and ability to anticipate and meet customer needs.

- ◆ Internal-Business Perspective
  Internal business-related performance measures focus on processes that have the greatest impact on customer acquisition and retention and on achieving financial objectives. Also included is the identification of new processes in which the organization must excel to meet customer and financial objectives. In summary, the balanced-scorecard internal business process objectives highlight the processes that are most critical for the success of an organization's strategies.

- ◆ Innovation Perspective
  While traditional performance measurements focus on the delivery of current products and services, the balanced scorecard approach includes a focus on the innovation process, the long-term of value creation. It is these longer-term

processes that derive future financial performance and assure the continuing success of the concern. Included in the long-term perspective are new product and new customer development and the development of new processes and systems for delivery of value to customers.

Business Process Reengineering (BPR)

Michael Hammer and James Champy define business process reengineering as "the fundamental rethinking and radical redesign of business processes and organizations to achieve dramatic improvements in critical, contemporary measures of performance, such as cost, quality, service, and speed."[6] The message here is that the level of performance improvements is dependent upon the degree of changes you are prepared to make. BPR focuses on radical changes and dramatic improvements, since incremental improvements are not classified as BPR.

BPR techniques could be used to take advantage of enabling technologies. Businesses must learn how to use these techniques.[7] They must stop automating chaos, and they must learn how to reengineer their environments to maximize the potential for using information technologies effectively. This is possible if and when organizations stop believing that technologies are a panacea and start learning how to use them as strategic tools.

Automated Information Management Corporation (AIM), an information technology and management consulting company in Ontario, Canada, designed a BPR methodology, which they have been using effectively for the last several years[8] (Figure 23–3).

This methodology has a broader perspective, with the focus being on improving productivity and proficiency on a continuous basis, optimizing the business processes, taking advantage of technologies, and capitalizing on the skills and expertise of personnel. It describes an integrated, enterprise-wide approach to renewing services through optimizing the current business practices and applying information technology to amplify overall performance.

---

6. M. Hammer and J. Champy, *Reengineering the Corporation,* HarperCollins, New York, 1993, p. 32.
7. Ali, Mir F., "Stop Automating Chaos," *Electronic Commerce World,* November 1995.
8. Information from Automated Information Management Corporation on their BPR methodology is used with their permission.

FIGURE   23–3

An Example of BPR Techniques

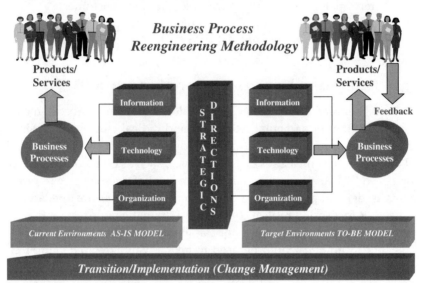

Source: Based on Information from Automated Information Management Corporation.

This methodology is transformed based on the following concepts and philosophies:

- ◆ Information engineering to treat information as a strategic resource
- ◆ Activity based costing/management (ABC/M) methods to cost activities, products, and services
- ◆ Alternative service delivery (ASD) methods to ensure that service delivery analysis is based upon all options, internal and external
- ◆ ISO 9000 to adopt the three elements of documenting the business processes, following the documented business processes to operate the business, and auditing to ensure the accuracy and consistency of these processes
- ◆ Total Quality Management to follow business objectives, performance measurements, production and delivery, skills

requirements, management role, organizational structure, and authority

This methodology provides:

+ *Flexibility:* The methodology can be customized to meet specific business requirements, the intention being to produce the best results and make necessary changes without jeopardizing objectivity.

+ *Consistency:* Duplication, overlaps, and redundancy among business processes can be eliminated, removing the bottlenecks and ensuring smooth information flow.

+ *Relevancy:* Relevancy can be sustained in linking, merging, and eliminating business processes to improve overall productivity and proficiency.

Methodology Overview

The methodology consists of four phases:

Phase 1: Current Environments (AS-IS Model)

The integrated approach reflects the recognition that the business must be dramatically reassessed to live within shrinking budgets. This phase is designed to document and cost the current activities and practices through working sessions, meetings, interviews, and documentation. As a result, the AS-IS business, information, technology, organizational models, and various matrices are developed in the modeling tool. The observations made during this phase are documented and communicated to the next phase.

The following are defined for each documented business process:

+ Corporate definition for function, process, and activity
+ Service/product being supported by process
+ Internal/external clients
+ Resources consumed (costs)
+ Current technology (systems, networks, etc.) being used
+ The information flow associated with each process
+ Organizations involved in each process and their role (organizational structure)
+ Geographic location

- Any regulatory or administrative authorities exercised
- Level of service

Phase 2: Strategic Directions   This phase is designed to work with senior management within the organization to define the mission, vision, goals, objectives, strategic drivers, critical success factors, performance measures, etc. to establish the strategic directions for the subsequent phases. It also includes conducting the SWOT analysis to determine organizational strengths, weaknesses, opportunities, and threats. This strategic direction will help to establish the parameters for the target environment that the TO-BE model will attempt to meet. This phase is done in parallel with phase 1.

Phase 3: Target Environments (TO-BE Model)   The work perspective is to establish the business rationale for the products and services, then determine how the products will be produced and service will be delivered to the clients. Based on the observations made and senior management input in the previous phase, models and matrices are created by conducting the following analyses:

- *Conduct effectiveness and efficiency analysis.* Each business process is tested to determine whether the process is supporting the mandate (effectiveness) and is being done efficiently. The answers to these questions will help us to flag each business process accordingly—i.e., does not support mandate = no reason to continue performing.
- *Conduct seamless services analysis.* All business processes are reviewed to determine the possibility of delivering services/ products to clients through a single window, eliminating functional barriers. This requires redesigning the way services are now provided, including focusing on client service and client satisfaction. Opportunities and issues identified through client/stakeholder focus groups will be analyzed in this activity.
- *Conduct streamlining analysis.* The process from client to delivery of the services/products is minimized. This will require realignment of staff functions, from task-oriented to service-oriented, and potential reinvestment in staff training and new client-oriented service delivery activities.
- *Conduct choices analysis.* Wherever possible, clients will have options as to how services are provided and delivered. This

will require new investments and regular reviews of clients' needs, with the potential for new opportunities for innovation on the part of staff, lower costs for service delivery, and improved choice of clients.

♦ *Optimize process flows.* Each valid business process is reviewed, evaluated, and optimized vertically and horizontally, with opportunities for reengineering identified. This includes the identification of methods/techniques improvements, elimination of unnecessary activities, identification of outsourcing opportunities, identification of activities for merging/grouping, exploration of revenue generation opportunities, etc.

♦ *Review best practices.* Relevant best practices from similar organizations are searched and reviewed to identify and apply lessons learned by other organizations.

♦ *Identify and analyze revenue generation and partnering opportunities.* Opportunities for generating revenues from service delivery models, assets, and partnerships will be identified and incorporated into the TO-BE model, where applicable.

♦ *Identify technology opportunities.* Automation opportunities to further streamline business processes and integrate business information will be identified to support the redesigned business processes.

As a result, a TO-BE model is created, including the business, information, technology, and organizational sub-models. Performance indicators are set up for each redesigned process.

Phase 4: Implementation/Change Management

A final analysis is conducted to identify the recommended changes required to bridge the gap between the AS-IS models and the proposed TO-BE models. Models and business cases are assessed to determine the final process, information technology, and legislation realignments required. Recommendations are developed to deal with the organizational realignment, identifying the organizational structure and training requirements to support the proposed TO-BE model. Legislation roadblocks are analyzed and documented to include an assessment of potential for influencing the legislation and the course of action necessary for pursuing the roadblock.

The proposed changes are analyzed against the AS-IS ABC model to determine (quantify) the potential impact on the current cost structure and the potential efficiency gains. The proposed TO-BE model is also analyzed against the Strategic Direction Phase (2).

The proposed TO-BE model is then analyzed to identify implementation considerations, issues, and plans. These elements are assessed to produce a high-level implementation strategy for the identified opportunities, identifying key activities, potential costs, timelines, and inhibitors.

Total Quality Management (TQM)

Total quality management (TQM) can be defined as "a philosophy and system of management focused on customer satisfaction."[9]

It is no secret that Joseph M. Juran has contributed a great deal to TQM. He raised and discussed questions on the contribution of quality in reducing costs and improving standards in 1951 in his *Handbook*,[10] which has become an essential reference work on TQM. He was invited to Japan in 1954 along with W. Edwards Deming to speak to Japanese senior managers on the importance of planning, organizing, and managing quality programs.

Juran's approach to quality control and its management is two-sided:

- The company's mission in terms of fitness for use through providing products or services that conform to customer specifications, plus issues of reliability, availability, maintainability of customer service, etc.

- The role of senior managers in providing leadership, providing the required resources, encouraging awareness and participation, and developing systems of policy, goals, plans, measures and control for quality.

Quality, according to Juran, has to be controlled at each stage of the process but should not be implemented as just a mechanical process. It should be aimed at controlling:

9. M. R. Leenders and H. E. Fearon, *Purchasing and Supply Management*, 11th ed., Irwin, 1997, p. 164.
10. J. M. Juran, *Quality-Control Handbook*. 1st ed., McGraw-Hill, New York, 1951.

♦ Sporadic problems or costs (defects and product failure, scrapped materials, labor wasted, usage for rework, repair, dealing with customer complaints)

♦ Costs dealing with chronic problems (prevention and control)

Alan S. Morris defines TQM as an integrated approach to quality that operates in all parts of a company and encompasses a style of management aimed at achieving the long-term success of a company by linking quality with customer satisfaction.[11]

Morris further notes that TQM requires that the quality of the company's product should be the company's number one priority and that there should be an ongoing commitment to progressively increasing quality still further. To be successful in this, it is essential to achieve the total involvement of all personnel in a company and foster a common commitment to quality that is shared by everyone. Everyone must understand what level of quality is required of him or her and be motivated to produce it. It is extremely important that high quality be achieved in all areas of a company. Islands of quality here and there are of no use at all.

Morris suggests that at the departmental level within a company, it could be very useful to ask every member of the department the following questions:

♦ What process are you involved in?

♦ What are the key measures of performance for the process?

♦ How do you monitor performance using these measures?

♦ What can you do to improve performance?

Morris also suggests a further useful annual exercise consisting of construction of a flowchart of the processes that each department is responsible for and asking the following questions concerning the processes:

♦ Why do we carry out each operation?

♦ Is each operation necessary?

♦ Can the process route be simplified?

---

11. A. S. Morris, *Measurement and Calibration Requirements for Quality Assurance to ISO 9000*, John Wiley & Sons, New York, 1997.

Quality Circles

The concept of quality circles originated in Japan in the 1960s. The Japanese were very much committed to improving and perfecting their quality control techniques. Quality circles came into existence as a result of these efforts. The first three quality circles were registered with the Japanese Union of Scientists and Engineers in 1962.

John S. Oakland[12] defines quality circles as a group of workers doing similar work who meet:

- Voluntarily
- Regularly
- In normal working time
- Under the leadership of their "supervisor"
- To identify and analyze

Depending upon the level of support and commitment from senior management, quality circles can help accomplish the objective of improving the quality of products and services.

Oakland identifies the following four major elements in a quality circle organization:

- Members
- Leaders
- Facilitators
- Management

Members are employees who have been taught basic problem-solving and quality-control techniques, and can identify and solve work-related problems.

Leaders are usually the immediate supervisors of the members who have been trained to lead a quality circle.

Facilitators are the managers of the quality circle initiatives. They bear the primary responsibility for the success of the quality circle concept in an organization. They coordinate training and circle meetings, and form the link between the circles and the rest of the organization. Ideally, a facilitator is an innovative teacher who also has the abilty to communicate with all levels and parts of an organization.

---

12. J. S. Oakland, *Total Quality Management: The Route to Improving Performance*, Nichols Publishing, East Brunswick, NJ. 1993.

Management support and commitment is necessary to the success of quality circles. Management must be willing to accept that the real experts on task performance are those who actually perform the work.

Morris also notes that quality circles can be a very useful method of attaining quality ideals in a manufacturing company. Discussion that takes place at periodic meetings of the quality circles can fulfill several functions:

1. It ensures that thinking about quality maintains a high profile throughout the company.
2. It provides a feedback mechanism whereby breakdowns in or difficulties with a quality system can be reported and suggestions for improvement made.
3. By everyone being given a personal involvement in achieving high quality, an atmosphere is generated in which people have pride in their work, understand the reasons for the quality control procedures implemented, and are fully committed to their operation.

Benchmarking

Benchmarking is a continuous process of measuring performance of products, services, and practices against the desired levels of performance and bridging the performance gap by implementing effective business strategies. Benchmarking enabled troubled corporations in the 1980s to conduct comprehensive surveys to monitor customer satisfaction. These corporations used Japanese best practices as a target to improve their products and services. David T. Kearns, chief executive officer of Xerox Corporation, defines benchmarking as "the continuous process of measuring products, service, and practices against the toughest competition or those companies recognized as industrial leaders."[13]

Harrington defines benchmarking as

a never-ending discovery and learning experience that identifies and evaluates best processes and performance in order to integrate them into an organization's present process to increase its effectiveness, efficiency, and adaptability.[14]

---

13. H. J. Harrington, *Business Process Improvement*, McGraw-Hill, New York, 1991, p. 218.
14. Ibid.

A generic benchmarking process includes the following six steps:

1. The process or activity to be benchmarked is determined, those who will be involved in the benchmarking are identified, and a flowchart of how the work is currently being done is constructed.

2. Research is conducted to find out what is currently known about the process or activity that is being benchmarked, including checking with in-house experts and using library sources, customer surveys, and industry publications.

3. Additional data are collected on the benchmarked process or activity through visits to other companies, interviews, and questionnaires.

4. The findings are evaluated and decisions are made regarding how to use the information.

5. The data are applied and adapted to the benchmarked process or activity.

6. The changes are institutionalized and made part of the ongoing operating process.

Harrington further notes that the benefits of benchmarking far outweigh the effort and expense and identifies benefits that include:

◆ Improvement in customer satisfaction
◆ Identification of best processes
◆ Improvement of existing processes
◆ Identifies your competitive position
◆ Can transform complacency into an urgent desire to improve
◆ Helps set attainable but aggressive improvement targets
◆ Prioritization of improvement activities
◆ Contributes to creation of continuous improvement culture

Statistical Process Control[15]

A common approach to controlling manufacturing quality and preventing defects in finished products is *statistical process control*. It consists of several concepts or techniques that can be used first to determine the

---

15. While this section is included in the supplier section of the chapter, these techniques are equally usable by purchasing organizations for control of their processes.

capability of a process to produce the desired quality and then to monitor the process and identify and eliminate causes of process variation.

Determination of process capability consists of obtaining the acceptable range or tolerance (e.g., for the size of a part) for a particular process or operation and then comparing that to the production capability range of the process. This will reveal whether the range of the process is within the range of the specification or tolerance. A process capability index (C_p) can be calculated to make this comparison.

If the averages of the specification range and the process capability range are not the same, the process is considered to be "not centered," but may still be usable. Another index, the C_{pk} index, can be used in such situations to indicate process capability. This index combines the tolerance and centering comparison.

Once the process is in production, control charts called X bar and R charts can be used to monitor the process and identify developing problems and out of control operations. The X bar chart consists of the average values of periodic production samples plotted on a graph that also shows the specification mean, upper and lower specification limits, and upper and lower control limits. If the sample averages indicate a trend away from the mean or exceed the control limits, corrective action may be needed to keep the process in control and avoid the possibility of exceeding the specification limits. The R chart is a plot of sample ranges. An increase in range may also indicate the need for corrective action to keep the process in control.

QA TOOLS AND TECHNIQUES FOR BUYERS

A Typical Purchasing Model

Figure 23–4 represents a typical purchasing model. This model illustrates the interfaces between a purchaser and supplier:

+ Purchaser sends to supplier a *request for quotes.*
+ Supplier responds back to purchaser, providing the requested *quotes.*
+ Purchaser sends a *purchase order* to supplier indicating the products and quantity.
+ Supplier ships the *merchandise plus packing slip/services* to the address indicated on the purchase order.
+ Supplier mails an *invoice* to the purchaser for the merchandise shipped.

F I G U R E   23–4

A Typical Purchasing Transaction

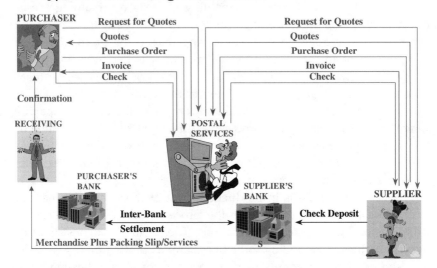

Source: Adam Management Consulting.

- ◆ Purchaser gets a *confirmation* from the department within the company that received the goods or services.
- ◆ Purchaser authorizes the payment and a *check* is sent to supplier.
- ◆ Supplier deposits the *check* into the company account.
- ◆ An *inter-bank settlement* takes place and the supplier's bank charges the amount of that check to the purchaser's bank. The amount is eventually debited to the purchaser's account.

This is a very generic model, but it covers all major activities associated with the procurement of any goods or services in any organization. The purpose of this model is to provide a base for comparison with a typical electronic commerce model, which will be discussed in the next section.

A Typical Electronic Commerce Model

We all know that electronic commerce is becoming a reality every day. Those who think that technologies are simply going to go away are mistaken. Electronic commerce will continue to grow to the point that any

F I G U R E   23–5

A Typical Electronic Commerce Transaction

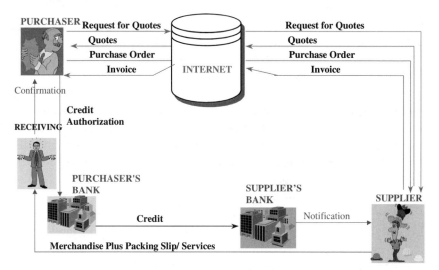

Source: Adam Management Consulting.

supplier or purchaser who chooses not to be a part had better be pre-pared to go out of business.

The U.S. Department of Commerce reported, in *The Emerging Digital Economy* in May 1998, the following statistics, which give an idea of the growth:

- *Business to business*

1996	$ 2.6 B
1997	$ 5.6 B
1998	$ 16.0 B
2000	$300.0 B

Other statistics include:

- 97% of all large corporations are now connected to the Internet.
- 41% of small businesses are on the Net.
- 46% of Web sites are profitable.
- Dell Computers does 5M orders per day on their site.

Figure 23–5 represents an electronic commerce environment. Postal services have been totally replaced by the Internet. This eliminated major delays, interruptions, and inefficiencies that were associated with the purchasing process. Internet tools like Purchase Pro[16] are available in the market at a reasonable subscription rate to take advantage of technologies. These tools help minimize the front-end process—request for quotes, submission of quotes, and issuance of purchase order—from several days to hours. This process is called electronic data interchange (EDI).

In an electronic commerce transaction the payment process is speeded up, eliminating significant inefficiencies. As can be seen in Figure 23–5, a credit authorization from a purchaser to its bank, a transmission of credit to supplier's bank, and a notification to supplier replaced the total time-consuming process of issuing and depositing the check. This process is called electronic funds transfer (EFT)

However, how would a purchaser know whether the merchandise or service delivered to the respective department met the expected level of quality? The answer to this question is dependent upon the kind of mechanism in place in the company to check and report on quality. Such a mechanism needs to be created and implemented. The following three sections discuss the relevant topics on the subject. They will provide you with a basic understanding that could help you to design and implement a quality assurance mechanism in your organization.

Key Quality Assurance Ingredients

Morgan notes that purchasing departments have spent much of the past decade laying the foundation for continuous quality improvement.[17] Today, with much of that foundation work completed, many are looking ahead to the next ten years. Morgan also observes that these organizations envision a structure built on the following five key components: skills, documentation, cultural changes, reorganization, and planning.

- ♦ *Skills:* Purchasing departments and their suppliers must improve their understanding of manufacturing and supply processes. There also is a need for more training in areas

---

16. Purchase Pro is an Internet software tool designed to help purchasers to prepare and send RFQs to a selected group of suppliers, receive response back from suppliers, and issue a P.O. to order the desired goods and services. It does not deal with issuance of invoices or receiving payments. Source: www.purchasepro.com.
17. J. Morgan, "The 5 Key Ingredients," *Purchasing,* January 16, 1997, pp. 40–42.

including quality, controls, preventive maintenance, and advanced technology.

♦ *Documentation:* Processes and procedures must be better documented. Responsibility for measurement and testing is migrating to suppliers. This trend requires improved supplier evaluation systems, processes, and documentation.

♦ *Cultural changes:* In order to achieve the level of quality assurance that is required by the marketplace, many companies will have to implement changes in culture such as greater flexibility in their relationships with suppliers and customers. Other developments such as increased integration of suppliers into design and planning will also require cultural changes.

♦ *Reorganization:* Procurement reengineering will also likely require greater information sharing within the organization and with suppliers. Also required will be greater participation of purchasing personnel in product design and process planning.

♦ *Planning:* Purchasers will be more involved in strategic planning as procurement decisions affect quality. Insourcing/ outsourcing decisions and supply base reduction will require more consideration of long-term capabilities of both supplier and purchasing organizations.

Morgan observes that one of the most basic problems for many procurement operations over the past ten years has been the need to relate quality to products and processes. Instead of looking at purchasing from outside sources in terms of fulfilling needs, procurement professionals found they had to begin to look at products and processes in terms of how design, but especially manufacturing, practices affected quality.

In many cases, just taking this leap in approach was slow and often difficult. Aside from the obvious political problems involved in challenging traditional and accepted practices, procurement professionals had to take totally new approaches in dealing with goods coming in from outside supply sources.

Quality Assurance Methodology

Elena Epatko Murphy indicates that "quality planning has come a great distance in recent years. It used to be a stilted process where departments that normally did not work together threw in their input once a year and returned to their separate functions."[18] This has changed as companies have realized that, to stay competitive, departments must work together year-round. Murphy further comments: "All strategy-oriented functions now contribute information from their daily quality processes to develop a plan for the company's long-term quality goals."[19] She also observes that purchasing has emerged as a leader in quality planning because it already acts as a link between the internal organization and suppliers.

Murphy indicates the following four examples of effective quality planning processes that really work:

- Know your market
- Pick good suppliers
- Give good suppliers guidance
- Measure supplier's performance

Quality Assurance Policy

It is critical in the interest of any quality assurance initiative that a policy be established to provide the overall guidelines. The following demonstrates the structure of a policy for purchasing goods and services:[20]

The Queensland (Australia) Government's quality assurance policy, approved by Cabinet on October 28, 1996, states:

1. Policy:
Government agencies shall not require quality assurance for purchases valued at less than $10,000 except by Ministerial direction.

For purchases valued at $10,000 or more, Government agencies will examine the level of risk associated with that purchase and specify quality assurance requirements depending on the level of risk [in Box 23–1]:

Government agencies will help facilitate recognition of industry/professional systems and standards for the purposes of this policy.

2. Scope of Quality Assurance Policy:
This policy applies to all government departments and statutory bodies as defined in the *Financial Administration and Audit Act* for the purchase of all

---

18. E. E. Murphy, "Purchasing's Daily Work Supports Long-Term Planning," *Purchasing,* January 16, 1997, pp. 59–60
19. Ibid.
20. Source of the material in this section: www.qgm.qld.gov.au/purchasingpolicy/quick-guide/qags-pl.htm.

B O X   23-1

Low Risk	No quality assurance required.
Moderate Risk	Selected elements from a Quality System Standard or approved industry/professional systems or standards to be specified.
High Risk	Quality System Standard or approved industry/professional systems or standards to be specified.

products or services except real property. Covered under this Act are purchases from:

♦ Manufacturers, stockists, agents, merchants and distributors (including suppliers of overseas product);

♦ Construction contractors;

♦ Services, suppliers and contractors including the suppliers of professional and technical consultancy services, suppliers of maintenance and repair services and suppliers of on-going routine services to agencies.

3. Approved Quality Assurance Systems:
Queensland Purchasing maintains a database of approved quality assurance systems and standards. This database includes approved:

♦ Quality System Standards
♦ Quality Assurance based product certification schemes
♦ Industry Association Quality Assurance Systems or Standards
♦ Industry Specific Quality Assurance Systems or Standards
♦ Professional Association Accreditations

4. Responsibilities:

4.1 Government Agencies:
It is the responsibility of Government agencies to:

♦ Ensure the level of risk associated with a purchase is assessed correctly and that the appropriate quality assurance requirements are specified

♦ Ensure that suppliers meet the specified quality assurance requirements for a purchase

♦ Ensure officers who specify, purchase or evaluate offers have adequate training in the quality assurance requirements of the *State Purchasing Policy*

♦ Where appropriate, establish their own trained and registered quality system auditors and evaluators

♦ Counsel their suppliers on the Quality Assurance Policy

♦ Ensure adherence to the Queensland Government Quality Assurance Policy

4.2 Suppliers:

Suppliers tendering to government agencies are required to understand the quality assurance requirements and satisfy these requirements where they are specified. It is also the responsibility of suppliers to demonstrate that they meet specified quality assurance requirements.

CONCLUSION

We all know that technology has changed the way we do business today. In the last few decades we have gone through some gradual and not so gradual changes that have impacted our lives and businesses tremendously. They have impacted business structures, refined interfaces, and redefined basic business values. Most importantly, they have affected the attitudes of the parties involved in conducting business with each other. As a result, the perception of buyers is changing. They are no longer perceived as arrogant people with money and unlimited demands but no patience. At the same time, technology is putting pressure on suppliers to produce and deliver their goods and services faster, more quickly, and more cheaply. It is no secret that technology such as electronic commerce has become a survival tool for suppliers.

Current practices and future technological trends have created a very difficult situation for suppliers as well as purchasers. It has become critical for the success of any supplier to understand that they cannot afford to compromise the quality of their goods and services in the competition to produce and deliver faster, more quickly, and more cheaply. They must understand the necessity not only to achieve and meet the minimum requirement for quality, but also to try constantly and consistently to exceed the level of quality in their goods and services in order to gain the competitive edge. At the same time, it has become absolutely clear that it would do purchasers no good to just sit back and continue to demand quality from suppliers without giving any thought or communicating their ways to measure quality.

This communication gap has caused some unbelievable problems in the past. The good news is that both purchasers and suppliers have realized that technology has also created some strategic opportunities for them to work together as partners. They acknowledge the need to upgrade their knowledge and skills to deal with issues related to quality, as well as the need to establish partnerships to tackle the quality issues together.

Purchasers began to feel obligated to communicate and train suppliers to make them understand quality needs and requirements. Some companies established training centers that were open to suppliers and company employees. But whether or not their companies used formal training schools, purchasers soon found that it was up to them to guide suppliers in developing an understanding of what is involved in a quality culture.

Some companies have defined and provided training for suppliers on such quality techniques and tools as statistical process control, measurement systems analysis, advanced product quality planning, failure mode effects analysis, product part approval process, tooling and equipment quality systems requirements, self-assessment procedures for production part quality systems, and tooling and equipment.

As part of their efforts to upgrade supplier understanding of quality issues, many companies have also stressed how quality affects the competitiveness of products and corporations.

The bottomline is that suppliers must realize that they are selling not just goods and services, but relationships, and these serve as an insurance policy for purchasers. The relationships they are establishing with each other, and the professional atmosphere they are creating, in order to understand each other's culture, will enable them to produce quality goods and services that can not only measure up to but exceed expectations.

CHAPTER 24

Value Analysis

Editor
Lawrence J. Clark, C.P.M.
Purchasing Manager
Burleigh Instruments

OVERVIEW

In today's business climate, purchasing is considered a significant team member critical in helping the modern corporation succeed in the marketplace. Integration with marketing, engineering, and production is critical if companies are to get quality products released in the shortest possible amount of time. Speed to market, cost reduction, and improved design depend on teamwork. Value analysis is a technique that brings the various departments together to work for a common goal that is important to their company. In recent years this process has been pushed forward in the product life cycle by combining it with the ideas of *design for manufacturability* (or, for nonmanufacturing situations, *design for execution efficiency*). Thus, value analysis has changed from an afterthought in the design process to a strategy in design development. It attempts to eliminate *unnecessary cost* at the outset, rather than trying to reduce it later. Although value analysis originated and is often associated with manufacturing, it is also applicable to nonmanufactured products such as services.

HISTORY

Value analysis originated at the end of World War II in order to deal with material shortages. Substitutions had to be made, and in many cases the replacements were more suitable. Larry Miles of General Electric wanted to carry this into future designs as a cost reduction–product improvement strategy. With Roy Fountain, an electrical engineer, Miles, a purchaser, developed the first value analysis plan. In 1952 they organized workshops to train GE employees in various plants. These extensive workshops typically involved 40–60 hours of training. Initially, value analysis was considered strictly a purchasing tool. Now it has moved forward in the product life cycle to combine with *value engineering*. Gradually it has expanded to cover other functions, such as engineering and marketing. As it evolves, it is being used earlier in the product life cycle and in businesses outside of manufacturing.

BENEFITS

The benefits of value analysis are extensive and far exceed any cost associated with the program. There is a potential for:

♦ Reduced labor costs
♦ Lower cost of goods
♦ Improved quality
♦ Better performance
♦ Increased customer satisfaction
♦ Preservation of scarce resources
♦ Increased profitability

THE BASIS OF VALUE

Definitions

Note: The various concepts and use of the term *product* throughout this chapter should be interpreted as also applying to nonmanufactured products such as services in addition to physical products. The purchaser of services is concerned with efficiency of service execution and the end result of the service and should keep those concepts in mind throughout the chapter.

♦ *Value Analysis:* Value analysis is the organized and systematic study of every element of cost in a part, material, or service to make certain it fulfills its *function* at the lowest possible cost.

Value analysis also employs techniques that identify the functions the user wants from a product or service; it establishes by comparison the appropriate cost for each function; then it causes the required knowledge, creativity, and initiative to be used to provide each function for that cost.

- *Value engineering:* The terms *value analysis* and *value engineering* are used synonymously in this chapter, and *value analysis* will be used to represent both concepts. Generally speaking, however, value engineering can be thought to be applied early in the design process, as opposed to later in the product life cycle, after several production runs have been completed. Because value analysis or value engineering is strictly a team effort, the freedom to make suggestions by both engineering and purchasing is necessary. Purchasing must question engineering specifications, and engineering must question purchasing practices such as sourcing and award decisions based on price.

- *Concurrent design:* Concurrent design centers around the consideration and inclusion of product design attributes such as manufacturability, procurability, reliability, maintainability, schedulability, and marketability in the early stages of product design. To achieve this, design engineers work with purchasing, manufacturing, and marketing, as a *cross-departmental team*, in the areas of developing specifications, interchangeable parts, and part substitutions. It bears a close resemblance to value analysis and value engineering in that it involves a multi-departmental group working together to reduce cost. In many organizations it appears that value analysis programs have evolved into concurrent design programs.

For a manufactured product example, see Box 24–1. For a nonmanufactured product (service,) see Box 24–2.

Functions—Primary and Secondary

The key to value analysis and value engineering is to understand how a part fulfills its function. For instance, the *primary function* of a watchband is to hold the watch to the wrist. It can perform this work whether

B O X   24-1

THE WELDED CAN

This is an example of a value analysis project that came about in an effort to reduce lead time and improve speed to market for a new product. The product was a scanning tunneling microscope. The function of the head, shown below, was to *enclose* the *probe and sample*. Additional benefits were realized in cost, customer maintainability, and faster release to market.

Before Value Analysis
A. The custom-size unfinished steel-drawn can is purchased from a manufacturer. Lead time is eight to twelve weeks due to manufacturer's production schedule.
B. At the sheet metal fabricator the cutouts and holes are machined or milled into the formed can. It is difficult to fixture and hold the part because of material flexing and the rounded corners. Machining adds three to four weeks to the lead time.
C. The can is painted and silk-screened. Rounded corners make it difficult to align silk-screened registration marks. One to two weeks is added to the lead time.
D. The cover is inspected and shipped. Total lead time at this point is 13 to 19 weeks. There are frequent rejections due to dimensional accuracy problems.

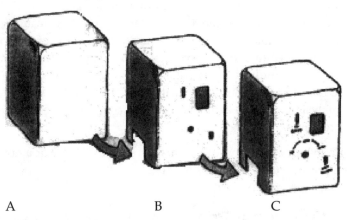

A   B   C

After Value Analysis
A. The raw material is changed to aluminum sheet, eliminating the steel-drawn can, saving lead time and expense.

B. The aluminum sheet is sheared, and holes and slots are punched instead of machined. A slot is added to facilitate customer removal of the cover without removing the knob, providing easier maintenance. Punching is inexpensive and faster than machining. Also, holes and slots are easier to locate on flat sheet as opposed to rounded, flexible can.

C. The material is bent to shape.

D. The seams are welded and ground to a smooth finish.

E. The can is painted and silk-screened. New lead time is four to six weeks total. Total cost of the part is reduced by about $8.00. Product maintenance is simplified.

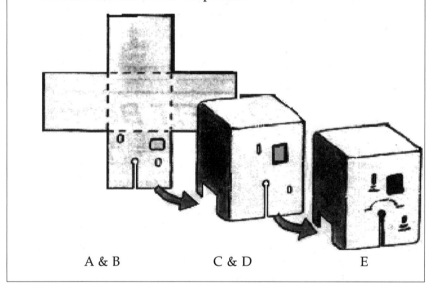

A & B   C & D   E

it is plastic or gold. A *secondary function* may be to allow the watch to be worn during participation in sports. If this is the case, then the soft plastic band would be more appropriate than the gold-plated band. The plastic band holds the watch on the wrist comfortably and at lower cost and is safer to wear. There are other examples. For a jewel case for a compact disc, the primary function is to *protect* the *CD*, and the secondary function may be to *hold* the *jacket* that helps sell the CD.

Function is that which the product or service must do to make it perform and sell. For example, a knife *cuts material* and a thermometer *measures temperature*. Defining the function by using just two words, the

B O X 24–2

OFFICE CLEANING SERVICE

This is an example of a value analysis project that came about in an effort to reduce the cost of office cleaning.

Before Value Analysis
Company X had a contract to clean offices that had been in place for a number of years. The specifications for what was to be done, how it was to be done, and how often it was to be done were very general and vague. Other than cleaning being required five nights per week, the rest was pretty much up to the contractor. Discussions with the cleaning contractor revealed that each office was vacuumed, all work surfaces dusted, and trash containers emptied nightly. Additional work was done nightly in restrooms and hallways. Basically all cleaning chores were repeated each night. Company X's purchaser contacted several purchasers in other companies who had office cleaning contracts and found that the current cleaning cost was above what most others were paying and that most other purchasers had more detailed cleaning specifications in their contracts than did Company X.

After Value Analysis
It was determined through experimentation that vacuuming of offices was not required nightly and that dusting of work surfaces also was not needed every day. Vacuuming was changed to every third night and dusting to once per week. Other tasks were also similarly spread out. By alternating which parts of the office received the various treatments, the contractor was able to carry out the revised schedule with fewer personnel. The purchaser for Company X prepared and competitively quoted a new contract that explicitly stated what the various cleaning tasks were and when and how they were to be done. Company X realized an acceptable level of cleaning at a significantly reduced cost.

verb and the noun, prevents an attempt to apply more than one simple job at a time to the part being analyzed. It is important to note that while function definitions describe the desired result, they do not define the means to achieve the end. There are always several choices one can make on how to proceed. A complex product or process may have several functions and even subfunctions. Function analysis is performed so that the function of the product or service can be fully understood. The product or service is described as a number of word-pairs, verb and noun, rather than the product, service, or process itself.

Value

Value can be defined as the lowest end cost at which the function can be accomplished at the time and place and with the quantity required. Value has no direct relationship to cost. Some items that cost less than a similar product accomplish the function in a superior manner. For example, a premium paid for overnight shipping increases the cost of a product but probably does not add to its value. However, it is important to consider value in the customer's eyes. Value analysis is a technique that lowers cost while maintaining worth from the end user's perspective. It does not cheapen the product.

Value Analysis in Action

Probably the best way to understand value analysis is to look at a case of it being used. A good example is a humidifier that goes from a metal to a plastic drip pan. The function of the drip pan is to *hold water* as it drips from the condenser coil. A plastic drip pan can *hold water* as well as a metal one, but there is value in making the change. Plastic is cheaper, quieter, weighs less, and does not rust. It will not dent or scratch as easily. The substitution of plastic in this case resulted in lower cost without lowering quality from the customer's point of view.

Checklist: Test for Added Value in a Product or Service

Fifteen questions to ask about the product or service being considered:

1. Does an item, component part, or phase of service contribute value to the product?
2. Is the cost proportionate to the product's usefulness?
3. Does the product have secondary functions or phases that can be broken out?
4. Has the product's function changed over time?

5. Does the product require all its features, parts, components, or phases?

6. Do original specifications or standards still apply?

7. Can specifications or standards be changed?

8. Is there a better replacement or method available for the intended use?

9. Can the product or item be eliminated?

10. Can a useful part be made, or a different aspect of service be employed, at a lower cost?

11. For a product, can a standard part be found that will accomplish the function at a lower cost?

12. Is the product produced using proper tooling, considering the quantities used?

13. Can another dependable supplier provide the product for less? Or can you make the item or provide the service more cost-effectively yourself?

14. Can you work with your suppliers to reduce cost?

15. Can long lead times be reduced, allowing product to get to market faster?

Selecting a Product or Service to Be Value-Analyzed

To make the most of value analysis techniques, it is important to give consideration in selecting the products, parts, processes, or services to be analyzed. You want to look at items that can give you dollar returns on your efforts. It is best to start with components that have a high dollar value. Here is a list of things you can look for:

1. High annual dollar value or expense

2. Intricacy or complication in design

3. Low yields or high scrap expense

4. Labor-intensive or time-consuming processes

5. Complex processes with many operations

6. An assembly that can be reduced to a single part

7. Parts that can be standardized, or used in several applications

8. Obsolete or hard-to-obtain components

9. Older raw materials that have had better substitute materials on the market in recent years

10. Items with inconsistent quality or performance

THE PURPOSE OF VALUE ANALYSIS

The cooperation and participation of other departments, such as marketing, engineering, and production, are important to the success of any value analysis effort. In order to optimize teamwork among the various departments, management should be involved. To win management's cooperation, it is important to convince them that value analysis will maintain or improve quality while reducing costs. It is important to link value analysis to a product's success in the marketplace. Value analysis helps to improve a product's performance, quality, marketability, maintainability, and reliability. It also assists in getting products to market quickly.

Quality

A decision as to suitable quality must involve *technical quality* and *economic quality*. Regardless of the degree of technical suitability, the item must be procurable at a satisfactory cost on a continuing basis. So, economic quality includes technical quality and also cost factors and availability as well. Reappraisals of the material, product, and process selected are necessary from time to time because applications, competition, and customer expectations do change. Quality must be maintained or enhanced, otherwise any savings will be inconsequential as sales and reputation decline.

Performance

No matter how attractive or solidly built, if the product does not function efficiently, it will not sell. In value analysis, the goal is equal or improved accomplishment of the function at a lower cost. In some cases, cost may be increased to achieve better performance or reduce maintenance costs and thereby improve product marketability.

Marketability

The primary aim of business is to produce products or services that find a ready market and provide a reasonable profit. All items must have the necessary degree of sales appeal, whether in:

- Effectiveness of operation
- Efficiency of operation
- Low repair or maintenance costs
- Esteem value

Value analysis recognizes that marketability must be maintained or improved.

Maintainability

Maintainability is an important feature affecting the total end cost of a product to a customer. Regardless of the initial quality of components and initial marketability of the product, if a value analysis study results in increased maintenance costs for the customer, any savings realized will sooner or later be wiped out by decreased sales and loss of goodwill.

Reliability

It is equally important that the required *reliability* of a product be preserved or improved by the value analysis recommendation. Suppose an electrical relay performed perfectly for half its expected life and then malfunctioned, shutting down a production line. Suppose a commercial water heater functioned perfectly 98% of the time! What would happen to customer goodwill, and to profits?

Teamwork and Speed to Market

Because of the cross-departmental nature of value analysis, it only makes sense that it would be combined with concurrent design principles and moved forward in the product life cycle. Design, working together with manufacturing and purchasing, can make many of the value substitutions before the release of a new product. This not only gets the product to market faster but saves money by avoiding costly redesigns and downstream waste in procurement and assembly. The cooperation among departments improves the manufacturability of the product. With product development working simultaneously with purchasing and assembly up front, many procurement and manufacturing issues are resolved by the time a product is released. In modern economies the first products in the marketplace are often the most successful.

THE PROCESS OF VALUE ANALYSIS

Value analysis should follow an organized application of specific techniques. The goal is to follow a plan similar to the way a scientist follows procedural steps in an experiment. In the completion of complex operations, having an method to follow is important. To finish with a quality product, a contractor follows a blueprint, a writer follows an outline, and an assembler uses a bill of material. The key is to follow a systematic plan to get the best results from value analysis in the shortest amount of time.

Value analysis is easiest to implement in companies where the cost of goods or services is an issue. Intense competition in the marketplace tends to drive the task of adding value and avoiding excess cost. Competition also drives the concept of moving value analysis forward in the design process. Speed to market with new products is important in the face of intense competition and shortened product life cycles.

Work within a Team

Value analysis is a team effort. The different departments working alone cannot do as well collecting information and making proposals affecting others. Best results are achieved in a team environment. In small companies where the lines between departments may be loosely drawn, an informal work group might be effective, as long as issues are looked at from all points of view. It is important to include representation from marketing (customers), engineering, design, service, production, purchasing (suppliers), and quality. Purchasing often takes the lead, performing the initial cost analysis on the target product and selecting items with economic feasibility for investigation. Teams should report successes—particularly to senior management. Regular reporting of cost savings and product improvements not only lends credibility to the effort but can encourage others to join or form a value analysis team.

Value Analysis Job Plan

The job plan is the organized application of specific techniques in order to achieve the best results. A rational sequence of events is followed in identifying value and reducing cost without diminishing quality. Traditionally, it was considered important to follow formal procedures to the letter. Now, especially in smaller organizations, procedures are being followed on a more casual basis. On small or simple projects, informal techniques can be effectively used, especially where team members have previous experience with value analysis. Although it varies with size and type of enterprise, a typical job plan includes the following steps:

- Preparation
- Information
- Analysis
- Creation
- Synthesis
- Development
- Presentation
- Implementation
- Follow-up

Preparation Phase

Before starting the study, the team lists all areas that will be improved by the assessment's results. They should list any roadblocks they expect to encounter and any action plans to consider in order to overcome obstacles. These lists must be updated as the investigation continues. This procedure helps to limit unfortunate surprises later in the execution or implementation phase. The team can then select the product that will most benefit from cost reduction and improvement. An item challenged by new competition in the marketplace is a good candidate, as is an item that has a high dollar impact on a company's revenues. The team should review all the components of a product and sort them by cost. Typically, it pays to review the high dollar items first. Each item is assessed carefully for its function, and ideas are presented, perhaps by brainstorming, for ways to substitute better materials, components, or processes. Finally, an estimate is made of annual savings that will be achieved through the value analysis improvements made. This is a tangible way to measure the project's success.

Information Phase

The objective of the information phase is to gather relevant information and to make known opportunities for improvement. This phase includes:

+ Establishing performance perimeters
+ Determining customer acceptance
+ Gathering meaningful costs
+ Obtaining details of manufacturing methods or processes
+ Determining quality aspects
+ Defining objectives
+ Analyzing costs
+ Performing a Pareto analysis to separate the significant few items from the trivial many
+ Defining functions and developing a function logic diagram
+ Allocating costs to functions
+ Focusing on opportunity areas or problem statements upon which to apply creative efforts

The team should accumulate bills of material, cost information, assembly procedures, and other relevant facts. Typical questions at this phase include:

+ Should we compare machining to casting costs?
+ Will plastic substitute for metal on that component?
+ Is there an easier or quicker way to put that assembly together?
+ Can we add customer services without increasing the labor involved?

Prepare a list of questions that will need to be answered in the attempt to reduce unnecessary cost. Involve others from outside the team in searching for knowledge; for example, a machine operator, a supplier, or even a customer.

Analysis Phase

The objective of the analysis phase is to evaluate ideas and select those worthy of development. Steps in this phase include:

+ Listing advantages and disadvantages for each idea
+ Estimating the impact on cost, performance, and quality

- Selecting approaches with the best yield for resources required
- Comparing against objectives

In this phase the question is, "What will the changes cost?" Estimate the dollar value of each proposal. Select those ideas that reduce cost but do not negatively affect value in the customer's eyes. The parts and costs for a product or service should be broken down into functional areas, and the cost associated with each area should be identified. Total cost should be compiled, which may require some estimates of hidden cost. For a more accurate estimate, use actual costs rather than standard costs. Items that must be gathered at this phase include supplier's input, prices, order lot sizes, drawings or design specifications, and information about manufacturing methods.

Creative Phase

The objective of the creative phase is to generate a large quantity and variety of unjudged ideas. The creative phase should include the following steps:

- Writing down all ideas for each stated opportunity area or problem statement
- Using generic terminology to enhance generation of different means to accomplish goals
- Calling upon outside experts, consultants, or suppliers

At this time various techniques are applied using the information gathered above. Here the question "What else will do the job?" is asked. Creativity is important in evaluation of the function, or job, a part performs. Avoid dismissing ideas offered by team members. Usually all suggestions are recorded, then the team reviews the suggestions and picks those most likely to succeed. During this phase, as ideas and concepts arise, the team leader may ask someone in the group to champion specific ideas or concepts. If no one volunteers, the idea or concept may be dropped. Those who do volunteer are charged with investigating the feasibility and economics of the idea or concept. This champion concept can result in a series of solutions that are likely to be implemented.

Development Phase

The objective of the development phase is to expand selected ideas into workable value improvement proposals. It includes:

- Developing ideas into decisions
- Engineering or redesigning, with enhancement of good points and strengthening or elimination of weak points
- Determining how to design, produce, alter, and ensure quality
- Consulting suppliers and specialists
- Determining total system impacts
- Preparing the implementation plan

Presentation Phase

The objective of the presentation phase is to obtain the approval, support, and resources necessary for implementation, including:

- Combining proposals into reports for distribution
- Presenting value improvement recommendations with their anticipated financial and nonfinancial impacts
- Obtaining necessary commitments and resources

Implementation Phase

The objective of the implementation phase is to obtain results from the improvement proposals. Steps include:

- Following the established implementation plan
- Conducting regular management reviews
- Applying value techniques to resolve problems
- Documenting results

Follow-up Phase

The objective of this phase is to track the progress of the effort. Here you will apply precise evaluation techniques and measure savings. Figure out how much you are saving per part and multiply it by annual use. Total up all the savings on all the product's parts and report entire reduction in cost. This is how the value analysis team shows it is successful and worthwhile to the organization.

Approaches to Value Analysis

The most common approach for a company to applying value analysis is to create a value analysis committee composed of representatives from marketing, design, procurement, and production. This committee operates most effectively when it employs the workshop method in reviewing possible value analysis opportunities. The workshop approach encourages free discussion and exchange of ideas on how the function of the various items studied can be performed at a lower cost. Value analysis workshops have led to a number of refinements of the basic principles and procedures.

In recent years many companies have moved the value analysis forward in the product life cycle. Historically, value analysis was applied at the mature stage of a product's life. This was the point where competing products had established themselves in the market. It was felt that the mature stage was a good time to lower costs to stay ahead of rivals in the marketplace. In today's economy that theory does not work so well, especially with products like the personal computer. Many product life cycles have been shortened dramatically. By the time the competition catches up, it is time to be designing a new product, not fixing the old one. Concepts like Total Quality Management (TQM) and concurrent design compel manufacturers to consider releasing high-quality products quickly. Typically, the first product in a particular market gets the largest share and keeps its leadership role, especially if it is a correctly designed, quality product. Getting marketing, manufacturing, and design to work together on the front end helps to avoid expense and to speed the release of new designs.

Creative brainstorming is the process of stimulating an uninhibited flow of ideas, however outlandish they may seem at first, from members of the value analysis team. In such sessions, negative thinking, i.e., expressing skepticism or derision about another team member's ideas, is not permitted. The theory underlying this approach is that nothing keeps a person's mouth sealed so much as the fear of being laughed at. Another rule is to record all ideas, no matter how foolish they may seem at first. Judgment is deferred until later phases of the analysis after all propositions have been considered carefully.

Leapfrogging is a technique of value-analyzing comparable products in a company's line to identify their best features and characteristics. These are combined into a hybrid or fused product that, in turn, is value-analyzed to bring additional creative ideas from the team. This process has, in some cases, enabled a company to enter a new market with a superior product that is priced competitively.

Value Analysis and Concurrent Design

Many organizations have combined value analysis and value engineering into one operation and applied it with concurrent design principles. Concurrent design centers around the consideration and inclusion of product design attributes, such as manufacturability, procurability, reliability, maintainability, schedulability, and marketability, in the early stages of product design. To achieve this, design engineers work with purchasing, manufacturing, and marketing as a cross-departmental team in the areas of developing specifications, interchangeable parts, and part substitutions. This bears similarity to value analysis in that a cross-departmental team works together to reduce cost and improve the product. However, concurrent design principles lack the systematic, somewhat scientific approach in avoiding cost. In many companies it appears that value analysis programs have evolved into concurrent design programs.

There are several benefits to the concurrent design approach, including reduced cost of goods, nimble release of new product to market, and wares or merchandise more in touch with customer requirements. Often as much as 70% of the cost of manufacturing is determined in the design stage. For example, once a mold for a part is built and paid for, cost reduction is difficult to achieve on that part due to the sunk costs for tooling. The bulk of production savings come from improvements in design rather than savings in material, labor, or overhead. Therefore, it makes sense to look closely at a product for cost reductions as it is being developed.

The best way to avoid costs in a product early on is to bring in the downstream departments of production, purchasing (including suppliers), and marketing for their input before the design is finalized. Organizations can accomplish this by having regular design review meetings, which include members of all departments, right from the beginning of a new project.

Purchasing professionals can contribute to design in many ways before it is fixed. In developing specifications, purchasing may help a designer revise tolerances and features. This is accomplished by reviewing plans with potential suppliers. For example, a machine shop might recommend new materials that hold tolerances better than those originally specified, resulting in lower fabrication costs. Purchasers can often recommend parts that meet functional requirements at a lower cost. In one instance a lower-cost diode laser, recommended by a supplier at design-review meeting, replaced a helium–neon laser in a portable sighting device. This substitution reduced the cost by several hundred dollars and the weight by several ounces.

Purchasing is often in a position to recommend *interchangeable* or common parts. It already knows what it is buying for other products. Making some of these parts common to several products reduces inventory and increases the benefits of larger lot size buying. A classic example is Eli Whitney's use of exact replicas of any part on a rifle to enable mass production and accompanying reduction in costs. Whitney's demonstration to the War Department of disassembling, mixing parts, and reassembling rifles resulted in increased sales. Part *standardization* is important. Efforts should be made to utilize off-the-shelf rather than custom parts to perform a function. Standardized parts typically have shorter lead times, lower prices, and better warranties. In addition, salvage values are usually higher for standardized parts, in case the project changes. Purchasing is in a good position to take the lead in implementing value analysis techniques in the forward design meetings.

SUMMARY: STEPS TO TAKE IN SETTING UP A VALUE ANALYSIS PROGRAM

Value analysis achieves the greatest benefits when it is implemented as a *continuous improvement* process. A purchasing professional can follow the steps below to get a value analysis team working in his or her company.

Step One: Obtain senior management approval. A value analysis program will not work if the climate does not exist for cultivating an ongoing group. A management sponsor, such as a president, vice-president or general manager, must be identified to oversee the program. The sponsor should have corporation-wide responsibility and authority and be committed to the program. The sponsor provides motivation and funding, evaluates the proposals, and makes decisions on implementation.

Step Two: Identify a value manager. The value manager receives direction and objectives from the management sponsor, organizes workshops, and administers the program. The value manager should also identify projects for value analysis, and track and report the value improvement progress.

Step Three: Appoint a workshop facilitator. The workshop facilitator instructs team members in value analysis principles and techniques and leads the team in applying them to a specific project. The facilitator must have an in-depth knowledge of value analysis principles and methods and how to apply them. He or she must have a sense of where and how to uncover improvement opportunities and the ability to manage a multidisciplined team. The facilitator should be able to guide the members in stimulating creative output, without being viewed as a source of solutions.

Step Four: Integrate the value program with other improvement programs. Many organizations have some improvement programs such as concurrent design, TQM and Just-in-Time. These programs should be integrated with value analysis under the banner of improving competitiveness through value. Objectives should be aligned with organizational goals.

Step Five: Plan for implementation. It is crucial to do this from the start. The plan should be documented, with a description of how value improvement recommendations are to be evaluated. Resources must be made available to accomplish the approved recommendations.

Step Six: Obtain cross-functional support. A value analysis program requires cross-organizational support—it needs to be a program in which all organizational elements have a role and a commitment.

Step Seven: Select a project. A prudent plan of action is to begin simple and then move to more sophisticated projects, choosing ones that tie into strategic objectives. Value analysis study projects are usually identified by management insight or through the use of organization diagnostics. For each project it is imperative that the specific objectives and scope be clearly stated and understood. Although value analysis can be applied to almost any area, typical projects include products, production processes, and/or other information processes that have problems such as:

- High cost
- Unsatisfied needs
- Redundancy or unnecessary functions
- Repetitive problems (multiple bottlenecks)
- Waste (time, effort, money, material)
- Complexity of time or consumption

Step Eight: Select a team. Once the project is defined, select a team representing the elements of expertise necessary to address the project.

Team members should be capable, respected, and able to obtain the support of their departments; they should also have an unbiased viewpoint. Choose a team leader from the group.

Step Nine: Collect data. Information for analysis should be collected, with the value manager, the facilitator, and the team leader working together to identify what is required. The nature and extent of the data depend on the project and the objectives, but they typically include facts on cost, resources consumed, cycle times, suppliers, and any known problems. Customer or field data may also be required. The team leader has overall responsibility to see that the data is collected but may delegate the actual collection to various team members.

Step Ten: Conduct the workshop. The value manager and facilitator work together on workshop preparation, making arrangements for items such as meeting facilities, equipment, and letters of invitation. The workshop should be a full-time commitment during which the participants need to focus their attention on the project without having their thoughts interrupted by other commitments.

Step Eleven: Implement approved projects. Approved recommendations enter into the implementation stage. Sponsors should hold monthly or bimonthly implementation progress review meetings at which those responsible for implementation report their progress and problems.

Step Twelve: Recognize and reward success. It is important for management sponsors to realize that implementing value improvements can be frustrating work. An important role of the sponsor is to support and encourage those working on implementing value improvements.

Step Thirteen: Track and record the benefits. Shifting priorities or changing management can have an impact on an ongoing value analysis program. Should the program come under scrutiny, success and continuation can be achieved by the keeping of well-documented records of audited savings and other benefits.

Step Fourteen: Repeat the procedure. Project selection is an ongoing process. As soon as the first project moves into implementation, the next project and workshop should be taking form.

BIBLIOGRAPHY

Carbone, J. "Value Analysis: For Some More Important Than Ever." *Purchasing,* June 20, 1996, pp. 33–34.

Farrell, P. *Aljian's Purchasing Handbook,* 4th ed. NAPM, McGraw-Hill, New York, 1982.

Mazel, J. L. "New Value Analysis Emphasizes Greater Supplier Involvement." *Supplier Selection and Management Report*, Management & Administration, Inc., New York, Issue 96-4, April 1996.

Miles, L. D. *Techniques of Value Analysis and Engineering*. McGraw-Hill, New York, 1972.

Miller, J. "The Evolution of Value Analysis." *NAPM Insights*, February 1993, pp. 13–14.

Morgan, J. "Where Has VA Gone." *Purchasing*, June 1, 1995, pp. 34–37.

Mudge, A. E. *Value Engineering, A Systematic Approach*. McGraw-Hill, New York, 1971.

Napoleon, L. J. "Reaping the Benefits." *NAPM Insights*, December 1993, pp. 26–27.

Raia, E. "Taking Out the Cost." *Purchasing*, June 4, 1992, pp. 41–57.

———, VA Contest Winners." *Purchasing*, June 3, 1993, pp. 55–64.

Stundza, T. "Purchasing Evolves into Supply Management." *Purchasing*, July 17, 1997.

"Value Analysis Contest." *Purchasing*, June 2, 1994, pp. 33–39.

"Value Analysis Report 1991." *Purchasing*, vol. 110, June 6, 1991, pp. 61–71.

ADDITIONAL READINGS

Brown, J. *Value Engineering: A Blueprint*. Industrial Press, 1992.

Clark, L. J. "Understanding and Applying Value Analysis and Value Engineering." *NAPM InfoEdge*, December 1997.

Fowler, T. C. *Value Analysis in Design*, Van Nostrand Reinhold, New York, 1990.

Shilito, M. L., and D. J. DeMarle, *Value: Its Measurement, Design and Management*, John Wiley & Sons, New York, 1992.

A Practitioner's Guide to Forecasting

Editor
Michael P. Niemira
Vice-President and Senior Economist
Bank of Tokyo-Mitsubishi, Ltd.
Research Department (New York) and
Adjunct Professor of Economics
New York University
Stern School of Business

INTRODUCTION

What is forecasting and why must business engage in the process? Forecasting is the prediction of some future event, condition, or level of some relevant variable so as to reduce risk over the forecast period or horizon. It is more than just picking a statistical technique and applying it. It starts from some theoretical perspective or framework—even if the theory is loose. Forecasting requires data, which often, in turn, requires finding the data. And sometimes the data are not quite what you really want. Forecasting requires an analysis of those data and the development of some preliminary hypotheses, which ultimately are tested by statistics and judgment. There is no right or wrong way to forecast. The ultimate judgment of the efficacy of the method used will depend on what actually happens.

Forecasting is an art, and the art comes from using the simplest, most cost-effective technique for the situation. Statistical forecasting models cannot replace basic judgment. On the other hand, statistics should not be ignored, since they will help to guide, shape, and generate a forecast. In one sense, forecasting also is similar to storytelling. You need to tell a good story with the projections.

OVERVIEW OF THE FORECAST PROCESS

Why does a purchasing executive need to forecast? The answer is simple: The role of purchasing is changing; purchasing is becoming less concerned with the transaction and more concerned with supply management. Not surprisingly, this expanded role for the purchasing professional also requires expanded activities, such as forecasting. Number three on the list of 18 purchasing/supply executive issues identified in *The Future of Purchasing and Supply: A Five- and Ten-Year Forecast*,[1] was *strategic sourcing* as a driver of supply chain management initiatives. A 1992 survey of members of the National Association of Purchasing Mangement as reported by Wisner and Stanley (1994) found that, "while most purchasing departments placed a relatively high level of importance on forecasting, judgment-based forecasting techniques were heavily relied upon and methods of forecast improvement were not widely employed. Additionally, forecasting by purchasing departments was found to be a relatively recent phenomenon. The findings also revealed that purchasing departments may not be taking full advantge of the many forecasting and forecast improvement techniques available."[2] The implication is fairly obvious: Increased importance of strategic sourcing will require increased and improved forecasts of requirements.

"Back of the envelope" forecasting will no longer serve the purchaser's need. A more formal treatment of the forecasting process and a more reasoned forecast are fast becoming critical for supply management. The starting point in this undertaking is to develop a crisp forecasting strategy, which may include a healthy dose of judgmental forecasting. The information from the National Association of Purchasing Management's manufacturing and nonmanufacturing business surveys also can play a key role in this forecasting process.

Many tasks are involved in the forecasting process, but without a doubt the most important step is to set the forecast strategy or guidelines for the analysis. Only after this is done will the remaining steps in the forecast process make sense. The entire forecast process can be summarized by the following steps:

---

1. A joint research initiative of the Center for Advanced Purchasing Studies (CAPS), the National Association of Purchasing Management (NAPM), and A. T. Kearney, Inc., Arizona State University and Michigan State University 1998.
2. Wisner and Stanley, p. 22.

- *Step 1: Determine the objective of the forecast.* At the start, the forecaster must determine: (a) what will be forecasted, (b) the periodicity (monthly, quarterly, yearly, and so forth), (c) the length of the forecast horizon, and (d) what statistical techniques, if any, are most applicable for the data and forecast horizon.

- *Step 2: Determine what data are available and get them.* Often the most time-consuming aspect of the forecasting process is finding the data needed and if necessary cleaning them up. Data from internal company sources and/or published government and private sector data will often be used. Company data may contain missing observations or an occasional "bad" data point, which must be accounted for *before* the analysis begins.

- *Step 3: Look at the data.* Before any statistical technique is applied, the forecast practitioner would be wise to graph the data, in various forms—levels, growth rates, and so forth—to understand how the data behave. Ask yourself questions about the data: (a) Did anything special occur during the data period that you are looking at (Was there a recession? Did a supplier have a special promotion in place? Was the value of the dollar against foreign currencies rising or falling? Were interest rates rising or fallen? etc.), (b) Is the data pattern linear (a straight line), seasonal, cyclical, or some combination? and (c) Is there some reason to expect the pattern to be vastly different in the future? The answer to these questions will shape other parameters in the forecast exercise and help to determine the appropriate statistical technique that would be most suitable for the data.

- *Step 4: Choose a forecast method and apply it.* This task is to apply a statistical technique—if that is the most appropriate technique for the forecast given the data—or to rely on surveys, consensus forecasts, or "bootstrapping" a forecast— or simply to use judgment. Error analysis should be used to evaluate any quantitative method. How much error was there over the estimation period? How much error was there in the out-of-sample or "holdout" test period? Did the forecasting method capture a turning point? Did the forecasting method capture a seasonal pattern? The purpose of this chapter is to acquaint you with various forecast techniques that might be applied and why, but the details of each forecasting technique are beyond the scope of this article. Table 25–1 offers some guidelines for selecting an appropriate forecast method based on the data.

♦ *Step 5: Generate a forecast and monitor it.* Once you are satisfied with the forecasting method and evaluation of its forecasting errors, the final step is to generate a forecast. If the forecast is acceptable and accepted, a formal tracking scheme should be in place so you can alert yourself to any likely deviation from the forecast path.

♦ *Step 6: Present the forecast.* In presenting the forecast, be sure to tell a story. The numbers are not the story, nor is the *technique* used to forecast. The story explains the logic for the forecast and why you think that forecast is plausible.

ASSEMBLING DATA: INTERNET PROVIDES A NEW RESOURCE

Not that long ago, economic data for analysis and forecasting purposes were difficult to find, hard to understand, or, from a purchasers' stand-point, too much of a diversion for the purchaser to waste time with "economic statistics." In one sense, the NAPM Manufacturing *Report on Business®* (ROB) solved that problem for the purchasing community with "one-stop" shopping for a wide range of manufacturing data. The ROB contains qualitative data on new orders, production, supplier delivery times, raw material prices, employment, and so on, and with those survey data it is easy to monitor the overall manufacturing cycle.

Although the ROB manufacturing business survey data continue to play that same role, the surrounding economy has evolved into the Information Society. Government and private sector data—for the United States and for world economies—are readily abundant today. However, today's business environment requires more skill to transform those data into useful information than ever before.

Table 25–2 provides a partial listing of some U.S. and foreign statistical sources that are available through the Internet. These Internet sites often are a starting point for finding data and often have a glossary or descriptions of the data available on them. The regional Federal Reserve Banks can be a useful source for regional data as well. The Bureau of

T A B L E 25–1

Some Guidelines for Picking an Appropriate Forecasting Method Based on the Data

Type of Data Pattern or Type of Data	Description of Data Profile	Types of Suitable Techniques	Data Requirements
Seasonal	Repetitive seasonal pattern from year to year	• Time-series decomposition • Winters' exponential smoothing • Regression-based models with seasonal qualitative (dummy) variables	At least three years of data to assess the seasonal pattern
Cycles	Cycles of varying or fixed duration extending at least 13 months	• Analog or pattern models • Leading indicators • Regression-based sine–cosine models • Spectral analysis	At least three cycles
Trend growth rate or level	A visual straight line	• Exponential smoothing • Moving averages • ARIMA models • Regression-based trend models	Depends on method applied and forecast horizon. ARIMA models tend to need more data than other methods shown.
Trendless (stationary) in growth rate or level	A visual straight line essentially without any upward or downward slope	• Exponential smoothing • Autoregressive time-series models • ARMA models	Depends on method applied and forecast horizon. ARMA models tend to need more data than other methods shown.
Mixed	A combination of the patterns, including seasonal, cyclical, and trend components	• Regression-based causal models • Neural network models	Depends on forecast horizon. At least three years of data are necessary.

T A B L E 25-1

Continued

Type of Data Pattern or Type of Data	Description of Data Profile	Types of Suitable Techniques	Data Requirements
Probability	Data bounded by 0% to 100%	◆ Regression-based logit or probit models ◆ Survival or hazard models ◆ Threshold models ◆ Hidden Markov models	Depends on duration of event horizon and number of events.
Qualitative evaluation or outcomes	States or regimes, for example, "buy," "sell," or "hold."	◆ Regression-based qualitative models ◆ Neural network models	At least three years of data are necessary, which span the regimes
Shifting volatility	Data exhibiting greater or lesser standard deviation over time	◆ Regression-based ARCH models	Sufficient data to reflect change in series volatility
Unknown	Too few data observations to determine pattern	◆ Judgmental forecasting ◆ Surveys of expert opinion	Whatever is available

T A B L E   25–2

Internet Sources of Financial and Economic Data

Sources of Data		Internet Location
Central banks	Federal Reserve Board	www.federalreserve.gov
	Bank of Canada	www.bank-banque-canada.ca
	Bank of England	www.bankofengland.co.uk
	Bank of Japan	www.boj.or.jp
	Deutsche Bundesbank	www.bundesregierung.de
Federal Reserve banks	FRB of Boston	www.bos.frb.org
	FRB of New York	www.ny.frb.org
	FRB of Philadelphia	www.phil.frb.org
	FRB of Cleveland	www.clev.frb.org
	FRB of Richmond	www.rich.frb.org
	FRB of Atlanta	www.frbatlanta.org
	FRB of Chicago	www.frbchi.org
	FRB of St. Louis	www.stls.frb.org
	FRB of Minneapolis	woodrow.mpls.frb.fed.us
	FRB of Kansas City	www.kc.frb.org
	FRB of Dallas	www.dallasfed.org
	FRB of San Francisco	www.frbsf.org
U.S. Government	U.S. Department of Commerce	www.doc.gov
	U.S. Bureau of the Census	www.census.gov
	U.S. Department of Labor	www.dol.gov
	U.S. Bureau of Labor Statistics	www.bls.gov
	Employment & Training Admin.	www.doleta.gov
	U.S. Department of Agriculture	www.econ.ag.gov
	Joint Economic Committee	www.house.gov/jec
	U.S. Bureau of Transportation Statistics	www.bts.gov

T A B L E   25–2

Continued

Sources of Data		Internet Location
Other financial data sources	Investment Company Institute (mutual fund data)	www.ici.org
Business cycle indicators	Conference Board— Cyclical Indicators	www.tcb-indicators.org/
	Economic Cycle Research Institute (ECRI)	www.businesscycle.com/
	Foundation for International Business & Economic Research (FIBER)	www.emgmkts.com/fiber/ fiber.htm
International organizations	United Nations	www.unsystem.org
	European Union	www.europa.eu.int
	OECD	www.oecd.org
	IMF	www.imf.org
	World Bank	www.worldbank.org
Foreign statistical sources	Australian Bureau of Statistics	www.statistics.gov.au
	Statistics Canada	www.statcan.ca
	German Federal Statistics Office	www.statistik-bund.de
	Japan Economic Trade Organization	www.jetro.go.jp
	Japan Economic Planning Organization	www.epa.go.jp
	UK Office of National Statistics	www.ons.gov.uk
Purchasing organizations and other data sources	National Association of Purchasing Management (national data and links to local affiliate data where available)	www.napm.org

T A B L E   25-2

Continued

Sources of Data	Internet Location
Cahners' Purchasing Online	www.manufacturing.net/ magazine/purchasing/
APICS	www.apics.org/
Dun & Bradstreet (Resource Center)	www.dnb.com/resources/ menu.htm
SVME Purchasing Managers' Index for Switzerland	www.de.credit-suisse.ch/ economic_research/pmi/ index.html
CIPS (UK)	www.cips.org/
Links to Other Purchasing Sites	www.napm.org

Labor Statistics Internet site is the source for wholesale and consumer price indexes that might be used in cost-of-living adjustment (COLA) contract clauses.

A TOOL KIT OF TECHNIQUES

Once the forecasting objectives are set and the data requirements met, the analysis stage begins. The initial analytical step is to statistically summarize the data.

Simple statistics, such as standard deviation and averages, and plotting of the data will provide the purchaser with a quick means to assess the key data characteristics. It is essential to know the characteristics of the data that you are trying to forecast before attempting to forecast. You should evaluate any data series that you might be interested in forecasting based on at least three data characteristics: (1) volatility, (2) trends, and (3) cycles. Ask yourself: How volatile are the data? Are they dominated by a trend? Is the trend linear (that is, does it follow a straight line) or nonlinear (such as increasing at a faster pace or a slower pace)? Can you see a cycle in the data? How variable is that cycle, if it exists? Should the data be seasonally adjusted? Are there outlier observations that should be explained? One simple rule to judge an outlier is to plot the data; the outlier would be inconsistent with the broad pattern of the remaining data. Another way to determine outliers is to define an outlier as an observation that falls outside two standard deviations around the mean of the distribution of observations.

Once those simple descriptive characteristics are determined, the next hurdle is to choose a forecasting method that is best suited for those data patterns. As a rule of thumb, the KISS principle is often followed in helping to choose the appropriate technique. KISS stands for "Keep It Sophisticatedly Simple"; it suggests that simple is better. However, that does not mean you should ignore a more sophisticated forecasting technique if there is an expectation that the forecast accuracy would be improved. All forecasting decisions require tradeoffs between the time, cost, and accuracy of a forecast, which will set the boundaries of the forecasting framework.

Again, Table 25–1 presents a bird's-eye view across a range of forecasting techniques suitable for various types of data and data patterns. Only a few of those basic techniques can be demonstrated, and hence references are provided at the end of this chapter that will lead the purchaser to more detailed descriptions of each of these techniques.

Although many of these forecasting methods shown in Table 25–1 can be calculated in spreadsheet software, such as EXCEL or Lotus 1-2-3, often it is more efficient to use specialized forecasting software for the computational and data manipulation ease. A list of many of the most common software packages can be found on the Internet at www.stata. com/links/stat_software.html.

Judging the Accuracy of a Forecast Method

Implicit in the selection of the "best" forecasting technique is some measure of forecast accuracy. All measures of forecast accuracy assume some underlying loss function, which allows one to determine the cost of an error and, in turn, what an acceptable amount of error might be. The most common measures of forecast accuracy are the *mean squared error* (MSE) and the *root mean squared error* (RMSE)—which is the square root of the MSE—with *symmetric loss*. The mean squared error is calculated as the cumulative sum (designated as Σ) of the difference between the actual observations and the forecasts and that result raised to the second power (squared) and divided by the sample size (designated as $"n"^3$) as follows:

$$\text{MSE} = \frac{\Sigma(\text{Actual}_t - \text{Forecast}_t)^2}{n}$$

The root mean square error measure is calculated as:

$$\text{RMSE} = \sqrt{\frac{\Sigma(\text{Actual}_t - \text{Forecast}_t)^2}{n}}$$

Hence, in comparing models, the forecasting approach with the lowest MSE or RMSE would be preferable, other things being equal.

At times, however, it might make sense to define your accuracy measure based on *asymmetric loss*. By that it is meant, for example, that the cost of buying too much of an item might be greater than the same magnitude of error from buying too little of that item. Hence, in this example the costs associated with the forecast error are not the same for being too optimistic versus being too pessimistic. In this example the MSE (or RMSE) measure might be defined only in terms of when the Actual value minus the Forecast observation is negative.

Finally, these same historical accuracy measures, which are used to judge the relative superiority of a forecasting approach, also can be used to track the forecast as actual data become available. If the error is growing relative to its historical average error, then that might be used as a signal to revisit the existing model.

Forecasting Methods: A Sampling of Approaches

To give the flavor of some forecasting methods, the basics of five techniques will be explained and/or demonstrated. These five techniques include:

1. Exponential smoothing
2. Composite leading indicators

---

3. There is a fine line of distinction here. As a summary statistic, the n equal to the whole sample size is a logical choice for determining the average. However, in the context of a statistical model, based on random variables and their accompanying probability distributions, the terms *biased* and *unbiased* come into play and an adjustment of $n - k$ would be appropriate in that formula. The use of $n - k$ is determined by the *degrees of freedom*, which is defined as the number of independent data points (n) minus the number of parameters estimated (k).

3. Pattern model projections
4. Scenario building
5. Regression methods

Most of these techniques also can be used in combination with each other

The Basics of Exponential Smoothing

Exponential smoothing is a method of extrapolating recent trends into the future such that the latest patterns/data are weighted more heavily. This technique is most applicable for a short-term trend projection; it must be recognized that any exponential smoothing formulation will not capture causal relationships but extrapolate from past patterns alone. The selection of the type of exponential smoothing to use (single, double, triple parameter) will be determined by the pattern of the data. Exponential smoothing also can account for seasonal patterns (using what is known as Winter's method). The mechanics of generating a forecast using exponential smoothing are relatively simple.

We will demonstrate what is known as double exponential smoothing (or one-parameter linear exponential smoothing). This method incorporates an "adjustment" rate factor with a "linear trend" coefficient. The nature of exponential smoothing is an algorithm to adjust the forecast to recent data with the computational objective to determine the "optimal" adjustment and linear trend growth rates. This can be done automatically in some forecasting software or can be done manually, where the adjustment parameter is selected by "trial and error" and the forecast accuracy based on that parameter is judged by minimizing the sum of the square error or some other accuracy criterion in order to determine the "optimal parameter."

The formulae needed to compute double exponential smoothing are:

Single smoothed estimate: $\qquad S'_t = \alpha Y_t + (1 - \alpha)S'_{t-1}$ (25–1)

Double smoothed estimate: $\qquad S''_t = \alpha S'_t + (1 - \alpha)S''_{t-1}$ (25–2)

Level adjustment: $\qquad L_t = 2S'_t - S''_t$ (25–3)

Trend component (slope): $\qquad T_t = \left(\dfrac{\alpha}{1 - \alpha}\right)(S'_t - S''_t)$ (25–4)

Forecast equation: $\qquad F_{t+k} = L_t + kT_t$ (25–5)

where Equations 25–1 through 25–4 are used to determine the historical performance for the smoothing coefficient, α, and Equation 25–5 is used to pivot off of the last actual data point to come up with either a one-period ahead historical estimate or an n-period ahead forecast. The subscript t indicates the time period, and k is the number of periods the forecast is from the last actual observation. The equations denoted by S' and S'' are the intermediate-step calculations for the single and double exponential portion of the process, L is an estimate of the level of the data at time period t, and T is the estimate of the trend portion of the process.

A demonstration of this technique to forecast annual purchases is shown in Table 25–3. Keep in mind that the benefit of this technique—in whatever variation—is that it is simple to apply and does not require a lot of historical data. Some computer spreadsheet programs, such as EXCEL, have a built-in routine to perform exponential smoothing.

Composite Leading Indicators

One of the best-known applications of a composite leading economic indicator is the measure that is compiled and released by the Conference Board (and includes NAPM's supplier delivery time diffusion index as one of its components). A composite index, as the name implies, is a basket of indicators that are selected based on specific criteria. For the Conference Board's leading indicator, the criterion was the ability of the individual components to anticipate cyclical turning points in the U.S. business cycle. Another composite leading indicator that purchasers may be familiar with is the Cahners Early Warning Indicator (CEWI), a composite index of data on housing starts, stock prices, and the inverse of the three-month Treasury bill rate of interest.

Leading indicator composite indicators exist for international economies as well. Some composite leading indicators are produced by governments and international organizations, such as the Organization of Economic Cooperation and Development (OECD) for its member countries, or individual governments, such as Canada, the United Kingdom, the Netherlands, and Japan. Others are compiled by private or public research groups, such as a composite leading economic indicator for Mexico published by the Dallas Federal Reserve Bank. Broad-based consistent sets of international leading, coincident, and lagging indicators are compiled by the Economic Cycle Research Institute (ECRI) and the Foundation for International Business and Economic Research (FIBER).

When the potential cyclicality of an industry or economy takes on heightened significance, so do cyclical indicator composites, since most

TABLE 25-3

Double Exponential Smoothing Example for Alpha = 0.80

Year	Purchases (Millions)	Single Exponential Smoothing	Double Exponential Smoothing	Level	Trend	Forecast	Squared Error
1985	$150	$150	$150				
1986	$175	$170	$166	$174	$16	$174	$1
1987	$165	$166	$166	$166	$0	$166	$1
1988	$180	$177	$175	$179	$9	$179	$0
1989	$178	$178	$177	$178	$2	$178	$0
1990	$145	$152	$157	$146	($21)	$146	$2
1991	$140	$142	$145	$139	($12)	$139	$0
1992	$150	$148	$148	$149	$3	$149	$1
1993	$170	$166	$162	$169	$14	$169	$1
1994	$190	$185	$181	$190	$18	$190	$0
1995	$200	$197	$194	$200	$13	$200	$0
1996	$220	$215	$211	$220	$17	$220	$0
1997	$250	$243	$237	$249	$26	$249	$0
1998	$265	$261	$256	$265	$19	$265	$0
1999						$285	$1
2000						$304	
2001						$323	
2002						$342	
2003						$361	

1985–1998
Mean Squared
Error (MSE)

Continued
Double Exponential Smoothing Example for Alpha = 0.80

Trial and Error Method for
Selecting Alpha

Alpha	MSE	
0.35	$69	
0.45	$33	
0.55	$20	
0.65	$12	
0.75	$3	
0.80	$1	← Smallest Error
0.85	$4	
0.90	$17	
0.95	$46	

simple trend forecasting methodologies do not forecast turning points very well. Leading cyclical turning point indicator composites often are used externally to any formal statistical model as a judgmental input but can be used directly in a regression model.

Pattern Model Projections

Pattern models, also known as analog models, are used when a repetitive pattern is suspected to be emerging. This type of model uses relevant averages from prior experiences to extrapolate from that pattern into the future. Pattern models tend to be common for seasonal pattern projections or cyclical forecasting.

In essence, this technique has three steps:

1. Array the data for each segment from a common event point (such as a business cycle turning point date or the date a new model or product was introduced)

2. Index each array from that common point in time (the event— such as that turning point date)

3. Extrapolate from the historical pattern (or relevant subset of it) into the future by pivoting off of the last actual value of the episode.

This is demonstrated in Table 25–4 for projecting industrial production of business supplies. This type of data can be used by purchasing in historical market analyses of items that have cyclical production patterns.

Regression Methods

The simplest statistical regression technique, known as *ordinary least squares*, is a standard feature of most spreadsheet software and is included in such programs as EXCEL and Lotus 1-2-3. A statistical regression relates the dependent or forecast variable to an independent variable or set of variables such that the regression algorithm minimizes the sum of squared errors. A practical introduction for interpreting some of the standard regression model statistical output is found in McLagan[4] and Diebold.[5]

4. D. L. McLagan, "A Non-econometrican's Guide to Econometrics." *Business Economics*, vol. 8, no. 2, May 1973, pp. 38–45.

5. F. Diebold, *Elements of Forecasting*, South-Western Publishing, Cincinnati, Ohio, 1998.

T A B L E 25-4

Pattern Model Projections Based on Cyclical Turning Points (TP) and Months from TP for Industrial Production of Business Supplies. (Index, 1992 = 100)

Step 1: Array Data for Each Segment from Turning Point Date

Turning Point Date	Values at Turning Point	TP + 1	TP + 2	TP + 3	TP + 4	TP + 5	TP + 6	TP + 7	TP + 8	TP + 9
Apr 1960	30.525	30.736	30.384	30.419	30.173	30.032	30.138	30.138	29.609	30.067
Dec 1969	52.190	52.128	51.721	51.983	51.743	51.650	51.540	51.742	51.315	51.667
Nov 1973	62.467	61.930	60.845	60.996	61.242	61.396	61.347	62.475	61.787	61.996
Jan 1980	74.680	74.167	74.784	72.854	72.025	71.569	71.605	72.442	73.232	72.994
Jul 1981	75.965	75.427	75.158	74.644	75.050	75.198	76.571	76.502	76.383	76.332
Jul 1990	101.339	101.166	100.727	101.079	100.229	101.004	102.535	101.454	99.032	98.158
May 1998 (T)	113.743	112.909	112.519	112.258	112.327					

TABLE 25-4

Continued

Step 2: Index All Data Segments to 1.0 at Turning Point (Divide Value at Turning Point by Itself; Divide Subsequent Periods of Specific Array Data into Value at Turning Point)

Turning Point Date	Turning Point Value (Indexed)	TP + 1	TP + 2	TP + 3	TP + 4	TP + 5	TP + 6	TP + 7	TP + 8	TP + 9
Apr 1960	1.000	1.007	0.995	0.997	0.988	0.984	0.987	0.987	0.970	0.985
Dec 1969	1.000	0.999	0.991	0.996	0.991	0.990	0.988	0.991	0.983	0.990
Nov 1973	1.000	0.991	0.974	0.976	0.980	0.983	0.982	1.000	0.989	0.992
Jan 1980	1.000	0.993	1.001	0.976	0.964	0.958	0.959	0.970	0.981	0.977
Jul 1981	1.000	0.993	0.989	0.983	0.988	0.990	1.008	1.007	1.006	1.005
Jul 1990	1.000	0.998	0.994	0.997	0.989	0.997	1.012	1.001	0.977	0.969
May 1998 (T)	1.000	0.993	0.989	0.987	0.988					
1960–1990 Average	1.000	0.997	0.991	0.987	0.984	0.984	0.989	0.993	0.984	0.986

Step 3: Extrapolate Current Cyclical Pattern Using Average 1960–1990 Pattern

Turning Point Date	Turning Point	TP + 1	TP + 2	TP + 3	TP + 4	TP + 5	TP + 6	TP + 7	TP + 8	TP + 9
May 1998 (T)	113.743	112.909	112.519	112.258	112.327	111.872	112.521	112.930	111.955	112.194
		←——— Actual ———→		←——————— Forecast Based on Average Pattern ———————→						

T = Tentative Turning Point Date

Regressions can take two distinct forms: *explanatory* or *time series*. In the explanatory form, the regression model can be designed to capture a theoretical "cause and effect" relationship between the forecasted variable and the set of explanatory variables. It should, however, be pointed out that there are classic examples of statistical regressions that are just "statistical fits" without any theoretical or realistic cause-and-effect linkage. Be on guard not to fall into that statistical trap—think about the causal relationship before estimating any relationship and check that the regression results show the appropriate "signs" for each independent variable. For example, if you expect that demand will move inversely with interest rates, then the sign on the independent variable should be negative.

Regression models also can be of the time series form. Some of the popular pure time series models are the autoregressive moving average (ARMA) models, which are applicable to trendless data, and the autoregressive integrated moving average (ARIMA) models, which are applicable to data with a trend, but the trend is removed by various levels of period-to-period differencing.

There are various special statistical problems that occur in the application of the regression method. One such special problem is when there is changing statistical volatility of the dependent variable over time, which violates a basic assumption of ordinary least squares estimation. Although there are simpler ways to account for this statistical problem (such as reformulating the explanatory variable or segmenting the interval into more uniform periods), one state-of-the-art method is known as the autoregressive conditional heteroskedasticity or ARCH models. ARCH models essentially estimate the changing volatility in the dependent variable, as well as the underlying statistical relationship. To explore these more advanced statistical estimation methods, see the references at the end of this chapter.

Scenario Analysis

"What if" analysis can be used in conjunction with other forecast techniques or as a stand-alone method. In essence, the purchaser would set up likely alternative paths for some relevant variable and forecast based on those alternative inputs. A simple application of this method to forecast the price of copper wire bar is demonstrated in Box 25–1. This type of forecast is useful for examining a range of possibilities (in this case for the price of copper wire bar) based on several possible rates of change of an underlying factor (in this case the growth of the economy).

B O X   25–1

SCENARIO ANALYSIS–COPPER WIRE BAR PRICE FORECASTING

Statistical Relationship:

Copper Prices = 0.60 + 0.05 × (Real GDP Growth)

(Cents per Pound)

Scenario 1: Slow Growth (Real GDP less than 2.0%)

Copper Prices:	0.60 + 0.05 × Real GDP Growth	
(20% Likelihood)	−1.0 =	$0.55
	0.0 =	$0.60
	1.0 =	$0.65

Scenario 2: Moderate Growth (Real GDP greater than 2.0% but less than 3.0%)

Copper Prices:	0.60 + 0.05 × Real GDP Growth	
(55% Likelihood)	2.0 =	$0.70
	2.5 =	$0.73
	3.0 =	$0.75

Scenario 3: Slow Growth (Real GDP greater than 3.0%)

Copper Prices:	0.60 + 0.05 × Real GDP growth	
(25% Likelihood)	3.5 =	$0.78
	4.0 =	$0.80
	4.5 =	$0.83

Weighted Forecast: 0.20 × (Scenario 1) + 0.55 × (Scenario 2) + 0.25 × (Scenario 3)

Midpoint Forecast   0.20 × ($0.60) + 0.55 × ($0.73) + 0.25 × ($0.80) = $0.72

For this example, it is assumed that the purchaser is given information that there is a 20% chance that the economy will grow by less than 2.0% in the subsequent year, a 55% chance that the economy will grow by between 2.0% and 3.0%, and a 25% chance that growth will exceed 3.0%. Based on historical analysis, the purchaser might have a statistical relationship between the price of copper wire and real GDP growth. Then, based on some plausible growth rate combinations, the purchaser might develop a range of price forecasts for copper wire and a weighted average (based on the probability of the outcome) could be used for the overall forecast.

Combining Forecasts

A common method for generating a forecast is to pool various forecasts that were developed using different techniques or models. The simplest method of pooling forecasts is to average the forecasts. Another method is to use a weighted average where the weights are derived based on the historical accuracy of the models. The weights are calculated using the mean square errors and the standard deviations and the weighted average of the two forecasts (designated as from model A and B) is given as:

$$\text{Composite Forecast} = W(A)^* \, F(A) + W(B)^* \, F(B), \text{ where}$$

$$W(A) = \left(\frac{\text{MSE}(A)}{\text{SD}(A)}\right) \div \left[\left(\frac{\text{MSE}(A)}{\text{SD}(A)}\right) + \left(\frac{\text{MSE}(B)}{\text{SD}(B)}\right)\right],$$

$F(A) = $ the forecast from approach A,

$$W(B) = \left(\frac{\text{MSE}(B)}{\text{SD}(B)}\right) \div \left[\left(\frac{\text{MSE}(A)}{\text{SD}(A)}\right) + \left(\frac{\text{MSE}(B)}{\text{SD}(B)}\right)\right],$$

$F(B) = $ the forecast from approach B

The designation $\text{MSE}(n)$ is the mean squared error for $n = A$ and B, and $\text{SD}(n)$ is the standard deviation of approach A and B, respectively. An example of combining forecasts is shown in Table 25–5.

FORECASTING WITH THE NAPM SURVEY DATA

The NAPM surveys for the manufacturing and nonmanufacturing sectors provide purchasers with "one-stop shopping" for data. These data can serve many purposes, including current tracking, cyclical forecasting, and even simple year-ahead forecasting. But the starting point before using these data is to understand them.

Each participant in the NAPM survey panels answers the survey questions, that measure orders, production or shipments, employment,

T A B L E 25-5

Combining Forecasts Based on MSE and Standard Deviation

Period	Actual (1)	Model A Estimate (2)	Model A Error (Col.1– Col. 2) (3)	Model A Squared Error (Col. 3 Squared) (4)	Model B Estimate (5)	Model B Error (Col. 1– Col. 5) (6)	Model B Squared Error (Col. 6 Squared) (7)
1992	1452	1500	–48	2304	1475	–23	529
1993	1545	1500	45	2025	1525	20	400
1994	1458	1500	–42	1764	1425	33	1089
1995	1475	1500	–25	625	1499	–24	576
1996	1588	1600	–12	144	1600	–12	144
1997	1625	1600	25	625	1610	15	225
1998	1701	1700	1	1	1685	16	256
1999	1745	1750	–5	25	1725	20	400
		MSE (Model A)		939.1	MSE (Model B)		452.4
		Std. Dev. (Model A)		885.1	Std. Dev. (Model B)		277.8

Weight (A) = MSE(A)/Std. Dev. (A)/[[MSE(A)/Std. Dev. (A)] + (MSE(B)/Std. Dev. (B)]]

= 0.39

Weight (B) = MSE(B)/Std. Dev. (B)/[[MSE(A)/Std. Dev. (A)]+(MSE(B)/Std. Dev. (B)]]

= 0.61

Composite Forecast = 0.39 × Forecast(A) + 0.61 × Forecast(B)

TABLE 25-5

Continued

Year	Composite Estimate	Error	Squared Error
1992	1484.8	−32.8	1072.6
1993	1515.3	29.8	885.1
1994	1454.3	3.8	14.1
1995	1499.4	−24.4	594.9
1996	1600.0	−12.0	144.0
1997	1606.1	18.9	357.2
1998	1690.9	10.2	103.0
1999	1734.8	10.3	105.1
MSE (Combined)			409.5
Std. Dev.			373.6

Year	Composite Forecast	Model A Forecast	Model B Forecast
2000	1740.3	1725	1750
2001	1790.3	1775	1800
2002	1797.0	1800	1795
2003	1815.3	1800	1825
2004	1842.9	1824	1855
2005	1866.0	1852	1875

prices, supplier delivery time, and so forth, based on an evaluation of *higher*, *lower*, or *unchanged* compared to the prior month.

Based on the percentage of the sample responding higher, lower, or same for each question, each question is summarized as a *diffusion index* (DI) following the convention of adding the percentage of the sample rising (or slower, for supplier delivery) plus one-half of the percentage of the sample responding "same" or "no change." The diffusion index can range between 0% and 100%. Some regional purchasing manager association surveys prefer to report their results as *net difference indexes* or *net percentage rising* (NPR). The NPR is simply the percentage of respondents reporting higher minus the percentage reporting lower. The net difference, which is bounded by $+100$ and -100, is related to the diffusion index as follows: $NPR = 2 \times (DI - 50)$, where DI is the diffusion index. Similarly, the identity can be reformulated as: $DI = 50 + (NPR/2)$. The choice of which formula to use for expressing the direction of survey change is arbitrary.

It can be shown mathematically that diffusion indexes will move in lockstep with the percentage change of its components, if the responses are weighted by the size of the industry contribution. Hence, the resulting figures that are reported by NAPM can be viewed as a "percentage-change" type of variable for orders, production, and the other categories.

The NAPM national composite index for manufacturing business activity is compiled as a *composite diffusion index*, which is called the *Purchasing Managers' Index* (PMI). It is based on a weighted average of new orders, production, employment, supplier delivery time, and inventories. The manufacturing PMI composite index is assigned the following weighting scheme:

$$PMI = 0.30 \times (\text{New Orders}) + 0.25 \times (\text{Production}) + 0.20 \\ \times (\text{Employment}) + 0.15 \times (\text{Supplier Deliveries}) + 0.10 \\ \times (\text{Inventories}).$$

The NAPM manufacturing survey has a long and distinguished history extending back to the early 1930s. Therefore there is a considerable amount of data to work with for forecasting. The NAPM nonmanufacturing report's summary measure is the business activity measure, which is more limited in scope than the composite PMI but serves as a focus of current activity. However, because of the limited amount of historical data from the nonmanufacturing survey (the historical data begin in mid-1997), it will take time to be able to use these data in a structured statistical or cyclical forecasting model (but their time will come).

The APICS Business Outlook survey is another purchasing-manager survey for the United States. It is currently based on about 100 manufacturing firms. The first APICS survey was taken in December 1992 and first became available publicly beginning in September 1993. The APICS summary measure is compiled as an arithmetic average of the current conditions component and the future conditions component. The current conditions component is an average of five components: (1) manufacturing shipments, (2) employment, (3) industrial production, (4) inventory stocks, and (5) unfilled orders. The future conditions component is an average of: (1) durable goods new orders (excluding aircraft and defense), (2) production plans, (3) the actual-to-desired inventory/sales ratio. The Society describes the compilation of the APICS indexes as follows:

> First, we calculate the percentage change in any given series for each company. These are then weighted by the size of the company, and a total weighted percentage change is calculated. These figures are then seasonally adjusted. The result might show, for example, a 0.5% gain in industrial production, a 2.1% increase in shipments, or a 0.3% decline in employment. These percentage changes are then converted to an index number format for ease of comparability. A value of 50 for each individual component means that variable is unchanged from the previous month. A maximum value of 100 means the increase is as large as the biggest expected monthly gain; that figure is based in large part on the biggest gain that has occurred at any time since 1980. A minimum value of zero would mean the decline is as large as the biggest expected monthly drop.

For example, if the shipments average increase was up 2.3% for the month and the maximum monthly increase was 3.8% over the historical period (based on government data), then the index value would be calculated as $50 \times (1 + 23/38)$, or 80.3. The APICS historical data set is relatively short but can still be used as another purchasing perspective.

Finally, numerous purchasing manager surveys now exist around the world—for the United Kingdom, Germany, and Switzerland, to name just a few. Unfortunately, most of those series are relatively new, which means that it will take some time to be able to use those data for more extensive statistical research.

Harnessing the Manufacturing Data for National Forecasting

The NAPM manufacturing survey data can be harnessed for simple forecasting needs or in conjunction with other data for more elaborate forecasting. Those data can be used to forecast (1) business cycle turning points, (2) the overall pace of economic growth, and (3) what the price measure implies for inflation.

Tracking the NAPM PMI as a Turning Point Indicator

Several critical threshold levels of the PMI have significant implications for the economy. The key threshold levels in the PMI are (1) the cyclical high, (2) 50%, (3) 42%, and (4) the cyclical low.

History suggests that the NAPM PMI is a reliable forecasting indicator of a *growth cycle turning point* (also sometimes referred to as the "growth rate cycle" or a "mini-cycle"). A *growth cycle* encompasses the *business cycle* concept of absolute increases and decreases in the level of output, employment, and other measures of business activity, and turns down prior to the upper turning point in the business cycle. A committee of the National Bureau of Economic Research (NBER) designates the "official" peak and trough dates in the U.S. business cycle, and researchers at the NBER also have developed a growth cycle chronology for the United States. (A chronology for the U.S. business cycle and a brief discussion of the growth cycle can be found on the Internet at www.nber.org/cycles.html, and international turning point dates can be found in the reference material section of the Economic Cycle Research Institute, which is located on the Internet at www.businesscycle.com.)

Over the last 40 years, the NAPM PMI led growth-cycle peaks by seven months, on average, and led growth cycle lows by three months. Hence, the PMI is a sensitive measure not only of business cycle turning points but also of slowdowns and accelerations in the expansion phase of the cycle.

A reading of 50% or less is the second threshold level to watch for in tracking manufacturing activity. The 50% threshold is, by definition, the point at which an equal percentage of the respondents to the survey say business conditions are better as say they are worse. As such, the 50% point is significant from a psychological standpoint, as well as being a signal of potentially more weakness to come. On average, the PMI has fallen below 50% two months before recessions have begun (with a range of fourteen months lead time in 1990 to a 10-month lag in 1973). However, the PMI also has declined below 50% when the manufacturing sector itself experienced sector weakness that may not have spread into the nonmanufacturing sector.

The statistical relationship between the NAPM PMI and quarter-to-quarter percentage changes (at annual rates) in real GDP (GDPQQ) between 1988 and 1998 is given in Equation 25–6a:

$$\text{GDPQQ} = 0.276 \times \text{PMI} - 11.692 \qquad (25\text{--}6a)$$

$$R^2 \text{ (adjusted)} = 0.344 \qquad \text{Sample Period: 1988--1998}$$

This relationship suggested that when the PMI equaled 50.0% it was consistent with a 2.1% pace of real GDP. Also over that same period, the PMI had to fall below 42.5%, and not just 50%, in order to signal a widespread contraction in the broader economy. The threshold reading in the PMI that historically is consistent with an absolute decline in real GDP was determined based on this simple statistical regression, but remember that the threshold level will change over time. These are changeable rules of thumb because the PMI measures manufacturing activity only and the service-sector industries tend to be less cyclical and/or lag manufacturing activity. (As noted above, the historical data for the NAPM nonmanufacturing survey currently are too short to use for cyclical analysis or in a regression model. Over time, however, those non-manufacturing measures should find greater use in the forecast process for the national economy.)

During a recession, the PMI generally continued to decline until it reached 34.8%, on average (lowest, 29.4% in 1980, and highest, 43.6% in 1961). Once the PMI turned around, it has taken an average of four months to cross above 44%, which generally has occurred simultaneously with a business cycle low. Finally, the PMI has never declined below 44% without signaling a "growth cycle" (which is a simple "slowdown" in the pace of activity) or business cycle downturn (which is an absolute decline in economic activity). However, it is very difficult to distinguish between these two types of national cycles based on the manufacturing data alone.

Using the NAPM PMI to Predict Year-over-Year Real GDP and Industrial Production

The relationship between industrial production growth and the NAPM PMI is statistically tight. On average, the PMI leads year-over-year changes in industrial production by two months. The estimated relationship between industrial production growth on a year-over-year basis (IP) and the PMI lagged two months is shown below. Over the 1978-98 period, the PMI explained nearly 75% of the fluctuation in industrial production.

$$\text{IP} = 0.506 \times \text{PMI}[-2] - 23.4 \qquad (25\text{--}6b)$$

$$R^2 \text{ (adjusted)} = 0.739 \qquad \text{Sample Period: 1978--1998}$$

This statistical relationship suggests that the PMI must exceed 46.2% to be consistent with flat industrial production growth. Alternatively, when the PMI is at 50%, that has been consistent with 1.9% growth in production (that is, $[.506 \times 50] - 23.4$). Figure 25–1 presents this relationship graphically.

Although it may be conceptually risky to associate the PMI with real GDP, since GDP covers services and structures in addition to goods output, the fact is that the PMI anticipates real GDP growth (year-over-year) reasonably well with a lead time of one quarter. This year-over-year relationship is statistically more reliable than the quarter-to-quarter growth counterpart described above.

$$GDP = 0.292 \times PMI[-1] - 12.3 \qquad (25\text{–}6c)$$

$$R^2 \text{ (adjusted)} = 0.690 \qquad \text{Sample Period: 1978–1998}$$

The estimated quarterly GDP/PMI relationship suggests that a PMI reading of 42.0% has been consistent with no change in real GDP growth. Additionally, a 50% PMI reading has been consistent with 2.3% real GDP growth. The real GDP growth – PMI relationship associated with this equation is summarized for selected values of the PMI in Table 25–6.

F I G U R E   25–1

Forecasting Industrial Production Growth Based on the PMI

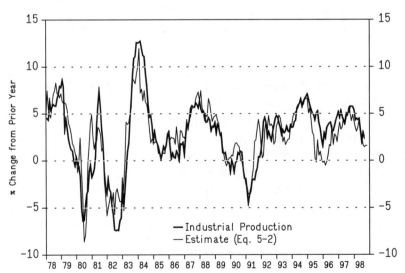

T A B L E   25-6

Real GDP Year-over-Year Growth Implications from the NAPM PMI

PMI	59.0	58.0	57.0	56.0	55.0	54.0	53.0	52.0	51.0	50.0	49.0	48.0	47.0	46.0	45.0	44.0	43.0	42.0	41.0	40.0
Real GDP Growth (%)	4.9	4.6	4.3	4.1	3.8	3.5	3.2	2.9	2.6	2.3	2.0	1.7	1.4	1.1	0.8	0.5	0.3	0.0	−0.3	−0.6

The key limitation of using the PMI to forecast some of the broader macroeconomic indicators is the short leadtime. Nonetheless, the PMI provides an excellent guide to what is currently happening.

Although the PMI offers limited insight into longer-term growth prospects, it is still possible to use it to forecast beyond the near term. However, as is true of every forecast, the longer the forecast horizon, the more uncertainty is associated with it. With this caveat in mind, the PMI could be used to project year-ahead growth using the following annual relationships:

$$IP = 0.519 \times (YEAREND[-1] - NAPM[-1]) + 2.38 \quad (25\text{--}6d)$$

$$R^2 = 0.659 \text{ (adjusted)} \qquad \text{Sample Period: 1978--1997, Annual}$$

where IP is annual industrial production growth, YEAREND is the December NAPM PMI index for the prior year, and NAPM is the annual average PMI, also for the prior year. The use of the December level of the NAPM PMI minus its annual average serves as a momentum indicator, that is, if the year ends higher than the annual average that suggests positive momentum will continue and vice versa. Similarly, an estimated equation also can be derived for real GDP, which is shown below.

$$GDP = 0.329 \times (YEAREND[-1] - NAPM[-1]) + 2.71 \quad (25\text{--}6e)$$

$$R^2 = 0.627 \text{ (adjusted)} \qquad \text{Sample Period: 1978--1997, Annual}$$

where GDP is annual real GDP growth. These two equations allow for a longer-term view.

The Price Diffusion Index—A Leading Indicator of Industrial Inflation

The NAPM business survey committee is asked each month to judgmentally average the prices that they paid for commodities and to indicate whether prices rose, fell, or stayed the same compared to the prior month. A number of studies have shown that the diffusion index compiled from this question is a leading indicator of turning points in the inflation cycle. For month-to-month forecasting, one study showed that the price diffusion index explained a relatively high 59% of the fluctuation in one-month-ahead estimates of changes in the Producer Price Index for intermediate materials and supplies (SOP code 2100).

The Unfolding of the Business Cycle Through the NAPM Business Survey

The NAPM survey provides a relatively complete picture of manufacturing activity. Hence, at different stages of the business cycle, different measures are worth dwelling upon. For example, coming out of a recession, one would expect that the new orders diffusion index would perk up first followed by production. Supplier leadtimes would tend to lengthen, suggesting that business activity is firming as well, although the greater adherence to JIT inventories and the closer partnership of suppliers and customers are likely to limit the cyclical information from this measure in the future. As the economy continues to improve, employment and inventories should notch higher. With a lag, prices will begin to reflect the strengthening economy. Similarly, the NAPM survey can be used for watching the unfolding of a slowdown or recession. New orders would be an early indicator of weakness in the economy, which tends to spread to supplier delivery times, production, and prices. Generally, the economic weakness will show up in the employment and inventories diffusion indexes last.

Short-Term Forecast Barometer

One very near-term barometer of future business conditions that can be calculated from the purchasing manager survey detail is the difference of the new orders and inventories indexes, which conceptually is similar to a ratio of a leading indicator to a lagging indicator. The Purchasing Management Association of Oregon (PMAO), for example, presents such a monthly index with their monthly survey, which has been dubbed their monthly *forecasting index*. Statistically, the correlation between the PMI and the difference between the national measures of new orders and inventories is highest with a one-month leadtime, which means that the same methodology used by PMAO can be applied to the national data. Based on this methodology, a simple one-month-ahead forecasting relationship can be derived as follows:

$$PMI = 0.832 \times PMI[-1] + 0.292 \times FCINDEX[-1] - 7.431 \quad (25\text{-}6f)$$

$$R^2 \text{ (adjusted)} = 0.864 \qquad \text{Sample Period: 1980–1998}$$

where FCINDEX is the forecast index, which is expressed in a similar fashion as the PMI and is calculated as: (New Orders − Inventories)/2 + 50.

CUSTOMIZE YOUR FORECAST APPLICATION USING NAPM SURVEY DATA

There are numerous ways to blend the NAPM survey data with industry forecasting. The simplest way would be to replace the GDP or industrial production variables in Equations 25–6a through 25–6e with the counterpart industry production series. Doing this customizes the data to the purchaser's industry. An example of that approach for the chemical industry industrial production (IP-SIC28) might look like the following for a year-ahead projection.

$$\text{IP-SIC28} = 0.526 \times (\text{YEAREND}[-1] - \text{NAPM}[-1]) + 2.44 \quad (25\text{–}7)$$

$$R^2 \text{ (adjusted)} = 0.541 \qquad \text{Sample Period: 1978–1997, Annual}$$

The forecasting performance of that model is shown in Figure 25–2.

FINAL THOUGHTS AND SUGGESTIONS ON FORECASTING

It is difficult for a survey article to address every possible forecasting application, and there will be times when you will face a new set of

F I G U R E   25–2

Forecasting Chemical Industry Production with the NAPM Survey

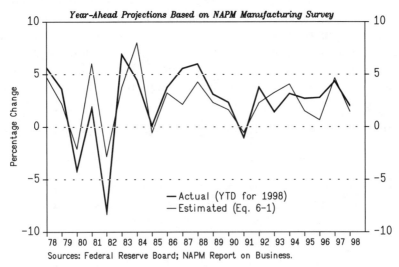

Sources: Federal Reserve Board; NAPM Report on Business.

circumstances. It will be useful then to ask: Has anyone else encountered this problem and how was it handled? A good place to look for help is the *Journal of Business Forecasting: Methods and Systems* (for information see: www.ibforecast.com/jbf/)—a forecasting journal for the practitioner—and the Journal's associated organization, the Institute of Business Forecasters.

So why must purchasers forecast? Because there is no alternative. But there are plenty of alternative forecasting techniques to choose from and a vast array of data to work with. This guide to forecasting has sketched out the why, the way, and the how of forecasting, but it has only scratched the surface.

ADDITIONAL READING

Ellis, D., and J. Nathan. *A Managerial Guide to Business Forecasting*. Graceway Publishing, Flushing, New York, 1990.

Makridakis, S., S. C. Wheelwright, and R. J. Hyndman. *Forecasting: Methods and Applications*, 3d ed., John Wiley & Sons, New York, 1998.

Niemira, M. P., and P. A. Klein. *Forecasting Financial and Economic Cycles*, John Wiley & Sons, New York, 1994.

Pindyck, R. S., and D. L. Rubinfeld. *Econometric Models and Economic Forecasts*, 4th ed., McGraw-Hill, New York, 1998.

Thomopoulos, N. T. *Applied Forecasting Methods*, Prentice-Hall, Englewood Cliffs, N.J., 1980.

Wisner, J. D. and L. L. Stanley, "Forecasting Practices in Purchasing," *International Journal of Purchasing and Materials Management*, Winter 1994, pp. 22–29.

Wright, G., and P. Goodwin, eds. *Forecasting with Judgment*, John Wiley & Sons, Chichester, U.K., 1998.

CHAPTER 26

Inventory Management

Editor
Mark S. Miller, C.P.M., CIRM
Manager Materials Control
Case Corporation

An average company's investment in inventory represents 25% to 40% of its invested capital. To effectively manage inventory is a challenge that requires balancing the conflicting objectives of inventory management. Some of these conflicting challenges in inventory management include:

1. *Never run out of anything.* Marketing encourages high inventories so that the product can be shipped to the customers quickly. "You can't sell from an empty wagon."[1]

2. *Never have too much on hand.* Finance wants low inventories to improve cash flows, lower taxes, and lower the requirement for borrowing. "Inventories are the graveyard of American business."[2]

3. *Buy more inventory to reduce prices.* Purchasing and manufacturing wants to buy or make large quantities to keep prices low. "Why don't we make plenty of them—we can always use them."[3]

The challenge of the inventory manager is to balance inventory costs, customer service requirements, and quantity price break advantages. Through the practice of sound inventory management techniques,

---

1. G. W. Plossl, and O. W. Wight, *Production and Inventory Control*, Prentice-Hall, Englewood Cliffs, New Jersey, 1967, p. 47.
2. Ibid.
3. Ibid.

a balance can be found to provide good customer service and make additional cash available. This section will review the basic concepts of inventory management and conclude with ten techniques that can be used to reduce your costs through inventory management.

OBSTACLES TO GOOD INVENTORY MANAGEMENT

There are many obstacles to good inventory management, including:

- Bad records—either bad past demands or poor inventory records
- Lead time inconsistencies
- Quality problems
- Ineffective supply chain management
- Marketing promotions without warning
- No control of surplus and obsolete inventory
- Volume buying/hedge price increases
- Large surprise orders, poor forecasting
- Overemphasis on cost controls
- Overemphasis on customer service
- Poor supplier deliveries

By recognizing these obstacles, the inventory manager can take actions to remove them.

FUNCTIONS OF INVENTORY

It is important to understand the different functions that inventory serves. There are four:[4]

1. *Anticipation inventory* is built up looking forward to a future event, such as high seasonable demand, a special promotion, vacation shutdowns, or disruptions in production caused by plant moves or labor problems.

2. *Fluctuation inventory:* Reserves or safety stocks carried to compensate for sales or production delays that cannot be accurately forecasted. Sales may average 50 units per week,

---

4. Ibid, p. 50.

but some weeks' sales reach twice that figure. Bottlenecks may result in manufacturing lead times that vary greatly. Fluctuation inventory is needed to ensure good customer service in an uncertain environment.

3. *Lot size inventory:* Set-up costs, hedge buying, and price quantity breaks often make it necessary to buy larger quantities than are actually needed. Items that are obtained in larger quantities are classed as lot size inventory.

4. *Transportation inventory:* The inventory that results from a supply chain with multiple locations. Transportation inventory is the goods that are in transit from one location to another.

CLASSES OF INVENTORY

Another way to segment inventory is to class it according to condition during processing. The classes of inventory are:

1. *Raw material/purchased parts inventory:* The inventory that is purchased outside and brought into the manufacturing process. This class includes steel, castings, purchased components, and other raw materials.

2. *Work in process inventory:* The partially processed inventory in the plant. This type includes components or subassemblies that are being worked on or are between operations in the factory.

3. *Finished inventory:* Finished product waiting for sale or distribution to the customer.

4. *MRO inventory:* Supporting materials needed for maintenance, operating, and supplies. These include items such as tools, office supplies, and shop towels. The control of MRO inventories is often neglected.

IMPACT ON THE BOTTOM LINE

It is important for the inventory manager to understand the financial impact that is involved in his function. The impact of inventory management is seen in both the balance sheet and the income statement.

If the funds to purchase the inventory are borrowed, the interest expense is shown on the firm's balance sheet. On the balance sheet, under the current assets section, inventories are usually broken down into raw materials, work in process, and finished goods.

B O X   26-1

INCOME STATEMENT

		Base		$10 less inventory
Sales		300		300
Cost of goods sold				
Material purchases	100		100	
Labor	50		50	
Overhead	40		40	
Change in inventory	0		(10)	
Total COGS		190		180
Gross profit from sales		110		120
Expenses		50		50
Net income		**$ 60**		**$ 70**

Inventory also appears in the company's income statement included in the cost of goods. If the investment in inventory is reduced, the net income is increased. Note in Box 26–1 that for every dollar the inventory is reduced, net income is also reduced by a dollar.

The benefits of reducing inventory must also be weighed against the impact on customer service. Poor customer service can result in lost sales, a bad reputation, and falling market share. The perfect solution is to reduce the investment in inventory and increase customer service. At the end of this chapter we will discuss ten techniques that can reduce inventory and maintain or increase customer service.

MARGINAL INVENTORY COSTS

Many costs can be associated with inventory. Inventory must be paid for, stored, received, counted, controlled, insured, and taxed, and can be stolen, spoiled, or damaged. Many textbooks have attempted to estimate the cost of carrying inventory. Most estimates for inventory carrying costs range from between 10% to 25% of the inventory value. See Table 26–1.[5]

---

5. G. J. Zenz, *Purchasing and the Management of Materials* 7th ed., John Wiley & Sons, New York, 1994, p. 55.

T A B L E   26–1

Inventory Carrying Costs

Category	% Ranges
Interest cost	6–15
Obsolescence/deterioration	2–8
Storage	0–5
Insurance	1–4
Taxes	1–3
Total carrying cost charges	10–35%

Care should be taken in defining inventory costs to include only variable costs. Costs for ordering and storage are often included in inventory carrying costs, but these items are often fixed and are not affected by a reduction of inventory.

COMMONLY USED PERFORMANCE MEASURES FOR INVENTORY MANAGERS

Inventory management is balancing the cost of inventory and the required customer service level. The inventory manager is thus measured by performance in regard to customer service and inventory cost.

Common Measures of Customer Service

- Percent of orders shipped on time
- Backorders—orders not shipped on time
- Percent of fill—measure of lines filled compared to lines entered

Common Measures of Inventory Performance

- Inventory turn rate—sales divided by inventory
- Day's supply of inventory—inventory divided by average daily demand
- Current ratio—current assets divided by current liabilities

* Cash flow—change in inventories and receivables
* Return on assets—profit divided by assets times 100

ORGANIZING THE INVENTORY FUNCTION

In many companies the purchasing and inventory functions work for different departments, use different systems, and are not integrated. The goals of the buyer and inventory analysts often conflict, as can be seen in Box 26–2.

A change in the organization that aligns the purchasing and inventory functions under one department can reduce many of these conflicts. This is basic to the materials management organization concept.

Another method that many companies are using is to establish a "buyer/planner." The advantage of the buyer/planner is that it removes the possibility of conflict, since one person is managing both. The disadvantage is the wide range of knowledge and extensive training needed to perform both functions.

FORCASTING FUTURE DEMAND

A basic tool of the inventory manager is forecasting what the demand will be. Forecasting involves looking at past demand, considering other pertinent information, and predicting what would happen in the future. All businesses need to forecast items such as sales, material prices, exchange rates, prices, and labor availability. Sales and marketing in most companies are responsible for the sales forecast, but the inventory

B O X   26–2

CONFLICTING GOALS

Buyer	Analyst
Cost reduction	Inventory turns
Price variance	Inventory investment
Sources of supply orientation	Internal operating orientation
Commodity-focused	Product-focused

manager is often responsible for driving the sales forecast down to the individual item level and forecasting the inventory needed.

Forecasting requires quantitative skills. These are mathematical and computer skills that take historical demand, recognize a pattern, and establish the forecast. Forecasting, however, also requires qualitative skills. These are the reasoning and judgment factors that adjust the mathematical forecasts.

Demand History

Forecasts are generated based on either independent or dependent demand. Dependent demand is driven down from the forecast of the final product. Items such as subassemblies, component parts, and raw materials are ordered based on dependent demand. Independent demand is for finished products that stand by themselves. Forecasts are only as good as the past demand they are based. Remember these issues in regard to the quality of the past demand:

1. *Beware one-time events.* One-time events such as special promotions, quality problems, and modification programs all can cause a surge in demand that will not repeat. Demand filters are useful tools for removing unusual circumstances or errors in the past demand from influencing the forecast.

2. *Orders versus shipment timing.* Demand is often recorded at order entry time versus the time the product is actually shipped. Customer orders are often adjusted or canceled after order entry. Caution must be taken when forecasts are based on order entry demand.

Five Principles of Forecasting

There are five basic principles of forecasting that the inventory manager must remember.[6]

1. *Forecasts are always wrong.* Forecasts are a look at the unknown future. Meteorologists learn quickly that forecasts are not

---

6. J. R. T. Arnold, *Introduction to Materials Management*, 2d ed., Prentice Hall, Upper Saddle River, New Jersey, 1996, pp. 192–193.

always correct. In forecasts of future sales the prediction will never be perfect. No matter how much money and time you spend on a forecasting system, it will never be perfect. The trick is to minimize the amount of forecast error.

2. *Measure and improve forecasts.* Measure your forecast accuracy and work to reduce the error rate. Several methods can be used to measure forecast error: tracking signals, filter trips, trend versus average, and demand versus forecast.

3. *Forecasts are more accurate for families.* It is easier to forecast families or groups of products than individual items.

4. *Forecasts are more accurate closer in.* The near future has more certainty than the distant future. We expect the next few weeks to be about the same as now, but our view of next year is cloudier. That is the advantage of short-lead-time versus long-lead-time parts.

5. *Low-volume/erratic parts are hardest.* The more demand history that is available and the higher the volume, the better the forecasts. Computer programs do a good job of forecasting high-volume parts. Low-volume/erratic parts are very difficult to forecast.

Quantitative Models

Many quantitative models are available to forecast based on past demand. Some common terms that are used in most quantitative models are shown in Box 26–3.

Several quantitative forecasting models can be used. Many programs compare many different models and select the best forecast. Some of these common demand patterns are shown in Figure 26–1.

Some common mathematical models that are used are:

1. Least squares/regression model
2. Box Jenkins
3. Winters model

For low-volume or erratic demand parts, a simple forecast method will give results that are as good as those from a sophisticated model. These simple models include:

1. Forecast equal to history
2. Forecast equal to average of past history

B O X   26–3

FORECAST MODEL TERMS

Level = average forecast per period

Trend = adjusts the level either up or down

Seasonal index = Recognizes a seasonal demand pattern

Standard deviation = Measure of forecast fluctuations

Mean absolute deviation = Measure of forecast error

Exponential smoothing = Forecast updating method that shortcuts
creating a whole new forecast

F I G U R E   26–1

Common Demand Patterns

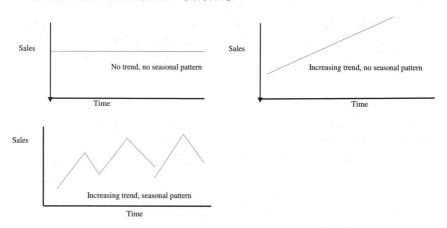

SAFETY STOCK

Safety stock is a quantity of inventory that is over and above expected demand. See Figure 26–2.

Safety stock is carried to protect against unexpected fluctuation in demand or supply. In a perfect world, safety stock inventory would not be needed, but forecasts, schedules, and suppliers are never perfect, so

FIGURE 26–2

Safety Stock Diagram

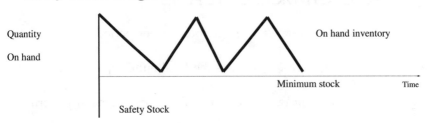

safety stock is carried to protect customer service. See Box 26–4 for a listing of the reasons safety stocks are held.

Many factors should be considered in determining what level of safety stock to carry.

1. *Forecast error.* The more forecast error, the higher the level of safety stock needed to ensure there will be no stock outs. Parts with lumpy demand patterns are the hardest to forecast and thus usually will have the most forecast error.

2. *Frequency of reorder.* The more often an item is reordered, the greater the safety stock needed. When you order once a year you have a great quantity of extra stock on hand, but if you order hourly you have no buffer stock to protect against errors.

BOX 26–4

REASONS FOR SAFETY STOCK

- Erratic demand
- Increase in customer service
- Long lead times
- Unpredictable suppliers
- Poor quality
- Forecasting error
- Poor recordkeeping

3. *Service level desired.* There is a direct relationship between service levels desired and the amount of safety stock needed (Figure 26–3).

4. *Lead time.* The longer the lead time, the more safety stock is needed. If the lead time is long, it takes longer to react if the forecast changes or the supplier has a problem.

SYSTEMS TO CONTROL INVENTORY

Hundreds of different systems and computer programs on the market can be used to control the flow of inventory. Discussed in this section will be the popular systems shown in Box 26–5. It seems clear from the list that inventory professionals love to use acronyms.

ABC Analysis

ABC analysis is a system that ranks part numbers by the extended cost times annual usage. ABC analysis is based on principles developed by an Italian economist, Vifredo Pareto, in 1896. Pareto developed the theory that 20% of a country's population does 80% of the work. ABC or Pareto analysis shows that a "vital few" account for the majority of the activity. The value of ABC for the inventory manager is that the inventory of the vital few constitutes the only items that need to be reviewed closely. Figure 26–4 summarizes how ABC analysis can be used in inventory management.

F I G U R E   26–3

Trade-off Between Service Level and Safety Stock

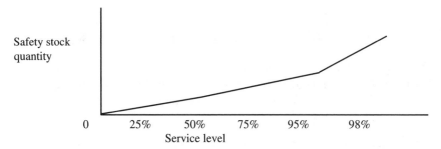

B O X   26-5

POPULAR INVENTORY MANAGEMENT SYSTEMS

- ◆ ABC
- ◆ EOQ (Economic order quantity)
- ◆ MRP (Materials resource planning)
- ◆ ERP (Enterprise resource planning)
- ◆ JIT (Just-in-time)
- ◆ Reorder point system
- ◆ DRP (Distribution resource planning)

F I G U R E   26-4

ABC Analysis

A items   B items   C items

70%
value
10%
Items

                              20% value   10% value
                              15% items   75% items

Review manually   Some attention   Trivial many
Order often   Computer controlled   Computer ordered
Count often   Order less often   Order large quantities
Low safety stock   Medium safety stock   Large safety stock
Continual expediting   Preventative expediting   No expediting

The Economic Order Quantity(EOQ) Formula

A popular approach for calculating the quantity to order in the EOQ formula. EOQ determines the least cost quantity, at which acquisition costs equal the cost of possession (Figure 26–5).[7]

---

7. R. G. Brown, *Advanced Service Parts Inventory Control*, Materials Management Systems, Norwich, Vermont, 1982, p. 128.

F I G U R E   26–5

Chart of EOQ Formula

The following is the EOQ formula:

$$Q = \sqrt{\frac{2(A \times S)}{I \times C}}$$

A = Annual usage in units
S = Ordering cost in dollars per order
I = Annual carrying cost percent
C = Cost per unit in dollars
Q = Order quantity in units

To use the EOQ formula, the inventory manager must input two key variables: variable ordering cost and the variable inventory carrying cost per period. The variable cost to place an order should be obtained from purchasing. Some factors to consider are displayed in Table 26–2.

It is important to recognize the limitations of the EOQ formula:

T A B L E   26–2

Variable Ordering Cost Example

Expenditure	Variable Cost per Order
Clerical/buyer labor	$10.00
Forms/stamps/envelopes	$ 2.50
Handling/inspection	$ 2.50
Accounts payable processing	$ 5.00
Total cost per order	$20.00

1. *Demand must be relatively constant and known.* If one-time demand or short shelf items are involved EOQ will not give a good recommendation.
2. *The item is purchased in lots or batches.* EOQ is not useful in a Just-in-Time or "pull"-type system.
3. *Order costs and carrying costs must be known.* You cannot use the EOQ formula if ordering or carrying costs are not known.
4. *Lead times are constant.* If lead times fluctuate, EOQ should not be used.

Materials Requirements Planning (MRP)

MRP is a computerized inventory management system that integrates the scheduling and controlling of materials. Joseph Orlicky, Oliver Wight, and George Plossl are credited with developing MRP. The basic elements of MRP are:

1. *Master production schedule (MPS).* The master production schedule is the plan of what should be built by a production plant. The MPS is developed from input from the sales forecast. MRP is only as good as the MPS.
2. *Inventory status.* Another key ingredient of MRP is an accurate record of the inventory. Inventory accuracy is essential to MRP.
3. *Bills of material.* A bill of material is a structure of all the raw materials, parts, subassemblies, and production operations that are involved in producing an end item. An accurate bill of material is necessary to explode the MPS into its components.
4. *Component lead time.* The lead time of every item in the bill of materials must be known. The component lead time is offset so the required parts are available when needed.

Figure 26–6 shows the essential elements of MRP.[8]

Manufacturing Resource Planning (MRP 2)

The shortcoming of MRP is that it is a closed-loop manufacturing system that does not get feedback from several key areas: capacity, shop floor

---

8. F. G. Moore and T. E. Hendrick, *Production/Operations Management*, 7th ed., Richard D. Irwin, Homewood, Illinois, 1997, p. 483.

F I G U R E   26–6

Essential Elements of MRP

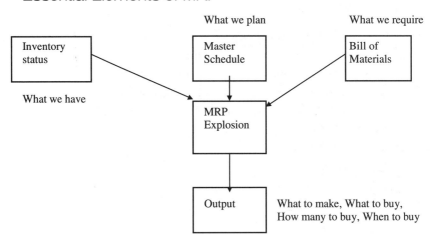

control, purchasing, or finance. MRP2 is the next generation of MRP. It gets feedback from these key areas and is designed to give "what if" capability.

Enterprise Resource Planning (ERP)

ERP is a complex software system that integrates a company's distribution network, marketing, finance, and field service in addition to MRP2 features. ERP moves MRP closer to a customer-based "pull" system from the "push" lot size system that it is usually portrayed as. ERP is an expensive and complex system. Care should be taken in selecting, justifying, planning, and implementing an ERP system.

Just-in-Time (JIT)

JIT is a philosophy that can assist in the control of inventory. Taiichii Ohno and Shiheo Shingo of Toyota are credited with developing JIT. JIT is a "pull" system that is launched by a signal further down the supply chain. Products are built and move to the assembly line at the precise time they are needed for production.

JIT is a manufacturing system that uses a trigger (Kanban) to signal when products are needed. *Kanban* is the Japanese word for *sign* and is the trigger used in JIT. Kanban uses standard lot sizes and returnable containers with a Kanban card attached. For JIT to work, the following characteristics are necessary:[9]

1. *Flexible manufacturing:* Short set-up times
2. *Close communications* throughout the supply chain between suppliers, manufacturing, and the customer
3. *Continuous improvement:* The Japanese word for improvement is *Kaizen* which strives to eliminate waste in production processes
4. *Perfect quality*
5. *Inventory accuracy*
6. *Accurate demand with no fluctuation*
7. *Few bill of materials levels*
8. *Flexible labor*
9. *Employee involvement, quality circles*
10. *Standard parts*

Reorder Point

A simple reorder point inventory management system is useful in many situations. In a reorder point system a quantity is determined at which inventory is replenished. An order quantity can also be established. Thus the reorder point and the order quantity become the minimum and maximum stocking levels. When the minimum level is reached, the inventory is replenished to the maximum level. Figure 26–7 shows a "saw-tooth" diagram that displays a reorder point system with safety stock.

There are advantages and disadvantages to the reorder point system.

Advantages	Disadvantages
Excessive stock is avoided	EOQ not considered
Back up stock is available	Tends to be automatic
Easy to understand	Quantity discounts not considered
Performance easy to check	Order quantity not defined

9. T. E. Vollmann, W. L. Berry, and D. C. Whybark, *Integrated Production and Inventory Management*, Business One Irwin, Homewood, Illinois, 1993, pp. 276–279.

F I G U R E   26-7

Reorder Point with Safety Stock

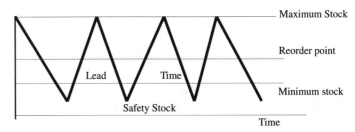

COMPARISON OF EOQ/REORDER POINT, MRP, JIT[10]

	EOQ/Order Point	**MRP**	**JIT**
Type of demand	independent or dependent	dependent	dependent
Demand used	historical	actual/MPS	actual
Time phased	no	yes	yes
Computer required	optional	yes	optional
Clerical effort	minimum	moderate	heavy
Low inventory	fair	good/ excellent	excellent

Distribution Resource Planning (DRP)

DRP is a system that forecasts and distributes the product to warehouses in the distribution network. DRP determines the needs of your lowest level in the network. Its benefits include:

1. The ability to plan resources needed to pick, pack, and receive product
2. Better response to changes in warehouse demand
3. Improved customer service at your local warehouse
4. Better planning of transportation needs and costs
5. Reduced inventory by better forecasting

10. D. W. Dobler, and D. N. Burt, *Purchasing and Supply Management*, 6th ed., McGraw-Hill, New York, 1996, p. 541.

F I G U R E 26–8

The Supply Chain

supplier → plant → warehouse → dealer → customer

COST REDUCTION USING INVENTORY MANAGEMENT

Good inventory management frees up cash that your company can use to invest in future opportunities. Purchasing plays a key role in reducing inventory costs. The following ten inventory management techniques can be used by purchasing to reduce costs.

One: Better Communications in the Supply Chain

The supply chain is the network by which products and services are moved to the customer (see Figure 26–8).

Many companies have found that improving communication links in the supply chain means that inventory can be reduced at the same time that customer service can be increased. Traditionally there is duplicate safety stock at each step of the supply chain. Improving communications with each partner in the supply chain means that duplicate safety stock can be eliminated.

Two: Negotiate Lower Supplier Lead Times

The buyer, working with suppliers to reduce lead times reduces inventory in two ways:

1. Forecasting improves because they are more accurate in the near future.
2. Less safety stock is needed as a result of lower lead times.

Lead times consist of as much as 95% idle time and 5% the actual production time needed to make the product.[11] Purchasing should ask

---

11. N. Kobert, *Managing Inventory for Cost Reduction*, Prentice Hall, Englewood Cliffs, New Jersey, 1992, p. 192.

the suppliers for a breakdown of the components of their quoted lead times. Work with the suppliers to reduce the idle time and reduce their lead time.

Expand the view of lead time beyond the supplier to the lead time in the entire supply chain. Look at the time required to receive, inspect, transport, and deliver products to reduce supply chain lead time.

Three: Standardize to Reduce Inventory

Many benefits are derived from buying standard products, including:

- *Lower prices:* Buying large quantities of standard products instead of small quantities of special products will lower prices.
- *Lower process costs:* The fewer part numbers, the lower the number of purchase orders, receipts, bin locations, and processing costs that will be necessary.
- *Fewer quality costs:* Fewer part numbers means fewer items to inspect and lower the chances of quality problems.
- *Lower inventory costs:* Fewer items with greater quantities makes forecasting more accurate. Less safety stock is required and thus inventory costs are lowered.

See Box 26–6 for a listing of the three steps that can be taken to standardize.

B O X   26–6

STEPS TO STANDARDIZE

1. *Use industry standards:*
   - ISO—International Standards Organization
   - National Bureau of Standards
   - SAE—Society of Automotive Engineers
   - ANSI—American National Standards Institute
2. *Classify parts:* So duplicates of similar parts can be identified
3. *Form a standardization committee:* To make sure new product are developed with standard parts

---

Four: Reduce Surplus and Obsolete Inventory

The easiest way to increase inventory turns without risking customer service is to purge from your inventory the unneeded surplus or obsolete inventory. The first challenge is to identify the surplus and obsolete inventory. The next step is to form a team to investigate ways to get rid of it. The following are methods the committee can consider for doing so:

+ Use it elsewhere within your firm.
+ Return it to the supplier.
+ Sell it to other companies.
+ Sell the inventory to employees.
+ Promote and sell at a discount to your customers.
+ Donate it to charity.
+ Scrap it.

Five: Improve Forecast Accuracy

By improving forecast accuracy, you an reduce the amount of inventory. The following are suggestions to improve forecast accuracy:

+ *Measure forecast accuracy.* You can't improve forecasts if you don't measure them. Measure and track how accurate your forecasts are.
+ *Use model switching programs.* For high-volume parts, pick a system that uses several forecasting models (least square versus Winters) and selects the forecast that gives the best result.
+ *Allow for seasonal forecasting.* Use a system that recognizes seasonal patterns.
+ *Variable safety stocks.* Pick a system that calculates a variable safety stock per forecast period versus a system that uses the same safety stock for each period. A variable safety stock allows a smaller safety stock in low-forecast periods and higher safety stocks in high-demand periods (see Figure 26–9).
+ *Forecast at the lowest level.* Forecast to the lowest level in the supply chain and pull the forecast up the chain. If each level in the chain forecasts independently, much inventory duplication

F I G U R E   26–9

Variable Safety Stock Graph

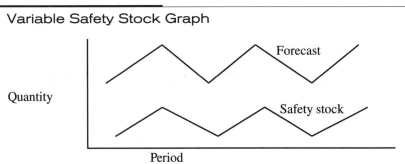

can exist. The closer the forecast is to the customer, the better it will be.

Six: Challenge Supplier Minimum Order Quantities (MOQ) and Price Quantity Breaks

Supplier minimum order quantities and price quantity breaks contribute to a buildup of inventory. MOQs and quantity price breaks are usually a result of supplier cost of setting up a job. Work with suppliers to reduce set-ups. If set-ups can't be reduced, negotiate with suppliers an annual commitment agreement in which the supplier can build in a large lot, but holds the stock and ships in smaller quantities.

Seven: Negotiate More Frequent Deliveries

The more often a part is delivered, the less average inventory there is (see Figure 26–10).

F I G U R E   26–10

More Frequent Deliveries

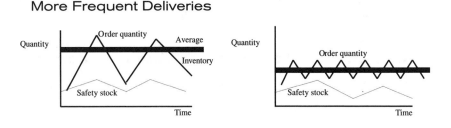

The average inventory is reduced by the ordering of smaller quantities more often.[12] The example below shows how increasing the average order frequency of the class A and B reduces the average inventory.

Class	Frequency	Average Inventory	New Frequency	New Average Inventory
A	Monthly	2 weeks	weekly	0.5 weeks
B	Quarterly	6 weeks	monthly	2 weeks
C	6 months	24 weeks	6 months	24 weeks
Average Inventory		3.7 weeks		1.9 weeks

Eight: Improve Supplier On-Time Delivery

Poor supplier delivery necessitates carrying large amounts of safety stock to compensate to achieve the desired customer service level. Purchasing has the opportunity to work to improve supplier delivery and reduce inventory. The buyer can take the following steps to improve on-time delivery:

- *Measure supplier performance:* Find a method to measure track and report supplier on-time performance. If it isn't measured, you can't improve it.
- *Communicate how it is measured:* Get together with suppliers and make sure they understand how you measure their delivery. Many variables need to be clarified, including: window used, ship date or receipt date, how calculated, and how short-lead-time orders are counted. Make sure your supplier understands how you measure on-time delivery.
- *Set Goals for Suppliers:* Meet with the suppliers and set goals for on-time delivery.
- *Recognize superior supplier performance:* Recognize suppliers who achieve their on-time delivery goals.

Nine: Let Suppliers Manage Your Inventories

Many popular programs are used in which suppliers manage and hold inventory for customers. Among these are:

---

12. Ibid, p. 145.

◆ *Vendor-managed inventory (VMI):* Supplier performs the inventory management function for the customer.[13]

◆ *Point of sale (POS):* The supplier reacts to customer demand and replenishes warehouses or retail outlets.

◆ *Consignment stocking:* Supplier retains ownership of the inventory, even when it is in your facility, until it is used.

◆ *Supplier stocking:* Supplier carries back-up stock and ships Just-in-Time.

All of these programs require purchasing to work with suppliers to help develop a plan to reduce inventory. The successful supplier-managed inventory program is not just a program to transfer inventory to the supplier. Rather, the goal should be to get the supplier's help in reducing duplicate and redundant inventory in the supply chain.

Ten: Recognize the Value of Inventory Reduction

Inventory reduction is critical to making your company financially successful. Recognize the importance of inventory reduction by:

◆ *Getting everyone involved:* Teach the importance of inventory reduction. Form a team that focuses on inventory reduction. Get suppliers, engineering, manufacturing, finance, and marketing involved in the team.

◆ *Crediting inventory reduction as a cost reduction:* Often, inventory reduction is not recognized as a legitimate cost reduction. Credit inventory reduction as a cost reduction and you will reinforce its importance to your organization.

ADDITIONAL   READING

Viale, J. D., *Inventory Management*, Crisp Publications, Menlo Park, California, 1996.

---

13. D. V. Landvater, *World Class Production and Inventory Management*, John Wiley & Sons, New York, 1997, p. 113.

CHAPTER 27

Legal Aspects of Purchasing

Editors
Constance Cushman, J.D., C.P.M.
Martin J. Carrara, J.D., C.P.M.

LAW AND THE PURCHASING PROFESSIONAL

Legal principles, statutes, and rules permeate the daily activities of purchasing professionals. They establish the purchaser's power to act and make purchases on behalf of the company. They form the framework for every purchase transaction and every contract with suppliers, determining whether or not an agreement is enforceable in court and what remedies are available if it is breached. In many ways they govern even routine administrative actions of purchasers, their suppliers, and their internal customers. Every professional purchaser needs a command of basic legal concepts and a knowledge of relevant statutes.

Sources of Law: Common Law and Statutory Law

The basic legal concepts that provide the framework for commercial transactions in this country come from *agency law* and *contract law* in the context of a market economy based on principles of free and open competition. Both agency law and contract law originated in the ancient English *common law*, which is a body of legal principles based on historical customs, reason, and justice that developed over time as courts made decisions on a case-by-case basis. The common law in this country continues to evolve through the ongoing development of case law. In deciding cases, judges look to prior judicial decisions for established precedents and make adaptations only to account for changing conditions and societal needs.

Over the years, in many jurisdictions, the principles of common law or case law have been codified in statutes. Statutory law consists of written rules of law enacted by legislatures at the federal, state, or local level, which may either formalize or override the rules of common law, or address issues that the common law never dealt with. Going beyond common law, lawmakers have developed many regulatory systems to achieve a variety of purposes, from protecting competition to safeguarding workers and preserving the environment. While judges cannot change statutory laws, they do interpret these laws when their application to the facts of a particular case is unclear.

The U.S. Constitution prescribes the areas of law that are within the jurisdiction of the federal government, leaving the balance of law within the purview of the individual states. Much of commercial law, including contract law, is left to the states; however, because the Constitution gives the federal government authority over interstate commerce and to ensure equal protection of the laws for all Americans, a myriad of federal statutes (including antitrust laws, health and safety laws, labor laws, and environmental laws) impose requirements and constraints on the purchasing professional.

In addition, the realities of global commerce bring to bear not just our own country's laws, but those of other countries and of international bodies. Treaties between sovereign states bind their participants to apply agreed-upon rules to commercial transactions across national boundaries.

All of these—common law, case law, statutes at all levels of government, court interpretations of statutes, and international treaties—weave together to create a legal system which makes contracts enforceable or not, sets out the mechanisms for enforcement, and dictates what purchasers can and must do as they contract with suppliers.

AGENCY LAW

In business, typically individuals act on behalf of companies for which they work, and their actions are governed by the principles of agency law. Agency law establishes the power and authority whereby a purchasing professional acts on behalf of the employer. It also establishes the duties and ethical responsibilities of the purchaser, so that in many ways agency law is the bedrock of purchasing professionalism.

Agency Law and the Authority of the Agent

The law of agency simply says that when one person acts as an *authorized* agent of another, the acts of the agent become those of the person for whom the agent is acting—usually called the "principal." All corporations, being invisible, intangible, and existing only in contemplation of the law, must act through agents. Therefore, most purchasing people and salespeople are agents of their companies. If agents act in the manner in which they have been authorized to act, the company is bound by their commitments. If agents act beyond the scope of their authority, the company is not bound and the agent may be personally liable for any commitments made.

Problems usually arise with the definition of *authorized*. There are three types of authority, each legally effective.

The first is known as *actual* or *express authority*. Some call this "job description" authority. It is what the company says the employee could do, either in express oral statements or in writing. It is often the job description, the statement of what the individual has been hired to do for the company. Purchasers have express purchasing authority; salespeople have sales and marketing authority; and engineers have design and engineering authority. When employees take action or make statements that lie outside their express authority, they do not bind the company.

Then there is *implied authority*, which is authority implied by the law to make it possible for the agent to carry out the express types of authority. For example, if a company expressly authorizes an individual to enter into contracts with suppliers on its behalf, necessarily the individual may seek quotes, enter into discussions, and reach agreement on terms and conditions. Otherwise it would not be possible to enter into contracts. All agents in the company have both express and implied authority.

Finally, the law also recognizes the concept of *"apparent authority,"* which is the authority the law cloaks a person with because of the way the principal acted toward third parties. Even if an employee does something outside of his or her authority, the employer, who is the principal, can retroactively approve or ratify that conduct. A pattern of ratifying unauthorized actions creates "apparent authority" because it gives outsiders a valid expectation that such conduct is allowed. If written company policy gives only the purchasing department express authority to enter into contracts with suppliers, but the accounts payable department routinely pays invoices for supplies or services ordered by personnel outside of purchasing, it has effectively given these nonpurchasing personnel apparent authority to make these purchases. This is the practice commonly known as "back-door procurement."

In a company with a highly centralized purchasing organization, lines of express or actual agency authority are usually well defined in written policies and are fairly well adhered to. In a decentralized setting, written policies are often less complete or current, and employees and their suppliers often rely to a greater extent on apparent authority. Reengineering the purchasing function, or introducing new technologies such as procurement cards or electronic contracting, often causes companies to reexamine and redefine their purchasing lines of authority, often rewriting their policies and procedures. When they do so, they are invoking the principles of agency law.

In summary, buyers must be concerned with two aspects of agency authority:

1. How can we run our company's procurement activities to ensure that purchases are made only by individuals with express purchasing authority, and so avoid, or at least reduce, "back-door procurement?" Up-to-date written policies spelling out which job titles carry purchasing authority are best because they establish actual or express authority. In addition to formal policies, there needs to be a program of internal education and communication so all company employees know, and are periodically reminded about, what they can and cannot commit to. Programs aimed at telling suppliers whom they can and cannot deal with are also useful but should be a second line of defense.

2. When we negotiate with suppliers, how can we make sure the agreements are enforceable? The best way is to be alert to situations where salespeople may be exceeding their authority. Where you think that may be the case, ask the salesperson to reduce to writing any express representation he or she makes and include that on your purchase order. In very important

cases, you might ask that the contract be signed by the vice-president for sales of the supplier.

Agency Law, the Duties of the Agent, and Purchasing Ethics

With the powers or authority a principal confers on his agent, go duties and responsibilities. Because the principal places his trust in the agent to act in his place, the agent has a fiduciary duty to act solely in the best interest of the principal. The word "fiduciary" comes from the Latin word for "trust" or "faith." The agent must "stand in the shoes of" the principal, acting on behalf of the principal, with only the principal's interests in mind. Personal or private interests of the agent must not influence the decision at all. And it is not just the principal's financial interests that the agent must serve. The agent must at all times act within the law and in good faith toward third parties when acting on behalf of its principal. The agent must do nothing that would cause the principal to be exposed to accusations of unfairness, sharp practice, or wrongdoing—certainly not criminal wrongdoing. These fiduciary obligations exist whether the agency relationship is one of express or apparent authority. They are the essence of purchasing ethics standards—and the standard of behavior is admittedly a very high one.

Because ethical requirements are rooted in agency law, agency law provides solutions for some seeming ethics dilemmas. When a possible problem of conflict of interest arises, so that a circumstance exists that might make a buyer seem to be less than completely independent of his suppliers (for example, that a buyer is related to one of the company's suppliers), the ethical problems can often be cured by disclosure to the company of the details, accompanied by the company's consent to the arrangement. By consenting to the arrangement, the principal expressly authorizes the agent to continue to represent him in the matter. The principal has declared the belief that its best interests are served by continuing the arrangement, and has expressly authorized the conduct.

Over the years, and generally in response to situations where people seriously violated their fiduciary and ethical responsibilities, legislatures have passed laws creating criminal and civil sanctions for certain unethical behavior. Similarly, because individuals often need more explicit guidance concerning their fiduciary and legal obligations, over the years companies and professional associations have tried to spell out these requirements, and they often incorporate the legal standards into their formal ethics policies. As a result, corporate ethics policies, the NAPM's *Principles and Standards of Purchasing Practice*, and state and local laws overlap with each other in many respects. Sometimes the differences can be confusing.

For example, the laws on bribery say essentially that if a purchaser takes *anything* of value that might sway the buying decision, however trivial it might be, it is a bribe. But since bribery is a crime, in order for the state or government to prosecute it there must be some criminal intent. Most ethics policies, however, assume that a payment of anything substantial to the buyer will affect the buyer's decisions and would be unethical, whether or not there is any bad intent, but they allow minor or trivial gifts or favors. The mid-1980s saw increased concern with bribery and ethics in the government contractor area. Therefore the rules are more stringent and the enforcement more rigorous if a buyer is purchasing items for use in connection with a government contract.

Similarly, the antitrust laws regulate the actions of both individuals and companies to preserve fair competition. Buying on the basis of reciprocity is often against company policy, and it could also be illegal under the antitrust laws if such a policy results in the lessening of competition or the restraint of trade. Favoring one supplier over another for reasons other than price, quality, and service may be unethical and may create serious legal concerns if there is a government contract in the picture. Agreeing with other buyers not to do business with a certain supplier can be unethical and is a boycott and restraint of trade under the antitrust laws.

What all this comes down to is still the same basic standard: an agent must act solely in the interest of his principal and of no other person, including himself; and the agent must do nothing that would cause the principal to violate the law or act unfairly toward its trading partners. Good common sense, alertness to situations that can "look bad," and full disclosure and discussion with management and legal counsel about questionable situations are very good ways to remain inside both legal and ethical boundaries.

CONTRACT LAW

Most of the day-to-day activities of purchasers involve the law of contracts. Every purchase is a contract between the buyer and the supplier, governed by the principles of contract law. Like agency law, contract law originated in the common law of England. It is a body of law that is left to the states, not the federal government, to address. Generally speaking, the law of the state where the contract is formed and per-formed will apply to that contract, but the growth of interstate and global commerce has meant that the law of contracts has been shaped to a very large degree by a process of developing uniform statutes that are de-signed to codify common law principles in a consistent manner from state to state within the United States and even across national bound-aries. The most notable example is the Uniform Commercial Code, or UCC. It is the product of extensive work, over several decades, by the National Conference of Commissioners on Uniform State Laws (NCCUSL) working together with the American Law Institute (ALI). By the late 1950s a version had been developed that eventually saw wide-spread adoption by the states.

Article 2 of the UCC applies to the sale of goods, which until fairly recent times was the dominant context of interstate trade. In making decisions in cases involving the sale of goods, courts look first to the written rules of the UCC as adopted in the state whose law applies to that contract, and then to case law when the UCC rules require inter-pretation or do not answer the specific question at hand. The UCC does not apply to contracts for services, which until recently tended to be much more local in nature. Courts look to case law to resolve disputes in this area, although they may apply UCC rules by analogy to contracts for services. Where a contract is for a sale of both goods and services, courts make a determination as to which—the goods or the services—is predominant. If the contract is predominantly for the sale of goods, then the UCC will be applied. The common law will be applied where services comprise the predominant part of the contract. This may appear confus-ing, and so it can be, but bear in mind that because the UCC codified common law principles of contracts, the essential concepts are fairly con-sistent for goods and services.

It is important to understand that, although the UCC is a set of rules governing commercial transactions, the UCC itself is *not* law. Each state chooses whether to make changes to the model text before enacting the statute that governs transactions in its jurisdiction, so there may be variations in the statutory provisions as well as in the judicial interpre-tations of the UCC from state to state. In a dispute between contracting parties from different states, in the absence of an express provision pro-viding which state's laws shall govern, the court hearing the dispute will make that determination based upon its own conflicts of laws rules.

The UCC is under constant review in an effort to keep it current with changing commercial realities. For example, for many years the drafters have been trying—unsuccessfully—to codify the law of services contracts in a similar manner to Article 2's provisions on the sale of goods. Much of what companies large and small contract for these days does not neatly fall into the old categories of "sale of goods" and "services." Instead we see software license agreements where the owner sells not the product but only the right to use the software in restricted ways, or systems development contracts mingling hardware, software, services and "expertise." Also, in the past decade, the explosion of information technology and electronic commerce has generated a great many commercial transactions for which the old rules are out of date—they just don't fit. The NCCUSL and the ALI have been collaborating for several years to draft legal rules to govern information technology and electronic commerce transactions. Originally intended to be a new section of the UCC—Proposed UCC Article 2B—the drafters decided to promulgate these rules for adoption by the states as a stand-alone Act known as the Uniform Computer Information Transactions Act (UCITA). Their discussions, current status and most recent drafts can be accessed on-line at www.2BGuide.com.

International Contract Law

In the context of international contracts, the laws of the different countries whose businesses are trading with each other come into play. Each country has its own contract laws, but to foster predictable and reliable business dealings a great many countries have joined together by treaty to create a common body of contract principles, the United Nations Convention on the International Sale of Goods (CISG), to govern international transactions. Just as states do with the Uniform Commercial Code in the United States, countries must voluntarily decide whether to be bound by the CISG. It applies to international sales contracts between parties in countries that are signatories (the United States is a signatory), unless the contracting parties specifically "opt out." This means that if you enter into a contract with a company located in a country that is also a signatory to the CISG, the CISG applies to your contract unless your written agreement expressly states that the CISG does not apply. A provision saying, for example, that the law of New York governs a particular international contract between two parties whose countries have signed the CISG will have the effect of making the CISG apply, since the treaty provisions signed by the United States are the controlling law in every state. While the CISG was modeled on and largely resembles the UCC, significant provisions vary. For this reason, it is important to be sure what law applies, and what it says, when you are contracting with businesses in other countries.

Other laws and treaties have bearing on international contracts. These include the various international trade agreements, the import and export laws (including quotas and customs duties) of the different countries, the banking, currency exchange, and credit laws, tax laws, and commercial bribery laws. A discussion of these provisions is beyond the scope of this chapter. Many excellent references exist, which are listed in the Appendix.

CONTRACTING WITH SUPPLIERS

The sections that follow discuss general principles of contract law, much of which are the same whether the UCC applies or not. Specific references to the UCC are made where the UCC provides clarification of or actual changes in common contract law principles. Remember: the specific details of the law may vary depending on how the UCC has been adapted when enacted by the legislature in your jurisdiction.

Definition of Contract

A purchase is a contract between the buyer and the supplier. A *contract* is a promise or set of promises that creates obligations that may be enforced in a court of law. Courts enforce a contract in two general ways: (1) specific performance or (2) money damages. When ordering specific performance, a court is directing the breaching party (the party that failed to fulfill its promise) to do what it promised to do, and practical considerations often make such an order difficult to enforce. Therefore, money damages are much more typical. Money damages are the payment of money by the breaching party to the nonbreaching party as compensation for the injuries suffered by that party as a result of the breach. They are intended to put the nonbreaching party in the same position it would have been in had the breaching party fulfilled its obligations under the contract. But before making any order, the court will examine whether there is a valid contract to enforce.

The Essentials of a Valid Contract

Four essentials must be present to create a valid and enforceable contract: (1) agreement, (2) made by competent parties, (3) concerning legal subject matter, and (4) supported by mutual consideration.

1. *Agreement.* In order to enter into an agreement, the parties must "mutually assent" to the same terms. This is often referred to as reaching a "meeting of the minds." Mutual assent is typically manifested through the process of *offer* and *acceptance*, in which one of the parties makes an offer to enter into a contract and the other party accepts that offer, thereby creating a contract (if the other essential elements of a valid contract are present). Offer and acceptance are discussed in greater detail below.

2. *Competent parties.* In order for a contract to be enforceable, it must have been made between parties with both the legal capacity and the authority to form a valid contract. Incompetency (i.e., lack of such legal capacity) arises where, at the time of entering into the contract, one of the parties: (1) is a minor, (2) suffers from some mental infirmity, or (3) is under the influence of drugs or alcohol. In many states, majority (i.e., the time when one is no longer a minor) is reached at age 18, but in some it is reached at age 21. Most contracts involving incompetents are *voidable* at the incompetent's option, which means that the incompetent has the choice of either enforcing the contract or acting as if no contract had ever been made. Both parties to a sales contract must also have the necessary authority to contract (see the previous discussion of *agency*). All competent individuals have the authority to contract for themselves. A corporation, however, must be represented by an agent who contracts for it. The purchasing officer is an agent of his or her organization and customarily possesses the authority to contract for it, although such authority may be— and typically is—restricted by the principal.

3. *Legal subject matter.* The subject matter of a contract must be lawful for the contract to be enforceable in a court of law. The subject matter cannot be immoral, against public policy, or outright illegal. Contracts that are illegal are void, which means that the contract is considered never to have existed at all. Commodities that require a license to procure, hold, or use, or services that require the service provider to be licensed to perform such services, cannot be the subject of an enforceable contract unless the parties have the requisite licenses.

4. *Mutual consideration.* To be enforceable, a contract must be supported by mutual consideration passing between the parties. Consideration is what distinguishes promises that will be enforced from those that will not. *Consideration* is defined as something of value that is bargained for. It is a performance or a return promise, and it may be in the form of a gain or a detriment. It may be a promise to do something that one is not obligated to do (such as a promise to purchase goods or services from a certain supplier), or it may be a promise not to do something that one has a legal right to do (such as an agreement not to compete). A promise to buy goods or services and a promise to sell goods or provide services are sufficient consideration to support each other. The common law was very strict in insisting that consideration be passed between the parties if there was to be an enforceable contract. Modern contract law and the UCC have relaxed these rules to some extent. Although courts will not enforce a contract that does not provide for mutual consideration, courts do not measure the equality of each party's consideration. That is left for the contracting parties to evaluate in their negotiations when forming the contract. Past consideration, which is a promise made by one party *after* the other party has already performed, may not be used to enforce a contract because it is not bargained for and does not induce the other party's act or promise.

If a valid contract exists, the court will next examine what the terms and conditions are in that contract, and the facts concerning what each party has done, to determine whether and how to enforce the contract.

Creating the "Agreement": The Contract Formation Process

A required choreography, a certain set of steps and exchanges, must take place in order to bring a contract into existence in the eyes of the law. Sometimes they take place in one conversation or exchange of documents. In other cases they take place over a long period of time with extended negotiations, and then are reflected in a master document that both parties sign to indicate that they are "in agreement." Either way, every contract will reflect the presence of these steps. Understanding them equips the purchasing professional to perform them smoothly and to exercise his or her rights in an effective and timely manner.

Offer

The first step to be taken in the formation of a contract is for one of the parties to make an offer. An *offer* is an unconditional promise by the maker, communicated to the other party, promising to enter into a contract under certain conditions if the other party accepts the offer. The party making the offer is called the *offeror*, and the person to whom the offer is directed is known as the *offeree*. Since an offer invites acceptance by the offeree, it gives the offeree the power to form a contract.

To be valid, an offer must be definite and precise and must be made with the intention of that party being ready and willing to enter into a contract with the other party. This intention of the offeror is determined under an objective standard, which means that a determination is made whether a "reasonable person" in the position of the offeree would have believed that the offeror intended to enter into a contract when the offer was made. Thus, an offeror cannot void the contract by claiming that the offer was made in jest. Offers generally must be made to a definite person and contain a definite quantity to be valid offers. If a purported offer is anything less than a complete indication of a willingness to enter into a contract with the offeree, it is only an "invitation to do business." Invitations to do business do not have the legal effect of an offer and cannot ripen into a contract—they do not invite acceptance. Thus, advertisements, catalogues, and price sheets issued by a supplier are generally not considered offers to sell, but merely invitations to purchasers to make an offer to buy. Similarly, a request for quotation issued by a buyer is not an offer to buy, but merely an invitation to do business.

A purchaser may be either an offeror or an offeree. A purchaser might be the offeror by saying or writing, "I will buy 12 gross of your #2 pencils at $14 per gross" to a pencil manufacturer. That would make the pencil manufacturer the offeree. Or the pencil manufacturer could first say to the purchaser, "I will sell you 12 gross of my #2 pencils at $14 per gross." The pencil manufacturer is then the offeror and the purchaser is the offeree. In negotiations between a buyer and a supplier, it is not uncommon for both to make several offers before an agreement is reached. In such instances both the buyer and the supplier act at times as offeror and as offeree.

Four possible fates may befall an offer. An offer may: (1) *lapse* due to the passage of time; (2) be *rejected* by the offeree; (3) be *revoked* by the offeror; or (4) be *accepted* by the offeree. The first three of these possibilities result in the termination of the offer. Only acceptance, the fourth possibility, will result in the formation of a contract.

Termination of Offer

Lapse

An offeror may specify a time limit within which the offer must be accepted, and if it is not accepted by the offeree within that time period, it will have expired. Thus, an offer that states, "this offer is good for 10 days" may not be accepted on the eleventh day or beyond. Offers are effective when they are received by the offeree. However, if the offer states it is good for a certain time period from a date specified in the offer, then the time period for acceptance begins to run from that date. If no time limit is specified, the offer will expire after a reasonable time period. UCC Section 1-204 provides that a "reasonable time" depends upon "the nature, purposes and circumstances of such action." An offer that is communicated verbally, such as in a telephone conversation between a supplier and a purchaser, is generally considered to have terminated at the conclusion of the conversation, unless the offeror states otherwise.

Rejection

An offer may be rejected at any time before acceptance by the offeree. Once an offer is rejected by an offeree, it is terminated and cannot be renewed by the offeree. It can only be renewed by the offeror. A verbal rejection can reject an offer. However, any rejection must be communicated to the offeror before it is effective. Thus, a rejection that is mailed to the offeror is not effective until the offeror receives it. A counter-offer by the offeree is treated as a rejection of the offer and the making of a new offer by the original offeree to the original offeror. Thus, an offeree who makes a counter-offer can no longer accept the original offer.

Revocation

Revocation of an offer is the act of the offeror. The common law allowed an offer to be revoked at any time before it was accepted, no matter how it read. Revocation was allowed because the offeror received no consideration from the offeree to keep open the offer. Therefore the offeror was free to revoke at will. For the sale of goods, the UCC provides an exception to this general rule that an offer is revocable any time prior to its acceptance. Section 2-205 provides that an offer made in a signed writing by a *merchant* that expressly states that it will be held open cannot be revoked. (A "merchant" is defined in Section 2-104 as one who deals in goods of the kind—thus suppliers and purchasers are merchants.) Such offers, referred to as "firm offers," remain open, and therefore subject to acceptance by the offeree, for the time period specified in the offer or, if no time is specified, for a reasonable time, but not to exceed three months in either event. A revocation must be received by the offeree before it is effective.

Acceptance of Offer

It is at the point of acceptance of an offer that a contract is formed between the parties. Acceptance must be made by the offeree to whom the offer was made, and it must be made in the manner prescribed in the offer. The offeror is deemed the "master" of his or her offer and may specify the required means for acceptance of the offer. Section 2-206 of the UCC states that an offer may be accepted in any reasonable manner unless otherwise stipulated in the offer; however, an attempt by an offeree to accept by any other means than that specified by the offeror will be invalid.

An offer may invite acceptance by: (1) the making of a return promise by the offeree or (2) performance by the offeree.

An offer that looks for a promise in return results in what is known as a bilateral contract. In a bilateral contract, there is an exchange of promises between the parties and each party is obligated to fulfill its promise to the other. For example, suppose party A (the offeror) says to party B (the offeree): "I will pay you $500 if you agree to paint my house this weekend." If B accepts this offer and promises to paint A's house this weekend, then that promise is the acceptance by B of A's offer and a bilateral contract is formed in which both A and B are obligated to keep their respective promises. If B does not paint A's house over the weekend, B will be in default of the contract and A will be entitled to recover from B damages A might have suffered as a result of B's breach.

Alternatively, an offer may invite acceptance in the form of a performance by the offeree, forming a unilateral contract in which only the offeror has made a promise. Returning to our example, now suppose that A said to B: "I will pay you $500 if you paint my house this weekend." Note that A did not ask B to promise to paint her house. At no time is B obligated to paint A's house, but if B does paint A's house this weekend, it is that performance that is the acceptance by B of A's offer.

A unilateral contract will be formed in which A is obligated to keep her promise to pay B the $500.

UCC Section 2-206(1)(b) provides that an order for prompt or current shipment is viewed as an offer that invites acceptance either by a prompt promise to ship or by prompt shipment. For illustration, let us return to the example where a purchaser makes an offer to a pencil manufacturer in the form of a purchase order to buy 12 gross of its #2 pencils at $14 per gross. If the pencil manufacturer accepts the purchaser's offer by promising to sell that quantity of pencils to the purchaser at that price, such as by returning an order acknowledgement, then a bilateral contract is formed and both parties are obligated to make good on their promises. If, however, the supplier responds to that offer by shipping the pencils, then it is this act of shipment that constitutes acceptance and creates the unilateral contract obligating the purchaser to keep its promise. Note again that with the unilateral contract in the latter example, the offeree/supplier was never obligated to ship, but once it did ship, that performance formed a unilateral contract that created an obligation on the part of the offeror/purchaser.

Under common law, an acceptance is valid only when it is a "mirror image" of the offer, which means that it unconditionally accepts all of the terms of the offer. A nonconforming acceptance is a counter-offer. A counter-offer is a *rejection* of the original offer and is itself a new offer, giving the other party (the original offeror) the power to accept the counter-offer. Modern business forms have made mirror images difficult to achieve. A purchaser's purchase order and a supplier's proposal to sell or its acceptance of an offer to buy will usually contain preprinted terms and conditions that are written in the party's favor. The chances of such forms being mirror images of each other are, of course, minimal. This has led to the problem known as the "battle of the forms," where the buyer and seller exchange preprinted forms in the hope of forming a contract on their own terms without attempting to reconcile the differences of their respective terms through negotiation.

UCC Section 2–207, titled "Additional Terms in Acceptance or Confirmation," attempted to eliminate the battle of the forms. The first part of the section says that an acceptance, if "definite and seasonable," can act as an acceptance even though it states terms additional to or different from those offered. The primary requirement here is that it must be very close to an acceptance, i.e., all the basic terms are in agreement and only minor differences exist between the forms.

The second subsection deals with the additional terms in the acceptance. Between merchants, such additional terms become part of the final contract unless (1) the offeror has insisted that acceptance can include only the terms of the offer, (2) they materially alter the contract, or (3) the offeror has previously objected to any additional terms or objects to them within a reasonable time after receiving the acceptance. No mention is made here of different terms because they are deemed to have been objected to because they are different.

The third subsection handles offers and acceptances that do not make a contract under the first subsection, but the contract is performed by the buyer and the seller. If a disagreement arises between the parties after the goods have been delivered, the papers exchanged by the parties (the purchase order and the supplier's proposal or sales acceptance) are laid side by side and compared. Those terms on which the parties agree are included in the final contract. Additional terms proposed in the acceptance will be included if they qualify as immaterial under subsection 2, discussed above. Those terms on which the parties disagree are discarded, and the appropriate UCC sections that deal with that subject matter will be substituted. That would constitute the contract put together by Section 2-207 that would be used to decide the disagreement between the parties. Although Section 2-207's purposes are laudable, it sometimes creates more problems than it solves. Section 2-207 is helpful in solving the battle of the forms but does not give us clear-cut guidelines as to when an acceptance is "definite and seasonable" and when it is not. If purchasers want to be sure regarding the terms that will govern a transaction, it is advisable that they negotiate the terms up front. Many purchasers accomplish this by negotiating a "master agreement" with suppliers with whom they will have ongoing purchases. The master agreement sets forth the terms and conditions that will govern subsequent orders, which incorporate the terms of the master by reference.

In the majority of jurisdictions an acceptance is effective when it is sent by the offeree, not when it is received by the offeror, since it is at this point in time that a meeting of the minds occurs and, thus, a contract has been formed. This affects revocation of an offer because an offeror *cannot* revoke an offer where the offeree has already sent an acceptance (because the offer has already been accepted at the time the acceptance was sent) even though the offeror has not yet received the acceptance. This is sometimes referred to as the "mailbox rule" because the acceptance is considered effective when it is dropped into the mailbox.

Oral Contracts and Writing Requirements

As said above, every contract will reflect the process of creating an agreement through the exchange of offer and acceptance, much of which typically takes place in conversations. The next question is, how much of this agreement must be in writing? Some types of oral contracts are enforceable, but certain types of contracts require written evidence of the existence of the contract in order for the contract to be enforced in a court of law. This requirement for a "writing" has its roots in an English statute known as the "Statute of Frauds," which was intended to prevent fraudulent claims. Under common law, contracts that cannot be completed within one year from the time that the parties entered into the contract must be evidenced by a writing to be enforced. Note that the rule speaks of contracts where completion within one year is *impossible*. Even if it is unlikely that a contract will be completed within one year, if it is possible that it may be, then it does not fall within this rule. UCC Section 2-201(1) provides that any contract for the sale of goods of $500 or more is not enforceable "unless there is some writing sufficient to indicate that a contract for sale has been made." It is not necessary for the parties to have entered into a formal written contract to satisfy these writing requirements. The writing does not have to be in any particular form, provided that it identifies the subject of the contract and indicates that a contract has been made, states with reasonable certainty the essential terms of the contract, and is signed by the party against whom enforcement is sought. The writing requirement may be satisfied by a memorandum, or by taking multiple documents together to evidence that a contract had been formed. The writing does not prove the contents of the contract—one must still prove that in court. It simply establishes the fact that a contract was made, and this opens the courtroom door to the party seeking enforcement of it. Section 2-201 also provides that partial payment or part performance establishes the fact that a contract was formed, and no additional writing is necessary in such a case.

Modification

Once a contract has been created, any change to the substance of the agreement, the terms and conditions of the contract, is in effect a new contract. Common law rules require consideration to pass between the parties in order for an agreement to modify an existing contract to be enforceable. For the sale of goods, UCC Section 2-209 states that the parties may modify an existing contract with no consideration. However, any modification of a contract involving the sale of goods where the contract as modified is valued at $500 or more must be in writing to satisfy the statute of frauds. A modification may also require a writing if the original contract has a provision that requires changes to be in writing in order to be effective.

Contract Terms and Conditions

So far, we have discussed the choreography, or what we might call the mechanics, the nuts and bolts, of how a valid contract is put together so as to be enforceable in a court of law. All of that is merely the preliminaries, for of course the content of the agreement will establish just what the parties expect to give and receive by way of the contract. The content is reflected in the contract business terms and conditions. Some of these are standard terms that purchasers will want to include in every contract. Lawyers refer to these as "boilerplate" because they can be recycled from contract to contract almost as though the contract were being manufactured on an assembly line. Even boilerplate should be reviewed to be sure it is appropriate in a particular contract. Other terms and conditions might be described as "special" because they are drafted with the particular contract needs in mind. Still other terms, such as warranties, become included in the agreement by operation of law, although the parties can modify them to a certain extent.

Warranties

A warranty is an assurance of the existence of some fact or a promise that some fact will exist in the future that is given by one contracting party to the other. When one party makes a warranty, the other party may rely upon that warranty and may recover damages—i.e., hold the warrantor liable—should the fact prove to be untrue. In a way, warranties are terms that the law puts into the contract in the interest of fairness. There are two general types of warranties: express and implied.

Express Warranties

Under common law, statements of fact made by the supplier create express warranties. These statements must relate to facts and cannot merely be opinions. UCC Section 2-313(1) provides that express warranties are created by the supplier by: (a) a promise or affirmation of fact, (b) a description of the goods, or (c) a sample or model, which is part of the basis of the bargain with the purchaser. The warranty in the latter two cases is that all the goods will conform to the description, sample, or model. Section 2-313(2) states that the supplier does not need to use the words "warrant" or "guarantee" to make an express warranty, but the statements made must pertain to facts and cannot be merely opinions.

Implied Warranties

Implied warranties are created by operation of law, rather than by any statements made by a party. For services, the common law in many states provides an implied warranty that the work will be performed in a "good and workmanlike" manner. For the sale of goods, the UCC provides the following implied warranties:

+ *Implied warranty of merchantability* (Section 2-314). This is an assurance that the goods will be of average quality and will be fit for ordinary purposes for which they are generally used.

+ *Implied warranty of fitness for a particular purpose* (Section 2-315). This is an assurance that the goods are suitable for the particular use intended by the purchaser, which arises only where a supplier knows of a purchaser's intended use for the goods and the purchaser relies upon the supplier's recommendation in selecting the goods.

The UCC also provides three additional warranties, although it does not term them "implied warranties." These warranties, nevertheless, are created by operation of law and are also often referred to as implied warranties or as "constructive warranties." They are:

+ *Warranty of title* (UCC 2-312(1)(a)). This is an assurance that the supplier has legal title to the goods and has the authority to transfer such title to the purchaser.

+ *Warranty of freedom from encumbrances* (UCC 2-312(1)(b)). This is an assurance by the supplier that there are no liens on or security interests in the goods.

+ *Warranty against infringement* (UCC 2-312(3)). This is an assurance that the goods do not infringe upon the patent or other intellectual property rights of any third party.

Disclaimer of Warranties

Warranties may generally be disclaimed (i.e., negated) by "clear and conspicuous" language in an agreement. UCC Section 2-316(1) denies effect to any disclaimer of an express warranty that is inconsistent with express warranty language. This means that if you have both words or conduct of warranty and words or conduct of disclaimer that are inconsistent, the language of warranty will override the disclaimer. Implied warranties may also be excluded by use of clear and conspicuous language. However, Subsection 2-316(3)(a) requires specific use of the words "merchantability," "as is," or "with all faults" in order to effectively disclaim the implied warranty of merchantability. Subsection 2-316(3)(b) points out that there is no implied warranty with respect to an obvious defect if the buyer has had the opportunity to examine the goods and fails to notice an the defect. However, that rule does not apply to hidden defects. Additionally, Subsection 2-316(3)(c) provides that implied warranties may be excluded or modified by course of performance, course of dealing, or usage of trade. Course of performance refers to the conduct of the parties under a particular contract, course of dealing refers to a sequence of prior conduct by the parties, and usage of trade is the practice widely accepted in a particular trade or industry.

UCC "Gap Fillers"

The common law of contracts is built on the principle of "freedom of contract," which provides that the parties to a contract are generally free to choose the contents of their contract. The UCC generally adopts this principle of freedom of contract, providing in Section 1-102 that the "effect of provisions of this Act may be varied by agreement. . . ." However, the UCC will supply certain provisions in the event that they are not specifically addressed by the parties. In the absence of express terms in the contract, these default rules of the UCC, sometimes referred to as "gap fillers," will automatically apply to the agreement. The following paragraphs discuss the UCC treatment given to quantity, delivery, price, and payment terms.

Quantity

Every contract for the sale of goods must contain provision for a fixed or determinable quantity of the item. The UCC will *not* insert a quantity term if the parties have not themselves agreed to the quantity. In effect, if the parties have not agreed to a quantity term, they really have not had a "meeting of the minds" and thus do not have a valid contract. It is noteworthy to remember from the earlier discussion on offers that, to be valid, offers generally must be specific as to quantity. The common law insisted that the quantity in a contract be fixed, but subsequent interpretations and UCC Section 2-306 countenance what are known as "requirements contracts." A requirements contract enables the purchaser to contract for the quantity of the item that the purchaser will require for a specific period or for a specific project without having to specify the precise quantity. The supplier is given prior usages or reasonable estimates of the total need to serve as a guideline in making the selling price offer. The purchaser is obligated to purchase all or some agreed percentage of her or his requirements of that item from that supplier, and the supplier is obligated to sell all or the agreed percentage of the purchaser's needs to the purchaser.

Delivery

Delivery terms in a contract specify: (1) the time and place when the supplier has completed its performance under the contract; (2) when risk of loss passes from the supplier to the purchaser; and (3) which party bears the expense of the transportation. If the parties do not specify the place of delivery in their agreement, UCC Section 2-308 provides that "the place for delivery of the goods is the seller's place of business" unless the parties know that the goods are located in some other place, in which case that other place is the place for delivery. Therefore, the default rule is that the purchaser is obligated to pick up the goods at the supplier's location or at some other location where they may be located.

However, it is most common for the parties to intend that the supplier will ship the goods to the purchaser's location. The UCC provides for the use of the F.O.B. ("free on board") trade terms as a simple method for specifying the place of delivery. Section 2-319 defines two F.O.B. terms: (1) F.O.B. place of shipment and (2) F.O.B. place of destination. When F.O.B. place of shipment is specified, the supplier's performance is completed when it delivers the goods into the hands of a common carrier for shipment to the purchaser's location, and the purchaser is responsible for the transportation costs. Additionally, under Section 2-509(1)(a), the risk of loss passes to the purchaser when the goods are delivered to the carrier. F.O.B. place of destination means that the supplier's performance is not completed until the goods are delivered to the purchaser's location. It requires the supplier to bear the cost for transportation, and, under Section 2-509(1)(b), risk of loss remains with the supplier until the goods arrive at the location specified by the purchaser.

In addition to these F.O.B. terms, purchasers involved in sourcing from foreign suppliers should be familiar with the "Incoterms" promulgated by the International Chamber of Commerce. They provide trade terms for international shipments.

Price

It may surprise some purchasers to know that they can form a valid contract even if the parties do not provide for the price. Price is, of course, an important component of any purchase contract, but some purchases are made without a price showing on the contract or purchase order, and price need not be included to make the contract valid. UCC Section 2-305(1) provides that, absent a specified price, the price shall be "a reasonable price at the time for delivery."

Price adjustment clauses are often used in longer-term contracts to provide for future variations in price due to changes in the supplier's costs for raw material. In this manner, suppliers do not have to cover in the original price quotation all future potential cost changes that may or may not occur in their raw material costs during the contract term. An adjustment clause permits both the buyer and the seller to keep the price of the contract at a current *level*. An adjustment clause, drawn properly and fairly for both parties, can provide for price increases ("escalations") or decreases ("de-escalations") as the market may dictate. The clause should also specify the base index that will best reflect price changes in the commodities involved in the supplier's product. And, finally, the adjustment should be applied to a predetermined percentage of the total price, such percentage reflecting the ratio of the amount of the critical raw material included in the supplier's product to the *total cost* of the product.

Payment

Section 2-310(1) provides that unless otherwise agreed, "payment is due at the time and place at which the buyer is to receive the goods." Note that the purchaser's payment obligation is tied to its *receipt* of the goods, even if the agreement provides for delivery F.O.B. place of shipment. This means that although the supplier will have completed its performance obligation when it delivered the goods into the hands of the common carrier, the purchaser is not obligated to perform (i.e., pay for the goods) until a later time. Section 2-511 further provides that tender of payment by the purchaser is a condition to the supplier's duty to tender and complete delivery. Section 2-507 makes tender of delivery of the goods a condition to the purchaser's duty to pay for them. These two sections operate to render the duty to deliver and the duty to pay concurrent conditions. The end result of all of this is that the default payment rule under the UCC is cash on delivery. Purchasers typically negotiate for credit terms at the time of contracting with the supplier. This includes a credit period after receipt of the goods and possibly a cash discount for prompt payment of the invoice within a specified number of days after the material has been received. The credit period and the cash discount period come only to those who ask for and get them from the supplier.

PERFORMANCE OF THE CONTRACT

Performance of the contract is the fulfillment of the obligations undertaken by the parties when they entered into the contract. The failure to perform any contractual obligation, without legal excuse, may result in a *breach* of contract, giving rise to remedies for the other (nonbreaching) party.

In a contract for services under common law, the obligation of the seller is to perform in the manner and time frame agreed and that of the buyer is to accept performance and to pay in accordance with the contract. A breach arises where there is a partial or total failure to perform or where there is some defect with the performance. If the breaching party has "substantially" performed, the breach is deemed immaterial. An immaterial breach is merely a "partial" breach, which may entitle the nonbreaching party to money damages but does not discharge that party from its obligations. The determination of whether a party has substantially performed is dependent upon the facts of the particular situation, and in making this determination, courts will generally consider the following factors:

+ The hardship on the breaching party if a total breach is declared

+ The extent to which the breach deprives the nonbreaching party of the expected benefit of the contract

+ The amount of benefit that has been bestowed on the nonbreaching party

♦ Whether the breach was inadvertent or intentional

♦ The likelihood that the party will be able and willing to cure the breach

For the sale of goods, UCC Section 2-301 states the general performance obligations of the parties as follows: "The obligation of the seller is to transfer and deliver and that of the buyer is to accept and pay in accordance with the contract." The supplier is obligated to make timely delivery of conforming goods, and the purchaser is obligated to receive the goods, inspect them for compliance with the contract description, formally accept them, and pay for the goods. These obligations will be discussed more fully below.

Delivery of the Goods

Under UCC Section 2-503(1), the supplier is required to "put and hold conforming goods at the buyer's disposition." *Conforming* means that the goods are "in accordance with the obligations under the contract" (UCC Section 2-106(2)). If the contract is a "place of shipment"-type contract, then the supplier tenders delivery by placing the goods in the hands of a common carrier (UCC Section 2-504). In a "place of delivery"-type contract, the supplier tenders delivery when it makes the goods available to the purchaser at the particular destination point (UCC Section 2-503(3)). Section 2-503(1) also requires the purchaser to "furnish facilities reasonably suited to the receipt of the goods."

Under UCC Section 2-513, the purchaser has the right to inspect the goods before accepting or paying for them. The purchaser must check the exterior of the containers or cartons after the delivery of the goods to make certain that no apparent damage was done to the goods during the delivery process. The carrier will want a receipt signed by the receiver indicating that no apparent damage has occurred. If there has been apparent damage, that fact must be noted on the carrier's receipt, and the carrier's representative must be given the opportunity to inspect the goods and the packaging material. The party to the contract that had the risk of loss for safe transit must file the appropriate claim with the carrier.

Acceptance of the Goods

Acceptance must be distinguished from receipt of the goods. *Acceptance* is a legal act indicating that the purchaser acknowledges that the delivered goods conform to the contract. To make certain of this fact, the goods must be inspected for quality. Note that this inspection is in addition to normal receiving inspection for damage during shipment. The purchaser has the right to inspect the goods for compliance with the contract description before accepting the goods. However, the purchaser under a C.O.D. shipment or a financing shipment may have to pay for the goods before inspection can be accomplished. Thus, payment may occur before acceptance because purchaser is not required to "accept" the goods until they have been inspected and meet the purchaser's approval. The purchaser accepts the goods if: (1) the purchaser signifies to the seller that the goods are accepted, (2) the purchaser fails to give the seller notice of rejection within a reasonable time after receipt of the goods, or (3) the purchaser uses the goods or otherwise acts in a way that is inconsistent with the seller's ownership (UCC Section 2-606).

Payment

If the goods or services have been furnished in accordance with the contract requirements, the buyer is obliged to pay, in the manner and time frame the contract specifies.

Failures of Performance

If the party that is obligated to furnish goods or services does not do so in accordance with the contract terms, and without a valid reason, it has breached its contract. But this does not automatically mean that the other party must go to court to seek enforcement of the contract. Rather, several avenues are available in the ordinary course of business and are recognized under the law of contracts.

Rejection of the Goods

If inspection discloses any variance from the contract description, the purchaser may reject the goods under UCC Section 2-601 by accepting the whole, rejecting the whole, or accepting any commercial units. The UCC has adopted the "perfect tender" rule, which means that the purchaser may reject the goods for any reason, however slight. The supplier must be notified of the rejection and given the reasons that the delivery is being rejected. A purchaser who fails to particularize any defect loses the right to claim damages for that defect. After notice of rejection is received, if the time for performance by the supplier has not yet expired, the supplier is given an opportunity to "cure" such defects by making another conforming delivery or curing the defects in the original goods within the contract time (UCC Section 2-508). Upon rejection of goods, the purchaser is under a duty to give reasonable care to the goods, subject to the supplier's disposition of them.

Revocation of Acceptance

What happens if the purchaser discovers a defect after acceptance of the goods? If the defect "substantially impairs the value of the goods" to the purchaser, UCC Section 2-608 allows the purchaser to revoke the acceptance and reject the goods under either of the following conditions:

1. The purchaser was aware of the defect when the goods were accepted, but the purchaser accepted on the reasonable assumption that the defect would be cured.

2. The purchaser was not aware of the defect at the time of acceptance due to the difficulty of discovery of the defect or due to the supplier's assurances.

This section provides that the purchaser must notify the supplier within a reasonable time from when the defect was discovered or should have been discovered by the purchaser. Failure to give this notice will cause the purchaser to be barred from any remedy.

DISPUTE RESOLUTION

Once goods have been rejected, or a prior acceptance has been revoked, for a valid reason, the buyer is no longer under any obligation to make payment. Sometimes this is the end of the matter, because the other party realizes its error and does not claim payment. But if payment has been made and not returned, or if other adverse consequences have resulted from the breach, or if the supplier disagrees that the goods or services were defective or claims that it was not given the proper notices or opportunity to cure the defect, the resulting dispute will likely end up in court.

In the same fashion, for services contracts, when all goes well the contract document is simply the roadmap to performance, clarifying the expectations and guiding the behavior of its parties. But circumstances change and documents are imperfect, either because something is left out or because the language can be read in more than one way. Often the parties to a contract find themselves in disagreement about what performance is required, and they resolve their disagreements either by clarifying the contract terms terms voluntarily themselves or by turning for interpretation to the courts or to some form of alternative dispute resolution. In other cases, there may be no real difference of understanding, but circumstances make performance more costly or more difficult for one of the parties and that party chooses to walk away from part or all of the agreement. Left in the lurch, the aggrieved party can either accept, renegotiate, or sue—taking its adversary to court.

At this point, after reviewing the merits of the case, the court will consider what remedies to order. But any resort to court must be made in a timely manner.

Statute of Limitations

A Statute of Limitations is an act of legislature that fixes the time period in which a party must seek to enforce its rights. After this time has elapsed, the aggrieved party is barred from bringing any legal claim against the other party. For the sale of goods, UCC Section 2-725 sets the Statute of Limitations at four years, which means that a legal action for breach of a contract for the sale of goods must be brought within four years from the time that the breach occurs. In many states, the Statute of Limitations for breach of a contract for services is six years.

Remedies

The basic remedy for breach of a contract is "compensatory damages," which are damages paid to the injured (nonbreaching) party in order to put that party in the position it would have been in if the contract had not been breached. This is sometimes referred to as giving that party the "benefit of the bargain." Damages are awarded to compensate for actual injuries resulting from the breach. Compensatory damages include "general damages," which are money damages for the diminution in value caused by the breach, i.e., the difference in value between what was received and what should have been received had the contract not been breached. They also include "special damages," which are damages for injuries caused indirectly by the breach, provided that they were reasonably foreseeable at the time that the contract was entered.

Breach by the Purchaser

When the supplier has performed and the purchaser fails to make payment when it is due, the supplier has the right to sue for the contract price under the common law and under UCC Section 2-709. For the sale of goods, the supplier may also recover "incidental damages," which are the seller's costs associated with transportation, care, and custody of the goods, etc. (UCC Section 2-710).

Breach by the Supplier of a Contract for Services

Where the failure to perform by the supplier is trivial and innocent and the cost of correcting the work is unjustified, the purchaser may recover compensatory damages equivalent to the diminution in value between the performance as delivered and the performance actually contracted for. For example, if a contractor installed a different manufacturer's pipe than was called for in the contract, but it was of the same grade as the pipe specified, the contractor will have substantially performed because the deviation, while intentional, was trivial. The measure of damages will be the diminution in value, if any. It simply would not make any sense to require the contractor to tear apart the structure, rip out the installed pipe, and install the specified brand of pipe.

Where the breach by the supplier is intentional and the defect is so great that the supplier has not substantially performed, the remedy for the breach may be the cost for completing the performance or the cost for correcting the performance.

Breach by the Supplier in a Contract for the Sale of Goods: Delivery of Nonconforming Goods

When the purchaser has accepted nonconforming goods shipped by the supplier, the UCC provides the following remedies:

- *General (direct) damages* (UCC 2-714(2)). The difference between the value of the goods as delivered and their value had they been delivered as provided in the contract.
- *Incidental (special) damages* (UCC 2-714(2). The costs associated with receipt, inspection, storage, and transportation of the goods.
- *Consequential (special) damages* (UCC 2-715). These include any losses realized as a result of the breach that the supplier had reason to know about at the time of contracting, including economic losses such as lost profits, and any damage to property or personal injury resulting from the breach.

Breach by the Supplier in a Contract for the Sale of Goods: Failure to Deliver

UCC Sections 2-711 and 2-712 provide that when a supplier fails to make delivery, the purchaser may "cover," which means the purchaser may buy the goods from another supplier and recover the difference between the price paid to that supplier and the contract price with the original supplier. Alternatively, the purchaser may recover damages measured by the difference between market price and contract price (without having actually to purchase replacement goods). In either case, the purchaser may also recover incidental and consequential damages.

Alternative Dispute Resolution

Court proceedings are expensive, time-consuming, and adversarial. They erode or destroy the communication and cooperation needed for successful buyer–supplier relationships. When disputes arise, by far the best practical course for those wishing to continue doing business together is for the parties to deal with each other directly and to clarify or update their contract. When this is possible, it keeps costs down and helps ensure successful completion of contract performance. Contract provisions can help support informal resolution of disputes by setting up effective mechanisms for contract administration.

Sometimes it is not possible for parties to resolve their disputes themselves. Each is wedded to its own position and has a hard time seeing the merits of the other side. To help keep costs down and speed up decision-making, parties now often seek ways to make their contracts enforceable without resorting to litigation in the courts. They do this by including in their contract documents specific provisions spelling out alternative dispute resolution (ADR) mechanisms that they agree will bind the parties should a dispute arise. Such ADR mechanisms commonly include mediation, arbitration, and mini-trial.

Mediation is a mechanism to bring in a neutral, trusted third party who helps clarify the issues and facilitates a voluntary resolution of the dispute. Mediators do not make binding decisions, and if mediation is not successful, the parties may go on to court or arbitration, whichever the contract provides.

Arbitration is more formal and typically results in a binding decision. The contract document will spell out procedures for selecting an individual or panel of arbitrators and for presenting the controversy to the arbitrator for a ruling. The arbitrator's ruling ordinarily cannot be appealed to court, unless the agreed procedures were not followed. For this reason it is very important to spell out in the contract what rules will govern the arbitrator and what, if any, law the arbitrator must follow in making his decision.

Either a mediator or an arbitrator may suggest a mini-trial, or a formal presentation of evidence and arguments by both sides in the dispute. If the setting is a mediation, this formal presentation sometimes helps the parties see the merits of the other side and fosters a settlement of the dispute. In an arbitration, it provides a structure for the panel or decision-maker to learn all the facts and hear the positions of the parties before making a decision.

The contract language adopted by the parties at the outset can help them deal with disputes in other ways as well. When courts or alternative adjudicators consider contract disputes, they must determine a number of threshhold issues before they can turn to the particular facts involving performance or breach of the contract. These issues include: Is this the correct forum for resolving the dispute? What law applies to the contract and performance questions under dispute? Are the correct parties before the court? Have all the formalities required to invoke the court's jurisdiction been complied with? and Has the dispute been brought to court in a timely manner? In their contract documents, parties can and should address each of these threshold matters. Thus, for example, the parties can agree that disputes will be presented to the courts in the home state of one of the parties and that that state's law will be used to decide the dispute. Or, in an international contract, they could agree that the CISG will govern and that an arbitrator will hear the dispute following the procedures established by an organization such as the American Arbitration Association (AAA). If the parties do not clearly address these issues in their contract documents, whatever court is presented with the case must invoke legal principles to decide these questions first. This process will increase the time and cost of litigation, and, in addition, the decision may not be what any of the parties would have wished.

Once it has resolved the threshold questions, the adjudicator can consider the merits of the case by reviewing the contract text, the facts concerning contract formation and performance, and the applicable law. The parties will present factual evidence by way of witness testimony, documents, and perhaps other physical evidence, such as samples of the items purchased. The records kept by the purchasing department will play a critical role in establishing the facts at trial, including intent of the parties where the contract language is ambiguous and the circumstances of performance or breach. The factfinder will draw inferences not just from what the records contain, but from what they have left out. Incomplete or damaged records will lead to adverse findings against the party that should have kept the records.

Following the principles described elsewhere in this chapter, the adjudicator will decide whether there was a valid contract; if so, what were its terms and what exactly do they mean; whether on the facts presented there has been a breach, and if so, what the remedy should be—to order performance or to provide for payment of damages, and in what amount. By having a clear understanding of their rights and obligations under the UCC, common law, and other statutes, buyers and sellers can develop contract documents and contract administration protocols that make disputes, if not easy, then at least easier, to resolve.

After considering the evidence on all these questions, the court or arbitrator will make a formal decision, usually with findings of fact and conclusions of law, and will issue a formal judgment stating the substance of the remedy. Parties can appeal court decisions and some arbitration rulings to higher courts, and still more time may elapse before the case results in a final judgment. The winning party must then invoke yet another judicial mechanism to enforce and collect on the judgement.

REGULATIONS AFFECTING PURCHASERS

The old expression "there oughtta be a law" captures the idea that for every wrong, there must be a remedy, and the remedy might well be a statute. Over the years, American lawmakers have responded to a great variety of problems with detailed laws spelling out what people and organizations must do to correct the problem, with paperwork requirements to ensure compliance, and with penalties for not complying. The "granddaddy of them all" for purchasers is the body of antitrust laws, responding to the great monopolies of the early Industrial Revolution and establishing the principles of free and fair competition that are at the heart of American domestic commerce. In addition, laws addressed to issues of fair labor practices, occupational safety and health, nondiscrimination on the basis of race, age, or gender, affirmative action contracting policies, equal opportunity for individuals with disabilities, and a myriad of environmental concerns all establish regulatory schemes that impose requirements on those entering into contracts. Professional purchasers must familiarize themselves with these regulatory requirements in order to help their organizations comply.

Antitrust Laws

The antitrust laws (the Sherman Act, the Clayton Act, and the Federal Trade Commission Act) prohibit agreements that create unreasonable restraints of trade. Since all contracts restrain trade to some degree, the question before the court in most antitrust litigation is whether a contract does so unreasonably. A full trial on all relevant issues is often necessary, and the results are often difficult to predict. However, there are some fairly clear rules.

Agreements on pricing are illegal. Do not agree with fellow buyers (whether or not they are competitors) on any aspect of pricing.

Reciprocal agreements may be anticompetitive if they foreclose a substantial amount of trade. Therefore, as a general rule, do not agree to buy any products on the basis of a reciprocal agreement on the part of the supplier to buy your firm's product.

Exclusive dealing arrangements may also be anticompetitive. An agreement to purchase all your requirements from a single source could be anticompetitive if your company accounts for a substantial amount of the total market for that product. Similarly, an agreement to purchase all the output of a certain company could be anticompetitive if that company accounted for a large share of the amount of that product available. Exclusive dealing arrangements of a substantial nature should always be reviewed by the company's legal counsel.

The Robinson–Patman Act prohibits a company from charging different prices for the same product to two different buyers if that difference would have an adverse effect on competition and is not justifiable. In general, purchases of items used in your business (such as office supplies) cannot affect competition. If one company gets a lower price on office supplies than another, typically this will not be a big enough factor in the total cost structure to have any effect on the sales prices of its own products. However, getting a lower price than a competitor on items your company resells (such as a buyer acquiring a commodity for resale) could have such an effect. Likewise, if you have reason to believe suppliers are charging your competitors more than they charge your firm, consultation with the company's legal counsel may be appropriate. The Robinson–Patman Act also prohibits a buyer from "knowingly inducing" a supplier to sell its product at a lower price than the supplier charges the buyer's competitors. "Knowingly inducing" are the key words in this section of the law.

Other Key Regulatory Laws

Purchasers should be aware that there are a number of other laws that affect how they deal with suppliers. Detailed treatment of these laws is beyond the scope of this chapter. Purchasers, nonetheless, must be generally aware of their existence and should seek appropriate legal counsel for guidance in these areas. Following is just a small sampling of some additional regulatory laws affecting purchasing.

Labor and Employment Laws

Laws in this area govern how purchasers may obtain and interact with contracted labor. Often the parties' actions will override the express language of the contract. For example, it is not enough for a contract for temporary labor to state that the relationship is that of an "independent contractor." In some cases the actions of the purchaser may be deemed to create an employment relationship, obligating the purchaser to provide employee benefits for the contract workers. Some laws, such as regulations issued by the Occupational Safety and Health Administration (OSHA), dictate safety precautions that must be taken, both by the contractor and by the purchaser that is obtaining the contracted services.

Environmental Laws

Environmental laws issued by the Environmental Protection Agency (EPA) and other administrative agencies affect how purchasers may obtain, handle, and dispose of certain materials categorized as hazardous. These laws may impose *criminal* penalties as well as civil penalties, and may impose penalties upon individuals as well as their employers. Hazardous materials laws also require certain labeling and communications to employees who will be coming into contact with the materials.

For additional information regarding these and other regulatory laws affecting purchasing, refer to the references listed in the Appendix.

ELECTRONIC COMMERCE

Any aspect of commercial transactions that once were performed face to face or through the exchange of documents written on paper and signed in ink can now be conducted exclusively by electronic means and at a distance between parties that never see or speak to each other. In the most extreme examples, companies can buy and sell in large quantities instantaneously through Internet transactions conducted by electronic agents acting without direct human intervention, with no paper document or inked signature at any point, from order to delivery to payment. Closer to home, ordinary people buy everything from gas to groceries using credit cards and do their banking in the middle of the night by computer, and in this sense it is hard to find any commerce these days that is *not* electronic. The enormous time and money savings generated by these technologies yields great competitive advantage, and it is no wonder that organizations are pressing forward without waiting for the laws to be spelled out. Company representatives make commitments by telephone, fax, or e-mail, and their business counterparts perform and receive payment, assuming that things will work out and that the laws will catch up when they have to.

Just as interstate and global shipping and trade created new circumstances that required the law to change and adapt, so too have information and communication technology advances outpaced developments in the laws governing commercial transactions. As in the past, generally accepted business practices sometimes become codified in statutes; some laws develop in the context of court cases when judges try to make a fair decision after things go wrong. What seems to be happening today is similar to what has happened over the centuries: businesspeople make business decisions based on practicality and common sense, sometimes taking risks in order to make money; and courts, legislatures, and uniform laws commissions look to the fundamental principles of the old laws and try to make them work in the new settings.

A few examples illustrate some of the major issues.

Under common law and the UCC, to be enforceable in court, certain contracts must be evidenced by a writing signed by the party (or the party's authorized agent) against whom enforcement is being sought. This requirement protects against fraud and mistake. In today's digital world, the requirement for a "writing" is being replaced by a requirement for a "record" (which could be entirely electronic), and the signature requirement is being met by elaborate "authentication" mechanisms to ensure that the parties to the electronic transaction actually are who they appear to be and that the "record" of the transaction has not been tampered with during transmittal. Other authentication mechanisms increasingly supplement or substitute for signatures in the credit card and electronic banking environment at the retail and consumer level: knowing your mother's maiden name or the first or last digits of your social security number. Encryption technology provides electronic means to keep records effectively "under seal" as though they were physically locked in a sealed container, protected from any alteration—just like old-fashioned original paper documents with initials on every page.

Or take the basic concept that a contract is formed when there is an "offer" and an "acceptance" in substantially identical terms, between competent parties and for a legal purpose. If both parties have established the required electronic systems, an electronic purchasing agent following programmed instructions can browse an on-line catalog, identify the required product, place the order, and even send payment; on the other side, the electronic seller's agent can process the purchase and order delivery. The required "meeting of the minds" is entirely figurative, but the contract transaction has taken place.

Now consider what happens when problems in performance arise. In today's world we can expect that even with a traditional paper contract agreement, many communications between the parties take place electronically during the course of performance, and that some of them actually modify terms of the original contract as the parties tried to work matters out. If the dispute is presented to a court to adjudicate, the electronic communications will likely become evidence in court, possibly on an equal footing with the original paper contract document.

What about the Internet purchase that goes wrong? Is the contract governed (for purposes of court decisions) by the law of the state where the buyer lives, or the seller, or the Internet service provider? Will the contract be viewed as one for goods, or services, or a mixture? Or (as with Internet sales of software) will it be interpreted as a license, not a sale at all? Will a court find that the bugs in the software were a breach of warranty? What about the disclaimer that the purchaser never had a chance to read?

Courts are even now wrestling with these and a myriad of other issues that electronic commerce presents. It is hoped that the aforementioned Uniform Computer Information Transactions Act (formerly known as Proposed UCC Article 2B) will bring uniformity to how many of these issues are handled.

Well-advised purchasing professionals will not wait for model statutes and court decisions. A better approach is to develop standard forms of agreement for the company's electronic trading partners, to serve as a master contract or umbrella agreement for all electronic transactions. In much the same way as any blanket agreement that is executed using purchase orders or releases, such a master contract can spell out agency authority and limits, set up authentication protocols, identify electronic order, delivery, acceptance, and payment methods, state any warranties or disclaimers, and select dispute resolution procedures, including applicable laws.

This is not a novel approach. It underlies all the electronic transactions that ordinary people execute every day, which make us take electronic commerce so much for granted. Our credit cards or checkbooks were not issued until after we signed a master agreement with paragraphs of fine print, some repeated on the back of every monthly statement. Web pages that support on-line shopping summarize the company return policies and shipping terms and often contain disclaimers. The software we download cannot be run until our mouse-click says we accept the restrictions of the license agreement. Nonetheless, such trading partner agreements must be drafted with the same level of care that goes in to any "partnering"-type agreement.

CONCLUSION

As this chapter has shown, the purchasing activity involves many areas of law. The various rules are often complex, and detailed treatment is beyond the scope of this chapter. The purpose of this chapter is simply to raise the purchasing professional's awareness of the various laws affecting the performance of their duties. This should help purchasers to recognize potential problems before they materialize, so that purchasers will know when they should seek appropriate legal counsel. This will help purchasers and their employers avoid many legal disputes and help them to obtain optimum outcomes when such disputes are unavoidable.

A P P E N D I X

BOOKS

Purchasing Manager's Desk Book of Purchasing Law, Third Edition
Prentice Hall 1998
Donald B. King, James J. Ritterskamp, Jr. ISBN 0-13-671462-5

Ritterskamp Views the Law: A Collection of Legal Articles for Today's
Purchasing Manager
NAPM 1995
James J. Ritterskamp, Jr.; Edited by Gaylord Jentz, J.D.

Purchasing and the Law—A Self-Study Workbook
NAPM 1997
Helen M. Pohlig, Esq.

A Short Course on International Contracts
World Trade Press 1999
Karla J. Shippey, J.D.
ISBN 1-885073-55-0

Legal Aspects of International Sourcing
Business Laws, Inc. 1986, 1997, 1998
ISBN 0-929576-09-8

Guide to the International Sale of Goods Convention
Business Laws, Inc. 1986, 1996, 1997
ISBN 0-929576-33-0

Incoterms 1990
ICC Publishing 1990
ISBN 92-842-0087-3

Complying With the Foreign Corrupt Practices Act: A Guide for U.S.
Firms Doing Buisness in the International Marketplace
American Bar Association Section of Business Law 1994
Donald R. Cruver
ISBN 1-57073-015-6

WEBSITES

Business Laws, Inc.
www.businesslaws.com

International Chamber of Commerce (ICC)
www.iccwbo.org

Pace Univ. School of Law Institute of International Commercial Law
www.cisg.law.pace.edu

American Bar Association (includes a comprehensive listing of ABA publications on business and commercial law, international trade, environmental regulations, technology, and ethics, as well as a comprehensive set of links to other law-related sites)
www.abanet.org

Guide to the Uniform Computer Information Transactions Act
(The Website Formerly Known as The 2B Guide)
www.2BGuide.com

Investment Recovery

Associate Editors
Richard Antus, CMIR
Manager, Investment Recovery
GTE Supply

William Boan, CMIR

Ron Brooks, CMIR
Central Zone Manager
Weyerhaeuser Company

Gary Colgrove
Manager of Resource Recovery
3M Company

Richard Cuniberti, C.P.M., CMIR
Supply Manager, Resource Recovery & Ecology Services
BASF Corporation

Carolyn Jackson, CMIR
ARCO Western Energy Company

Dennis Knutz, CMIR, ASA
Director, Investment Recovery
Weyerhaeuser Company

Roland Kotcamp, C.P.M., CMIR
Director
Niagara Mohawk Power Corporation

Michael Rhodes, CMIR
Corporate Investment Recovery
Virginia Electric & Power Company

William Yerkey
General Manager, Investment Recovery
Union Carbide Corporation

Coordinated by:
The Investment Recovery Association
Jane Male, CAE, Executive Director
With special thanks to Carolyn Jackson, CMIR, for her coordination
of the project.

INTRODUCTION

Every company or other type of organization, at some point, becomes involved in dealing with idle assets. An asset is defined as "anything having value," and when determined to be no longer needed, it becomes an idle asset. As more and more landfills reach capacity, companies must find economic ways to dispose of their nonhazardous solid wastes. Investment recovery (IR) is simply defined as a program to identify, reuse, sell, or otherwise dispose of idle assets and nonhazardous solid wastes generated through the operation of your company's normal business. An investment recovery program is a key function in support of a company's strategic asset management program.[1]

Each company setting up an IR program has, as its basis for doing so, certain objectives or goals in mind. The IR objectives of a company could be to:

1. *Improve* short-term cash flow, inventory level reduction, and space utilization
2. *Eliminate* environmental problems
3. *Recover* part of the cost of idle assets
4. *Strengthen* earnings through reduction or avoidance of operating costs
5. *Support* company strategic asset management program

Most companies with successful IR programs have several things in common. The companies have either established a separate investment recovery department or assigned administration of the IR program to a specific group (i.e., materials management, purchasing department). The investment recovery department would normally be a key support organization in a strategic asset management program that includes disposing of idle assets.

This chapter will begin with a discussion of the administration and management of IR and then cover what are perhaps the two most important aspects of IR, management of surplus inventory and marketing/disposal of surplus. In addition, the related subjects of facilities liquidation or dismantlement, recycling, safety and environmental involvement, and corporate donations are also included.

---

1. A resource: The Investment Recovery Association is a group of companies committed to the exchange of information about adding value to the IR process when disposing of a company's idle assets and nonhazardous solid wastes. The association has a common history of successful programs. This common history of "What works, What doesn't" is available through the association and its members.

ADMINISTRATION OF INVESTMENT RECOVERY

A major consideration for the administration of a successful investment recovery program is the selection of an organization or personnel with the highest standards of integrity. The personnel selected to administer the IR program must be determined, enthusiastic, above reproach, and dedicated to the premise that their honor and that of the program rest solely in their day-to-day interactions with others, both inside and outside the company. Remember, you market your integrity in every contact you make. Management controls the budget and objectives of the IR department and provides direction that determines the success or failure of the function as perceived by the company. IR management should participate in capital planning meetings and be as proactive as possible.

The objectives of a good IR department should complement the company objectives. To be successful, IR decision-makers must know and understand the company's current and evolving objectives when establishing and administering an IR program.

For example:

1. If one company objective is to improve short-term cash flow, it would not be prudent to hold items for a year without trying to secure cash from the sale of those items.

2. If objectives include cost avoidance or inventory-level reduction and the company is more interested in getting rid of items than in the amount of money to be received for them, delay in getting rid of items is not acceptable.

With company objectives in mind, normally the IR department's primary objective is to maximize the salvage value when disposing of idle assets in a timely manner and to limit company liability in the disposal process.

The identification of idle assets by the IR department is the first step in the investment recovery process. IR survives on the old adage "One person's trash is another person's treasure." Other factors that are essential to a successful IR department are appropriate and timely measurement and reporting of IR results to management, inventory control, documentation, authorization, clearly defined workflow processes, service agreements with internal customers (if applicable), and budget planning.

At this point it might be productive to talk about timely management feedback and internal service agreements. Everyone has heard that "the squeaky wheel gets the grease." This adage should be amended to "the squeaky wheel gets the grease—or gets replaced." Although it is important to demonstrate the value of IR in the company, it is just as important to give the credit for this success to others. In this way the IR function loses nothing, improves relationships, gains credibility, and does not look like a "glory-hog." If the IR function exports the credit and imports responsibility, people will be standing in line to sing the praises of IR. But first they will need information to form the verses. Reporting the results openly will provide that information. Blowing your own horn sometimes sounds a little off key. Let others do the horn-blowing; the music is much sweeter!

MANAGEMENT OF INVESTMENT RECOVERY

The success of an investment recovery function depends on the following:

- ♦ *Visible senior management support:* Recent benchmarking of top-performing IR departments indicates that visible support by the senior management team (SMT) adds significantly to the success of the function. The IR manager must show the SMT that services and benefits provided by the IR function add value and are in line with company and operating unit's (client's) goals. Senior management legitimizes the IR function, adding credibility and implying and/or directing operation of the company personnel at large. They provide the budgetary approvals and direction that help establish objectives for the IR function.

- ♦ *Strong working relations with other departments:* Investment recovery functions cannot succeed in a vacuum! The lines of internal communications are the virtual lifelines for an IR function. The existence of open internal lines of communication between IR and other departments is a byproduct of successful establishment of an IR program.

The people in the legal department should become IR's best friends. They are the ones who will keep IR activities free from legal complications. The best attorney in the world is worthless if not consulted or, when consulted, ignored. Staff attorneys are there to provide assistance and expertise to keep complications from becoming legal issues. Probably the best staff attorney is one who never has to go to court. Open and frank discussions with legal counsel, before the fact, will avoid lots of problems down the road. IR activities deal with the Uniform Commercial Code (UCC). The name implies uniformity, but in fact the provisions of the UCC are subject to interpretation by the state court having jurisdiction. If you are in business in Oklahoma, for example, and dealing with a buyer in Georgia, which court has jurisdiction? What if the purchaser was in business in Louisiana? If you cannot answer these questions off the top of your head, do not feel inadequate. Ask your staff attorneys for guidance—they will be glad to help and you will be thankful they did. Attorneys are the best source of information regarding warranties, indemnification, agency, misrepresentation, right to cure, liability, and all types of terms and conditions. If you are not capable of giving a lecture on each of these topics, you had better make good friends with the legal department.

Groups whose support and cooperation will be particularly instrumental in determining the success of your IR function are the engineering, accounting, and safety and environmental departments. Developing procedures, as mentioned earlier, can be very time-consuming and frustrating. The easiest way to avoid these problems is to get as many different departments as possible involved at the beginning. By including more people in establishment of procedures, IR professionals can ensure that their procedures are responsive and that the attitudes of others have been properly addressed.

The best source of technical information is often the engineering department. They are the best source for equipment and material specifications, the date the items were purchased, as-built drawings, operating parameters, and possible alternative uses for most equipment your company owns.

Engineers generally have a lot of power in determining when it would be acceptable to utilize surplus instead of new. This reuse philosophy can provide an unexpected new market for your surplus—your own company. It is fundamental that your company's engineering department be apprised of your IR activities and, more importantly, that their help and support be engaged.

No successful IR function exists without the cooperation and support of the people in the accounting department. These are the people who help document your function's contribution to the bottomline. Just as importantly, the accounting staff will help you establish procedures that will allow you to capture and document costs and contributions. Determining who will pay those costs and who is to be the beneficiary of those contributions is not a function that anyone should perform without input from accounting. Your procedures must complement fundamental accounting policy, and there probably should be a systematic method for those groups supplying the surplus to share in the rewards.

The procedures established at the beginning of your IR activity need not be all-inclusive. Once a good rapport is developed with the accounting people, they will probably assist you in developing procedures that are needed to allocate the revenues you generate for the company. In some cases it can take more than a year to develop procedures in detail. During this time little or no IR is taking place. To some, a year without contribution means the last year. We recommend that you contact a company in your industry that already has an IR department and see if they can share some of the basic procedures with you. You can always modify them to fit your company's specific operating criteria.

Relationships with the safety and environmental department will be discussed in the section below on Safety and Environmental Involvement.

In addition to management support and relationships with other departments, other keys to a well-managed IR function include:

- Highly trained IR professionals
- Sound practices and processes
- Database management
- A diverse marketing approach
- Credible performance measurements and communications

One primary function of the IR group is the evaluation of surplus assets. This establishes the fair market value, the true value of an internal transfer, and sets recovery expectations for a sale to third parties. These evaluations require *highly trained IR professionals* and cannot be made by persons unfamiliar with and/or untrained in IR. The trained IR professional also understands contracts and contract law, environmental compliance, sound safety practices, project management, marketing, and sales negotiations, all of which are important to IR success.

Every successful IR team must also employ *sound business practices and processes*. All of the processes should be documented, and improvement goals should be established annually. The IR group should team with other internal service groups in the development and improvement of the processes.

The collection and distribution of facts and data about surplus machinery and equipment must be clean, concise, and accurate. To achieve this requires *database management*. A purchaser, either internal or external, must have sufficient and accurate data to make a purchase decision. Steadfast rules must be developed and maintained for categorization and data collection for both surplus inventory and customers.

A *diverse marketing approach* including internal reuse marketing and a mix of direct sales to end users and dealers, sealed bids, donations, auctions, and brokerage and consignment sales may be employed to market a diverse mix of assets. Trades and long-term contract sales can provide good returns with a minimum of effort for commodities that have predictable quantities. Some items may have to be disposed of or scrapped. A well-managed IR group will also think of its internal customers in two ways. They will treat them as clients as they take their surplus to the open market, and as customers while searching for a place to redeploy the asset. A well-managed and advertised internal marketing plan provides the highest return on the company's investment.

An IR department's success is directly linked to its credibility. *Credible performance measurements and communications* are an absolute requirement. An IR department's charter must be agreed upon and put down in writing. The charter should spell out the types of surplus materials and equipment that IR will and will not handle. It should also outline the services IR will be responsible for, such as internal transfers, external sales, building demolitions, and plant closures. Clear performance measures must be established with the senior management team, IR's supervisor, and its clients. These measures should be quantifiable and easy to calculate. In those cases in which a judgment call must be made, have the client set the value. Credibility is paramount. A good performance benchmark is the benefit-to-cost ratio published by the Investment Recovery Association. Clear and consistent communications to your key clients of the progress towards your goals and your financial contribution will serve to maintain the support needed to sustain a healthy and constantly improving IR function.

SURPLUS INVENTORY MANAGEMENT

Surplus assets can be divided into a vast number of categories. A nonexhaustive list of categories would include:

- Equipment and machinery
- Maintenance supplies
- Byproducts and waste
- Raw product
- Excess inventory
- Buildings and land

A review of these categories makes it easy to imagine situations where assets in each of these categories could become surplus.

Among the keys to a successful IR program is an accurate and current inventory of surplus assets. While the need for an up-to-date inventory is obvious, the actual management may be difficult due to the dynamic nature of the inventory and the fact that in many cases the assets are spread over a number of geographic locations. Following are a number of practices that will assist with the management of the surplus asset inventory.

One of the most important keys is a *system of numbering or coding each individual asset*. Each item must have an individual code, specific to that item only. The item code may be numeric or alphanumeric, depending on the individual company's needs. The code may include a numerical sequence for tracking the item, digits to indicate the date the item was entered into the inventory, a code to specify geographic location, an indicator of the type of process the asset was used in, or a combination of some or all of these options. The configuration of the item code is not as important as the individuality of the code as it relates to a specific item.

Collection of information on the asset is also critical. The information contained in the inventory database must accurately represent the asset, since both internal and external customers will rely on this information when making purchasing decisions. The large variety of assets, and the need to have information specific to a type of asset, require flexibility in the database. Clearly the type of information needed to market a lift truck is different from that needed for a centrifugal pump. Following, however, is information that should be collected and entered into the database on the vast majority of assets:

- Capacity (lifting, GPM, CFM, PSIG)
- Condition
- Date of manufacture
- Date of purchase

- Fixed asset number
- Location
- Model number
- Original equipment manufacturer (OEM)
- Original purchase price
- Power requirements (HP, voltage, Hz, phase)
- Serial number

Additionally, it is important to have the date the asset was placed into the system so that aging data can be reported. A number of off-the-shelf database management systems are available that provide the power and flexibility to meet these requirements.

Data on the *physical condition* of items is subjective and frequently leads to disagreements between buyer and seller. For this reason it is suggested that definitions of condition be developed and shared with internal and external customers.

The discussion above relates primarily to the collection and input of data on the surplus assets. Just as important is the removal of the item following the disposal. Many IR professionals have included the *ability to archive the data for later reference*. This allows an individual to get historical data on specific items that may be of assistance when developing a marketing plan. Other data that may be useful to track are the type of disposal (redeployment, sale, scrap), sale or transfer price, potential customers, and data on the final purchaser.

One final key to the management of an inventory is the *integrity of the data*. While the types of information needed will vary from business to business, the integrity of the data must be protected and the database kept current. It is recommended that the data be input at a single source to ensure that the data remain useful and the database remains functional. If, for any reason, data will be entered by a number of different individuals or at various locations, standard nomenclature and other controls should be developed to maintain the consistency of the information.

PROCESSING REQUESTS FOR DISPOSAL

Someone comes to you with a trade in deal on a piece of equipment. One of the first things you as an IR professional would want to know is what the item is worth, its fair market value (FMV). You should know your company's approval procedures, who has what authority limit, and get the required authorization before committing to a sale. If you have received payment for an item before obtaining the proper approval, delay removal until authorization is obtained. Authorization should always be in written form. This authorization is probably the first potential stumbling block for the IR professional. It should be mandatory on any request for disposal. A request for disposal and a notification form may be two different documents or one document with both functions. One function informs you of assets available for disposal, and the other gives you permission to dispose of them. Do not confuse the two. Figures 28–1 and 28–2 are examples of combination surplus report (notification form) and asset disposition request (disposal approval).

DISPOSITION OPTIONS

The fact that a company generates surplus does not indicate that the company is poorly managed. How that company deals with the issue of surplus directly relates to the overall capability and responsibility of its managers.

It is IR's responsibility to ensure that policies and procedures for the disposal of surplus and obsolete equipment, materials, and supplies include the IR function and that those procedures are properly identified and available to the various operations within your company. Your efforts, as an IR manager, to make this information available will place you in the disposal loop and guarantee your company the opportunity to improve bottom line financial performance. The first step in the disposition process is making sure personnel know what to do when they identify surplus materials

In addition to the information previously listed under Surplus Inventory Management, other details are also important. Below is a partial list of additional facts IR personnel should strive to obtain once equipment, materials, or supplies are determined surplus:

- ◆ How stored
- ◆ Intended use
- ◆ Maintenance records
- ◆ Market value
- ◆ Reason for discontinuing use
- ◆ Drawings or specs

F I G U R E   28-1

Surplus/Idle Asset Routing Form

SURPLUS/IDLE ASSET ROUTING FORM
(See reverse side for instructions)

I.R. No.: _____ Quant.: _____   Date: _____

I. GENERAL INFORMATION

Originator: _____ Department: _____ Phone: _____

Location: _____ Division: _____ Cost Ctr.: _____

Item Name: _____ Asset No.: _____

Status (circle): In-Service   Idle   Surplus   Other: _____

Type (circle):   Fixed Asset/Capital   Expense Item   Raw Material   Other: _____

II. DETAIL INFORMATION

Mfgr: _____ Model: _____ Ser. No.. _____

Capacity/Size: _____ Design Ratings (Temp/Pres): _____

Weight: _____ Dimensions: _____

Age: _____ Matl's of Constr.: _____

Motor: HP: _____ Volt/Ph/Cycle: _____ RPM: _____ Encl: _____

Condition (Circle):   New   Unused   Good   Fair   Poor   Other: _____

Location: _____ Repairs Req'd: _____

Reason Goods are Surplus: _____

Comments: _____

III. ACCOUNTING

Book Values: Gross: _____ Net: _____ Purch. Price: _____

IV. IR COORDINATOR

Category Code: _____ Required Removal Date: _____

Work Needed (Circle):   Clean   Asbestos   Dismantle   Refurbish   Other: _____

Est. Removal Cost: _____ Est. FMV/Min. Accpt: _____

Recommend (circle):   Transfer   Sell   Donate   Scrap   Other: _____

Final: Transferred   Sold   Donated   Scrapped   Other: _____

To: _____ S.A. (or P.O.) No.: _____

V. APPRROVALS (sign and date)

Originator: _____ Dept. Head: _____

Maint/Eng: _____ Saf/Env: _____

Controller: _____ I.R. Coordinator: _____

_____ Title: _____

_____ Title: _____

Rejected By: _____ Reason: _____

White: IR Coordinator   **Canary: IR Manager**   **Pink: Accounting**   **Gold: Originator**

F I G U R E   28–1

Continued

Instructions For Surplus/Idle Asset Routing Form

1. When an item becomes surplus or idled indefinitely the 'asset owner' (originator) calls the local investment recovery (IR) coordinator who assigns an IR number and sends the form to the originator.

2. The originator completes Sections I. and II. with the best available information. This may require the involvement of other departments such as maintenance, engineering, purchasing, etc. The originator then obtains the required approvals to release the asset for transfer or sale. If more extensive evaluation is warranted (eg. test for asbestos), it should be noted on the form prior to forwarding to the site Safety/ Environmental Dept. Photographs should be included whenever possible.

3. The Safety Environmental representative(s) signs the form as a record of receiving it and forwards to the site Accounting Department. If the item is a known safety/environmental liability then he has the option of rejecting in Section V.

4. The Accounting Department notes that the asset has been declared surplus and adjusts book values accordingly. Gross and net book values are then entered in Section III. If the purchase price of the asset is available it should also be entered. It is then forwarded to the local IR coordinator.

5. The IR coordinator enters the item into his site inventory, and then establishes the fair market value (FMV), required removal date, minimum acceptable selling price, and recommended disposition in conjunction with the asset owner. Copies of the completed form are then distributed.

6. When the final disposition of the item has been determined it is noted in section IV. For tranfers show receiving location, cost center, and purchase order numbers. For external transactions show company name and sales agreement (S.A.) number. Copies are then redistributed to original copyholders including P.O. or sales agreement forms.

- ◆ Spare parts
- ◆ Book value

Certain assets could have even more information related to them. The successful IR professional will have positioned himself or herself to be part of the disposal decision process so he or she knows when assets will become available. Being part of the process enables him or her to acquire all of the information available prior to the time of disposal, if required.

Once these materials are identified, research must begin to determine what should be done with them. Items that are potential candidates for repair or remanufacturing should be segregated. This could eliminate the expense of new purchases and shorten delivery time. Potential repair and remanufacturing shops should be inspected and qualified to ensure that they comply with industry standards.

F I G U R E   28–2

Surplus Equipment Report and Asset Disposition Request

SURPLUS EQUIPMENT REPORT and
ASSET DISPOSITION REQUEST

DATE

GP 8639 (8-90)

DIVISION #	DIVISION NAME	TYPE OF OPERATION	LOCATION (CITY, STATE)

1. EQUIPMENT DESCRIPTION

DESCRIPTION OF EQUIPMENT

MANUFACTURER	MODEL NUMBER	SERIAL NUMBER	QUANTITY

YEAR MANUFACTURED	CONDITION OF EQUIPMENT	SPARE PARTS ☐ YES ☐ NO	DRAWINGS/MANUALS ☐ YES ☐ NO

2. PROPOSED DISPOSITION

☐ SALE $_____   ☐ OTHER_____

☐ TRANSFER $_____   Corporate Investment Recovery Consulted? ___ Yes ___ No

3. TO BE COMPLETED BY THE FACILITY CONTROLLER

ASSET AMOUNT $	RESERVE AMOUNT $	NET BOOK $
	AS OF (DATE)	
GUIDELINE CLASS YEAR SUFFIX	EQUIPMENT NUMBER, IF APPLICABLE	

4. APPROVALS

Obtain approvals in the following sequence. Refer to the Financial Handbook if you have any questions.

1. ORIGINATOR	DATE	5. REGIONAL/GROUP MANAGER (AS REQUIRED)	DATE
2. ENGINEERING MANAGER	DATE	6. CORPORATE INVESTMENT RECOVERY MANAGER	DATE
3. FACILITY CONTROLLER	DATE	7. VICE PRESIDENT (AS REQUIRED)	DATE
4. FACILITY MANAGER	DATE		

5. INVESTMENT RECOVERY

ITEM NUMBER	CATEGORY CODE NUMBER	ESTIMATED MARKET VALUE

6. DISPOSITION OF EQUIPMENT

☐ SOLD $_____   ☐ SCRAPPED

☐ TRANSFER $_____   ☐ ABANDONED

☐ TRADE-IN $_____   ☐ DONATION

WHITE - INVESTMENT RECOVERY   YELLOW - FACILITY CONTROLLER   PINK - ORIGINATOR

Below is a decision sequence to maximize recovery, beginning with the most advantageous outcome and ending with the least desirable alternative. Refer also to Figure 28–3.

- *Use*
  - Redeploy
  - Repair and redeploy
  - Convert and redeploy
- *Return*
  - Return to original equipment manufacturer
  - Return to source
- *Sell*
  - Remarket
  - Employee sale
  - Reclamation of parts
  - Recycle
  - Scrap or scrap for salvage
- *Trade*
  - Trade it in for merchandise
  - Trade it in for services
- *Donate*
- *Dispose*

FIGURE 28–3

Decision Sequence to Maximize Recovery

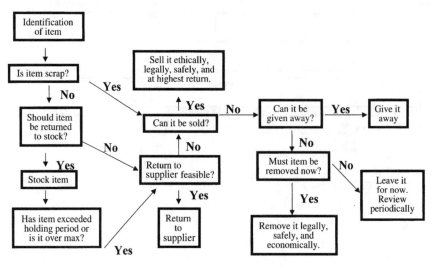

Use

Review all material identified as obsolete, surplus, or scrap to determine if it can be reassigned to any other area within the company before the material is made available to a third party. Many times an item declared surplus in one area of the company could be used in another area or location without any change to the item whatsoever, and an additional new purchase of the item can be avoided. Lack of intraorganization use of surplus occurs in many companies with multiple locations because of lack of communication, reluctance to cooperate, perception that surplus is somebody else's rejects, or an innate belief that new is always better. Once the IR professional overcomes these obstacles, the concept of reuse can be nurtured until reuse becomes the first option of operating divisions.

To help the situation, IR personnel should identify the personnel responsible for the purchase of various types of material and arrange to make surplus material lists available to them whenever these items become available. Whenever possible, personnel responsible for technical support or maintenance of the items should also be made aware of the available product. The following example can be used to illustrate the need for redeployment of surplus and used assets.

Example: Item X is purchased for $10,000 with a normal life of 10 years. Department A uses X for five years. Department A changes its operation, eliminating the need for X. X is now surplus, with a current market value of $5,000. Department B is about to begin a new operation that requires item Y at a cost of $15,000. If Department B can be persuaded to use X instead of Y, the remaining life of X, five years, can be recovered and the new cost of Y can be avoided. The argument can be made that $5,000 is lost by not selling X. When the $5,000 lost sale is subtracted, the net cost avoidance is $10,000. Given the choice of $5,000 income or avoiding an expense of $15,000, what would most bosses do?

Return

Oftentimes surplus items are the result of changes in planning or unforeseen changes in operation that result in unused assets. Many times the item can be returned to the manufacturer or dealer. There may be a restocking fee associated, but many times a restocking fee can be reduced through negotiation. Remember, the manufacturer or dealer has thorough knowledge of the item and a client list to which it can sell the item without exposing itself to additional risks. However, the cost of the restocking fee should be compared to current market value of the product.

Sell

Once it has been determined that the item cannot be used within your company or returned to the manufacturer or distributor, the process of selling it outside your company should begin. An item of no use to the company may be in high demand from other users within the same industry or other industries. For example, it may possible to recover the entire cost of the product by selling it to another company in your industry. There are used equipment dealers and brokers who specialize in this type of item. These dealers would be purchasing the item for resale to a third party. Identifying the end user and eliminating the dealer's commission would ensure higher profits. An item is worth more to the person who is purchasing for use than it is to a purchaser who plans to resell.

When you are selling products to resellers, it is important to know the companies you are dealing with and have them understand and adhere to your company's rules and restrictions concerning proprietary information, logo restrictions, and hazardous material disposal processes. To avoid potential litigation problems, it is IR's responsibility to ensure that these rules will be followed until the next end user has the product in use. This is particularly important if the items you sold contain hazardous material.

Trade

Selling an item or trading one are essentially the same. In some situations trading an item can have tax advantages that could enhance the overall return. Surplus can be traded for other goods or services. In some instances it would not be uncommon to gain more in operating costs than in income from a sale. For example: I have a valve with a current market value of $5,000. Company Z has offered $5,000 cash or $6,000 in valve reconditioning. I have idle equipment reconditioned on a regular basis and use Company Z as one of my regular shops. Both sides win in this situation. I gain another $1,000 in profit and Company Z is guaranteed more of my regular work.

When trading, make certain the item to be received has value equal to or greater than the amount received through selling the item. In addition, make sure that the item to be received will fulfill an immediate or short-term need. Don't trade for an airplane when you need a bicycle.

Donate

Sometimes an item cannot be reused, but rather than sell or trade it, the company sees benefit in donating the item. In most cases the decision is made through a recommendation from the IR professional. A similar decision could be made when it is more economical to give it away than to spend funds to make it ready for sale or trade. To ensure that the right decision is being made, compare the costs to make ready for sale against the anticipated return from the sale.

Disposal or Scrap Sale

The decision to dispose of a product creates a whole new set of issues. Some items cannot be allowed to enter the open market and therefore cannot be sold through normal channels, if at all. Many items your company uses every day may be considered hazardous and must be disposed of in accordance with state and federal environmental and safety regulations. Government regulations control the disposal of many items, and the list continues to grow. An IR professional must be aware of regulations regarding disposal of any surplus the company generates, strive to ensure that all relevant guidelines are followed, and ensure that documentation is retained that proves compliance by the company.

Most chemical processing companies are able to extend the life of many chemicals used by their companies by segregating and recycling chemical wastes. Make sure you research all available options.

Scrap sale is similar to selling surplus as a usable item. The difference is that the item is sold for the material it is made of instead of for what it does. Scrap sales are usually in terms of weight or volume rather than items. Environmental and safety considerations apply equally to scrap sales as to other forms of disposition.

Outsourcing

There are companies available to dispose of anything, but at a cost. Using an external company is usually considered the least desirable option because of the cost associated with it. However, by effectively managing this function, the IR professional can keep these costs to a minimum and generate potentially huge cost avoidance benefits in the future. Also, in companies that do not generate large volumes of surplus or generate surplus only occasionally, outsourcing may be the most cost-effective solution to provide an IR program.

MARKETING OF USED AND SURPLUS ASSETS

A general marketing strategy is composed of two elements: the target market and the marketing mix. The "target market" is the group of customers to whom the investment recovery professional attempts to disposition the used and/or surplus assets. The target markets for IR efforts, in order of priority based on typical highest return potential, are (1) internal customers, (2) original supplier, and (3) other external customers. With regard to internal customers, the objective is redeployment of assets within the organization/company for a cost avoidance/cost savings. Internal areas should include your local area as well as other company locations, international locations, and affiliates. If redeployment is not viable, then the second target market approach is to seek asset return arrangements to the original vendor. The third target market default is to focus on sales to other external customers.

In regard to the marketing mix element of a marketing strategy from an IR perspective, the appropriate development and application of the four basic variables (product, place, promotion, and price) is essential to a successful IR program.

Key IR considerations for the *product* variable include (1) accurate descriptions/assessments of the physical goods and (2) warranty issues. See the Surplus Inventory Management and Contract Execution and Administration sections of this chapter for discussion of these considerations.

One popular misconception is that IR has little control over what "product" will be turned over for dispositioning. In fact, proactive investment recovery groups assist in the identification of existing used and/or surplus assets through physical site surveys. Furthermore, at the opposite end of the supply chain, proactive IR functions assist in minimizing the unnecessary generation of additional surplus through participating in capital planning meetings and providing historical input to requisitioning organizations on frequently surplused materials.

With respect to the *place* variable, particular emphasis in the investment recovery arena would be on storage and transportation. Where are the assets physically located? Is there a centralized area for IR assets? Are the assets located at multiple facilities? Who will be responsible for transportation—the customer or the IR function? At what point does title to the goods change hands? In the marketing of the product, all of these considerations and more should be clearly identified and understood by both the seller and the purchaser.

Perhaps the heart of marketing for IR is the *promotion* variable of the marketing mix. Two primary considerations for IR related to this variable are advertising and methods of sale.

Common advertising methods include publication of excess lists, catalogs, advertising insertions in trade publications and on Internet sites, utilization of brokers, e-mail, newsletters, flyers, and word of mouth. With the advent of the Internet and intranets, an increasing number of investment recovery groups are developing and utilizing their own Web sites for access by internal and external customers. IR professionals informally "network" with each other through professional trade associations such as the Investment Recovery Association.

Another effective means of advertising is more appropriately called "publicity." For example, customer satisfaction often leads not only to repeat business, but also to "free" word of mouth recommendations to other potential customers, and recognition of IR efforts is extremely important in "getting the word out." For example, management reporting of cost savings achievements with credit given to the appropriate party (not the IR function) will enhance further investment recovery success opportunities.

These are just a few of the common advertising media used today. Innovative IR professionals are constantly finding other ways to seek out the market for their wares.

The second consideration of promotion is method of sale. The IR professional uses a variety of methods. When each method should be used depends on the circumstances. Common methods of sales and brief descriptions of each follow.

Auction sales can be an effective and exciting method of dispositioning use and/or surplus assets. Auction companies can be contracted to perform any or all parts of the sales process, from sorting and staging the material, to preparing and mailing bid catalogs and brochures, to conducting the auction, to collecting payment from the buyers, to performing load out of the materials. Auction companies typically work on a percentage commission of gross sales basis. Auction sales allow the seller to set a specific date for sale and quickly liquidate assets. Auction sales are conducive to consolidation of assets from multiple locations.

Auctions do not always have to be on-site. Slide auctions are also popular. Color slides of the material for sale are shown to buyers at a more convenient off-site location. In both instances purchasers are encouraged to view the material in person at an appointed time prior to auction. Auctions can also combine the equipment from several different companies. Typically, auctions are billed as "absolute auctions," meaning that every item in the sale will be sold to the highest bidder regardless of the bid. This can be a two-edged sword. "Absolute" implies that if there are limited bidders on a particular item in the sale, the bidders might be able to buy the item at less than market value. Thus, the burden is on the seller to ensure that the contracted auction company has the advertising expertise to attract the right potential bidders to the sale so that there is healthy competition for every item in the sale. In some cases the seller can set a minimum price on specialized equipment.

Bartering is one of the oldest forms of trade. It basically amounts to purchasing goods or services with other goods or services, rather than currency. Bartering is not a widely used method by IR professionals, but opportunities may arise.

Broker agreements are similar in concept to consignment sales. IR professionals may choose to enter into a contractual arrangement with brokers who have expertise in locating "ready, willing, and able buyers" for used and/or surplus assets. In contrast to a consignment agreement, in a broker arrangement the broker does not take physical possession of the used and/or surplus assets. Brokers typically work on a percentage commission of gross sales basis.

With *consignment sales*, a contractual agreement is executed with another party (legally referred to as the "consignee") to accept used and/ or surplus assets on consignment for sale. The consignee is typically sought on the basis of expertise and availability of resources to more effectively market particular used and/or surplus assets. The consignee takes physical possession of the assets, markets them, and pays the consignor the agreed amount for the assets upon successful sale by the consignee to a third party. A specific time is usually set for marketing. For protection of the consignor, in the event that the consignee loses or damages the assets, the consignor should file a UCC1 (Uniform Commercial Code Form 1).

With *fixed price sales*, the IR professional sets the price for the used and/or surplus assets. Typical avenues for offering these assets are publication in catalogs and/or advertising insertions in various publications. Some IR operations actually run retail stores for public sale of assets. The assets included in such retail operations tend to be high-volume assets with a relatively low market value.

As the title implies, *negotiation price sales* entail actual negotiation of a sales price with a prospective buyer for use and/or surplus assets. A key consideration in utilization of this method is the expertise of the IR professional in the art of negotiating and determining market values.

Open bids are accepted at any time. Some companies accept offers on assets they were not aggressively trying to dispose of simply because someone called to inquire.

A *pool partnership* is a variation of a consignment arrangement. Basically, the consignee purchases surplus from multiple consignors, warehouses the surplus, and sells it back on demand to any of the consignors. Thus there is a surplus sharing arrangement of some basic asset (e.g., wire and cable) amongst multiple companies that is facilitated by a consignee for a fee arrangement. This method reduces waste, eliminates surplus generation, and utilizes excess assets more effectively. In the example of a wire and cable pool partnership, in typical arrangements another benefit would be that the consignee could buy back exact lengths for a particular project rather than having to purchase bulk minimum quantities such as an entire reel.

With *sealed bid sales* a bid package is sent out to a list of qualified and specific potential buyers with a limited description of sale inventory. Bidders are encouraged to view the merchandise before submitting a bid, but this is not mandatory. A limited time is allowed for submission of bids. Bids are opened and witnessed at a designated time and date, as noted in the package. Sealed bids help to ensure an ethical, confidential bid process. Large quantities of items can be sold at one time and to more than one buyer. An example of bidder terms is shown in Figure 28–4.

International sales can be profitable also. Some Third World countries are not financially able to buy new and are interested in out-of-date technology. The U.S. Department of Commerce has many ways to assist in developing international markets. For example, it publishes an Export Yellow Pages that helps in contacting foreign markets. For an export programs pamphlet put out by the U.S. Government Resources, dial 800/USA TRADE. It includes a list of officers of commerce.

Dealing in international sales transactions will entail more emphasis in certain aspects such as prequalification of potential buyers, licensing, language barriers, and financial and transportation arrangements.

F I G U R E 28–4

Supplemental Terms for Request for Bids

SUPPLEMENTAL TERMS FOR REQUEST FOR BIDS

_____

1)   Bids shall be submitted no later than _____ to:

_____
_____
_____
_____

For overnight deliveries:

_____
_____
_____
_____

2)   _____ reserves the right to reject any or all bids, to accept
     other than the highest bid, to accept all or part, and to waive irregularities and informalities in any
     bid.

3)   Buyer   shall   not   reassign   its   interest   or   title   to   goods   until   removed   from
     _____   property   without   the   express   written   consent   of
     _____.

4)   Payment shall be made by certified check or bank money order in U. S. Dollars prior to any removal
     of goods from _____ property and such removal shall be scheduled with and witnessed by
     _____ personnel or their assignee. Removal of goods from any facility shall be
     subjected to a routine inspection at the exit from _____ property.

5)   All sales are subject to sales or use tax, to be added to the purchase price, unless the buyer has
     provided _____ with the appropriate tax exemption certificate.

6)   Successful bidder is required to complete the attached indemnification form prior to being allowed to
     remove any equipment from _____ property.

7)   Bidders are invited to inspect the material offered by contacting _____ at the
     address above or by phone at _____.

8)   Unless specifically stated otherwise, all items are offered on a WHERE-IS, AS-IS basis with no
     warranties of any kind accompanying the goods. Buyer has been given the opportunity to inspect the
     material/equipment prior to submission of his bid and by such submittance has agreed to accept the
     material/equipment with any and all faults that should be reasonably determined by such an
     inspection.

9)   All bids become the property of _____. It is understood by all
     concerned that _____ retains the right to accept or reject any bid for any
     reason, accept other than the highest dollar bid, waive irregularities in any bid, negotiate with the
     higher bidders, and rebid the offering for any reason.

There are international trade consultants and brokers who can assist in the transactions for a fee.

The fourth and final variable of the marketing mix is *price*. The IR professional must know how to assess the value of the use and/or surplus assets that are to be disposed of. There are multiple "values" of any particular asset, including, but not limited to, book value, scrap value, replacement value, and fair market value. The appropriate assessment of a combination of these values forms the basis for the price. It is important to know what will generally provide the greatest and best use of an asset. Know what options are available.

FACILITY LIQUIDATION AND DISMANTLEMENT

The dismantlement/demolition of a facility or unit of a facility is the final step in the liquidation of the personal property asset(s) declared surplus to the needs of the entity.

IR's role normally begins when the facility or unit has been declared surplus and ends when the final disposition and/or dismantlement of the facility is complete. Between these two elements are a number of work processes to perform to maximize the return and keep the demolition and remediation costs at a minimum. When a facility has been surplused, IR works with management to evaluate the situation to arrive at the "one best" way to sell and/or reuse the assets. Their goal is to maximize the return at the lowest overall cost. The three processes normally used in the disposal of facility assets are:

1. *Sell the facility as a whole*, including spare parts, with the intent that the facility will be "match marked" and moved to another location at the new owner's expense. This process typically returns the most income to the owner at the least cost, but usually takes considerable amounts of time to find interested parties and consummate a sale. The new owner may do some final demolishing after the removal.

2. *Dismantlement*. This process identifies the valuable assets that owner and IR desire to retain to either sell or reuse internally. Assets are identified prior to the bidding process. All assets are clearly identified, not only in the specifications for the work but also physically by color coding or tagging. Valuable assets for sale or reuse should not be limited to the equipment,

but should include materials such as valves, electrical wiring, motors, high-value stores inventory, scrap metal(s), and other items that the recoverer feels can produce more value than the contractor will give credit(s) for. Normally, the identified assets retained by the owner are removed by the contractor during the course of the work. Unwanted assets become "razed property" and become the property of the contractor upon signing of the contract.

3. *Demolish for scrap only.* In this case, the equipment and materials are demolished and sold as scrap with the assets becoming razed property for the contractor. This method normally generates the least return but is the most expedient. In some cases, when the facility contains unusual volumes of high-value metals, i.e., copper, stainless steel, etc., the contractor(s) will pay for the privilege of demolishing the site for the metals they recover.

The first thing you need to do when a facility is approved for demolition is to get a list of what is included and what is specifically excluded and of any preparatory work, such as remediation. You cannot get an appraised value without knowing what equipment is included. How do you know what potential safety and environmental impacts will apply if you do not know what equipment there is at the start? If asbestos and/or lead paint is prevalent, the issue should be addressed of how the remediation will be done. Will the demolition contractor be required to perform the remediation, or will it be done by others prior to the demolition? A list is mandatory. If at all possible, check the facts yourself. This becomes increasingly important if the facility you are liquidating is in reality a part of a multiplant facility.

A demolition project site is no different from a construction site. If something serious should happen on a construction or demolition site, you could still have the responsibility and the legal liability to keep things under control and ensure that any investigation complies with your company policy. Consult a lawyer for clarification. Criminal or civil charges can be brought against you or your company for any incident due to willful negligence of the contractor.

In all cases and whenever possible, individuals familiar with the facility should be retained until the demolition is complete. Their knowledge is invaluable not only to the contractor, but also to the owner, to ensure that the work is done in accordance with the contract and that all safety and/or work issues can be answered so as not to create undue safety hazards or delays for the contractor.

Contracting for demolition/dismantlement is typically done using one or a combination of three types of contracts. These are:

1. *Lump sum contract.* Scope of work is defined by IR or others, including what will or will not be retained by owner. The contractor keeps all property not identified by owner as razed property and submits a fixed price for the performance of the work. In this instance either the owner pays the contractor or the contractor pays the owner. Normally, lump sum is the best way to contract for the work.

2. *Cost plus a fixed fee contract.* Typically used when either the scope of work cannot be clearly defined and/or the owner retains all the scrap equipment and materials to be sold. All costs of the work are borne by the owner, plus a percentage fee above the cost is added as contractor profit. This is a good method when the work is not clearly defined and many changes in the work are expected.

3. *Time and materials contract.* Used as in 2, but in this case the contractor adds a profit and overhead percentage to the actual hourly labor rates. Owner pays rental costs on the required equipment and also a percentage markup on materials and supplies. T&M contracts are an excellent contract method for small-dollar demolitions (under $200M), and also when the scope is not well defined or when time is of the essence. Typically, an annual agreement is developed for this type of work with one or two contractors.

If IR is responsible for demolition contracting, an "approved" contractors' list should be developed and maintained. A contractor questionnaire is developed and sent to the prospective contractors. Typical items that are reviewed include:

- Name of contractor
- Address of contractor
- Financial strength
- Work experience over past five years
- Type of work performed
- OSHA incident rates

- Proof of insurance
- Past citation(s) or violation(s) history
- Tax exemption certificate
- Employee training programs
- Union/non-union
- Verifiable references
- Other

Demolition bids are really no different from any other bid for services that your purchasing department solicits. Many of the problems that occur with demolition contracts can be avoided through an effective bid effort.

The contractor list should be reviewed annually and updated information obtained to ensure that the prior-approved contractors remain on the approved list. Also, new potential contractors should be sent information and evaluated as the need arises.

Following is a checklist for successful performance of a dismantlement or demolition by IR is:

1. Define what assets are at the site, their value, and what the owner will retain.
2. Develop a disposal plan.
3. Address any remediation issues.
4. Ensure equipment is clean and ready for reuse or demolition.
5. Decide on the method of contracting: lump sum, T&M, etc.
6. Develop a "specification for the work" and an invitation to bid.
7. Select contractors for bidders.
8. Bid the work and have contractor site visit(s).
9. Evaluate the bids.
10. Award contract.
11. Follow work progress.
12. Dispose of equipment retained by owner.
13. Complete project; evaluate contractor's performance.

RECYCLING

Every organization produces material wastes. Offices produce waste paper. Factories, which are designed to produce products, often produce as much waste as final product. We should all be working to reduce these wastes to minimal levels, but some levels of disposal seem inevitable.

What remains, if handled properly, may turn out to be an unexpected cash bonus to your company in the form of direct sales and reduced costs. But first you have to think of it not as waste, but as by-products with potential value in the marketplace.

Although your organization may have hundreds of waste streams, you will want to narrow your focus to the ones that have the greatest opportunities for significant return. Value in the marketplace is defined by three variables: the inherent value of the material, its purity, and how much of it there is. Start with those materials that likely have some value, that are not contaminated and can be segregated, and that have sufficient volume to interest commercial buyers. Since the advent of the environmental movement, organizations have been looking at their waste streams with much more attention, so it is likely that someone in your organization already knows what is being disposed of and how. Common recyclables are paper and corrugated cardboard, glass, and metals of all kinds. Recycling of these materials has been part of these manufacturing processes since the 19th century. The oil crisis of the 1970s encouraged the recycling of petroleum-based materials, including plastics, organic solvents, and other chemicals.

In all cases, the return you will get for any recovered material is dependent upon its purity. Systems need to be set up in your organization to separate the recyclables. Do not forget the people as a part of such systems. They must be appropriately educated. Recovered materials can no longer be thought of as just another part of the trash. They have to be thought of as other products. That is, they are raw materials for those who receive them, and must be treated accordingly.

Another issue affecting your return is the marketplace. The recyclable markets, like raw material markets, are highly subject to world economic forces. Oil prices, regional economic cycles, and regulations all have significant impacts on prices. At this writing, the Asian economic slowdown, the world oil glut, and forced recycling by European Union directives have combined to raise supply while lowering demand, thus leading to long-time low prices for most recyclable commodities. But all markets turn around. Never count future income on either extreme of prices. Use long-term averages, and be sure to include the cost savings from not having to pay for landfill or incineration as part of the positive cash flow.

There is one way to avoid fluctuation in the recyclables markets— return the recycled material to the original process as an input raw material. This will not only guarantee you a reliable customer (yourself) but will provide you with an even greater return. If the recycled material can be used, it will reduce the need for buying virgin material, and the savings will almost always be greater than what can be returned from selling it.

There are, of course, many materials that are nearly impossible to recycle, including mixed or otherwise highly contaminated materials. Either the cost of cleaning them up or separating them is too high or, in some cases, the technology is not yet available. If it is not possible to use the material as is, disposal will have to be considered.

If the inherent energy content of such material is significant, the material may be a candidate for energy recovery. Many utility companies have set up energy-capturing incineration processes. These are usually safe alternatives to landfill that could be lower in cost and leave no long-term environmental legacy.

Mixed materials in the waste stream are usually the result of the original product design. If such material can be eliminated in the design stage, it will not show up in manufacturing. The role of the recovery specialist is not to tell designers how to design products. If a mixed material is needed to give the product its unique properties to win in the marketplace, so be it. But often material selections are made as part of the design process that are not critical to product performance. It is here that the recovery specialist can have an impact. The job is to educate the designers as to the issues and then to be available to provide ongoing consulting help when the designers need it. With particular design projects, the recovery specialist can assess the recycling potential of both the process byproducts and the product itself. Such judgments can be made only with knowledge of the recycle market and associated technical issues. When the assessment is done well, the findings may uncover the possibility of environmental marketing claims, giving the product even greater advantages in the marketplace.

Among the responsibilities of the recovery specialist is protecting the organization. This includes getting good value for the asset and ensuring that both its reputation and markets are protected.

The best way to get the best value for recyclables is to follow the markets. Market indices are published for recovered paper, glass, and metal commodities. Few such indices exist for recovered plastics and hydrocarbon solvents. Tracking virgin raw material prices is helpful, but sometimes they do not correlate well with the recycle market. A metal scrap disposal process is a recycling program with which many people are probably familiar. When setting up a contract for such a program, be sure to base pricing on a verifiable metal industry index such as American Metals Market or Comex and require verifiable indepent weight tickets for quantities sold.

If you have large, consistent streams of materials, use an open-bidding process to find the market prices. Make sure you know as much as possible about those to whom you award the business. Price is important, but it is not everything. Service—that is, picking the material up when promised—may be even more important in the manufacturing setting. Imagine a large factory scrambling to figure where to put the waste when the high bidder doesn't show up.

You must also have the confidence that the buyer will use the material as agreed. Otherwise you may have even larger issues with which to deal. Some of the waste materials you handle may be semifinished goods or rejected final products. Clearly, if not sold with appropriate usage restrictions, they could find their way into the same markets as your company's products. Besides reducing sales, this could damage the organization's credibility and quality image. This is especially true when your brand name is on the material. Such goods should ALWAYS be sold with a written agreement as to how they cannot be used. And then follow up, track the material, visit the purchasers' facilities to ensure compliance, review the paper trail, and visit trade shows to look for "leaks." Sell particularly sensitive materials to only one buyer. You then know to whom to turn if there are leaks.

It is obvious that with many kinds of hazardous materials great caution must be taken. Work only with well-qualified contractors with solid reputations. Even though the dangers of nonhazardous materials are less, they are still present. If a fly-by-night buyer abandons some waste materials after "cherry-picking" the high-value materials out, your organization will likely be liable for the cleanup. You could probably argue the legal issue—after all, the buyer assumed the cleanup responsibility when he bought it. But it is unlikely that you could win the negative publicity or community relations issue.

SAFETY AND ENVIRONMENTAL INVOLVEMENT

Some of the safety and environmental laws you need to have a working knowledge of are OSHA, CERCLA, RCRA, and HMTA.

The Occupational Safety and Health Act (OSHA) requires employers to provide for safe and healthful working conditions and work practices. OSHA also requires development of handling, labeling requirements, and safety precautions for hazardous materials. Another mandate requires employee health recordkeeping where there is potential for worker exposure to hazardous materials, and the development and enforcement of maximum permissible levels for contaminants in workplace air.

The Comprehensive Environmental Responsibility, Compensation, and Liability Act (CERCLA), commonly called "Superfund," regulates the cleanup of releases of hazardous substances into the environment and cleanup of inactive, contaminated waste sites. It covers hazardous substances found in the Clean Water Act, Clean Air Act, Resource Conservation and Recovery Act, and Toxic Substance Control Act. CERCLA is intended to cover all chemicals and materials produced and establishes a national contingency plan.

The Resource Conservation and Recovery Act (RCRA) is a cradle-to-grave system that requires closed-loop documentation on a specified list of materials found to be hazardous to human health or the environment. This documentation responsibility is placed on the generators and transporters of hazardous materials as well as the facilities that store, treat, and dispose of these substances. RCRA establishes a manifest or tracking system and standards for generators, transporters, and treatment storage and disposal facilities.

The Hazardous Materials Transportation Act (HMTA) provides for regulation of hazardous materials transported by air, rail, highway, pipeline, and water.

Most of us do not feel adequate when operating in the environmental arena solely on our own knowledge. Laws are built for specific hazardous materials, cases, and situations. It is important to consult a qualified expert, for your protection as well as your company's, when dealing with environmental issues. Such expertise may reside in your in-house environmental, legal, or transportation departments. In addition to in-house resources, the regulating government agencies as well as qualified third-party consultants and contractors can be resources on environmental law and procedures.

Whose safety and environmental rules should take precedent: federal, state, local, or your company's? The answer is your company's because they are obligated to follow existing laws. If you comply with company rules, you are complying with the rest of the rules as far as the company is concerned.

As stated previously, there are so many safety and environmental laws you could not be aware of, or have a working knowledge of, that is important to seek professional safety and environmental assistance. It would be wise to get to know your safety and environmental department. These folks are well versed in the laws and upcoming legislation concerning safety procedures, hazardous waste, carcinogens, and handling of controlled materials that affect how business is done. Federal safety and environmental regulation is a topic on which you may not be up to speed, but someone in your company should be, and that someone is the people that make up the safety and environmental group. Their role is to assist you in compliance matters.

It is not wise to take off on your own when you have access to people with a wealth of safety and environmental knowledge who are willing and able to provide informed guidance in safety and environmental issues. Compliance reduces operating costs by reducing the probability of violations and fines due to noncompliance.

We have all heard of "deep-pocket" rulings where a corporation is held liable for a large hazardous waste cleanup even though the firm's contributing percentage of the site's total contamination is minor. This usually happens when the waste site's owner or other waste generators are financially bankrupt or insolvent. If your company's safety and environmental people are involved when needed, chances are the deep pockets will not be yours. In addition to in-house resources, an ever-growing number of companies can offer expert consultants on U.S. safety and environmental regulations and cleanup procedures. The Department of Transportation (DOT) and the Environmental Protection Agency (EPA) are two sources of information. The DOT regulates transportation of chemicals and other hazardous and nonhazardous substances. The EPA is the federal agency with environmental protection, regulatory, and enforcement responsibility. The EPA administers the Clean Air Act; Clean Water Act; Federal Insecticide, Fungicide, and Rodenticide Act; Resource Conservation and Recovery Act; Substance Control Act; and other federal environmental laws.

These laws are tough, but there are regulations that you should adhere to even before them. You answer directly to your company and may be acting as an agent for your company in transactions involving hazardous materials. Certain statutes provide for personal liability and you personally could be found in violation of federal U.S. or Canadian provincial law. An investigation could find that you violated company rules that led to the determination of your being in violation of those laws. If you see something that does not look right, consult with a professional and let them determine proper handling, documentation and disposal procedures.

Let's turn our attention to hazardous waste. With today's cradle-to-grave responsibilities for hazardous waste, companies live under a perpetual cloud of liability. The laws that pertain to the disposal of hazardous waste can generally be found under RCRA for disposals in the United States and under provincial statutes in Canada.

A key element and current trend in solving a company's environmental problems is the discovery of new ways to minimize waste and reuse and recycle material used in the production process. This is an area where IR can be a big contributor.

SALES CONTRACT CONSIDERATIONS

An example of a surplus sales agreement is presented in Figure 28–5. Some particular surplus sales contracting considerations include confidentiality, restriction of use of item sold, indemnity, warranties, condition of item, inspection and payment, cancellation of sale, buyback, safety rules and regulations, and hazardous waste and environmental compliance.

Confidentiality and Limitation of Use

Assume that you have sold something to company A. If you wanted to protect your technological advances that may be discernible from the item you sold, you can, in the sales contract, restrict company A's transferring title of the item to another party. There are also ways to limit the use to which someone can put an item that they have purchased from your company. Your attorney can assist you in developing appropriate confidentiality and restriction of use clauses for your particular situation.

Indemnity

Indemnity is the section of a contract that usually refers to someone protecting you from a liability to which you might be exposed. The seller should make the buyer responsible for any injury, illness, death to any

F I G U R E   28–5

Sale Agreement

SALE AGREEMENT

THIS SALE AGREEMENT is dated the _____ day of _____ , 19 _____ , between

_____
"Seller," and _____

_____ "Buyer" (include Company Name and address).

1. Buyer hereby purchases from Seller the following property: _____

_____

_____

_____

"Property".

2. The purchase price is _____ ($ _____).

3. WARNING! ANY PORTION OF THE PROPERTY AND/OR ANY CONTAINER THEREOF, WHICH BUYER MAY HEREAFTER RECEIVE FROM SELLER MAY BE OR MAY BECOME (BY CHEMICAL REACTION OR OTHERWISE), DIRECTLY OR INDIRECTLY, HAZARDOUS TO LIFE, TO HEALTH, OR TO PROPERTY BY REASON OF TOXICITY, FLAMMABILITY, EXPLOSIVENESS OR FOR OTHER SIMILAR OR DIFFERENT REASONS, DURING USE, HANDLING, CLEANING, RECONDITIONING, OR DISPOSAL. No limitation in this broad warning shall bind Seller unless the limitation is expressly made in writing by Seller's Division Vice President. No additional specific warning shall be deemed to limit this broad warning, and if the additional specific warning is inadequate, all of the terms and conditions of sale hereinbelow set forth shall still apply, even if the inadequacy of the specific warning was due to negligence on Seller's part and no course of action on Seller's part shall be deemed to limit this broad warning.

4. The terms and conditions of this sale shall be as follows:

(A) NO WARRANTIES. The Property is sold, "AS IS, WHERE IS, WITH ALL FAULTS." THERE ARE NO EXPRESS WARRANTIES EXCEPT THAT SELLER OWNS THE PROPERTY. NO WARRANTIES, INCLUDING, BUT NOT LIMITED TO, WARRANTY OF MERCHANTABILITY OR WARRANTY OF FITNESS FOR A PARTICULAR PURPOSE, SHALL BE IMPLIED.

(B) RISK OF LOSS. Buyer assumes all risks of loss after delivery by Seller.

(C) INDEMNIFICATION. BUYER AGREES TO INDEMNIFY SELLER AND TO HOLD SELLER HARMLESS AGAINST ANY AND ALL LIABILITY COST AND EXPENSE (including reasonable attorneys' fees) TO ANY AND ALL PERSONS FOR INJURY, SICKNESS, AND DEATH AND FOR PROPERTY DAMAGE ARISING OUT OF THE HANDLING, TRANSPORTATION, STORAGE, USE, RESALE, OR DISPOSITION OF THE PROPERTY, WHETHER OR NOT DUE TO THE NEGLIGENCE OF SELLER, arising after delivery by Seller to Buyer and whether arising out of strict liability, negligence, warranty or any other cause of action.

(D) WARNING BY BUYER. Buyer agrees to give warning of any possible hazard to any person or persons to whom Buyer resells, gives or delivers the Property or whom Buyer can reasonably foresee may be exposed to such hazard whether or not in the containers in which the Property was delivered to Buyer or Seller.

(E) REMOVAL OF _____ MARKS. Buyer agrees to remove any and all   trademarks, labels, distinctive markings and designs which may appear on the Property, the packaging material or the container therefore at the time of delivery of same to Buyer, and to refrain from making and use of such trademarks, labels, distinctive markings and designs.

(F) PAYMENTS. All payments are to be made in full by certified check or cashiers check, upon   execution of this Sales Agreement and before shipment of the Property or pick-up by Buyer, unless otherwise agreed upon in writing between Seller and Buyer.

(G) FORCE MAJEURE. Seller shall not be liable for its failure to perform hereunder due to any contingency beyond its reasonable control, including acts of God, fires, floods, wars, sabotage, accidents, labor disputes or shortages, governmental laws, ordinances, rules and regulations, whether valid or invalid (including, but not limited to priorities, requisitions, allocations, and price adjustment restrictions), inability to obtain material, equipment or transportation, and any other similar or different contingency.

F I G U R E   28–5

Continued

(H) <u>SHIPMENT TERMS.</u> Unless otherwise specified, the place of delivery of the Property to Buyer shall be at the Seller's premises where the Property is located. Unless specifically excluded under subparagraph 4(N), Buyer shall pay all costs of preparing the Property for shipping and loading.

(I) <u>CONSEQUENTIAL DAMAGES.</u> IN NO EVENT AND UNDER NO CIRCUMSTANCES SHALL SELLER BE LIABLE FOR ANY INCIDENTAL OR CONSEQUENTIAL DAMAGES.

(J) <u>TAXES.</u> Buyer agrees to pay, at the time of sale, all applicable sales or use taxes or other taxes, charges, or fees required to be paid or collected by Seller by reason of this sale, or to provide Seller with valid exemption certificate. In the event that Buyer either fails to pay the tax or other charges as agreed above or fails to provide a valid exemption certificate, Buyer agrees to indemnify and hold Seller harmless from any liability and expense by reasonof Buyer's failure.

(K) <u>INSURANCE.</u> Buyer shall not move, load transport or otherwise handle the Property on Seller's premises without first having obtained insurance coverage satisfactory to Seller. Such insurance shall include Workers' Compensation, Employer's Liability, Public Liability (Bodily Injury, Property Damage and Contractual Liability) and Automotive Liability (Bodily Injury and Property Damage) Insurance. Certificates of Insurance evidencing the aforementioned insurance coverages shall be furnished to and shall be approved by Seller. Buyer shall comply with Seller's plant safety rules. Seller may, at its sole option, waive this insurance requirement.

(L) <u>MODIFICATION.</u> Buyer understands and agrees that (a) no modification or waiver of the Warning contained in Paragraph 3, above, shall be effective unless made in accordance with that Paragraph, and no modifications of the terms and conditions of sale setout in this Paragraph 4 shall be effective unless made by an authorized representative of Seller in writing addressed to Buyer and specifically referring to this document; (b) no course of action on the part of the Seller shall be deemed to modify the Warning or the terms and conditions of sale, and (c) Seller's acknowledgement or acceptance of anything in writing from Buyer which is in conflict with the Warning or the terms and conditions of sale and any subsequent delivery of items shall not constitute a modification or waiver of the Warning or these terms and conditions of sale.

(M) <u>GOVERNING LAW.</u> This instrument shall be construed according to the laws of the State in which the property is delivered to the Buyer.

(N) <u>ADDITIONAL TERMS:</u>

_____

_____

_____

_____

_____

IN WITNESS WHEREOF, the parties have signed this Sale Agreement.

SELLER   BUYER

Company Name: _____

Division/Location: _____   Company Name: _____

Signature: _____   Signature: _____

Title: _____   Title: _____

persons, damage to property, and liability for pollution contamination from spills, leaks, discharges, improper storage, and transportation.

Warranties

Contract terms and conditions should include no express or implied warranties. The Uniform Commercial Code identifies four specific types of warranties:

1. Warranty of title
2. Implied warranty of merchantability
3. Implied warranty of fitness for a particular purpose
4. Express warranty

Warranty of title implies that you own the goods and have the authority to sell. If you imply that the goods are in fair market condition and can be used for their intended service, that is an implied warranty of merchantability. An implied warranty of fitness for a particular purpose might come into play if the buyer is relying on your expertise in providing goods to do a particular required job. Express warranties are those specifically stated in the sales agreement, such as size, capacity, and model.

Condition of Item

Make sure your purchaser knows that the goods are sold "as is, where is" and the condition of the goods is as reported and inspected (unless in order to make a sale or secure a higher price you are willing to agree to support some particular condition of the material or to relocate the material for the purchaser).

Inspection and Payment

When the removal of goods is involved, limit any potential problems by having the buyer inspect the premises where the goods are located and familiarize themselves with removal conditions. Personal inspections can help eliminate many misunderstandings. Be specific on payment terms. Payment should be made before any goods change hands. Most companies prefer certified checks, cashier's checks, or money orders, unless they are dealing with a reliable party with established credit. The seller is responsible for reporting and remitting all tax due to states, whether or not the tax is separately billed to the purchaser. Taxes normally are due to the state in which delivery is made.

Cancellation Clause

Another important section in your terms and conditions should be a cancellation clause. Reserve the right to cancel the sales contract if performance by the buyer to pay and/or take possession is not undertaken within a reasonable amount of time or the performance is not satisfactory.

Buy-Back Clause

There are situations where the seller's experience indicates that occasionally an internal need for the sold material arises shortly after the sale. To protect against such events in those situations, the seller should try to get the buyer to agree to a clause that allows the seller to repurchase the material, with the buyer's agreement, within 30 days or some reasonable time, at the price at which it was sold plus any expenses the buyer incurred in removing or handling the material.

Safety Rules and Regulations

Make it a part of your contract to state that a purchaser shall perform work in a safe, workmanlike, and efficient manner. In cases where the purchaser will be working on the seller's premises, request a certificate of insurance evidencing that the purchaser, at minimum, maintains worker's compensation, comprehensive general liability, and automobile liability insurance policies. The purchaser should comply with all the seller's site rules and safety regulations and act at his own costs and risk and in no way an agent or employee of the seller. Seller should be specific on when and how removal of the good is to be made. Make sure any changes to your contract are in writing.

Hazardous Waste and Environmental Compliance

A very important section of your contract should be a hazardous waste and environmental compliance clause. This clause should obligate the buyer to be compliant with all federal, state, and local laws dealing with the environment, hazardous materials handling, and human health. This clause should also warn the purchaser of any potential environmental hazards involved in the equipment or material itself and/or in the removal of the equipment or material and of the purchaser's duty to warn others of any potential hazards.

CORPORATE DONATIONS

There are a number of national and local nonprofit organizations that compete for corporate donations of money and surplus items. These charities support a wide variety of worthy causes.

Used cafeteria furniture for a homeless soup kitchen, furniture for a crisis and counseling center, copy machines for the associations in support of the handicapped, are some examples of what can be provided for your own communities.[2]

Donations are another area of concern to the IR professional. Number one, they remove an item from the list of items from which we are expecting a return. Granted, every company has its own philosophy when it comes to donations, but it is important that you do not do anything that jeopardizes the options available to your company. This leads to number two, the fact that as IR professionals we do not deal with donations nearly often enough to be experts at it. Before agreeing to donate anything, one of the first things you should verify is proof that the organization has been granted an exemption status. In order to obtain exemption status, an organization must file an application and meet certain requirements. All companies that make contributions to a charitable organization are able to claim deductions for these donations on their federal income tax.

The U.S. federal code that applies to charitable donations is 501(C)3. For Canada the applicable section of the Canadian Income Tax Act is 110.1.

Common sense must be used in all such dispositions to minimize liability and to avoid donating specialized items not intended for use by the general public or giving away items needed by or of value to your company at another location. The positive recognition your company will receive in the community outweighs in most cases the financial benefit. Put some thought and effort into donations. The recognition your IR program receives from your company and the community, plus the personal satisfaction you derive, might surprise you.

Donations must also be consistent with your company's authority policy. It is important for you to know who has what approval authority and the transaction limits. It is customary to receive a written request for the donation as well as a letter acknowledging the receipt of your donation from the nonprofit organization.

---

2. R. Cuniberti, "Local Charitable Donations," *IRA-News Journal*, March 1990.

ADDITIONAL READINGS

Byrns, R., and G. Stone. *Microeconomics* 6th ed., HarperCollins, New York, 1995.

Cuniberti, R. "Local Charitable Donations." *IRA-News Journal*, March 1990.

Dollar, W. *Effective Commercial Negotiations.* DOLLAR Group, Houston, 1995

Russell, W. G. *Life Cycle Accounting Increases Return on Assets.* Coopers & Lybrand, 1994.

CHAPTER 29

Managing Budgets and Operations

Editor
Henry F. Garcia, C.P.M.
Director of Administration
Center for Nuclear Waste Regulatory Analyses

OVERVIEW OF BUDGETING

In government or business, the two primary functions of managers are planning and controlling operations. Budgeting involves all levels of management and remains integral to the successful execution of these two functions. Fundamentally, a budget is a plan, expressed quantitatively, that specifies how resources will be acquired and used during a specific period of time. The time dimension should be unique to the planning horizon(s) employed by each public or private sector organization, and it should be designed to accommodate the organization's particular needs and characteristics. Budgeting by a government entity is driven primarily by the need to allocate scarce resources, funded by revenue collected from taxes and fees, among its organizational components. Government entity expenses are restrained by available funds (revenue). Since business revenue depends on sales, there is no limitation or constraint on revenue. The allocation of scarce resources and availability of funding are thus not the driving force behind business budgeting. Sales revenue assumes certain costs and expenses necessary to generate this revenue. A business, however, should correlate its revenue with its expenses, which can be achieved without necessarily minimizing expenses.

Government or business managers should protect and improve the financial performance and position of their organizations, consistent with

741

the conduct of business. Traditionally, government managers demonstrate financial performance through the effective allotment of scarce resources to the delivery of requisite services (defense/safety, social services, and infrastructure) and the efficient use of approved funding. Further, they maintain the entity's financial position by the productive use of fiscal policy or bond rating. Business managers, on the other hand, usually manifest performance through earning a reasonable profit and sustaining a positive cash flow for the organization. They retain the firm's position by efficiently using capital assets and effectively meeting liquidity and solvency requirements. Thus, proper budgeting not only emphasizes the "best management practices," but stresses the financial bottom line regardless of sector.

Budgeting is a systematic and formalized approach for performing significant phases of planning. It involves developing and applying long- and short-range plans, along with their corresponding objectives and goals, and establishing a system of organization-specific periodic performance reports and follow-up procedures. Examples of budgeting as it affects the performance of these functions are presented below.

In the public sector, a city presents in its five-year budgetary plan and annual budget how it will apportion its revenue among safety (e.g., police and fire protection), social services (e.g., childcare and alcohol/drug rehabilitation), and infrastructure maintenance (e.g., city streets, recreation facilities, and public buildings). The city council receives periodic reports on departmental activities and may ask the mayor or city manager to create/modify operating procedures to mitigate problems associated with service delivery. In the private sector, a cruise line uses its fiscal year plan and budget to meet operating expenses, match staffing and equipment with projected cruise demand, and allocate capital improvement funds among competing needs. Examples of competing needs are expansion of its fleet or improvement of its on-land facilities. This cruise line employs periodic reports to evaluate managerial performance and offers bonuses to mangers who meet or exceed their budgets' profit objectives and goals. Operating procedures, specifically those involving performance incentives, may be revised to accommodate changing expectations.

BUDGETING FOR OPERATIONS

Essentially a collaborative process, budgeting requires that managers from all parts or levels of the organization (divisions, departments, and units) contribute knowledge and experience of their particular activities and responsibilities toward the integrated development of a comprehensive or master budget. The budget at each part or level constitutes the summation of all the budgets at the next-lower part or level, in addition to the costs and other budget items associated with the management of that particular part or level. Moreover, a summary of information is presented at each part or level upward. The organization's budget represents a consolidation of budgets that match its structure, because each of these parts or levels has an organizational structure within it.

To illustrate, consider a national distribution firm whose sales division is responsible for selling a number of dissimilar products in various geographic regions. The initial budgets come from each of the branches (units). All of a single region's branch budgets are then consolidated into that individual region's (department) budget. The budgets from all regions, plus those for sales administration (overhead), are combined into the sales division's budget. Concurrently, the budgets of other divisions of the firm are constructed in the same manner. Ultimately, the firm's budget is the amalgamation of all divisions, departments, and units. This budget, provided in a mixture of financial and activity formats, supplies the information used by senior management to effectively manage the firm.

The purchasing department, too, offers its budget along with the others. Purchasing may have operating units responsible for securing certain goods and services in each region. These units present their decentralized budgets for incorporation into the centralized purchasing budget. For example, the interrelationship of the merchandizing budgets affects purchasing operations, since purchasing is responsible for acquiring merchandise for sale by the sales division of the firm.

BUDGETING PROCESS

A budget is the pivotal point of planning. Budgets aid organizational management in planning, primarily for the following year, offering a sense of reality to the organization's strategies and objectives and providing a vehicle for monitoring business operations and, where applicable, profit performance. Budgeting is a management exercise. Since a budget inherently considers an uncertain future, managers recognize that external factors beyond their control often influence the success or failure of the final budget. Because many managers are evaluated on their performance against the budget, they may not be motivated to submit challenging and realistic budgetary data or information. Managers usually present a conservative budget that will gain certain approval. This "gamesmanship" makes budgeting a psychological process, revolving around the intrinsic competition and conflicts among participants from the organization's divisions, departments, and units. The budgeting process, then, should take a behavioral approach to moderate this tendency while planning the best performance realistically achievable consistent with the organization's strategies and objectives.

Managers (division, department, and unit) should communicate objectives, establish operating parameters, set labor and capital resource needs, examine requirements and expectations, consider assumptions, provide variance flexibility, and provide feedback. Like other managers, the purchasing manager should focus on objectivity and concentrate on real opportunities and problems, rather than on "games." Moreover, purchasing managers must deal realistically with uncertainty and uncontrollability, while eliminating these as causes of confusion, and dedicate themselves to promulgating effective strategies with attainable objectives. Essentially, managers must "think it through" before initiating the budgeting process.

The budget process, then, should use a bottom-up approach, especially when managers are initially involved. Managers at each level understand the priority of objectives, recognize the presence of opportunities, anticipate the possibility of problems, and comprehend the process for allocating limited resources. They expect the budget to be analyzed, adjusted, and approved by the next level(s) of management.

Budget preparation in the public sector can commence one year prior to submittal of the final budget. In the private sector, preparation usually begins three or four months before the organization's fiscal year starts. Although varying among organizations within each sector, budgeting involves four essential steps:

1. Budget forms and instructions are distributed to all managers.
2. Forms are completed and submitted to the next level of management.
3. Individual budgets are transformed into the appropriate terms and consolidated into one organizational budget.
4. Final budget is reviewed, modified (if necessary), and approved.

Initially, budget forms are disseminated to lower-level (unit or department) managers either on paper or electronically (diskette, local area network, or organizational intranet). These forms and their accompanying instructions contain the detailed schedule for the organization's budget process; the assumptions and ground rules applicable throughout each part or level of the organization; the general objectives and priorities for budget preparation; and any changes in procedures from the previous year. Managers prepare their budgets, based on the instructions and general guidance, and submit them on the forms provided. Management, whether line or staff, performs the transformation and consolidation of these lower-level budgets. These budgets are then configured into the financial format used by the entire organization. This transformation and consolidation step becomes integral to the exercise of review, modification, and approval—the final step in the budgeting process. Managers at every level reconsider, change, and accept the individual budgets as they transform and consolidate them for the next level of management to approve. This iterative process culminates with the final review and adoption of the organization's budget by the ultimate approval authority.

The purchasing department develops its own budget and uses that together with the organization's budget. In the exercise of its responsibilities, this department maintains access to the organization's master budget, including all sub-budgets, to ensure that purchasing does not "commit" or "encumber" funds in excess of those approved (budgeted) for securing goods or services from each division, department, or unit within the organization. Moreover, the purchasing department can use these budgets to schedule delivery of goods or performance of services to coincide with funds available for payment of such goods and services during each fiscal period.

TYPES OF BUDGETS

Before the various types of budgets are delineated, it is important to recognize their utility to each part or level of organizational management in protecting and improving the financial performance and position of the organization. A budget is useful to all levels of management, especially senior management, to

- ◆ Implement long-range (strategic) and short-range (tactical) plans, ensuring that the whole organization is moving in the same direction
- ◆ Coordinate the organization's business, ensuring that the entire organization focuses on accomplishing these plans
- ◆ Anticipate results and needs, envisioning the consequence(s) of fiscal and operational actions and the requirement(s) for resource allocation

- Determine budgetary reliability, comparing planned estimates with actual expenditures
- Control costs and activities, allowing management to review all spending relative to the master budget or a particular sub-budget and requiring justification for any proposed activity in these budgets
- Measure performance, permitting each level of management to evaluate adherence to the budget affected by changing organizational priorities and business conditions

Senior management should prepare a master budget, consisting of integrated sub-budgets, to summarize planned activities. A master budget is based on organization-wide forecasts, estimates, targets, and predictions. Its nature and scope will vary with divisional, departmental, or unit characteristics. To provide flexibility, a master budget may contain optimistic, expected, or pessimistic estimates. The master and all sub-budgets must interrelate. The following types of budgets represent components of or complements to the individual sub-budgets and reflect specific purposes for these sub-budgets.

- *Activity-based:* Delineates the expected costs for specific activities or functions
- *Add-on:* Reviews previous years' budgets and adjusts them for current requirements
- *Bracket:* Offers a contingency plan where costs are predicated at higher or lower amounts than the base figures
- *Capital:* Lists key long-term, fixed-asset expenditures
- *Cash:* Relates the expected cash inflow with outflow for a stated time period; assists the managers with maintaining cash balances in relation to organization needs; avoids idle cash and possible cash shortages
- *Financial:* Examines the financial condition of the division, department, or unit
- *Fixed:* Presents budgeted amounts at the expected capacity level without adjustments for unexpected changes in division, department, or unit resource allocations
- *Flexible:* Allows for variances in organizational activities and unanticipated changes in labor and capital resources
- *Incremental:* Estimates budget increases in percent or dollars without considering the master budget

- *Operating:* Defines the total cost of products produced and services provided—the operating aspects of the organization
- *Program:* Allocates funding based on cost/benefit, risk, and, where applicable, expected rate of return,
- *Strategic:* Integrates strategic planning and budgetary control
- *Stretch:* Reflects optimistic projections primarily of revenues
- *Supplemental:* Provides additional funding for items not included in the existing budget
- *Target:* Categorizes major expenditures and compares them to division, department, and unit objectives

Managers, especially at the lower levels of the organization, should be aware of these budget types and apply a bottom-up approach to their development. These budgets may be applicable to or consistent with particular sub-budgets and used to manage the planning and control of division, department, and unit activities.

BUDGET APPLICATIONS

Division, department, and unit managers collaborate with the purchasing department in the development of their sub-budgets for securing goods and services. In some organizations, purchasing prepares the budget for acquisition of goods and services for the entire organization in addition to preparing its own departmental budget. Through the careful development and judicious application of their budget, purchasing managers improve the operational efficiency and effectiveness of their organizations. These managers can enhance services in the public sector or increase profits in the private sector by following their budget when selecting appropriate source(s) for and ensuring timely delivery of quality goods and services.

Purchasing managers are responsible for securing quality goods and services from the most responsible supplier(s) at a fair price and on a timely basis. They should use the master budget and all relevant sub-budgets to guide and bound the exercise of this responsibility. For example, purchasing managers can use budgetary variance analysis to adjust service or product pricing, inventory costing, and delivery timing. Moreover, these managers set quality and quantity standards before establishing a corresponding unit price for a good or service. These standards are based on the managers' knowledge of price data and market conditions.

BUDGET PREPARATION

Organizational managers, including the purchasing manager, should prepare comprehensible and attainable budgets. They should use innovation and flexibility to meet unexpected occurrences. Irrespective of the type, budgets can fulfill their potential through the following requirements.

Budgetary planning should be accomplished within the framework of the organization's strategies, objectives, and goals. Managers should establish a planning continuum leading from these strategies, objectives, and goals to the finished budget. In establishing this continuum, they should scrutinize inside controllable as well as outside uncontrollable factors that affect budgetary performance, identify critical factors that influence the success of the plan, consider producing a one-page summary strategy statement, and provide preliminary budget numbers. Budgetary assumptions, whether developed by lower-level managers or accepted from senior management, should deal realistically with the uncertainty and uncontrollability associated with these outside factors. These assumptions should be explicit so that all "interested parties" understand which factors are controllable and subject to performance assessment/improvement and which are uncontrollable and must be responded to by managers on an ad hoc basis. The importance of establishing appropriate assumptions lies in the rational process of identifying and recognizing how these factors influence management decisions.

The budget format for each part or level within the organization should readily identify financial and performance variances throughout the year and provide information on the potential benefits and consequences of management actions. This format should emphasize cash flow instead of revenue or sales, focus on total costs instead of burdens and ratios, and relate outputs to activities and actions. Of course, the best format for any organization depends on the specific purpose of that organization.

Budgetary content should furnish the most likely numerical predictions of next year's revenue/sales and expenditures. Because the budget addresses the future, the numbers that represent expected performance are estimates. Managers should ensure these numbers are the most probable and meaningful estimates possible. Good content, based on direct data, trends, or models, requires the proper planning for and a clear understanding of the organization's expected output. Direct data and trends must be time-sensitive because service or product demand is not constant and conditions causing the trend will change. Models are approximations, but they are a better source of predictions than inaccurate direct data or trends, particularly for organizations that can benefit from statistical and probability analyses.

The budget process should encourage excellence and continuous performance improvement from all parts or levels of the organization. Because obstacles to best performance are arrayed against this objective, a specific technique is required. Gap analysis, an effective technique for this purpose, begins with identifying a parameter of concern (e.g., cash flow or total costs) known as gap dimension. Next, the desired goal for this parameter is projected with the expected status quo result, the consequence of continuing to perform activities in the same way. Defining the extent or magnitude (dimension) of a parameter of concern involves determining the gap or difference between these two projections. Finally, action programs are developed to close the gap. This budgeting technique is used to decide and plan the most important actions throughout the organization for at least the following year. Gap analysis focuses the organization's attention on achieving important results from the application of these action programs.

Budgetary flow and attention to details require the dedicated efforts of management from all parts or levels of the organization. Effecting a coherent, efficient, and timely process flow suggests two stages to tie everything together. In the first stage, "thinking it through," managers complete the budgetary plans, communicate the organizational strategies, and develop the requisite action programs. The main output of this initial stage is a preliminary budget, which is easier to change if budgeted results (numbers) are inconsistent with organizational plans, strategies, or programs. In the second stage, "crunching the numbers," managers generate details of the final budget for each part or level of the organization. These details should be carefully organized to ensure accuracy, agreement, and acceptance throughout the organization. Managers should follow all budgetary guidance, include all elements of cost for any given activity, and seek approval of all budgets from each part or level of the organization.

Preparing the budget for each part or level, with subsequent assimilation into the master budget for the organization, involves the following steps.

1. *Review strategies, objectives, and goals.* Managers should set individual division, department, or unit objectives and goals to ensure consistency with those of the organization.

2. *Plan the work.* Managers should understand the nature and scope of their division, department, or unit activities; identify the expected output from the conduct of these activities; and establish a schedule for accomplishment.

3. *Define needed resources.* Managers should establish realistic estimates for revenue/sales and expenditures and determine the necessary capital and labor resources to achieve individual division, department, or unit objectives and goals.

4. *Generate accurate budget numbers.* Managers should produce numbers that reflect, to the extent possible, the experience-based estimates of expected activities in each division, department, or unit to conform with organization strategic or tactical plans.

5. *Present the budget/secure approval.* Managers should agree on a uniform method for presenting and "selling" their division, department, or unit budget to senior management responsible for the master budget.

Proper budget preparation contributes to good management and organizational performance. It offers an effective vehicle for dissemination of fiscal information, incorporation of plans and strategies, and promulgation of an assured attitude for management decisions. Moreover, it promotes prudence and control in the exercise of all activities as well as reasonable and timely reaction to the problems and surprises affecting all organizations.

BUDGET ANALYSIS AND REVISION

Budgets are dynamic models of estimated revenue/sales and expected spending. They must be reviewed periodically to ensure the relevance of planned estimates and modified accordingly to reflect actual expenditures. Variance analysis involves a mathematical comparison of two sets of data examining the differences between revenue/sales estimates and actual spending. It can be used to gain insight into the underlying causes of a variance. Planned estimates are treated as the base or reference point, while the actual expenditures are regarded as the point of departure.

An acceptable tolerance range (e.g., percent) should be fixed. It should be contingent on the objectives and operating parameters set for each division, department, or unit and for the entire organization. The range must be based on assumptions and expectations used and the extent of uncertainty and uncontrollability associated with outside factors.

With the application of this range, managers can determine permissible tolerances between:

+ Estimated revenue/sales and actual spending for any fiscal period or year
+ Actual results of the current fiscal period and those of a prior period
+ Estimated year-to-date revenue/sales and actual spending for the present fiscal year

Managers should compare actual expenditures with planned estimates for controlling operations. If expenditures differ from estimates to an extent beyond the acceptable tolerance range, managers are responsible for making or recommending the necessary revision(s) to the particular budgets.

Moreover, managers should understand the underlying causes of a variance. Poor planning and estimating, errors in reporting, uncontrollable factors, and certain management decisions may cause variances. Managers should pay special attention to variances for which the underlying causes are not known. Since variances are interrelated, their net effect should be considered. For example, the production department may show a favorable variance indicating lower unit cost of producing a particular item. Conversely, the inventory department may experience an unfavorable variance resulting from the higher cost of holding excess inventory of this item unless it is already sold.

Division, department, or unit budgets, especially those sections pertaining to the acquisition of goods and services, affect the purchasing department. In the conduct of its activities, purchasing usually is responsible for closely monitoring these budgets to ensure compliance with budgetary limits for securing goods and services for the organization. If the procurement of a good or service exceeds the limit for the specific budget cost category, the purchasing department should contact the division, department, or unit to secure the proper authorization to either ignore the limit or modify the budget, as required. Depending on the policies, procedures, or practices of the organization, purchasing may be empowered to make the necessary adjustments to individual budgets.

PURCHASING DEPARTMENT BUDGET

Like other parts or levels of the organization, the purchasing department produces a budget. Because purchasing is an overhead department, its budget usually reflects only indirect operational costs. Contingent on sector identity and organizational practice, this budget may include such cost categories as merchandise for resale; materials for in-process inventory; maintenance, repair, and operating items; capital equipment; and other materials and supplies. To the extent that it includes these cost categories, the purchasing department's budget is interdependent with the other parts or levels of the organization. Purchasing collaborates with each division, department, and unit to secure the proper inputs to their budget. As mentioned, the purchasing department usually monitors the expenditure of funds for the acquisition of goods and services for the entire organization.

CONCLUSION

In government or business, budgeting involves all levels of management in the systematic and formalized approach to the successful execution of the planning and controlling functions. A budget results from a plan that defines how resources will be acquired and used during a specific time horizon. It not only represents a strong management tool, but stresses the financial bottom lines of the public and private sectors. Essentially a collaborative and iterative process, budgeting requires all parts or levels of the organization to integrate their budgets with the master budget. The purchasing department participates in this process by contributing its budget for assimilation into the master budget.

Purchasing should seek a proactive role in the development and implementation of all the organization budgets, especially those involving the acquisition of goods and services. In a previous section, the sales division identified the purchasing department as responsible for acquiring merchandise for resale. The purchasing department should collaborate in the development of the organization's other budgets to ensure that it recognizes the available funding to secure goods or services for each division, department, or unit within the organization.

The purchasing department should have responsibility and authority to monitor budget consumption for goods and services from each division, department, or unit of the organization. Irrespective of budget type, purchasing uses the budgets from each part or level of the organization, including its own, to plan and control the expenditures for acquired goods and services. In planning and controlling these expenditures, purchasing managers can use budgetary variance analysis to make requisite adjustments to these budgets. Such adjustments are based on these managers' knowledge of and experience with source selection, price data, market conditions, and established quality standards.

The purchasing department retains a pivotal position in using primarily the materials and supply budgets from other organizational groups to control spending. Purchasing is a vital resource to the organization in preparation and implementation of the master budget and the associated division, department, or unit sub-budgets.

CHAPTER 30

Marketing Purchasing and Supply

Editor
Alvin J. Williams, Ph.D.
Chair and Professor
Department of Management and Marketing
University of Southern Mississippi

INTRODUCTION

The purchasing and supply management field continues to undergo noteworthy change. Changes in both external and internal business environments encourage constant review of what purchasers do and how they execute their responsibilities. A review of the supply management landscape makes it apparent that a critical success factor throughout the organization is marketing acumen. Supply managers who are successful over a sustained period of time employ marketing skills in various facets of organizational work. Given the pivotal role that marketing plays in initiating and maintaining key internal and external linkages, it is incumbent upon supply managers to master the rudiments of marketing and the purchasing and supply management applications of marketing. The following sections detail marketing's role in contributing to supply management effectiveness.

CHANGES IN PURCHASING ENCOURAGING A MARKETING ORIENTATION

More and Varied Internal and External Linkages

Increasingly, purchasing professionals are required to interface with a wider array of organizational and nonorganizational members than ever before. This is referred to as the "boundary-spanning" function of purchasing.[1] Purchasing literally spans the boundaries of every single function in the organization. Each interaction with a given function may require differing levels of marketing expertise. The marketing approach used in managing relationships with technical areas differs from that used in nontechnical categories.

Compressed Time Frame for Decision-Making

The constrained time parameters surrounding supply management decisions necessitate a stronger marketing orientation. Marketing encourages purchasers to focus more quickly on key issues by targeting the needs of other persons, teams, or functions in the organization.

Increased Focus on Value-Added Perspectives

As purchasers think more about adding value throughout supply chain relationships, marketing's significance increases. Value is added when purchasers identify innovative ways to reduce total costs, improve processes, increase overall performance, and otherwise make contributions to the purchasing effort. Marketing assists in accomplishing these ends.

Heightened Definition of Customer Satisfaction

Purchasers have to become more marketing-oriented because customers have higher expectations in terms of service, value, and general performance. Both internal and external partners seek more and better responses from purchasing. With rising expectations, marketing allows purchasers to have a stronger focus on real customer needs and expectations.

Greater Attention to Internal and External Partnering

Marketing is an integral component of the partnering process. As more and varied partnerships are formed, marketing's significance increases. Effective partnerships and alliances demand certain marketing acumen

---

1. R. Monczka, R. Trent, and R. Handfield, *Purchasing and Supply Chain Management*, South-Western College Publishing, Cincinnati, Ohio, 1998, p. 133.

B O X   30-1

WHY SUPPLY MANAGERS SHOULD UNDERSTAND MARKETING

- ♦ Improved understanding of managing and facilitating exchanges
- ♦ Enhanced capacity to identify and service internal and external "market segments"
- ♦ Stronger communications links with all relationship partners
- ♦ Better understanding of value creation and delivery
- ♦ Encouragement of a more macro-oriented perspective of the supply management function and its role in the organization

for success. As the complexity and nature of relationships vary over time, purchasers will continue to focus on sharpening marketing skills as a means to enhance performance. Specific reasons why and how purchasers can benefit from marketing are detailed in Box 30–1.

WHAT MARKETING IS AND IS NOT

For purchasing and supply managers to get the greatest benefit from marketing efforts, it is essential that they understand the boundaries and scope of the concept. All too often marketing is seen as a thoughtful advertising, promotion, or communication strategy designed to have basically a public relations-oriented focus. This is a limited view. A more comprehensive view is that of marketing as the "process of planning and executing the conception, pricing, promotion, and distribution of ideas, goods, and services to create exchanges that satisfy individual and organizational goals."[2] Marketing is an integrated process of creating and facilitating exchange concerning tangibles and intangibles (ideas). In a basic way, marketing is a philosophy, a call to organizational action, a way of thinking, and a perspective on managing various exchange processes. It is not one action or a series of disjointed actions, but a cohesive,

---

2. *Dictionary of Terms*, American Marketing Association, Chicago, Illinois, 1995.

well-conceived approach to understanding and responding to the needs of multiple audiences, internally and externally.

Occasionally in organizations, specific marketing-like actions are undertaken sporadically and this is perceived as marketing-oriented. However, a few isolated behaviors such as customer satisfaction surveys and newsletters only scratch the surface of the potential contribution of marketing to overall supply management effectiveness. For best results, supply managers should develop and implement an integrative marketing effort over a sustained period of time.

WHY PURCHASERS SHOULD UNDERSTAND MARKETING

Improved Understanding of Managing and Facilitating Exchanges

To be effective, purchasers have to know the fundamentals of the exchange process and how various actions can influence that process. An examples is knowing what types of relationships to develop with both individuals and teams in the firm. The nature of an exchange or a relationship in the health services industry may vary immensely from that in the steel industry. Understanding the peculiarities in exchange processes is a critical ingredient in successful purchasing.

Enhanced Capacity to Identify and Service Internal "Market Segments"

The ability to classify or categorize internal and external partners as "market segments" allows purchasers to think of these as distinct customer units with identifiable needs and expectations. Thus, purchasing strategies can be tailored to match the requirements of different groups. This systematic approach to handling customers increases effectiveness.

Stronger Communication Links with Others in the Organization

Marketers think in terms of integrative communications mechanisms to convey the thoughts and intentions of the sender (within the context of the needs of the receiver). Key questions in assessing how purchasing communicates with others include: What is the most effective medium to share purchasing's purposes with clients? What communications strategy ought to be pursued to ensure solid, long-term results concerning either internal or external customers? If purchasers fail to communicate properly with significant others, everything else is affected negatively. Major repercussions can result from poorly conceived and executed communications strategies.

Better Understanding of Value Creation and Delivery to Various Partners

The essence of marketing is the creation and delivery of value. If purchasers adopt a marketing perspective, they are likely to be more innovative and entrepreneurial in viewing the supply management function and its multiple possibilities in value creation.

Allowance for a More Macro-Oriented Perspective on the Purchasing Function and Its Role in the Organization

Frequently purchasers are accused of being micro-oriented, territorial, and myopic in orientation. These views get in the way of seeing the "big picture" and understanding purchasing's contribution to the overall vision. If purchasing fails in conceptualizing this broader angle of its role in the organization, countless opportunities to contribute to the firm are lost.

THE EXCHANGE CONCEPT AND MARKETING AND PURCHASING PROCESSES

Exchange is at the core of what both marketers and purchasers do. Exchange relationships allow parties to acquire what they do not have, whether something tangible or intangible. The three basic types of exchange are: restricted, generalized, and complex.[3] Restricted exchange is basically a two-party relationship whereby A gives to and receives

---

3. R. Bagozzi, "Marketing as Exchange," *Journal of Marketing*, vol. 39, October 1975, pp, 32–39.

from B. There is a real focus on achieving and maintaining equity in the relationship. It is based on a *quid pro quo* notion. For example, if purchasing gives to manufacturing, then manufacturing in turn must give something (tangible or intangible) of perceived equal value. The something of value might be time, attention to the request, or other actions demonstrating the importance of the request.

On the other hand, generalized exchange occurs when A gives to B, B gives to C, and C gives to A. There is no reciprocation, and both giving and receiving are in one direction. While this approach does not characterize typical exchange processes experienced by purchasers, it does offer a useful perspective. Only when units in an organization fail to recognize their interdependence do they approximate generalized exchange.

The final concept, complex exchange, characterizes a process of mutual relationships among at least three partners. This is symbolized by both A and B giving to each other and B and C giving to each other and so on. A good example of this is a supply chain consisting of customers, retailers, distribution centers, assemblers or manufacturers, first- and second-tier suppliers, and others. This scenario involves a full range of exchanges that are complicated and quite interwoven.

From a purchasing management perspective, it is important to understand the type of exchange relationship involved and the actions required to facilitate the actual exchange process. Managerially, if purchasers can identify the nature and parameters surrounding the exchange, then the probability of a successful relationship is enhanced.

STAGES OF MARKETING EVOLUTION— PURCHASING AND SUPPLY MANAGEMENT IMPLICATIONS

Practitioners embrace marketing concepts and ideas at different levels.[4] The levels represent varying commitment to different aspects of marketing and management and, in fact, reflect different philosophies of marketing. The levels of marketing orientation are:

---

4. C. Lamb, J. Hair, and C. McDaniel, *Marketing*, 4th ed., South-Western College Publishing, Cincinnati, Ohio, 1998.

+ Production
+ Sales
+ Marketing

Within firms, those organizations and functions that adhere to the production orientation phase of commitment focus attention on their own strengths and not on the real needs of the customer. They identify and take into consideration customer needs as secondary concerns in the marketing and management processes. This approach does not consider whether the strengths and assets of the unit really match the expectations of various partners. How is this related to supply management? Assume purchasing deals with all other units on a very technical level because this is their strong point. They issue reports that are rather technical and quantitatively sophisticated. However, what is really needed is a descriptive, qualitative perspective on some purchasing-related issue. The production orientation suggests that purchasing will continue to focus on technical concerns, that being what they do best, and neglect the real information needs of internal partners. It is important to capitalize on strengths, but not to the point of ignoring the needs of key customers, internally or externally.

Firms or units with a sales orientation focus on assertive sales techniques to persuade others of the merits of their products or their position on issues. Their attention is primarily on selling ideas as opposed to finding out what service customers want and then providing it. Too many organizations and functions equate selling with marketing. The "selling" of the purchasing function is shortsighted because it encourages efforts to get other units in the firm to accept purchasing "as is" without any adjustments. It is an inwardly focused orientation targeting purchasing's needs without full consideration of other units.

At a different level of commitment is a marketing orientation, which has an outward focus on the needs, wants, preferences, and expectations of specific customer groups. Different market segments are identified and a marketing program is designed to meet the individual expectations of value of those groups. This is much more of a "rifle" approach in targeting narrow categories of concerns and developing programs, products, processes, and systems to fully match what they need. In short, if purchasing practitioners are really marketing-oriented, they establish "value propositions" for each set of internal and external partners. These value propositions identify strategies and means to accomplish them. Purchasing's behavior is synchronized with the real needs of its allied groups within the total supply chain. There is a greater level of sustained responsiveness to the core concerns of manufacturing, engineering, research and development, customer service, marketing, and other internal groups.

In reality, the degree of marketing orientation can be viewed as a dynamic continuum. On one end is a production orientation with a limited focus on customer needs, and on the opposite end is a marketing orientation that expresses a clear leaning toward customers. Purchasers with a solid marketing focus are on track to satisfy overall organizational goals.

WHAT IS THE MARKETING CONCEPT?

The marketing concept is a philosophy of business that has the following tenets:

♦ Customer orientation
♦ Integrated marketing and systems perspective
♦ Long-term focus
♦ Commitment to profitability and/or return on investment (in whatever terms it is measured)

Customer Orientation

A customer orientation entails visualizing ideas, concepts, and processes from the vantage point of other partners. When purchasing is really customer oriented, it embodies the values, spirit, and nuances of other groups in order to serve their needs better. Part of this understanding involves knowing the expectations, concerns, challenges, and reservations of other partners. When purchasing makes a genuine, sustained effort to include the details of other groups into the context of decision-making, the result is stronger marketing and thus more effective purchasing. Another important contributor to a marketing orientation is purchasing's comprehension of the evaluation and reward system of other internal and external partners. Evaluation and reward systems govern the actions and behaviors of groups. Partners in accounting, finance, sales, production, customer service, engineering, and other areas are frequently measured by different variables and therefore have totally different perspectives on the same issues. All of these things collectively create a subculture unique to particular functions. If purchasing is to be effective, the various subcultures within the organization must be understood and managed.

Integrated Marketing and Systems Perspective

For marketing to be an effective instrument for attaining supply management objectives, it must be conceptualized and practiced from a holistic viewpoint. If marketing is viewed as a series of isolated, short-term, static actions, the results will be disappointing. On the other hand, if purchasers view marketing as an integrated system of processes, outcomes are much more likely to be positive. A myopic view of marketing entails focusing on selling and other forms of communication to convey purchasing's points of view or other types of exchanges. A broader view entails undertaking a close review of the partners' needs, expectations, and problems and then developing a comprehensive program to address the focal point of the exchange, the value involved, appropriate communications strategies, and the mechanics of delivering the desired exchange. This is a much wider posture from which to approach marketing-based decision-making in purchasing and supply management. All elements of the marketing process are thus integrated and woven into a consistent fabric capable of enhancing effectiveness.

Long-Term Orientation

Decisions made from a strict marketing angle pinpoint long-term results and not short-term solutions. Marketing-oriented purchasing decisions that reflect longer time horizons are likely to be more consistent with the mission of the organization and will yield higher returns. Short-term decisions that reflect expediency may not be in the sustained interest of all supply chain members or internal partners. When delivering value, purchasers should have the intent of influencing longer time frames.

Commitment to Profitability or Return on Investment

When is a partnership profitable? How can purchasing determine return on investment regarding an internal or external partnership? In both instances, purchasing has to look at the ratio of benefits (tangible and intangible) to the sacrifice necessary to receive the benefits. Purchasing professionals invest time, expertise, and other resources in order to get satisfied customers. Marketing-oriented purchasers are committed to achieving customer satisfaction within the defined "profitability" parameters. There has to be ample return for the input of purchasers in order to have extended viability. Different purchasing organizations have varying means of assessing the nature of the input/output ratio in relationships with other units.

CREATING VALUE THROUGH MARKETING (INTERNALLY AND EXTERNALLY)

Purchasing creates value through marketing by being sensitive to the full range of needs of partners. Value creation is a dynamic and moving target that forces constant assessment of organizational behaviors leading toward mission attainment. Purchasers create value by being innovative in approaching such concerns as cycle time, supplier reductions, global sourcing, technology issues, collaborative teams, outsourcing efforts, commodity strategies, process mapping, and purchasing systems and processes. Whenever purchasing implements any program or processes in the above areas or in others, then, from the viewpoint of its partners, value is created. There are multiple paths to value creation in purchasing. Successful purchasing organizations identify these paths and pursue them with focus, determination, and energy. Marketing-oriented purchasers are assets targeted toward continuous enhancement of people, products, and processes.

THE MARKETING PROCESS AND SUPPLY MANAGEMENT EFFECTIVENESS

Purchasing managers have direct responsibility for conceptualizing, planning, and implementing marketing processes. The better the process is understood, the more effective the marketing outcomes. Below are the phases of the marketing process with corresponding supply management implications.

Understanding the Real Mission of the Organization

The organization's mission is the foundation on which all other efforts are initiated. It basically identifies the *raison d'être* of the firm and provides considerable guidance in terms of resource priorities and allocations. It defines the orientation and philosophy of the firm. A market-centered organization is likely to be more customer-focused and is more likely to place higher levels of importance on customer-related concerns. Supply management functions in such organizations are likely to be more oriented toward taking the extra steps required to be responsive to internal and external partners.

Setting Marketing-Oriented Goals for Supply Management

Marketing-oriented goals are those that define purchasing's existence and purpose from the perspective of the units served and the overall organization. Examples of these types of goals are:[5]

- ♦ Developing formal contracts and supply strategies to ensure the flow of materials required to support production and operations
- ♦ Developing and implementing purchasing and supplier performance measurement systems
- ♦ Effectively managing the supply base while improving supplier performance
- ♦ Establishing real-time information systems with suppliers
- ♦ Establishing an organizational structure that is adaptive and responsive to dynamic market conditions
- ♦ Developing strong relationships with internal customers
- ♦ Working with suppliers to develop or gain access to leading-edge technology

Goals developed around customers are more sensitive and responsive to the ever-changing needs, both internally and externally. They ensure consistent and targeted attention to important elements of the organization.

Collecting and Analyzing Market-Based Information for Decision-Making

Supply managers make an array of decisions concerning a plethora of areas. The quality of the decision-making is influenced by the caliber of data. Supply managers cannot be marketing oriented without having a

---

5. Monczka et al., op cit., p. 17.

systematic approach to data collection, analysis, and dissemination. Timely information is required from every internal and external customer group. The various types of data and data collection methods that might be useful to supply managers are:

1. Primary data
2. Secondary data

Primary data are collected directly from specific groups for select purposes. The information is in fact gathered for the first time. These data may be collected through surveys, personal interviews with internal customers, focus groups, e-mail interviews, and telephone conversations. It is important to match the type of data needed for purchasing decision-making with the method of collection. If there is a need for in-depth information, a focus group may be convened to sort out key concerns. If limited information is needed on a wide range of topics, a survey is useful. Regardless of the method, primary data can make rich contributions to how purchasing professionals interface with other units.

Secondary data have been collected previously for a variety of purposes. Some of the most common sources of this information include: internal records, trade and industry associations, government data, and on-line databases. The secondary information used should be consistent with the problem or concern. Internal records may provide insight into purchase history, purchasing trends with particular suppliers, and related information. Trade association data is industry-specific and provides an overview of occurrences in a certain area that can influence purchasing decision-making.

The better the quality of information, the more marketing-oriented purchasers can be. Without consistent, reliable input, decisions are haphazard and not truly reflective of the dynamic circumstances affecting relationships at all levels inside and outside the organization.

Developing Marketing Strategies for Supply Management Success

There is no one best marketing strategy for purchasing organizations to pursue. Rather, there is an array of options from which to select. Purchasers must understand their markets and choose approaches to meet the unique requirements of different groups.

How to Identify Target Markets

Purchasing has numerous target markets inside and outside the organization. To identify both major and minor targets, purchasing should pinpoint all of the interactions it has with particular groups and chart the frequency of exchanges and their value. For example, in a manufacturing environment, purchasing's interface with production partners might be more frequent and valuable than its interface with the legal department. Even though all relationships are potentially valuable, at select points in time some are more valuable than others. Each group (target) has a different set of needs at different times. However, there are certainly commonalities within and across groups that are stable over time.

Target groups of segments may be based on many variables within the organization including benefits sought, need structures, functional culture, usage rate, cost factors, size, power, and location. Customer groups seek different benefits, have varying need structures, operate in diverse cultures functionally, have varying rates of product use, incur cost differentials, and have distinct size, power, and location demands. All of these individually or collectively can be determinants of market segments in the firm and within the supply chain. An alternative perspective on viewing segments or marketing focal points is to analyze personal characteristics, team characteristics, variations in purchasing criteria, and purchase importance. The key question for all segmentation efforts is, "On what basis should needs be subdivided to allow purchasing maximum leverage in providing the greatest value-added contribution?" This question is the essence of purchasing's challenge in identifying its markets.

Product/Service Strategies

A product is anything given or received in the exchange process. It may be a tangible product, an idea or concept, or some blend of the two. What products do purchasers have and how do they impact overall effectiveness? Purchasers' offerings may include negotiating skills, technical knowledge, interpersonal talents, conflict resolution skills, team-oriented approaches, managerial expertise, legal prowess, and a host of others.

For maximum effectiveness, purchasers must combine skills and talents into a "custom-made bundle" to match the requirements and expectations of disparate target markets. Purchasing's adroitness in bundling its talents is a key measure of effectiveness. Purchasing creates its products on demand from various customer groups. For example, if key quality issues are surfacing, purchasing amasses the related skills to correspond to the issue. This is the product that purchasing markets to its customers.

Communication Strategies

Once purchasing has identified the needs of the various target groups, it has to develop integrative strategies to communicate effectively with the segments. In particular, purchasing has to "speak the language" of the group. For communicating with senior management the approach is quite different than for communicating with the information systems team.

With top management, the following has been suggested as a communication approach:[6]

1. Understand senior management's vision, strategies, and concerns (ask questions, observe, study senior management's history, learn their system, understand their values).

2. Speak a common language (focus on purchasing from senior management's perspective, use their terminology to describe purchasing challenges and opportunities, measure functional progress and achievements in the context of senior management's concerns and the organization's goals, regularly orient purchasing professionals to management's thinking, values, and goals).

3. Market purchasing through multiple means in ways understood and respected by top management (create visibility, design special reports targeted to this customer group, communicate continuous improvement, indicate specific instances of value-adding behavior at both the micro and macro levels, and present examples of customer-driven strategies).

In all the communications efforts an integrative focus is critical. All communications mechanisms (personal, nonpersonal) should complement and reinforce each other. A "sales pitch" to a particular segment should be strengthened by corresponding memos, newsletters, visual displays, position papers, and so on. The resultant effect is really greater than the sum of the individual communication efforts.

---

6. W. Bunker, "Speaking the Language of Senior Management," National Association of Purchasing Management, *NAPM InfoEdge*, May 1995, pp. 4–5.

Pricing/Value Strategies

The pricing element of marketing has a different context than that normally used by consumers. When considering pricing in a organizational sense, one is looking at the value associated with facilitating the exchange between parties. If purchasing is developing a marketing strategy aimed at particular customer groups, it has to put some perceptual and/or real value on the interaction. This might be measured in time spent, resources used, opportunity costs, and other tangible and intangible means. An objective measure of cost might include labor hours involved, computer and technical resources used, and related variables with some identifiable nature to them. More subjective measures of costs might include power, prestige, and other variables that are strictly perceptual in nature. The critical question becomes "What does each party give up in order to get what it wants?" If purchasing markets ideas and concepts to engineering, the "total cost" of doing so is included in the assessment and measurement of value. Greater short-term costs may be involved in marketing to senior management, but the long-term dividends are likely to be higher. The costs of marketing to supply chain partners may vary among constituents at any given point and within groups across time. Thus, purchasing develops separate marketing programs to reach different segments within the firm and in the supply chain. If purchasing adopts a value-based approach to pricing, it will focus on the needs and demands of the customer targets and the value expectations they have. If purchasers are really long-term oriented in marketing, a life cycle costing method of looking at exchanges is useful. What are the real costs for the duration of the exchange? Answers to this question can guide purchasers' thinking in conceptualizing and designing workable marketing strategies. A different value is placed on each of the exchange relationships. The way the exchange is valued varies with time, people, and situations. It is dynamic and requires constant review.

Distribution/Logistical Issues

Distribution covers a wide range of marketing concerns, including location, time, situation, modality, and context. Some of the key questions associated with this aspect of marketing are:

- Where should the marketing effort take place (locally, regionally, with a certain group or target)?

♦ What time frame should be used for maximum marketing impact? (The timing of a particular effort can ensure either success or failure. For example, if purchasing times a marketing move to follow a merger or major organizational restructuring, the results are likely to be different than during a period of relative corporate tranquility.)

♦ What is the right situation in which to present a marketing effort? Should ideas be presented to top executives and then be allowed to filter down, or should a grass-roots approach be pursued?

♦ Should the marketing effort be presented from a factual, technical, financial, conceptual, or basic approach or some combination of the these?

Given the almost infinite variety of ways and means to convey marketing strategies, the choice process becomes critical. The choice of distribution approach is contingent on customer needs and expectations, the nature of the product, and other requirements dictated by the situation.

All of the elements of the marketing effort—product, promotion (communications), pricing, and distribution—must be woven into a cohesive, coherent process aimed at the needs of customer groups. Each element has a pivotal role to play in marketing success. Frequently the promotion element is elevated in importance above the other components. But to pursue that logic is shortsighted and myopic. Sustained success in marketing is derived from a careful blending and mixing of elements to match challenges and opportunities associated with exchange processes.

EXECUTION OF MARKETING STRATEGIES FOR SUPPLY MANAGEMENT SUCCESS

Conceptualizing marketing strategies for supply management is an important step. However, equally critical is the appropriate execution of strategy to reach internal and external partners. The best plans with poor implementation fail to reach the mark. To ensure some modicum of success, an action plan is required. Very simply, this involves asking, relative to the marketing plan: Who? What? When? Where? How? The responses to these queries force marketing-oriented supply managers to address, in some detail, the critical success factors and will allow the development of a deployment strategy that will be useful in executing the plan. In particular, human, financial, time, and other resources can be matched with key elements of the strategy. The adroitness with which resources are matched with marketing opportunities is a major determinant of success.

Execution of the marketing-oriented purchasing effort is in part dependent upon:[7]

1. Ensuring that well-defined and specific goals for the effort exists (this provides focus and direction)
2. Properly assigning resources to ensure appropriate outcomes
3. Building and developing the interpersonal relationships and informal networks required to smooth the exchange process

PERFORMANCE MEASUREMENT AND ASSESSMENT

Were the marketing goals attained, and how do you know? Measuring results is a key element in any strategic effort, and marketing is no different. Exchanges with internal and external partners vary in terms of objectives, and there are thus variations in associated measurement techniques. Examples of changes desired by purchasing are:

- Changes in the level of customer satisfaction experienced by partners (as measured by surveys, direct responses, reduction in complaints, etc.)
- Changes in behavior of customers (quicker response time, improved accuracy and adequacy of responses, etc.)
- Reduced conflict or friction among teams (increased synergy, more cohesiveness, and greater sense of purpose)
- Reduced costs, improved return on investment, improved communication, and lessened resource requirements

Whatever the measurement units or approach, sustained consistency in the assessment process is essential for continuous improvement.

---

7. W. Schoell and J. Guiltinan, *Marketing: Contemporary Concepts and Practices*, 5th ed., Allyn and Bacon, Boston, 1992.

Marketing strategies used by purchasers should be reviewed and analyzed for both effectiveness and efficiency. If there is an integrated decision support system regarding marketing efforts, there will be a greater probability of success in the application and use of marketing in the performance of purchasing and supply management functions. Thus, information, in whatever form, is key to determining how well the process was executed and the results received by the parties involved.

EXAMPLES OF MARKETING APPLICATIONS FOR SUPPLY MANAGEMENT

Internally, marketing can be applied to the following exchanges:

- Other functions within the organization
- Different levels/layers of management
- Concepts, ideas, perspectives, etc.

Externally, applications are appropriate for:

- Suppliers (all tiers)
- Distribution centers (and other intermediaries)
- Retail institutions
- Final customers
- Horizontal partners (purchasing consortium members)

SAMPLE MARKETING PLAN[8]

Executive Summary

Overview of the plan for marketing the idea, product, service; the investment needed; anticipated results.

Introduction

Product

The idea to be marketed is the increased value-worthiness of the supply management function in an ever-dynamic and turbulent competitive environment.

---

8. Adapted from W. Cohen, *The Marketing Plan*, 2d ed., John Wiley & Sons, New York, 1998.

Sample Scenario

Assume you are the supply management director at a 500-bed, comprehensive healthcare facility in a medium-sized city in the southeastern United States, with annual purchases exceeding $100 million annually.

Situational Analysis

This includes, if applicable, information on demand and demand trends for the product (service or idea); social and cultural factors; demographic/socioeconomic variables (Who are the key decision-makers? What are their key characteristics?); economic and business conditions (Does the state of the economy influence how the product or idea is marketed either externally or internally?); financial environment; technological influences; political concerns; legal and regulatory influences.

Also included is the competitive environment (What are the competing products, services, ideas, etc.? What are the relative advantages/disadvantages of their offering or perspective?).

Another important component is the current organizational environment. Considerations here include: products/services; marketing strength; structure of the organization; assessment of decision-making style, power, control, culture, values, and team orientation; assessment of other resources, including financial, human, supply, and customer franchise.

Sample Scenario

The situational variables important in marketing the value-worthiness of the supply function to top management are varied. Demand trends would indicate considerable projected growth of healthcare services based on the changing demographics in the United States. With increased growth and a corresponding increase in competitive response to these needs, the organization has to reassess the strength of all of its key components. Strong supply management acumen is one of the foremost assets required to battle competitors and provide efficient and effective healthcare service to an ever more selective array of customers. In addition, very strong influences from the technological, regulatory, and financial environments are assured.

The hospital leadership is dominated by conservative, technical bureaucrats with a penchant for the status quo. The purchasing function is viewed as an important but transaction-oriented unit. Purchasing successes are recognized, but in a limited, myopic way.

Target Audience(s)

What individuals or groups are the focal points of the marketing effort? What are their characteristics and how might those influence the development and execution of a marketing strategy?

Sample Scenario

The primary target audience in the hospital is the executive committee, which consists of the CEO, CFO, medical chief-of-staff, and two very influential external members. The secondary audience is the second tier of managers and directors (at the same reporting level as the supply management director). For each audience a thorough analysis of its individual and collective needs, expectations, and motivations is required. As much detail as possible in this category provides considerable input into developing a marketing strategy.

Problems and Opportunities

What are the major opportunities and problems confronting the hospital and the healthcare industry, nationally and locally? This includes a traditional SWOT Analysis (strengths, weaknesses, opportunities, threats).

Sample Scenario

The major opportunities include improvements in return on investment, more effective resource utilization, and chances to enhance overall patient satisfaction. The key threats might include injuring current relationships among the two target groups, the remote possibility that supply management might be promising more than it can realistically deliver (and the corresponding effect on credibility), and the general uncertainty associated with new and bold initiatives in tradition-laden healthcare organizations.

Marketing Objectives and Goals

What are the specific goals of the marketing effort in both quantitative and qualitative terms?

Sample Scenario

Specific goals include the following:

1. To enhance the level of perceived value-added contribution of supply management by the executive committee by 25% over the last fiscal period (as determined by surveys, interviews, etc.).

2. To increase the visibility of supply management accomplishments in key purchasing performance areas (cost effectiveness, supplier performance, inventory management, strategic initiatives, and consortium arrangements) over last year.

3. To increase the variety of media used to reach the executive committee, in an attempt to communicate better the breadth and depth of supply management's contributions.

Marketing Strategy

What is the optimal combination of resources in matching the product (service or idea), communications methods, pricing (value), and distribution concerns to satisfy marketing goals?

Sample Scenario

The product (idea) is to enhance the perceived value-adding potential of purchasing to the executive committee. This intangible requires attachment to something that is perceived as tangible to gain maximum effectiveness. Purchasing's specific contributions to each of the key areas of the mission, vision, and strategic goals are important. This approach is one that top management can relate to.

The communications strategy is essential. Share the message via direct and indirect and subtle means, including reports, charts/diagrams, independent third-party assessments of purchasing's contributions, and various financial-oriented information. Indicate changes and trends over time and purchasing's impact. All of these things must be communicated in a certain way to meet the personal and group needs of top managers. Certain managers are deductive and others are inductive, and they like receiving information in a form consistent with their style.

From a pricing perspective, what is the value of the contributions that purchasing offers? Is there a specific dollar amount or a qualitative understanding that purchasing has made a positive difference in the hospital's standing?

Distributionwise, it is important to time the strategy, to use certain means and mechanisms to convey the ideas, and to use situational variables and approaches to facilitate getting the message across.

Marketing Tactics and Implementation

How will the strategy be implemented? What tactics are likely to be successful and why?

Sample Scenario

Purchasing could enlist the collective assistance of other units in the hospital in sharing its message. Others sometimes can make a stronger case for recognition than the function in question, their case being seen as less self-serving.

Purchasing might do some interorganizational benchmarking and use methods to promote purchasing that have shown promise in nonrelated industries.

Any number of options are at purchasing's disposal in terms of "how" to convey the message to the executive committee. They may be both short- and long-term in nature, with varying degrees of sophistication.

Assessment, Evaluation, and Summary

It is essential to review the results of any marketing effort. What happened and why? Findings from the assessment effort become key ingredients for planning and executing future programs.

Appendices and Supporting Materials

What complementary documentation is needed to reinforce the strategy and increase the probability of goal attainment? The choice of materials or data is directly dependent on the needs and requirements of the target group. If they are technical in orientation, prepare materials accordingly. If the market segment is more qualitative and descriptive, provide materials to meet those specifications.

B O X   30–2

HOW CAN PURCHASING BECOME MORE PARTNER FOCUSED?

- ◆ Develop a partner-centered mission and vision.
- ◆ Conduct internal "market" research.
- ◆ Institute customer-based marketing training and development.
- ◆ Learn from sales reps from supplying firms and others.
- ◆ Learn from your own internal marketing team.
- ◆ Develop internal and external market segments based on needs, motivations, expectations, etc.
- ◆ Review best practices in marketing of industry leaders and others.
- ◆ Review and map processes periodically.

SUMMARY

Marketing is an integral factor in supply management success. The level of supply management excellence is in direct proportion to the marketing acumen of its decision-makers. Since marketing is so critical, it is incumbent upon supply management professionals to practice it and to practice it well. The diverse applicability of marketing concepts bodes well for purchasing practitioners. These concepts work in dealing with both internal and external partners in a wide variety of situations and scenarios. As purchasers become more partner-focused (Box 30–2), heightened performance expectations ensue.

The most important thing for purchasers is to think in marketing-oriented ways when engaging in exchange relationships. Marketing thinking is a key precursor to sustained accomplishments in the ever-competitive world of supply management. The creative nature of marketing forces purchasers to approach problems and solutions from different perspectives. It allows the benefit of multidimensional thought and action in elevating purchasing effectiveness in a wide range of organizations with disparate missions. Marketing is not a cure-all for what ails the supply management function, but it does provide an insightful frame of reference from which to approach purchasing and materials management challenges now and into the next century.

CHAPTER 31

Supplier Performance Evaluation

Editors
Michael Harding, C.P.M., CPIM
Harding & Associates

Mary Lu Harding, C.P.M, CPIM, CIRM
Harding & Associates

Measurements drive behavior. Supplier measurements define the criteria for acceptable performance, monitor performance over time, and lead both parties to take action based upon the data. The *only* purpose for collecting data is to act on what it says; the evaluation process should include actions to be taken when performance is unacceptable, acceptable, or superior. Data assists purchasers in assessing supplier performance objectively.

The real work of purchasing is to determine what the organization values and to define the parameters of the measurement system. When properly defined, the measurement system assists in the creation of a supply base that best serves the business needs of the organization. First, purchasing must define what it wants for specific results. If price is the most important measure, low price is what the company will get. Delivery, quality, low inventories, and profitability will be distant seconds.

Supplier performance evaluation is inextricably linked to purchasing's performance evaluation. As purchasing is evaluated, so it will measure suppliers. Both aspects of these measurements will be discussed in this chapter.

TRADITIONAL MEASUREMENTS

Commonly, organizations (users and software providers alike) rely on the time-honored measures of price, delivery, and quality, in that order.

While the traditional methods of calculating these measurements have some inherent problems, they will be reviewed first, and then alternative measurements will be discussed.

PRICE

How do you know when you have gotten the best price? Several thorny issues can arise in determining an appropriate measure of price. One involves the use of standard cost accounting. In companies using a standard cost system (primarily manufacturing), a standard price is established internally for each item before the beginning of the fiscal year and is in place for the year. Differences between the internal standard price and actual prices paid are measured as variances. A standard cost system establishes a consistent valuation for inventory and helps determine the cost content of the end product. However, standard cost systems become counterproductive when price variances are used as a measure of purchasing's or a supplier's effectiveness.

In many organizations, purchasing, being in the best position to predict future prices, establishes the standard costs. When variance to standard is also a measure of purchasing performance, political games often result. What defines success? If ending the year with favorable variances is defined as success, purchasing has an incentive to set high standards. Actual prices less than standard cost can then be easily achieved, and purchasing is successful. If both favorable and unfavorable variances are bad, and achieving the standard is the only success, then hitting the number at any cost will be the resulting behavior—even if that means walking away from a cost-saving opportunity or exerting destructive pressure on suppliers.

Using standard costs as a measure of purchasing's or a supplier's performance does not work very well even in the most enlightened environments. Commodities can experience market moves in price that cannot be predicted a year in advance. If actual prices go up, purchasing and the supply base look like they are performing badly when that may not be the case. If prices go down, they look like heroes. In neither case is the price change due to any creative efforts from purchasing or the supplier.

Other cost accounting systems measure actual price variances from the last price paid, a budget amount, or an engineering estimate. The belief is that if purchasing and suppliers provide prices as expected, the buying company will have acceptable and predictable costs. A standard or budget cost becomes a stake in the ground from which movement can be measured.

Comparison to a target is a comforting measure of price for those who are not involved in the negotiations. For example, general management and finance are sufficiently distant from the price-establishment negotiations that it is difficult for them to tell how well the job was done. Was the result the best that could be obtained? Comparing the result to a target is one way that these noninvolved people can measure the result. However, problems arise in establishing the validity of the target costs and in the behavior that hitting an artificial number creates. Those doing the actual work know what can be achieved. Focus on hitting an artificially established number can blind them to what is really desirable or possible, creating destructive behavior and suboptimum results.

There are several methods of price measurement that will foster appropriate behavior in both purchasing and the supply base better than variance to a standard or target cost. These include measurement of price trends, cost savings/cost avoidance, contribution to profit, and affordable cost.

PRICE TRENDS

A trend measurement is always better than a spot measurement or performance to a preset target because it shows context and history. Rate of change (slope) and degree of variation are readily apparent. Trends also do not foster political games as does hitting an artificial number.

To measure price trends, plot time on the x-axis and price on the y-axis. The slope of the resulting data shows the rate of change of a supplier's prices. Data can be plotted for individual items or in aggregate showing a whole commodity or all of a supplier's items. For determining goodness, the trend can be compared to industry averages or to affordability. An example is shown in Figure 31–1.

COST SAVINGS

Measurements drive behavior. If the behavior desired is suppliers and purchasers getting creative to control prices, then consider measuring that activity. A good way to do that is to measure cost savings and cost

F I G U R E   31–1

Price per 1000, P/N 84732-1. From Able Corporation.

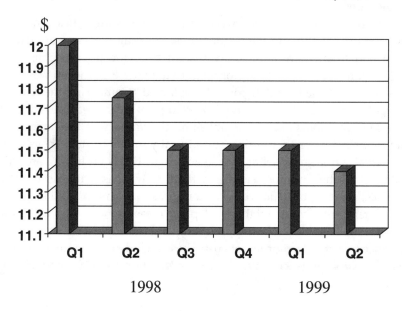

avoidance. If the rules for measurement are established appropriately at the beginning, they are less prone to games than standard cost variances.

Since standard or target costs are artificial numbers, measure cost savings against prior *actual* costs. Request that the following data shown in Table 31–1 be captured and reported with each savings claimed.

These data allow the savings to be audited, which is very important for internal credibility. It also proves that the savings has substance.

T A B L E   31–1

Cost Savings Report

1. Prior price:	Contract or PO #	Date	Quantity	Unit Price
2. New price:	Contract or PO #	Date	Quantity	Unit Price
3. Extended dollar savings				
4. Brief description of what was done to achieve the savings				

Comparing the quantities will show that the savings was not due to simply reaching the next volume price break. Price and date can be plotted on trend graphs. A description of what was done to generate the savings provides the information to credit creative effort and good ideas. These good ideas may also be transferable to other purchasers and commodities, and they provide the basis for rewarding talented purchasers and suppliers. (Caution: be careful not to give away one supplier's good ideas to their direct competitors or ethics problems as well as supplier disenchantment may result.)

Credit purchasing and suppliers with the extended dollar amount saved. If the savings is on one purchase order only, the extended dollars are the unit price difference multiplied by the quantity on the purchase order. If the price change is permanent, credit the difference in price multiplied by the average annual quantity used. After a year's credit, the new price becomes the norm. Accumulate the total savings by supplier, by purchaser, and as a grand total so that it can be publicized internally to generate recognition for purchasing and for good suppliers.

COST AVOIDANCE

Cost avoidance is the remission of charges that are legitimate—that purchasing negotiates away and the supplier agrees to waive. Examples include legitimate penalty charges, set-up charges, and cost increases. Since the higher price was not paid, documentation of the starting point is all the more important. Request that the following data be captured and reported with each avoidance claimed:

1. Documentation of the charges from the supplier
2. Documentation of the final settlement of the charges
3. Total dollar savings
4. Description of what was done to achieve the savings

Appropriate documentation will allow for an audit to insure that facetious data is not being used. If your organization is wary of cost avoidance or has had a history of abuse, keep cost savings and cost avoidance figures separate until credibility can be reestablished. Measuring and crediting cost savings and cost avoidance sends a message to purchasers and to suppliers that cost issues matter and individual efforts are recognized and rewarded. Documentation of what was done to achieve the savings provides the basis for training of all purchasing staff in what is possible. Joint efforts to control costs between purchasing and suppliers can result in a deeper level of relationship.

CONTRIBUTION TO PROFIT

An objective of business is to produce a profit. Regardless of a company's other objectives, if it does not produce a profit, it will not continue to exist for long. Top management is typically measured and rewarded based on the company's profit performance. Everyone else is measured and rewarded based on cost control. Top management has a better deal. They have the latitude to make decisions that improve profitability. An important measure of purchasing's and a supplier's cost effectiveness is their contribution to profit. When purchasing measures and reports contribution to profit, general management is better able to understand the value that purchasing contributed to the company.

To determine contribution to profit:

1. Obtain a costed bill of material for an end product or service. The costed bill of material represents the material cost content in the end product.
2. Record all price changes to components in that bill of materials.
3. As purchasing reduces the cost of some components in the bill of material, the total cost content will decrease.
4. As prices increase on other components, the total cost content will increase.
5. The net difference in the total material cost content becomes purchasing's contribution to the profitability of that product.

Using the bottom line of total material cost content as a measure of effective price control gives purchasing needed flexibility to look for genuine opportunities and not get sidetracked working areas with little or no opportunity. Suppliers can be measured on genuine level of performance rather than against an artificial target. For example, a good supplier may negotiate for a price increase based on legitimate increases in their costs beyond what they can absorb. If they work together with you to keep the increase to a minimum and to cut costs wherever possible, they can get some degree of credit for cost containment and level of effort even if the price increases somewhat. Another commodity may have more opportunity for cost reduction. Purchasing is measured on the sum total of all items, which is a more balanced measure.

DELIVERY

On-time delivery is a major concern for everyone in the buying organization. However, measuring true delivery performance is not a simple process. In most organizations using computer-generated data, delivery performance calculations compare the due date on the purchase order to the receipt date as recorded by receiving.

Data integrity can become a major issue. Dates kept current will increase the supplier's acceptance of their calculated delivery performance. A shipment (expedited by purchasing) delivered before its original due date (as requested) will be recorded as early (and possibly subject to refusal or return) if the original due date is not changed in the purchaser's system. The supplier will be penalized in delivery performance for doing what was requested. If due dates are not well maintained, the performance measurement rapidly loses credibility with suppliers, and if bad data are used against them, relationship damage may result. (A second area to monitor for data integrity is receiving. A backlog on the docks can also create inaccurate delivery data.)

What is the appropriate due date against which delivery will be measured? Some use the suppliers' promised delivery dates, while others use the requester's need dates. Using the supplier's promise date increases the likelihood that the date will be met (increasing delivery predictability), but the buying organization's needs may not be served. Need dates may change as schedules change, but using them provides a more accurate reflection of supplier flexibility in meeting actual customer demands.

The next definition required to establish a delivery performance measurement is what constitutes "on-time." What window of time is appropriate for your organization? For organizations with many deliveries and tightly scheduled unloading docks, on-time may be a 30-minute period during which this supplier's truck is scheduled to unload. Other examples include the due date plus or minus nothing, the due date plus or minus one day, up to five days early but no days late, within the week, etc.

Once delivery expectations have been defined and the on-time window identified, delivery performance is calculated as an attribute measurement. The delivery date as recorded at receiving is compared to the on-time window. Either it was delivered within the window or it was not. Every delivery is measured and determined to be on-time or not-on-time. Delivery performance is calculated as:

$$\frac{\text{Delivery}}{\text{Performance}} = \frac{\text{Deliveries "on-time"}}{\text{Total number of deliveries}} \times 100 = \% \text{ On-time}$$

A third consideration in maintaining a valid delivery performance measurement is FOB point. For shipments sent FOB origin, the supplier "delivered" the goods when they loaded them onto the carrier at their facility. If there were delays in transit, the buying organization owns both the goods and the problem. If the supplier is measured on dock receipt date, they have every right to challenge the legitimacy of the measurement. Manual back correction can be time-consuming. Deliveries shipped FOB destination do not have this problem, since delivery measurement and transfer of ownership are at the same point.

QUALITY

Most organizations track the quality of incoming material, recording supplier, purchase order number, item number, and lot number of an incoming item and whether it passed or failed any quality checks. They tally the number of lots rejected from each supplier and compare them to the total number of lots received yielding a percentage, often called the "reject rate." They should also notify purchasing when there is a supplier quality problem. Histories can be developed that accumulate problem information by supplier, by part number, and by print or specification revision.

Incoming inspection results do not provide a complete picture of a supplier's quality performance. Latent defects, line fall-out, or random failures may not be apparent until the product is well into the manufacturing process or even in the hands of the final customer. Some software systems, such as the more advanced versions of MRPII, can accumulate supplier-assignable errors throughout the process and report the results to purchasing and to quality. Until such complete reporting of quality failures, including customer returns and complaints, is achieved, the supplier quality picture is incomplete and possibly distorted.

Capture data as far into the life of the item as possible, and make certain that suppliers understand the scope of the data collection involved in reporting their quality performance. If the only information available is from incoming inspection or the initial user, understand that only a portion of the errors will be detected and reported.

A system that gathers additional quality data from work in process, final test, and the customer would be more desirable. Data from these sources must distinguish supplier-assignable errors if they are to be used in a supplier evaluation process. Rules for determining responsibility for the error must be clear in order to maintain the integrity of the process and the perception that responsibility is fairly assigned.

Correlation of measurements between the supplier's and purchaser's quality systems is a major issue in establishing a valid quality measurement process. Are the two organizations measuring the same thing? Are they using the same measurement methods? It is fundamental to the credibility of the quality rating system and its results to ensure that the two quality systems are compatible and capable of yielding the same results.

COMBINING THE DATA

Often a single total numeric score is calculated with which each supplier can be compared against others. A cut-off score can be determined as a threshold of performance at which the buyer begins to ask if the supplier requires assistance or should be deleted from the qualified supplier list.

Purchasing must define acceptable performance by category. For example, purchasing may decide that:

1. 95% of invoices must not exceed standard or target cost.
2. 90% of lots received must pass incoming inspection without objection.
3. 85% of lots received must be "on-time."
4. An accumulated score of 90% (95 + 90 + 85 = 270/3) is acceptable performance.

Purchasing may also add subjective input to the process, including:

♦ Causes of low performance: For example, unclear specifications, commodity price changes, etc. (to add sanity to the numbers).

♦ Maintaining balance: It may not benefit the purchaser to have a supplier who is 100% in price and delivery and only 70% in quality.

♦ Allowing time: To meet with low-performing suppliers to determine causes and possible turnaround strategies.

♦ Making certain that a critically important but low-performing supplier is not automatically dropped.

This combination of data and cut score provides a basis for discussion with current and potential suppliers about expected versus actual performance. Performance can be monitored, definitions can be negotiated, and issues will arise that promote healthy discussions between purchasing and suppliers. The cut score may be reviewed periodically to ensure that it reflects the purchasing organization's needs.

THE QUESTIONING

Many organizations question whether price, delivery, and quality *alone* are the right measures of supplier performance. They are desired results, but will the traditional measures produce those results? That is:

♦ Is price performance against a preset standard, budget, or estimate a sign of goodness? Is a standard cost established nine months ago relevant in today's market?

♦ If a critical item is required in one week, but the supplier promises and delivers in four weeks, did the supplier deliver on time?

♦ Incoming inspection will discover catastrophic errors. Random and latent errors will only be found by the process or the customer. Is incoming inspection the proper place to measure supplier quality performance?

♦ Even if the goals of price, delivery, and quality are met, will the buying organization meet its profitability goals?

Predictable supplier performance may no longer be sufficient. More advanced measures include:

1. Affordable prices in a changing market
2. Delivery of goods and services when needed
3. Quality tracked through the process and as perceived by the end customer

AFFORDABLE PRICES

The ability to meet the cost needs of the organization should be the measure of success for purchasing and suppliers. Cost reductions, process improvements, redesigns, and material substitutions, as well as the acceptability of quoted prices, can all be measured against what is affordable.

The process to determine what is affordable must start with the marketplace. The steps are as follows:

Step 1. Marketing and sales must determine at what price the product will yield the desired sales volume and market position. For example, a company must price its product at $75 to achieve its desired market position.

Step 2. Financial analysis breaks down the selling price into its major components: desired profit margin, labor, overhead, materials, and any other major cost factors. The example selling at $75 may break down as: profit margin = $10, labor = $10, overhead = $25, and material cost = $30. The affordable total price for all material content is now estabished.

Step 3. Product design staff produce and verify a costed bill of materials.

Step 4. Purchasing uses the costed bill of materials and the affordable total price target, derived from the market price, to work with suppliers to develop prices that allow their company to produce a profitable product. If purchasing can obtain all the components on the bill for $30, the company's desired margins can be achieved. If purchasing can buy the materials for $28, they have contributed an additional $2 per finished unit to profit. Individual prices of the components are irrelevant; only the total matters.

In order to contribute to profit, purchasing must know what is an affordable price.

F I G U R E   31–2

Affordable Prices. Once an Affordable Price has been
Established, Purchasing and the Supplier Begin to Re-
duce Cost/Price Based on a Business Need. Their
Progress can be Reported in this Chart. Once a Price
Goes Below the 100 Mark, Purchasing and the Supplier
Begin to Contribute to the Profit of the Buying Com-
pany.

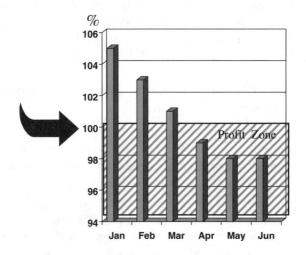

DELIVERY WHEN NEEDED

Similarly, delivery should not be driven by the suppliers' comfortable
leadtimes. Suppliers' response times to customers must conform to the
customer's requirements, not the other way around. Delivery to quoted
leadtimes is not acceptable performance if those dates do not meet the
customers' needs. Traditionally purchasers have compensated for long
leadtimes by increasing inventories. The cost associated with this practice
is no longer affordable. If the purchaser must respond to the customer
in 10 days, suppliers have less than ten days to deliver the required
materials. Only "need" dates have any meaning.

TRACKING QUALITY

Supplier quality must be judged by total performance throughout product life. Good quality results in customer acceptance of the product with

F I G U R E   31-3

Supplier Delivery Performance. The Only Two Dates that Matter are NEED and DELIVERED. Where the Two Match, There is Acceptable Delivery. Data May be Displayed by Major Part Number or by Averaging All Part Number Deliveries on a Periodic Basis or by Dollars of Goods Purchased. Be Aware that Averaging Can Hide Performance Problems. Need May Also be Expressed in Terms of Hours.

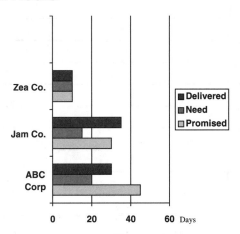

minimum investment by the producer to ensure that quality. It does a purchasing organization little good if the purchased materials pass incoming inspection and latent defects appear in the final product in the customers' hands. Create a process that tracks supplier-assignable defects throughout the production process and reports that information to purchasing so that corrective action can be taken with suppliers.

Data from these new measures may be analyzed by part number (especially for large-dollar items), by supplier (aggregating all part numbers provided by a supplier), or by purchaser and supplier (see Figures 31-2, 31-3, and 31-4).

This information gives purchasing the required tools to move suppliers to a point where they not only meet their customers' needs but begin to contribute to their customers' profitability. Once their needs are met, customers can begin to reduce their investment in hedge inventories and quality overhead.

F I G U R E   31–4

Supplier Quality Chart. Supplier Assignable Errors. A Log–Log Chart May be Used to Normalize the Data Presented. The Small Numbers Represent the Highest Cost to the Buyer's Firm—Those Items that have Value Added to Them When the Fault is Discovered. The Highest Cost to the Company, However, is When the Customer Finds the Fault.

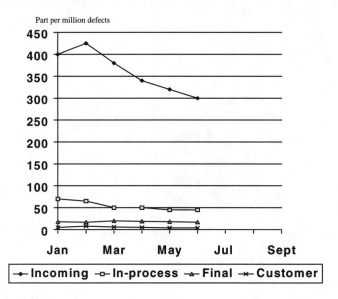

A BETTER PLACE

There is a point beyond common measurements that embraces the intent behind the measure. If suppliers perform to real market needs, operating costs improve, and that also contributes to profit.

INVENTORY

Consistent, on-time, when-needed delivery creates a financial benefit just as the failure to meet delivery requirements creates a cost. A large portion of that cost is inventory. The longer the supplier leadtime and the greater the uncertainty of delivery, the more inventory the customer will carry as insurance. Generally Accepted Accounting Practice (GAAP) calls inventory an asset. However, it can also be a hindrance to cash flow if it exceeds an affordable level. Most organizations believe that the cost to carry inventory is relatively low (about 20% per year), primarily based on the cost of money (interest rates) plus taxes, insurance, space, and obsolescence. However, if one calculated *all* the overhead costs, the true cost to carry inventory would be much higher, as shown in Table 31–2.

A more comprehensive view of the cost to carry inventory has led companies to question their dependence on it. Many are now factoring the cost of inventory into their purchase decisions. For example: Acme Drill Company carries one week of inventory for each week of supplier leadtime for steel. They have three suppliers of steel and calculate inventory carrying costs at 75%. Usage is 5,000 lbs. per year, and Acme's standard cost is $12.50. Purchasing requested quotes for a new high-speed steel rod size and received the information shown in Table 31–3.

If purchase price variance is a heavily weighted measure, purchasing may be inclined to buy from Able to stay within the standard cost

T A B L E   31–2

The Cost of Carrying Inventory[1]

Recognized Costs	Approximate % Per Year
Interest rate of money	~10%
Taxes (vary from state to state)	~5%
Insurance	~3%
Space (occupancy and utilities)	~5%
Obsolescence reserve	~7% (to 20%)
	~30%
Unrecognized Costs	
Personnel (warehousers, inventory controllers, etc.)	~15%
Capital equipment (fork lifts, racking, etc.)	~7%
Computation costs: Hardware + transactions (counting, sorting, moving, issuing, receiving, reconciling)	~3%
Secondary quality costs (reinspection)	~10%
Rework, handling damage, addiitonal loss	~10%
	~75%

[1] M. Harding and M. L. Harding, *Purchasing*, Barron's, 1991, p. 205

T A B L E   31-3

Original Quotations Received

Supplier	Price	Lead Time
Able Corp.	$12.25	10 weeks
Baker Co.	$12.65	7 weeks
Couch, Inc.	$13.10	2 weeks

T A B L E   31-4

Quotations Adjusted for Inventory

Supplier	Inventory Factor	Total Cost*
Able Corp.	$12.25 (.015 × 10)	$14.09
Baker Co.	$12.65 (.015 × 7)	$13.98
Couch, Inc.	$13.10 (.015 × 2)	$13.49

*Quoted price + [Quoted price × 1.5%/week × number of weeks]
1.5%/week = 75% ÷ 50 weeks/yr

and create a favorable variance (knowing full well that added inventory will be required), but if price is adjusted for the cost of inventory, the results change, is shown in Table 31–4.

When the total price, including inventory, is used to make the decision, suppliers quickly understand that they must compete on leadtime as well as price.

THE COST OF QUALITY

Since the 1980s, an increasing number of companies have been calculating the *cost of quality* (also called the *price of nonconformance*). Advanced companies seek the root causes of quality problems at all stages of their business and know the associated costs. (Activity-based costing [ABC] has been helpful in this effort.) When the cost of supplier-assignable errors (see Figure 31–4) is understood, these costs can be added into the quoted price to determine cost of quality. Cost of quality includes the following internal costs:

- Inspection
- Sorting
- Added inventory
- Scrap
- Rework
- Poor yields
- Repairs
- Premature failures
- Warranty work
- Added handling
- Added space
- Administrative costs
- Nonfunctional tests
- Longer leadtimes
- Lost reputation
- Lost sales
- Delayed revenue

Note that many of these costs can also be applied to services. The costs of quality are not limited to physical products. For a nonphysical product such as a transportation service, if the service is not performed on time or if the shipment is lost or damaged, significant costs in addition to the cost of the transportation will be incurred (e.g., product repair or replacement, loss of customers, consequential costs to customer of not receiving the shipment on time).

MEASURING TOTAL COST IMPACT

Price, delivery, and quality can be combined into a single measure of contribution to profit (expressed in dollars). For example: A purchaser obtains 1,000 widgets at $5 each. The affordable price is $4.75, but $5 was the best the purchaser could obtain. Delivery is promised in eight weeks, but the widgets are needed in three weeks. After receipt and incoming acceptance, 27 are found defective at final inspection, and three defective widgets find their way to the end customer. See Table 31–5.

T A B L E   31–5

Total Cost Impact

Profit/⟨loss⟩ on the buy	$0.25	×	1,000	=	($250)
Late delivery (5 wks × 1.5%)	$0.375/unit	×	1,000	=	⟨$375⟩
Cost of finding 27 defects	$8.00/unit	×	27	=	($216)
Cost of customer's repairs	$26.00/unit	×	3	=	⟨$ 78⟩
Gain or ⟨loss⟩ of profit					⟨$919⟩

A total loss of $919 on the purchase of 1,000 widgets equates to a loss of $0.919 each, so the effective price paid was $5.92 each.

Measurements drive behavior. Measuring both purchasing and suppliers on all cost factors and contribution to profit frees purchasers to make business decisions rather than price decisions, and the buying company will reduce its costs.

PUTTING IT ALL TOGETHER

In addition to price, delivery, and quality, organizations measure many other attributes of supplier performance. *Anything* that adds to the total cost of the item or service can be a part of the performance measurements, including policy issues that the purchasing organization values in suppliers. Since the array of issues spans a diverse spectrum, it is useful to have a common denominator so that a bottomline result can be calculated and used to compare a supplier's performance to both their own past performance and the performance of other suppliers. Money is a good common denominator. When all issues are translated into their dollar impact, the sum of all measurements represents the supplier's total cost to the organization.

Issues that organizations measure generally fall into three categories: cost, performance, and policy. Cost issues include price plus any other ancillary costs that the purchaser will ultimately pay, such as transportation cost, set-up charges, and so on. Performance issues include delivery, quality, leadtime, inventory, and any other measure of performance the buying organization chooses to include, such as responsiveness or flexibility. Policy issues include those attributes that the buying organization values in suppliers and wishes to foster or reward, such as disadvantaged business status, recycled content in the product, socially responsible practices of all kinds, and so on.

CALCULATING TOTAL COST

Total cost is the sum of all cost, policy, and performance factors that the purchasing organization wishes to measure. Since purchase decisions are frequently made on the basis of unit price, a good way to measure total cost is to calculate it per unit also. Unit Total Cost is the purchase price amended by the addition of all other factors (translated into their per-unit monetary impact).

Cost issues are the easiest to include because they are stated in monetary terms from the beginning. All that is required is to convert the ancillary charges into their per-unit impact. To do that, divide each charge by the number of units over which it applies. A "unit" is the unit of measure in which the price is quoted: each, roll, dozen, etc. For example, if transportation charges are $14.95 and there are 100 units in the shipment, then the per-unit transportation cost is $0.15 each.

The financial impact of performance issues can be determined exactly or approximated. Organizations that use activity-based cost systems may have calculated the cost of dealing with rejected material, supplier leadtime, or nondelivery. If exact figures are available, use them. If they are not available, approximations can be used. Performance evaluations are primarily used for comparisons: comparing a supplier's performance to their previous history to measure improvement or comparing suppliers to each other to make sourcing decisions. When the purpose is comparative, approximations derived from the same formula will suffice.

Estimates are acceptable as long as they are *relatively* valid. A formula for approximating performance can be considered valid as long as:

♦ It makes sense—it is relevant to the issue the organization wants to measure and can be calculated without undue difficulty.

♦ It can be applied across suppliers and used to validly differentiate performance.

COST OF NONDELIVERY

If the supplier delivers the goods early, you will pay for them sooner and carry the inventory longer. If the supplier delivers late, you will

T A B L E   31–6

On-Time Delivery Calculations Example

Factor	Able Co.	Baker Co.	Charlie Co.
Quoted price	$10.00	$11.50	$12.00
Nondelivery penalty	+1.50	+1.27	0
(1-OT)	(85% OT)	(89% OT)	(100% OT)

consume people's time to replan the materials schedule and/or expedite delivery. If the lateness is chronic, you may carry safety stock inventory, and you may have to alter your production schedule. All of these cost an organization money. Calculating the actual dollars of expense would be time-consuming and would vary with each situation.

A simple method for incorporating the cost of nondelivery into total cost calculations is to use the *non*delivery performance percentage as a price adder. For example, if Able Company delivers on time 85% of the time, then they are not on time 15% of the time (Table 31–6). Multiply Able's quoted price by 15% and add that amount to the base price as the cost factor for their delivery performance. The better their delivery performance, the lower the cost adder they bear. Since each supplier bears the result of its own performance, this is a fair way to differentiate between suppliers.

COST OF NONQUALITY

The actual costs of nonquality include the overhead costs of the incoming inspection organization, the reject materials stockroom, the administrative expense of a materials review board, and the cost of the materials return process. They also include rework expense and quality fallout from the production processes due to defective or marginal incoming materials. An organization that uses activity-based costing may have calculated the costs of quality into a separate cost pool. If so, that becomes a good base for allocating quality costs back to suppliers in proportion to the consumption of those resources that each item represents.

If actual cost numbers are not available, use the measure of percent defective components or percent reject shipments as a price adder in the

T A B L E   31–7

Quality Calculations Example

Factor	Able Co.	Baker Co.	Charlie Co.
Quoted price	$10.00	$11.50	$12.00
Nonquality penalty	+1.30	+0.92	0
(% Reject)	(13% rejects)	(8% rejects)	(100% quality)

same manner as the nondelivery percentage. For example, if 8% of Baker Company's shipments are rejected, then Baker's price is multiplied by 8% and that amount is added to the base price to compensate for your costs of handling nonquality goods. The higher the supplier's quality, the lower the cost factor they bear. Since each supplier bears the costs derived from its own performance, this is a fair relative measure of quality (Table 31–7).

LEADTIME

Leadtime is a performance factor. Items with a leadtime of four weeks will be managed differently than those with a leadtime of 12 weeks. Long-leadtime items limit your flexibility in changing your schedule to accommodate changes in the business. They may also be a major driver of safety stock inventory. Since measurements drive behavior, measuring leadtime as a cost factor also sends a message to the supply base that leadtime matters and less is better.

To derive a formula for the cost of leadtime, start with the cost of carrying inventory stated as a percent per year. Divide that by 52 to obtain the percent per week. Determine whether that formula is strong enough to send the appropriate message to suppliers about how much you value leadtime reduction. If it does not carry the weight you deem appropriate, increase the percentage per week until the weight is appropriate. Formulae of 1–2% per week are typical. Once the appropriate percentage has been determined, apply it by multiplying the percentage by the supplier's quoted leadtime and adding the result to their quoted price as the performance factor for leadtime (Table 31–8).

T A B L E   31–8

Lead Time Calculations Example

Factor	Able Co.	Baker Co.	Charlie Co.
Quoted price	$10.00	$11.50	$12.00
Leadtime penalty	+1.00	+1.04	+0.84
(1%/wk)	(10 weeks)	(9 weeks)	(7 weeks)

SUBJECTIVE PERFORMANCE MEASURES

Subjective performance characteristics, such as responsiveness or flexibility, matter, and they can be measured if you are willing to find a way to quantify them. To do that, first define what you mean by the term—for example, *responsiveness*. There may be two aspects: a responsive attitude, in which the supplier is open and willing to listen to your requests, and responsive actions in which the supplier either did or did not do what you requested.

Secondly, devise a method to track performance. How many requests for flexibility were made? To how many of those did the supplier respond appropriately? Eventually, all measurements must be defined and tracked. If there is no agreement on definition or no desire to track performance, the characteristic cannot be measured, and using it for supplier evaluation while definitions are mushy will open the door to disagreement and potential chaos.

Almost any performance measurement can be calculated as a percentage: how many occurrences were there in total, and in how many of those did the supplier respond well? Percentages can be applied as price adders by calculating that percent of the quoted price and adding it into the total. Remember to use the percent *non*performance.

INCLUDING POLICY FACTORS

Policy factors are those issues that an organization wishes to foster or recognize in the supply base, such as disadvantaged business status, recycled material content, consentual reciprocity, and compliance to social policy standards. Compliance to a policy is usually an attribute measurement: either suppliers comply with the policy standard or they do

T A B L E   31–9

Social Policy Calculations Example

Factor	Able Co.	Baker Co.	Charlie Co.
Quoted price	$10.00	$11.50	$12.00
Recycle $Award		−0.58	−0.60
(−5%)	NO	YES	YES

not. To incorporate any policy factor into supplier measurements, the following steps are necessary:

1. Define the policy factor.
2. Define what constitutes compliance.
3. Define how much the organization values the issue.

To define organization values, ask the policy's sponsors (usually general management), "If all other measurement factors were equal, up to how much more would you be willing to pay to incorporate this issue?" The answer creates a measure of value. It does not mean that the organization will necessarily pay any more; it simply defines a limit. Once the limit has been defined, it can be used for measurement.

In unit total cost calculations, if the supplier complies with the policy issue, credit the supplier's price with the amount of the defined limit. This creates a positive incentive for the supplier to comply (Table 31–9).

UNIT TOTAL COST

When all measurement factors have been defined and the dollar impacts calculated, add them together with the price to obtain unit total cost. Table 31–10 shows an example.

In this example, cost factors, performance factors, and policy factors are all evaluated in dollars and can be compared to each other as well as across suppliers. Unit total cost can be used to select suppliers and measure their changing performance over time.

If a supplier is new, and there is no history of performance, request that the supplier provide at least three references (specific name and telephone number) to other organizations who purchase this specific

T A B L E   31-10

Unit Total Cost Calculations Example

	Factor	Able Co.	Baker Co.	Charlie Co.
Cost factors	Quoted price	$10.00	$11.50	$12.00
	Shipping	+0.09	+0.07	0
	($/Qty)	($8.98/100)	($700/100)	
	Discounts	−0.20	−0.06	−0.12
	(prompt pay)	(2% 10 net 30)	(5% 10 net 30)	(1% 10 net 30)
Performance factors	Nondelivery	+1.50	+1.27	0
	(1-OT)	(85% OT)	(89% OT)	(100% OT)
	Nonquality	+1.30	+0.92	0
	% reject	(13% rejects)	(8% rejects)	100% quality
	Leadtime	+1.50	+1.04	+0.84
	(1% wk)	(10 weeks)	(9 weeks)	(7 weeks)
Policy factors	Recycle		−0.58	−0.60
	−(5%)	No	Yes	Yes
Unit total cost		$13.69	$14.16	$12.12

product. Contact them. Ask them what they measure and how (to get an understanding of the validity of their measurements). Then ask them how this supplier has performed over the last year. Although a supplier can provide extraordinary service to customers once in a while, it is very difficult to do that for multiple customers consistently. If the information provided by these references is consistent, it is a reflection of the operating system by which the supplier does business, and you can be reasonably sure that the service you experience will fall into the same range.

USING UNIT TOTAL COST

A total measurement plan such as unit total cost accomplishes several business objectives:

1. It allows disparate issues to be combined into a coherent measurement plan.

2. It provides a method by which all groups within the organization can have access to the supplier selection and measurement process, ensuring that their issues are included.

3. It makes clear the basis on which suppliers are selected and retained, educating everyone about how the decisions are made.

4. It gives the supplier clear information about what issues matter and how they are weighted, so that suppliers understand what comprises good performance.

Often for the first time, suppliers have specific information about how their performance affects their competitive position, what they can do to compete, and how much improving performance is worth to them.

MEASURING SERVICE SUPPLIERS

When services are rendered, there can be a host of subjective assessments as to their quality, timeliness, and cost-effectiveness. Quantifying performance can thus be a challenge. In order to have something against which to measure service performance, it is imperative to document expectations up front. The various forms of services can make measurement more difficult. Some of those difficulties include:

♦ Users may be uncertain of the final product at the time the order is placed.

♦ User expectations may be unrealistic or unclear.

♦ Both users and providers make assumptions.

♦ Personal service may vary based on personalities (e.g., physician, consultant).

♦ Job definition may change in the middle of the work.

♦ People within either organization may change during the work.

♦ The unforeseen may occur.

♦ Funding may change.

Purchasing's job is to assist all parties to define their performance expectations, costing formulas, and acceptance criteria. These should be clearly spelled out and incorporated into the purchase order. For example, an order for product development services might incorporate the following:

1. What work is to be done? Define the project and its scope.
   ◆ Design a new shoe sole that will last three years in average use.
2. Who will do the work? Specify the people and skills.
   ◆ Mr. W. B. Anderson and three "A"-level polymer engineers.
3. What is the time frame?
   ◆ Work will begin on September 1, 1999, and conclude with a finished product on or before May 1, 2000.
4. Progress reporting.
   ◆ Written progress reports will be submitted by the 28th of each month to Vice-President K. L. Beep and meetings will be held on the 5th of each month to review status.
5. What are acceptance criteria? When will both parties know work is completed?
   ◆ Blueprints and specifications will document a product that meets the three-year criterion. Three samples will be submitted to K. L. Beep.
6. What legal issues need to be covered?
   ◆ We will own all patentable features of the new sole, and you will assist us to obtain the patents.
7. How are changes approved and documented? Plan for changes in time, scope, and costs. Provide a process to accommodate and document inevitable changes.
8. How are costs determined?
   ◆ Project effort $200,000
   ◆ Hourly rate (hours to be documented) $40/hr
   ◆ Machine hours (to be documented) $90/hr
   ◆ Materials as invoiced................................ actual cost
   ◆ Overtime .... not allowed
   ◆ Estimated project cost............................... $350,000
9. How will the money be paid?
   ◆ Costs will be itemized and invoiced monthly. The last $50,000 will be paid upon successful testing of the sole—no later than June 25, 2000.

Once the criteria are defined, measurement may be recorded as either attribute (yes/no) or variable (numeric) data. It is important to track all the major issues:

How did the supplier perform against these criteria?

	Yes	No
Was the new sole produced?	X	
Were the specific talents utilized?	X	
Was date commitment met?	X	
Were costs and estimates met?	X	
Were the agreed-upon reporting and documentation procedures followed?		X

Regardless of the type of service, up-front agreement on deliverables will provide the criteria against which to measure performance.

SUMMARY

Measures drive behavior. A good measurement system will engender the desired behavior in both purchasing staff and suppliers and will lead to the desired business results. To develop a good measurement system:

1. Define the desired business results.
2. Define what behavior will generate those results.
3. Construct measurements that will measure that behavior. (Be careful to think through what people will do as a result of the measurement. Misplaced measurements can produce unproductive behaviors.)
4. Make the measurement as simple as possible, numeric, and preferably translatable into dollar effect.
5. Allow all the people in the organization who have a vested interest in suppliers to participate in the measurement establishment process. (Quality, new-product development, materials management, production, and purchasing all have issues to measure and want a say in how suppliers are performing for them.)
6. Make the measurements clear to suppliers so that they know what is expected of them and how their performance will be measured.

7. *Act* on the results of the measurements. Use them to drive
   business decisions.

BIBLIOGRAPHY

Harding, M. L. "Creating Your Own Supplier Evaluation Formula," *Purchasing Today®*, November, 1997, pp. 12–13.
——. "Understanding Total Cost of Ownership," *NAPM InfoEdge*, vol. I, no. 14, August 1996.
Harding, M. "Purchasing Performance Measurements on the Leading Edge," *NAPM InfoEdge*, vol. 2, no. 5, January 1997.
Harding, M. and M. L. Harding, *Purchasing*, Barron's Press, 1991.

PART FIVE

Item and Industry Practice

Many purchasing and supply concepts, processes, practices, and techniques are more or less equally applicable across the entire spectrum of products, services, industries, environments, and situations. We have tried to provide a broad variety of such topics in the other sections of this sixth edition of *The Purchasing Handbook.* Some items and industries, however, because of the nature of the items purchased, the characteristics or requirements associated with their purchase, the purchasing environment or situation in particular buying industries, or some combination of these or other factors, contain unique aspects that merit special consideration. As an example of a special purchasing situation, purchasers in process industries, such as chemicals and petroleum, have found that much of the available information, guidance, and training material on purchasing and supply management is directed at either manufacturing or manufacturing support industries. Relatively little material or attention has been devoted to process industries or other purchasing environments where most purchases are for either capital equipment or services. Similarly, as an example of special purchase item requirements, until recently relatively little attention has been focused on the unique problems and opportunities involved in buying MRO (maintenance, repair, and operating) materials.

To ensure adequate coverage of these types of subjects, this edition of *The Purchasing Handbook* contains this section on item and industry practice. In this section, specific chapters are devoted to purchasing of raw materials and commodities, MRO materials, software and intellectual property, capital assets, services in general, construction services, and transportation and related services. Also, specific chapters are devoted to the special purchasing environments and requirements found in service industries, process and extractive industries, and public and not-for-profit organizations.

Purchase of Raw Materials and Commodities

Editor
Frank Haluch, C.P.M.
President
Haluch & Associates Ltd.

DIFFERENT PURCHASING

Buying raw materials and commodities is different from buying services, component parts, or fully manufactured products. Raw materials must meet the needs of many processing technologies as the material passes through the manufacturing process. For example, in the production of a steel fabrication, the material must be formed, welded, and finished. Each of these process technologies requires different material characteristics for optimal processing. Leading-edge companies attempt to measure total processing costs (effectiveness), not workstation costs (efficiency). This approach optimizes the system cost rather than attempting to define material specifications that favor one process over another and thus result in higher total processing costs.

To achieve the lowest total cost, a buyer needs to work across all process technologies required to produce a product. Most important is the early involvement of suppliers in design. The role of the purchaser is to help the business make wise decisions by assisting such functions as design engineering, manufacturing engineering, and shop operations in assessing trade-offs, so that the lowest total cost is achieved.

PHYSICAL AND MECHANICAL PROPERTIES

The purchaser needs to understand the cost relationships between the physical and mechanical properties as well as those between acquisition price and processing costs. Physical and mechanical properties are as illustrated in Box 32–1.

Commodities

Commodities can be crude or refined products such as oil, chemicals, minerals, ores, and agricultural products that are used as the building blocks for other products. Physical properties are usually more important than mechanical properties in the purchasing of commodities. There is a significant cost impact on the processing of a commodity, depending on its purity and the types of the impurity present. Impurities may affect the time needed to process the material as well as impact its yield. Analysis of the effect of various types of impurities on the cost of processing has resulted in purchasers establishing bid factors for various types of impurities.

Raw Materials

Raw materials are products that have been converted from commodities into standard products (steel sheet, plastic resins, rubber compounds, and aluminum tube). As a rule, raw materials are more sensitive to mechanical properties. The amount and type of impurities are also important considerations when buying raw materials, but for different reasons

---

B O X   32–1

Physical:

♦ Density
♦ Coefficient of thermal expansion
♦ Thermal and electrical conductivity

Mechanical:

Engineering properties relate to how the material reacts in a specific application.

than is the case with commodities. Impurities have an impact on performance characteristics such as strength, hardness, notch sensitivity, grain structure, electrical properties, machinability, and finishing.

GLOBAL EVENTS IMPACT PRICE AND AVAILABILITY

The sources for many raw materials and commodities have always been outside the boundaries of North America. Until the early 1960s, though, many buyers and sellers were not concerned with world events. Such things were interesting but not really relevant to their business. However, after two oil crises and the assault on the U.S. marketplace by foreign companies, buyers and sellers have become more sensitive to global events.

DEVELOPING A MATERIAL RESOURCE PLAN

For the raw materials and commodities that are key to the business, it is wise to prepare an annual material resource plan. A raw material or commodity may be key for a variety of reasons, such as the amount of spend, its percentage of total product cost, limited sourcing possibilities, and high "switching costs."

A material resource plan needs to include the following:

1. Current world demand along with trend analysis (short and long term)
2. Worldwide capacity (current, future, and ease of increasing/decreasing production)
3. Major producers (new entrants, mergers, and potential exits)
4. Criticalness of current technology to your product
5. Relationships that cause the market to work smoothly (e.g., production in one industry segment that generates a byproduct that is the feedstock for another item)
6. Threats:
   A. Production shutdowns:
      (1) Labor unrest (strikes, slowdowns)
      (2) Union contract expiration dates
      (3) Weather (floods, drought, earthquakes)

    B. Government:
      (1) Environmental regulations
      (2) Political environment
      (3) Interest rates
      (4) Currency fluctuations
      (5) Trade restrictions
    C. Market actions, e.g., potential cartel formation such as the Organization of Petroleum Exporting Countries (OPEC) or mergers/acquisitions
  7. Analysis of current supplier(s)
    A. Management (competency and depth)
    B. Technology (R&D expenditures)
    C. Financial status (e.g., financial ratios) and Z-score analysis (predicts bankruptcy)
    D. Product and process improvements (patents and manufacturing technologies)
  8. An annual forecast of your firm's needs

Packing and shipping of raw materials and commodities require close attention by the purchaser. Many raw materials and commodities require special vehicles or containers to move them from the supplier to the purchaser. Also, barge or rail may offer the most economical way to move them. The buyer must know the availability of rail sidings or barge facilities. It is also helpful to know the capacity of on-site cranes and storage tanks. In some cases, the cost of transportation may exceed the purchase price of the raw material or commodity and therefore logistics can become an important factor in the buying decision.

COMMUNICATION OF MATERIAL NEEDS

Although material requirements planning (MRP) has been a significant productivity tool, its application in the area of raw materials and commodities can pose difficulties. The unit of measure is the cause of the problem. Consider wire, for example: the bill of material often specifies the gauge, type of insulation, and number of inches needed per unit. Wire is generally purchased by the pound and shipped by the reel. Clearly many opportunities exist for ordering and usage errors.

Wire is a rather simple example, but what about requirements for paint and grease? What about materials that have large minimum purchase quantities and are used under many different part numbers? Purchasers need to work with systems analysts and engineers to create conversion tables for developing effective conversion rules of thumb.

WHAT IT IS CALLED IS IMPORTANT

The method chosen to describe a requirement to suppliers will affect both the price paid and the type of material received. Use of a brand name means that the purchaser is relying on the manufacturer to supply the same-quality material, lot after lot. However, this approach may lock out potential product improvements brought out by competitors. Using industry standards provides a wider choice of potential suppliers but at the same time introduces more variability into the system. Industry standards generally state material characteristics in terms of maximums or minimums. Thus two materials that meet an industry standard may behave very differently during processing. Often the best way to ensure that the material purchased meets both your firm's and the end customer's needs is to develop a material specification that defines both physical and mechanical properties.

HAZARDOUS MATERIAL

Some raw materials and commodities have been designated as hazardous materials. A purchaser should not rely exclusively on the seller to ensure that this type of material is packaged and shipped properly.

LARGEST SOURCE OF UNFAVORABLE COST VARIANCE

In many industries, raw materials represent the largest single source of variable cost. Those costs also have the potential of being the largest source of unplanned, unfavorable cost variance. As such, they can dramatically impact a firm's contribution margin (sales price − variable cost = contribution margin). Changes in variable costs can have a large impact on operating income. One study reported that a 1% change in the variable cost had a 7.8% impact on operating income.[1] Total cost systems can begin to bring together the cost of waste caused by a supplier, such as quantity (over and under shipments); delivery time (early and late); quality (PPM (parts per million defects); CpK (a measure of process capability to meet a specified standard and centering of the process relative to the standard); 6σ (which means that 99.7% of a product is within the quality standard); and processing losses. A tool has also been developed for measuring the amount of waste generated by a supplier as its material passes through the value-added conversion process. With this type of total cost tool, purchasing decisions can be made on the basis of costs versus purchase price.

THE COST OF QUALITY

A *Fortune* 100 company has documented that approximately 70% of the firm's quality problems come from purchased materials. This fact, coupled with Ison's law of 10 (the cost to find and fix a defect is 10 times the initial cost—for example, if an item costs $10 at the subassembly level, it will cost $100 at the assembly level and $1,000 at the product level to find and fix the problem) should motivate firms to focus resources on ensuring that defect-free material enters the production process.

SPECIFYING AND VERIFYING QUALITY

Chrysler Corporation identified that 20–80% of its quality problems came from lack of clear communication between the purchaser and the seller. Poor quality of raw materials and commodities affects the entire manufacturing process. The quality of the end product is totally dependent on starting with good raw material. The first action to take is to ensure that the material that was ordered is the material that was delivered. This can be achieved though either: (1) testing the incoming material (a non-value-added activity); (2) asking the supplier to submit data as evidence that what it shipped is what you ordered; or (3) contracting for guaranteed certified quality. A supplier, in guaranteeing the quality, is agreeing not only to cover the replacement cost of defective material but

---

[1] M. V. Marn and R. L. Rosiello, "Managing Price, Gaining Profit," *Harvard Business Review*, vol. 70, September–October 1992, pp. 84–94.

also to pay all costs incurred in finding and replacing the defective material.

INVENTORY COSTS

One tends to think of inventory costs in terms of the cost of heat, space, insurance, and the cost of money. To be sure, raw materials and commodities may take up significant amounts of space and capital. However, what one does not always see is that technology, design, and manufacturing innovations are being locked in place. Inventory restricts the rapid changeover as either customer needs or technology changes. We are now in the era of time-based competition. Many markets are shifting from high-volume, low-mix to low-volume, high-mix with fast response. In fact, some customers are willing to pay significant premiums to have products delivered almost instantaneously. Therefore, management needs to think of cost of inventory in terms of the dynamics of the customer marketplace as well as the production side of the equation.

In addition, a purchaser needs to keep in mind that carrying cost often averages 2–3% per month of the value of the inventory. That means that it costs $240,000 to $360,000 per year to carry $1 million of inventory. Well-managed firms such as Honda of America Manufacturing, Inc. have learned to turn inventory by the hour. Purchasing and the entire firm need to learn to strike a cost-effective balance between meeting customers' needs and having low inventory carrying costs.

ORGANIZING FOR PURCHASING

Purchasing decisions are driven by three factors: (1) the ability to forecast requirements, (2) the number of divisions in the firm using the material, and (3) commonalty of specifications within those divisions. Depending on how these three factors interrelate, a purchaser may be forced to buy in the spot market or may have the opportunity to contract for their requirements.

ELECTRONIC AUCTIONS

A number of companies are using the Internet to source commodities and raw materials. The benefits from this type of sourcing approach are the ability to make your requirements known globally versus locally; to create a competitive environment; to provide suppliers with immediate feedback on their pricing decisions; and to allow sellers to prune themselves from the bidders list without the need for a purchaser to intervene. In the future this process may result in the in the development of a large number of electronic trading pits where industrial purchasers and sellers match supply with demand on a daily basis.

The auction process is normally conducted through a company that specializes in providing this type of service, such as FreeMarkets OnLine, Inc. and GE Information Services. They assist the purchaser in developing a "competitive bidding event."

PURCHASERS RESPONSIBILITIES FOR INTERNET AUCTIONS

Purchasers are responsible for preparing the requests for quotations (complete drawings, proven technical specifications, identified critical quality characteristics, schedules, etc.) to be available on-line. Additionally, purchasers must organize the bid package into logical groups to facilitate the bidding process and monitor the real-time competitive bidding event, and must establish the rules of the game:

- Identify supplier pre-qualification requirements and the process for meeting them.
- How will business be awarded (including reservations)?
- Will target prices be published (highly recommended)?
- Will the current low bid be published to all bidders?

SUPPLIERS RESPONSIBILITIES

Suppliers are responsible for being prepared to bid during the competitive bidding event. This means they have downloaded the request for quotation, passed all of the qualification and prescreening hurdles, and analyzed the RFQ for business and are prepared to submit bids.

The electronic auction works through software that integrates the buyer and sellers so that everyone appears to be in the same room (except that the sellers do not know the name of the company that is bidding, just the price they have bid). Each provider runs its competitive bidding events differently, so it important to review their products carefully prior to scheduling a competitive bidding event.

LESSONS LEARNED

As one can imagine, mistakes have been made as purchasers have attempted to utilize this technology. Some of the lessons that have been learned are:

♦ Rigorous supplier prequalification is critical; it is the key to success.
♦ You should get electronic bid packages on-line early.
♦ You should double- and triple-check all data for accuracy.
♦ Target prices ensure success.
♦ You should oversell and overeducate your suppliers on the initial event.
♦ You should make sure suppliers understand the "rules."

CONTRACTING FOR SIMILAR REQUIREMENTS

Contracting involves more than requesting bids and awarding the business to the lowest price bidder. Contracting for raw materials and commodities requires input from engineering, the use of trial runs, and a great deal of cooperation among purchasing, engineering, and operations. As a rule, successful contracting is achieved through the use of multifunctional teams. The first step is to level the playing field, i.e., to rationalize the specifications that are currently being used to purchase the material. The next step is to determine which suppliers' material meets the new specification. And the final step is to schedule small runs to ensure that all members of the contracting effort are able to use the material. After these are completed, the contracting team will be prepared to analyze the bids and select a source.

POOLING COMMODITY REQUIREMENTS

A commodity used by a number of company locations may lend itself to the pooling of requirements. Large companies often establish pools for commodities such as copper, silver, gold, plastic, and fuel. Pool buying operates on the principle that it is less expensive for one specialist to execute the buy, with input from users, than to have several purchasers duplicate each other's efforts. A pool differs from a contracting group in that a pool takes ownership of the commodity and then distributes materials to pool participants. Generally, items in the pool are bought from commodity exchanges, enabling the pool manager to use the market to balance risks and take advantage of price averaging in a fluctuating market. Pooling also permits the transferring of material to outside suppliers so that the cost advantage of pooling is leveraged. Outside suppliers charge only for the cost of their processing or fabricating operations.

SPOT MARKET PURCHASES

When requirements cannot be forecast with reasonable accuracy, a buyer is forced into the spot market and must pay the current market price. Buyers who know the ins and outs of the market will fare better than those less skilled. Timing of spot market purchases is often critical.

ANALYSIS OF REQUIREMENTS

The availability of a recognized industry specification does not mean that the item is generally available for purchase. The proliferation of metal grades and alloys in earlier years, for example, has caused significant problems for producers and users alike in some industries. Care needs to be taken in defining the specification. Keep two things in mind: (1) how many suppliers are willing and able to supply the material, and (2) what are the minimum quantities that will be ordered during the production life of the product? If the specifications are so particular that few suppliers are interested in supplying the item, or the quantities are so small that it is uneconomical to produce the item, long waits and special charges may be incurred.

YIELD DETERMINES VALUE

A story has been circulating about how the retail outlet Banana Republic purchased old military uniforms during its start-up years. Since the firm could not travel around the world buying old army uniforms on an individual basis, they bought uniforms in bulk by the pound. The Banana Republic founders apparently worked out a rule of thumb that converted the weight of the various types of clothing into pieces of clothing. This enabled the firm to know how much could be paid per pound and still allow a profit when the individual pieces of clothing were sold. In other words, Banana Republic had developed a yield formula, which worked very well until one clever general loaded rocks in with the uniforms. This event changed the firm's buying practices. Nevertheless, this scenario is a good example of how a business bought something by the pound and resold it by the piece. When the general put rocks in the box, he changed the yield, making it necessary for Banana Republic to develop a new yield formula.

Commodity and raw material buyers face the same problem. Yield is affected by dimensional characteristics (length, width, thickness), density, flow rates, and purity. If purchasing decisions are based merely on the price per unit of measure quoted by suppliers, one may be surprised when the *actual* cost of the purchase is calculated.

The examples cited in the following paragraphs show how the concept of yield can be applied in different situations to determine which supplier is offering the best value. The information necessary to perform this analysis may not be located in the purchasing department or collected in a central location; however, as the use of *total cost management* increases, this type of analysis will be performed to increase the productivity of a particular process.

Theoretical Weight

Steel sheet is a good example of a commodity that is purchased by the ton with parts made from it measured in pieces. Any time the production control unit of measure is different from the purchase order unit of measure, the potential always exists for some form of waste to enter the financial equation. If the expected yield is not realized, a bargain price obviously becomes less attractive. This situation is illustrated in Box 32–2.

Examination of the results in Box 32–2 shows that use of supplier A's material generates the opportunity for a $2.69 lower cost per part ($26.56 − $23.87); this reduced unit per cost stems from A' s larger part yield per ton. This is true even though A's price per ton of steel is $100 more than supplier B's. Analyses that convert suppliers' selling prices into internal cost measures provide great insight into the most advantageous buying decision (see Chapter 19).

Plastic Resin

Plastic resin is another example of something that is bought and used by the pound but accounted for on the basis of a cost per finished piece.

B O X   32–2

YIELD CALCULATIONS FOR TWO SUPPLIERS

- Theoretical sheet weight = thickness × width × length × density
- Cost per sheet = cost per ton/number of sheets per ton
- Cost per part = cost per sheet/number of parts per sheet
- Number of parts per sheet = 15

	Supplier A	Supplier B
Price	$2,650/ton	$2,550/ton
Thickness	0.53″	0.60″
Width	30.00″	30.25″
Length	60.00″	60.50″
Density (pounds/cubic inch)	0.2833	0.2833

Supplier A
- Theoretical sheet weight = 0.53 × 30.0″ × 60.0″ × 0.2833 #/cu. in. = 270.27 #
- Number of sheets per ton = 2000/270.27 = 7.4
- Cost per sheet = $2,650/7.4 = $358.11
- Cost per part = $358.11/15 = $23.87

Suppler B
- Theoretical sheet weight = 0.60 × 30.25″ × 60.50″ × 0.2833 #/cu. in. = 311.08 #
- Number of sheets per ton = 2000/311.08 = 6.4
- Cost per sheet = $2,550/6.4 = $398.44
- Cost per part = $398.44/15 = $26.56

In fact, the *total* cost of a plastic part is a function of a number of factors: the cost of the resin, the scrap rate, and the machine cycle time to form the part. If the raw material's density is high and its thermal characteristics (how it fills the mold and how quickly it cools) are slower than those of another resin, the total cost may be greater than the savings generated by the use of the other material.

Chemical Reactions

Manufacturing processes considered to be chemical reactions are also subject to yield analysis. The purity or types of contaminant may slow the process and affect the purity of the output. Both of these conditions affect the cost. Increasingly, purchasers are developing formulas that assign bid factors to specified properties and impurities in the raw material they buy.

The Key: Identify Critical Characteristics

Identify the critical characteristics that affect the rate at which the raw material or commodity is processed. Also, ask what impact physical or mechanical properties have on the function of the end product. Then apply the principles of value analysis to both the processing characteristics and end customer needs. This approach ensures that the focus will be on characteristics that generate increased *value* rather than on the price of the time purchased.

SUPPLY MARKETPLACE

The sources for many raw materials and commodities have always been outside the boundaries of North America. Before the 1960s, a few developed countries competed for most of the world's resources. However, as other countries joined the industrialized world, the pricing and availability of many raw materials and commodities have become increasingly tied to events occurring outside the United States.

CHARACTERISTICS OF THE SUPPLIER MARKET

Types of Products

For purposes of market competition, products can be classified as either standardized or differentiated. A standardized product is exactly like those produced by all the other producers of that product. For example, farmer Wilson's potatoes are just like farmer Jones's potatoes as far as the product is concerned, so price is the only consideration. Sellers of standardized products know that the market is very sensitive to price because it is relatively easy for buyers to comparison shop.

A truly differentiated product is different in some respect from all the other producers' products. That is, the product has some feature that no other product has. However, many producers try to make buyers think that their product is differentiated when in fact there is little or no difference. The primary way to make a standardized product appear to be differentiated is through the use of advertising and promotional activities. One must not be fooled by this ploy. Examine the characteristics of the product closely to determine whether the differences are real and important.

Market Structure

The supplier marketplace can be divided into four groups, made up of suppliers that operate under conditions of (in order of most to least competitive): perfect competition, imperfect competition, oligopoly, and monopoly. When one is trying to get the best price, it is helpful to understand the market structure within which the supplier is operating. Knowledge of the market structure helps a buyer know how prices are set, whether price concessions may be possible, and how to approach getting the best price. For a list of characteristics, pricing strategy, types of products and examples, and the highest-value purchasing activities for each group, see Table 32–1.

Perfect Competition

There are more goods than purchasers. Under this condition the marketplace dictates the deal. The purchaser merely needs to keep abreast of what is happening in the marketplace, because the marketplace will serve up the best value by the actions of all the purchasers. Thus, a purchaser is able to achieve a solid value with little or no effort. Again, purchasers need to use available resources to determine the physical and mechanical properties of the material being bought and buy from suppliers that fit the profile.

Imperfect Competition

Neither the purchasers nor the sellers are able to dominate in the marketplace; together they generate a deal. The value of the deal depends

T A B L E 32-1

The Supply Marketplace Structure Continuum

	Perfect Competition	Imperfect Competition	Oligopoly	Monopoly
Characteristics	Large number of suppliers that desire your business Market controls price	Small number of suppliers that desire your business Purchaser can control price	Limited number of suppliers Sellers control price	One supplier No substitutes Supplier controls price
Seller's pricing strategy	Sells at market price	Sellers try to differentiate products and thus price	Sellers follow market leaders	Sets price that maximizes profit but does not provide an incentive for alternatives
Types of products and examples	Agriculture (commodity exchanges) Standards (fasteners, bearings, paper)	Make to print (job shops)	Steel, copper, plywood, automotive, farm and construction equipment, computer equipment	Patent owners (pharmaceuticals) Copyright owners (software)
Highest-value purchasing activity	Hedging and forward buying	Analyzing cost drivers Knowledge of supplier's processes	Analyzing cost drivers Determine weakest competitor and offer long-term contract in exchange for concessions	Analyzing cost drivers Identify potential substitutes Redesign the product to use other material

823

on the resources they are willing to invest and the length of the contract. The key to generating value in this type of market is the ability of the parties to solve problems. Solving problems requires that both parties understand how the processes work and what is undesirable and what is desirable.

Oligopoly

Except possibly in a price war (which is usually caused by economic recession, a surplus of items, or some political crisis), it is very difficult to get price concessions from an oligopolistic firm, especially if the product is standardized. This happens because if a supplier's competitor hears about a price reduction, the competitor will also reduce its price (competition often knows of such a price reduction on the day the reduction occurs). When the word spreads, all competitors tend to reduce price to meet the competition. As a consequence, all suppliers end up selling about the same volume that would have been sold without the price decrease. This results in a reduced profit for all. Obviously, such an approach is hardly a winning strategy for suppliers, and therefore oligopolistic suppliers always try to avoid direct price competition.

Monopoly

A monopoly may exist as result of having a producer having a patent, a special license agreement from a patent holder, a trade secret, or just luck in no other producer having decided to compete with them. The best approaches to a monopoly are to find a substitute material, redesign the product to eliminate the need to buy from a monopolist, or produce the item in-house.

INFORMATION DATABANKS

Wise buyers of raw materials and commodities keep track of the state of their markets. They usually monitor such activities as:

+ Worldwide demand
+ Worldwide consumption
+ The major user (by industry, company name, or both)
+ Current technology
    + Extraction
    + Processing

♦ The interrelationships that cause the market to work smoothly, e.g., production in one industry segment may generate a byproduct that is the feedstock for another item
♦ The interrelationships that cause market disruptions
    ♦ Weather
    ♦ Labor
    ♦ Interest rates
    ♦ Currency fluctuations
    ♦ Government interventions

The maintenance of such data helps a purchaser be more effective in developing effective purchasing strategies and tactics.

SPECIALTY VERSUS FULL-LINE PRODUCERS

In recent years there has been a movement away from large, concentrated, integrated producers of many materials. Small-scale specialty producers are emerging, such as mini-mills. Mini-mills produce steel products within a very narrow range. Using the latest technology, they produce steel products less expensively and with more consistent quality and usually are more responsive to customer needs. The mills fit the new manufacturing paradigm: low volume, high mix, and fast response. In a competitive market that increasingly is being driven to shorter manufacturing cycle times of small lots, specialty manufacturers are becoming a greater force in the marketplace. Faster delivery of smaller lot sizes adds value for the purchaser because it reduces total costs and improves customer service.

BUYING FROM THE PRODUCER OR FROM THE DISTRIBUTION SYSTEM

Most people feel that buying from the producer is the most cost-effective option. This is both true and false. A cost analysis should be conducted to determine the appropriate level of the distribution system for each item purchased. Conducting such an analysis is the only way to determine whether to buy from the distribution systems or the producer.

SELECTION OF SUPPLIERS

The supplier selection process is even more important today than in the past. With the arrival of time-based competition and the ongoing reductions in the length of product life cycles, the supplier is becoming a key element in the competitive advantage equation. In time-based competition (sometimes referred to as "short-cycle production"), strategic suppliers are involved with the buying firm at the design stage. Their manufacturing processes and quality systems have been prequalified, and the buyer is certain to receive 100% defect-free material when needed.

It is critical that the buying team (representatives from design, manufacturing, engineering, quality, marketing, and purchasing), in designing a supplier selection process, define the selection criteria in both macro and micro terms. Macro considerations are important from the standpoint of determining the technological and business requirements that potential suppliers must meet. The notion that all suppliers are capable of being a supplier to a specific business is no longer valid. The needs of a particular business are very specific and, to some extent, rigid (customer-driven requirements). The need today is to find a close fit between the purchaser's needs and the seller's capabilities. The concept of "go" and "no go" is a good description of the selection process that many companies use today.

In micro terms, once a supplier passes the go/no go screen, the next step is for the purchaser to determine the value-added content of the offering. For this to be done, characteristics such as commodity experience, product differentiation, shared technology interests, market access potential, advanced quality systems, research and development, and distribution systems need to be examined. The criteria for supplier evaluation will differ for each commodity and raw material. The criteria will also change as the purchaser's business strategy changes, and this might be conditioned by the extent to which the end product has progressed through its product life cycle.

When making comparisons of suppliers, construct a matrix to aid in the organization and evaluation of data for each supplier, as illustrated in Box 32–3.

INFORMATION REQUIREMENT

There are many sources of information about companies. The source listed in the following sections provide a wealth of information about

B O X   32–3

EXAMPLE OF A SUPPLIER SELECTION MATRIX–FACTORS TO CONSIDER FOR EACH SUPPLIER

Go/No Go Factors*	Value Factors**	Price
Specifications	Product differentiation	1 = High
Commodity experience	JIT manufacturing	2 =
Quality systems	Process control	3 =
Lead time	Responsiveness	4 = Low

*U = unsatisfactory, M = meets needs, E = exceeds needs,
**1 = adds little value, 2 = significant value, 3 = very significant value

raw materials and commodities. In today's environment, with changes occurring at an increasing rate, purchasers must become learners, applying principles of continuous improvement to gathering information concerning the materials for which the purchaser has responsibility. The purchaser should be tracking and communicating the changes in the supply marketplace as well as searching for suppliers of new technology needed for the next generation of products.

NONDOMESTIC OPPORTUNITIES

U.S. purchasers have been slow to exploit the opportunities available from nondomestic manufacturers. Knowing who to contact has been a major problem. Today there are numerous sources of good information on nondomestic source. The U.S. Department of Commerce publishes specific information on materials imported into the United States by country of origin. The Department also publishes world trade reports and overseas business reports that contain information on specific companies and maintains country and region desks to assist Americans in doing business overseas.

Annual and semiannual trade shows are excellent places to meet new suppliers and to see new technology. Such shows as the semiannual Leipzig and Hanover Fairs in Germany and the biannual International Exhibition of Chemical Engineering in Paris are excellent to attend.

International directories such as *Trade Directories of the World* (Croner Publications, New York), *Fortune 1000 Foreign Companies,* and *World Marketing Directory* (Dun & Bradstreet, New York) are valuable sources of information concerning nondomestic producers. Foreign consulates and embassies also have catalogs, organized by industry, that give information on specific companies.

Most foreign countries have embassies in Washington, D.C., and some consulates are located in major North American cities. Representatives of these countries are happy to assist anyone who wants trade information about their country.

PRICING

Sources of Pricing Information

There are many sources of current commodity price information. *The Wall Street Journal*, the *Journal of Commerce*, and *The New York Times* publish cash, futures, and option pricing on various agricultural, metals, and petroleum products. The U.S. Department of Agriculture is another excellent source of information on agricultural products. Industry publications such as *Metals Week* by McGraw-Hill and *The Paper Trade* by the Lockwood Trade Journal Company are also excellent sources of pricing data for metals and paper.

Commodity Prices is a "must" book for anyone buying a wide variety of commodities. It references sources of pricing information from Abaca to Zonarex and more than 5,000 other agricultural, commercial, industrial, and consumer products in between the two extremes.

Changing Pricing Patterns

In the past, commodity pricing normally followed the same pattern as the economy. Prices tended to fall as the economy lost momentum and manufacturers reduced their inventories. Prices rose as the economy gained strength and manufacturers increased finished goods inventories. Time-based competition and a Just-in-Time manufacturing philosophy, however, tend to dampen the normal strong order demand that is usually seen as an economy begins an upturn. Therefore, in the long run, the pricing of many raw materials now appears to be based more on the cost of production. This is particularly true of raw materials that have lost their differentiation over time and since have become true commodities.

Evaluating Prices

What drives price? Demand? The cost of raw materials? The cost to process? Is it a labor- or capital-intensive process? Understanding how a material or a raw material is produced is the first step in understanding price. Understanding the industry structure provides information that is useful in evaluating prices, particularly in evaluating requests for price increases. It is also helpful to understand how standard materials are classified and how their properties differ. This information may well suggest substitution possibilities.

During the oil crisis of the mid-1970s, many salespeople justified their request for a 10% price increase by the fact that the cost of petroleum had gone up 10%. What the salespeople did not tell the buyers was that petroleum made up only 20% of the cost of product. This means that a 10% increase in petroleum prices should have had only a 2% impact on the selling price. Perceptive buyers need to understand these cost relationships.

Developing cost models for one's major commodities and raw materials is an excellent way to gain an understanding of the dynamics of the marketplace. The models need not be perfect. Capturing the basic cost elements that drive price is more important than the model being complete. The next step is to determine how controllable or uncontrollable the cost factors that drive prices really are. In the case of a capital- or labor-intensive product, the producer has a lot of control over the cost of production. However, if a product is raw material-intensive and the material is purchased in either a monopolistic or a free market, the producer's control over the cost of production is significantly restricted.

Controlling Price Escalation

Partnering has been seen by many firms as an answer to the question of price determination because it promotes the concept of suppliers opening their books to reveal their cost structure while the buying firm discloses how much it could afford to pay for the material. On the surface this seems like a reasonable approach to the determination of a fair price. This works well where the quoted market price is higher than that at which a company is willing to sell or the seller is not a cost leader and needs increased volume to reduce its unit costs. The purchaser and seller can work together to reduce the cost of production throughout the sharing of technology. Under these conditions the cost take-out can be significant.

However, what should the purchaser pay if, during these joining efforts to reduce costs, the transaction price in the marketplace drops below the cost of production and the purchase is to be made from the lowest price producer? Does the purchaser continue to pay the partner on the basis of cost plus profit? Or should the partner be required to meet competition? What about the windfall profit that can be made if the price of the product does drop because the purchaser and all competitors do not pass along lower prices to their customers? Should the partner share in these windfall profits? Because of these and similar questions, a purchaser should be cautious in tying the purchase price to a producer's cost.

Hedging

Futures markets provide the opportunity for buyers to transfer the risk of price increases to the marketplace. This is accomplished through hedging, which involves a material purchase in the spot market coupled with a simultaneous offsetting sale of a futures contract.

Box 32–4 is an example of a perfect hedge. In this example, the selling price was changed to reflect the exact change in materials cost so there was neither a net loss in Case A or a net gain in Case B. Unfortunately, perfect hedges do no occur in reality. The price fluctuation in the cost of raw materials usually is not *immediately* reflected in the price of the finished good, and buying and selling commissions need to be factored into the raw cost of hedging transactions. Obviously, there must be a spot and a futures market for the commodity you wish to hedge. However, for the right commodity, hedging is an ideal way to transfer the risk associated with the price uncertainty into the market place. The goal in hedging is to stabilize price, not to generate profit. Playing the market for profit is called speculating. Most purchasers are not empowered, nor should they be, to speculate.

QUALITY

Pitfalls of Using Industry Quality Standards

Industry standards, or market grades, that only define minimums or maximums of certain attributes are useful, but can be risky specification

B O X   32–4

CLASSIC MARKET HEDGE

Actions Today

1. Buy in the spot market 2,000# @ $1.00/# and use the material in production
2. Sell in futures market *futures contract* for 2,000# @ $1.00/# for delivery 90 days from now.

Actions 90 Days from Today

Case A: Buy 2,000# in the spot market to settle the futures contract @ $1.20/#. Generates a $400 loss.

Case B: Buy 2,000# in the spot market to settle the futures contract @ $0.90/#. Generates a $200 gain

Net Results

	Futures Contact	Sale of Goods	Net Dollars
Case A	−$400	+$400	0
Case B	+$200	−$200	0

to use. Defining characteristics this way may expose a buyer to two potential problems. By defining only an upper or lower limit, the variability of a characteristic can change as long as there is not more than or less than the stated amount of change. In either case, this instability may cause the conversion process to generate unexpected variation.

MRO Materials

Editor
Jack Barry
President
E-time, Inc.

INTRODUCTION

Maintenance, repair, and operating supplies and materials, otherwise known as MRO, make up a usually significant and sometimes substantial part of the total materials and services purchased by a company or other organization. In some cases MRO amounts to as much as 20% of total purchases. Every industry and organization uses some form of MRO, from office supplies to lubricants to cutting tools to pipe fittings to cleaning supplies, to mention only a few MRO items. While every organization buys MRO and in many it is a significant purchase, only relatively recently has management focused attention on how to better manage the MRO buy. This chapter will discuss what MRO is, the improvement potential available from better management of the purchasing and supply of MRO items, traditional MRO procurement, some "new" approaches to managing the MRO buy, and a general approach to developing and implementing improvement of MRO supply management.

WHAT IS MRO?

MRO is a major area for potential improvement in purchasing and supply management. MRO is in every industry; up to 20% of all purchases are for materials and services that never go into the finished product.

These items account for 70–90% of the purchase orders, shipment expense, and invoices processed. MRO is a significant expenditure for all companies across a wide range of industries.

Indirect materials, commonly called MRO, are typically parts and supplies that do not go into the finished product; for example, fasteners, hand tools, and lab supplies. In 1997, U.S. companies spent over $500 billion for MRO materials purchased through over 60,000 distributors (see Figure 33–1), and the administrative costs, shown in Figure 33–2, are excessive. In most companies, the indirect administrative costs and processes to acquire MRO are rarely visible or tracked in any cost accounting report.

The marketplace is complex, with multiple buying channels. See Figure 33–3.

Typically, the materials and services included in the general definition of MRO are:

1. Electrical and mechanical (includes repair parts, apparatus, and equipment, plus those materials to support capital projects)
2. Electronic (parts and equipment and computers and peripherals)

F I G U R E   33–1

1997 MRO Distributor Sales ($Billion)

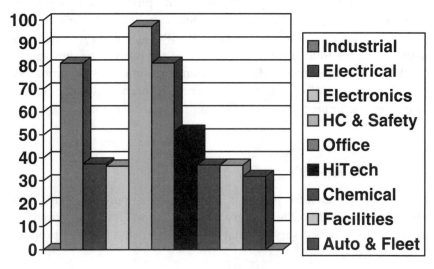

F I G U R E   33–2

Transport, Administrative, and Logistics Costs

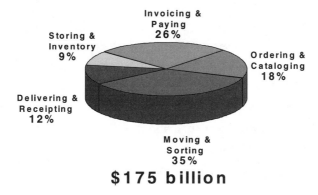

$175 billion

F I G U R E   33–3

Multiple Buying Channels

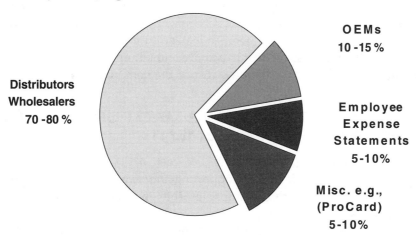

3. Professional equipment (includes laboratory equipment and supplies)

4. Industrial supplies (includes general maintenance supplies)

5. Safety and healthcare equipment, parts, and supplies

6. Machine shop supplies (industrial machinery, equipment, and tools)

7. Office supplies and equipment

8. Chemical supplies and equipment

9. Vehicle and fleet parts, equipment, and supplies

The marketplace is nondifferentiated, with thousands of suppliers and millions of purchasers accounting for over 75% of purchases, transport, storage, inventory SKUs, and accounts payable transactions. It has substantially long, non-value time delays and hidden costs.

Suppliers are concerned with

♦ High and long receivables

♦ High cost of order management

♦ High financial risks

while purchasers are concerned with

♦ High materials costs

♦ High administrative costs

♦ High levels of nonstandards

Over half of all MRO transactions account for less than 2% of total procurement. It is now becoming recognized that for many of the MRO or indirect purchases, at an average expenditure per transaction of less than $50, with an average cost to acquire and administer of over $65, the acquisition cost is higher than the cost of the item purchased.

POTENTIAL TO IMPROVE MRO PURCHASING AND SUPPLY MANAGEMENT

There is significant potential to reduce cost in the extensive administrative and manual processes supporting the acquisition and management of MRO. For many companies the processes are broken! See Figure 33–4.

Over the last 20 years, much of the focus of procurement professionals has been on improving the quality, service, and cost of purchased strategic production materials through:

♦ Supplier base reduction

♦ Supplier partnerships

♦ Supplier certification

♦ JIT programs

♦ Gain sharing

F I G U R E   33-4

MRO Practices and Processes

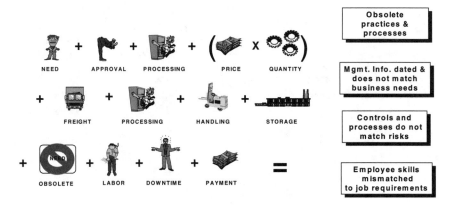

Similar advances have not been made in the area of MRO procurement. Conventional wisdom was that MRO was not very significant.

In the past, companies have attempted to manage the MRO market by choosing either a control or a convenience approach. Both approaches have failed. Success requires better financial and operational controls *and* increased user convenience *and* consistency of processes and infrastructure—one without the other fails. The marketplace, both providers and users, is looking for convenience, consistency, and control solutions to link the users, suppliers, carriers, and other stakeholders.

Many companies have been frustrated in their attempts to manage the low-volume, infrequently used, and nonstandardized items that make up MRO. Research, however, has found that there is considerable opportunity to both reduce net costs and substantially improve the quality and service to internal operational users.

Companies, therefore, do have the opportunity for immediate cost reductions based on redesigned MRO procurement processes. This can include utilizing the increasing power of information technology and electronic means of doing business, as well as reengineering MRO purchasing processes.

Companies who duplicate those innovations will have the potential to realize cost reductions and operational productivity improvements, as shown in Table 33-1, plus substantial savings in acquisition, administrative, operational, and performance costs.

T A B L E   33–1

Savings

	Short Term (less than one year)	Long Term (over one year)
Major and minor materials	5–8%	10–15%
Professional and business services	5–15%	15–25%
Employee support and benefits	3–5%	10–15%
Transportation and travel	2–4%	10–15%
Support and administrative materials and supplies	5–10%	15–20%
Reduced cost of acquisition		20–40%
Improved operational efficiencies		10–25%
Improved inventory turnover		200–300%
Reduced cost of supplier base management		30–40%

All the above improvements have been achieved by companies without major investments or negative impact on service, quality, or supplier relationships. Indeed, support and quality have been enhanced in key areas.

TRADITIONAL APPROACHES TO MRO SUPPLY MANAGEMENT

In many organizations the traditional approach was for purchasing to largely ignore the supply of MRO or relegate it to a very low-priority status. In such cases almost anyone could buy MRO from anyone they chose, and few controls were imposed. Reasons for this convenience approach included:

+ Other things were more important.
+ The dollars spent for MRO were too small.
+ There was scattered responsibility for the various categories of MRO.
+ Operations and maintenance service requirements were all-important and superseded any potential purchasing improvement.

In other organizations a control approach was used that required every MRO item to be requested in writing on a requisition form from which a purchasing person would buy the required item. This approach often required large purchasing staffs to place all the individual MRO orders. Reasons for this control approach included:

+ Complete transaction control was desired.
+ MRO processes were dictated by other policies.

Other characteristics of and reasons for traditional MRO supply approaches included:

+ Large inventories of MRO items on hand if needed
+ Supplier limitations
+ Suppliers, users, and management unwilling to change
+ Support infrastructure not available, e.g., communication facilities such as the Internet, electronic data interchange (EDI), and e-mail, and procurement card technology

NEW APPROACHES TO MANAGING MRO PURCHASING AND SUPPLY

Most of these approaches are new only in the sense that only in recent years have they begun to be used by large numbers of organizations. Pioneering companies and organizations have used some of them for many years. Unfortunately, terminology in purchasing and supply management is not always precise, and therefore some of the approaches described here may be described elsewhere using different names or characteristics. The intent here is to provide a selection of approaches that are used and can be considered. Approaches discussed below include:

+ Supplier partnerships or alliances
+ Integrated supply
+ Just-in-Time
+ Supplier city
+ Distributor cooperatives
+ Buyer cooperatives
+ Use of lead suppliers or outsourcing

These approaches are not mutually exclusive and are often employed in combination. For example, an integrated supply arrangement usually involves some form of partnership or alliance agreement and also includes Just-in-Time delivery of required items. The following discussion will briefly describe the approaches and indicate where they can be applied.

Supplier Partnership or Alliance

This type of arrangement is usually a single-source agreement, is not a legal partnership, and requires at least one, and more often three to five or more, years of commitment. A partnership or alliance may involve investment by the buyer or supplier or both in special facilities and/or training to implement the agreement, and will usually include requirements for joint improvement efforts and cost and benefit sharing. Inclusion of a dispute-resolution mechanism in the written partnership or alliance agreement is recommended because of the length of the agreement and the interdependence that is created.

Partnerships and alliances are often applied to large-cost or high-volume items as well as to items on which purchasing spends a large amount of time due to difficulty in obtaining the items or to a large volume of requests for the items. Items that have high price volatility are also often considered for these long-term agreements

Integrated Supply

Integrated supply consists of one supplier having responsibility for the supply of all materials in a particular product line. For example, if a company now has three suppliers for electrical MRO items, an integrated supply arrangement would have only one supplier for electrical MRO items, and that supplier would have to obtain or arrange for supply of items not previously in their product lines. Integrated supply sometimes assigns to the integrated supplier all responsibility for purchasing, inventorying, and delivery to the user in the purchaser's facility of all items included in the agreement. Often the supplier may operate on the customers premises, perhaps operating a warehouse that formerly was operated by the customer.

Integrated supply is often applied where there are large numbers of individually purchased products and many miscellaneous items can be obtained from one source. MRO is therefore usually an ideal candidate for application of integrated supply.

Just-In-Time

Just-in-Time usually implies that the buying organization maintains no inventory and that the supplier delivers whatever has been agreed upon just as it is needed by the purchaser's employees. Delivery may be made once or more per day from the supplier's stock, depending on level of usage and type of material. For example, some maintenance materials may be delivered four times per day, while office supplies may be delivered only once per day. In particularly high-usage situations where the supplier does not operate on the customer's premises, the supplier may place one of more employees on the customer's premises to function as combination suppliers and purchasers and provide communication and coordination between supplier locations and purchasing company personnel.

Just-in-Time is applied where large quantities of material are purchased from one supplier, usually involving frequent orders. A high level of coordination between purchaser and supplier firms is required for successful operation.

Supplier City

A supplier city consists of one supplier from each of a number of purchased product lines co-located near the purchaser's location or near a large complex that includes multiple purchasers. Normally each supplier would provide all purchasing and supply management services for their products. The concept is similar to integrated supply but potentially includes multiple product lines and multiple customers.

The supplier city concept obviously requires either a very large customer operation or a large complex of several customers facilities located near each other.

Distributor Cooperative

A distributor cooperative consists of a number of separately owned and geographically dispersed distributors of various industrial products agreeing to work together. The member distributors agree to cooperate in inventorying and selling all products they collectively carry and represent. The result expands the ability of each member distributor to provide a greater variety of products and provides one-stop shopping for buyers of the various items that are collectively offered. However, local inventory may not be available for all items.

Distributor cooperatives can be used to gain access to a broader variety of supplies and materials than that normally carried by one distributor. Distributor cooperatives can also be useful in providing a broad range of product representation and availability in locations remote from supply centers where local distributors are few. Distributor cooperatives are also a way to obtain a national agreement with local representation for a large company with many and widely scattered operating locations.

Buyer Cooperative

A buyer cooperative is somewhat the reverse of a distributor cooperative. Several buyers agree to pool their purchase of particular product lines in order to obtain improved pricing, service, or availability. The actual buying of pooled items may be done by members' employees as part of their jobs, or, in the case of large cooperatives, a separate staff may be set up to do the cooperative buying.

Buyer cooperatives appeal to relatively small buyers of common items who are co-located within a relatively small geographical region and are interested in a cooperative buying approach. Cooperatives can be and are also used for larger purchases, but as an individual organization achieves sufficient volume to obtain the maximum price and service benefits on its own, the added coordination needed to use the cooperative diminishes in appeal.

Lead Supplier or Outsourcing

Use of the lead supplier or outsourced method of procurement implies that one supplier has total responsibility for the supply of one or more purchased product lines. Any products not carried by the lead supplier must be purchased by them. This approach differs from integrated supply in that the buyer relinquishes all day-to-day control for purchasing and supply management of the designated product lines.

Use of lead supplier or outsourcing is appropriate where the buyer no longer wants to do the buying internally and wants no day-to-day involvement in the supply of the items. Often this type of agreement is used for noncritical items, items bought only occasionally, items bought in small quantities, or items bought in great variety—in other words, in situations where the risk of giving up control is low.

DEVELOPING AND IMPLEMENTING IMPROVED MRO SUPPLY

A successful approach to improving MRO supply management is called high performance business process redesign. It focuses on *supply chain purchasing* support required by key business processes as defined by internal users. The process includes five types of actions:

1. *Segmenting* MRO procurement into rational commodity groups and adopting segment specific strategies and tactics
2. *Consolidating* requirements to gain volume leverage
3. *Shrinking* the supplier bases dramatically to gain additional volume leverage
4. *Establishing* long-term partnerships with suppliers in order to create a framework for continuous improvement
5. *Eliminating* transaction-intensive activities to reduce administrative costs and focus procurement personnel on managing critical user and supplier relationships

Some of the activities involved in implementing these actions include:

1. *Rationalize the supplier base* through drastically (over 75%) reducing in the number of suppliers and engaging in significantly expanded roles with the remaining suppliers to reduce cost and improve quality and service.
2. *Sell back* excess and obsolete *inventories* to the original suppliers at a potential range of 65–85% of original cost on possibly 35% or more of the total inventory investment.
3. *Eliminate* noncritical and transaction-intensive activities, replacing them with more cost-efficient and responsive processes, including the use of third-party procurement and logistics service providers (with resultant potential of 60% reductions in inventory levels).
4. *Automate* low-dollar and low-volume transactions, which currently may account for over 70% of procurement, receiving, and accounts payable and receivable activities, to reduce transaction costs and eliminate non-value process cycle time and personnel (potential of over 70% reduction in administrative cost).
5. *Identify* any gaps in collective and individual procurement effectiveness both within internal structure and against

competitors, suppliers, emerging technology, and other
world-class organizations.

6. *Quantify* the expected benefits and do cost/benefit analysis.

7. *Build consensus* on improvement and implementation plans.

8. *Identify* the actionable tasks to achieve cost reductions, quality
   improvements, and operational efficiencies.

9. *Specify* the reengineered and redesigned procurement
   processes that will support the improvements sought.

10. *Develop* the long-term implementation plans that will allow
    purchasers to realize continuous improvements in MRO
    procurement.

Four fundamental concepts should be applied in developing improved MRO supply management:

1. *User driven:* Requirements must be driven by the user. Users
   should be accountable for usage and inventory. Users must be
   partners in the supplier selection process. The performance
   measurement for procurement should reflect users' needs.

2. *Supplier partnerships:* Long-term, full-service sourcing
   agreements should be the standard. The number of suppliers
   must be substantially reduced. Remaining suppliers must be
   full partners in aggressive cost reductions and gain/risk
   sharing. Suppliers must play an active role in forecasting
   requirements and reducing inventory investments.

3. *Lean environment:* Noncore and noncritical transaction-based
   activities must be eliminated. Information must be a realistic
   substitute for inventory.

4. *Central role:* Purchasing must facilitate increased user and
   supplier interactions. The coordination of supplier evaluations,
   consolidated requirements, and company-wide agreements
   must be a primary responsibility.

USE OF ELECTRONIC COMMERCE IN MRO PROCUREMENT PROCESSES

The Internet and the complete capabilities of an electronic commerce
marketplace are dramatically changing the way successful organizations
buy goods and services, and MRO in particular.

Companies that have not yet done so must develop an electronic business infrastructure that is both platform-independent and compatible with and accessible by existing and proposed enterprise resource planning (ERP) financial systems applications. With this technology, companies and other organizations can realize benefits in the following areas:

♦ Validation and control of receipts at any point
♦ Reduced costs and tighter controls of financial accounting
♦ Access to electronic commerce cataloging and ordering
♦ Integration with existing and new financial systems, e.g., Oracle, SAP
♦ Lower costs from suppliers based on reducing their costs
♦ Higher levels of and conformity to financial and operating standards
♦ Effective control of supplier selection and pricing

TWO EXAMPLES

Company A Is a Division of a Major U.S. Auto Manufacturer

The three key features of Company A's MRO procurement strategy are:

1. 100% use of full-service, primary suppliers
2. Accounting for 100% of inventory until use
3. Elimination of purchasing and receiving functions

Company A has two supplier categories: primary supplier and second tier supplier.

Primary suppliers	Company A has one supplier for each major commodity group, such as: cutting tools & abrasives, oils & lubricants, power transmission, and others. Each primary supplier has an "evergreen" contract in place.
Second-tier suppliers	When an indirect material item falls into a primary supplier commodity category but is not in the primary suppliers product line, the item is purchased from a second-tier supplier by the primary supplier for company A.

Key to Company A's MRO procurement system is the structure of the supply base. Company A's philosophy is that 100% of its business will be placed with the 22 primary suppliers. Less than 50 purchase orders per year go to other suppliers.

Number of suppliers	♦ One primary supplier for each major commodity group. ♦ 22 full-service suppliers. ♦ Support by second-tier suppliers.
Contracts	♦ "Evergreen" contracts in place.
Inventory	♦ Supplier acts as indirect material inventory crib for Company A.
Purchasing	♦ Supplier does Company A's purchasing role with second-tier suppliers.
Technical support	♦ Supplier experts in Company A plant Identify opportunities for improved materials and procedures.
Continuous improvement	♦ All supplier reps and indirect material group meet regularly on continuous improvement activities.

Primary Supplier Functions

1. Act as a central indirect material inventory crib for Company A.
   - ♦ One supplier has a dedicated Company A warehouse of 25,000 square feet and 20 people.
   - ♦ Another allocates 38,000 square feet to Company A and carries 135 days of inventory
2. Serve as Company A's purchasing department for second-tier suppliers.
   - ♦ The price Company A pays for the second-tier item is increased only by a transaction cost paid to the primary supplier.
3. Provide in-plant technical support.
   - ♦ Supplier technical experts in the Company A plant provide constant support for proper application of materials and identify opportunities for improved materials and procedures.
   - ♦ Primary suppliers provide a 24-hour emergency telephone support, but they report that this service is rarely used.

Company A has 22 MRO suppliers.

♦ Level of purchases outside of 22 suppliers is very low.

♦ Last year Company A placed 50 P.O.s outside, mostly for exceptional, nonordinary, large purchases.

♦ Total transactions are about 5,000/month.

♦ Company A makes it difficult to order from other suppliers; full P.O. paperwork is required.

Company A developed an EDI system to communicate with each of the 22 suppliers.

The basis of the Company A system is to account for and track *all* inventory through to the *point* and *time* of use.

Location	Inventory is primarily stored at team stations.
	A small amount is in central inventory.
Accountability	Inventory is tracked until usage.
	Team accountability is being established.
Levels	Presently feel levels are "too high" due to inefficiencies and "padding" at start-up.
Supplier inventory	Full-service suppliers hold 4–6 months of inventory in co-located warehouses.

Company B Is a Major U.S. Parts Manufacturer

Company B has restructured its entire purchasing organization over four years.

♦ Conversion from a centralized to a decentralized purchasing system.
  ♦ Reduced the total number of suppliers from 1,500 to 600.
  ♦ End user bypasses corporate purchasing for the acquisition of both materials and contract services with reduced cycle times.
  ♦ Corporate purchasing provides value-added services, e.g., supplier city, and negotiation of master purchasing agreements and service contracts.
  ♦ Perrmac software system facilitates the complete ordering process from order to receipt and payment.
♦ Plants run 24 hours a day, seven days per week.
♦ Purchase approximately 6,000 different MRO items.

- ◆ Master purchase agreements are monitored by the purchasing department using mutually agreed-upon performance measures
  - ◆ Leadtime
  - ◆ Number of rejections (wrong part or damaged material)
  - ◆ Quantity and price
  - ◆ Annual cost reduction of 10% in any combination of Company B and supplier operating costs.
- ◆ All service contracts are entered into online system.
  - ◆ Contract terms and conditions
  - ◆ Customized in any manner
  - ◆ Blanket P.O. # is created for corporate-wide acquisition of services.

- ◆ Supplier city has been established for primary MRO suppliers.
  - ◆ One-stop shopping
  - ◆ Delivery four times a day
  - ◆ Computer link-up with barcoding of each shipment for receipting
  - ◆ Currently 5 suppliers approved, with a goal of 15
  - ◆ Long-term, mutually advantageous relationship established (20 years)
  - ◆ Reduced lead-time, inventory, and cycle times.

Company B has experienced significant benefits from restructuring.

- ◆ Transaction time from request to P.O. reduced from 30 days to 2 hours.
- ◆ Invoices ready to pay in 36 hours.
- ◆ Supplier qualification and selection completed in three months.
- ◆ 88% of requests require no approvals.
- ◆ 100% of invoices paid at P.O. price upon receipt.
- ◆ Delivery four times per day from suppliers in supplier city.
- ◆ Discounts 100% taken.
- ◆ Inventory reduction for steel 43%.
- ◆ Corporate purchasing staff reduced from 36 to 22.
- ◆ Corporate purchase orders went from 3,000 to 20 per week.
- ◆ Field-authorized purchase orders replaced the difference.

Company B established a set of basic principles for their purchasing philosophy.

- Continual improvement and change are required by *suppliers and employees.*
- Getting the end user the material or service is the only goal.
- *The only measure that matters is the corporate bottomline.*
- The mundane is handled by the system; people then have time to work the "big hit" items.
- Suppliers are *partners,* and they are the key to continuously lowering costs
- Authority as well as responsibility are put into the hands of those using it. Anyone can see where the costs are being spent.
- The logistics group (materials and purchasing) is accessible and committed to adding value to the company
- MRO commodities are different and require different approaches in a broad sense.
- Having real-time cost data available is essential.

Other innovative companies have achieved dramatic results in a wide variety of private and public sector companies by Redesigning their MRO purchasing processes. See Table 33–2.

T A B L E 33-2

MRO Improvement Results

Company Example	Process Redesigned	Focus of Redesign	Selected Results
U.S. Railroad	Maintenance procurement process	Transformation Focus on user-friendliness, cost reduction, and employee value-added activities	Identified $34 million annual recurring benefits
Federal Government Agency	Acquisition process	Privatization Apply industry best practices to acquisition process	Developed a new vision to support expansion
Automotive Vehicle Manufacturer	Indirect and maintenance material purchasing and material management	Cost and effectiveness Develop a vision for new MRO procurement process	Identified potential savings of $160 million
Federal Government Agency	Transportation supplier/carrier consolidations	Consolidation Apply industry best practices to acquisition process for transport carriers	Reduced the number of carriers and simplified work processes which reduced processing time by 5 days and saved over $30M
U.S. Chemical	Supply chain organizational effectiveness	Purchasing redesign Establish organization and processes to achieve volume advantage and operational control	Achieved $33 million cost reductions within 16 months

Company Example		Process Redesigned	Focus of Redesign	Selected Results
Consumer Goods		Maintenance supplier consolidation process	Volume advantage Design and implement supplier consolidation process to leverage volume and improve service	Reduced supplier base from over 6,000 to less than 100
International Telephone Company		Capital expansions MRO procurement	Material availability Design and establish the business processes and stakeholder services	Increased material availability from below 45% to over 85% with net cost reductions of over $65 million
Petroleum Company		Purchasing accounts payable	User requirements Focus on user material requirements for field and headquarters	Utilized user-directed procurement, resulting in systems effectiveness and cost reductions of over $200 million
Worldwide Automotive Manufacturer		Business simulation supporting acquisition process of small purchases	Technology Application of communication technology to speed the bid and award processes	Purchases cycle time reduced by over 80% and both administrative and material cost reduced
Steel Manufacturer		Purchasing maintenance production	Process changes Eliminate delays and duplicate operations	One-time savings of $5 million plus current savings rate plan for $77 million over the next three years

T A B L E 33-2

Continued

Company Example		Process Redesigned	Focus of Redesign	Selected Results
Healthcare Provider		Supplier management cost reduction	Cost and efficiency Design processes to achieve cost reductions at multiple hospitals	Reduced major material costs, inventory and assets, supplier base, all at faster cycle time and better customer service levels
Mail Order Retailer		Distribution and purchasing network	Rationalization Reduce the waste in procurement and distribution networks	Reduced network by 70% at a 30% cost reduction
U.S. Insurance Company		Procurement and delivery processes of support materials	Transformation Apply best practices and internal customer measurements	Greatly reduced cost, inventory, and cycle time with major increases in availability
U.S. Navy		Acquisition processes of small purchases	Technology Utilize commercially available communication technology to speed the bid/award processes	Reduced small purchase cycle time by over 80% and both administrative and material costs reduced

Company Example		Process Redesigned	Focus of Redesign	Selected Results
Automotive Vehicle Manufacturer		Accounts payable	Cost and effectiveness Develop a new process for "evaluated receipts" and paperless payments	Implemented imaging to replace manual and paper processing of accounts payable
International Chemical Company		Transportation supplier/carrier consolidations	Volume advantage Design joint approach to carrier negotiations to achieve volume benefits without service dilution	Carrier base was reduced over 60% with 25% reduction in rates
U.S. PetroChemical		Supplier accreditation process	Safety and reliability Design accreditation to leverage the supplier and improve operations	Focused 80% of MRO with less than 60 suppliers and outsourced utility and transportation bill paying
Tobacco Company		Promotional materials purchasing and distribution	Supplier consolidation Reduce supplier base and process cycle time. Outsource noncritical tasks	Outsourced the largest and most successful consumer promotion. Over $250 million savings with an over 35% increase in availability

T A B L E   33-2

Continued

Company Example	Process Redesigned	Focus of Redesign	Selected Results
U.S. Telephone Company	Supplier and purchasing performance metrics	Performance Metrics Redesign and validate metrics to evaluate supplier and purchasing performance	Won the Malcolm Baldridge Award with special notice of the measurement criteria for internal user customer service
U.S. Water Utility	Supplier management cost reduction	Cost and efficiency Design processes to achieve cost reductions at multiple sites	Reduced material costs by over $30M and reduced excess inventory by over $70M and reduced supplier base and faster service cycle time
International PetroChemical	Supply chain management	Reengineering Design and implement consolidation of purchasing, material planning, and logistics	P&L impact exceeds $100 million with 50% staff reduction plus installation of major client–server MIS
Paper Manufacturer	Procurement process effectiveness	Procurement redesign Design and establish a world-class paperless procurement process	Reduced admin. costs by 50% or $3.5M; cycle time by 70%; and cost of materials by $20 million

CHAPTER 34

Software and Intellectual Property

Editor
Leslie S. Marell
Attorney at Law
Law Offices of Leslie S. Marell

The successful acquisition of software and other technology requires knowledge of various types of legal principles. These principles are drawn from a number of areas of the law, including the law of contracts, employment, and intellectual property.

Part One of this chapter will introduce the concept of intellectual property and provide an overview of the four principal types of intellectual property. Part Two will apply these intellectual property principles to software acquisition as well as identify and discuss the key issues involved in the acquisition agreement.

PART ONE: WHAT IS INTELLECTUAL PROPERTY?

Intellectual property consists of products of the human intellect that have economic value. Examples include software, books, music, movies, photographs, artwork, records, and inventions.

Intellectual property is "property" because over the past 200 years or so a body of laws has been created that gives owners of such works legal rights similar in some respects to those given to owners of real estate or tangible personal property. Intellectual property may be owned and bought and sold the same as other types of property.

There are four principal types of intellectual property law:

1. Trade secret law
2. Copyright law
3. Trademark law
4. Patent law

Trade Secret Law

Under the Uniform Trade Secrets Act, which many states have adopted, a trade secret is information or knowhow that: (1) is not generally known in the business community, (2) provides its owner with a competitive advantage in the marketplace, and (3) is treated in a way that can reasonably be expected to prevent others from learning about it. Trade secrecy is based on a simple idea: By keeping valuable information secret, one can prevent competitors from learning about and using it.

The information can be an idea, written words, formula, process or procedure, technical design, customer list, marketing plan, or any other secret that gives the owner an economic advantage. Trade secret law protects the owner of the confidential information against unauthorized use, copying, or disclosure. However, in order to protect the confidential information, the holder of a trade secret must do more than put a confidentiality notice on his or her materials. He or she must actually maintain the secrecy of them. This requires, among other things, that the recipient of the information agree in writing to maintain the secrecy of the confidential information.

The reward for developing and maintaining a trade secret is that it may last forever; however, others are merely prohibited from misappropriating it. Anyone is free to develop the same information independently.

Unlike copyrights and patents, which are governed by federal law, trade secrecy is not codified in any federal statute. Instead, it is made up of individual state laws and is based on statutory and common law and contractual provisions. However, the protection afforded to trade secrets in every state is much the same.

In order to ensure that a company's trade secrets remain confidential, all recipients of the trade secrets should sign a nondisclosure agreement. Simply making a document "Proprietary" or "Confidential" may not be enough to legally require that the recipient keep the information confidential.

A nondisclosure agreement is a document in which a person who is given access to trade secrets promises not to disclose them to others without permission from the trade secret owner. Using nondisclosure agreements consistently is the single most important element of any trade secret protection program.

Copyright Law

A copyright is a form of protection provided by the federal laws of the United States (and most other countries) to those who create what the law refers to as "original works of authorship." Copyright protects only the *expression* of an idea, concept, or discovery in a computer program, book, or movie; it does not protect any ideas, concepts, or discoveries embodied in the work. In fact, the U.S. Copyright Act states that "In no case does copyright protection for an original work of authorship extend to any idea, procedure, process, system, method of operation, concept, principle or discovery. . . .'"

Copyright is a grant of certain exclusive rights to authors in order to allow them control over how the work is used. Under current law, a work is automatically protected by copyright as soon as it is "fixed in any tangible medium of expression." Neither use of a copyright notice, publication of the work, nor registration is necessary to secure the copyright.

Copyrights provide their owners with the exclusive right to reproduce, display, perform, distribute, and prepare derivative works from the copyrighted work. The owner has a monopoly on his or her fixed expression of an idea, but does *not* have a monopoly on the idea itself. Others are free to independently create even an identical work and to make whatever use they wish of the ideas embodied in the copyrighted work.

In the case of copyrighted software, the user has the right to:

♦ Use the software for its intended purpose
♦ Make a copy of the software for archival purposes
♦ Make a copy of the software if such copy is a necessary step in the use of the software in conjunction with a computer

Copyright protects all kinds of original works of authorship, including literary works (including software programs, computer databases and software documentation), motion pictures, photographs, graphic works, sound recordings, choreographic works, and architectural works. If someone wrongfully uses material covered by a copyright, the copyright owner can sue and obtain compensation for any losses suffered, as well as an injunction (court order) requiring the copyright infringer to stop the infringing activity.

Before 1989, all published works had to contain a copyright notice (the © symbol followed by the publication date and the copyright owner's name). This is no longer necessary in the United States. Even so, it is always a good idea to include a copyright notice on all works distributed to the public.

Until October 1998, works created on or after January 1, 1978, had a term of the life of the author plus 50 years. In the case of *works made for hire* (see definition below), the term was 75 years from publication. Legislation enacted in October, 1998 has extended these terms for an additional 20 years.

Ownership of Copyrights

As a general rule, the creator of a work owns the copyright. This means that when a company retains an independent contractor to develop, design, or create a work, the independent contractor, *not the company*, will initially own the copyright to the work. *Works made for hire* are an important exception to the general rule. If a work is created by an employee as part of his or her job, the law considers the product a work for hire, and the employer will own the copyright. If the creator is an independent contractor, the works will be considered works for hire *only* if: (1) the parties have signed a written agreement stating that the work will be a work for hire *and* (2) the work is commissioned as a contribution to a collective work, a supplementary work, an instructional text, answer material for a test, an atlas, a motion picture, or an audiovisual work. *Thus, unless there is a contractual agreement to the contrary, and the work fits within one of the above categories, the independent contractor owns the copyright.*

Note that the above list is very limited. The items likely to be purchased such as software computer programs, photographs, catalogs, and designs, are not listed. Merely including the "work-made-for-hire" language is not enough to ensure that your company obtains ownership to the copyright in most cases.

In order to effect a transference of the copyright ownership to your contract, you should have a contract that includes language in which the independent contractor transfers ("assigns") the copyright in the creation to your company. See Exhibit 34–1 for example language of an independent contractor assigning his or her copyright rights in the work to the company.

E X H I B I T   34–1

COPYRIGHT ASSIGNMENT

This Agreement is made this _____ day of _____, by and between [Insert Consultant's name] with offices located at _____ (the "Assignor") and [Insert Your Company Name] with offices located at _____ (the "Assignee").

WHEREAS, Assignor has prepared, written, created, or developed certain materials or works pursuant to Assignee specifications entitled [Insert Project Name], (the "Work");

WHEREAS, Assignor desires to transfer entire ownership of the copyright in the Work to Assignee;

IT IS THEREFORE agreed between Assignor and Assignee as follows:

1. Assignor hereby grants, transfers, assigns, and conveys to Assignee, its successors and assigns, the entire title, right interest, ownership and all subsidiary rights in and to the Work, including but not limited to the right to secure copyright registration therein and to any resulting registration in Assignee's name as claimant, and the right to secure renewals, reissues, and extensions of any such copyright or copyright registration in the United States of America or any foreign country;

2. Whether the copyright in the Work shall be preserved and maintained or registered in the United States of America or any foreign country shall be at the sole discretion of Assignee;

3. Assignor hereby confirms that Assignee, and its successors and assigns, own the entire title, right, and interest in the Work, including the right to reproduce, prepare derivative works based upon the copyright in the Work, distribute by sale, by rental, lease, or lending or by other transfer of ownership; to perform publicly; and to display, in and to the Work, whether or not the Work constitutes a "work made for hire" as defined in 17 U.S.C. Section 201(b);

4. Assignor agrees that no rights in the Work are retained by Assignor;

E X H I B I T   34—1 Continued

5. Assignor agrees to take all actions and cooperate as is necessary to protect the copyrightability of the Work and further agrees to execute any documents that might be necessary to perfect Assignee's ownership of copyrights in the Work and to registration;

6. All terms of this Agreement are applicable to any portion or part of the Work, as well as the Work in its entirety;

7. This Agreement constitutes the entire agreement between the parties hereto; this Agreement supersedes any prior oral or written agreement or understanding between the parties;

8. This Agreement has been interpreted under the United States Copyright Law; but will be litigated or prosecuted under the laws of the state of _____.

Assignor	Assignee
By: _____	By: _____
Title: _____	Title: _____
Date: _____	Date: _____

Trademark Law

A trademark is any visual mark that accompanies a particular product or line of goods and serves to identify and distinguish it from products sold by others and to indicate its source. A trademark may consist of letters, words, names, phrases or slogans, numbers, colors, symbols, designs or shapes, or combinations of any of these. Common trademarks include COKE, LOTUS 1-2-3, an apple with a bite taken out of it, and FORD HAS A BETTER IDEA. As a general rule, to be protected from unauthorized use by others, a trademark must be distinctive in some way.

A tradename is the formal name of a business but is not protectible as a trademark. A tradename is used to identify a business for such purposes as opening bank accounts or paying taxes. However, a tradename may be protected as a trademark when it is used to identify and distinguish products or services sold in the marketplace. State statutes and common law provide protection for a business entity's tradename.

There are other more specialized marks under the trademark category. They include:

Service mark: A mark used to identify and distinguish services

Collective mark: A symbol, word, phrase, or other identifying mark used by members of a group for goods they produce or services they perform

Certification mark: A mark used for the purpose of certifying various qualities of products or services

Protection of trademarks is granted under common law, which is that body of law developed from court decisions rather than from state or federal statutes. Greater protection is secured through federal or state registration, but is it not necessary. The federal statute governing trademarks is known as the Lanham Act and grants many important benefits not available at common law.

Patent Law

The U.S. Patent Act states:

> Whoever invents or discovers any new or useful process, machine, manufacture, or composition of matter, or any new and useful improvement thereof, may obtain a patent therefore.

A patent is an official document issued by the U.S. government or other government that describes an invention and confers on the inventor a monopoly over the right to make, use, or sell the invention for a certain number of years. This monopoly gives the inventor the right to stop anyone else from making, using, or selling his or her invention—even if independently developed—for a limited term of years. In the United States, patents require periodic renewal by the inventor and can extend for a maximum of 20 years beginning on the filing date of the application (for patents filed after June 1995). Where available, patent protection is so strong that it takes the place of both copyright and trade secret protection.

In order to be patentable, the invention must meet several basic legal tests and be sufficiently "innovative." Generally, in order to obtain a patent, the invention must meet each of the following criteria:

- *Novel:* Unique compared to previous technology in one or more of its elements

♦ *Nonobvious:* Surprising to a person with ordinary skills in that technology

♦ *Useful:* Possessing a sufficient degree of utility

In the United States, a patent is obtained by submitting an application and fee to the U.S. Patent and Trademark Office (USPTO). Once it has received the application, the USPTO assigns an examiner who is knowledgeable in the technology underlying the invention to decide whether the invention qualifies for a patent and what the scope of the patent should be.

Most software is not sufficiently novel or nonobvious to qualify for a patent. However, the tendency of the USPTO with respect to issuing software-based patents now is more favorable than it was five years ago with respect to software programs that:

♦ Run computers that in turn run machines that then make something you can touch or identify—for instance, a two-dimensional picture plotted as a three-dimensional picture

♦ Use an algorithm to translate one set of numbers into another where the second set of numbers is used for diagnosis or analysis—for instance, when numbers produced by analog measurement of an earthquake are digitally manipulated to analyze the earthquake

Each of these four types of intellectual property may be used to protect different aspects of software, although there is a great deal of overlap. The purchaser should be aware of their application to software in order to construct a meaningful software acquisition agreement.

PART TWO: ACQUISITION OF SOFTWARE

The Software License

The owner of a copyright, trade secret, or patent in software may assign (transfer) or sell all rights in the software program. Alternatively, the owner of the software may license specific, limited rights to one or more licensees. Most computer software contracts today grant the party acquiring the software a "license" to use the software, rather than transferring ownership through the purchase process.

A *license* is the permission by the owner of the software to another to use the software, or exercise a certain privilege without granting any ownership interest. The two parties to the license are the *licensor*, who grants to another (the licensee) certain limited rights to possess and use software, and the *licensee*, who acquires the right from the owner (the licensor) of the software to possess and use the software, subject to the terms of the license agreement. A licensee obtains no ownership rights in the copy of the software that he or she receives.

The software license agreement is a key document between the software supplier and the software user because it may control the relationship between the parties for a lengthy period of time. The supplier has spent a great deal of time and money in developing a sophisticated software package. Therefore, it is critical for the supplier to be able to limit access to its valuable asset. From the user's viewpoint, he or she must understand what is in fact being purchased and the restrictions on the use of the computer program.

The following are key issues to address in a software license agreement.

Type of License

Exclusive or Nonexclusive Mass-marketed software will generally be licensed on a nonexclusive basis. With custom software, however, competing interests come into play. On the one hand, the user will want to acquire either all rights or an exclusive license to restrict its competitors from acquiring and using the software. On the other hand, the vendor will want to market the software to others in order to recoup its development costs and make greater profits.

Scope of Use The scope of the license defines the approved user, the equipment upon which the software can be used, the business location where the software can be maintained, and any limitations on business applications. This key element goes to the very core of the agreement between licensor and licensee. Typically, the supplier will want to limit the user to installing the licensed software on only one piece of computer equipment. An inexperienced user often does not realize that the license is restricted to a single computer installation. When seeking to expand use of the licensed software to another system or location, the user may unexpectedly discover that additional licenses are significantly more expensive than initially estimated. If a licensee has subsidiary or affiliate operations, it is advisable for the license to provide that the software may be used by those operations.

The following are examples of the different types of licenses and their scope of use:

+ *Corporate or enterprise:* Licensee may utilize the software on any CPU anywhere within the corporation.
+ *Site:* Licensee may utilize the software on all CPUs at a physical location.
+ *CPU:* Licensee may use software only on one computer.
+ *System:* Licensee may use software on all seats in a department accessing one server.

Term, Renewal, and Termination

Term   The effective date of the license will be specified in the agreement or will be the last date that a party executes the license. The termination date could either be unspecified (a perpetual license) or specified (a limited-term license). The user must be assured of receiving a license for a sufficient time period. Generally, if the license is for a short, fixed time period (e.g., one year), the user will be required to pay an additional fee to renew the license.

If the license is perpetual, the user will generally pay a one-time license fee and then be permitted to use the license in perpetuity thereafter. Even with a perpetual license, however, the licensor will want to have the ability to terminate the license in the event that the user breaches the license agreement.

Renewal   If the license is a limited-term license, the agreement may include a renewal provision. Typically, however, suppliers use automatic renewal or "evergreen" provisions. The following is an example of an evergreen provision:

> This Agreement shall automatically renew for successive one (1) year periods unless terminated in writing by either party at least thirty (30) days prior to the expiration of any one year period.

A contract tip for licensees: Users who want to reevaluate the software license every year should insist that renewal occur only upon payment of the renewal license fee. In addition, the user should reserve the right to terminate at any time.

Termination   *Protecting the user upon termination.* Unexpected termination of a software contract can severely impair the licensee's ability to process its business, particularly in the case of software that performs a crucial function of the licensee's business operation. Therefore, the termination provision should be drafted in a manner to protect the user from unexpected terminations and provide necessary assistance from the licensor in order to implement an orderly transition to another software system.

Provisions for termination by either party should be specified. In the event of an alleged breach of the agreement by the licensee, a reasonable notice period and an opportunity to cure or dispute the alleged breach should be provided. This will avoid a situation where the licensor terminates the software with little or no warning or for a reason that the licensee disputes, leaving the licensee with no software and little time to replace it.

The user may seek to restrict the vendor from attempting to disable the software. The following is a sample provision:

> Licensor warrants that the Software does not contain any code that will, upon the occurrence or the nonoccurrence of any event, disable the Software. If any such code is present, Licensor agrees to indemnify Licensee for all damages suffered as a result of a disabling caused by such code.

No termination upon bankruptcy. A provision such as the one in Section 11 of the Software Source Code Escrow Agreement contained in Exhibit 34–2 should appear in the license to prevent unforeseen termination of the right to use the software upon bankruptcy of the licensor.

Termination assistance. Often, transition to another software program will result in the need to transfer the existing data to another format. In such a case, the licensee may require the technical assistance of the licensor since the transition may require specialized knowledge of the former system possessed only by the licensor. In any type of termination setting, whether in a default or nondefault scenario, such assistance should be provided for in the license agreement.

Acceptance/Rejection

Acceptance is a key event in a software contract. The purpose of an acceptance provision is to ensure that the software delivered and installed does in fact operate in accordance with all specifications and contract requirements. If the software does not operate as required, the licensor should have the right to reject the software, send it back, and receive a full refund of payments made. Significant to proper acceptance are (1) detailed functional and design specifications and (2) detailed acceptance test plan.

Acceptance should be the triggering event for the following:

♦ Final payment to the licensor

♦ Commencement of warranty period

♦ Commencement of support and maintenance obligations

One key to successful software testing is to conduct testing of each module of a software system and then conduct system or integrated testing. The development of a comprehensive test plan is critical to determining whether the software has met the acceptance criteria.

Fees and Terms of Payment

Fees   It is important to identify what is and is not included in the license fee and what is encompassed in any additional fees. Types of fees include license fees (one-time, annual, or monthly), installation fees, training fees, and maintenance fees.

If there are annual license fees, users should insert a price protection clause into the contract. This is accomplished by putting a maximum limit on the annual rate of increase. The following is an example clause:

> The annual maintenance fee is subject to change by Licensor following the end of the one-year period upon ninety (90) days' prior written notice to Licensee; provided, however, that such maintenance charge shall not be increased more than one in any one-year period and in no event shall any increase exceed ___% of the maintenance charge applicable to the preceding year.

Terms of Payment   There are two methods of payment:

1. Lump sum:
   A. Payment on execution of agreement
   B. Payment upon delivery/acceptance of the software
2. Progress payments:
   A. Purpose: To tie payments to successful completion of benchmarks or delivery schedule
   B. Sample payment benchmarks for large systems:
      ♦ Execution of license
      ♦ Detailed specifications approved
      ♦ Completion of preliminary testing by supplier at its site
      ♦ Completion of preliminary testing by supplier at user's site
      ♦ Training of user
      ♦ Delivery of software documentation

+ On-line system implementation
+ Completion of final integrated acceptance test
+ Final acceptance

Warranties

Express Warranties   An express warranty is a promise or statement made by a seller regarding the quality, quantity, performance, or characteristics of something being sold. The software licensor, in making an actual promise about how the software will work, whether orally or in writing, is making an "express warranty." While an express warranty can be created by using words such as "warrant" or "guarantee," there are no magic words necessary to create a warranty. Representations made by salespeople, sales literature, statements at product demonstrations, proposals, manuals, and specifications can all constitute express warranties. Express warranties can last for any period of time, from a few months to the lifetime of the software.

Licensees often seek an express warranty from the licensor guaranteeing that the software is free from defects and will meet the functional and design specifications established. Another common express warranty is a guarantee that the software will not infringe any third party's copyright, patent, or trade secret rights.

In order to ensure that the express warranty is enforceable, it is important that all promises about the software be written into the contract. If these promises (including reference to the licensor's proposal) are not included in the contract, they will likely *not* be binding on the licensor.

The following are express warranties the licensee should consider including into the license:

+ Warranty of software performance
+ Warranty of good title
+ Warranty against disablement
+ Warranty of compatibility
+ Warranty against infringement
+ Warranty of Year 2000 compliance

The following is an example licensor warranty clause:

Licensor warrants that the Software is free from material defects and will operate substantially in accordance with the documentation listed in Exhibit 34–1 for twelve (12) months following acceptance by Licensee.

If, at any time within the twelve (12) month period, the Software is considered by Licensee not to be in conformance with this warranty, Licensee shall promptly notify Licensor of such nonconformance. Licensor shall respond as required in the Error Correction section of the Paragraph entitled "Maintenance."

If a nonconformance is not corrected within thirty (30) days of the original notification to Licensor, or if an acceptable plan for correcting the nonconformance is not established during such period, Licensee may, by giving Licensor written notice thereof, terminate this Agreement and return all copies of Software to Licensor or verify in writing that the Software has been destroyed and Licensor shall refund to Licensee all fees paid by Licensee pursuant to this Agreement.

Implied Warranties   In every commercial transaction involving the sale of goods, certain representations by the seller are assumed to be made, even if no words are written or spoken. These representations are implied by state laws based on the Uniform Commercial Code (UCC). In the past, a number of courts have disagreed on whether software qualifies as a "good" governed by these state UCC laws, but today the trend appears to be that the UCC applies to off-the-shelf and custom software sales and license transactions.

There are four implied warranties:

1. Implied warranty of title
2. Implied warranty against infringement
3. Implied warranty of merchantability
4. Implied warranty of fitness for a particular purpose

Disclaimer of Warranties   There is no requirement that the licensor provide any warranties at all. The implied warranties (and any express warranties) may be expressly disclaimed by the licensor.

Training
A comprehensive, well-thought out training plan may be important, particularly with large, complex integrated systems. Key issues to address are:

- How much will the training cost? (What is included in the license fee?)
- How many employees can be trained?

- What is the course curriculum? (Importance of reviewing the training course)
- How many instructors?
- Where will training occur?
- When will training occur?
- Who will pay for travel and provide training facilities?

Maintenance and Support

Response and repair times should be specifically stated as well as all the licensor's support and maintenance obligations, such as providing bug corrections, modifications, and enhancements.

Confidentiality

If the user will be providing the software licensor with any of its trade secrets, such as business procedures, customer lists, computer programs, and the like, the license should include nondisclosure provisions.

Assignment

The supplier's license agreement will undoubtedly have a restriction on the licensee's right to assign (transfer) the license to a third party. If there is a possibility that the user will outsource the operation of its data processing function, the user should carve out an exception to the restriction against assignment. The following is an example clause:

> Upon advance written notice to Licensor, Licensee may assign this Agreement, at no charge, to a parent, subsidiary, a company acquiring the interests of Licensee, or a successor in interest carrying on the business of Licensee. In addition, Licensee shall have the right, at no charge, to assign this Agreement to a third party who assumes the responsibility of Licensee's data processing function.

The Source Code Escrow Agreement

If a software supplier goes out of business or simply stops maintaining the software, this will cause great harm to the licensee. In the case of a computer system, the user's system may be rendered virtually useless. The user may be forced to obtain a replacement source, the cost of which could be substantial.

The source code is the code used by the software developer to create the software. It is typically in a different computer language than the object code (the language the licensee uses to "read," install, and use the software) and is considered to be valuable proprietary information belonging to the licensor. Without the source code, the licensee cannot perform regular maintenance on the system.

On the one hand, the source code (relating to software) will be a trade secret of the software supplier, and the supplier will be reluctant to provide it to third parties. However, the user will want to make sure that the software will be maintained no matter what happens to the vendor.

One approach to resolving the interests of both licensee and licensor is to establish an escrow account into which the source code is deposited. As the name implies, this involves having the software owner deposit a copy of the source code (and appropriate documentation) into "escrow." This device is used, for example, in purchases of real estate, where the buyer does not want to pay until he or she gets the title and the seller does not want to transfer title until he or she gets paid.

Problems with Escrow Agreements

Bankruptcy   Under the federal bankruptcy laws (which take precedence over state laws and private contracts), the bankruptcy trustee has no obligation to turn over the escrow data to the buyer unless such a clause is specifically included in the escrow agreement. Therefore, a clause similar to the one found in paragraph 11 of Exhibit 34–2 should be included in the escrow agreement:

Defining Events of Default   Events that trigger the licensee's access to the source code are usually termed "events of default." In order to avoid disputes that will delay distribution, these events must be listed very specifically. They may include:

◆ Filing of bankruptcy by licensor
◆ Licensor going out of business
◆ Failure of the licensor to maintain the software
◆ Discontinuance by licensor of production of software
◆ Failure of licensor to maintain the software in a timely manner
◆ Consistent quality problems

Source Code Must Be Current   If the source code is not current, it will likely be useless. Therefore, it is critical that the source code in escrow be periodically reviewed to ensure currency. The simplest approach in the contract is to put a provision in the escrow agreement requiring that the licensor maintain the information in escrow as current. However, this could be the least effective method if the licensor does not comply. It will be important, therefore, that the agreement provide that the licensee be able to monitor compliance. Another approach is to require that the escrow agent (or independent third party) monitor the source code to ensure that it reflects the current state of the software.

Delays   If the licensee claims an event of default and the licensor says there is not, the escrow agent will be subjected to various demands. So that this potential can be addressed, escrow agreements are typically drafted to allow for arbitration to resolve disputes. While arbitration is generally less costly and speedier than a court case, the process may still be time-consuming.

One approach to speed up the process is to require an expedited arbitration where both parties agree that the arbitration will take place in a certain way and within certain time frames. In addition, the parties can agree that the escrow agent also act as the arbitrator.

For example language requiring the licensor to establish an escrow account and defining the events of default, see Exhibit 34–2.

E X H I B I T   34-2

SOFTWARE SOURCE CODE ESCROW AGREEMENT

This Agreement is entered into and effective as of the _____ day of [Insert Month, Year] by and between [Insert Your Company's Name] having its principal place of business at [Insert Your Company's Address] (the "Licensee") and [Insert Supplier's Name] having its principal place of business at [Insert Supplier's Address] (the "Licensor") and [Insert Escrow Agent's Name] having its principal place of business at [Insert Escrow Agent's Address] (the "Escrow Agent").

Background:

Licensor has granted a license to Licensee to use certain computer software pursuant to the terms and conditions of a Computer Software License Agreement (the "License Agreement") attached hereto as Exhibit A; and

The uninterrupted availability of all forms of such computer software is critical to Licensee in the conduct of its business; and

Licensor has agreed to deposit in escrow a copy of the source code form of the computer program (the "Software") included in the Software System covered by the License Agreement, as well as any corrections and enhancements to such source code, to be held by Escrow Agent in accordance with the terms and conditions of this Escrow Agreement.

The parties agree as follows:

1. DEPOSIT

Licensor has concurrently deposited with Escrow Agent a copy of the source code form of the Software (the "Source Code"), including all relevant commentary, explanations, and other documentation of the Source Code (collectively "Commentary"). Licensor also agrees to deposit with Escrow Agent, at such times as they are made, but not less than two (2) times per year, a copy of all revisions to the Source Code or Commentary encompassing all corrections or enhancements made to the Software by Licensor pursuant to the License Agreement or any Software maintenance contract between the parties. Promptly after any such revision is deposited with Escrow Agent, both Licensor and Escrow Agent shall give written notice thereof to Licensee.

E X H I B I T   34—2 Continued

2. TERM

This Escrow Agreement shall remain in effect during the term of the License Agreement and any Software maintenance contract between Licensee and Licensor. Termination hereof is automatic upon delivery of the deposited Source Code and Commentary to Licensee in accordance with the provisions hereof.

3. DEFAULT

A default by Licensor shall be deemed to have occurred under this Escrow Agreement upon the occurrence of any of the following:

(a) if Licensor has availed itself of, or been subjected to by any third party, a proceeding in bankruptcy in which Licensor is the named debtor, an assignment by Licensor for the benefit of its creditors, the appointment of a receiver for Licensor, or any other proceeding involving insolvency or the protection of, or from creditors, and same has not been discharged or terminated without any prejudice to Licensee's rights or interests under the License Agreement within thirty (30) days; or

(b) if Licensor has ceased its ongoing business operations, or sale, licensing, maintenance, or other support of the Software; or

(c) if Licensor fails to pay the annual fee due to Escrow Agent hereunder; or

(d) if Licensor fails to or is unable to maintain the Software as required by the License Agreement; or

(e) _____(__) months after Licensor notifies Licensee in writing of its intent to discontinue the marketing, manufacturing, or support of the Software. Licensor agrees to provide Licensee with not less than twelve (12) months written notice of its intent of any such discontinuance.

(f) the sale of all or a substantial portion of Licensor's business to a third party who is in the business of selling any of the same or similar products as Licensee ("Competitor"); or if Licensor enters into a cooperative arrangement with a Competitor which is the functional equivalent of such an acquisition or merger or consolidation; or

(g) if any other event or circumstance occurs which demonstrates with reasonable certainty the inability or unwillingness of Licensor to fulfill its obligations to Licensee under the License Agreement, this Escrow Agreement, or any Software maintenance contract between the parties, including, without limitation, the correction of defects in the Software.

E X H I B I T 34–2 Continued

4. NOTICE OF DEFAULT

Licensee shall give written notice to Escrow Agent and Licensor of the occurrence of a default hereunder, except that Escrow Agent shall give notice of the default to Licensee and Licensor if same is based on the failure of Licensor to pay Escrow Agent's annual fee. Unless within seven (7) days thereafter Licensor files with the Escrow Agent its affidavit executed by a responsible executive officer stating that no such default has occurred or that the default has been cured, then the Escrow Agent shall upon the eighth (8th) day deliver to Licensee in accordance with Licensee's instructions the entire Source Code and Commentary with respect to the Software then being held by Escrow Agent.

5. GRANT OF LICENSE

In the event of a default, Licensor grants Licensee a nonexclusive, nontransferable, royalty-free license within the United States to use, reproduce, modify, maintain, or have maintained the Source Code for the sole purpose of maintaining the Software; provided, however, that during the term of this Agreement and thereafter, if an event of default does not occur, Licensee shall not be entitled to such license.

6. TECHNICAL ASSISTANCE

Licensor shall provide Licensee with such technical support and assistance at the rates set forth in Exhibit _____ as Licensee may require in connection with the support of the Software.

7. COMPENSATION

As compensation for the services to be performed by Escrow Agent hereunder, Licensor shall pay to Escrow Agent an initial fee of [Insert Dollar Amount], payable at the time of execution of this Agreement, and an annual fee in the amount of [Insert Dollar Amount], to be paid to Escrow Agent in advance on each anniversary date hereafter during the term of this Agreement.

8. LIABILITY

Escrow Agent shall not, by reason of its execution of this Agreement, assume any responsibility or liability for any transaction between Licensor and Licensee, other than the performance of its obligations, as Escrow Agent, with respect to the Source Code and Commentary held by it in accordance with this Agreement.

E X H I B I T   34–2 Continued

9. TESTS

Upon written notice to Licensor and Escrow Agent, Licensee shall have the right to conduct tests of the Source Code held in escrow, under the supervision of Licensor, to confirm that it is the current Source Code for the Software running on the Hardware specified in the License Agreement.

10. CONFIDENTIALITY

Except as provided in this Agreement, Escrow Agent agrees that it shall not divulge or disclose or otherwise make available to any third person whatsoever, or make any use whatsoever, of the Source Code or Commentary, without the express prior written consent of Licensor.

11. NO TERMINATION UPON BANKRUPTCY

The parties acknowledge that this Source Code Escrow Agreement is an "agreement supplementary to" this Development and License Agreement as provided in Section 365(n) of Title 11, United States Bankruptcy Code (the "Code"). In any bankruptcy action by Licensor, failure by Licensee to assert its rights to retain its benefits to the intellectual property encompassed by the Software pursuant to Section 365(n) of the Code, under an executory contract rejected by the trustee in bankruptcy, shall not be construed by the courts as a termination of the contract by Licensee under Section 365(n) of the Code.

12. NOTICES

All notices or other communications required or contemplated herein shall be in writing, sent certified mail, return receipt requested, addressed to another party at the address indicated below or as same may be changed from time to time by notice similarly given:

If to Licensor:

If to Licensee:

If to Escrow Agent:

13. ASSIGNMENT

Neither this Escrow Agreement, nor any rights, liabilities, or obligations hereunder, may be assigned by Escrow Agent without the prior written consent of Licensee and Licensor.

E X H I B I T 34–2 Continued

IN WITNESS WHEREOF, the parties have executed this Escrow Agreement as of the date first set forth above.

Licensee	Licensor
By: _____	By: _____
Title: _____	Title: _____
Date: _____	Date: _____

Escrow Agent

By: _____
Title: _____
Date: _____

KEY TERMINOLOGY

ACCEPTANCE: The customer's written notification to the supplier that the product meets the acceptance criteria agreed to by the parties. This is a key contract clause in a development and IP contract.

ASSIGNMENT: The transfer or sale of property or of rights granted by a contract. In general, rights granted by contract may be assigned, unless the contract expressly prohibits assignment.

COPYRIGHT: The exclusive right granted to "authors" under the U.S. Copyright Act to copy, adapt, distribute, publicly perform, and publicly display their works of authorship, such as literary works, databases, musical works, sound recordings, photographs, and other still images, and motion pictures and other audiovisual works.

DAMAGES: The compensation owed to the nonbreaching party to recover any financial loss or injury caused by a breach of contract. Compensation designed to make an injured party to a contract "whole."

DAMAGES (CONSEQUENTIAL): Damages that arise from the occurrence of special circumstances not ordinarily predictable. Those losses that are a result of a breach but are not direct and immediate. Examples of consequential damages are lost sales or profits, loss of interest, damages to property, and personal injury damages.

DAMAGES (LIQUIDATED): The sum that a party to a contract agrees to pay if he or she breaks some promise. Liquidated damages clauses specify the dollar amount due upon breach of the contract and are the only damages to which the injured party is entitled.

DEFAULT (BREACH): The omission or failure to perform a legal or contractual obligation.

DEFENDANT: The individual or business entity being sued in a lawsuit.

DISCLAIMER: The disavowal of a right given to a person. A contract clause used to limit the seller/licensor's liability to the buyer/licensor for breach of a warranty.

ESCROW: Agreement between a buyer/licensee, seller/licensor, and escrow agent that sets forth the rights and responsibilities of each party. Property is delivered to the escrow agent to be held by the agent until the happening of a contingency or performance of an event, and then by the agent delivered to the buyer/licensee.

ESCROW AGENT: An escrow company specializing in Software Source Code escrow, a commercial bank, insured by the Federal Deposit Insurance Corporation in the business of providing escrow services, or another entity providing escrow services.

INDEMNITY: Reimbursement. An undertaking by one party to reimburse a second party upon the occurrence of a predefined loss. An insurance policy is a classic example of an indemnification agreement. The indemnity clause typically found in a license agreement obligates the copyright owner to indemnify the licensee for any loss incurred by the licensee as a result of a lawsuit filed by a third party against the licensee over ownership of the software.

INFRINGEMENT: A violation of the rights of a copyright, patent, trade secret, and/or trademark owner; an unauthorized use. When someone copies software without permission of the copyright owner, or uses a trademark without the permission of the trademark owner, he or she has committed an act of infringement.

INJUNCTION: A court order directing a party to a lawsuit to do or refrain from doing something.

LICENSE: Permission to do some particular act, or exercise a certain privilege without possessing any ownership interest.

LICENSEE: The party who acquires the right from the owner (the licensor) of the software or content to possess and use the software or content, subject to the terms imposed in a license agreement. A licensee obtains no ownership rights in the copy of the software—or other content—that he or she receives.

LICENSOR: The party who grants to another (the licensee) certain limited rights to possess and use software or other content.

MISAPPROPRIATION: The theft or improper use or disclosure of the trade secrets of one party to another.

NONDISCLOSURE/CONFIDENTIALITY AGREEMENT: An agreement that secret information disclosed by its owner will be kept confidential and not disclosed to anyone else.

PATENT: A grant of exclusive rights issued by the U.S. Patent Office that gives an inventor a 20-year monopoly on the right to "practice" or make, use, or sell his or her invention.

PLAINTIFF: The person who brings suit against someone, the defendant, whom the plaintiff believes is responsible for doing him or her harm.

REMEDY: Relief (or rights) given to the nonbreaching party by law or by contract.

TERMINATION FOR CONVENIENCE: A contract clause that permits one or both parties the right to terminate the contract before the scheduled expiration date without giving any reason. *Note:* General contract law and the Uniform Commercial Code DO NOT automatically give either party this right.

TRADEMARK: Any word, name, symbol, or device or any combination adopted and used by a manufacturer or merchant to identify his or her goods and distinguish them from those manufactured or sold by others.

TRADE SECRET: Any secret formula, pattern, device, or compilation of information that is used in one's business and that gives an advantage over competitors who do not know or use it.

TRIAL USE AGREEMENT: An agreement whereby the Licensee has the opportunity to evaluate the product prior to entering into a definitive purchase or license agreement.

UNIFORM COMMERCIAL CODE (or UCC): A body of law governing the sale of goods, banking transactions, and security interests, among other things; it has been adopted (with minor variations) in all states in its entirety except Louisiana. All sales of goods, such as the sale of computer hardware, are governed by the Uniform Commercial Code.

WARRANTY: A promise made by the licensor that the article sold has certain qualities; a statement of fact regarding the quality, fitness, or character of goods sold made by the licensor and relied on by the buyer. A specification written onto a purchase order or other contract document is an example of a warranty.

WORK MADE FOR HIRE: A copyrightable work of authorship that is either (1) a work prepared by an employee within the scope of his or her employment or (2) a work specially ordered for use as a contribution to a collective work, as part of a motion picture or other audiovisual work, as a translation, as a supplementary work, as a compilation, as an instructional text, as a test, as answers for a test, or as an atlas, if the parties agree in a written document that the work shall be considered a work made for hire.

CHAPTER 35

Capital and Its Impact on the Organization

Editor
Bruce J. Wright
President
B. Wright & Associates and Total Systems, Inc.

WHAT IS CAPITAL?

There are many definitions of capital and the use of capital in an organization. The idea of capital is discussed and debated by many people and organizations. There is a basic premise that capital only goes where it is invited and remains only if made to feel welcome. This is very true when considering the purchase of capital assets.

Capital is another word for money or value, and *expenditure* denotes the trade of money or value for something else of value. This in a direct sense is the definition of a capital expenditure. This is probably why there is such a broad application of the term in organizations. Accounting has attempted to apply their own definition by making capital expenditure synonymous with depreciable asset. In today's world of management accounting, this is not a true definition of the term. Capital expenditure is more aligned with the term *fixed asset* in today's world. A fixed asset is any asset that lasts more than a year, with an impact on shareholder value, and is considered by management worth controlling. This is much broader than the current accounting definition. That definition is determined by each organization relative to time and value related to materiality. Relative to time, the government has issued ADRs (asset depreciation ranges) for all types of equipment that might be used in an organization. These ADRs, however, start at three years. This means that if an asset (that might be very costly) has a life of less than three years, the organization has the option of expensing the asset rather than depreciating it. On the value side, companies are allowed to set what they feel is material in accounting for depreciation related to an asset. In some companies this is as low as $500, while in others it may be as high as $5,000 and in some rare instances even more if agreement of auditors and taxing authorities is obtained. Most companies are currently at a level around $1,000. This assessment of materiality affects the accounting process, but it doesn't necessarily reflect the desires of management. Normally management will want to keep track of any asset that is significant to the outcome of the organization mission and is not included in an inventory process.

Some other business definitions of capital assets are:

+ Renovation of worn or obsolete production, distribution, or service facilities or the replacement of these facilities

+ New production, distribution, or service facilities or expansions of a product or product line

+ Research and development, improved working conditions, or investments that might be required by the government through regulations to improve the health and welfare of workers or the community

+ Any material expenditure of money that extends the economic life of current assets

The definition of a capital expenditure really comes down to the organization and the way it looks at the use of funds. There are several very general accounting definitions, but within reasonable bounds the decision is left to the individual organization. It is important in purchasing that we determine the policies of management related to capital spending and then model the organization of the purchasing group after this.

When purchasing a capital asset, purchasers should be ready to make sure that the money they are spending will return value to the organization they are involved with and also to the shareholders of the organization. The placing of value in the organization is a partnership between the purchaser and the user of the asset. The user must provide a means of use for the asset that will return to the organization through revenue generation, cost saving, or cost avoidance that will exceed the cost of the capital that purchasing must use in obtaining the asset. The only exception to this is assets that must be purchased because of laws or regulations or are part of a strategic mission.

IMPACT OF CAPITAL ASSETS ON THE ORGANIZATION

Capital assets are the tools by which an organization works and creates value. The improper decisions in a capital process can be very detrimental to the organization. In today's world, there is a movement to use the value of the capital assets purchased as a measure of management performance. In the use of value-added evaluation, a capital charge is taken before the benefit to the shareholder is calculated, and management is limited in bonuses until the cost of capital taken on the capital base is achieved.

In all organizations, the application of capital assets is important to the success of the organization. As more and more organizations become automated and computers become more and more a focus of the organization, the application of the relationship of capital assets to the success of the company in all types of organizations becomes more important. Organizations must exercise care in selecting their capital asset base to avoid damaging the ability to compete and support the organization's mission and the flexibility required in servicing customers and markets.

CAPITAL EXPENDITURE ENVIRONMENT

Successful capital expenditures depend upon four conditions:

1. *Timing:* Usually the saying "Strike while the iron is hot" applies. Timing of capital expenditures can mean the difference between success and failure.
2. *Direction:* Proper direction of a capital expenditure is imperative if budgets and deadlines are to be met. Capital buys must reflect the strategic planning of the organization.
3. *Support:* This means both top management and supervisory support. Without proper support, failure is assured.
4. *Coordination:* Coordination of capital expenditures is required to make sure full use is given to resources available and employed by the organization.

Purchasing should be involved from the strategic planning process of a capital buy. This is often not the case, but where it is, there is normally a much better result achieved in the buy process. There is a balance that must be struck in a capital buy; this is the balance between the technical side of the buy and the business side of the buy. If the technical side of the buy is completed before the business side is undertaken, we are often left in a position where the asset fits the situation technically but we miss the opportunities of negotiation of price, delivery, warranty, service, and many of the other values of the business side of the buy where purchasing is focused. On the other hand, if the business side is undertaken before the technical side is ready, we can get a piece of equipment that fits the values of purchasing but does not fit the form and function required for success in the strategic position of the organization. There must be a balance in the business and technical side of the buy, with the business side leading. This leadership is normally seen in the negotiation of terms and conditions and the initial sourcing of the supplier at the point of planning for the buy. The terms and conditions of the buy should not be on the back of the purchase order, where they are often found in organizations. They should be separated and placed up front in the buy. The terms and conditions are the standard terms and conditions that define the playing field for both the supplier and the purchaser and should be handled when the sourcing process is first initiated. This is when the purchaser is in the best negotiating position, when the supplier is not yet in a position of being a supplier for the organization. It is best to initiate contact with suppliers by negotiating terms and conditions and getting them out of the way so that an alliance is formed and the rest of the purchase can take place without problems in how the two parties will conduct their business.

CAPITAL CONTROL

The control of capital depends on the development and use of reliable methods of assessing the impact of projects on the profits of the company. There must be adequate coordination of the direction of the company to ensure continuity of the company's capital spending program. Misdirected capital spending increases operating costs and ties up needed funds, which many times reduces profits and creates unneeded excess capacity. Failure to make good capital decisions at the right time can increase product cost and jeopardize a company's competitive position.

Capital invested in the right place at the right time will increase a company's strength and competitive position and provide the basis for effective strategic planning.

THE ENTERPRISE RESOURCE PLANNING MODEL

The planning part of an organization normally includes five planning thrusts: strategic plan, capital forecast, revenue forecast, cash forecast, and operating forecast. These must be coordinated and related to the operating process so that they will translate into actions that move the organization forward. These plans should be dynamic rather than static. In the past, companies have set their plans once a year and then set about to execute those plans. In this type of environment, many times the plans are set and then put away until the results are in, when they are brought out and it is just coincidence if they are achieved or exceeded. It seems in many organizations that every year starts with an exercise called "SURPRISE." Everyone is surprised if the revenue forecast coordinates with the capital forecast and the operating forecast supports the strategic plan. To be really effective, the planning cycle must be a dynamic process that continues through time and is not limited to the artificial constraints of an accounting year or period.

The enterprise resource planning model is a model (see Figure 35–1) of information flow and coordination in an organization. This process is divided into three areas: planning, actual, and historical. This process allows us to make sure that everything we do within the organization is connected and has purpose and that the various elements of the process do not just hang out as islands or territories in the organization.

CAPITAL PROCUREMENT, EVALUATION, AND CONTROL TOOLS

The capital procurement process (see Figure 35–2) deals with the right-hand side of the enterprise resource planning model.

The ability to achieve success and fulfill the conditions of capital procurement, evaluation, and control depends on the use of the proper tools related to the process. These tools are as follows.

Strategic Plan

There are generally two methods used when senior management performs their strategic planning responsibilities: intuitive–anticipatory

F I G U R E   35-1

The Enterprise Resource Planning Model

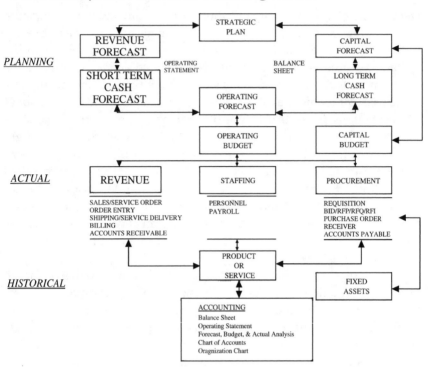

planning and formal systematic planning. Both are important and must not be underestimated. In many corporations, there are conflicts between these two approaches because different thought processes are involved in completing them. However, formal planning cannot be done without management intuition. Correctly tailoring the accounting and information systems to support the managerial characteristics of looking ahead and anticipating the future will help managers improve their intuition. The strategic plan must be an analysis of the opportunities and challenges presented by the internal and external environment of the business. The strategic plan is the process of setting goals and then analyzing the various processes that will allow the organization to accomplish those goals. The interaction and information that supports the strategies of the organization come from the capital forecast and the revenue forecast. These two forecasts give management the insight into where revenue will be generated and where capital must be invested to make the

F I G U R E   35–2

The Capital Procurement Process

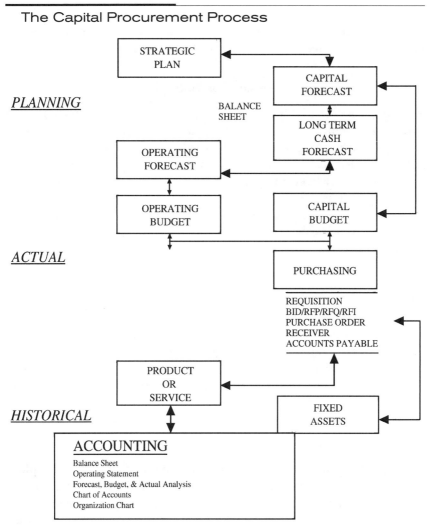

organization capable of taking advantage of the opportunities of the industry. The strategic plan provides the framework for the formulation of a good capital, revenue, and operating forecast. The strategic plan takes into consideration as many long-range external and internal factors as possible, and it reflects the thinking and desire of senior management as to the position of the company in the future. The planning horizon for the strategic plan should be such that decisions are made with as much flexibility as possible. This horizon is usually based on the capital intensity of the firm, the firm's ability to maneuver, and the points listed above. The greater a firm's ability to maneuver or the more volatile the industry, the shorter the strategic planning process.

Capital Forecasting

The capital forecast is the second step in the capital procurement cycle and one of the most important tools in controlling capital and optimizing the expenditure of capital funds. This is because the wise use of capital is the basis for accomplishing the strategic plan. It is also the basis for determining how large an operating force will be needed to support the effort required to achieve the goals and objectives of the strategic plan as a result of capital projects and the ongoing requirements of the organization. It gives an indication of the firm's potential production and therefore sales. Several other areas are served by a formal capital forecast. Some of these follow.

Forecasting Cash Requirements

Capital forecasts assist in forecasting the timing and amount of cash required and thus enable corporate management to plan for additional financing if required. Plans can also be made to defer or abandon certain projects if insufficient funds are available or if the costs would exceed the amount that management is willing to invest in capital expansion. Such revisions can be made before operating units go to the trouble and expense of compiling the details of their operating forecast.

Determine Operating Targets

The capital forecast is most useful in apprising management of the plans of their operating personnel for cost reduction, product/service improvement, additional capacity, or new products or services. The necessity of preparing a forecast of capital requirements forces managers to make more realistic appraisals of their overall goals and objectives. Procurement should be involved here in determining the industry position on general availability, suppliers, lead times, and sourcing possibilities.

Elimination of Duplication

A formal capital forecast helps to avoid such duplication as similar capital projects being undertaken by two operations. It also lessens the possibility that an operation may be permitted to purchase a capital asset that is available elsewhere within the company.

Project Priorities

A capital forecast is essential in selecting and assigning priorities to projects, the sum total of which usually far exceeds the funds available.

Most companies require that proposed projects be rated as to their degree of urgency or desirability. They will generally fall into three broad categories:

1. *Must projects:* Projects that affect the continued operation of the company; management usually has no choice about whether they will be done or not. Often they are needed to satisfy a regulatory requirement or an emergency replacement of existing capacity. In addition, there are special projects, sometimes called *pets* or strategic projects, that in no way reflect a return on investment but are the perks of management. These might include a corporate airplane, corporate yacht, or other projects that are included in the image of the organization rather than the operation.

2. *Want projects:* Projects that provide some type of real improvement and are desirable from their risk reward position. These are projects that show low risk and high return and will be of direct benefit to the bottom line of the company. One hopes the bulk of the projects in an organization will fall into the want category.

3. *Wish projects:* Projects that carry either a high risk or relatively low reward for the company. These are projects that may be out of the company's operational expertise but may show a high reward potential. Normally these projects are undertaken only after the first two categories are exhausted.

Compatibility with Company Objectives

The capital forecast, as part of the enterprise resource planning model, makes it easier to detect projects that are not compatible with the strategic plans of the company. Many times, parts of the strategic plan will remain confidential to the point that operating management will not be fully aware of their impact. A formal forecast enables management to eliminate or defer any projects that are at cross-purposes with the strategic plan.

Operating Forecasts

Operating forecasts are the coordination point of the effect of capital forecasts and revenue forecasts. Generally this process contains the most recognized steps in the planning cycle. An operating forecast is the basis of the operational planning and control system. It provides the plan by which management will attain the company's goals. It is a forecast that will carry the operational figures on a dynamic basis. It will also provide a tool for recording the assumptions related to the forecast and the operating effect of management and capital decisions.

The operating forecast is normally made up of two sets of information: deterministic information and probabilistic information.

Deterministic Information

1. *Strategic Plan:* This is the set of information that provides management with the opportunity to set "par" for the organization in establishing goals and objectives that will be carried out by the organization.

2. *History:* History provides the trends and relationships that will allow us to project a good forecast on a moving basis. The historical information is usually represented by trends and causal relationships. The causal relationships are often called *ratios* by the accounting group.

3. *Industry:* Industry information is used to predict what will happen as a result of influences outside of the organization. Industry information is usually related to the trends of industry and the success of other organizations within the industry. The measure against the success of other organizations is called *benchmarking.*

4. *Geopolitical:* This is a review of the political and regulation environment that the organization finds itself in and the ability to work within the boundaries of this environment both internally and externally.

Probabilistic Information

Management perception comes in two thrusts:

- ◆ Magnitude
- ◆ Confidence

Operating management should be able to review the direction of events and input their perception to this direction in these two areas. In fact, operating management should have the ability and responsibility to communicate the assumptions by which the figures in the forecast could change, and they should provide the relative range of the change, where the information is critical to the outcome of the organization segment. Confidence can only be expressed in terms of probability and ranges. There are two types of ranges in a capital buy: the revenue range and the cost range. Because a capital expenditure is always evaluated on a cash in, cash out basis, these ranges naturally deal with cash in (revenue) and cash out (cost), with purchasing coordinating the cash out in the purchase process and the operating management coordinating the revenue generation or the cost savings.

Operating forecasts provide the final step in forecasting the timing and amount of cash required. The operating forecast, along with the revenue budget, staffing budget, purchasing budget, and the capital budget, coordinated with the operating flows of information, provide the tools necessary to keep close control on cash requirements and capital expenditures. At this point the request for capital should be completed and evaluated. For this process to be completed, the outflows of cash must be brought together with the inflows of cash and the resulting effect on the organization evaluated.

Appropriation Request

The appropriation request is used by the project sponsor and purchasing to submit the capital request in detail and transfer the project from forecast to budget. Funds are committed to the project only after complete review of the appropriation request. The appropriation request is reviewed at the levels of management required and determined by the dollar limit of approval given to each management level. Large projects would require the approval of the president and board of directors, while small-dollar outlays could be handled by a line manager. Purchasing should be involved with the initial information gathering to determine possible prices, deliveries, and other factors that will affect the ultimate buy. Purchasing should be careful to protect the integrity of the buy related to competitors and others in the industry.

Capital Budget

The capital budget provides management a tool that assists in appraising the relative merits of projects proposed and controlling the funds that are approved for the purchase of the capital equipment and services involved. Once a project is approved to the capital budget, it should be in a position where purchasing can go ahead with final sourcing and negotiation of terms and conditions with potential suppliers.

CAPITAL ACQUISITION REQUIREMENTS

The process involved in establishing a successful capital acquisition process depends on the success of the following processes:

1. *Creative search for investment opportunities:* This is the first step in the capital expenditure program. A company must give ample opportunity to its managers to identify the best capital investment opportunities.

2. *Long-range plans and projections for the company's development:* This is the step called strategic planning. This is the process of upper management that develops a plan for the growth and position of the company, given the company's resources, the market, and the company's financial condition.

3. *Forecast and study of demands for funds:* A good program for the determination of the sources and uses of funds for the company is essential for success in a capital investment program.

4. *Correct yardstick of economic worth:* There are many methods of determining the return on the investment in a capital project, and each has positive and negative points. (ROI alternatives will be discussed below.) Each company must decide what constitutes the correct yardstick and then use it consistently.

5. *Realistic estimation of economic worth of projects:* This includes the subjective (ranking according to management outlook) and objective (ranking according to return on investments tools) determination of a project worth.

6. *Standards for screening investment proposals:* This includes the establishment of some type of "hurdle rate" and levels of approval that are consistent with company size and direction. The hurdle rate and approval levels should be set with

company goals, economic circumstances, and risk taken into consideration.

7. *Expenditure controls by comparison of authorizations and specifications:* This is the control imposed during the outlays of funds to make certain that the expenditures do not get out of control.

8. *Candid and economically realistic post-completion audits:* The audit is probably the most important of the steps in ensuring that the capital program will remain viable over a long period of time.

9. *Investment analysis of candidates for disposal:* This step is to make sure that past investments are still performing according to the needs of the organization.

10. *Forms and procedures:* This step is company-dependent and should be determined after the needs and requirements of the company and management are determined.

CAPITAL ASSET EVALUATION

In the evaluation of an asset, the project sponsor and purchasing must coordinate in establishing the cash flows that will effect the outcome of the purchase. The first premise that must be understood is the corporate purpose or objective. The corporate purpose or objective is to maximize, as far as is possible in the presence of uncertainty and imperfect information, the long-run wealth of the company's owners. This criterion underlies all decisions about optimal asset, financial, and operating structures.

The maximization of shareholder wealth is not the only purpose in business, but it should be one of the dominant ones. The maximization of shareholder wealth should be in relationship to the strategic plan and long-range health and survival of the corporation.

The maximization of business return to shareholders depends on a balance of resources, both capital and operational, with the potential of gaining profit or position in a given marketplace. This is accomplished by maintaining a balance in the strategic planning process between long-range use of capital and current requirements of operating processes. Along with this, close monitoring and analysis of actual results and projection of these results to test forecast thinking is essential in this process.

GENERAL CAPITAL ANALYSIS

When a good capital forecast and budget process are part of the coordinated planning cycle, it is easier to detect projects that are not compatible with the strategic plans of the company. Many times, parts of the strategic plan will remain confidential to the point that operating management will not be fully aware of their impact. A formal forecasting process with an appropriation process enables management to eliminate or defer any projects that are at cross-purposes with the strategic plan.

The general categories of projects are those the organization *must* do, those they *want* to do, and those they desire to do but, for reasons of risk or fit, will undertake only if ample capital exists for the musts and wants.

HURDLE RATE

A hurdle rate is the rate of return on investment in capital that will ensure continuing operations and provide a desired level of return for the shareholder. The starting place in determining the hurdle rate is understanding the present cost of the capital. The cost of capital is the return required by those that provide the capital utilized, in order to keep them happy. Example: A bank requires a certain interest rate before they will lend money. The interest rate required by the bank is the cost of that type of capital.

The second factor in the determination of shareholder return is return on invested capital (sometimes called ROIC). This is determined by looking at the performance of the company related to the capital invested by the shareholders.

COST OF CAPITAL

The cost of capital is the average rate of earnings that investors require to induce them to provide all forms of long-term capital to the company. Operationally this cost is the weighted average cost of the various classes of the long-term capital, i.e., long-term debt, preferred shareholders' equity, and common shareholders' equity.

Components of the Cost of Capital

The following is a breakdown of the components and an example that will illustrate how the cost of capital is calculated:

Long-Term Debt		500,000
Preferred Shareholders' Equity		200,000
Common Shareholders' Equity		
Common Stock	300,000	
Paid in Surplus	100,000	
Retained Earnings	300,000	
Total Common Equity		700,000
Total Capital		1,400,000

Weighted Average Cost Method

This method examines the various components of the capital structure and applies the weighting factor of after-tax cost to determine the weighted cost of capital. The following examples will show the formation of the weighted average cost of capital.

Long-Term Debt

There are two considerations when looking at long-term debt:

1. The present cost of debt
2. The availability of the financing method

Long-term debt includes bonds, mortgages, and long-term secured financing.

Bond Cost

Let's say we can issue bonds with face values of $100 per bond and it is estimated that the bond will generate $96 net proceeds to the company after discounting and financing costs. The normal interest is $14, or approximately $9 after taxes (assuming a 35% tax rate). To obtain the cost, we divide the after-tax interest by the proceeds:

$$\frac{\$9}{\$96} = 9.375\%, \text{ which is the after-tax cost of bond financing}$$

Mortgage and Long-Term Financing Costs

Our banker has informed us that our long-term rate is two points over prime. Prime is currently 10%, which puts our lending rate at 12%. With a 35% tax rate it comes to a 7.8% cost. Our banker has informed us that our mortgage rates are presently 11%, which would give us an after-tax cost on mortgage money of 7.15%.

Weighting the Cost of Long-Term Debt To weight the cost of long-term debt, we take the average of the costs of long-term debt, which would give us

$$\frac{7.8\% + 7.15\%}{2} = 7.48\%$$

and multiply the long-term debt ($500,000) by that factor, which will give us a weighted average cost of $37,400.

Preferred Stock Costs

We must take the present market value or an estimate of that value less discounts or finance costs and divide dividends or cash flow per share by this value. Example: Preferred $100 per share less $2 finance costs or $98.00 proceeds. Cash flow or dividends on preferred are $11 per share.

$$\frac{\$11}{\$98} = 11.2\% \text{ after-tax cost of preferred}$$

Weighting the Cost of Preferred Stock To weight preferred stock, we multiply the after-tax cost of 11.2% by the preferred stock (200,000) which gives us $22,400 weighted average.

Common Equity Costs

Common equity has three components: common stock, paid-in surplus, and retained earnings. From the stockholder's viewpoint, all three are costs. If retained earnings are used in the business, the stockholders cannot use them elsewhere to earn money, and therefore they carry an opportunity cost.

Common Equity Valuation

Stockholders invest because they expect to receive benefits equivalent to what they would receive on the next-best investment when risk is considered. Stockholders look forward to two benefits from common stock:

1. Current operating performance
2. Capital appreciation from growth

The valuation of common equity must take into consideration both the present and future earnings of the stock.

Weighting the Cost of Common Equity   We consider the present market price of the stock less issuing costs—e.g., $100/share less issuing costs of $15 or proceeds of $85 per share. This is divided into the future earnings per share estimated by investors or reliable analysts. If we use $12 per share, then the weighted cost will look like this:

$$\frac{\$12}{\$85} = 14.1\% \text{ after-tax cost of common stock}$$

Using the 14.1% and the total common equity of 700,000 we have $98,700 weighted average.

Total Weighted Average Cost of Capital

A summary of the three components gives us the weighted average cost of capital. The formula for figuring this is as follows:

Long-term debt	500,000 × 11.2% =	37,400
Preferred stock	200,000 × 11.2% =	22,400
Common equity	700,000 × 14.1% =	98,700
TOTAL CAPITAL	1,400,000	158,500

$$\text{Weighted average cost of capital } \frac{\$158,500}{\$1,400,000} = 11.3\%$$

Use of the Cost of Capital

The 11.3% weighted cost of capital serves as one input into the formulation of the hurdle rate or the basis of evaluation of the capital expenditure. We know that we should not accept any situation that earns less than 11.3% after tax. This figure actually forms a *minimum* goal for management to exceed in performance of the organization to provide a return to the shareholder related to the shareholder expectations and the expectations of the other holders of capital. This completes one of the factors in establishing our hurdle rate.

The other factor that we would not be willing to violate for a long period of time would be return on invested capital (ROIC). Every organization has investors that have put money into the organization either through loans or through an equity position, and each of these individuals or organizations wishes a return on their invested capital. This is a ratio that is fairly easy to obtain, and it gives the investor or any other interested party a good gauge, over time, of the health of the organization.

The formula for ROIC is a ratio represented as follows:

$$\text{ROIC} = \frac{\text{Operating Income before Interest and Taxes}}{\text{Total Liabilities} + \text{Equity} - \text{Current Liabilities} - \text{Accruals} - \text{Reserves}}$$

This ratio should normally be higher in a service organization than in a manufacturing firm because of the difference in the level of the asset base required in manufacturing versus service and the higher risk level in the service industry brought on by easier entry from the outside.

Letting this ratio trend lower will jeopardize an organization's ability to return value to investors through the use of the capital invested.

In addition to the bases provided by the cost of capital and/or the return on invested capital, other factors must be taken into account before we finally come to a hurdle rate for the evaluation of capital equipment. The following is a list of these factors.

1. *Zero return projects:* Some projects must be undertaken for other reasons than the maximization of shareholder value. These fall in the areas of complying with government regulations, civic responsibilities, work responsibilities, and work quality improvement. Another area that might be considered a must is management pets. The first type of project might include smokestack scrubbers, pollution control devices, or other non-revenue-producing projects. The second type of project might include a corporate aircraft or yacht. Our hurdle rate must be high enough to compensate for this type of project. An evaluation of the percentage of our total capital outlay that will go to this type of project will help determine the effect of zero return projects on the overall requirement for capital and the effect on the return on invested capital.

2. *Replacement projects:* Many times we will be faced with replacing worn out equipment just to maintain our market position. These projects will usually show a fair return on investment, but often this return is below our current cost of capital or return on invested capital. Because of this, other projects must make enough return to make the overall rate of return either equal to or above the cost of capital and the return on invested capital.

3. *Overhead:* Because the evaluation of a capital expenditure is based on incremental cash flow based on the project itself, there is normally no consideration in the project itself for overhead. This is added to the hurdle rate to make sure the return covers the portion of overhead that should be supported by this project.

4. *Relative risk:* Another factor in our hurdle rate is the risk factors of the projects we expect to undertake. As the risk increases, it is natural that we would expect to receive a greater return for that risk. Most companies will set a minimum hurdle rate for prime projects and then increase that rate according to the risk of that project relative to prime projects.

Hurdle Rate

After evaluation of the above factors, we can settle on a hurdle rate or series of hurdle rates, depending on our approach. Generally most companies find the addition to cost of capital or ROIC to get to the hurdle rate to be about 4 to 6 points for must projects and another 4 to 6 points for estimating errors and management reach. Another approach is to take 1.5 times the cost of capital and add it to the cost of capital to make sure the project makes the grade. This is by no means a scientific standard, and each company should come to its own determination of what their hurdle rate should be to achieve the desired stability and long-term health in the organization.

FINANCIAL RETURN ANALYSIS

Methods for evaluating capital expenditures vary from rough rule of thumb or visual inspection techniques to sophisticated discounted cash flow methods. It is very important that we recognize the advantages and limitations of each of the various techniques in common use today.

It should be remembered that mathematical analysis of capital expenditures is only a guide to investment decision, not the decision itself. Also, the precise nature of the results of quantitative analysis can obscure errors made in the formulation of the original problem. Care must be taken to apply the procedures consistently to all projects. Further, it is extremely important that all cash flows relevant to a project be identified and entered into the computations, even if this involves making several estimates. Normally, in a return analysis, the purchasing group and the operating group should work together in establishing the cash flows. Purchasing should determine the cost of the business side of the capital expenditure, and the project sponsor should determine the operating costs and savings and the resultant excess cash flows.

Management should be aware of the assumptions implicit in the calculation method being employed, including limitations as well as advantages of those methods. It is understood that with "must projects" purchasing will try to make the best business decisions related to obtaining the asset and accomplishing the requirement of the asset usage. There is no use in evaluating the must projects by the hurdle rate, because it is known that they will not accomplish a return on the investment required. The goal is to keep the cash requirements to a minimum and still accomplish the requirements of the project.

All other projects are normally evaluated using a combination of the following five methods, which gives management input to the decision process related to the asset.

The examples used in this section are all based on a simple project with a life of three years plus the investment year with the following flows. This is Project E in the capital evaluation calculation example at the end of the section.

Year	Outflows	Inflows
Investment Year	(1,000)	0
Year 1	(800)	1,200
Year 2	0	400
Year 3	0	900

Nondiscounting Investment Evaluation Techniques

There are two basic nondiscounting methods used in evaluating capital expenditures: accountant's rate of return and payback. These techniques use cash flow data without any direct attempt to adjust for the time value of money.

Advantages:

1. Simple to calculate
2. Based on easily understood ideas and produce "apparently" useful answers

3. Can be used as coarse screening devices to pick out high-profit projects that are so clearly desirable that they require no refined return estimates and to reject quickly those projects that show such poor promise that they do not merit thorough analysis

Disadvantages:

1. No consideration for the timing of cash inflows and outflows
2. No consideration for the timing of tax savings based on the decision to expense part of an investment outlay or from writing off capitalized costs over the life of the project
3. No consideration for the cost of capital

The Accountant's Rate of Return

The accountant's rate of return may be defined as the percentage yield that the income anticipated from a project will earn on the investment. Some of the variety of possible ways to calculate this measure are:

1. (Total profit)/(Average investment)
2. (Average annual profit)/(Total investment)
3. (Average annual profit)/(Average investment)

A definition of the factors used:

Total profit = Total net inflows − Total net outflows

Average annual profit = Total profit/Number of years in project life

Average investment = Nondepreciable portion
$$+ \ (1 - \text{tax rate})(\text{depreciable portion})$$

An example of accountant's rate of return using the example above would be:

Total profit (inflows − outflows) = $2,500 − $1,800 = $700

$$\text{Average annual profit} = \frac{\$700}{3} = \$233$$

Average investment = 0 + (1 − 0.34) ($1,800) = $1,188

The accountant's rate of return in each case would be:

$$\text{Method 1:} \quad \frac{\$700}{\$1,188} = 58.92\%$$

$$\text{Method 2:} \quad \frac{\$233}{\$1,800} = 12.94\%$$

$$\text{Method 3:} \quad \frac{\$233}{\$1,188} = 19.61\%$$

Use of the Accountant's Rate of Return   If there are no constraints, select all projects above an arbitrary rate of return cutoff; if there are budget constraints select projects with the highest rates of return.

Advantages of Accountant's Rate of Return   This method gives a cash on cash return without taking the time value of money into consideration. It may be a more accurate measure for long-term projects that have high returns in later life.

Disadvantages of Accountant's Rate of Return

1. It depends heavily on arbitrary accounting rules and does not distinguish between cash flows and accounting allocations.
2. The use of averages in the calculation of cash flows compounds the problems of timing individual cash flows.
3. The three techniques listed to calculate the return can produce different rates of return for any one proposal, leading to uncertainty as to which method is best.
4. It ignores the time value of money and uneven flows of money.

Payback

Payback is the year (or fraction of year) at which the sum of the outflows of cash equals the sum of the inflows of cash, or the year (or fraction) at which the sum of flows equals zero.

Example of payback:

Year	Outflow	Inflow	Net Flow	Cumulative Flow
0	1,000	0	(1,000)	(1,000)
1	0	400	400	(600)
2	0	400	400	(200)
3	0	900	900	700

Explanation: Investment is made in year 0, resultant inflows occur in years 1, 2, and 3. Cumulative flow turns positive in year 3, therefore payback period is between 2 and 3 years. At the end of year 2 cumulative flow is 200 negative. Net flow for year 3 is 900 positive, therefore it takes 200/900, or 2/9, or .22 of year 3 to reach payback. Payback period is thus 2.22 years.

Use of Payback   If no budget constraints, accept all projects with payback period less than some arbitrary cutoff period; if budget constraints exist, select projects with the shortest payback period. Care should be taken in using this decision tool that long-term survival is not compromised by short-term gains.

Advantages of Payback

1. It concentrates on cash flows early in the life of the project. Payback is useful for appraising risky investments because cash flows can be estimated with some certainty in the early life of a project.

2. It is an adequate guide for companies with poor liquidity positions, i.e., with high outside cost of capital and severely limited internal cash-generating ability in comparison to a high volume of profitable investment opportunities.

Disadvantages of Payback

1. It does not consider earnings after the year of payback. This may lead to rejection of highly profitable projects that produce revenue streams later on.

2. Payback measures the liquidity of a capital investment program and not profitability over the project's economic life.

3. It does not provide results that can be measured against current rate of return on investment for the company or the cost of capital.

4. When major outflows occur in more than one period, there is a possibility of confusing results.

Discounting Investment Evaluation Techniques

The three major techniques most widely used for taking into consideration the time value of money are internal rate of return (IRR), excess present value index, and net present value.

Advantages of Discounting Methods

1. The timings of investment and cash flows are weighted so as to reflect the differences in the value of near and distant cash flows.
2. Discounting concentrates on cash flows and does not include arbitrary accounting allocations.
3. Total economic life of the project is considered.
4. Timing of tax savings is reflected.

Disadvantages of Discounting Methods

1. Management is not, in general, as familiar with discounting as with the more commonly used nondiscounting methods.
2. The precise nature of discounting calculations often obscures the difficulty of making annual cash flow estimates and the many assumptions implicit in the calculation method to arrive at such estimates.

Internal Rate of Return (IRR)

This method has many different names, including return on capital employed, discounted cash flow, return on capital, and return on net capital. The definition of IRR is that rate of return that would discount all cash flows of the project to zero (for an example of IRR, see Table 35–1). We compare this rate to our hurdle rate for the class of project to determine the worth of the project to the company, and we also compare this rate

T A B L E   35–1

Example of IRR: (Trial and Error Method) Example

	Cash	Factor	@ 20%	Factor	@ 30%	Factor	@ 27%
Inv. Year	(1,000)	-0-	(1,000)	-0-	(1,000)	-0-	(1,000)
Year 1	400	*0.8333	334	*0.7700	308	*0.7850	314
Year 2	400	*0.6944	278	*0.5925	237	*0.6175	247
Year 3	900	*0.5787	521	*0.4556	410	*0.4878	439
Total	700		132		(45)		0

* Present value factor of $1.

to the cost of capital to make sure that the project will return to the shareholders and others that hold capital interests.

The exact return would be 27.14%, but again, beware the exact because the cash flows are really only guesses. In fact, this would be a good time to look at the ranges of expenditure and the ranges of returns and evaluate the return based on those ranges.

Use of IRR   If there are no constraints, choose projects with rates of return above the hurdle rate. If there are budget constraints, choose projects with the highest rate of return.

Advantages of IRR   It is strictly comparable to the hurdle rate and the cost of capital ratios, so the relationship between indicated rate of return and the value of money to the company is apparent.

Disadvantages of IRR

1. It is assumed that all future cash flows can be invested at a rate identical to the original rate for the project.
2. When periodic net inflow and net outflow are staggered over time, there may be more than one yield rate that satisfies the condition of discounting all flows to zero.
3. There is no direct way of evaluating projects for which only the costs can be stated, e.g., mandatory projects such as smokestack scrubbers.

Excess Present Value Index (EPVI)

This is an index derived from comparing the present value of outflows to that of inflows (see Table 35–2). It is used to rank and compare proposed investment projects. The higher the project index, the more profitable or desirable the project.

Use of EPVI   If there are no constraints, choose projects with an EPVI greater than 1. If there are budget constraints, choose projects with the largest EPVI.

Advantage of EPVI   The EPVI may be used as an index of investment profitability; therefore, place all alternative opportunities on a comparable easy-to-understand basis.

T A B L E   35–2

Example of Excess Present Value Index

Formula:

$$EPVI = \frac{\text{Net Inflows Discounted at Hurdle Rate}}{\text{Net Outflows Discounted at Hurdle Rate}}$$

		Actual	@ 20%	Actual	@ 20%
Inv. Yr				(1,000)	(1,000)
Year 1	0.8333	1,200	1,000	(800)	(668)
Year 2	0.6944	400	278		
Year 3	0.5787	900	521		
Total		2,500	1,799		(1,668)

$$EPVI = \frac{\$1,799}{\$1,668} = 1.08$$

Disadvantages of EPVI

1. There may be problems in defining the expenses associated with the investment.
2. The two types of flow must be discounted separately.

Net Present Value (NPV)

This is the sum of net cash flows, discounted by the hurdle rate (for an example of NPV, see Table 35–3).

T A B L E   35–3

Example of the Net Present Value

	Cash	Factor	@ 20%
Inv. Yr	(1,000)	*0.0000	(1,000)
Year 1	400	*0.8333	333
Year 2	400	*0.6944	278
Year 3	900	*0.5787	521
NPV			132

Use of NPV   If there are no constraints, choose all projects with a positive NPV; if there is a budget constraint, choose projects with the largest NPV.

Advantages of NPV

1. Cash flows are discounted at the hurdle rate or at the minimum acceptable rate of return on capital investment.
2. It involves only one discounting sequence.
3. The method makes a minimum of implicit assumptions.
4. NPV calculates directly the amount of discounted contribution to a firm's profit, which is the logical quantity to be maximized.
5. Risk can be factored in with relative ease by raising or lowering the hurdle rate according to the risk of the project.
6. Investment projects of different types (replacements, new investments, "required investments") can be evaluated using NPV and can be strictly compared.

Disadvantages of NPV   None, other than those listed under general disadvantages for discounting methods.

Steps in a Project Evaluation Program

1. Establish a hurdle rate.
2. Determine the evaluation techniques to be used (you may use more than one).
3. Rank the projects available.
4. Make the decisions that will make the project evaluation meaningful.
5. Complete a capital request for transfer from forecast to capital budget-making process.
6. Set the criteria and timing for post-completion audits and determine audit criteria.

Table 35–4 illustrates the problem with using just one of the evaluation methods. Notice that all five projects have the same investment or cost of acquisition. The variation is in the cash flows after the acquisition of the asset. It can be seen that depending on the adjustment of the cash flows, each of the projects can come up number one. For this

T A B L E   35–4

Example of Capital Evaluation Calculation

	Revenues and (Investment Outlays) Example Information			
	Time Period			
Project	-0-	-1-	-2-	-3-
A	(1,000)	25	50	1,600
B	(1,000)	1,100	100	100
C	(1,000)	1,000	325	50
D	(1,000)	400	400	850
E	(1,000)	$400*	400	900

* $1,200 Inflow–($800) Outflow = $400

	Accountant's Rate of Return (On Average Investment)		Payback Period		Yield Method (DCF) (IRR)		Excess Present Value Index*		Net Present Value*	
Project	Rate	Rank	P.P.	Rank	Yield	Rank	EPVI	Rank	NPV	Rank
A	45.0%	1	2.58	5	19.2%	5	0.98	5	(21)	5
B	20.0%	5	0.91	1	24.5%	4	1.04	4	44	4
C	30.0%	3	1.00	2	28.3%	1	1.09	2	88	3
D	43.0%	2	2.24	4	25.7%	3	1.10	1	103	2
E	26.0%	4	2.22	3	27.1%	2	1.08	3	133	1

*@20% Cost of Capital

and other reasons, we suggest that the organization use at least payback period, IRR, and net present value (NPV).

For the evaluations above to be applied, it is imperative that a good job of revenue and cost evaluation be completed. This is often termed *life cycle value analysis.*

LIFE CYCLE VALUE ANALYSIS

Simply stated, life cycle value analysis estimates the total revenues and costs related to an individual project, including acquiring, installing, using, maintaining, and, in some instances, removing and disposing, and the revenues or cost savings that will be generated as a result of the process. In reality, it makes sense to pay a somewhat higher price for an item if it has greater productivity gains and lower maintenance cost than an alternative item from another source. Life cycle value analysis provides a sensible alternative to the emphasis on low acquisition cost only. Its use has recognition and support from many organizations, including Coca-Cola and Intel.

Eleven essential steps are involved in the determination of the life cycle value analysis for a project:

1. Determination of purchase and installation price
2. Establishment of operating profiles
3. Establishment of utilization factors
4. Identification of revenue elements
5. Identification of critical revenue elements
6. Identification of cost elements
7. Determination of critical cost elements
8. Calculation of costs at current incremental values
9. Escalation of current labor and material costs over the life of the project
10. Discounting of all costs and revenues to a base period
11. A summation of all discounted and undiscounted costs and revenues

The project should be shared by purchasing and operating management with the assistance of accounting. It is often best to utilize a range process with life cycle valuation with a modeling technique to determine the probability of success (exceeding the hurdle rate), the business exposure involved (business worst position related to business best position), and where operations and purchasing should spend their time to improve the value through revenue enhancement or cost reduction. Companies are using Monte Carlo modeling to accomplish this evaluation.

PURCHASING'S ROLE IN THE ACQUISITION OF CAPITAL EQUIPMENT

The role of purchasing in the capital process is to provide the business side of the purchase. This process relates to the ten rights of purchasing. The buyer must optimize the following "right" areas:

1. Capital asset
2. Place
3. Time
4. Price
5. Quality
6. Quantity
7. Warranty
8. Service
9. Terms
10. Contract

Ideally, purchasing should be involved from the strategic planning process right through to the disposition of the asset after the productive life is over. However, in most cases this is not possible. Factors such as culture, past practices, and tradition may inhibit the buyer's participation in some areas of the acquisition process. It is vitally important that the buyer coordinate the ten rights of purchasing.

Right Capital Asset

This is the process of review of specifications, drawings, and statements of work for clarity and competitiveness. Coordination with users on the requirements of the technical side of the purchase is important to start as soon as possible.

Right Place

This process relates to supplier sourcing and coordination of the place of the purchase with the rest of the procurement processes. Finding and developing possible sources of supply is an ongoing and important function in the area of capital equipment purchasing. Normally the time span between capital evaluation and requisition is fairly short, and the more we can do in preparing for the actual purchase, the better off we will be.

One of the important parts of supplier sourcing and time processes in many capital acquisitions is a supplier visit. It is important that the buyer understand and qualify the supplier before the bid and contract process takes place. This is the time when the buyer should introduce the company's terms and conditions to the supplier and make sure that the supplier is willing to comply with the terms and conditions stated or that differences are negotiated at this point in time. There are several other reasons why a purchaser would visit a supplier before the actual purchase of the equipment.

The purchaser should determine:

1. Can the supplier deliver?
2. Does the supplier have the equipment to complete the order?
3. Does the supplier have the workforce and equipment to meet the desired delivery date?
4. Is the supplier involved in programs such as value analysis, TQM, ISO 9000, or other quality or value programs, and how will this affect their ability to handle our order?

In addition, the purchaser should make contacts that will assist in troubleshooting and preventing or resolving problems when they occur.

Supplier visits provide the purchaser education. Valuable insights into an industry or a procedure may be gained through a supplier visit, and thus visits to every new source may not be necessary.

Courtesy would dictate that notice be given to a supplier before you burst upon the scene. A proper warning of your intent to visit allows the people involved to coordinate their schedules to allow all interested parties to be available, such as technical people, sales managers, and so on. Furthermore, a previous announcement of your intent to visit allows the company to put its best foot forward.

Right Time

Time relates to the coordination of the purchase with the requirements of the organization. This is where the statement "strike while the iron is hot" fits.

At the beginning of the process it is good to provide each one of the prospective suppliers with a booklet of the terms and conditions. These terms and conditions are usually found on the back of the purchase order or as part of a contract, which is probably the worst place in the world to have them. Terms and conditions should be agreed upon before the contracting process is ever started. This way the groundwork will already be laid and the process of developing a good working relationship can begin right up front.

An overview of the project should be given, and a discussion should be conducted on how it fits into the overall plan and purpose of the company. This step follows and is a natural extension of the terms and conditions and the presentation of our organization.

Another timing factor is the coordination of timing of installation, production, and other time constraints of either the supplier or the user of the equipment. This also relates to the management of project records and status, including:

1. Bid/RFP/RFQ/RFI processes
2. Purchase contract issue
3. Authorizations
4. Changes and adjustments
5. Expediting log, including final receipt and acceptance

Right Price

This is often thought of as obvious in the purchase process. However, the balance of monetary value against the rest of the rights is very important in a capital acquisition to optimize both use and shareholder value.

Right Quality

Quality is perceived by the parties involved. It is very important that the purchaser understand the quality requirements so that there is again a balance of the quality against the price and the other elements involved.

Right Quantity

Although there is not a question of quantity related directly to the purchase, this relates to the quantity of spare parts and where they will be maintained and any other quantity such as quantity of time for training or time for support.

Right Warranty

Warranty is often a negotiable item related to price and quality. Again, it is a balancing process.

Right Service

Service with capital equipment is very important. Many times a negative service contract will be included. This means that payment for service will depend on up-time of the equipment. The supplier will receive the most from the contract if the equipment is always in top operating condition.

Right Terms

This right deals with both shipping terms and payment terms. Payment terms could include progress payments, while shipping terms should determine when the title of the equipment transfers.

Right Contract

The right contract will address the following areas, at a minimum:

1. The clarity of specifications, drawings, and statement of work and inclusion of this in the contract
2. The expected level of performance of the equipment and personnel involved and the remedies if performance, including quality, does not occur
3. The expected schedule of performance to meet delivery requirements of the organization and the relationship of maintenance and spare parts to the operation
4. Warranty, guarantee, and service agreements, including action to be taken if defaults occur
5. The price and payment schedule relating to all parts of the equipment and services to be delivered as a result of the contract

It is obvious that the issues in the contract and in the ten rights of the procurement process must be coordinated with the capital team prior to preparation of a Bid/RFP/RFQ/RFI; again during the analysis process; and finally during the preparation and execution of a negotiation plan.

NEGOTIATION

Negotiation should be the least troublesome method of settling disputes and/or establishing agreement. Negotiation may be exploratory and serve to formulate viewpoints and delineate areas of agreement or contention. It may aim at working out practical arrangements. The success of negotiation depends upon whether (a) the issue is negotiable (that is,

you can sell your car but not your child); (b) the negotiators are interested not only in taking, but also in giving; are able to exchange value
for value; and are willing to compromise; and (c) there is a trust level
between negotiating parties. If there is not an element of trust, then there
will be a plethora of safety provisions and protections that will render
the agreement unworkable.

Here is an excellent definition of negotiation from the U.S. Air
Force:

> A mutual discussion and arrangement of the terms of a transaction or
> agreement. Negotiation is the use of argumentation and persuasion, not to
> win an argument, but to resolve issues—not an individual issue—but the
> whole problem. Negotiation is not the process of giving in or mutual sac-
> rifice in order to secure agreement. It is an attempt to find a formula which
> will optimize the interests of both parties.

It is a specialized process of communication called "bargaining,"
by means of which a purchaser or a supplier reach agreement on the
issues involved that will reflect a balancing of the interest of the two
parties. Negotiation is the application of facts and logic supported by
the strengths of a bargaining position to achieve valid and necessary
business objectives. Procurement by negotiation is the art of arriving at
a common understanding through bargaining on the essentials of a contract, such as delivery, specifications, prices, and terms. Because of the
interrelation of these factors with many others, it is a difficult art and
requires the exercise of judgment, tact, and common sense. The effective
negotiator must be a real shopper but not a haggler, alive to the possibilities of bargaining with the seller. Only through an awareness of relative bargaining strength can a negotiator know where to be firm or
where he or she may make concessions in position. Simply put, negotiations must result in an agreement that is acceptable to both parties.

Control of Negotiations and Supplier Relations

For a number of reasons it is an inherent function of purchasing to maintain careful control of negotiations and supplier relations:

1. A purchasing department negotiator's effectiveness is greatly
   weakened if he or she is not recognized as the person to deal
   with at the very beginning. Suppliers quickly smell out the
   fact that the negotiator does not have full authority, no matter
   how carefully he or she tries to hide this fact. Purchasing
   should control all contracts with suppliers.

2. In negotiation with suppliers over prices or other conditions, unwise disclosures can be very harmful to the company's interests. Other departments are asked to confine their discussions with suppliers to specifications and performance and leave price and all other matters to the purchasing department unless they are specifically asked by the representative of that department in charge of the negotiations to get into other areas.

3. Effective supplier relations are necessary to achieve assurance of supply and protect the company's position and reputation.

Negotiation Goals and Objectives

Major goals must incorporate the following items:

1. Obtain fair and reasonable price and performance criteria.
2. Get the supplier to agree to performance against milestones and time deadlines.
3. Persuade the supplier to give maximum cooperation throughout the agreement.
4. Develop a sound and continuing relationship with competent suppliers.

The preceding are possible objectives to consider when negotiating. These objectives should be considered in light of the end results desired in the agreement.

Negotiation Timing

1. Always. Not necessarily for price, but for something. In every part of a capital buy process, whether by phone, P.O., or formal contract, the purchaser should negotiate for something: delivery, renewal terms, service, dating, etc. A fringe benefit of this for the purchaser is the practice in negotiating.
2. Where technical discussions are required for a full understanding of the nature and function of the capital item.
3. Where quotes have been received but all seem to be excessive in price, unsatisfactory in delivery, or not close enough to specifications.
4. Where prices are fixed but astute bargaining will enable a purchaser to obtain "fringe benefits" from a supplier.

What Makes a Good Negotiator

1. Clear, rapid thinking
2. Good self-expression
3. Ability to analyze and recognize windows of opportunity
4. Impersonality
5. Patience
6. Ability to consider the other person's ideas objectively
7. Tact, poise, and self-restraint
8. Good sense of humor

Planning and Preparation for Negotiation

Spend the time in preparation—it is the best investment you can make. Know the supplier, the people who will be present, and those with whom they will consult during negotiations (engineers, etc.). Spend four to six hours in preparation for every hour you will spend in negotiation with suppliers. Practice with dry runs and simulations with your people. Anticipate every argument they might bring up. Try to guess every position they might possibly take.

Decide on your objectives and the order in which they will be negotiated. It is best not to start with the main point first, as this will leave no place for the negotiations to go. Make sure you determine the following:

+ *Musts:* Absolute minimum requirements and any legal considerations.
+ *Wants:* Desirable items—set ranges for these, i.e., target and walk position as well as supplier's perceived minimum.
+ *Wishes:* Giveaways or trades for wants.

Plan the issues for discussion and their order. Plan and rehearse your tactics. Prepare questions that are difficult for them to answer with a yes or no. Make sure you know and appreciate your own strengths and weaknesses. Prepare for some stall techniques, such as bathroom breaks, open-ended questions, and information searches. In summary, know your business, your supplier, and your requirements.

Your Team

When you establish your negotiating team, several things should be kept in mind:

1. A negotiator and note taker should be identified (may or may not be leader).
2. Act as the host. Make arrangements for telephone, messages to and from the room, refreshments, etc. (Creature comforts are up to you.)
3. As host, introduce people as they enter; be the first to stand, the first to introduce yourself, etc. Identify the players and their parts. Make sure you point out your note taker.
4. Plan the seating and indicate to people as they arrive where they are to be placed. Perhaps see that note pads, pencils, water, etc. are in place.
5. As hosts, you and your people should radiate a convivial mood and a cordial atmosphere conducive to effective negotiating.
6. The person who starts the meeting is the leader of the meeting. It should be the purchasing company, not the supplier. Make it you (it is your money).
7. Agree on a stopping place.
8. Prepare and use an agenda and have all team members review it.
9. Some writers suggest that after the adjournment of the final negotiating session the participants all meet over dinner. Indeed, the session (if successful) has been the culmination of the beginning of a successful and profitable relationship for both sides.

Be patient. Remember, most settlements occur shortly before the deadline. Beware of quick settlements, which usually result in extreme outcomes. Beware of panic at a deadline. Skilled negotiators make smaller concessions as deadlines approach.

During the final phases of negotiation, the purchasing team should have in mind the type of financing that will be used to acquire the asset. It should be kept in mind, however, that the acquisition decision should be separate from and not dependent on the financing decision.

LEASE VERSUS BUY ALTERNATIVES

What is a lease? What is the difference between an operating lease and
a capital lease? The answers to these basic questions can be given from
an economic, legal, SEC, accounting, financial, IRS, or industry point of
view. Which is right? The answer depends upon the needs of the person
asking the question. For the sake of this definition we will rely heavily
upon the accounting definitions given by the Financial Accounting Standards Board (FASB), since the Board governs the accounting practices of
virtually all public corporations. Then too, reliance will be placed upon
IRS terminology and classification because taxes are such a crucial element in any decision concerning leases.

In general, a lease is viewed as a contract between a lessor (owner
of an asset) and a lessee (user of an asset) where the lessor grants the
temporary possession and use of an asset to the lessee. This is usually
for a specified period less than the asset's economic life at a fixed periodic charge (rental charge/lease payment). However, even though a contract labeled as a lease might contain these characteristics, it will not
necessarily be considered a lease from an accounting or IRS point of
view.

FASB Accounting Definition of a Lease

The Financial Accounting Standards Board, in its Statement No. 13 on
"Accounting for Leases," divides all leases into two basic classifications:
a capital lease and an operating lease. A capital lease is not really considered a true lease at all, but rather is a *sale* of equipment from the
lessor's viewpoint and a *purchase* to the lessee; whereas an operating
lease is a true lease from both the lessor's and the lessee's viewpoints.

Capital leases can be further subdivided into three types of leases:
a sales-type lease, a direct finance lease, and a leveraged lease where the
lessee wants to use as little of the organization's money as possible.

According to FASB Statement No. 13, "If at its inception a lease
meets one or more of the following four criteria, the lease shall be classified as a capital lease by the LESSEE. Otherwise, it shall be classified
as an operating lease."

1. The lease transfers ownership of the property to the lessee by
   the end of the lease term.
2. The lease contains a bargain purchase or bargain lease renewal
   option.

3. The lease term is equal to 75% or more of the estimated economic life of the leased property.

4. The present value at the beginning of the lease term of the minimum lease payments equals or exceeds 90% of the fair market value (FMV) of the leased property at the inception of the lease (the FMV of the property to be reduced by any investment tax credit or energy credit retained by the lessor prior to determining the 90% base).

The lessor's discount rate shall be the implicit rate in the lease.

The lessee's discount rate shall be its incremental borrowing rate unless implicit rate in the lease can be determined and that rate is lower.

Criteria 3 and 4 are ignored when the beginning of the lease term is within the remaining 25% of an asset's economic life. This situation occurs when used assets are leased during the last 25% of their economic lives.

If none of the aforementioned criteria are met, then the lease is considered a true lease and is referred to as an *operating lease*.

Lease and Purchase Cost Evaluation

To facilitate the identification of pertinent lease costs, the format in Table 35–5 subdivides leasing costs into direct and indirect costs. Direct costs are generally the initial, subsequent, and terminal financial costs that form an integral part of the lease. Indirect costs are represented by executory and other miscellaneous costs that are not integrally related to the lease but are incidentally related, such as taxes and insurance.

Costs of purchasing an asset with the proceeds of either an installment loan or with internally generated cash will be categorized in the same manner as leasing costs. The purchase decision format appears in Table 35–6.

Explanation for Lease Versus Buy Analysis

1. Some leases require delivery and installation charges to be paid by the lessee.

2. Security deposits are sometimes required to be paid in advance to give the lessor additional collateral security and compensate the lessor for any excessive wear and tear on the leased asset at the time of its return to the lessor.

TABLE 35-5

Lease Cost Format

	Amount	×	Tax Factor	×	P.V. Factor	=	Total
Add direct leasing costs:							
Initial costs						=	
Advance rental payments	___	×	___	×	___	=	___
Security deposit	___	×	___	×	___	=	___
Lease origination fee	___	×	___	×	___	×	___
Subsequent costs:							
Lease payments	___	×	___	×	___	=	___
Excess use charges	___	×	___	×	___	=	___
Lease termination costs							
Exercise of purchase option	___	×	___	×	___	=	___
Add indirect leasing costs:							
Sales tax in advance	___	×	___	×	___	=	___
Sales tax with payments	___	×	___	×	___	=	___
Insurance expense	___	×	___	×	___	=	___
Maintenance	___	×	___	×	___	=	___
Fuel costs	___	×	___	×	___	=	___
Accounting costs, etc.	___	×	___	×	___	=	___
Total present value of costs to lease							
Deduct leasing benefits:							
Depreciation tax shield	___	×	___	×	___	=	___
Return of security deposit	___	×	___	×	___	=	___
Total present value of leasing benefits							$ ___
Net present value of leasing							$ ___

T A B L E 35-6

Purchase Cost Format

	Amount	×	Tax Factor	×	P.V. Factor	=	Total
Add direct purchasing costs:							
Initial Costs							
Down payment	___	×	___	×	___	=	___
Service charge	___	×	___	×	___	=	___
Sales tax	___	×	___	×	___	×	___
Compensating bank balance	___	×	___	×	___	=	___
Subsequent Costs							
Periodic payments	___	×		×	___	=	___
Purchase Termination Costs (none normally)							
Add Indirect purchasing costs:							
Insurance expense	___	×	___	×	___	=	___
Maintenance	___	×	___	×	___	=	___
Fuel costs	___	×	___	×	___	=	___
Replacement costs	___	×	___	×	___	=	___
Additional facility costs	___	×	___	×	___	=	___
Accounting costs, etc.	___	×	___	×		=	___
Total present value of costs to purchase							
Deduct purchasing benefits:							
Return of compensating balance	___	×	___	×	___	=	___
Interest tax shield (per assumptions)							
Depreciation tax shield (per assumptions)							
Total present value of purchasing benefits							$ ___
Net present value of purchasing:							$ ___

3. Percentage rentals are based upon a fixed percentage of the lessee's gross revenue in excess of a base amount. The percentage rentals are generally paid by the lessee in addition to the normal periodic rentals.

4. The amounts of some lease payments are tied to increases in the prime rate or in the consumer price index.

5. Should the lessee expect usage of the equipment beyond that allowed in the lease, excess use fees will be charged by the lessor.

6. At the end of the lease term, one of several alternative actions will be taken, depending on the terms of the lease and the needs of the lessee. The equipment may be purchased by the lessee.

7. At the termination of the lease, the contract might require the lessee to pay a penalty for excess use (e.g., mileage on trucks beyond a specified maximum) or for repairs and maintenance required to bring the equipment up to a specified working order and condition. Should the lessee anticipate such additional costs, they should be included as costs under the lease alternative.

8. In net leases, executory costs such as sales tax, property tax, insurance, and maintenance are required to be paid by the lessee.

9. Replacement costs are incurred when equipment is obtained from the lessor to replace equipment temporarily out of service due to extraordinary breakdowns.

10. Under certain full-service leases, fuel costs can be minimized. For example, many Ryder Truck leasing agreements provide for the purchase of fuel from company outlets at prices below retail. With rising energy costs, these savings could become a decisive factor in the lease-versus-buy decision.

11. Compared to purchasing equipment, leasing the same equipment generally requires substantially less accounting and bookkeeping.

12. Miscellaneous costs are those expenses that are unique to the leasing of particular types of equipment. For example, some equipment requires special licenses and permits—e.g., trucks used in interstate commerce.

13. Sublease income expected from the lessee's anticipated leasing of the equipment to others should be deducted from the lease costs.

14. In the event the lessee does not expect to receive a refund of the security due to anticipated excess wear and tear of the equipment, such loss becomes a future noncash tax deduction.

15. In many cases, it is more advantageous to the purchaser of equipment to capitalize costs of delivery, installation, closing and service fees, and licenses and permits. Such capitalization allows the purchaser to take energy credit on the capitalized costs. Moreover, these costs can be subsequently depreciated, resulting in additional tax benefit.

16. At times banks and other financial institutions also require security deposits in addition to a down payment when loaning on an installment purchase. Such a deposit is not tax deductible to the purchaser.

17. Compensating bank balances are cash deposits required to be held in the purchaser's checking account with the banker–lender. Since the cash outlay is held by the bank without any payment of interest, it represents a nontaxable outflow in the initial year and a nontaxable inflow at the time the loan is paid off.

18. Recent installment loan agreements have provided for payments that increase as the prime rate increases. Therefore, forecasting of future prime rates is required.

19. In order to keep installment loan payments to a minimum, some banks allow the purchaser to pay a large balloon payment at the end of a loan term. This type of loan structuring makes the installment loan very comparable to leases that require large guaranteed residuals to be paid at the end of the lease.

20. Ownership of equipment oft times entails costs that would not ordinarily be incurred under a full-service lease. For example, spare parts and supplies inventories must be maintained to support equipment maintenance, etc. Significant added costs of ownership are represented by these incremental support costs. Should any of these support costs represent capital expenditures, these should be added to the

initial cost of purchasing. Later on, these capitalized costs would result in depreciation tax shields available to the purchaser as benefits of ownership. Remember to add only those costs that are incremental, i.e., those variable costs that will be incurred only as a result of purchasing the equipment.

21. Equipment that is owned qualifies for depreciation under IRS rules. Depreciation results in tax savings that are equal to the income tax rate multiplied by the annual depreciation charge.

22. Interest is included in the installment loan payments listed above as a purchasing cost. Since interest is tax deductible, it results in a tax savings equal to the interest paid times the tax rate.

23. If the equipment is assumed salvaged prior to the end of its economic life in order to make the purchase alternative equivalent to the shorter-term lease alternative, the salvage proceeds represent a savings. However, such proceeds must be adjusted for tax consequences. If the equipment is salvaged for more than its book value (tax basis or undepreciated value), taxes must be paid equal to the tax rate times the gain (ignoring any capital gain opportunities). Should the salvage value be less than the book value, a tax benefit would be earned in an amount equal to the loss times the tax rate. In either case, the additional tax expense or benefit must be deducted or added to the salvage value.

CHAPTER 36

Services and Nontraditional Goods

Editor
Henry F. Garcia, C.P.M.
Director of Administration
Center for Nuclear Waste Regulatory Analyses

OVERVIEW

In the same way that the 1851 Great Exhibition at the Crystal Palace in London, England symbolized manufacturing's triumph over agriculture, the 1957 launch of Sputnik by the Soviets coincided with the beginning of the post-industrial society. Today, knowledge and information services account for over 70% of the U.S. Gross Domestic Product. Some economists predict that in the first decade of the 21st century, services will represent 90% of the U.S. economy and the progressive transformation away from manufacturing and toward services will be well established.

Traditionally, purchasing professionals have been engaged in purchasing raw materials; subassemblies; supplies; maintenance, repair, and operating (MRO) items; and manufacturing-related capital equipment. Despite their often peripheral involvement in the acquisition of various services, these professionals should demonstrate their capacity for enhancing profits in the private sector or benefits in the public sector through a better understanding of the methods and mechanics of purchasing services and nontraditional goods (SNG). The procurement of SNG demands greater appreciation for and comprehension of the generally labor-intensive nature of services, the technology and inherent training required for use of capital assets, and the market determinants involved in outsourcing and retailing. For example, purchasing professionals can apply opportunity-cost and benefit-cost analyses to the purchase of SNG by evaluating the return on investment or the return on assets from engaging a service provider, selecting a capital asset supplier, or favoring outsourcing or retailing over in-house production.

TYPES OF SERVICES AND NONTRADITIONAL GOODS

Private and public sector organizations buy several types of services and nontraditional goods for use in their operations and administrative functions for the short and long term. A categorization of these services and goods can be found in the Consumer (CPI) and Producer (PPI) Price Indexes. For the purposes of this chapter, however, services are categorized as follows:

- *Facilities:* Design, construction, janitorial, maintenance and repair, moving/storage, environmental, pest control, landscaping, and security
- *Logistics:* Inventory, traffic and transportation, salvage and reclamation, and warehousing
- *Communication:* Information technology, video-teleconferencing, photography, publication, television, public relations and advertising, and telephone
- *Employee:* Employment and relocation, outplacement, fringe benefits, training and counseling, uniforms, cafeteria and vending, travel, and entertainment
- *Business:* Accounting and audit, financial and brokerage, architectural and engineering, market research, auctioneering, consulting, and legal

Similarly, nontraditional goods are categorized as follows:

- *Capital goods:* Business and computer equipment, and physical plant and equipment
- *Resale:* Outsourced items and wholesale/retail items, including original equipment manufacturer (OEM)

These types of services and goods do not constitute an all-inclusive listing. For example, purchasing professionals may be asked to secure testing services and shop instrumentation for an organization.

RESPONSIBILTY FOR PURCHASING SERVICES AND NONTRADITIONAL GOODS

Purchasing SNG requires familiarity with the nature and scope of different service types; comprehension of the technological characteristics of capital assets, including requisite training; and knowledge of the market mechanisms inherent in outsourcing and retailing. Usually the purchasing department depends on the expertise of individuals in the operating divisions/departments of an organization to identify competent sources for SNG as well as factors influencing the acquisition of resale items. These individuals support the mechanics of source selection and the decision to purchase outsourced items and/or wholesale/retail items. In addition, they often participate in the evaluation of these providers of services or purveyors of nontraditional goods.

A 1995 study entitled *Purchasing of Nontraditional Goods and Services*[1] by the Center for Advanced Purchasing Studies (CAPS), a program jointly sponsored by NAPM and Arizona State University, found that in the 116 organizations responding to its survey, individuals in the operating divisions/departments were responsible for spending 59% of the organizations' total purchase dollars. The study examined the responsibility for acquiring such goods and services in three sectors (manufacturing, service, and government). Comparing the organizations' total purchase dollars in each sector, this study revealed that the purchasing department accounted for 48% in the manufacturing sector, 22% in the service sector, and 49% in the government sector.

This study corroborates the higher rate of growth in the purchase of SNG throughout the various sectors of the U.S. economy. It can be inferred that purchasing departments can enhance profits in the private sector or benefits in the public sector through more effective involvement in the procurement of these services and goods.

PREPARATION FOR PURCHASING OF SERVICES AND NONTRADITIONAL GOODS

Since the influence of service delivery and nontraditional good utility can exceed the impact of the dollars spent, purchasing professionals

---

1. H. E. Fearon, *Purchasing of Nontraditional Goods and Services,* Center for Advanced Purchasing Studies, Tempe, Arizona, 1995.

should demonstrate the necessary credentials and qualifications to identify, select, and evaluate sources for these services and goods. These credentials and qualifications should permit them to thoroughly understand
the essence and extent of the services to be purchased; the technology,
coupled with the necessary user training, intrinsic to the efficient application of acquired capital assets; and the market factors encouraging the
outsourcing of certain services or items and retailing of select OEM products. Moreover, these professionals should be completely familiar with
the execution of applicable financial analyses and the conduct of relevant
operations management methods employed in the decision to secure certain services, select specific capital assets, or subscribe to outsourcing or
retailing over in-house production. Purchasing professionals should exhibit the necessary capacity and credibility preparatory to their assuming
a leadership role in the selection of SNG.

For many organizations, the majority of total SNG purchases were
not made by the purchasing department, as indicated by the chief executive officers and agency heads in the 1995 CAPS study. These officials
should provide an appropriate environment for SNG acquisitions and
seek a proactive involvement by the purchasing department. A collaborative approach, specifically the use of cross-functional teaming and strategic partnering, should be implemented to purchase services and nontraditional goods. This approach allows the purchasing department to
effectively gain the integrative support of the organization's operating
divisions/departments, especially in making award decisions. With this
support, purchasing can complement its capability and confidence in the
identification and selection of responsible and competent sources for the
purchase of SNG as well as the recognition of those market determinants
affecting the acquisition of resale items. Moreover, the purchasing department can choose those strategic partners that will improve the organization's profits or benefits, contingent on sector identity.

PROCESS FOR PURCHASING SERVICES AND NONTRADITIONAL GOODS

The employment of cross-functional teaming permits each team member
from the stakeholder operating divisions/departments of the organization to offer his/her discipline expertise to ascertain whether selecting
specific providers of services or purveyors of nontraditional goods is
proper under current budgetary or qualified source constraints. If such
constraints exist, these team members can use their expertise and familiarity with competent professionals or firms to improve the possibility

of mitigating these constraints. Prior to developing a request for proposal (RFP) along with its statement of work (SOW) or product specifications, however, the typical cross-functional team should carefully define any prerequisites for identifying, qualifying, and selecting competent service providers or goods purveyors. Some of these prerequisites include:

♦ Determining the requirement for their expertise and the rationale for not using in-house capacity

♦ Discovering the existence of any potential conflict of interest and the need for executing a nondisclosure agreement

♦ Deciding on the expected duration of any resultant contract and the costs associated with the nature of the required expertise and the existing budget

♦ Defining the managerial levels of the oversight and approval authorities

♦ Describing the delivery requirements consistent with the SOW or product specifications

After delineating these prerequisites, the team members responsible for identifying, qualifying, and selecting these competent service providers or goods purveyors should:

♦ Describe the key business issue or problem (i.e., the nature and scope of the project) and establish the requirement for, and the feasibility of, hiring a service provider or goods purveyor to provide special support

♦ Determine the desired result from the project and clarify the operating limits of support needed in this particular project

♦ Document any interdependencies and identify all stakeholder groups (i.e., staff working with the potential provider or purveyor on this project)

♦ Develop the estimated resources, time, and costs for executing this project

♦ Decide on the requirements for communicating the provider's or purveyor's project activities (i.e., pre- and post-project expectations and delivery methods)

Subsequent to taking these steps, the cross-functional team can begin identifying, qualifying, and selecting a competent professional or firm.

Regardless of their familiarity with responsible and competent providers or purveyors, team members should begin a thorough search of various sources from whom to solicit a proposal. Locating these professionals or firms involves:

- Checking similar organizations with like requirements that have employed these professionals or firms in the conduct of their project activities and soliciting referrals and recommendations from these and other organizations, competitors, and suppliers
- Researching published directories (e.g., *Consultants and Consulting Organizations Directory* and *Thomas Register of American Manufacturers*) and listings (e.g., Better Business Bureaus and Chambers of Commerce)
- Accessing professional and trade associations (e.g., *Encyclopedia of Associations* and *National Trade and Professional Associations of the U.S.*)
- Participating in regional and national trade shows to identify those providers and purveyors with specialized skills
- Researching organizations on the Internet

After identifying potential service providers or goods purveyors, the cross-functional team can start qualifying those professionals or firms that have been found.

The qualifications of each provider or purveyor will form the basis for selecting the most appropriate professional or firm to satisfactorily resolve the key business issue or problem in collaboration with core staff in the stakeholder divisions/departments. In the qualification process, team members should:

- Consider the size and scope of the key business issue or problem as well as the expected expertise for its resolution
- Evaluate not only the experience and credentials but also the management and interpersonal skills of each provider or purveyor for compatibility with the purchasing organization's culture and practices
- Establish whether each provider or purveyor has the available labor and capital resources to meet project milestones on-time and within budget
- Present a briefing to the potential service providers or goods purveyors, as may be appropriate, to explain the origin or background of this issue or problem, provide the rationale for

engaging these professionals or firms to resolve the issue or
problem, and identify the organization's staff with whom they
would work

After completion of the qualification process, the cross-functional
team can start the selection process. Team members should use their
collective proficiency to craft a detailed RFP addressing the nature and
scope of the key business issue or problem and defining the performance
criteria, quality specifications, budgetary ceiling, and delivery schedule
requirements.

The RFP should include clearly defined specifications, performance
expectations, and acceptance criteria to ensure that all parties, particularly responding providers, or purveyors have an understanding of the
complete requirements for the acquisition. Failure to adequately define
these specifications, expectations, and criteria may result in the buying
organization paying too much or not securing the appropriate services
or nontraditional goods for the intended applications. Moreover, inadequate specifications can lead to restraint of competition, technological
innovation, and quality improvements.

The most important part of the RPF is the SOW (the specifications).
As with design or performance specifications used in the purchase of
commodities, a SOW can be design- or performance-based. A design-
based SOW states not only what is required but also how that requirement will be fulfilled. It is used when the purchasing organization wants
strict control over the particular methodology used in performance of
the work specified in the SOW. This control, however, can contribute to
higher direct costs, restrictive competition, and higher indirect (administrative) costs associated with compliance monitoring. Conversely, a performance-based SOW describes the nature and scope of the issue or problem as well as the preferred outcome resulting from the performance
criteria, quality level, budgetary restraint, and delivery schedule frequency. It allows the provider or purveyor the maximum flexibility to
select the most cost-effective and efficient methodology to accomplish
the work.

A clear, accurate, and thorough SOW will determine, to a great
extent, the potential for a provider or purveyor to satisfactorily complete
the objectives of the resultant purchase order or contract. Further, it will
provide the expectant emphasis on price, quality, and delivery in addition to technical or professional excellence, supplier-furnished creativity,
and timeliness of reporting interim progress or final delivery of the SNG.

When crafting the SOW, the team members should have a complete understanding of all factors influencing the execution of this SOW together with the precarious balance between protecting the buying organization's interests and promoting supplier creativity during the critical proposal preparation and post-award performance periods. Moreover, the team should be aware of possible misinterpretation of the SOW by all affected parties and take the proper measures to solicit feedback from these groups. After the RFP with its SOW has been "approved" by all affected parties, the proposal package is ready for submittal to the provider(s) or purveyor(s). Contingent on the buying organization's requirement for soliciting competitive proposals, the RFP will be conveyed to the select recipient(s).

Following receipt of these proposals, these team members employ their expert knowledge and considerable experience to examine each proposal for the most technically sound and innovative approach to resolve the organization's key business issue or problem, consistent with the provisions stated in the RFP. The team can make an informed recommendation to the purchasing department of the best source for contract award. Then, purchasing can begin the analysis/confirmation process by using the same methodologies associated with commodities or product source selection, with some modifications. This process includes the utilization of as many analytical techniques as are practical for the specific procurement. The following analyses can be employed.

- *Cost analysis:* An analysis of the cost for each component of the service or nontraditional good as it impacts the quality and total price of such service or good
- *Value analysis:* An analysis of the nature and scope of the proposed service or good relative to the defined requirement and cost
- *Life cycle costing:* An analysis of the total cost of the service or good, including all operating and follow-on expenses, throughout the life of the service delivery or volume of the good
- *Project management:* An analysis of post-award administrative activities through the use of Gantt charts, PERT/CPM systems, and the like to monitor and control schedule, cost, and quality, especially in service contracts

After conducting the appropriate analyses, the purchasing department, in collaboration with the cross-functional team members, makes the overall final contract award decision, consistent with the RFP's SOW and other stated requirements. This fulfills the buying organization's objective of providing the greatest expected value for the organization from selection of the most responsible and competent provider of services or purveyor of nontraditional goods.

Subsequent to choosing the most appropriate provider or purveyor, the cross-functional team should recommend that senior management consider establishing a strategic partnering agreement with the chosen professional or firm. Such an agreement would not only meet the organization's immediate needs but also provide the organization with competent and long-term support for its specific issues or problems. Further, a strategic partnering agreement would create an interdependent and mutually beneficial business relationship conducive to meeting the organization's profit or benefits objectives.

Many major organizations, even those in the public sector, are reducing the number of service providers and goods purveyors with whom they do business. Several of these organizations are developing strategic partnering agreements with one or a few professionals or firms. Credibility and continuity of support are joining price as important factors in choosing providers of services or purveyors of nontraditional goods. As these providers or purveyors demonstrate their concern for their client's best interests, the price for their services or goods becomes less a factor than trust and commitment as a strategic partner.

Establishing a partnering agreement with the most appropriate professional or firm involves:

+ Defining the organization's profit or benefits objectives and the anticipated role of the provider or purveyor in the satisfaction of such objectives
+ Allowing the potential professional's or firm's knowledge of the organization's requirements to facilitate the appropriate response to the organization's RFP
+ Establishing a functional awareness and specified knowledge of each partner's requirements and expectations for addressing the organization's demands
+ Matching the potential professional's or firm's technical strengths with the organization's performance expectations

The resultant agreement or alliance should demonstrate a strong commitment to achieving mutual benefits to both parties, based on open communication, reciprocal support, and trust. Moreover, this agreement or alliance should show an appreciation for the operational advantage available to each partner and the bilateral support for any adjustments to the underpinnings of the agreement or alliance.

SELECTION OF THE PROPER PURCHASING VEHICLE FOR ACQUIRING SERVICES AND NONTRADITIONAL GOODS

The purchasing department should employ a logical purchasing process for the procurement of SNG. In the context of creating strategic partnering agreements or alliances, purchasing should eschew, whenever possible and permitted by governing law or regulations, competitive bidding and espouse negotiated procurements to secure such services or goods. Generally, the comparison of professional service quality and expertise is not amenable to price competition, and the delivery of services does not exhibit the same characteristics as those for commodities or products. On the other hand, certain types of services or nontraditional goods can be purchased through competitive bidding. These include janitorial and uniform services, capital equipment, and resale items. Typically, the choice between competitive bidding and negotiated procurements can depend on:

♦ The nature of the competitive environment (the number of service providers or goods purveyors by geographic region and their relative dominance of the market in that region)

♦ The type of service or nontraditional good—their distinguishing characteristics

♦ The need for continuity of service delivery or goods volume that would suggest establishing a strategic partnering agreement with one or more select providers or purveyors

Given a good competitive market, however, a negotiated procurement usually permits the productive application of good business judgment coupled with a focused analysis of pricing. Nevertheless, purchasing should be cognizant of the possibility and desirability of engaging in strategic partnering, obviating the use of competitive bidding, with providers of these types of services and kinds of nontraditional goods.

Purchasing professionals should pursue establishing blanket orders, open-end orders, or systems contracts as the appropriate vehicles for acquiring SNG. Other similar vehicles (i.e., consulting services contracts and standardized industry contracts) may be used for this purpose. Releases against these blanket orders, open-end orders, or systems contracts permit individuals from the user divisions/departments to initiate a procurement action without involving the purchasing department. Purchasing, however, retains the responsibility and authority to make any modifications to these orders or contracts. These procurement vehicles allow the purchasing department the time to demonstrate its professionalism in source selection and contract negotiation and administration. Ultimately, the type and scope of service delivery or the kind and volume of capital/outsourced goods will determine the choice of the most appropriate purchasing vehicle.

LEGAL IMPLICATIONS RELATED TO PURCHASING SERVICES AND NONTRADITIONAL GOODS

Purchasing's proactive involvement in the areas of SNG acquisitions is affected by myriad laws and regulations applicable to the purchase of various types of services and nontraditional goods. The legal aspects relating to the execution of a purchasing professional's responsibilities are more clearly visible in the public sector, which relies on the Federal Acquisition Regulations, state statutes, and local ordinances in formulating any one of the previously mentioned acquisition vehicles, including the terms and conditions stated in the boilerplate of each procurement. In the private sector, however, the Uniform Commercial Code (UCC), except in the state of Louisiana, applies to contracts for the purchase of goods (primarily commodities and products) but does not pertain to contracts for services. Service contracts are governed by the body of common law. In mixed contracts, such as the purchase of nontraditional goods, the applicable law is determined by the predominant purpose of the contract. For example, the UCC applies to the purchase of capital equipment but does not apply if the major focus of the contract is the procurement of installation services. Here, common law would apply.

Especially in specific types of services, certain federal legislation may affect a contract for service delivery. Some of the major applicable Acts include:

- ◆ Clean Air and Water Act

- Privacy Act
- Prompt Payment Act
- Americans with Disabilities Act
- Contract Work Hours and Safety Standards Act
- Service Contract Act
- Davis–Bacon Act
- Fair Labor Standards Act
- Walsh–Healy Public Contracts Act

Other legislative and regulatory provisions that may affect a contract with a service provider or goods purveyor include:

- Patent and copyright infringement
- Provisions for insurance or bonds protective of the buying organization
- Limitation of liability and indemnification or "hold harmless clauses"
- Royalties allocation and reporting
- Inspection rights, rights of rejection, and title to property
- Warranty of title and implied warranty of merchantability
- Order cancellation, breach of contract, and liquidated damage provision
- Use of highly underutilized businesses
- Affirmative action and equal opportunity
- Stop work orders

Purchasing professionals should research and be familiar with considerations involved in the development of specific procurement vehicles to ensure that all applicable laws and regulations have been included. They should request a legal review of all contracts before finalizing them with either the service provider or goods purveyor.

SUPPLIER PERFORMANCE EVALUATION ASSOCIATED WITH PURCHASING SERVICES AND NONTRADITIONAL GOODS

Unlike traditional supplier evaluation methods, evaluation of the performance of services providers or goods purveyors should employ the same collaborative approach, using cross-functional teaming, involved in the process for purchasing SNG. This approach does not rely on establishing performance-rating standards but applies well-defined performance criteria, already established in the qualifying process prior to contract award, as the basis for such an evaluation. Team members provide input to the determination about each provider's or purveyor's conformance with such criteria.

Performance should be monitored at periodic intervals and appropriate action taken to resolve significant issues identified during the period of performance. Previous performance history, either with this organization or others that may have provided a reference, can provide tangible guidance in the conduct of an objective evaluation. To the extent practicable, such evaluations should be quantified primarily for two reasons: These evaluations are usually more objective and precise and feedback to the provider or purveyor is typically more meaningful and motivating. Regardless of the quantitative or qualitative nature of the evaluation method, scheduled performance evaluations are an important part of the post-award administration of a contract. These evaluations typically contribute significantly to the maintenance of good supplier relationships, which in turn promotes efficient and effective service delivery or nontraditional good utility.

CONCLUSION

The purchase of SNG is a challenging responsibility for purchasing professionals, regardless of sector identity. As stated previously, the purchasing of SNG requires a greater appreciation for and comprehension of the generally labor-intensive nature of services, the technology and necessary training required for use of capital assets, and the market mechanisms involved in outsourcing and retailing. The resultant service delivery and goods utility can affect the attitudes and productivity of supplier and purchaser alike.

The development of an effective RFP, with its well-defined SOW or product specifications, for SNG is often more difficult than the creation of an RFP for a commodity because of the disparate nature of the various types of services or nontraditional goods. Additionally, selection of a service provider, which necessitates knowledge of the firm and the professionals performing the work, is a more thorough process, implying the application of a cross-functional team approach. Evaluation of a proposal for services thus involves some dependence on qualitative judgments and quantitative assessments. Hence, solid familiarity with cost analysis is essential to the effective selection of the proper provider or purveyor.

The choice of the most appropriate purchasing vehicle for securing these types of services or nontraditional goods suggests the use of blanket orders, open-end orders, or systems contracts. These are more complex purchase contracts than conventional purchase orders, and require uniquely specific SOWs or product specifications as well as contract clauses or the boilerplate peculiar to the nature of the service or good. Similarly, criteria for performance evaluation may be more subjective and exposed to a different level of scrutiny by more individuals (cross-functional team) in the purchasing organization than may be the case in commodity purchasing.

Purchasing professionals have a distinct opportunity to demonstrate their competence and capabilities in buying SNG. Through the use of cross-functional teaming, they can enhance their visibility and credibility among the various divisions/departments of the organization and assume the responsibility for spending a larger percentage of the total purchase dollars.

CHAPTER 37

Construction Services Procurement

Editor
Bruce J. Wright
President
B. Wright & Associates and Total Systems, Inc.

ELEMENTS IN CONSTRUCTION PURCHASING

Construction purchasing is unique in many ways, not the least of which is the uncertainty of the purchase. In construction, innumerable types of contractors supply many kinds of construction services. Each contractor has its own unique character and technical talents, but they all have one thing in common—high uncertainty. Where there is high uncertainty, two options are present: risk and opportunity. Contractors manage high risks and opportunities related to intellectual property, labor and craft problems, human motivation, jurisdictional disputes, weather conditions, material coordination, and job complexities.

Construction purchasing is infrequent for most purchasers. At best the purchasers have a working knowledge and a good background in purchasing services. However, most contract for new facilities or construction only infrequently. The customary procurement methods and policies often are very different from those prevailing in the world of construction.

In purchasing for manufacturing or service operations, the description of the good or service to be purchased is usually definable and reasonably precise, with other elements of the purchase measurable and controllable. Purchasers are normally accustomed to dealing with prices that can be questioned and analyzed and then agreed upon. One of the important focuses in today's general procurement is the establishment of policies and procedures that tend to provide for consistent, long-term relations with suppliers where continuing analysis of price and cost is frequently conducted, computing rather precisely the amounts of raw material, labor, and production resources; support costs; and technology costs that are required to produce the quality product the end customer desires.

Construction contractors perform their services for an organization according to a set of criteria generally known to the contractor but first-time and one-time to the purchaser. This adds to the uncertainty of the purchase and requires tools that will measure that uncertainty as well as solidify the desired outcome of the relationship. Most organizations have gone to contracting for deliverables rather than time and materials with a set profit margin and only cost changes after the contract is agreed upon. Some elements are controlled by neither purchaser nor supplier, such as weather and government regulations.

CONSTRUCTION PROJECT PROCESS

The construction project process generally follows the following flow:

- ◆ Strategic plan
- ◆ Capital evaluation
- ◆ Request for proposal
- ◆ Bid/request for quote
- ◆ Negotiation for deliverables
- ◆ Purchase order (contract)

Strategic Plan

Normally the construction project process starts with a strategic decision to expand, update, or otherwise change or increase operating capability. Management should determine the focus and outcome of this project relating to the customers, shareholders, and employees. With this start, it is also important to evaluate the expectations of other groups of people that will be affected by the project, such as suppliers, government, community, and other groups that have expectation in the outcome of the project. It is very important in a construction project to manage expectations and optimize their outcome so that when the project is completed it will not only be accepted but also supported by all concerned.

Capital Evaluation

The next part of the process is the general evaluation of resources available to support the project. This includes monetary capital, people capital, and market capital. Monetary capital deals with the range of expenditure anticipated by management. People capital relates to the personnel from both purchasing and user areas that will be dedicated to the project. Market capital determines the expected shareholder position as a result of the project. It should be understood that this is an initial look, so the ranges of commitment could be wide and varied.

Request for Proposal

With most construction projects the purchasing organization does not have the information or the expertise to establish a bid or quote process directly. Consequently, most organizations will go through a request for proposal. This process is now deemed to be a request for intellectual property with recent legal changes, and it should be treated as such. Oftentimes an architectural firm will be used first to establish the elements of the construction and the desired quality and structural integrity. This is often called a two-step buy. The first step is to get the architecture firm to create the requirements, and the second step is for the purchaser to take those requirements and go to general contractors to have them bid or quote on the requirements.

In the second step it is important to understand the relationship of the request to the outcome of the process. When a request for proposal is sent out to multiple parties, care should be taken to agree to a confidentiality or secrecy agreement at the time of the proposal to protect both parties. From the purchaser's point of view, care should be taken not to use either the information of the proposal or the company information for purposes other than the construction without the express approval of the purchasing organization. Likewise, the proposer does not want the information in the proposal used by either the purchasing organization or other parties for gain outside of the proposal. Care should be exercised to make sure that ideas from one proposal are not arbitrarily provided to other proposers without the rights to those ideas first being acquired. When the rights to ideas are acquired, care should be taken to make sure that an agreement for the use of the proposal is signed by both parties.

Three levels of agreement are normally used in a proposal process:

1. **License to use:** If no other stipulation is agreed to by both parties, the purchaser, upon the purchase of the proposal, has license to use the information internally only in the purchasing organization. This is normally sufficient in a construction project except where ideas or software will be included in subsequent operations. When this is desirable, the second level of agreement should be undertaken.

2. **Right of resale:** When intellectual property will be used in a product or service produced by the construction, an agreement should be made related to the right of resale. Normally the proposer will want a royalty arrangement, while the purchaser would be better off if they can negotiate a bulk agreement. Whichever is established, the agreement needs to be part of the payment of services for the proposal.

3. *Right of copyright or patent*: The final state of agreement sometimes used is the right of copyright or patent. This means that the proposer turns over to the buyer all rights to copyright, patent, trademark, or service mark the ideas or property produced by the proposal and agreement. This is not often done, but it should be considered where the identification of the construction will become an integral part of the image of the organization.

In most cases the first level will be enough, but the purchaser should consider their position before the establishment of the payment for the proposal.

If the company that makes the proposal also becomes the general contractor for the project and will carry the construction to completion, then we would go directly to negotiation of contract and not make this a two-step process. However, this is not always the case and so the proposal step is very important.

Bid/Request for Quote

The bid or request for quote is the next step after management, users, and purchasers are satisfied with the direction, quality, look, and functionality of the project. Normally the bid or quote will go out to general contractors that will hire and coordinate the activities of subcontractors in completing the project. It should be understood that with the bid process, all parties are given the same chance to submit their best position the first time. Although this principle is often violated according to the ethics of a bid, it is not negotiable. All bidders should have the same possibility of success. With a quote, it is understood that the quote will be the starting place for the contractor and that negotiation will take place in all areas of the contract. If the purchaser does not have expertise or time, the bid process is often best. If there is some expertise and there is a desire to optimize value, the quote process is normally the best to follow.

ORGANIZATIONAL STRATEGY

A variety of construction contracting strategies should be considered in planning for a construction project. The construction purchaser, along with the other members of the management team, should carefully analyze the options at this point in the planning process to ensure selection of the organizational strategy that best suits the project. There are normally three strategies employed.

1. *"Turnkey."* The design approach, sometimes referred to as the "turnkey" method, involves the selection of a single firm to accomplish the complete design and construction of the project. Using this strategy, the purchaser delegates full authority and responsibility to the design builder. The purchaser typically provides the deliverables that the completed project is expected to meet—operating and performance characteristics, cost, site location, esthetic appeal, and schedule requirements, for example. In addition, the turnkey builder is sometimes obligated to meet other special requirements, such as matching an existing facility and using local materials and the architectural style and mechanical/ electrical systems or equipment preferred. Within these general specifications and requirements, the turnkey contractor must complete the project.

2. *"General contractor."* The "general contractor" strategy, sometimes referred to as the "traditional contracting" strategy, encompasses the use of a bid package, with a request for proposal, that has been developed by the buying organization's design staff or by an independent architectural/ engineering firm under a separate contract as indicated above. The bid is typically completed by several general contractors,

and the contract is awarded to the successful bidder for the
construction of the project. This strategy is most often utilized
for small to mid-sized construction projects. On some projects,
where a variety of trade skills is required, the general
contractor will, in turn, subcontract portions of the
construction work to other more specialized contractors,
sometimes referred to as "subs." The primary difference
between the general contract and the design-build strategies is
that in the general contract approach the design function is
accomplished by the purchasing firm or a separate design
organization.

3. *"Construction management."* In today's sophisticated
environment the "construction management" or team
approach is used. The term *construction management* has been
used to describe any variations and hybrid approaches to the
more conventional turnkey and general contract approaches,
borrowing concepts from both. Because of these variations in
definition, construction purchasers must ensure that they
understand exactly what is meant when analyzing a specific
proposal for construction management and look to writing the
agreement in relation to deliverables rather than general
objectives. Members of the construction management group
may or may not perform some of the construction work, or
supervise laborers, artisans, or other subcontractors. Clearly,
though, they do oversee each of the contractor entities that the
buyer has employed. The construction manager's staff is made
up of personnel experienced in project management,
scheduling, estimation of labor relations/jurisdiction,
engineering, purchasing/expediting, personnel management,
accounting, and performance measurement.

Negotiation for Deliverables

With a turnkey process, normally the negotiation for deliverables is left
to a general outcome bond. With the other two processes, a construction
manager is generally appointed in the purchasing group who will coordinate the efforts of the organization and the contractor with the time
frame for the project and ensure the final balance of the expectations of

the various groups involved. A key element of the construction manager's responsibility is working with the architect during design to ensure that all deliverable issues are adequately considered. Sometimes referred to as "pre-construction design," this involvement during the design work distinguishes a construction manager from a general contractor. Without question, this is an important advantage of the construction management organizational strategy. Proponents of construction management also point out that it puts the management team in position to oversee the specialty contractors, and at times even the general contractor. They believe that a general contractor often "wears blinders" when it comes to recognizing the need for improving performance. Of course, construction management involves an additional level of management, which costs an additional 1–5% of the total project cost. But it may be a real bargain if optimization of expectation of the outcome relates to the outcome of the project and increases the performance of all the operating units.

For years general contractors themselves have offered construction management services along with their general contractor duties. This generally is still the case. It can be difficult, however, for a general contracting firm also to serve as its own construction manager, because the firm's personnel often are too involved in the actual construction process to discern mismanagement.

The construction management or general contractor organizational strategy may or may not be the best strategy for a purchaser to utilize. There are other means of gaining the advantages that impartial, objective construction management can accomplish. First, the purchasing firm may have the expertise internally to do it; second, the general contractor may be willing and quite able to designate a construction management team that reports to a different part of the contractor's organization; and third, the architect/engineer may also be able to carry out this role.

Regardless of the strategy used, strong, effective construction management should be present that will have the responsibility for performing the management function of making sure that the deliverables and expectations are met. The construction management or general contractor concept will have an impact on the bidding/quoting contractors, and they should be aware, prior to the process, what the expectations will be.

From a review of the three major contracting strategies just described, several conclusions can be drawn. An analysis is presented in

Table 37–1. The following general comments are offered concerning specific characteristics:

1. *Significant purchasing firm involvement required.* The major effect of an organizational strategy or general contract is to dictate commensurate management involvement in project-specific activities. Depending on the subsequent assignment of responsibilities within the boundaries of any given strategy, the buyer's management involvement varies greatly.

2. *Contract pricing alternatives.* Although described in more detail later, pricing alternatives depend to a great extent on the establishment of deliverables and negotiation of prices on the deliverables. In the absence of any other influencing factors, such as the competitive nature of the contracting marketplace, completeness and firmness of design information, and general economic uncertainty, the ability to secure firm fixed price contracts increases and the scope of work decreases with each contractual performance period.

3. *Single contractor risk.* With the turnkey process, everything is placed in the hands of a single contractor. As the number of outside contractors in a project increases, the risk vested in any one contractor decreases. Potential negative impacts resulting from failure, termination, or inadequate performance

T A B L E   37–1

Contracting Strategies Relationship

Characteristic	Turnkey	General	Management
Issued contracts	Few	Moderate	Many
Size of contractor	Large	Mid-size or small	Large
Service scope	Extensive	Moderate or limited	Extensive
Scope definition at contract start	Preliminary	Extensive	Extensive
Contractor's project responsibility	Extensive	Moderate	Moderate or limited
Schedule flexibility	Extensive	Limited	Extensive
Scope change frequency	Low	High	Moderate
Price contingency	Large	Small	Moderate to large

from any one contractor are reduced when the total project scope is distributed among a number of outside organizations. The benefits of this spreading effect on risk must be weighed against the demands for increased management and control.

4. *Contractor control capabilities.* As the relative scope of work and company size increases, internal management and control capabilities typically improve. Larger design-build contractors usually maintain more extensive management and project control capabilities than do smaller, specialized contractors, which typically work on a restricted scope, within the environment of controls provided by others.

5. *Contract formation and administration requirements.* Two major factors influence the scope of contract management duties and the difficulties with which they are performed. These are the *organizational approach* selected by the purchaser and the *pricing alternative* used for each contract. Pricing considerations aside, contract formation and administrative efforts increase in direct proportion to the number of contracts issued for a given project.

Only by understanding the impact, features, and benefits of each strategy can a construction purchaser make a rational selection of a single strategy or develop an effective hybrid strategy, and then successfully implement the strategy chosen.

Purchase Order (Contract)

The purchaser–supplier relationship and related agreements in construction purchasing deal with situations not typically found in the industrial purchasing situation. The prospective construction service purchaser must be fully aware of all the issues and their related effect of the outcome before attempting to analyze the wide variety of contract pricing alternatives available. A brief description of the key contractual alternatives follows.

Fixed Price Types

Lump Sum Fixed   This is a single price commitment related to bid or quote specifications and drawings. Changes by the purchaser to the concept or scope of the job add to this total. All market cost increases are borne by the supplier, and the original price for the defined job is fixed. This pricing type is used primarily for small to medium-sized, well-defined projects and some large construction projects that are well defined and properly negotiated. Deliverables and design must be well established to avoid large contingencies in the price.

Lump Sum with Escalation   In addition to the contract price, escalation of labor and material costs are paid by the purchaser. This pricing type is also used on projects where design is well established but may involve an extended or loose schedule that inhibits the possibility of obtaining a fixed price or involves work in a highly volatile industry.

Fixed Deliverable Price   A dollar amount for each work deliverable described in detail; all segments of work added together constitute the entire project cost. The segment of work can be for worker hours of labor or for all material and worker hours or any other combination. This pricing type is used for a wide range of construction and contracting services: temporary office help, security services, construction materials, and so on; or for other trades work where quantities may not completely be established for the work in question.

Cost-Plus Types

The following five types of contract pricing alternatives are all cost-plus. In each one, the purchasing firm reimburses the contractor for all costs plus an overhead percentage (usually based on costs) plus a contractor's profit.

Cost-Plus, Fixed Profit   The contractor is reimbursed for all direct costs and for overhead and administration at a predetermined percentage of the labor costs. The contractor's profit is a fixed amount. The profit amount is altered only if the specifications and scope of the job are changed from the original contract agreement. This pricing type can be used for all types of construction in which there are insufficient design specifications to bid a pure fixed price, but the specifications are complete enough to avoid a percentage fee arrangement.

Cost-Plus, Percentage Profit   The contractor is reimbursed for all direct costs plus a percentage of labor costs for overhead and administrative expenses. In addition, a contractor's profit is calculated as a straight percentage of direct cost and overhead. This pricing type is used for construction contracts where work cannot be adequately defined to permit incentives or where the schedule is so tight that a prediction of work conditions is impossible to make. Obviously, this is a risky pricing arrangement for the purchaser.

Cost-Plus, Incentive Profit   The contractor is reimbursed for all costs of labor, material, equipment, and tools, plus a markup on all labor costs to cover administrative expenses, plus an *incentive* profit. The incentive profit is built around a target estimate as part of the contract, in the form of either a target worker-hour figure for the total job or a total dollar target of the cost of labor, materials, tools, and equipment. This type of contract often includes a floor of 60–70% and a ceiling of 110–135% of the target. If the contractor succeeds in billing under the target, they receive a percentage of this difference (usually a specified dollar amount for each hour of labor less than the target, until this figure, when added to the fee, reaches the ceiling). If the contractor exceeds the target, they lose a given amount per hour for all worker hours or costs above the target, until the fee has been reduced to the floor. This pricing arrangement can be used for all types of construction where the percentage of drawings and specifications completed prior to contract establishment is insufficient for a fixed price to be determined and yet sufficient for the contractors to create an accurate target.

Cost-Plus, Upside Maximum   The contractor is reimbursed for all costs, including labor, material, equipment, tools, overhead, and administration, plus a percentage markup on all labor costs and a markup for profit according to the contract schedule of prices. Each contractor on the final contract has three lump sum figures. The most likely figure is called the "target" lump sum, the second figure the "maximum," and the third figure the lump sum "floor." Contractors are paid for all their costs plus a percentage markup for overhead and a markup for profit up to floor (if costs plus overhead and profit are below the floor, there can be a purchaser/contractor sharing of savings). Any additional costs are paid, plus a percentage markup for overhead only from the floor to target; costs only are paid from target to maximum; the purchaser pays nothing above maximum. This pricing arrangement is used for any type of construction where the scope or specification definition is too vague for a guaranteed maximum price but sufficient to avoid a lesser type of incentive contract.

Cost-Plus, Guaranteed Maximum Price (GMP) or Fixed Price Incentive
The contractor is reimbursed for all costs, including labor, material, equipment, tools, overhead, and administration. In addition, they receive a percentage markup on all labor costs and a markup for profit based on the contract schedule of prices, up to a guaranteed maximum dollar amount. If the scope and specifications change during the course of the job, the purchaser and the contractor agree on a new guaranteed maximum; otherwise, the original maximum remains fixed. This pricing type is used for all construction in which a reasonable amount of engineering is performed and the scope is well defined.

Cost-Plus Reimbursable Fee Types
The following two types of contract pricing differ from cost-plus types in that the purchaser pays all direct costs and a fee to the contractor. The fee reimburses the contractor for all indirect costs, administrative overheads, and profit.

Cost-Plus Reimbursable, Fixed Fee
The profit and overhead stay fixed unless there is a major change of scope, and the contract allows for such profit and overhead alteration. The purchaser pays all direct costs as incurred.

Cost-Plus Reimbursable, Incentive Fee
This contract permits the contractor to alter the fee if the work is performed with fewer worker hours or at a lower labor cost than originally calculated. A target for total hours or total labor cost is established for the contract. If the contractor's actual labor cost is less than the target, the fee is increased; if the target is exceeded, the fee is decreased in accordance with a formula agreed on in the contract terms.

Time and Materials
This specialty type of cost contract is structured so that an all-inclusive labor rate is charged for every worker hour of work performed. The rate includes the labor cost, supervision, insurance, taxes, tools, field and home office expenses, and profit. The material factor is the actual cost of materials billed at the price paid by the contractor, less the trade, quantity, and cash discounts. This pricing arrangement is used frequently for pricing extra work that cannot be defined

well in advance or for field work where unknown requirements or conditions may surface during performance of the work.

SELECTING THE PROPER PRICING ALTERNATIVE

The numerous types of construction contract pricing alternatives simply reflect the fact that a wide variety of construction projects are carried out under greatly different operating conditions. Generally, there is no single pricing alternative that is best. The best choice varies depending on the various elements of the project. A key consideration in selecting the pricing alternative is the assignment of risk and the required management controls necessary to minimize risks. Many purchasers are using modeling techniques to assess the risks and opportunities of these types of processes.

THE USE OF MODELING IN CONSTRUCTION PURCHASING

What will that construction project cost? What will it cost to finish that construction job? How much will productivity increase if we install that new equipment in our plant? How many staff-hours will it take to design that new system? In other words, " What is your best estimate?"

Estimating is an integral part of planning, and we do a lot of it. Many of us seem to be on an "estimating merry-go-round." Much of our time is devoted to estimating costs, productivity, profits, and a multitude of other performance measures. And around and around it goes. It very much looks like "the business is estimating."

Doing a good job of estimating brings plaudits and profits. Doing a poor one can bring bankruptcy. It is not surprising, then, that we spend a lot of time and money on estimating. We harness rivers of data. We filter the data. We polish the data. We reflect upon the data. Then, finally, we make our selection of "the right number," holding it up for all the world to see. To all appearances, this number represents our best thinking. But does it? Almost never! Our best thinking can seldom be captured in one number. The sad fact is, no matter how good a job we do, there's one safe bet—the actual cost of the construction project will be different than our estimate. The question is, how much different is it likely to be? Often enough, it's very different, and we end up getting buried under a big cost overrun or having problems with a contractor cutting corners because of problems with the relationship of costs and profits.

Generally, when a cost overrun occurs, particularly a large one, a serious search is begun to pinpoint the reasons. Anyone who had anything to do with the estimate is likely to fall under suspicion. The problem, however, is one of method, not of man. Simply put, our traditional method of estimating construction projects often fails to cope with the realities of the modern world.

The Real World is Not a Spreadsheet

Although it may take the form of an electronic spreadsheet, traditional estimating is nothing more than the application of simple arithmetic. Each item in the estimate is described with one—and only one—number. To arrive at our bottomline estimate, we add, subtract, multiply, and divide these numbers as if they were absolutes (sometimes they take on an almost Biblical importance). But what you see is not what you get. The real world is not as neat and tidy as our spreadsheets. The real world is populated with probabilities and ranges of possibilities, not single-point numbers frozen in time and space just waiting for us to count on them with certitude. In fact, about the only thing we can count on is uncertainty. In other words, the real world is probabilistic. What we need is an analytical technique that comes to grips with this unavoidable fact.

This doesn't mean that our traditional estimating technique should be abandoned. It simply means that once we have completed the estimate, we need to apply an analytical tool which will give us the answers to such vital questions as: What is the probability of success (living up to expectations) in this construction project? If it gets bad, how bad can it get, and if it gets good, how good can it get? (Beware the use of best case, worst case scenarios.) Where should we direct management to spend time to take advantage of minimizing risk or increasing opportunity?

What's Critical and What's Not

Estimating is either conceptual or detailed in nature. If it is preliminary, for order of magnitude, it is classified as conceptual. If it considers low-level details, it is classified as detailed. Whether conceptual or detailed, estimating can be defined as the method we use to forecast the bottomline cost of a project, based upon our forecast of the value of each element that plays a role in determining that bottomline. The traditional estimate contains a "target" estimate for each such element. When all of these targets are combined in the proper arithmetic fashion, they produce a target estimate of the bottomline cost of the project.

The typical estimate has numerous elements. But Pareto's law (the law of the "significant few" and the "insignificant many") tells us that only a few are critical. It is this phenomenon that both sets up the problem and allows us to solve it. Since there are but a few critical elements, it is quite possible that a majority of them will go in the wrong direction and thus lead to a cost overrun. On the other hand, their small number allows us to concentrate our analytical energies on them to see how the project is likely to unfold. But which elements are critical?

In order to decide which elements in the estimate are critical, we first must decide what is critical as far as the project's bottomline cost is concerned. Specifically, what maximum variation in bottomline cost, caused by variation in a single element, are we willing to tolerate? That threshold value is called the critical variance of the bottomline. A substantial amount of empirical evidence indicates that this threshold occurs in the neighborhood of 0.5% in conceptual estimates and 0.2% in detailed estimates. (If the bottomline measures profit rather than cost, the threshold values are approximately 5% and 2%, respectively.) With this rule of thumb, if the bottomline cost of a project in a detailed estimate is $1,000,000, then the critical variance of the bottom line is $2,000.

The critical elements in the estimate can now be identified. Specifically, a critical element is one whose actual value can vary from its target, either favorably or unfavorably, by such a magnitude that the bottomline cost of the project would change by an amount greater than the critical variance. Thus, in the previous example of the $1,000,000 detailed estimate, any element in the estimate that can change the bottomline cost, either favorably or unfavorably, by more than $2,000 is classified as a critical element.

This rule of thumb has been successfully applied in hundreds of projects of all types. They ranged in size from $100,000 to $12 billion, and well over 90% of them had fewer than 30 critical elements each.

It is important to note that the deciding factor in determining criticality is an element's potential for variation, not its magnitude. For example, an element may account for a very large portion of the bottomline cost of the project but have very little or no potential for variation. In other words, the actual value of the element cannot be sufficiently different from its target, either favorably or unfavorably, to produce a bottomline change that is greater than the critical variance. Such an element is noncritical. On the other hand, another element may account for a very small portion of the bottomline cost but can vary from target, either favorably or unfavorably, by such a degree that the bottomline change would be greater than the critical variance. An element such as this is critical.

Uncertainty: Measure It to Manage It

In the real world, the actual value of a critical element can be any of hundreds or thousands of values. For example, if a critical element's target is 16,000 man-hours and its actual value can be anywhere between 14,000 and 20,500 man-hours, then, if we count only the whole numbers, the actual can be any one of 6,501 possibilities, only one of which is the target of 16,000 man-hours. Although there are relatively few critical elements, there is a tremendous number of ways in which their possible values can combine in the real world to produce the actual bottomline cost of the project. For example, if there are just ten critical elements, each with only ten possible values, they can combine in 10 billion possible ways to produce the actual bottomline cost. Is it any wonder our estimates are never right?

In a word, the problem is uncertainty. Uncertainties in the critical elements combine and cascade through the estimate to produce the uncertainty at the bottomline. If this uncertainty is to be dealt with effectively, it must be measured. We are accustomed to measuring all sorts of things. Why then don't we measure uncertainty, the biggest potential killer in most projects? The answer is simple: there has been no easy way to measure it, at least not until the advent of the personal computer.

Range Estimating in Uncertainty

Range estimating picks up where the traditional methods leave off—it tells us the possibility of having a cost overrun, how large the overrun can be, what to do now to eliminate or reduce that risk, and how much contingency to add to our estimate to reduce any residual risk to an acceptable level.

Range estimating does all this by breaking the problem down into its component parts. The uncertainty of each critical element is assessed, and then, with the use of a personal computer, these individual uncertainties are put together in such a way that the uncertainty at the bottom-line can be measured. Surprisingly, the entire process requires only a modest amount of effort. It must be emphasized that range estimating is not an estimating system. It is a decision technology that is employed as an adjunct to traditional estimating.

The Range

As its name implies, range estimating utilizes a simple but effective measure of uncertainty: the range. The range is specified by three parameters: the probability that the element's actual value will be equal to or less than its target, a lowest estimate, and a highest estimate. This is explained in the following example.

An element having a target of $10.05 has the following range: a probability of 75%, a lowest estimate of $7.80, and a highest estimate of $14.35. This means there are 75 chances in 100 that the actual value will be equal to or less than $10.05. (And, indirectly, it also means there are 25 chances in 100 that the actual value will be greater than $10.05.) If the actual value is equal to or less than $10.05, it can be any value from $10.05 down to $7.80. If the actual value is greater than $10.05, it can be any value from $10.06 up to $14.35.

As is apparent in this example, the probability parameter measures the likelihood of an underrun (and, indirectly, the likelihood of an overrun), whereas the lowest and highest estimates measure the degrees of potential underrun and overrun. The lowest and highest estimates form the boundaries of the range. The greater the uncertainty, the farther apart these boundaries and the broader the range.

Specifying the lowest and highest estimates follows a quantitative guideline. Specifically, the lowest estimate is set low enough that there is less than 1 chance in 100 that the actual value can be any lower. Similarly, the highest estimate is set high enough that there is less than 1 chance in 100 that the actual value can be any higher. In other words, the lowest and highest estimates lie beyond the 1st and 99th percentiles, respectively. However, as far as range estimating is concerned, the lowest and highest estimates serve as the outermost boundaries of the range. Looking at it another way, the range is nothing more than a contingency, one that considers potential underruns as well as potential overruns.

Some people have difficulty quantifying probabilities. In such cases, it is often helpful to elicit a qualitative assessment and then translate it into quantitative form. The first step is to ask if it is (likely, unlikely, equally likely as unlikely) that the element's actual value will be equal to or less than its target. In other words, what is the likelihood that the actual value will not overrun the target?

An answer of "equally likely as unlikely" means that the probability is 50%. "Likely" means that the probability is greater than 50% and its specific value must yet be determined. "Unlikely" means that the probability is less than 50% and its specific value must yet be determined. If the answer is "likely," the next step is to ask if it is (somewhat, very, highly, extremely) unlikely that the element's actual value will be equal to or less than its target. "Somewhat" suggests a probability of 40%, "very" 30%, "highly" 20%, and "extremely" 10%. Again, if there is difficulty in making a selection between two qualitative assignments, the corresponding midpoint probability should be used. Thus, if there is difficulty making a choice between "highly" and "extremely," then a probability of 15% is appropriate.

By assessing each critical element in the form of a range, we can better articulate our perception of the future—certainly much better than by mentally wrestling with all the critical elements simultaneously. When specifying the range, we take into account all foreseeable circumstances. This ability to look at critical elements in terms of extremes dampens undue optimism or pessimism and thus encourages realistic assessment of their uncertainties.

Furthermore, range estimating puts the critical element's target into proper perspective. The target is but a single number in a spectrum of possible numbers. The range, no matter how subjective it may be, is far more valuable for decision-making than any single number from within it—including the target. This makes six tons of sense. How could the target, a single number, be as valuable as the range from which it comes? Most of us understand this dangerous deficiency in single-point estimates and, if we are given a choice, make use of ranges to describe the future. Crudely put, by using ranges rather than single targets, we prefer to be approximately right rather than exactly wrong.

There are several PC-based programs that will allow the purchaser to create a model with the contractor. Most of the good construction management firms now use models in project management and evaluation of project processes. These programs are available on the Internet and from software providers.

CONTRACT CONTENT FOR PROTECTION OF THE PURCHASING ORGANIZATION

It is generally best to have two segments to the agreement between the purchasing organization and the contractor. The first is the terms and conditions agreement, which is executed up front during the capital evaluation phase. This provides an umbrella agreement that can cover relationships with the suppliers under any conditions. It should contain the boilerplate and only needs to be executed once. The other segment is the construction contract or contracts between the purchaser and the contractor. The makeup of typical terms and conditions and the construction contract can very well follow a general pattern including the principal segments described below.

Terms and Conditions Agreement

The Recital

It is good protection for the purchaser to describe carefully the parties to the contract, including the company's official location and name. The recital should include a fairly comprehensive description of the project, whether the contract is for specialty work or is a general contract for the entire job. The recital sets the position of the parties in the terms and conditions agreement and sets a standard for all contracts under its umbrella. It puts the burden on the contractor to perform the work in keeping with the purchaser's overall project expectations, whether specifically spelled out in later paragraphs or not.

Method and Manner of Performance

The status of the supervisors and the employees of the contractor must be specified, indicating that they are not employees of the purchasing organization and that the level of competence of the personnel will be subject to approval of the purchaser. This should also be done for any subcontractors or other personnel acquired by the general contractor. The contractor has an obligation to comply with all laws. They must also adhere to reasonable work practices so that adjoining property owners are not annoyed by noise, pollutants, or material hauling operations, etc.; establish adequate protection against fire, theft, and storm damage; and establish and enforce job practices relating to the safety and welfare of employees. This includes adequate training to ensure compliance with all federal, state, and local laws on safety and health.

The contractor must agree to perform its labor relations function in keeping with its labor contract agreement, consistent with actions in the purchaser's best interest. Any overtime practices or retroactive agreements with unions that would be to the purchaser's detriment should be limited to only those approved by the purchaser.

Taxes

A statement regarding the method of handling all taxes in the best interest of the purchasing organization is required. Taxation of construction equipment and some materials varies between states and between the owner and the contractor.

Accounting System

The purchaser should specify the accounting system to be used by the contractor so the final records are compatible with the firm's own system. The contractor should agree to safeguard the purchasing organization's rights with respect to the waiver of liens against the purchased property for any unpaid bills, including those to subcontractors and suppliers.

Changes

The contract should include a mutually agreed-upon system for establishing official changes to the contract. This includes changes in scope and changes in compensation for the contractor.

Assignment of the Contract and Subcontractors

The contract should definitely define the acceptability or unacceptability of the contractor or subcontractor assigning any of the rights of the contract to another third party.

Advertising

The purchaser should reserve the right to approve, prior to release by the contractor, any information about the project. This avoids misleading advertising and protects the purchaser from erroneous statements.

Force Majeure

Since contractors invariably insist on protection from job completion defaults occasioned by acts beyond their control (riots, strikes, acts of God, etc.), it is well to have the exact words of this provision agreed upon by both parties before the job starts.

Arbitration

The purchasing organization should have the privilege of specifying its desires about settlement of disagreements between the purchaser and the contractor through the use of courts of law or perhaps the arbitration process.

Governing Law

It is common practice to include a provision in the contract that says the contract, and the rights, obligations, and liabilities of the parties, should be construed in accordance with the laws of the state in which the purchasing firm is located, or perhaps where the facility is being built.

Equal Employment Opportunity

Without question, the contract should include provisions that require the contractor and all subcontractors to comply with U.S. Executive Order No. 11246, as amended September 24, 1965, and the rules, regulations, and relevant orders from the Secretary of Labor.

Binding Effect of Contract

Once the basic contract provisions are agreed upon, the contract should contain a clause stating that it is binding on both parties and their respective successors, assigns, subcontractors, heirs, executors, administrators, receivers, and other representatives.

Entire Agreement

A statement should be included to the effect that the terms and conditions and the contract, including all its appendices and amendments, constitute the agreements between the parties relative to the project or projects undertaken by the parties and that these agreements supersede any previous agreements or understandings.

Contract Elements

The Scope

A description of the individual contract being awarded. The work to be performed by the contractor should include all specifications, drawings, and other official documents. This includes applicable codes around which the proposal was made and the contract is being formed. It usually includes the technical specification and the general conditions of the contract.

Work to Be Performed by the Purchaser

To enable a complete meeting of the minds for both parties, it should be clear what support the purchasing organization customarily and specifically provides for the contract in question.

Acceptance by Purchasing Organization

This section defines the agreed-upon method by which the purchasing organization both partially and finally accepts the work. For some types of construction jobs, the purchaser needs to assume control of certain parts of the job before the entire job is completed; this is frequently the case when certain types of training are required. Both parties should also agree on the definition of what constitutes final acceptance before payment of any retained compensation.

Title to Work Ownership

A mutually satisfactory statement concerning the timing of the title transfer for the job is important; ownership of materials and equipment is particularly significant. Property taxes are levied by many states on the basis of ownership.

Compensation

The methods used to compensate the contractor must be described completely. This description should be prepared carefully to establish the most practical means of administering the contract, both in the field and the office. Construction contracts contain some provisions, such as retention of payment and partial payment for uninstalled but received goods, that are not normally present in purchase orders for materials and equipment. They are typical in construction contracts, however, and can be made very workable.

Schedule of Payments

The exact timing to which both parties have agreed for submitting invoices or approving deliverables if no invoicing is used and making payments should be stated in the contract. At times it is desirable to pay for some costs such as materials and equipment rentals on a monthly basis and for others such as salaries on a more frequent basis. Reimbursements by the purchaser for payments to subcontractors must also be scheduled.

Contracts that include a fee or separate profit usually define the payment schedule for the fee or profit. Incentive fee or profit contracts should hold back enough of the fee or profit to make necessary adjustments for contractor performance. A retention of 5–10%, depending on the size of the project, is usually considered reasonable. This "hold-back" is to help supply an incentive for the contractor to finish the job as early as possible and avoid errors or omissions.

Termination
When writing a termination or deferment provision to the contract, give careful attention to the numerous details of the physical movement of people and material and the ultimate costs of these activities. It is much better to do this prior to the start of work on the job.

Suspension of Work
It is customary for the purchaser to retain the right to extend the schedule of work to be performed or even to suspend the work and direct the contractor to resume work when appropriate, with equitable adjustment of the contract for added costs caused by the suspension.

Liability
Suitable indemnification of the purchasing organization and the "hold harmless" provision to be furnished by the contractor should be detailed in the contract. If possible, purchasers also frequently attempt to include a provision to the effect that the cost for any rework required due to lack of performance of the contractor will be borne by the contractor. Contractors usually accept this provision only up to the stated dollar limit.

Patent Infringement
The contractor should agree to protect the purchaser from any patent infringements by the equipment suppliers from whom the contractor buys and protect the purchaser against any suits because of contractor-created infringement.

Schedule for Performance of Work
It is the contractor's responsibility to schedule the various components of the job so that requirements can be met without planned overtime. Without a precise, yet realistic, schedule for performance of the work,

important completion dates may not be met and cost overruns may be experienced.

Progress Reports

Monthly (or more frequent) progress reports usually are required from the contractor. The specifics of this provision should be included in the contract.

Standard Construction Industry Contract Forms

Construction purchasers developing contract terms and general conditions for a construction project for the first time would do well to borrow a set previously used successfully for a similar type of project. The American Institute of Architects (AIA) has prepared many standardized contract and general condition forms. One in particular, AIA Document A201, *General Conditions of the Contract for Construction*, includes many of the protective features just discussed. It is also a familiar and accepted document by most construction contractors. When utilized with a project-specific supplemental document developed by the construction purchaser and legal counsel, this can be a very useful document for construction contracting purposes. AIA documents can be obtained by writing to the AIA at 1735 New York Avenue, NW, Washington, DC, 20006.

CONCLUSION

The entire cycle of construction purchasing is clearly an extremely demanding purchasing assignment. Yet, because of the infrequent timing and the magnitude of most construction jobs, the purchasing task is filled with opportunities to provide unique and effective service to the organization. It should be looked at as an opportunity, not a burden.

CHAPTER 38

Transportation and Related Services

Editor
M. Theodore Farris II, Ph.D., C.T.L.
Faculty
University of North Texas

Associate Editors
Deverl Maserang
Corporate Director Routing and Logistics
Pepsi Bottling Group

Terrance L. Pohlen, Ph.D.
Assistant Professor of Business Logistics
College of Business Administration
University of North Florida

James Tognazzini
Facility and Operations Manager
UPS Worldwide Logistics

INTRODUCTION

A 1991 report by the Center for Advanced Purchasing Studies (CAPS) entitled *Purchasing's Involvement in Transportation Decision Making*[1] revealed that over 50% of U.S. purchasing departments have the responsibility for inbound transportation services for their organization. Purchasing can make an outstanding contribution to profits by reducing delivery costs, improving carrier services, lowering inventory carrying costs, and helping to implement Just-in-Time (JIT) systems. This section addresses the buyer's role in purchasing transportation and related services.

From the mid-1970s to the early 1980s, interstate (movement between states) transportation was economically deregulated by the federal government. While a few states deregulated movement within their states (intrastate) in 1980, complete economic deregulation for all states

---

1. J. J. Gentry, *Purchasing's Involvement in Transportation Decision Making,* Center for Advanced Purchasing Studies, Tempe, Arizona, 1991.

occurred in 1995. The economic deregulation of the transportation industry has given buyers more options in selecting the transportation mode and carrier and opened pricing to free market forces.

REDUCING INVENTORIES BY REDUCING VARIABILITY

Reduction of lead times and variability can improve the ability of the firm to plan production on tight schedules, reduce the requirement for protective inventory, and reduce forecasting errors. The necessity to maintain large inventory stocks can be controlled if suppliers and carriers understand the lead-time requirements and work with purchasing to perform within these requirements. Use of express deliveries such as overnight or two-day air transportation can further reduce variability and lead time. Management of transportation services can help facilitate production flows and process improvements.

REDUCING TRANSPORTATION COSTS

Purchasing can influence a firm's bottomline by optimizing transportation services to meet the goals of the firm. Through effective planning and negotiating, purchasing may limit its carrier base and obtain better pricing and services from those carriers meeting the firm's service requirements.

COST TRADE-OFFS AND THE TOTAL COST CONCEPT

Purchasing transportation services requires the purchaser to consider a variety of cost trade-offs, including speed of delivery, accessibility, reliability, damage, inventory carrying costs, lot sizes, and theft. Higher transportation costs may be offset by greater savings in other areas. The purchaser must attempt to optimize service needs to achieve the lowest total cost.

JUST-IN-TIME, QUICK RESPONSE, AND EFFICIENT CONSUMER RESPONSE

For the Just-in-Time process to work effectively, carriers must provide transit time on extremely tight schedules. Deviation from these schedules

can result in substantially higher costs in the process. The carriers selected must be willing to negotiate tight schedules and provide a means
of information flow such as electronic data interchange (EDI) to allow
for tracing of inbound materials and confirmation of scheduled deliveries. The ability of purchasing to negotiate these selective services plays
an important part in implementing a Just-in-Time system. Supporting
quick response (QR) and efficient consumer response (ECR) activities
also require the same characteristics for outbound carriers.

FUNCTIONAL BOUNDARY SPANNING
The Integrated Team Approach

The establishment of a transportation program, no matter what the size
of the company, requires team commitment from within the company,
with information sharing and cooperation between a number of groups,
including senior management. The level of proficiency this program
achieves will depend upon the stability and long-term commitment
brought to the effort. The principles of transportation management are
the same in both large and small firms.

The transportation team typically consists of members from purchasing, transportation and manufacturing, marketing and sales, accounting, production planning, and warehousing. It is important to gain
the support of upper management before the team's activities are established. If upper management does not clearly understand the strategic
benefit gained from the effort, the improved service and the financial
gains may not materialize.

TERMINOLOGY
FOB Terms

If purchasing wishes to firmly establish its authority over shipments,
then freight terms must be specified on the purchase order. The most
common means of obtaining authority is to specify on the purchase order
that the goods are being bought *freight collect*. If a purchaser wants to
take title at the supplier's plant, then the terms *free-on-board* (FOB) *origin
collect* or *FOB shipping point collect* should appear on the order. The FOB
terms of purchase and the carrier payment terms are an important part
of the purchase contract and have a direct bearing on who can and
should exercise control over carrier selection and transportation costs.

The following summary of FOB and freight term (prepaid or collect) definitions and of legal responsibilities for both purchaser and supplier should prove helpful in avoiding controversies and uncertainties that occasionally arise. FOB terms may be broken into two components:

1. Title ownership (or the point at which legal title passes)
2. Responsibility for payment

Title Responsibility

- *FOB origin.* When *FOB origin* is used, the title, or ownership of the goods, passes to the purchaser from the supplier at the moment the goods are transferred to the carrier, with delivery to the carrier constituting delivery to the consignee from a legal point of view.
- *FOB destination.* When *FOB destination* is used, ownership of the goods is transferred at the receiver's dock, plant, or other designated place. The supplier is the owner of goods while in

F I G U R E   38–1

Common Carrier Terms

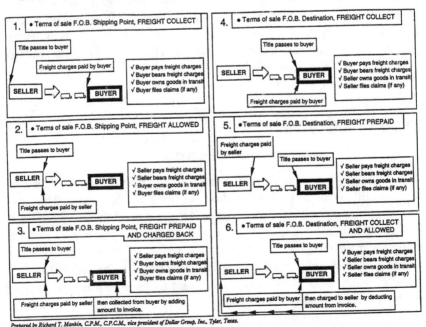

Prepared by Richard T. Mankin, C.P.M., C.P.C.M., vice president of Dollar Group, Inc., Tyler, Texas.

Reprinted with permission, National Association of Purchasing Management, *NAPM Insights*, November 1990, p. 7.

transit and is responsible for any loss or damage up to the time of delivery.

Payment Responsibility

The terms *collect* and *prepaid* are freight payment terms and designate where the carrier sends the freight invoice.

♦ *Freight prepaid. Prepaid* means the supplier will be invoiced by the carrier for the freight charges.

♦ *Freight collect. Collect* means the purchaser or receiver will be invoiced by the carrier for the freight charges. *Driver collect* means that the carrier will not release the goods until the charges are paid to the driver in cash or check. *Cash on delivery* or *collect on delivery* (COD) is the amount the shipper has directed the carrier to collect from the receiver at the time of delivery. A COD amount may or may not include the charges for freight.

♦ *Preferred terms of freight on purchases.* If the product is a private label or brand name of the purchaser's company, the purchasing firm usually wants the title to transfer at the origin so that it will own the goods while in transit. For this type of domestic purchase, the ideal terms are *FOB origin, freight collect.* For other types of purchases, many purchasers prefer to use *FOB destination, freight collect.* This places the burden of claims (loss or damage) on the seller and usually permits the purchaser to specify the carrier to be used.

♦ *FOB variations.* Many variations of these terms are used, based on mutual agreement or negotiation between the purchaser and the supplier. Some common modifications are *freight collect and allowed* (absorbed by supplier), *freight prepaid and charged* (added to the supplier's invoice), and *freight equalized* (with a named competitive shipping point). Any such special agreement does not change the legal stipulation that the title passes wherever designated in connection with the FOB terms.

International FOB Terms

Purchase of material *FOB destination* (delivered duty paid) makes the price comparison with domestic prices easy but does not reveal all the costs added to the price of the product FOB plant, *ex works* (after leaving the supplier's plant) in the foreign country. The ability of the purchasing firm to extract (or unbundle) all these costs in advance of purchase, make a decision to control the movement, and buy at point of manufacture may result in substantial savings to the firm. Most of the activities involved in transporting and importing materials involve firms other than the exporting firm. These firms all add their costs to the final product. The exporting firm adds these costs plus a markup for coordinating these exporting activities to the final price offered to purchasing. If the importing firm wants to avoid this markup and has the ability to negotiate with each party involved, potential savings can be realized.

ESTABLISHING TRANSPORTATION REQUIREMENTS

Analyzing the Transportation Requirements

Transportation costs are inversely related to speed of service. The more quickly the product must be delivered, the higher the transportation cost. Additional services such as special handling will also add to the cost. Analyzing your transportation requirements to determine exactly what level of service, at what speed of delivery, will help you to optimize your transportation expenses. In order to effectively negotiate with carriers, purchasing should first determine the transportation services that are required to obtain delivery of purchased goods, including determining the nature of the goods purchased (size, weight, density, characteristics such as hazardous or requiring special handling, packaging, and delivery schedules) as required by the firm. Physical characteristics such as shipment in bulk, in boxes or on pallets, in gas or liquid form, should be noted before the mode of transportation is selected.

Modes of Transportation

The mode of transportation (air, motor, rail, water, pipeline, intermodal (two or more modes), or small-package services) must be determined. After that, the shipping point or points for the goods must be identified, as well as the volume of goods that will be shipped from each shipping location. The volume shipped should include the total weight, average shipment size, and frequency of shipments.

LTL/LCL Versus TL/CL Carriage

Summarizing the volume of shipments (including weight and frequency from various suppliers located at the same or nearby shipping points to one or more destinations) makes it possible to establish volume "traffic lanes" that are useful in bidding or negotiating a transportation contract. The object is to identify the traffic lanes that exist for those commodities that can be transported by similar equipment, that is, van trailers, containers, trailers on flatcars, boxcars, air cargo containers of boxed or palletized freight, rail tank cars or tank trucks for liquid or gas shipments, and flatbed trucks or rail flatcars for large, heavy equipment that cannot be loaded in enclosed van or boxcar vehicles.

In choosing between truckload (TL) and less-than-truckload (LTL) carriers, a purchaser must pay close attention to the weight and volume (cube density) of shipment and packaging, especially when the weight of a shipment approaches truckload volume. The difference between LTL and TL rates is great; truckload rates usually are at levels well under the common carrier LTL published rates. Additionally, rate differences, often 10–20%, may exist between seemingly similar motor carriers.

Delivery Requirements

Delivery requirements such as one- or two-day delivery will influence the choice of mode and carrier. For example, small, frequent shipments that require follow-up or expediting could be hauled on a timely basis by a regional truck line for short distances, a truckload carrier or intermodal stack train for transcontinental distances, air freight for time-sensitive shipments, or air package for small packages. Each mode and carrier usually offers a different service and price based on the weight, distance, and frequency of the shipments. It is important for a purchaser to know the delivery requirements for each major type of commodity purchased and to discern the existence of traffic lanes created by the shipment patterns before negotiating the desired service between origin and destination points.

Additional Management Opportunities

A carrier's capability to provide the desired transportation service can be determined by researching the available carrier equipment, service schedules, geographic coverage, insurance, tariffs or price lists, and willingness of the carrier to participate in the firm's traffic requirements. This research is usually done by contacting carrier sales and operations personnel or by employing a transportation consultant.

A good place to start the analysis of a firm's transportation requirements is to look at existing records to determine whether traffic lanes already exist. Begin by examining the accounts payable invoice records for carriers already supplying services to the firm. This examination will show the total payments to carriers delivering collect to the firm. Also, freight charges on supplier material invoices should be summarized and added to arrive at the total cost of transportation. Adding outbound prepaid shipment charges to the total will enable a firm's total transportation buying power to be ascertained. It is possible to increase a firm's buying power by redefining the FOB terms of ownership and payment for freight. Working with the firm's transportation department, the purchasing manager can use this combined sum of shipments to consolidate the number of carriers and achieve a lower transportation cost or improve service to the firm. Statistics gathered can be analyzed to reveal suppliers and customers located within a specific proximity by comparing origin and destination zip codes. Matching shipments to a specific area with the firm's plant sites should disclose the total volume of freight moving from the origin area and thus the existence of a traffic lane. If transportation volume is very light or sporadic, then a traffic lane probably does not exist and other locations should be examined. If transportation volume is heavy, a traffic lane will exist and opportunities for consolidation of materials and reduction of freight costs should be pursued.

Freight bill analysis may employ the services of a transportation audit firm or a bank payment service. If asked, the audit firm will capture transportation statistics from the firm's paid freight bills, along with a pre-audit of the invoices, for correct application of freight rates by the carriers. Carrier invoicing has improved but still needs to be audited by trained rate specialists if the firm wishes to pay only the legal charges due the carriers. A rate or price audit should be performed for all carrier invoices, whether from a common or contract carrier.

Once the analysis of the firm's transportation requirements has been completed, selection of carriers may begin. Researching these requirements clearly will strengthen its negotiating position with the carriers and usually will generate better service and pricing arrangements with selected carriers.

CARRIER SELECTION

When the carrier to be named on the purchase order is to be identified, the first step is to determine the service that will best meet the delivery requirements. The mode of transport should be chosen first, then the specific carrier. A conscientious purchaser of transportation thinks constantly about what can be done to have materials delivered in a more economical and effective manner.

The cost of developing, implementing, and monitoring a carrier-selection process is significant but becomes minuscule when compared with the cost of not having a program. With tariff freedom and creativity in the pricing of transportation services, purchasers who control the carrier-selection process are able to obtain a lower total delivered cost for goods. The charges listed on the face of carrier billings may not represent the total cost, due to incentive discounts, rebates, loading allowances, and more complicated pricing structures.

Reliability, consistency, and flexibility are important considerations in studying carriers and modes of transportation. Purchasers can determine such characteristics during their investigations. In addition, determination of a carrier's financial stability is an important part of a purchaser's carrier-selection process. Since deregulation of the industry, many carriers have faced bankruptcy, and purchasers obviously should avoid these firms. Obtain a copy of the previous year's financial statement for each carrier to determine the carrier's assets and debt position. Consider how the carrier finances new equipment and other capital improvements. Look for strong revenues or whether the carrier is in financial difficulty.

One valuable barometer of a carrier's financial health is its claims record. Often one can predict which firm is in trouble by reviewing the speed and difficulty with which claims are settled. Generally, the quicker the settlement, the more secure the supplier of transportation services. The carrier's ability to handle claims quickly and efficiently should always be investigated.

The carrier's organization should be reviewed to indicate how long it has been in business, the number of employees in the company, how many pieces of equipment the carrier has, and the average age of critical equipment such as tractors, locomotives, or containers. Whether the carrier has additional equipment available for use during emergencies or peak periods should also be determined.

Carrier safety and hazardous material programs should be checked to indicate the carrier's commitment to federal and state regulations.

Records should be available revealing accidents, citations, cargo claims, and the amount of time scheduled for safety training. A carrier's training program will give a good indication of the emphasis on safety. Copies of manuals used to correct safety problems should be requested and how these manuals are made available to employees identified.

A perceptive purchaser should also look into a carrier's tracing program and determine whether the carrier has established an EDI or Web-based program for tracking shipments and equipment. The carrier's billing process should be reviewed and the percentage of inaccurate bills determined. The ability to invoice using EDI generally is an asset to the purchasing firm in helping reduce administrative and tracing costs.

It is important to keep in mind that the current trend is to enter into long-term partnering-type relationships with carriers. Companies entering into long-term relationships must take care in selecting their partners. Once a partner is selected and a relationship is established, much of the effort required to complete the above listed activities is minimized.

Carrier Classification

Transportation consultants have divided carriers into four types of service:

1. General-purpose carriers
2. Commodity-type carriers
3. Specialized carriers
4. Bulk carriers

General-Purpose Carriers

Although general-purpose in character, these carriers will often provide a unique service designed to fit a purchaser's specific requirements. Rates are a significant part of the evaluation process. The purchasing strategy should be to standardize the service required and then to use competitive bidding. An example is the carrier industry, which offers either common carrier or contract carrier service to fit the firm's needs. Contracts should be bid and made for one- to two-year periods.

Commodity-Type Carriers

These carriers include volume or commodity-type carriers offering no distinctive service. Because service is interchangeable, achieving the lowest rate is the overwhelming determinant in purchasing these services.

A purchasing strategy for this type of carrier and general-purpose carriers is to consolidate traffic with as few carriers as possible to apply volume leverage. Discussion of this strategy may be found under Managing LTL Shipments below. A good example is the LTL common carrier industry, which normally offers very similar service in scheduled traffic lanes between major urban areas. The services should be bid for periods of one year or more, depending on the bidding schedule of purchasing for its major suppliers.

Specialized Carriers

Specialized carriers are those that have developed specific services based on individual shipper requirements. An example would be carriers used by rigging companies that have trailers capable of handling outsized cargoes such as reactor vessels. These carriers should be selected and evaluated on the basis of the competitive advantage provided and the value added.

Bulk Carriers

An example of this type of carrier would be a tank truck carrier used to transport a hazardous material required for a manufacturing process. Rates are insignificant in dealing with such a carrier due to their specialized and often unique services. Purchasers should develop long-term fixed-price relationships based on mutual trust, shared risk, and reward.

Selecting Motor Carriers

The forces of federal and state economic deregulation have affected motor carriers. Deregulation resulted in a great expansion in the number of truckload motor carriers and a decline in less-than-truckload carriers through bankruptcy and consolidation. Many carriers used the economic regulatory changes to their advantage by focusing operations in specific market niches.

When negotiating with carriers, purchasing should know the carrier's traffic lanes, volumes, and discount schedule. Under certain circumstances, a knowledgeable negotiator can often obtain one rate level for all commodities (FAK-freight-all-kinds), and couple this with competitive discounts.

Selecting Air Carriers

Air freight, including small-package carriers, is viewed as "premium transportation." Its cost per pound is significantly higher than that of other transportation modes. At the same time, savings resulting from speed of delivery may outweigh the additional expense. Purchasers turn to air when shortened transit times or total control in transit is needed or small volumes are shipped. Small-package air carriers have become experts in consistent, efficient, cost-effective delivery of small packages. Purchasers should thoroughly consider the requirements prior to entering into agreements with air carriers. Issues such as "beyond" charges, nondirect points, insurance, and other add-on costs should be investigated. Studies have shown that many premium air freight shipments could have been shipped using lower-cost surface mode and still arrived within the needed time frame.

Selecting Rail Carriers

Movement by rail is recommended with most commodity-type items because they are bulky and are shipped in large volumes. Rail has always held a lead position as far as overall cost per unit weight. Shipping by rail costs less, especially large volumes over long distances, than by truck or air. Movement by water is usually least expensive but gated by accessibility. Truckload carriers are fierce competitors, especially for shipments less than 500 miles. A disadvantage of rail is that shippers may not be able to easily divert a carload of freight from one destination to another in case the desired unloading point changes. Also, obtaining goods in transit in cases of emergency may be inconvenient. These drawbacks must be weighed against the more consistent time schedule that rail provides. Potential damage is a consideration. If freight is not securely blocked and braced, load shifting can cause damage. Knowledge of the materials to be shipped is very important in such cases.

The majority of the rates used by rail carriers today are contract rates, indicating a predetermination of long-term need for rail equipment and services. Tariff rates, however, have not been totally abandoned by rail carriers. Shippers with facilities on only certain lines may be captive to available rail carriers.

Selecting Intermodal Carriers

Goods have been moved by use of one or more modes of freight carriers for many years. The intermodal transportation of goods started in the

1930s with "piggyback" and was considered an alternative to truckload transportation in the transcontinental market. In the 1980s, major technological advances brought substantial changes in the combined use of truck and rail equipment. The most dramatic technological breakthrough came in the form of the "container" and "stack" trains used to transport these containers from a ship at dockside to major inland markets. Instead of trailers with wheels being used, the container box was modified to be transported to customers on a chassis provided by the delivery carriers. The increase in efficiency and the reduced costs allowed the steamship lines and railroads to offer lower intermodal rates and faster service with much less damage by taking advantage of the inherent advantages of each mode of transportation. Purchasers should consider intermodal movements as an important alternative for any truckload or volume movement of materials to their firm.

The railroads still offer the traditional *trailer on flat car* (TOFC) or piggyback service. Service can be very cost-efficient where the rail carriers have a heavy volume of traffic to keep costs low. Purchasers should check with the appropriate rail carrier to see if such service is available. TOFC service could be a major factor in future domestic markets if the railroads find ways to improve the speed and cost of terminal transfers.

Not to be left out of intermodal transportation are the air cargo forwarders and their offers of deferred service using truckload carriers in place of and in combination with aircraft. The service matches the speed of air movements, at much lower rates, and should be considered when one is expediting inbound materials.

INTERNATIONAL CONSIDERATIONS

The principles of purchasing international transportation services are similar to those for domestic purchases. Volume and frequency of shipments, weight and size of each shipment, handling requirements, packaging, and hazardous restrictions play a large part in the final price paid for the transportation service.

Motor and rail carriers are the primary means of transportation for materials from Canada and Mexico. The purchase of materials from foreign countries involves finding a source for the material; arranging for domestic transportation from the manufacturing site to the point of shipment; paying export fees or value-added taxes, if any; arranging for transportation on an international carrier, usually a water carrier or airline offering cargo service; paying import fees (customs duties) if applicable; and arranging for domestic transportation to the point of use.

Foreign Distribution Companies

Negotiating with carriers for domestic transportation in some foreign countries may prove difficult for even the best purchasing or logistics manager. Purchasing should consider dealing with a distribution firm within the exporting country (found with the help of an import broker).

International Carriers

With most exporting countries it is possible to negotiate with an international carrier so that costs can be controlled. Purchasing must contact the carriers within the appropriate mode (water, air, rail, motor) to begin negotiations. It should be noted that prior to 1990, most domestic firms relied on the exporting firm selling the material to make transportation arrangements to the port of importation and tender the freight to domestic carriers. With the increase in speed and ease of communication and travel, a good purchasing department may be able to conduct much of this activity with its own staff or with the assistance of the international carrier and its import broker.

Major water carriers negotiate arrangements with domestic rail carriers to enable them to offer their customers door-to-door transportation from exporting country to final delivery at the customer's facility. If the importing firm has the volume to substantiate intermodal container shipments, the price for the transportation service can be quite low. If purchasing has a large one-time import shipment, it may wish to negotiate (with the help of its import broker) a nonconference water carrier to obtain the best price for the transportation. Nonconference carriers do not belong to the large cartels (called "shipping conferences") that publish tariffs and restrict activities among their members in order to charge higher prices. Some international air carriers and forwarders also offer pick up service in foreign countries and domestic delivery, including help with customs clearance. For small international shipments needed in a short period of time, these air cargo carriers can provide a valid alternative to the slower, less expensive water transportation service.

ESTABLISHING ROUTING

Listing on the Purchase Order

Whenever possible, purchasing should seize the opportunity to select the carrier. It is preferable to show the routing in a space provided on the purchase order form. The routing names the carrier or carriers that will handle the transportation services to the end user. If the purchase order covers a number of shipments or is a blanket purchase order against which a number of releases will be made, the supplier must understand that all shipments should be released to the carrier routing shown on the purchase order.

Routing Letters

An additional action to back up the routing on the purchase order is to send a routing letter to the customer service and traffic departments of the supplier. Often the routing on the purchase order may not be passed from the sales office to the department calling the carrier for pick-up of the purchased material. Such a routing letter should ensure that the correct carrier is used for the shipment, and it can be used as a confirmation of the routing instructions on the purchase order. The carrier routing instruction on the order creates a contract that can be enforced in case the supplier selects a different carrier offering different delivery service or price. Often the supplier will select a carrier based on pick-up convenience rather than on the best service and price to the customer.

ESTABLISHING PRICE FOR SERVICES

Three key variables are used to determine rates:

1. *Handling characteristics.* The carrier will begin the rating process by classifying the freight using a basis of 100. Commodities that are denser and easier to handle will receive a lower classification number. Less dense or difficult-to-handle commodities receive a higher classification number, which will be reflected in a higher rate.

2. *Distance freight is moved.* Rates increase at a decreasing rate as distance increases.

3. *Weight of freight.* As the total weight of a shipment increases, the cost per pound decreases. A shipper may lower total transportation costs by consolidating shipments with a carrier.

These three elements are combined to determine the rate. Rates are generally listed in cents per hundred pounds (cwt). Carriers began to make their tariffs available in electronic form during the late 1980s. The most common means is to provide a personal computer floppy disk containing class rates to their largest shippers. Other means include use of direct inquiry into a carrier's computer mainframe tariff base or use of the Internet. This is done with the use of a security code for each shipper to protect the carrier's confidential information. Purchasing should obtain these easy-to-use forms of tariffs once rates are negotiated with a carrier. A paper copy of each approved tariff agreement used by the buyer firm must be in its file. A file should exist at the firm's facility and also at the office of any pre-audit or post-audit firm used to verify and pay the carrier's charges.

Some express or small-package carriers publish their tariffs for their customers in the form of a rate sheet. These sheets are easy to use and should be kept on file in the purchasing office and in the rate auditor's office. The actual charges used are computed using the zone applied between origin and destination and the weight of the shipment. These charges often apply to small shipments and may be added to the supplier's material invoice if that is instructed by purchasing.

Pricing

When carriers price their service, they must consider the two pricing boundaries of:

1. *Cost of service pricing.* The lower pricing boundary is the price of service. While carriers can survive in the short run by covering their direct costs, over the long run they must cover both variable and fixed expenses. When you are quoted a rate below the cost of service, caution is advised to consider the long-term survival of your carriers, especially if you plan to maintain an ongoing business relationship.

2. *Value of service pricing.* The upper pricing boundary is the value of the service to the shipper. Pricing considers the ability of the freight to bear the higher cost. Rates per pound tend to be higher for higher-valued freight as the freight can more readily absorb the higher cost and still have shipping costs as a lower percentage of the total cost of the item. These higher rates are also held in check by free market forces.

The pricing model for transportation services may be broken into two components. The total of these charges represents the freight bill.

1. *Hauling charges*. Hauling charges represent the cost of physical movement of the freight from one point to another.

2. *Terminal and accessorial charges*. Terminal and accessorial charges represent the cost of loading and unloading and extra handling requirements of the shipment, including COD, delivery to congested areas, redirecting of deliveries, relabeling, or special equipment requirements. These charges will vary by region and class of trade. Each has "accepted practices" that greatly influence charges required or preferred.

NEGOTIATIONS

A purchasing manager should negotiate with a carrier's representative to obtain the lowest class of rates for shipping. A firm may use the services of a transportation consultant to negotiate the class of rates if the firm does not have a transportation manager trained in the classification structure for the material to be transported. This is an important first step because the class of rates for the material sets the level for all rates paid to the carrier.

Once the class of rates is determined, the next step is to obtain the most reasonable discount possible with the carrier. It is the combination of the class rate and the discount that actually determines the charge that the carrier will apply to its invoice once the freight is delivered. *Commodity tariffs* or *freight-all-kind* (FAK) rate tariffs may be negotiated with the carrier for repetitive movements of a given commodity between specified origin and destination points.

ESTABLISHING RULES

In the course of negotiating contracts, carriers may try to insert their rules tariffs in the contracts. There should be no mention of rules tariffs in a contract. These rules tariffs are incorporated into the carrier's bill of lading and can contain some pitfalls that should be avoided in a contract. Such pitfalls may include:

1. Late payment penalties that would force the buying firm to give up its discount

2. Liability limitations that carriers use to claim that freight moved at automatic released rates

3. Inadvertence clauses that state if the carrier inadvertently accepts freight with a value above a certain low limit, its liability will not exceed that low limit

4. Special damages incurred by the purchasing firm as a result of service failure by the carrier are exempted by the carrier tariff

5. Substitute service rules that allow the carrier to substitute other types of service any time it wants—unless purchasing specifically says no

CONTRACTING FOR TRANSPORTATION SERVICES

Contracts with carriers should be negotiated when the firm can generate a substantial and continuous movement of materials in a traffic lane that presents a carrier the opportunity to dedicate equipment to the movement and to offer rates that are profitable but substantially lower than rates found in common carrier tariffs. A contract can also be negotiated to meet the special needs of the purchasing firm, such as a one-time shipment that requires very specialized equipment (an outsized piece of machinery, for example). The purchaser should research existing common carrier class or commodity rates prior to starting negotiations with the carrier or use a transportation consultant or logistics firm with contract experience to assist.

Key Elements of a Transportation Contract

Purchasers should consider the following items when contracting for transportation services.

1. *Disclosure of goods.* Necessary for determining the value of materials shipped. Absence of notice to the carrier about specific goods permits the carrier to avoid paying for damages.

2. *Responsibility of goods.* Defines the basis of liability as well as the process for mitigating damages and claims filing procedures.

3. *Routing, mode, and method of transportation.* Eliminates the chance of the wrong methods or equipment being used.

4. *Responsibility for specification.* Designates which party is responsible for tractors, trailers, containers, and other equipment.

5. *Termination.* Details changes in rates—how, when, what notice is needed, what index they will be to, etc. Defines the escalation and deescalation clauses.

6. *Volume requirements.* Defines the minimum quantity or percent of tonnage of the shipper and the minimum of equipment to be supplied by the carrier.

7. *Scope of transportation.* Defines what transportation service is to be performed—who pays for what?

8. *Operational standards.* Defines safety standards, Environmental Protection Agency (EPA) and HAZMAT (hazardous materials) guidelines, equipment condition, and driver qualifications.

9. *Billing and payment.* Defines what documents will be used, CODs, what constitutes a bill, to whom it is sent, credit period offset damages, billing errors, and right of lien.

10. *Title of goods.* Defines where the title passes, claim responsibility, and other liability matters.

11. *Force majeure.* Defines acts of God and other situations beyond the control of either party.

12. *Conflict with government regulations.* How to handle state versus federal regulations.

13. *Applicable law.* Which state's laws will apply—the purchaser's or the supplier's.

14. *Assignability.* Will you allow it?

15. *Method of changing the contract.* In writing, and to whom?

16. *Notice.*

17. *Effect of failure to comply with the contract.* What constitutes a breach and what is the result of the breach?

18. *Method of resolving disputes.* Arbitration? Damages paid?

19. *Confidentiality.*

20. *Notice regarding carrier insurance.*

MANAGING LTL SHIPMENTS

For most firms, LTL shipments represent the majority of transportation shipments. Cost-reduction efforts should initially focus on LTL shipments. Consolidation of the carrier base and consolidation of shipments are the two most likely methods of cost reduction.

Carrier Reduction

Reducing the number of LTL carriers serving the firm increases shipping volume with the remaining carriers, increasing your importance as a customer. Reducing the number of carriers also relieves dock congestion and may establish closer relationships, simplify routing, tracing, filing claims, and the processing and payment of freight bills. The purchaser is more likely to get rate discounts based on volume and having the service needs fulfilled. Both sides benefit.

Shipment Consolidation

Rates taper with regard to the total weight shipped. The greater the weight shipped, the lower the cost per pound. Consolidation activity reduces rates and offers advantages of volume deliveries, such as less handling en route and less chance of misrouting loss or of damage. Consolidation may take the form of combining shipments into a truckload delivery. An LTL delivery could also be consolidated into a larger LTL delivery, take advantage of the rate taper, and achieve a lower cost per pound. It may be prudent to ask suppliers to consolidate each day's or week's material shipments.

Consolidation in an area where many of the firm's suppliers are located can also be used to gather individual supplier shipments on a daily basis and concentrate these shipments to individual destinations. Regional consolidation is best facilitated by a third-party logistics firm or a transportation broker with the facilities to gather and stage freight on its dock and shop at the direction of purchasing. A broker may ship to one destination with multiple stop-offs en route to the firm's various facilities. Compare the rates and stop-off charges to the multiple LTL charges that would be accumulated for individual shipments.

To determine what service is actually required, purchasing needs to fully discuss needs with manufacturing and warehouse. Delivery dates and supplier production schedules can be matched to determine the required carrier transit times. This will identify when to expedite and when to specify longer transit times. Consolidation and longer shipping times do lead to increased inventory levels, so be sure to evaluate the cost trade-offs and the impact on performance measurements.

MANAGING EXPRESS OR SMALL-PACKAGE SHIPMENTS

Purchasing is often under pressure to obtain next-day delivery. The ability to obtain this service depends upon the supplier's ability to ship the material the same or next day and the carrier's ability to deliver the next morning.

Air freight carriers that own their own planes and ground service are known as integrated carriers. These carriers offer various levels of service: same-day, next-day, second-day, or deferred service, which is slower and may even move by other modes of transportation such as truckload. Purchasing should know that these services are available and that the carrier uses other modes to reduce costs. The same air freight charges may apply even if the mode used is different than what is expected. Knowledge of the one- and two-day coverage areas of small-package carriers is important for attempting to reduce air freight charges.

Reducing Costs

It is important to note that one of the most economical ways to increase service and reduce cost is to know the carrier's service area coverage. Service area maps may be obtained from each carrier that highlight the number of days it takes a carrier to deliver a shipment to a destination from a given origin. The major carriers move most of their next-day and second-day air shipments using surface transportation. Depending upon various cutoff times by location, the purchaser can request late pick-ups and have the shipment arrive at the destination by the next day at ground rates.

Shipment Consolidation

Shipment consolidation, commonly known as "drop shipping," is an excellent method of reducing cost and receiving a unique level of service. The carrier will request the shipper to split the shipments into groups based on zip codes. These loads will then be sent to a drop location and processed through the carrier's system. One of the primary advantages of drop shipping is the potential for lower damage as a result of less handling by the carrier. In many instances, if the shipper has a large number of shipments to be shipped, transit times may be reduced. The loads may be moved by an expedited driver team and dropped into one of the carrier facilities, thus reducing the number of days in transit. There are currently models developed by the major carriers that can provide the shipper custom solutions to enable shipment anywhere in the continental United States in three days or less. These special types of services typically require a minimum number of shipments per day to qualify. Some carriers specialize in shipment consolidation for smaller shippers and are referred to as "consolidators." Consolidators provide various levels of service to assist the shipper in developing a consolidation program that best fits their needs.

Corporate Contracts

The best-known express carriers concentrate on transporting small parcels of under 150 pounds, but they also offer their services for much heavier weights. Their rates vary considerably, depending on whether the service is next-day or second-day. Also offering these express services are air freight forwarders that own no equipment but buy the services of other express carriers or use belly space offered by the major airlines. These forwarders also use the services of truckload carriers that provide next-day service within a specified time. The rates offered by all these express carriers are high compared with those offered by any other type of carrier. These carriers should be used with discretion, for their service can result in transportation costs that exceed the cost of the material purchased.

The largest small-package carrier is also an express carrier offering several levels of service—next-day, second-day, three-day, and ground (up to five days) to most destinations in the country. The rates for these services are fixed at known levels, except for the very largest of shippers. The rates offered by small-package carriers should be compared with those offered by other express carriers before the supplier is instructed to ship "prepaid and add." The small-package industry traditionally insists that shippers be billed for their services, forcing suppliers to add these freight charges to their material invoices. New conventions, however, allow for consignee billing or COD services.

The small-package service is a convenient means to deliver small packages weighing less than 150 pounds to most destinations within five service days. The rates for this service are listed on a rate sheet and are easy to calculate and add to the supplier's invoice. When purchasing requests that the supplier use small-package carriers, it should also ask the accounts payable manager to capture the freight charges added to all the commercial invoices received by the firm. The purchasing manager should know the total freight paid to small-package carriers through the *prepaid-and-add* system. An analysis of these charges and service may reveal opportunities to reduce these freight costs by having the supplier perform a dock consolidation or taking advantage of other programs offered by competitive carriers.

Other Types of Express Carriers

When purchasing next-day service, a purchaser should remember that many regional or intrastate LTL carriers offer next-day service to many of their customers. This daily service should be considered because of its reasonable rate level and the carrier's ability to match the service of any express carrier in its primary market. The truckload carriers can also provide next-day delivery, often to customers that are within 500 miles of their suppliers. This range may be extended to 1,000 miles by the carrier's using team drivers on its equipment. The air freight forwarders have long been aware of this service and have substituted it for that provided by air cargo carriers.

TRACING AND EXPEDITING

Shipments may require tracing or need to be expedited. The first step in tracing is to determine that the material was shipped and what carrier was used. The supplier's customer service office can supply this information. The date of shipment and the carrier's pro number (for a truck shipment) or waybill or car number (for a rail shipment) must be determined to successfully trace a shipment. A word of caution: if the shipping information is not available and purchasing is told that the material was shipped, a call should be made to the origin carrier to determine if a pick-up was actually made or, if by rail, if the car was pulled from the siding. If not, the supplier's sales department should be immediately contacted.

Once it has been established that the material is in transit, the carrier should be contacted to determine where the material is in its system and the carrier may be able to expedite the shipment. Most major carriers provide this information electronically by offering access to their computer systems by phone or computer modem or via a Web page. Tracing can be done by entering the customer's security code to gain access to the computer and then entering the correct inquiry code to locate the missing shipment or car. Not all carriers have EDI or Web-based tracking capability; in such cases, the more laborious method of tracing by phone must be initiated.

EVALUATION OF PERFORMANCE

The effort by purchasing to ensure delivery of materials when needed and to optimize inventories depends on the timeliness and reliability by the carriers. Many carriers now provide a monthly service report for a customer summarized by supplier and state of origin that may contain invoice information, shipment times, and delivery date information. For the contract carriers serving the firm with contracted transit times, a report should be submitted by the carrier summarizing all activity on a monthly basis or as requested by the purchasing department. If the carrier is not capable of performing this summary, the transit data will need to be captured by the receiving facilities and submitted for evaluation to purchasing.

The performance report should be reviewed in a timely fashion to ensure that actual carrier performance matches desired performance. Performance review should include the transit performance between the supplier's and the firm's facilities, equipment utilized, billing accuracy, claims occurrence, pick-up and delivery schedule performance, rate negotiation service, sales representative information and follow-up, and any new technology or innovative service offered by the carrier.

PAYMENT AND AUDITING FREIGHT INVOICES

The majority of firms, both large and small, still process their own freight invoices. This activity requires a check for duplicate billing and an audit of the rates. A common method to assess the effectiveness of in-house operations is to have several months' freight bills sent to a post-audit company for an audit after payment. A post-auditor takes a negotiated percentage of all claims paid by the carriers and returns the rest to the firm requesting the service. If the post-audit returns a considerable number of claims, action should be taken to employ a pre-audit firm and payment service to reduce the number of mistakes.

The cost of auditing services should be negotiated on bid as for hiring any other service. An audit summary report should be provided indicating the number of freight bills processed, the number of invoices reduced through the pre-audit, the number of duplicate bills received from each carrier, and the total amount owed to the pre-audit firm for this activity plus any special reports. Usually the cost savings resulting from freight invoice reductions and duplicate rejections will substantially exceed the cost of the auditing firm.

Shortened Statute of Limitations

Freight bill audits should occur on a regularly scheduled basis. The Negotiated Rates Act of 1993 limits the statute of limitations for freight bills to 180 days. Once an audit firm has been sourced, audits should be scheduled on a regular basis.

CLAIMS, ANALYSIS, AND PROCESSING

Over, Short, Wrong, and Damaged Goods

Managing shipments includes dealing with claims for over, short, or wrong goods shipped by the supplier or damaged goods delivered by the carrier. If either carrier or supplier fails in their efforts, purchasing becomes involved in the claims process. It is often difficult to distinguish between the need to file a claim against the supplier and the need to file against the carrier. Material delivered short can be the fault of either party. If the supplier shipped short, the claim will be against the supplier because the quantity inside the carton or package is short of the correct quantity. However, if the carton or package shows damage that may have allowed a quantity of material to fall out or be lost, the claim should be filed with the carrier. To help you assess responsibility, your dock personnel must note any damage to packages or quantities that are short when delivered by the carrier and attempt to assess the cause. Training dock personnel to properly receive material upon delivery by the carrier is very important if claims are to be successfully processed against a carrier.

Filing Claims

The carrier must make note of noticeable damage at time of delivery. A claim for concealed damage may be filed against the carrier but must involve inspection by the carrier's representative. For concealed damage discovered after the cartons are opened, it is necessary to set the cartons aside and have the carrier's representative come and inspect the damage. Pictures may be taken and kept as evidence of the damage. The carrier's inspection form left by the representative must be included with other documentation when the claim is submitted. It is the carrier's responsibility to acknowledge the claim and assign a number for claim processing. It is the purchasing firm's responsibility (FOB origin) to mitigate the damage done by the carrier in terms of making repairs to return the material to original condition. These repair costs will become the final amount of the claim. If no repairs can be made and the firm suffers a total loss, the entire value of the damaged shipment must be submitted as the claim value.

When first submitting the claim, it is best to submit the claim for the entire value of the goods until the actual repair costs are known. In this way, the claim can be submitted quickly and not delayed, possibly missing the legal limit for claim filing. Later submittal of actual repair costs will not diminish the validity of the claim. Claim forms can be obtained from all carriers. If no notation of damage or shortage is made on the carrier's delivery receipt at time of delivery, there is no basis for claim against the carrier if shortages are discovered later.

Losses

When goods are lost by the carrier, the carrier has the responsibility to communicate to the shipper and the receiver that the goods have been lost in transit. Unfortunately, most carriers are not very responsive in making this information available. The carrier's waybill number (if a rail carrier), pro number (if a motor carrier), or tracking number (if a small package carrier) must be obtained in order for a tracing action with the carrier to be initiated in an attempt to locate the material. Most suppliers usually will help in this process. If the carrier cannot find the material, a claim should be filed at once. If the material is permanently lost, the value of the claim will be the value of the material plus the value of the transportation service. The transportation charges on the freight bill can be used as the value of the transportation.

Overshipment

If a carrier delivers more material than is specified on the delivery receipt or invoiced by the supplier, purchasing should first inquire with the supplier to determine whether an intentional overshipment was made. If this is the case, the purchasing firm can choose to keep the extra material and pay for it or return it to the supplier. Any returns should be sent *collect*. If the carrier included material with the delivery that was not intended for the purchasing firm, the purchaser must notify the carrier to pick up the material and deliver it to the rightful owner.

OUTSOURCING TRANSPORTATION ACTIVITIES

Purchasing may desire to gain control of its transportation operations but simply not have the time or support personnel to devote to the task. If transportation services have not previously been managed (inbound, outbound, or both), savings will likely result. Companies lacking the resources to manage their transportation services should explore the opportunities of outsourcing these activities to a third-party provider.

Using Transportation Brokers and Freight Forwarders

A freight forwarder can consolidate many shipments for its customers to achieve substantial freight savings. The forwarder can perform the entire service of pick-up, transit, and delivery and should have facilities at both origin and destination to be effective.

Using Third-Party Providers

Another route to follow if the firm decides to outsource transportation services is to select a third-party logistics company to perform the day-to-day task of monitoring carrier activity. To eliminate the temptation to increase the freight bill to increase the return to the provider, it is best to pay an agreed-upon rate per shipment instead of a percentage of the freight bill. The contract with the provider should include a statement that the provider will receive no payment from the carriers as part of their agreement to provide transportation services for the firm.

TRANSPORTATION CONSULTANTS

Many purchasing managers have turned to transportation consultants to explore opportunities to improve areas in which they have little expertise. Consultants should possess the necessary experience in analyzing a firm's needs and constructing a program to gain control of the carrier selection and routing process. Often these consultants begin in the accounts payable area to gain an understanding of the freight charges being paid by the firm.

The selection of a transportation consultant is similar to the purchase of any service. Criteria must outline exactly which areas of the firm the consultant will work in and who will be in charge of the consultant's activities. As part of the firm's goals for the consultant, a stated reduction in freight charges for the same volume of freight should be agreed upon in advance by both parties. Also, a pre-audit and post-audit of all freight charges added to supplier invoices should be established. Traffic lane reports and carrier reports showing all activity by carrier should be developed so that purchasing has a monthly and annual summary of all transportation to use as a basis for further improvement in managing transportation.

Quality measurement is an important aspect to the purchasing function. The consultant should develop a series of reports to reflect carrier billing accuracy, transit times, claims volume and claims service, sales response, and an evaluation survey that can be used to gather input from all the firm's receiving facilities on carrier delivery service and overall performance. A file should be established for each of the firm's major carriers.

RELATED TRANSPORTATION SERVICES
Household Goods Movement

Selecting carriers for household goods involves much of the same preparation as for materials movement. The volume of moves for the forthcoming year should be projected by each department of the firm and totaled to arrive at an estimate of expenses for the movement of household goods. The carriers will want to know the volume of expected movements and the principal lanes of traffic in which the moves will take place.

If the firm desires to have the carrier pack all household goods and store these goods when required, this element must be included in the contract negotiations. Individual prices for each carrier activity must be established. Rates for furniture movement automatically include released liability to the carrier of 60 cents per pound, so additional insurance should be negotiated to provide full coverage. Special services, such as delivering goods to a second- or third-story building, should be defined and an accessorial price quoted by the carrier in the contract terms. The handling of claims and the claims process should be clearly defined. Any damage to an employee's personal property must be handled quickly and with a great deal of sensitivity. The total carrier liability for claims for each move and the terms and cost of the insurance policy should be stated in the contract. Some firms insist, as part of the contract, that, when moving household goods, the carrier utilize only drivers who are listed among the top 50% in terms of reliability and performance. The household goods carrier should also be expected to provide information on the new area where the employee and family will live. This service makes the transition for the family a little easier and aids the employee in starting the new job knowing the family is well situated.

Corporate Travel Services

Travel Policy and Requirements

To effectively negotiate with the passenger carriers, a manager must know the firm's travel policy and the expected travel requirements for the next year. Statistics for the past year may be gathered from the travel agencies presently handling the ticketing function and from accounting records of travel expenses paid to the firm's employees. Current travel budgets for all the firm's departments may be summed to project travel requirements for the coming year. Records of flights taken in the past will show the travel activity of employees, including origins, destinations, frequency of flights, and which airlines were used. Purchasing should seek airlines willing to offer lower fares in order to obtain most of the firm's travel business.

The manager should have the full support of top management when the company commits to a volume-based discount contract with a particular carrier. Employees need to be informed of the selected carrier and encouraged to make use of this carrier.

Air Travel

Preparation for a successful airline passenger program includes:

1. Consolidation of all travel under one travel agency
2. Accurate data on travel activities

3. Confidential handling of airline contracts
4. A strong travel policy, endorsed by top management, directing business trips to designated airlines.

The consolidation of company travel with one agency provides complete travel data by documenting where all company travelers go and capturing total volume statistics. It also provides necessary confidentiality by limiting the number of people who need to know the terms of the carrier contract. Airlines are extremely sensitive about discount contracts being kept confidential because their marketing tactics can be negated if they are known to their competitors.

CHAPTER 39

Purchasing in the Service Industry

Updated for Sixth Edition by
Joseph A. Yacura
Senior Vice President, Worldwide Procurement
American Express

Fifth Edition Editor*
Donna Lynes-Miller, C.P.M.
President, Arcop, Inc.

Fifth Edition Associate Editors*
Nancy C. Cummings, C.P.M.
Purchasing Manager,
American Airlines, Inc.

Gary C. Fraker, C.P.M.
Vice President Purchasing
Sportservice Corporation

John S. Nagle
Manager, Purchasing Maintenance, Equipment & Supplies,
American Airlines, Inc.

Charles E. Page, Jr., C.P.M.
Vice President,
Corporate Purchasing Division,
Dominion Bankshares Corporation

Alex J. Vallas, C.P.M.
Director of Materials Management,
Magee-Women's Hospital

Buying has been an integral part of commerce since the earliest days of trading. The buyers were also most likely the sellers, as they bought and sold necessities and treasures around the world.

When developing nations moved from agrarian to industrial economies, producers of goods began to recognize the need for sound buying

---

* Titles as of time of printing of the 5th edition.

practices. There most likely was not a purchasing executive with a well-defined job description, but someone within those early organizations recognized the bottom line benefits of efficient materials management.

The growth in the service sector of many economies is at a faster rate than in the manufacturing sectors. New services are being created at a rapid pace as parts of the developed countries move further away from a manufacturing to a service-based economy. These new service industries, along with less vertical integration in manufacturing companies, have elevated the importance of the service sector.

While manufacturing companies were defining and organizing the purchasing and supply function, service companies also were recognizing the need to formalize the purchasing function. This chapter discusses some of the purchasing techniques employed by companies in the service industry.

ORGANIZATIONAL STRUCTURE

Over the past several years, much attention has been given to the question of where purchasing should report in the organization. The answer is not consistent. Most purchasing executives value their position in the corporate hierarchy and would prefer to report to the chief executive officer (CEO) along with their marketing and operations peers. However, few do. Purchasing executives can be found reporting to marketing, finance, administration, or operations departments. In the service industries in particular, many procurement/supply management functions report to the chief financial officer (CFO).

The rationale for who reports to whom is more often a function of culture than of logic. We cannot and should not expect consistency. We should, however, expect the function to gain the respect it deserves and eventually report to the CEO.

One emphasis of American business in the 2000s will be on Total Quality Management (TQM) and creating value for the company and its customers. The main component of TQM is emphasis on team building. The team consists of the customer, the supplier, and the supply line management professional.

CHARACTERISTICS OF DEMAND

Service companies rarely experience stable demand for many of their product and/or service needs. Short life cycles and a boom-or-bust syndrome are the norms for items typically handled. Materials supporting products or promotions intended for limited duration are characteristic of the service industry, and the phrase "while supplies last" is frequently heard.

Variations on this theme may cover multiple deliveries, prior to or during the life of the item. Negotiating options for additional quantities with the most favorable terms, along with options to cancel the entire contract at some point, are issues to be considered by a forward-thinking purchaser who protects company interests.

The single most outstanding characteristic of these limited-life-cycle items is that their usages are based not on any past history but rather on market surveys, projections, and estimates, whose accuracy is based on some degree of conjecture. The purchaser's job becomes more difficult as he or she is forced to operate in gray areas.

Service industries have material needs that are as important as those of their manufacturing counterparts. While these items may generate a less pronounced financial impact, their results are no less important. Adequate supplies of computers, software, network routers, point of sale terminals, and test equipment are examples of critical items used by service industries. Adequate supplies of properly sized drinking cups, envelopes with accurately placed glue strips, and grocery bags in ample amounts are examples of inexpensive items on a unit-cost basis that, when missing, send the wrong message to customers. These are examples with more constancy in their usage, and a key to survival and prosperity in the service industry is the purchaser's ability to recognize the difference between these and their less stable counterparts. The buyer must utilize all available data in managing these items, including emphasis on inventory handling and cycle counting.

SUPPLIER SELECTION

Traditional points of evaluation in supplier selection include quality, service, and price. New areas for consideration in supplier selection for service industries include value attributes such as adaptability, ease of use, access, and compatibility. Although traditional buyer–seller relationships are changing, all aspects should be considered before a relationship begins. The work relationship carries the implication that the purchaser and seller are partners and have similar objectives and a level of mutual respect and understanding.

Any number of recent business articles reference this shift in outlook to "ongoing buyer–seller relationships." The concept of "partners" is not new, but it has not achieved the level in the United States that it has among our foreign competitors. The most vivid example is the combination of Fred Astaire and Ginger Rogers. Both were committed to achieving a common goal. Both were willing to practice and forgive the other's missteps while on their way to reaching success. The successful partner relationships of the 21st century will need these same basics as a foundation. Three elements cover these relationships: capability, capacity, and credit.

Capability

Simply put, can the supplier do what it says it can? Does it have the resources to perform? Can it summon the necessary subcontractor support? Does it have access to adequate raw-material sources? Does it have environmental problems that may interrupt any dealings? Are its engineering and design people up to the task? How do its service and training people measure up?

Capacity

Will the supplier do what it says it will? Can it perform to schedule? If a large commitment overloads the organization, who will decide which order goes first? Small suppliers trying to increase volumes may promise deliveries they cannot possibly make. Thorough research in this area may save needless supply interruptions.

Credit

The financial side of the service business is becoming increasingly important. Will the prospective company be around next month, next year, or five years from now? Leveraged buy-outs, acquisitions, spin-offs, and outright bankruptcies are quite common. The ability to see financial trouble ahead with your suppliers will save hours of looking for replacement sources. The ability to read, decipher, and understand a financial statement will pay great dividends. Know about performance bonds and their cost. Know the legal status of your key suppliers. Are they sole proprietorships, corporations, or partnerships?

PAYMENT METHODS

Payment terms are one of the most important topics negotiated by purchasing and supply professionals. Most major texts cover the subject adequately, so only a brief review will be given here. As these methods become fair game for negotiation, most purchasing professionals now include them on their agenda along with prices and deliveries.

Net/30 is one of the most widely used terms, indicating that net payment is due 30 days after receipt of goods. Somewhat less popular terms are *net/20* and *net/10*, covering times of 20 and 10 days, respectively. Different service industries sometimes have terms peculiar to that industry. The beginning purchaser should become acquainted with accepted industry terms before becoming involved in negotiations.

Discounted terms are attractive to both purchaser and supplier because both interests are served by increasing the velocity of cash. Again, industry peculiarities prevail and should be reviewed. The term *2%/10, net/30* indicates that the purchaser may discount the invoice by 2% if remittance is made in 10 days; otherwise the total amount is due in 30 days. A variation on this is *1%/10, net/30*. The paper industry continues to offer terms similar to these. In general, terms are limited only by the imagination of both purchaser and supplier.

The importance of discount terms lies in the value of the money being used. Not taking advantage of a 2%/10, net/30 invoice in effect borrows the invoiced sum from the seller at an annual gross percentage rate of 36½%, a handsome rate indeed, and one significant enough to make any corporate treasurer sit up and take notice. Even 1%/10, net/30 equals 18%, usually in excess of the prime lending rate. The power of discounts is obvious, and they should be kept high on the list of important factors considered by purchasing professionals.

International trade differs from domestic in a number of respects; one focus is on currency exchange. United States dollars are generally accepted worldwide and probably will continue to be. British pounds, Euros, and Japanese yen also are acceptable, depending on the wishes of the parties in any given transaction. The international department of a commercial bank is a good source of help about current values and exchange rates. This advice is sometimes free, even to new customers.

Electronic data interchange (EDI) is used by many organizations, and its unique characteristics offer some promise in breaking the paper logjam. Currently a number of purchasers and suppliers use EDI to transmit purchase orders, acknowledgments, releases, shipping confirmations, and related documents. They are sent through value-added networks (VANs), which are simply electronic switching stations or mailboxes. The mechanisms exist for purchasers and suppliers to transmit their funds similarly. Consumers can use their bank cards to withdraw money from automated teller machines practically anywhere, with their own accounts being charged. The mechanism to perform commercial transactions is similar and offers significant promise for both purchaser and supplier. These types of transactions obviously eliminate the clearing times involved with mailing checks.

Purchasing cards have also gained acceptance in recent years as an alternative payment vehicle. Some card systems provide considerable data capture that can be utilized by the supply line management organization to analyze what had traditionally been bypass activity around the supply line management organization. Some cards also have a "preferred supplier" capability. This selective capability can ensure contract compliance and prevent the card user from going to noncontracted suppliers.

With the cost of funding becoming more of a factor, every advantage must be leveraged, and a smarter use of funding can be an advantage. More favorable terms can be negotiated because electronic transactions guarantee that funds are available on the negotiated date—no more waiting for the postal service and checking postmarks to ensure that the purchaser observed the correct date for the discount! Purchasers and suppliers both may have something to gain by implementing EDI payment transactions.

Payment terms may prove to be a fruitful area for gaining concessions and even improving a supplier's performance. Negotiate payment terms in good faith and live up to what you agree to. Your overall leverage will increase as you become known as one with financial knowledge.

VALUE ANALYSIS IN THE SERVICE INDUSTRY

The application of value-analysis systems and techniques is more narrowly defined in service industries because, by their very nature, these companies are usually not directly involved in the engineering design and manufacturing of products. Consequently, studies are approached from the user, buyer, or consumer perspective. However, the ultimate objective is the same: to identify a function and determine the most economical and efficient method to accomplish that function by eliminating unnecessary costs that do not add value to the product or service being purchased.

Value-analysis techniques are not restricted to purchased goods and can easily be applied to improving the methods by which a service is provided. For example, when analyzing the function of taking temperatures, a hospital can evaluate numerous alternatives to determine the most efficient and economical method to accomplish this function. The process could involve examining and isolating the different costs associated with glass, electronic, one-time-use plastic, and battery-operated thermometers. Among the cost factors to consider would be nursing time associated with taking temperatures, theft and loss, cleaning and handling, breakage and usage, inventory and distribution, accuracy, and the possible effects of infection through cross-contamination.

PREPARING AND ANALYZING BIDS

Preparing and analyzing bids is a basic required purchasing skill for both industrial and service organizations. For example, American Airlines purchases and consumes enormous amounts of materials, products, and supplies and relies heavily upon many different outside service companies to support its worldwide operation. Accordingly, the purchasing practices employed by the company must be responsive, streamlined, and effective. They must ensure that all needed support is provided reliably and quickly while still achieving the best price and value for the corporation.

The competitive bidding process is the preferred and most commonly used method to establish competitive price levels and select suppliers for the products and services purchased throughout the company.

The bidding process may be utilized when the financial value of a transaction exceeds $20,000 or any other designated relative value. Items of a lesser value may be purchased directly from a reputable supplier without using a bid process. Sole-source items obviously are excluded, and determination of price fairness is left to negotiations. Figure 39–1 presents the criteria used to determine when to use the bid process.

The complexity of the bidding process varies widely, depending upon the value, nature, and availability of the item, product, or service to be purchased, e.g., standard finished goods versus custom-designed

FIGURE 39–1

Criteria to Determine When to Use the Bid Process

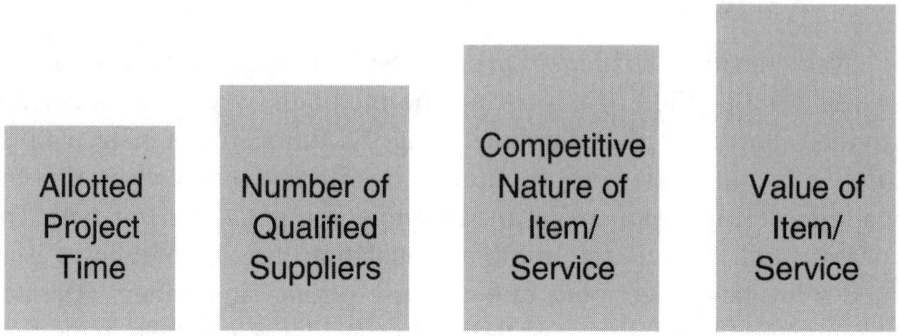

Allotted Project Time	Number of Qualified Suppliers	Competitive Nature of Item/ Service	Value of Item/ Service

items or specialized highly technical services. In all cases, careful attention must be given to developing practical and accurate specifications for the item or service to be sourced. This process requires close cooperation and a spirit of constructive teamwork between representatives of the organization requiring the item, the purchasing department, and the supplier community. Box 39–1 is a listing of the steps in one firm's bid process.

The statement "you get what you pay for" could be reversed to "you pay for what you get" when it relates to the importance of developing practical specifications. The users, purchasers, and suppliers all must clearly understand the function of the product or service in order to ensure that the item selected is of adequate quality to meet the need. Overspec-ing an item results in needless expense; the reverse also is true.

NATIONAL AND INTERNATIONAL CONTRACT ITEMS

Standardized goods and services that are commonly used throughout a national or international company are consolidated and competitively sourced by most corporate purchasing departments. They are ultimately placed on a national or international contract. This permits all user groups to requisition these items directly from the supplier at predetermined contract prices and terms without rebidding each time the item is needed. Nonstandardized requirements may be handled on an individual basis.

B O X   39-1

Example of the Flow of Preparing and Analyzing Bids (for American Airlines)

I. Need origination and specification
  A. Need originates from sponsor or user group.
  B. Purchasing assists with developing specifications and information concerning need, i.e., time frame requirements, volumes, and a picture of what, who, why, when, where, and how product or service is to be used.

II. Considerations
  A. Is product or service readily available?
  B. Consider whether to make or buy.
  C. Develop qualified supplier list.
  D. Obtain technical support or industry specs if available. Ask for engineering support if needed.
  E. Prepare final specifications.
  F. Prebid conference with qualified suppliers, users, etc. Consider partnership approach.

III. Preparation of bid packet
  A. Include specifications on product, volume requirements, shipping destinations, pricing structure needed, length of contract, and scope of service.
  B. Request supplier volume discounts or manufacturing methods which may decrease costs. Use expertise available by leaving open areas for consideration.

IV. Release of invitation to bid
  A. State response time needed, e.g., 1–2 weeks depending on complexity of bid for bid to be returned.

V. Document review and bid analysis
  A. Record the date the bid is received.
  B. Compare bid documents received with supplier bid list.
  C. Contact suppliers who have not responded with a bid document at bid closing to confirm their intentions.
  D. Authenticate bid content.
    1. Did bid actually address specifications and respond to *all issues*, and is it signed?
    2. Are volumes, prices, and extended value mathematically correct?
    3. Note any supplier comments, questions, issues, and recommendations outside the basic quotation request.

B O X   39–1

Continued

    E. Extensive analysis
      1. Prepare a spreadsheet to permit comparison of all standardized bid criteria.
      2. Determine if any bid prices appear too high or too low compared to others.
      3. Review subjective factors—geographical location, technical expertise, value-added services, special terms or services.
      4. Identify other issues beyond basic specifications whereby the supplier adds value or differentiation as compared to proposals of other bidders, i.e., increased warranty, barter.
VI. Final analysis and conclusion
    A. Prepare cost analysis from supplier cost data.
    B. Prepare price analysis and summary of all relevant issues.
    C. Conduct postbid conference plus address any open issues.
    D. Prepare bid award recommendation and financial summaries for joint review with management of the using department.
    E. Award contract to mutually (user and purchasing) agreed upon best-value supplier.

Note: If an irreconcilable dispute exists between the purchasing department and the user over best-value supplier selection, all financial data may be presented to an appropriate level of higher management for resolution. The using department generally retains final authority concerning supplier selection. This further reinforces the need for a spirit of teamwork, cooperation, and mutual respect between the using departments and the purchasing organization.

PRESALE AND POSTSALE SERVICE

The most important contemporary changes in most corporate purchasing departments are the recognition that *value* is more important than *price* and that *partner* is more important than *supplier*.

We no longer can conduct our business effectively in the adversarial, competitive bidding mode with a fraternity of cautious, guarded, self-interested suppliers who understand only their products, not their customer's operational requirements or the final customer's needs. Purchasing energies have been redirected to cultivate strategic, high-quality, full-service suppliers and to incorporate their strength, expertise, and assistance in our own *procurement* activities.

This involves a more open and candid exchange of information with potential suppliers and an expansion of service expectations to include much more than a simple description of the product requirement. The buyer–seller relationship goes beyond the mere selling and buying of the product or service. The relationship now encompasses presale services, such as engineering assistance and prototype testing.

The new relationship also includes expanded postsale services such as extended warranties, supplier warehousing of spare parts, final disposal of the product, and training. These services may continue until the product or equipment is ultimately retired. The modern complexities of doing business require that purchasers and suppliers work more closely than ever before and expand their product and service expectations and day-to-day working relationships. Examples of presale and postsale service expectations are:

- *Presale Service by Supplier:*
    1. Technical and engineering experience to determine product requirements
    2. Preliminary design work
    3. Consultation to assist in specification refinement and standardization
    4. Specifications customized to buyer's requirements
    5. Manufacturer prototype for testing
    6. On-site equipment testing prior to purchase
    7. Payment deferred until after equipment test period and user acceptance completed
    8. Trade-in options
    9. Equipment and inventory buy-back
    10. Control and monitoring of stock depletion by original supplier prior to new supplier taking over the contract
- *Postsale Service by Supplier:*
    1. Inventorying and stocking of spare parts

2. Maintenance of inventory at supplier warehouse and other designated locations and at the minimum and maximum stock levels agreed upon
3. Regionalized (close to user) stocking of critical items
4. Extended warranty beyond customary standard warranty
5. Exclusive, dedicated account representative
6. Technical training, seminars, workshops, and continuing education program for users
7. Ongoing equipment repair, modification, and service
8. User and inventory reporting for buyer requirements
9. Trend analysis reports
10. Market data and forecasting reports

PRICE INFORMATION SOURCES

Up-to-date, reliable pricing information for the service industry is available from a number of sources. An increasing source of product specifications and pricing is the Internet. Other, more traditional sources of specification and pricing information are sales personnel, hard copy catalogs, industry price reports, and specialty reports published exclusively for individual products and product groups. The total life cycle cost of the acquisition must also be taken into account when a product or service is being acquired. Distributor-supplied software for the operator's personal computer is also sometimes available, with updated pricing downloaded daily, weekly, and monthly. This information is then available at the touch of a button and can cover thousands of items.

Some information is available on a continuous basis, as for frequently traded commodities. This information enables the buyer to know the price at which a product is trading, both present and future. Examples in food service include coffee, sugar, edible oils, and orange juice.

PRICE EVALUATION

Purchasers continually ask the question, "What is this item going to cost?" The initial purchase price of an item is only a portion of the cost. Other factors must be weighed carefully when the purchasing decision is made. Factors such as quality, service, timing, terms, freight, handling, discounts, spoilage, yield, and inventory costs also should be considered. This list is not exhaustive; it represents only a few examples of items to be considered in evaluating pricing. Purchasing a product or service that saves 10% in purchase cost and raises internal preparation labor by 15% is obviously not a good decision.

Some products, such as alcoholic beverages, are controlled by federal, state, or city regulations. In many regions of the country, the purchaser may purchase on "deal" (negotiate a bargain) at certain times. Promotions and "post-offs" (discount from listed or posted prices) may be discounted up to 20%. The astute purchaser also must consider inventory carrying costs. With comprehensive, careful price evaluation, very favorable purchase decisions can be made.

New and better products are entering the marketplace every day, requiring that purchasers become better educated. Within the food service sector a head of lettuce may be purchased as is or with the core removed, for example. Further, it may be purchased cleaned and cored, diced, shredded, or sliced. The same base product, in multiple forms, bears a different price. What is the best product to fit a purchaser's particular need? Obviously the lowest purchase price is not always the correct buying decision.

An educated purchaser is essential in today's service industry. He or she must understand the needs of the customer and all factors of his or her business, as well as that of the suppliers. Only then can prices be evaluated effectively.

COST INFLUENCES

A good purchaser must recognize and understand technology, markets, products, and prices. Many factors influence prices, including technology curves, seasonal demand, perishability, and the social, political, and economic conditions of the producing region. For example, the growing season for fruits and vegetables may be heavily influenced by weather. Price relationships among crops, livestock, subsidies, tariffs, and quotas cause broad swings in a global market and can spell trouble for the unknowing buyer. Proper timing and anticipation can be influential for making a more profitable purchase.

Some flexibility may exist within the service industry, making it unique. If the cost of a purchased product is rapidly increasing, the operator can simply raise the selling price, reduce the portion size, or remove the item from the menu.

All purchasers should be responsible for forecasting the cost of products and services over short and long periods of time. This enables the purchasers to alert management regarding potential supply problems and price trends. A company's planning and production then may be restructured for greater profitability due to timely purchasing practices.

PRICE FLUCTUATIONS

Occasionally items may be negotiated at a fixed price for a set period of time. However, because of the dynamics of the marketplace, price fluctuations will occur for certain products or services. Supply and demand play a major role. Newer techniques in packaging, handling, processing, and storage have tended to stabilize prices for many product categories. However, many items will continue to have prices that are cyclical in nature and will rise and fall with the dynamics of the marketplace. Highly volatile products, such as fresh fish, fresh fruits, and fresh vegetables, may be priced daily or weekly, and the price will rise and fall with the market.

ESCALATION–DEESCALATION CLAUSE

Certain contracts for significant items over longer periods of time may contain escalation-deescalation clauses. This affords the purchaser continuity of supply while allowing the seller to review selling price, cost, and profit margins in the event that costs escalate. Conversely, if costs decline, the buyer may receive the benefit of reduced prices. There are various indices to which the product may be tied, and movement may be up or down based on a specific formula. Lastly, prices may increase or decrease by a specified percentage during fixed periods of time.

TYPES OF CONTRACTS

Many types of contracts are utilized in the service industry. Brief mention will be made of those types covered in other areas of this book, while programs distinctive to the service industry will be covered in more detail.

Fixed Price

Fixed pricing is probably the most frequently used method, covering all segments of purchasing. Obtaining a fixed price may be as simple as a buyer receiving quotes from two or three suppliers. In the simplest form, the purchaser determines the best price and buys the item from the respective supplier at a fixed price for a set period to time. This method may cover a one-time single delivery, or it may be structured for many products for delivery to multiple locations.

Fixed price with fluctuation within a range (or "corridor pricing") is another option that gives both purchaser and supplier the advantage of fixed pricing with flexibility. The price is fixed within a plus-and-minus range and may be tied to a given market or index. The price may be adjusted only if cost moves out of the designated range.

Cost-Plus Manufacturer Markup

Many purchasers find it advantageous to buy according to a cost-plus arrangement with manufacturers. Cost usually refers to that part of the price that includes materials, labor, packaging, and transportation charges. The plus may refer to G & A (general and administrative overhead), plant overhead, or profit. In some cases, the purchaser may allow certain costs to fluctuate if they are indexed. The profit add-on, on the other hand, may be fixed for the entire length of the contract. Table 39–1 gives an example of a cost-plus price formula.

T A B L E   39–1

Example of a Cost-Plus Price Arrangement
with Manufacturer

	Item Cost	Percent of Total
Cost (category A)*		
Raw materials	$ 65.00	65%
Packaging }		
Factory labor }	$ 15.00	15%
Salaried labor }		
Benefits }		
Cost	$ 80.00	80%
Add-on cost (category B)**		
G & A and plant overhead }		
Interest on capital }	$ 8.00	8%
Depreciation }		
Profit }	$12.00	12%
Total cost	$100.00	100%

*Category A may fluctuate.
** Category B may be guaranteed for the life of the contract.

Cost-Plus Distributor Markup

Wholesale distributors sometimes price according to a cost-plus markup arrangement. In this case, cost is usually the price paid by the distributor to the manufacturer, plus transportation charges. Cost may or may not include cash discounts and payment terms. The markup includes the distributor's cost of doing business, including cost of warehousing, administration, transportation, and profit.

The markup may be expressed as a percentage above cost or as a set fee per category. Care should be given to avoid percentage markups on high-priced, volatile items. An item may increase dramatically in price, but the cost of distribution should not rise commensurate with product cost. Alternative price options to percentage above cost are cents per pound above cost or dollars per case above cost. Table 39–2 gives an example of distribution markup options.

Market Price

This method is sometimes called "riding the market." Purchasers place orders as they are needed, paying the going price. This method is used by some purchasers to ensure the supply of goods. During periods of

T A B L E   39–2

Example of Distribution Markup Options (#193 USDA Flank Steak)

	Stable Market*	Rising Market**
A. Cents per Pound over Cost		
Cost per pound	$2.80	$3.50
Markup per pound	+0.20	+0.20
Selling price per pound	$3.00	$3.70
B. Percentage Markup over Cost		
Cost per pound	$2.80	$3.50
Markup (add 12%)	+0.34	+0.42
Selling price per pound	$3.14	$3.92

* Although cost increases in rising markets, the distribution markup remains stable with a fixed-fee approach.
** Both cost and distribution markup increase in a rising market when percentage markup above cost is used.

tight supply, this may give a purchaser a higher supply priority than other purchasers.

Guaranteed Sale

Consignment and guaranteed sale is used from time to time. The consignment is ongoing, and the guaranteed sale requires the purchaser to pay for the goods after they are used or resold. This method is utilized by buyers for new and untested products when the supplier is anxious to move products quickly into the marketplace and assume all risk.

Hedging and Cross-Hedging

Hedging and cross-hedging are used to protect cost. Future contracts are bought and sold for specific products, e.g., pork bellies and orange juice. Hedging is an effective means of stabilizing your product costs for a set period of time. In general, hedging is not employed by purchasers in an attempt to beat the market.

Equipment Included

Some product contracts are tied to equipment packages, which range from merchandising aids to sophisticated dispensing equipment. The equipment can be provided on a loan basis as long as the buyer uses that supplier's products. The supplier may include an extra markup on certain products to cover the cost of maintaining the equipment. These extra charges can be ongoing for as long as the purchaser has the supplier's equipment, or they can be structured for set periods of time, with title of the equipment passing to the purchaser at the term's end.

Discounts

A variety of discounts may be possible under the purchase agreement. These can take the form of label allowance, off-invoice pricing, free goods, freight pick-up allowances, advertising and promotional allowances, and payment terms.

1. Proof-of-purchase discounts are offered by many manufacturers. Purchase activity is submitted to the manufacturer on a periodic basis, and the supplier remits

accordingly. (For example, if the proof-of-purchase discount from supplier A is $2.00 per case to be submitted quarterly and a purchaser purchases 2,000 cases in a quarter, then the purchaser will receive a rebate of $4,000.)

2. Volume discounts and incentive allowances may be established according to plateaus. For example, if a certain amount of purchases are made within a set period of time, a given discount is given. In some cases, retroactive discounts (calculated back to the first dollar purchases) are given for reaching incentive barriers.

3. Off-invoice pricing and discounts may be offered from manufacturers to distributors and are available to the purchaser who negotiates effectively and tracks product flow.

4. Free goods generally are tied to higher purchase volumes and may be combined for multiple receiving areas; for example, buy 75, get 5 at no charge. (In this case, if one operation cannot handle buying 75, delivery of 25 can be made to each of three operations and they will receive 80 for the price of 75.)

5. Freight pick-up allowances may be realized when the buyer or distributor picks up the goods at the manufacturer's dock. An effective negotiator may receive reduced or no freight charges by avoiding commercial carriers.

6. Advertising and promotional allowances are offered on a one-time basis and on an ongoing basis. The skilled purchaser should negotiate for these discounts, especially when purchasing brand-name or retail-oriented items.

LAWS GOVERNING PURCHASING

It is not advisable to enter hastily into contracts for items that may be subject to government control. Laws may been enacted on a city, state, or federal level. Thorough research and the advice of counsel may be prudent. Here are two examples.

Federal Alcohol Administration Act

This act, passed in 1935, has four objectives:

1. To regulate interstate and foreign commerce in distilled spirits, wine, and malt beverages

2. To promote fair competition in the industry
3. To protect the revenue
4. To protect the consumer

Many states have enacted additional laws similar to this one. Trade practices normally are regulated by both federal and state and covers:

1. Exclusive outlet
2. Tied house
3. Commercial bribery
4. Consignment sale
5. Labeling
6. Advertising

A purchaser responsible for purchasing alcohol must be knowledgeable about these laws in all states where he or she operates. For example, one may be able to use signs to promote alcohol products in one state and not in the adjoining state. A thorough review of all regulations with your suppliers is advised.

Federal Aviation Administration

Federal Aviation Administration (FAA) laws impose significant purchasing restrictions on both the supplier and product sourcing functions relative to the procuring of aircraft, aircraft components and parts, materials used on aircraft, and certain service and outside repair functions. Once an aircraft is certified as airworthy by the FAA, all the parts and manufacturers of those parts receive *part manufacture authority* (PMA); accordingly, alternative parts cannot be substituted without approval and certification from the FAA. The FAA controls and regulations also apply to service companies engaged in aircraft overhaul and repair, flight crew operations, airport security services, and so on.

TRANSPORTATION CONSIDERATIONS

Transportation needs strategic planning as much as other purchasing activities do. It no longer is the simple task of identifying the lowest-cost commercial hauler.

Certain areas of the service industry deal almost exclusively with local suppliers who build the cost of transportation into the cost of the product. Most items include freight to the distributor. The buyer, in specifying products, should review quantities moving into the distribution network for the most effective total cost. For example, manufacturer A sells to distributor B in 2,500-pound quantities, while manufacturer C sells to distributor B in 40,000-pound quantities. The freight savings per pound from contracting with manufacturer C may be a better purchase decision, even if the purchase price per item from manufacturer A is lower. Piggybacking on other customer's purchases to obtain lower per-pound freight rates may save significant dollars.

Transportation within the airline industry encompasses primarily the movement of newly purchased materials, supplies, and equipment from the supplier's facility directly to a designated facility where the materials are ultimately to be used or to other strategic staging locations where the materials are temporarily stored and inventoried for subsequent redistribution to other locations for use as needed. The majority of these materials are transported from the supplier's facility via "bestway" (supplier is free to choose the mode and carrier) ground transportation to the nearest airport into which the airline has scheduled flight service. The materials then are transported to their ultimate destination via company-owned aircraft on a low-priority, space-available basis behind baggage, mail, and revenue cargo. The higher-priority "must ride" category is carefully controlled and virtually restricted to the movement of critical aircraft repair parts. The corporate philosophy always has been, "Why pay someone else to transport our material when we are in the passenger and cargo transporting business?" This is a sensible and practical approach when lead time is sufficient such that periodic nuisance delays resulting from space priorities can be tolerated.

Until recently, this approach provided adequate support to day-to-day operations. However, with the escalating demand for air travel, coupled with rapid expansion into the international arena, many airlines find that the once-available cargo space has been reduced. This has resulted in an increase in transportation delays and nagging product shortages. Many stocking points and locations have countered this problem by raising the reorder levels and increasing their local on-site product inventories to provide an added stock cushion to sustain operations during periods of high-revenue traffic.

This dynamic growth has created a need to look externally to solve distribution limitations and reduce added safety stock costs. One area of emphasis has been in searching for large suppliers who have multiple domestic and international facilities and efficient distribution networks. Another consideration is to expand the use of and dependence on international warehouse and distribution companies to serve as transportation brokers.

CHAPTER 40

Purchasing and Supply Management in the Process and Extractive Industries

Editor
Thomas A. Crimi
Supply Chain Team Coordinator
Texaco, Inc.

Associate Editor
S. R. (Randy) Dean
Supply Manager
BHP World Minerals/New Mexico Coal

INTRODUCTION

Processing and extractive industries such as chemical, mining, petroleum, and petrochemical share many functions with other industries, both manufacturing and service-oriented. However, in some important respects these industries are different from manufacturing and also from each other. This chapter focuses on the effects of those differences on purchasing and supply management responsibilities and activities in these industries.

THE NATURE OF PURCHASING AND SUPPLY IN PROCESS AND EXTRACTIVE INDUSTRIES

Purchasing and supply activities in process and extractive industries contrast sharply in some respects with those in a typical manufacturing company or a service company. First, compared to manufacturing, there may be no end product components to purchase at all, or if there are components and materials, they may be much smaller in number and variety than in a manufacturing organization, although purchase volumes may be enormous. In the mining environment, for example, almost all non-capital purchases are made to support the maintenance of mining equipment necessary for the extraction of ore or other materials such as coal. A small mining operation may require a warehouse containing over 20,000 catalogued items just to support the maintenance of operating mining equipment. Second, the importance of capital purchases frequently is much greater than in either manufacturing or service industries. Most of the process and extractive industries are very capital equipment-intensive. Mining, petroleum production, and chemical and other processing industries all use large quantities of capital to acquire and construct production and processing facilities and provide the equipment necessary to support the operation of the facilities. A third area of differentiation is the relative importance of purchased services. While this difference may be growing smaller with the increased utilization of outsourcing by most industries generally, in some of the process and extractive industries, purchased services can amount to over half of all annual purchase dollars.

The remainder of this chapter will discuss these and other key aspects of purchasing and supply in the process and extractive industries, including effects of location of activities and multiplicity of business sites, impact of technology, use of strategic sourcing and alliances with suppliers, effects of economic cycles, importance of MRO (maintenance, repair, and operating) items, capital purchases, and purchased services, the nature of inventory and materials management in these industries, use of global sourcing, and some miscellaneous trends.

LEASE AND ROYALTY OBLIGATIONS

In the petroleum exploration and production industry in particular, many operations are conducted on properties that are jointly owned by various entities, including private companies, government entities, and individuals. Some of these owners are compensated for their ownership in cash, based on the amount of production. Others elect to share in both the revenues and expenses on a percentage basis. Procurement activities can be affected by the lease or operating agreements that govern such situations. For example, such arrangements may include audit provisions or requirements for partner approval for certain purchases and for asset sales.

LOCATION OF ACTIVITIES AND MULTIPLICITY OF BUSINESS SITES

The extractive industries, such as mining and petroleum exploration and production, must necessarily operate where deposits exist of the materials they produce. Often these locations are far from markets and commercial centers. Sometimes (or often, in the petroleum and mining industries) operating locations are on the floors of oceans and lakes and in areas of tundra, deserts, and jungles. Many extractive industries operate in remote and sometimes hostile environments that may contain both environmental and political hazards and risks. The chemical and petrochemical industries, on the other hand, are more likely to be located in or near commercial or population centers. Because of the geographical dispersion of both raw-material deposits and processing and consuming centers, operating locations can be quite numerous. In the petroleum industry, for example, individual operating locations for any one company may number in the thousands and be geographically dispersed world-wide. Process industries that purchase their raw materials usually have fewer operating locations. However, their raw material suppliers are often agricultural or extractive industries that frequently do have numerous and dispersed locations.

Remote and sometimes numerous operating locations generate additional and special activities and challenges for purchasing and supply management that are not often present in industries that have few locations and are near commercial and population centers. For example, in remote locations for extractive industries, the purchasing and supply function must frequently procure and arrange for communications equipment and/or services, logistical services, and furnishing and operation of employee living quarters. Construction of maintenance, administrative, and living facilities at operating locations is common in the mining industry. Another challenge is the transportation of capital equipment, operating materials and supplies, and personnel from commercial centers to the remote location and transportation of the produced ore, petroleum, or other materials from the production site to processing and consuming centers. Providing for transportation service may itself generate additional supply requirements such as materials and construction services to build pipelines, roads, or railway and dock facilities. For international locations, packing, security, and transportation factors may be of equal or greater importance when compared to the quality and price of the material itself. Use of freight forwarders, security services, chartered aircraft or vessels, or other special transportation is often a routine aspect of supply management in the international operations of these industries.

A purchasing and supply manager, when faced with the problem of how to provide purchasing and supply management to dispersed or remote locations, particularly new operating locations, must first assess the location(s) in terms of infrastructure (transportation, commercial, political, and possibly residential), supply facilities and capabilities, available services, and nearness to supply centers. These factors must be evaluated in relation to the material and service requirements of the operation. From this assessment any deficiencies can be identified and a supply plan developed that addresses deficiencies and provides for all supply and transportation requirements, including construction, startup, and operation of the facility.

In some operations, such as petroleum exploration and production, because of their dispersion and often their relatively small purchase volumes, operating locations usually have some level of purchasing authority and responsibility—for example, small spot or emergency requirements, with strategic procurement activities conducted from a headquarters or other central location. Mining and process industry operating locations tend to be much larger and more usually contain a supply structure at each location, perhaps with global agreements as guidelines for procurement activities.

IMPACT OF TECHNOLOGY

Different technologies used in the various parts of process and extractive industries cause their purchasing focus to address specific aspects of each industry, such as exploration for ores, minerals, and petroleum, development and operation of mines and oil and gas production, transportation of the produced material, processing or refining, and marketing activities. One result of this focus has been the formation of strategic supplier alliances with primary product and process technology suppliers. As the technology used by these industries has developed and become more complex, it has required a tremendous amount of specialty item procurement and procurement of "engineered equipment" unique to a particular industry. At the same time, equipment quality has improved and reduced the need for replacement or back-up material.

The technology of communications has improved to facilitate immediate contact and the accurate transmittal of drawings, specifications, and equipment data. Remote locations, no matter where located on the globe, have virtually instant communication capability with any other global location via satellites and microwave technology.

Technology has also improved the purchasing process. Electronic commerce has enabled requisitioning, ordering/contracting, invoicing, and payment processes to become more efficient and to reduce ordering and delivery cycle times and inventories required. As a result of these capabilities, transaction costs have been and continue to be drastically reduced. Information technologies have also improved both tactical and strategic planning. This has enabled the concept of strategic sourcing to become more viable in these industries that tend to have long planning horizons and long-term project buying with large impact on many commodity families.

STRATEGIC SOURCING

Because most industries in the process and extractive group are mature industries and therefore are not experiencing rapid overall growth, they have relatively stable overall supply needs and have embraced strategic sourcing as a primary procurement enabler. These industries have become highly systematic in directing their purchasing and supply activities using plans to develop and manage supply bases that are consistent with their organizations' strategic objectives. The trend in many of these industries is, in effect, to create an extended enterprise by integrating suppliers into their long-term business processes. Strategic sourcing is also a central process within a larger industry trend towards supply chain management.

STRATEGIC ALLIANCES

Many process and extractive industries rely heavily on supplier alliances to provide domestic and global requirements for materials and services. The ability to share risks between suppliers and purchasers in areas such as developing new technologies and serving remote and/or hazardous locations is one reason for the attractiveness of strategic alliances to these industries. Alliances also fit well with a strategic sourcing strategy of concentrating on best-in-class suppliers to reduce total cost of ownership while maintaining competitive purchase prices. An example is leveraging MRO purchases through strategic alliances to reduce overall prices paid. Use of alliances is also consistent with significant personnel reductions that have taken place through reengineering in many of these industries. In addition, alliances are part of many organizations' plans to use suppliers as an "extended enterprise" to help further reduce overall supply chain costs.

In remote areas where the supply base is limited, it is becoming more common for competing companies to form alliances, cooperatives, and consortiums in order to use existing suppliers and to leverage overall purchasing capabilities for all companies. In the mining industry, for example, mines are creating supply alliances with primary customers (i.e., coal mines with power generators) in an effort to keep the overall cost of the customers' end product down and enable them to compete effectively in the customers' markets.

ECONOMIC CYCLES

Because many of the process and extractive industries produce basic commodity-type materials that are sold in global markets, economic cycles have a significant impact on their business, particularly on product demand and on prices they receive for their products. Although technology has enabled a reduction in the historically long lead times required to find and develop mines and oilfields or to design and construct new processing plants, lead times are still long relative to those in many other industries. In addition to the time required for design, procurement, and construction, environmental, governmental, and local issues can extend new projects by weeks, months, or years, depending on the project. These industries must therefore try to conduct a delicate balancing act with the objective of providing adequate supply, but not so much supply that, in economic downturns, they experience severe negative effects on prices of their produced products. Such a balancing act has been very difficult to implement in practice. One result has been the creation of cartels in several of these industries over the years in attempts to restrict supply and increase product price. Tin, diamonds, and petroleum are three noteworthy examples. Generally these efforts eventually fail and the additional supply attracted by artificially high prices causes market glut and depressed prices, sometimes for extended periods of time.

Another impact on the petroleum and mining industries has been caused by deregulation of the electrical power industry in the United States. The potential of increased competition has caused companies who were in only one area of the industry to diversify into various other areas, including exploration, production, transmission, and distribution.

The significance of these developments for purchasing and supply is that specialized supply communities that cater to the process and extractive industries also tend to wax and wane with the buying industry. In good times a seller's market often prevails, and in bad times a buyer's market develops. The swings in the petroleum industry from 1980 through 1999, for example, have brought two high-activity periods with accompanying seller's markets followed by two periods of very low activity and resulting buyer's markets.

MRO PROCUREMENT

The purchasing of MRO (maintenance, repair, and operating) materials is a significant part of purchasing in the process and extractive industries. MRO purchasing may account for only 20–25% of the purchasing spend in these industries, but it may use 75–80% of a procurement department's resources. There are opportunities to achieve significant savings in this area by using total cost of ownership analysis in conjunction with using major suppliers as alliance partners; i.e., the extended enterprise. Many companies have implemented consignment, supplier stocking, and outside-operated warehouse management programs in efforts to reduce personnel and inventories. "Distribution" companies have evolved that offer, through a consortium of suppliers, multiple product lines, warehouse management, and purchasing systems as a means to reduce total cost of ownership.

This extended enterprise approach applied to MRO purchases is a strong industry trend that enables firms to focus on consolidation of the supply base, better leveraging of purchase dollars, reductions in inventory, manpower, and transaction costs, and continuous improvement. All of these efforts can provide significant costs reductions and improvements in supplier service and the delivery of products. The strategic focus in the MRO area in these industries is characterized by firms identifying, developing, certifying, and forming alliances with global best-in-class suppliers for major groups of MRO commodities. A relative comparison of some characteristics of process and extractive MRO and typical manufacturing purchasing would likely yield differences shown in Table 40–1.

CAPITAL PURCHASING

In the extractive industries in particular, and also in some of the process industries, capital purchases sometimes dominate the overall purchases

T A B L E   40-1

Relative Situations Concerning MRO Purchases

	Industries	
Characteristic	**Process and Extractive**	**Manufacturing**
Cost controls	Low	High
Dollar value/order	Low*	High
Usage history	Low*	High
Purchaser expertise	Low	High
Administrative order cost	Same	Same
Number of purchase orders	High	Low
Number of suppliers	High	Low
Emergencies (frequency)	High	Low

Electronic commerce (EDI), auto-fax, and evaluated receipts have changed many of the transactions issues for MRO purchasing. Also, the use of automatic max/min MRP-type systems has drastically reduced personnel requirements in MRO warehousing. The trend toward alliances has also reduced the supply base in both groups of industries.
* High for the mining industry.

of materials because purchased components for the firm's produced or manufactured end products may be small, of little importance, or non-existent. For example, in the oil and gas-producing industries, most purchases are either capital materials to construct facilities and/or keep the physical plant, or oilfield operating, capital equipment, or services. In the mining industry, the majority of purchases are for the maintenance of large capital equipment and the purchase of that equipment. The product that is mined or otherwise produced from the earth includes few if any purchased ingredients.

The procurement of capital equipment differs from that of other materials in a number of respects, including the fact that often each purchase involves substantial amounts of dollars and takes place after a long purchasing cycle that may include design services and several levels of negotiations. In the purchasing of MRO materials, for example, a major alliance supplier may be selected on the basis of price, quality, logistics, and service overall for a broad range of products, and the business relationship is maintained with this supplier until there is reason to change. In contrast to this, for each major equipment purchase there will very likely be separate and long-term negotiations with diverse suppliers. Because of the specialized nature of much of the capital equipment, most capital maintenance items, such as parts, must be purchased from the original equipment manufacturer (OEM). In contrast to MRO purchasing, there is generally not an automatic continuing relationship with the same supplier, with some exceptions if the item is purchased on a regular basis.

Lead times for capital purchases are generally much greater than for other materials. Specifications also may be more flexible than those for other types of purchases. One factor affecting specifications is that the equipment options for the same functionality from alternative sources may vary in characteristics to some degree. One other differentiating factor in capital purchasing is that very often related equipment, spare parts, materials, and services may be required to be purchased along with the capital equipment. In situations where spare parts are held in inventory, it may be necessary to consider the cost of carrying spares if a decision is made to change OEM. Purchase decisions for capital should include the item price, costs of obsolescence and availability, and costs of carrying and/or changing inventories of spares. Standardization of capital equipment can contribute to reduced total cost of ownership through reduction of spare parts inventories. Repurchase surveys, installation services, and training services are additional major dimensions of capital purchasing.

PURCHASED SERVICES

Services procurement is substantially different from materials procurement. For example, services cannot be stored, and therefore availability and delivery timing of services have heavy weight in procurement planning and evaluation.

The major categories of purchased services in the process and extractive industries include technical, operational, mechanical, construction, professional, and transportation and related services. Historically, services in some of the extractive industries have been largely purchased at decentralized operating locations and by various parts of the organization. As the industries seek to improve leverage with suppliers through reducing numbers of suppliers, the tendency is to move to more central coordination and/or cross-functional team approaches to procuring services, and on a company-wide basis where applicable. There appears to be a strong trend toward using strategic alliances in services procurement as numbers of suppliers are reduced. Alliances with service providers can also be used to share development and operational risks in hostile operating environments. In some cases, materials and services are combined in one alliance arrangement.

Most services that are used by these industries are evaluated in a "make-or-buy" fashion to determine whether better value can be obtained by providing the service internally or by purchasing it through an outsourcing arrangement. Many services, such as maintenance, engineering and design, and administrative services that historically were provided internally, have been outsourced by many process and extractive companies.

INVENTORY AND MATERIALS MANAGEMENT

Inventory and materials management issues are significant in these industries where inventory carrying costs can range from 20–30% annually. Inventory levels are often driven by the cost of equipment downtime if repair parts are not available when needed. Inventories may include MRO and other operational support items that have not been put on a vendor-stocked, Just-in-Time delivery program. Other items that may be inventoried include raw materials, containers, packaging materials for some process industries, and certain capital equipment and equipment parts, including so-called long lead-time "insurance parts" for critical pieces of capital equipment. Most organizations do have very substantial Just-in-Time, supplier stocking, or integrated supply programs. Safety stock issues are usually minimal but may be dependent on the remoteness of the operation and the availability of parts and service. Cycle times are closely tracked to minimize inventory investment. Systems that track responsiveness to customer demand are used, particularly in the MRO materials supply area. The key objective for MRO supply are to get materials from the supplier directly to the location where needed, at the exact time needed, and in the quantity required. Electronic commerce technology has facilitated inventory reduction programs by improving communications content and speed and making possible delivery of materials within hours of the request for material.

Almost all of the process and extractive industries are 24-hour, 7-day operations. Inventories must be based on supporting that operating requirement. Wherever maintenance inventories are located or whoever owns them, availability when needed is critical.

GLOBAL SOURCING

A global scope to purchasing activities is not new to many process and extractive industries. Because of the location of raw materials or mineral or petroleum deposits, they have had to operate on a global basis for many years. However, as the world has become more developed and communications capabilities have improved, true global purchasing has become not only possible but necessary. Historically, most material, equipment, and service requirements might have been purchased in the United States, Europe, or Japan and shipped to wherever needed. Procurement cycles were long and much inefficiency had to be accepted. Today there are likely supply alternatives in a number of locations across the globe, and transportation and communications technologies have reduced the time required for the procurement cycle. Purchasing activities in a global context have also taken on additional meaning as the process and extractive industries have matured. An increasing number of domestic industrial manufacturers (e.g., sources of materials and equipment needed by process and extractive industries) have moved part or all of their operations overseas or established multiple locations in different countries. This move by manufacturers and suppliers has created an opportunity for global companies to better utilize alliances worldwide. In addition, a majority of large process and extractive industry members have exploration, production, mining, process, refining, or marketing operations in a number of different countries.

One of the major challenges of procurement in a global setting has to do with the significant variability in quality, service, dependability, and pricing from various sources of supply in different countries. A key challenge to the purchasing professional is to balance the advantages of global supply with the requirements of individual operating site requirements. The leveraging advantages of global alliances are sometimes outweighed by service and availability needs of operating locations. The impact of exchange rates also makes buying commodities in various markets a variable task that has to anticipate rapid changes in pricing due to currency fluctuations.

Countertrade activities can also be a significant factor in global sourcing due to capital requirements, logistical considerations, or host country requirements. Countertrade or barter activities are usually complex procurement arrangements, since the valuation process changes over time and objective and consistent pricing benchmarks are not easily established or tracked.

Given the current and developing capabilities of many industrialized or industrializing countries, global sourcing is a necessary part of developing a competitive supply base. Two key aspects of global business relationships are cultural and communication differences between buyers and sellers. Philosophy, political considerations, customs, and business practices also can create barriers to effective procurement activities.

Cost pressures are another reason for interest in global procurement opportunities. There are new competitors in traditional markets. There is new access to emerging markets. There are procurement opportunities to redefine the supply chain, redesign supply base relationships, and realign processes, people, and technology to enable the organization to sustain and maintain competitive advantage through effective global sourcing. Strategic sourcing has become, in many organizations, a "core competency" in which leading industry members have invested significant resources. These successful companies have utilized global sourcing to keep their organizations on the cutting edge of cost and technology by being able to realize breakthrough opportunities in locations all over the world. Procurement in this sense is perhaps best thought of as a global sourcing process with the objectives of maximizing leveraging advantages, improving services, and reducing costs.

MISCELLANEOUS TRENDS

A number of management trends are shaping current procurement processes in the process and extractive industries. A continuing increase in the utilization of cross-functional teams for sourcing and purchasing is one example. Early and immediate involvement of purchasing in planning and operations teams is necessary to achieve the best possible procurement contribution to development and operating activities. Along with this is the trend towards embracing best practices within the industry. Continuous improvement efforts permeate purchasing activities at all levels and are a permanent feature of many organizations' business process. Benchmarking of purchasing activities to compare one's own performance with that of peer organizations is becoming more commonplace, with CAPS (Center for Advanced Purchasing Studies) having a major role in assisting various industries' efforts. Some of the process and extractive industries for which CAPS has compiled benchmarks include chemical, mining, and petroleum.

In summary, the process and extractive industries in the early 2000s are characterized by redefinition of supply chains, evolution of supply base relationships, and realignment of parallel processes, people, and technology. In today's world, competitive advantage through procurement activities is a recognized objective and is sustained by advancing total cost of ownership concepts that focus on reducing exploration, mining, production, transportation, processing, and marketing costs, and promoting standardization while providing world-class service to internal and external customers. Consequently, the role of change management has increased significantly in these industries as they find themselves in the first years of the new millennium and its opportunities for new vision.

CHAPTER 41

Public/Private Purchasing

Updated for Sixth Edition by
Donald L. Woods, J.D., C.P.M.
State and Local Government Consultant
Las Vegas, Nevada

Fifth Edition Editors*
Stephen B. Gordon
Purchasing Agent,
Metropolitan Government of Nashville and Davidson County
Nashville, Tennessee

Richard L. Mooney, C.P.M.
Managing Associate
University Procurement Consulting Group

Fifth Edition Associate Editors*
Donald K. Carte, C.P.P.O.
Chief of Standards and Specifications
Purchasing Division, State of West Virginia

Joseph J. Finnerty
Procurement Consultant

Kevin J. Grant, C.P.P.O.
Procurement Manager, Department of Transportation
State of Arizona

Earl Hawkes, C.P.M.
Director of General Services
Clark County, Nevada

Thomas Logue
Senior Buyer, Public Schools System
Montgomery County, Maryland

G. B. Stephenson
Executive Director of Administration
Upper Occoquan Sewer Authority

INTRODUCTION

The not-for-profit sector is extremely diverse, encompassing public, quasi-public, and private organizations (hereinafter "public sector").

---

* Titles as of time of printing of the 5th edition.

Consequently, public purchasing is accomplished through systems that run the gamut from those that legally mandate stringent policies and procedures to those that resemble their more flexible counterparts in the profit-making sector (hereinafter "private sector"). This chapter seeks to explain how purchasing in public sector organizations differs from purchasing in a private sector context. It devotes particular attention to purchasing in medium-sized to large public sector entities as well as the quasi-public sector organizations. This focus is the result of at least two considerations. First, the purchasing done by these two particular types of public sector entities can be most clearly distinguished from that performed by private sector organizations. Second, purchases by public sector governments alone dwarf the purchases made by the other public sector entities. In 1998, total government consumption and investment expenditures amounted to about $1,500 billion in the United States.

The major points addressed in this chapter include:

♦ The context, roles, and responsibilities of purchasing in public sector organizations
♦ The purchasing cycle
♦ External and internal forces
♦ Organizational issues
♦ Ethical issues
♦ Professional development issues
♦ Operational issues

CONTEXT

How does the public sector purchasing function differ from the private sector purchasing function? In certain respects, the purchasing function in the public sector is similar to that in the private sector. The fundamental objective is to identify sources of needed materials and services and to acquire those items when needed, as economically as possible within accepted standards of quality. The purchasing function must be able to react quickly, effectively, and efficiently to the desired requirements, while policies and procedures must conform to sound business practice. Public sector purchasers utilize professional techniques and modern methods, and they employ professional purchasers and managers to ensure that the purchasing program fully supports their organizations' needs.

Even so, purchasing for public sector organizations differs in several respects from purchasing for private sector entities. Most important, public sector purchasing is a stewardship function because it involves the expenditure of someone else's money to support services and activities that a public sector official has decided, in advance, should be provided. In the case of public sector governmental entities and certain public sector hospitals and universities, the service demands (and the resources to satisfy those demands) emanate from the taxpayers. As a result, the public purchasing function has evolved into a highly controlled, yet open, process that is prescribed by a myriad of laws and ordinances, rules and regulations, judicial and administrative decisions, and policies and procedures. These requirements (which cover everything from who is authorized to purchase a particular item to who can and cannot supply the item) complicate and frequently delay the seemingly simple process of securing needed goods and services.

For example, whereas the purchasing department in a private sector firm can restrict bidding opportunities to as few firms as it wishes, a public sector organization generally must announce its intention to receive bids or proposals on a particular item and then allow as many firms as desire to submit an offer to do so. Purchasing departments in public sector entities not only give essentially every interested supplier equal opportunity to bid on a particular contract, but also grant a supplier the right to obtain any information (current or historical) that is available to its competitors. To be able to obtain what is needed when it is needed, while demonstrating proper stewardship, demands openness and legal compliance from the public sector purchaser.

Other kinds of public sector organizations have purchasing functions that are more like those in private sector industry. Public sector utilities, whose revenues are obtained from the sale of their products and services, are an example. Such entities are somewhat akin to private sector enterprises in that they are not tax supported. In fact, they may even contribute services in lieu of taxes to public sector governmental agencies in their service areas. Depending on their charter, some utilities have the latitude to conduct their purchasing function along the lines of private sector or investor-owned utilities, rather than as tax-supported agencies. Unlike public sector purchasing operations, utilities are able to restrict their bid list to a reasonable number of qualified firms using methods ordinarily employed in the private sector. Public sector utilities often have no requirements to advertise for competitive bids or to open bids to the public.

CATEGORIES OF PUBLIC SECTOR ORGANIZATIONS

The different types of public sector organizations are categorized as public, quasi-public, and private.

Public

The public sector includes federal, state, county, and local governments. It also includes some schools, universities, and hospitals that are run as public sector governmental entities, such as federal hospitals, state-controlled universities, and public schools. Purchasing in the public sector tends to be highly codified, with formal competitive bidding being the method of choice for determining source and price. Information regarding purchasing transactions generally is available to anyone who is interested, and purchasing operations are subject to close scrutiny by legislative bodies and the media.

Quasi-public

Quasi-public sector entities include public utilities; authorities that operate bridges, tunnels, transit systems, or ports; and colleges and universities that are state-related but have separate organizational structures and governing boards. For example, while utilities are subject to operating and rate-setting provisions set by public utility commissions, they are formed as public sector corporations with independent boards of directors. Likewise, many state-related universities are organized as corporations under constitutional provisions that place their management in the hands of independent boards of governors or regents. Purchasing in quasi-public sector organizations is often subject to statutory control and, like purchasing by public sector governmental agencies, is open to public scrutiny. Typically, however, purchasing policies in quasi-public sector organizations provide more operating flexibility than do those in public sector entities.

Private

Private nonprofit organizations include churches, charities, and private schools and universities. Such organizations are characterized by their relative independence from public sector governmental control. They have tax exemptions as charitable or educational organizations, and they are governed by independent boards of directors or trustees. In general, private nonprofit organizations are free to set their own purchasing policies that conform more to generally accepted business practice than to state or local statutes. Their purchasing affairs are not subject as much to public scrutiny as those of public sector or quasi-public sector organizations.

ROLES

The purchasing department in a public sector organization plays several roles that distinguish it from its counterparts in private sector organizations. These roles may include, but are not limited to, being:

- A supplier of often thousands of different types of goods and services for a wide variety of departments and agencies that in turn utilize those items to operate their departments/agencies or add needed infrastructure
- An implementer of policy that, in addition to promoting and securing maximum practicable competition through detailed, prescribed procedures, must also champion laws and ordinances that govern the purchasing function and may include minority business participation as well as environmental protection issues
- A marketer of business opportunities that must seek out as many potential supply sources as possible, accurately and attractively communicate needs to those potential sources, and maintain effective relationships and communication with both the successful and the unsuccessful offerors

SPECTRUM OF RESPONSIBILITIES

The responsibilities of the purchasing department in a public sector organization can be viewed in terms of both the specific products and services it supplies to their internal customers or end users and the various functions it discharges in the course of supplying those items.

Products and Services Purchased

Public sector purchasing departments typically purchase a large number and variety of products and services. Generally speaking, the items purchased are commercially available; that is, they can be purchased off the shelf without the need for custom design and manufacturing or major modifications. Obvious exceptions include items such as weapons systems for the Department of Defense, specialty vehicles such as fire trucks, construction, state-of-the-art research equipment (for universities), professional services, and specialty or customized hardware and software. A typical state government centralized purchasing department will, for example, purchase literally thousands of different items within the course of a single year. Among the items that account for a large part of purchasing expenditures are office supplies and equipment, computer hardware and software, telecommunications equipment, food, furniture, and vehicles. Public sector organizations also are turning increasingly to private sector companies for the provision of a variety of services.

Functions Performed

The purchasing department in the public sector organization performs several functions that support its fundamental mission of supplying goods and services to those who require them. These functions include:

- Developing, organizing, and maintaining formal lists of potential suppliers
- Assisting end users/internal customers in designing, researching, and preparing written, competitive solicitations or specifications and evaluating the offers received in response to the specifications
- Ensuring continuity of supply through coordinated planning and scheduling, term contracts, and appropriate levels of inventory
- Ensuring the quality of purchased goods and services through standardization, inspection, and contract administration
- Participating in decisions on whether to make goods in-house or buy from outside sources
- Documenting purchasing actions and making pricing or other nonproprietary data reasonably available to those requesting it
- Advising management, using department staff and others on such matters as market conditions, product improvements, new products, and opportunities to build goodwill in the local and business community

THE PURCHASING CYCLE

The purchasing cycle in a public sector organization (see Figure 41–1) encompasses a variety of tasks and responsibilities, beginning with the determination of a need for a product or service. For products, the cycle generally concludes with the consumption or disposition of the item. For services, it typically ends with final payment for services rendered. The three key phases in the cycle are planning, supplier selection, and contract administration.

Planning and Scheduling

Purchasing and their internal customers must work together in this phase of the process to ensure that needs for products or services are satisfied at the lowest total cost. This can mean, for example, agreeing on acceptable quality levels, consolidating requirements, deciding when and how to purchase, or determining whether to carry a particular item in inventory. In recent years, public sector purchasing departments have begun to move away from simply processing requisitions to assisting with better business solutions.

Value analysis, an important element of purchasing planning, is generally not formally applied as frequently by public sector purchasing departments as it is in the private sector. Among the exceptions are the life cycle cost bid evaluation formulas that enable purchasers to consider projected energy and maintenance costs in addition to price and salvage value when determining an evaluated bid price.

Consolidation of requirements and scheduling of acquisitions, two other key aspects of planning, are becoming more prevalent as public sector organizations automate their purchasing functions. Purchasing, or in its absence a lead department, should collect, maintain, and regularly analyze historical data for quantities purchased, frequency of purchases, unit prices per transaction, and supplier performance in order to determine the timing and method of procuring repetitively purchased items.

Planning and scheduling can be done manually or with tools that are readily available for use on personal computers.

Supplier Selection

Selecting suppliers or contractors involves several activities, including identifying potential sources, soliciting offers, evaluating offers, and making contract awards.

F I G U R E   41-1

The Purchasing Cycle (Including Planning and Budgeting of Requirements)

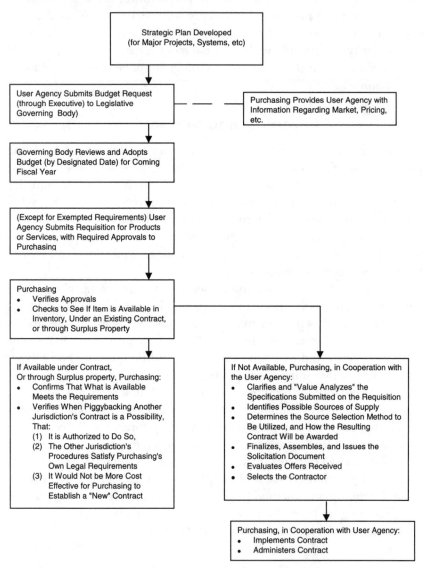

Identifying Sources of Supply

Most public sector organizations are required to obtain at least some competition on all but the smallest of purchases. Many are, moreover, required to formally advertise in newspapers of record. However, because formal advertisement is not an effective way to solicit bids, public sector organizations have relied upon bidders' mailing lists to produce an adequate number of responses. In order to ensure that only existing and interested firms are solicited, and to keep bidders' pricing as competitive as possible, public sector organizations may:

◆ Use a proven commodity coding system to organize the bidders on their list according to the specific products and services they sell

◆ Encourage or require applicants for the bidders' mailing list to sign up for only those specific items they intend to offer

◆ Develop and implement a procedure to purge from the bidders' mailing list those companies that do not respond to an established number of solicitations

◆ Continually seek out and develop new sources of supply, particularly in those areas in which only a few possible sources are known or are interested in selling to the entity

◆ Use an Internet Web site to inform potential suppliers of items purchased and to provide on-line signup for bidders

The so-called Texas commodity coding system is a popular system utilized by public sector organizations to classify their suppliers. It utilizes a three-digit class and a two-digit item to organize bidders according to what they sell. Other systems are the Standard Industrial Classification Code (SIC) and the National Institute of Governmental Purchasing, Inc. (NIGP) classification. Note that the SIC is being changed over to the North American Industry Classification System (NAICS), with most government statistics being published under the new system beginning from about 2001.

Public sector purchasing departments typically remove a supplier from the bidders' mailing list for a specific product or service after that firm has failed to respond to three successive solicitations for that item. However, such a firm nevertheless can respond to a solicitation for the item should it discover the bidding opportunity through other means. Even a supplier that has performed very poorly on previous contracts may submit an offer, but there is no assurance that its offer will be considered responsive and responsible. Quantitative scoring to evaluate suppliers can be done manually or with various computer programs. With computer-based purchasing systems and/or Internet-based solicitation, supplier performance and hence a company's eligibility to remain on a bidders' mailing list can be more easily be scored quantitatively.

Public sector purchasing departments add potential sources to their bidders' mailing lists through a variety of methods. These include printed resources such as the telephone book's yellow pages, industrial registers and directories, Internet searches, and networking with other purchasing departments, professional associations, and business development organizations. Many jurisdictions actively market their bidding opportunities through supplier promotion seminars. Because the public sector purchasing process typically is more complex than that of the private sector, suppliers often need to be convinced that selling to public sector organizations is worth the effort.

Soliciting Offers

The effectiveness of a public sector purchasing department is highly dependent on the amount and quality of competition its solicitation documents generate. An effective system for soliciting offers supports the use of the most appropriate source selection method as well as the most appropriate type of contract. It also promotes the adoption and use of standards that ensure the quality, content, and effectiveness of individual solicitation documents.

Although the terminology varies from entity to entity, the fundamental methods being utilized by public sector organizations can be found in the American Bar Association's Model Procurement Code for State and Local Government. Some additional information regarding these methods is provided in Box 41–1.

The types of contracts utilized by public sector organizations can be classified in several ways, including:

+ Fixed price
+ Definite or indefinite quantity
+ Whether or not there is a performance incentive for the supplier
+ A one-time requirement versus one covering a period of time
+ A purchase, lease purchase, or true lease

B O X   4 1 – 1

OBTAINING BIDS OR PROPOSALS

Although the terminology will vary from state to state and jurisdiction to jurisdiction, basic methods used in the competitive acquisition of supplies and services include competitive sealed bidding, multistep competitive sealed bidding, and competitive sealed proposals.

Competitive Sealed Bidding

Competitive sealed bidding is the method most often used by local governments for acquiring goods, services, and construction. It provides for award of the contract to the responsive and responsible bidder whose bid price is lowest, thereby making the bid evaluation process more objective than it is when competitive sealed proposals (see below) are evaluated.

Competitive sealed bidding, which *does not* include negotiations with bidders after bids are opened, is normally used when:

♦ Clear and adequate specifications are available.

♦ Two or more responsible bidders are willing to do business with the government in accordance with the government's requirements and criteria.

♦ The dollar value of the purchase is large enough to justify to both buyer and seller the expense associated with competitive sealed bidding. In many jurisdictions competitive bidding is legislative or policy mandated when the dollar value exceeds a specified threshold.

♦ Sufficient time is available for the solicitation, preparation, and evaluation of sealed bids.

Even though competitive sealed bidding is the easiest method to audit, there are certain circumstances under which this method may not be practical. Provided that they have the legal authority to do so, jurisdictions may find that multistep competitive sealed bidding, or requesting competitive sealed proposals, is more appropriate.

Multistep Competitive Sealed Bidding

Multistep (generally, two-step) sealed bidding is a variant of the competitive sealed bidding method. It may be used when a jurisdiction wishes to award a contract on the basis of price, but avail-

B O X   41–1

Continued

able specifications are inadequate or too general to permit full and free competition without technical evaluation and discussion. It is a multiphased process that combines elements of both the request for proposals method (in the first phases) and "regular" competitive sealed bidding (in the final phase).

The first phase consists of one or more requests for information, or unpriced technical offers. The second phase resembles competitive sealed bidding. Bidders who submitted technically acceptable offers in the first phase are invited to submit sealed bids based on their technical offers. The contract is awarded to the lowest responsive and responsible bidder. Multistep bidding, if used properly and within appropriate circumstances, can introduce price competition into purchases of complex items. But there is also a disadvantage in the limiting of competition in the second or pricing phase.

Competitive Sealed Proposals

If a jurisdiction has to purchase relatively new technology or a nonstandard item, it may choose to request competitive sealed proposals if its laws permit it to do so. Some reasons for going this route are:

♦ The contract needs to be other than a fixed-price type.
♦ Oral or written discussions may need to be conducted with offerors concerning the technical aspects and price of their proposals.
♦ Offerors may need the opportunity to revise their proposals, including price.
♦ The award may need to be based on a "comparative evaluation" that takes differing price, quality, and contractual favors into account.

Jurisdictions should be sure that they have the ability to use this approach fairly and effectively before they actually request sealed proposals. This method provides more flexibility than competitive sealed bidding, but it also allows more room for error.

Source: S. M. Cristofano and W. S. Foster, eds., *Purchasing, Management of Local Public Works*, International City Management Association, Washington, D.C., 1986. Originally published in National Institute of Governmental Purchasing, Inc., Public Purchasing and Materials Management.

The majority of contracts entered into by public sector entities are of the fixed-price type because most of the products and services purchased by these organizations are commercially available. Forms of fixed-price contracts, which typically are authorized for use, include firm fixed-price (the most common), fixed-price with escalation, and fixed-price with a performance incentive. Many state and local governments are using agreements for specific periods (term contracts) with estimated quantities. Application of information technology to the procurement function has enabled public sector purchasing departments to collect, manipulate, and analyze historical data easily.

Solicitations drafted by the public sector tend to be wordy, illegible, and difficult to understand, which can discourage the very competition and/or quality of competition required by the purchaser's employer. These problems can be overcome with new generalized employee training and by topic specific education in specification or contract writing as well as emerging purchasing skills and concepts.

Evaluating Offers and Awarding Contracts

Economy and fairness, two of the most fundamental goals of public sector purchasing, are brought together in the evaluation of quotes, bids, and proposals. Consequently, everyone involved in the purchasing process, including those who do the purchasing, those for whom goods and services are acquired (user), and the supplier community, must understand both the significance of the purchasing process and how it works.

The criteria that a public sector entity uses as a basis for awarding contracts vary, depending on the source selection method that is used. A contract that is to be established through competitive sealed bidding generally will be (and should be) awarded to the *responsible* bidder whose offer is *responsive* to the invitation for bids and is lowest in price. Hence the phrase "award to the lowest responsive and responsible bidder." A responsive offer is one that at a minimum *conforms in all material respects to the invitation for bids*. Factors that should be considered in determining whether the standard of responsibility has been met are provided in Box 41–2. Several examples of nonresponsive bidders are provided in Box 41–3.

The responsiveness of a bid or proposal is determined at the earliest opportunity after the document is removed from its sealed envelope. Only minor irregularities should be waived, and the determination of responsiveness *must* be objective, based on the criteria stated in the solicitation document. But buyers need to recognize that competition can

B O X 41-2

RESPONSIBILITY OF A BIDDER OR OFFEROR

A *responsible bidder or offeror* means a person who has the capability in all respects to perform fully the contract requirements, and the integrity and reliability which will ensure good faith performance. (*The Model Procurement Code for State and Local Governments*, Section 3-101)

Factors to be considered in determining whether the standard of responsibility has been met include whether a prospective contractor has:

♦ The appropriate financial, material, equipment, facility, and personnel resources and expertise, or the ability to obtain them, necessary to indicate its capability to meet all contractual requirements
♦ A satisfactory record of performance
♦ A satisfactory record of integrity
♦ The legal qualifications to do business with the entity
♦ Supplied all necessary information in connection with the inquiry concerning responsibility (*Model Code*, R3-401.02, Standards of Responsibility)

be restricted when extraneous criteria are included in the document's responsiveness requirements. Examples are mandatory pre-bids or walk-throughs, proof of insurance and bonds at time of submitting bid, and detailed work plans on how the project will be accomplished.

The responsibility of an offeror can be determined any time after opening of the bids or proposals but prior to the award process. Most entities have the legal authority to obtain the data required for assessing the capability of an offeror after bids or proposals have been opened. Although the determination of responsibility should be as objective as possible, it also may involve subjective elements reflecting the judgment of the purchasing officer. Under no circumstances should an offer or an offeror ever be evaluated on the basis of a requirement or a criterion that is not set forth in the solicitation document.

Decisions regarding more complex procurements by public sector organizations should be referred to evaluation committees.

B O X   41-3

EXAMPLES OF NONRESPONSIVENESS IN BIDDING

Responsive bidder means a person who has submitted a bid that conforms in all material respects to the invitation for bids (or request for proposals). (*The Model Procurement Code for State and Local Governments*, Section 3-101)

Examples of nonresponsive bidders include those who:

♦ Substitute their standard terms and conditions for those included in the solicitation document

♦ Qualify their offers in such a manner as to nullify or limit their liability to the jurisdiction

♦ Fail to conform with required delivery schedules as set forth in the solicitation or the permissible alternatives

♦ Qualify their prices in such a manner that the bid price cannot be determined

♦ Make their bids contingent upon their receiving award on other bids of theirs that are currently under consideration

♦ Make the purchasing authority responsible for determining that the bidder's products or services conform to the specifications

♦ Limit the rights of the contracting authority under any contract clause (National Institute of Governmental Purchasing, 1977)

Contract Administration

Contract administration historically has consisted of little more than following up on orders and inspecting incoming merchandise. Now, however, with many public sector organizations acquiring expensive high technology or relying on contractors to produce a variety of services, the function is receiving unprecedented attention. In order to make the best possible use of financial resources and to ensure the quality of services delivered by the organization, public sector purchasers should implement broad contract administration functions based on the objectives in Box 41-4. Many public sector organizations are using start-up conferences to initially ensure that contractual requirements are understood and that as many potential problems as possible are identified and addressed.

B O X   41–4

OBJECTIVES OF CONTRACT ADMINISTRATION

- Ensure that all necessary contractual requirements are spelled out clearly, correctly, and concisely
- Ensure that the staffs of both the public sector organization and the supplier understand their responsibilities under the contract
- Flush out and resolve as many potential problems as possible before the contract takes effect
- Check (after the contract becomes effective) to assure that the supplier provides goods or services in accordance with the contract
- Document problems and take the appropriate action to resolve and/or minimize their impact
- Take the lessons that are learned and utilize them (to the extent possible) to improve future contracting arrangements

Source: S. B. Gordon, "Purchasing," in J. Peterson and D. Strachota, eds., *Concepts and Practices in Local Government Finance*, Government Finance Officers Association, Chicago, 1991.

WHY PUBLIC SECTOR PURCHASING IS DIFFERENT

Several important factors make purchasing in public sector organizations different from purchasing in the private sector, including *external forces*, which are exerted by the institution's public/constituents, and *internal forces*, which emanate from the culture of the organizations themselves. These forces shape the way the purchasing function is organized, the way it responds to ethical issues, its staffing and professional development, and the way it handles a wide variety of operational challenges.

External Forces

All organizations are affected to some extent by such external factors as laws and regulations, political processes, and economic conditions. However, public sector organizations may be the champions when it comes to both the number and the diversity of external forces that must be taken into account when both policy and business decisions are made.

The external forces that shape the culture in public sector organizations, and that, in turn, mold the purchasing function, emanate primarily from the various constituencies of these entities. A significant number of these constituencies are highly organized—more so, for example, than the typical loosely knit consumers of industry's goods and services. In fact, some of these constituencies, including taxpayers and members of churches and associations, even play a formal part in the governance of the entities with which they are affiliated. Others, such as students and their parents, have a role in school governance. The effect is to make it virtually impossible for public sector organizations to ignore any of their constituency groups when making decisions.

Other constituencies, although not direct consumers of the services of a public sector organization, also seek to influence its decisions. In education, for example, state and federal agencies who supply education funds apply both academic and financial pressures. Foundations, donors, lending institutions, and state and federal agencies that "purchase" research and other services exert financial pressure. Accrediting agencies, professional societies, and educational associations impose their requirements. And all sorts of special interest groups demand a piece of the action. The news media like to have access to all communications and information, based upon the idea that these items are public property. Moreover, quasi-external forces, such as student factions, alumni associations, faculty groups, disadvantaged business organizations, and governing boards, seek to advance special agendas. Each constituent acts as though it owns a piece of the organization and possesses a right to participate in its governance and administration.

The actions of elected governing bodies, such as the U.S. Congress, state legislatures, county boards, city councils, and school boards, often have a significant impact on the purchasing function in a public sector entity. Certain policies, such as statutes that require the purchase of recycled or recyclable products, legislation that is designed to increase purchases from minority-owned businesses, and regulations that prescribe how hazardous products are to be acquired and disposed of, have a direct effect. Other policies, such as those that place strings on what can be purchased with a particular fund or require the purchasing function to account for its actions to community, accreditation, or student special interest groups, are less direct.

Dealing with all these external demands challenges purchasers in the public sector to manage their many outside "bosses" effectively.

Internal Forces—Organizational Culture

Culture is "the set of key values, guiding beliefs and understandings that are shared by members of an organization. It defines basic organizational values, and communicates to new members the way to think and act, and how things ought to be done."[1] Many internal forces join with environmental factors to shape the culture of a public sector organization and, in turn, to influence how purchasers do their job.

Commitment to Mission

It is public sector organizations' sense of mission that most distinguishes them from private sector entities. Whereas private sector organizations exist to generate income, public sector organizations seek to bring about change in society generally and in individual human beings particularly. The traditional mission of government, regardless of level, has been to promote the health, safety, and welfare of the citizenry. The product of a school, whether public sector governmental or private nonprofit, is a child who learns. Despite the often cumbersome policies and procedures under which they must operate, public sector purchasers must not lose sight of the mission of the organization in which they work.

Organizational Size

Most public sector entities, especially the larger ones, have bureaucratic characteristics. Such organizations "provide us with abundant goods and services, and . . . surprise us with astonishing facts . . . that are testimony to their effectiveness." They also are "accused of many sins, including inefficiency, irresponsibility, and the creation of demeaning, routinized work that alienates both employees and the people an organization tries to serve."[2] Regardless of the size of his or her organization, the public sector purchaser must be able to "work the system" *legally and ethically* in order to provide needed support to those who interact directly or indirectly with the organization. This can be especially difficult in larger,

---

1. R. L. Daft, *Organization Theory and Design*, 3d ed., West, St. Paul, Minnesota, 1989.
2. Ibid.

more bureaucratic organizations where the cultures tend to prioritize control, policies, and enforcement before considering service.

The Power Structure

The distribution of power within a public sector organization also shapes organizational culture and affects in several ways how the purchasing function operates. The public sector purchasing department is normally viewed as a mid-level provider of a support function, typically not possessing much clout within the entity. Consequently, purchasing management, which must rely heavily on top management support as well as on effective working relationships with other departments in order to achieve their objectives, generally cannot initiate or change policies and procedures without prior approval from their superiors or internal clients.

Internal Restrictions on What Can and Cannot Be Purchased

Because public sector organizations obtain their resources either from people who are taxed or from those who freely donate their personal wealth, there are usually constraints on what purchasing can and cannot purchase. These constraints are designed to prevent expenditures for goods or services that the entity's constituents might see as frivolous or luxurious. While it is usual for commercial businesses to want to appear successful and affluent to attract new customers, most public sector organizations tend to want to project an image of conservatism and frugality. Consequently, all forms of entertainment and purchases of decorative desk or office items are usually prohibited. Sometimes purchases of carpet, draperies, and wood furniture are also prohibited or limited to the very top levels of the organization.

Job Security

Because of the "here today/here tomorrow" attitude in most public sector organizations, the staff tends to be more stable than in the commercial sector. Public employee unions and civil service-type rules have left their mark on the way employees are hired, supervised, and terminated. There may be less money available for training and salaries than in the private sector, but it may be offset by the difficulty of measuring purchasing's contribution to the bottom line and the increased job security. Despite this, and in some cases because of it, the public sector can boast of having some of the most dedicated, talented, and committed staff available.

Goal Confusion and Difficulty of Measuring Output

In the private sector, it is common for firms to identify a relatively narrow market niche and then to develop policies, procedures, and strategies designed to enable them to accomplish their goals. In those enterprises, almost everyone knows what business their organization is in and understands the short- and long-range goals. They talk in terms of contribution to the bottom line and return on investment.

The business of public sector government, on the other hand, is usually much less clear. Although, for example, most can generally agree that universities are in the teaching, research, and public service business, few can agree on which objectives are more important, what mix is appropriate, or what strategies are the best to pursue to ensure top performance on each objective. For a public sector purchasing function, it could be low price overall, and could even be the accomplishment of a particular goal such as value buying a product that is environmentally safe or buying it from a disadvantaged business. Is it better to save money for a program by purchasing the lowest priced materials or to buy what the user is familiar with and produce savings through maximizing the user's efficiency and convenience? Because of this, it is very difficult to measure one's contribution to objectives that few, if any, of the participants can agree on. Purchasing managers in the public sector are often frustrated in their attempts to quantify their contribution and sometimes fail to justify their existence effectively.

ORGANIZATIONAL ISSUES

Legal Authority to Purchase

The authority for a public sector organization, particularly a governmental organization, to contract for goods or services is or should be defined in writing. In the case of a public sector governmental organization, this authority is, or should be, contained in a set of statutes, a charter provision, an ordinance, or some other form of law.

Although only two statutes provide the framework for federal government contracting, literally thousands of other federal laws affect the federal procurement process. Together, these statutes and laws create agencies; define roles and missions; authorize programs; appropriate funds; balance public and private interest; provide for methods of procurement and for contract award procedures; and promote fairness, effectiveness, and uniformity."[3] The federal enabling laws are supplemented by the Federal Acquisition Regulation (FAR). First effective on April 1, 1984, the FAR is designed to be a "single, uniform, simplified regulation governing the acquisition of supplies and services with appropriated funds for all federal executive agencies, both civil and military." The FAR is "designed for direct application by contracting officers and acquisition managers at all levels." However, agencies are "authorized to implement or supplement the FAR in a limited way and under restrictive conditions."[4]

Each of the 50 state governments has its own unique set of constitutional, statutory, and regulatory requirements that affect how the agencies, institutions, and offices of that state purchase. These laws incorporate (to varying degrees) provisions of the American Bar Association's *Model Procurement Code for State and Local Government.* The general effect of the incorporation of the *Model Procurement Code* has been to bring about a degree of standardization in terminology and practice among the state governments. Improvements based upon the *Model Procurement Code* also have given state purchasers greater flexibility and allowed them to be more responsive to operating needs, especially the more unusual ones.

The legal requirements affecting purchasing by the nation's 85,000 local governments are even more numerous and diverse in their form and content than those of the state governments. However, generally speaking, at least the general foundation for these requirements can be found in state law. Accordingly, these requirements, like the state government requirements, are increasingly being standardized by the adoption of various portions of the *Model Procurement Code* or its derivative, the *Model Procurement Ordinance.*

Purchasing authority in *private* and *quasi-public* nonprofit organizations flows from their governing boards. Generally speaking, the boards try to provide for as much latitude as possible in purchasing policies; yet public sector purchasers still are not as free of legal constraints as their counterparts in the private sector. Members, rate payers, and clients—like taxpayers—demand accountability. Moreover, the federal government, through Circular A-110 of the Office of Management

---

3. W. T. Thybony, *Government Contracting Based on the Federal Acquisition Regulation (FAR) and the Competition in Contracting Act,* 2d revision, Thybony, Inc., Reston, Virginia, 1987.
4. Ibid.

and Budget (OMB), has established minimum standards for purchasing systems in the nongovernmental, nonprofit organizations that obtain and spend federal money pursuant to federal assistance programs.

Public sector organizations of any type should consider using the *Model Procurement Code* as a basis for defining purchasing authority for the first time or for updating and improving what already exists. The key purchasing issues addressed in the model code include:

+ Organization
+ Source selection and contract formation
+ Modification and termination of contracts
+ Cost principles
+ Supply management
+ Legal and contractual remedies
+ Intergovernmental relations
+ Assistance to small and disadvantaged businesses
+ Ethics in contracting

Forms of Organization

Federal

The U.S. federal government is the largest purchaser in the world, with literally thousands of different buying offices spending a total of over $200 billion in 1998 to acquire goods and services. At departmental level, the Department of Defense is by far the largest purchaser (national defense items). The Veterans Department and the General Services Administration (GSA) also are major purchasers, appearing in the top division of a list that also includes such organizations as the U.S. Postal Service, the National Aeronautics and Space Administration, the Department of Transportation, and the Tennessee Valley Authority. A substantial proportion of the common-use goods and services utilized by civilian agencies and military departments is contracted by the GSA. Its four major subdivisions and their respective areas of responsibility are:

+ *Information resources management service.* The direction of government-wide programs for the procurement, management, and use of automated data processing and telecommunications equipment, software, and services
+ *Public buildings service.* The design and construction of buildings, as well as the planning of space, interior design, leasing of offices, and maintenance of offices

- *Federal supply service.* The supplying of thousands of common-use items ranging from paper and paper clips to cars, vans, trucks, and buses
- *Federal property resources services.* Sales of surplus land, buildings, and improvements that other federal agencies no longer need

The counterpart to the GSA within the Department of Defense is the Defense Logistics Agency (DLA). The DLA manages approximately 2 million general supply items for the military services. In addition, various commands within the departments of the Air Force, Army, and Navy are responsible for providing items related to their specific missions.

The federal government is not only the largest purchasing operation in the world, it is also probably the largest bureaucracy in the world. And it has purchasing functions that report to administrators at all levels. Virtually all who head up purchasing operations are civil service employees. At the highest levels, such as the centralized purchasing operations for a Cabinet-level department, the key individuals hold deputy director titles. At the lowest levels, they are clerks and technicians who wield limited decentralized purchasing power.

States

Although state laws vary significantly, most of them vest state purchasing authority in a central business unit or agency, generally a state department of general services or administration. This organization is usually headed either by an appointed official or high-level civil service employee who reports to an elected official, such as the governor or lieutenant governor, either directly or through another appointed official. The director of purchasing typically is a division head reporting to this department head. As more states incorporate provisions of the *Model Procurement Code*, state purchasing offices increasingly are delegating more day-to-day purchasing responsibility to using department staffs, retaining the right to pull back such authority if it is abused. In some states, certain universities and/or the Department of Transportation have legal purchasing authority equal to that of the central purchasing office of the state itself.

Counties

Depending on the size of a county and the state in which it is located, purchasing within that county will be governed by state law, local law, or both. Likewise, purchasing (even in a large county) can be very centralized, partially centralized, or completely decentralized. This depends on the number of constitutionally separate departments within the county and on the willingness of the heads of those units to cooperate with one another. The centralized purchasing function or, in its absence, the purchasing agency for the general government typically report to the chief administrative officer, a deputy administrative officer, or a finance or administrative services director. Variations occur where the head of purchasing reports directly to an elected official.

Cities

City purchasing operations and the reporting relationships of city purchasing managers are very sensitive to city size and the particular form of city government. For example, cities may be governed by aldermen, city councils, commissions, or simply by resolutions passed at town hall meetings. A mayor or city manager could be a city's chief administrative officer, and the city's purchasing manager could report to either. Generally, a municipal purchasing official will report to a director of administration or finance.

Colleges and Universities

Typically, both public and private colleges and universities are headed by a chief executive officer, called "president" or "chancellor." This official reports to a board of directors, governors, or trustees that sets institutional policy and controls the institution's funds and property. The board may be staffed by appointment, election, or a combination of the two. Typically the president or chancellor has two major subordinates who are responsible for the academic and administrative arms of the organization. The purchasing manager usually reports, either directly or through a materials manager or other intermediary executive, to the major subordinate responsible for the administrative arm.

Primary and Secondary Schools

Most medium- and large-sized school systems have a separate, centralized purchasing department. The head of purchasing typically reports to the superintendent or a deputy, who in turn reports to an elected school board.

Hospitals

Hospitals are organized very much like colleges and universities, with a director reporting to a governing board and the purchasing manager reporting to the director, either directly or through a materials manager or other administrative officer.

Utilities

The quasi-public entities, such as public utilities, municipal transit districts, and port and bridge authorities, generally have centralized purchasing organizations that acquire high-value equipment, purchase design and construction services, and establish standing agreements for common-use goods and services. However, because these organizations tend to have relatively far-flung or remote operations, varying degrees of decentralization are employed, with automated systems tying everything together for control purposes.

In any public sector organization, the chief purchasing official normally has the authority to develop and specify the detailed procedures to be used within both the central purchasing function and the operating agencies and departments that have been delegated limited purchasing authority. Typically, central purchasing officers are responsible not only for developing these policies and procedures, but for ensuring, through audits and management controls, that those policies and procedures are being followed.

Internal Organization of Purchasing Departments

Public sector purchasing departments generally are organized by customer department, commodity, or some combination of the two. The *departmental* orientation assigns groups of client departments to particular buyers; the *commodity* orientation assigns kinds or groups of commodities and services to the purchaser. Purchasing departments in most large public sector organizations use a commodity orientation, while purchasing functions in many of the smaller entities are organized along departmental lines.

The decision regarding which method to use is important because it has a pervasive effect on the department's efficiency, its effectiveness in meeting unique institutional goals, and the way it carries out its duties. Perhaps it is an oversimplification to say that departmental orientation favors service while commodity orientation favors efficiency, but there is at least an element of validity to that generalization.

The *commodity* orientation emphasizes purchaser specialization based upon unique product knowledge and is said to produce purchasers who are expert in a relatively limited spectrum of products and suppliers, are good technicians, and are most effective at producing savings.

This method is also said to be less user-friendly because user department personnel, requiring a wide range of goods and services, may have to deal with many different purchasers simultaneously.

Departmental orientation, on the other hand, is said to produce buyers who are highly loyal to their assigned client departments, whose expertise and product knowledge are more general, and whose knowledge of departmental business and personnel is highly developed.

Sometimes central purchasing department purchasers are physically located in the client departments to which they are assigned. These purchasers, sometimes known as *satellite purchasers*, naturally come to identify strongly with the client department; if these purchasers are correctly supervised and motivated by the purchasing manager, they can be very effective at performing both the required service and control functions in proper balance.

The key to the appropriate choice of organizational form lies in the organization's culture and the size and degree of specialization or personalization that is required. In the last analysis, the correct method is the one that works best in a given situation.

Centralization and Decentralization

A *centralized* purchasing function exists when the authority and responsibility for accomplishing all the purchasing and purchasing-related functions is assigned to a central organizational unit under the control of a director of materials management or purchasing. *Decentralized* purchasing exists when those functions are dispersed throughout the organization or are accomplished by departments that are not under the materials management or purchasing director's control.

As a practical matter, very few purchasing functions are either 100% centralized or decentralized. Even in the public sector, where the materials function is generally much more centralized than in the private sector area, complete centralization seldom exists. Rather, most public sector purchasing functions are hybrids, with certain authority and responsibility being assigned to operating units and the remainder centralized in an administrative unit.

The precise degree of centralization or decentralization that should exist in any organization cannot be determined by a standard formula or rule of thumb. An entity's objectives, culture, resources, and operating needs all play a part in determining what should be centralized and what can safely be decentralized.

Most arguments for centralization fall into the following four categories:

1. *Specialization.* This argument recognizes that those who have to perform two distinctly different functions, such as when purchasing is an incidental function in an operating unit, will often let the lesser function suffer. It also recognizes that most purchasing functions are unique and that unique knowledge must be possessed for them to be performed successfully. Centralization allows specialists to be employed and enables them to enhance their skills continually through practicing their specialty.

2. *Accountability.* Internal control considerations favor centralization. For example, it is generally agreed that a minimum number of people should have the authority to make financial commitments, and those people should be highly qualified. When authority is decentralized, accountability is easier to avoid.

3. *Objectivity of viewpoint.* Unlike personnel in operating units, central purchasing people tend to be motivated by what is best for the entire institution. They can combine requirements to reduce acquisition prices, and they can integrate functions to reduce operational and administrative costs. Centralized policies and procedures are more consistent and can be more evenly applied centrally.

4. *Administrative convenience.* A centralized purchasing function can usually interact more effectively with other centralized administrative functions and with outside constituencies, such as suppliers, governmental agencies, and auditors. In fact, the existence of an unduly centralized purchasing system will most certainly prove to be an impediment to obtaining and administering funds from outside sources.

Administrative officers who are concerned with cost containment, internal control, efficiency, and consistency of policies and procedures tend to favor more, rather than less, centralization. This is especially true when the need for cost containment and control is high, as with high-value or high-volume materials needs, and less so when centralization does not result in sufficient added value, such as the low-dollar acquisitions. Consequently, in the public sector, most purchasing is centralized in the main purchasing department or agency, with outlying operational units being authorized to acquire supplies and services of limited value.

Emerging trends that are increasing the efficiency of public organizations include allowing department staffs to place orders directly with the suppliers who are already under contract with their entity, and using credit cards or procurement cards in place of purchase orders.

ETHICAL ISSUES

Unlike most purchasers in the private sector, purchasers in the public sector (especially the governmental ones) live in a fishbowl. There is no way or place for public sector purchasers to hide. Their activities are open to public scrutiny as a matter of policy, if not law. Their constituents, whether taxpayers, students and their families, donors, or parishioners, typically believe they have an incontrovertible right to a voice in the way "their" funds are spent, and they demand that they be spent in a way that they perceive to be fair and unbiased by special interests.

Unfortunately, this does not make special interest groups go away. In government, elected officials are very accessible to their constituents. Indeed, they must be in order to represent effectively the people who elected them. Their constituents have certain justifiable needs, and their elected representatives must be committed to addressing them. But some of their constituents may have *special* needs, and some of those may not prove in the long term to be in the public interest.

At the same time that these elected officials are representing their constituents' interests, they are deciding many policy and budgetary matters that affect public organizations within their jurisdiction. Considering this, it is not surprising that elected officials sometimes exert political pressure on public purchasing departments. In fact, it is common in many jurisdictions for an elected official to contact the head of purchasing and express a viewpoint about purchasing matters. Because elected officials wield considerable political power, these viewpoints are not to be taken lightly.

While it is extremely rare for elected officials to request purchasing to do illegal or unethical things, it is normal for them to request special treatment for a constituent or group of constituents and to ask for favorable rulings in matters that are in the purview of the purchasing official. For example, the purchasing officer could be asked to favor a certain candidate for a job or a certain firm for a contract. Sometimes the purchasing officer is asked to favor groups of businesses, such as those owned by their minority constituents.

Not all of these influences prove to be actual problems, but all of them do provide purchasing and other officials with ethical dilemmas to resolve. To help guide their officials through this minefield, many jurisdictions have adopted ethics laws that assist the purchasing and other officials to identify the right decisions. The better programs are supported by training, and counseling is provided for those who require it.

In addition, professional associations that represent purchasers in the public sector (see Professional Development Issues, above) have developed ethics codes to define the profession's norms about the rightness or wrongness of certain actions and the appropriateness of the motives and ends of such actions. The codes also guide their members' actions when there are no applicable laws or institutional policies.

The special issues covered by purchasing codes of ethics are all based on three concepts: *impartiality*, *honesty*, and *loyalty*.

+ *Impartiality* means that the purchasers play no favorites. They treat all suppliers equally and do not discriminate on the basis of things other than value and the merits of each transaction.
+ *Honesty* means that the purchasers tell the truth in dealing with suppliers. They do not mislead them in the hope of getting a better deal. They must play fair at all times.
+ *Loyalty* means that the purchasers should be loyal to their employer first and should keep their business and personal lives separate. They must remain free from conflicts of interest.

Other than to help protect against inappropriate political influence, there are several important reasons why buyers, in general, should be particularly concerned with ethics. One has to do with protecting sources of supply. A purchaser's job is to acquire goods and services when needed and at prices and terms that are favorable to his or her employer. To be able to do this consistently, public sector purchasers must, at all times, be impartial and honest in their dealings with suppliers. Unethical treatment drives suppliers away or motivates them to retaliate for being mistreated, and neither result is desirable in a sector where maximum competition and fair play are highly valued.

Another important reason for being ethical has to do with the proper uses of power. Purchasers are uniquely powerful. They have *purchasing power!* They have the power to reward or punish suppliers by the way they spend their employers' money. They can *reward* by giving orders, by not being a tough negotiator, or by freely granting concessions. They can *punish* by withholding orders or by abusing suppliers in a variety of ways. Unethical purchasers may also attempt to use their "power" over purchasing's internal customers or users to extract cooperation or compliance. Strictly observing ethical guidelines helps buyers guard against abusing their power.

Purchasers are *agents*, and the law requires them to observe higher principles of conduct than ordinary employees. These are called *fiduciary duties*. Among them are duties that have ethical ramifications, including the duty of loyalty, the duty of accountability, the duty to inform, and the duty of confidentiality.

Finally, professional purchasers are anxious to protect their employer and their profession from unfavorable publicity. They know that the bad press coverage that results when they do not act ethically can be very damaging to professional and institutional reputations and can bring on additional laws and governmental control.

In general, any purchaser, and especially public purchasers, should avoid accepting gifts or favors of any kind from suppliers. They also should avoid intentionally misleading or mistreating a supplier in any way. Purchasers should avoid playing favorites among suppliers or treating one differently than they would another in a competitive situation. They should keep their business and personal lives entirely separate, avoiding conflicts of interest.

PROFESSIONAL DEVELOPMENT ISSUES

Purchasers in public sector organizations should possess the fundamental and specialized knowledge, skills, and abilities that are required of effective purchasers in any type of organization. They also should possess the unique knowledge and abilities that are required to function effectively within the specific context of a public sector organization. The general purchasing knowledge and understanding should encompass:

+ The overall procurement, supply management, logistics, and distribution process
+ Ethical principles applicable to purchasing and materials management
+ Commercial markets and how they function

- Business and trade practices, including their effect on manufacturing, distribution, and pricing
- Principles and practices of economics as they apply to markets and pricing
- Principles and practices of financial and cost accounting
- Principles of business and agency law, including the Uniform Commercial Code and its effects on the purchasing process
- Traditional, nontraditional, and state-of-the-art purchasing methods, including how and when they should be used
- Establishment and maintainance of good client and supplier relations
- Traditional internal control principles that apply to the purchasing process
- Automated systems that are most effective in improving the quality and efficiency of the purchasing function
- Government requirements that affect hazardous materials acquisition, use, and disposal, and safety requirements (e.g., Occupational Safety and Health Administration (OSHA)), as they relate to equipment and supplies
- Government requirements that affect the conduct of business and employment
- Customs regulations that affect the import and export of goods
- The international monetary system, including exchange rates, and principles and practices of offshore purchasing
- Traffic and transportation regulations that affect the cost of shipping goods from suppliers to the institution

The specific knowledge and understanding required of public sector purchasers includes:

- Proven principles and practices of public sector purchasing, as advanced by the professional purchasing associations
- Recommended statutory and regulatory coverage as set forth in the *Model Procurement Code for State and Local Governments*
- Applicable requirements for purchasing with third-party funds, including the requirements of the United States Office of Management and Budget as well as those of grantee agencies, foundations, and donors

- Ethical principles as they relate specifically to purchasing in a context where the openness and integrity of the process are of paramount importance

Of overriding importance is the fact that members of the purchasing staff must understand and be able to work effectively within the particular culture that makes their public sector organization uniquely different from other organizations.

Participation in Professional Associations

Purchasing professionals in public sector organizations should be encouraged to join and be active in the professional associations that serve the needs of purchasers in that sector. National organizations whose members predominantly are public sector purchasers include:

- The National Institute of Governmental Purchasing, Inc. (NIGP)
- The National Association of State Purchasing Officials (NASPO)
- The National Purchasing Institute (NPI), which is a District XII affiliate of the National Association of Purchasing Management (NAPM) specializing in government and institutional purchasers
- Rural Electric Utilities (REU), which is also an affiliate of NAPM's District XII
- The National Association of Educational Buyers (NAEB)

Other professional associations of interest to purchasing professionals in all sectors include:

- The National Association of Purchasing Management (NAPM)
- The American Society for Hospital Materials Management (ASHMM)
- The National Property Management Association (NPMA)
- The National Contract Management Association (NCMA)
- The Society of Logistics Engineers (SOLE)
- The Association of School Business Officers (ASBO)

Note: Several states have specific organizations, such as the California Association of Public Purchasing Officers (CAPPO) and the Carolinas' Association of Public Purchasing.

Certification

Several of the professional organizations offer professional designations that certify that the holder has demonstrated a prescribed level of knowledge in the field as well as satisfied certain other requirements. Two of these designations, the Professional Public Buyer (P.P.B.) and the Certified Public Purchasing Officer (C.P.P.O.), were developed specifically to address the needs of purchasers in governmental and quasi-governmental organizations. Both the P.P.B. and the C.P.P.O. programs are administered by the Universal Public Purchasing Certification Council, a certifying body jointly sponsored by the National Institute of Governmental Purchasing and the National Association of State Purchasing Officials.

The National Association of Purchasing Management (NAPM) offers two purchasing certifications that include requirements for knowledge of public purchasing concepts: the Accredited Purchasing Practitioner (A.P.P.) and the Certified Purchasing Manager (C.P.M.). The C.P.M. has been officially recognized as a broadly based professional standard by a group of other purchasing organizations, including the National Purchasing Institute and the National Association of Educational Buyers.

Additional designations include the Certified Professional Contracts Manager (C.P.C.M.) and the Certified Associate Contracts Manager (C.A.C.M.), offered by the National Contract Management Association, and the Certified Professional Logistician (C.P.L.), offered by the Society of Logistics Engineers.

Formal Education, Seminars, and Conferences

A large number of noncredit programs are offered for public sector purchasers by professional associations, universities, and other organizations. And college courses and degree programs in purchasing are becoming much more widely available today than they were just a few years ago. Such professional development programs not only are useful for the job-related knowledge and skills they impart, but they also prepare purchasers for professional certification and career advancement.

Professional Involvement

Interacting with one's peers on a regular basis is one of the most effective and relatively inexpensive approaches to professional development. This

can be done informally, or it can be accomplished through active participation in the professional organizations at the national, regional, and
local levels. Public sector purchasing associations are especially good
sources of information and knowledge because the purchasers in that
sector generally are not constrained by a fear of disclosing proprietary
information to a competitor.

OPERATIONAL ISSUES

Products and Services Procured

Although private sector firms and public sector institutions require many
of the same goods and services, the particular operating requirements of
most public sectors make purchasing in that environment unique. Most
public sectors do not manufacture a product and therefore do not have
the same large predictable requirements for materials. Additionally, most
of them have to acquire a number of unique products and services that
private businesses usually do not use.

An excellent example of the extreme diversity of goods and services
required by a public sector organization can be seen in requirements of
the typical large university. Most universities are like small cities—and
some are not so small. They have most of the same infrastructural needs
to support, and they have to provide access to all of the equipment,
supplies, and services needed to maintain that infrastructure.

In most cases, therefore, institutional purchasers must possess a
unique mixture of specialized market knowledge. As a consequence,
many institutions hire employees with specialties and group them together in teams with responsibilities for purchasing the commodities in
which they have expertise. For example, there might be a team responsible for furniture, furnishings, and food. Other teams might specialize
in computers and telecommunications equipment; medical, scientific,
and laboratory materials; or maintenance, repair, and operating products.

Unfortunately for purchasers in small public sector organizations,
the diversity of product and service needs is not directly proportional to
institutional size. Thus, in small organizations, a single purchaser, and
sometimes a general business officer who is also a purchaser, can be
forced into the role of jack-of-all-trades, dealing with the entire spectrum
of acquisitions.

As if diversity of goods and services were not enough to deal with,
the unpredictability of the requirements for quantity and quality is often

a major problem in public sector purchasing. In the private sector, manufacturing and distribution firms usually can program their purchases to support reasonably well-defined production rates or consumer demands. A significant proportion of goods and services needed in the public sector, on the other hand, can be difficult to predict. Unfortunately, this can make purchasing in these environments more reactive than proactive.

Another difference between the public sector and private sector is that in most private sector organizations a high proportion of material is requisitioned by the administration. It is purchased for stock or ordered by a material control group for the production process. By contrast, the bulk of public sector goods is requisitioned by hundreds of departments, offices, and projects using many applicable budgets. This requires institutional purchasers to deal with a multitude of internal clients, each sometimes a fiefdom unto itself, and most with their own unique styles and needs. This requires public sector purchasers to be particularly effective at developing good client relations.

Make-or-Buy Decisions, Privatization, and Outsourcing

Make-or-buy decisions involve judgments about which of the two alternatives should be used to satisfy a given need. In the case of goods, for example, both in-house and commercially operated machine shops can produce research apparatus for a department of a university. And the same is true with services such as vehicle pool management, maintenance operations, and trash collection. The objective is to arrive at a make-or-buy decision that maximizes utilization of the public entity's resources, strengths, and managerial capabilities and best contributes toward the attainment of its goals.

The need for a make-or-buy decision usually arises out of a desire for new goods or services or out of the unsatisfactory performance of an existing commercial provider. Performance problems can involve quality, timeliness of service delivery, or cost.

Make-or-buy concepts are often utilized in private sector business and may even result in the purchase of the manufacturing firm(s) that supply the goods that contribute to the ultimate product. But in the public sector there is very little application of the make-or-buy decision. When one does occur, it is probably done without input or advice from the purchasing staff.

Many times the user may try to avoid the budget process by requesting that a special desk, piece of equipment, or special service be provided by in-house staff, such as a carpenter, metal worker, or print press operation. If the final decision is left to the user, there will be little, if any, evaluation of the total cost to produce the item in-house versus obtaining it from the open market. Total cost application should include labor, employee benefits, parts, supplies, future training, maintenance, and liability.

The difficulty of a make-or-buy decision varies in direct proportion to the implementation costs and risks involved. Typically, the risk and cost are low when the institution already has the expertise and facilities necessary to provide the needed goods or services and the implementation is expected to be simple. For example, the risk is low when a small but unique electronic item is required and an electronics shop exists within the institution. High-risk, high-cost situations occur in opposite cases; for example, when an entity needs to establish a rapid transit system to move employees and visitors to and from remote neighborhoods and parking areas. In this example, the equipment, supplies, and operational costs are high; liability exposure is significant; and experienced rapid transit operators probably do not exist on the entity's staff.

Many make-or-buy decisions really end up in purchasing as an outsource or privatization project. When a *buy* decision is implemented, the purchasing professional, in effect, becomes the manager of the function, with the outside source providing the expertise, labor, and material. Thus, purchasing officials may have the same managerial interests toward the outside providers of goods and services as the other in-house executives have toward the in-house enterprises they manage. This, plus their specialized knowledge and professional abilities, is why purchasing and materials managers should actively participate in make-or-buy decisions.

Several states have laws that constrain public agencies, including state-related universities, from operating enterprises that compete with the private sector. In effect, these laws obviate many make-or-buy decisions. Even when such laws are not applicable, however, institutional competition with the private sector can still be a controversial issue. Therefore, the political ramifications of potential *make* decisions should be factored into the analysis before such decisions are finalized.

Bonding

Governmental organizations historically have been required by statute to mandate that bidders post bonds "as a part of the bidding and award process, and as applicable until completion of a contract" for construction and public works projects.[5] Bonds generally have not been legally required for equipment, supply, and service contracts, but there is a growing trend toward specifying performance and warranty bonds for goods and services. The principal types of bonds utilized in public sector purchasing include:

- Bid bonds, which afford an entity protection against an offer being withdrawn after bids are opened
- Payment bonds, which are utilized almost exclusively in construction contracts and require the contractor to guarantee payment to suppliers and subcontractors
- Performance bonds, which are intended to protect the owner/ entity against a contractor's failure to fulfill a contract
- Guaranty or warranty bonds, which ensure that the contractor will repair or correct defects after the project is completed

Cost and Price Avoidance Techniques

Public sector organizations rarely have sufficient resources to fund all the needed programs and services. Consequently, these organizations often look to the purchasing function to extend available resources by (1) reducing the total cost of goods and services purchased and (2) controlling the administrative costs of acquiring those goods and services. Popular techniques, which also are used in the private sector, include standardization, consolidation of requirements, scheduled buying, term contracting, and a variety of procedures that reduce lead times and sometimes allow entities to take prompt payment discounts. Public sector entities also cooperate with one another at the organizational level to obtain lower prices, reduce administrative costs, and otherwise seek to provide products and services at the lowest total cost. The methods utilized include:

- Cooperative purchasing, which encompasses a variety of arrangements through which two or more organizations purchase a product or service from the same contractor as a result of a single competitive solicitation

---

5. *State and Local Government Purchasing*, 4th ed., 1994, The Council of State Governments, Lexington, Kentucky.

+ Joint administrative (consolidated) purchasing, through which some or all of the purchases of two or more organizations are made by a purchasing office shared by those organizations
+ Group purchasing, through which participating entities take advantage of volume contracts established by a national or regional service, such as NAEB's Educational and Institutional Cooperative

When participating in such interorganizational arrangements, public sector purchasers should ensure that any third-party contract or agreement it uses has been established in accordance with all the requirements that apply to their particular purchasing program's policies and laws.

Socioeconomic Issues

The principal rationale for organizational programs that favor businesses owned by a particular segment of the population is to increase business awards to the preferred businesses. Since preferred business programs do not increase an organization's overall demand for goods or services, increases in awards to preferred businesses must be accompanied by decreases to businesses that are not so favored. This can raise constitutional issues and be very controversial, thereby requiring commitment, participation, and patience at the highest levels of management.

Most public sector organizations, even many private sector foundations and charities, enjoy the use of federal and/or state funds for a significant part, if not all, of their support. This subjects them to a variety of pressures regarding the kinds of social programs that should be supported. Also, most public sector organizations have important public service roles that obligate them to serve the needs and promote the interests of their local and state communities and citizens. Because of this, most public sector organizations are especially accountable for the social implications of how they spend their money. Important impacts for purchasing are programs that require formal or informal preferences to be extended to special groups of businesses, such as small businesses; those owned by socially and economically disadvantaged persons, women, or disabled persons; and sometimes businesses located in the organization's home states. Some of these formal and informal programs have been successfully challenged in the courts.

In-State and Local Preferences

These programs favor businesses that are located within a particular governmental jurisdiction. They vary in form from those that favor an in-state or local bidder, as in the case of a tie bid, to those that, for bid evaluation purposes, discount the bid price of an in-state or local bidder by a specified percentage. Reciprocal preferences, which penalize a supplier from another jurisdiction in proportion to the amount of preference accorded by that jurisdiction for its resident suppliers, are common. Preferences may be informal (a matter of practice) or formal (based in law). Application and enforcement can be very difficult.

Preferences for Small, Disadvantaged, and Women-Owned Businesses

Generally, these programs require that affirmative action be taken to increase awards to such businesses. Affirmative action always requires positive and creative efforts and sometimes calls for formal preferences to be applied to place targeted businesses at a competitive advantage. However, preferences have become somewhat problematic with the Supreme Court's *Croson* decision. In February 1989, the United States Supreme Court ruled in *Croson v. the City of Richmond, Virginia*[6] that racially based business affirmative action programs established without *prior findings of discrimination and "narrow tailoring"* as to the specific identity of targeted businesses were unconstitutional. Thus, *minority* business programs, especially those featuring set-asides (policies that set aside and reserve a certain percentage of awards for minority firms) and bid preferences (policies that allow a minority firm to bid a certain percentage higher than a nontargeted firm and still be considered the lowest bidder) have become subject to special constitutional scrutiny and challenge. As a result, many former *minority* business programs have been converted to *disadvantaged* or *small* business programs.

Generally, business affirmative action programs have four basic components: outreach, in-reach, compliance monitoring, and reporting:

♦ *Outreach. Outreach* is the term for reaching out into the community to identify qualified targeted firms and encourage them to become part of the institution's supplier base.

---

6. *J. A. Croson Company, Appellant v. City of Richmond, Appellee*, 822 F.2d 1355 (4th Cir. 1987).

Outreach is a business affirmative action's external marketing function.

♦ *In-reach.* "In-reach," a word coined to go with outreach, describes the process of reaching inside the institution to train, educate, and indoctrinate those on whom business affirmative action depends for its success. In-reach is the program's internal marketing function. In-reach activities consist of training and motivational activities for both purchasing and using department staff.

♦ *Compliance monitoring.* Some business affirmative action programs are two-tiered, particularly in the construction sector, where most of the work is done by subcontractors rather than prime contractors. Those programs require prime contractors to develop affirmative action subcontracting plans to accompany their bids. The terms of the invitations to bid often specify a minimum level of business affirmative action subcontracting plans to accompany their bids before these bids can be considered. In effect, this practice transfers a significant part of the business affirmative action responsibility from the buying institution to the prime contractor, who may or may not be appropriately aggressive in meeting, or making good faith efforts to meet, the goals of approved plans. The goal of the compliance monitoring function is to ensure that prime contractors comply with the terms of their business affirmative action contractual obligations.

♦ *Reporting.* The objective of the reporting function is to describe in accurate numeric terms the institution's business affirmative action performance. The need for accuracy and honesty in reporting cannot be overemphasized. If the numbers—both awards to targeted firms and the total base of expenditures—are not accurate or if they have been manipulated in any way to inflate the award percentage bottom line, the institution's credibility can be seriously and irrevocably damaged.

Automation

A majority of the purchasing functions in the public sector are at least somewhat automated and use computer and communications technology in the daily conduct of their business. However, the focus and the degree of automation vary greatly among organizations, with automation often meaning that an entity is able to generate a purchase order through its accounts payable system. By contrast, the more sophisticated systems eliminate much of the paperwork associated with the process and capture data that can be converted into a variety of useful management reports. These reports, which enable purchasing managers to make better planning and related decisions, are perhaps the principal benefit of automating the purchasing function. Typical reports provide information related to the type and frequency of purchasing actions, supplier performance, and staff productivity.

CLOSING

Although public sector organizations are diverse, purchasing in these organizations can be uniformly described as an accountable and outwardly visible process carried out by personnel who act in a stewardship capacity. Public organizations are the most regulated type of public sector entities, with their authority to act and decide generally spelled out in often detailed laws and regulations. Quasi-public sector organizations, although regulated somewhat less than public sector entities, are less constrained than the private sector nonprofit organization. Private sector, nonprofit purchasing tends to be much like private sector for-profit purchasing, with the major exception being the strong role played by the board of directors in the typical private sector nonprofit organization.

PART SIX

Purchasing and Supply Information Resources

Since 1915, the National Association of Purchasing Management (NAPM) has served purchasing and supply management professionals from around the world. From the national office in Tempe, Arizona, NAPM works with approximately 182 affiliated associations around the country to continually keep its members well informed, and always on top of the latest trends and developments in the field.

The information available from NAPM is extensive. The monthly Manufacturing and Non-Manufacturing *NAPM Report On Business®*, including the Purchasing Managers' Index (PMI) in the manufacturing survey, continues to serve as one of the key economic indicators available today. NAPM members receive this valuable report free in the pages of *Purchasing Today®* magazine, one of the many benefits of membership.

Members also enjoy discounts on a wide variety of educational products and services, along with reduced enrollment fees for more than 100 educational seminars held throughout the country each year. Topics cover the entire purchasing and supply management spectrum, from an introduction to purchasing to advanced purchasing strategies. Programs are available for senior executives as well as beginning professionals.

For executives interested in professional certification, NAPM administers the Certified Purchasing Manager (C.P.M.) and Accredited Purchasing Practitioner (A.P.P.) programs, enabling thousands of purchasing and supply professionals to continually test their abilities and keep their skills well honed. Members receive discounts on preparation materials and exam fees.

NAPM also publishes *The Journal of Supply Chain Management*, a one-of-a-kind publication designed especially for experienced purchasing and supply management professionals. Authored exclusively by accomplished practitioners and academicians, this quarterly publication targets purchasing and supply management issues, leading-edge research, long-term strategic developments, emerging trends, and more.

To provide a forum for educational enhancement and networking, NAPM holds the Annual International Purchasing Conference and Educational Exhibit in various locations throughout the United States each spring. Many of the top leaders in the purchasing and supply management field anticipate this unique opportunity for members and nonmembers alike to learn from each other and share success strategies.

To learn more about NAPM and the many ways it can help you advance your career, or to join online, visit NAPM on the Web at www.napm.org. In addition to general information, this expansive site features a vast database of purchasing and supply management information, much of which is available solely to members. You will find a listing of general purchasing and supply management references as well as an extensive article database, listings of products and seminars available, links to purchasing and supply related Web sites, a periodicals listing, other purchasing and supply organizations, and contact information for NAPM affiliates around the country.

For more information or to apply for membership via telephone, please call NAPM customer service at 800 / 888-6276 or 480 / 752-6276, extension 401.

Membership Application
National Association of Purchasing Management, Inc.

Members are encouraged to join a local affiliated association. To obtain information on the affiliated association closest to you and dues information, please call NAPM customer service at 800/888-6276 or 480/752-6276, extension 401. Applications can also be submitted via the Internet at www.napm.org.

Please check the appropriate box:
❑ New Member   ❑ Past Member   NAPM ID Number (if known) _____
❑ I am replacing the following current member in my company (If replacing a current member, send completed application to the affiliate.) Member Name _____ NAPM ID# _____

Dr. Mr. Mrs. Ms. Miss _____   ____   _____
    (please circle)   First Name   MI   Last Name

Title _____   Company Name _____
Please check the preferred mailing address:
❑ BUSINESS   ❑ HOME

City	State	ZIP Code	City	State	ZIP Code
Country		Postal Code	Country		Postal Code
E-Mail			E-Mail		

(   ) _____   (   ) _____   (   ) _____
  Business Phone Number**   Fax Number**   Home Phone Number **
                  **For international numbers, please include country and city codes.

Date of Birth (optional): ____/____/____
Industry Code (Choose a 3-digit code from the list provided on the back of this application): ___ ___ ___
Number of employees at your location (Please check one) ❑ under 100   ❑ 100-249   ❑ 250-499   ❑ 500-999   ❑ 1000+
Education (Check highest level completed): ❑ High School   ❑ Associate's   ❑ Bachelor's   ❑ Master's
❑ Other _____   ❑ Student (estimated graduation date): _____
Are you a C.P.M.?   ❑ Yes   ❑ No   Are you an A.P.P.?   ❑ Yes   ❑ No
Do you hold other professional designations? If so, please list:_____
Would you like to serve on a committee?   ❑ Yes   ❑ No
Are you involved in sales? If so, explain: _____

Option I	**Option II**
❑ **Regular Membership** (see back for details) I choose to become a member through (please provide affiliate name): _____	❑ **Direct National Membership** (see back for details) NAPM Dues (does not include affiliate benefits) $ _____ 270.00
For dues information and District/Affliate code, contact NAPM Customer Service at 800/888-6276 or 480/752-6276, extension 401.	**Option III**
	Regular Membership — Volume Discount Program (see back for details)
District/Affiliate Code (Code provided by NAPM): ___ ___ / ___ ___ ___	**Method of payment (U.S. Funds Only):**
Annual NAPM/Affiliate Dues: $_____	❑ Personal Check ❑ Company Check ❑ VISA
Administrative Fee: $_____ 20.00	❑ MasterCard ❑ American Express ❑ Diners Club
Affiliate Initiation Fee: $_____	Charge Card# _____
Other: $_____	Exp. Date __/__ Amount to be Charged $_____
TOTAL: $_____	Cardholder Signature _____

NAPM members receive *Purchasing Today*® magazine as a $12 portion and *NAPM InfoEdge* as a $12 portion of the national membership fee.
I agree to abide by the *NAPM Bylaws, Principles and Standards of*

Purchasing Practice, and *Statement of Antitrust Policy*, as stated on the back of this application. A copy of the *NAPM Bylaws* may be obtained by writing or calling NAPM Customer Service at the address and telephone number listed below.

Signature _____   Date _____

RETURN TO:	APPROVALS FOR AFFILIATE/NAPM USE ONLY	
	NAPM _____ Date _____	**PH 51**
	Affiliate _____ Date _____	
	Other _____ Date _____	

NAPM Use Only
Amount $ _____   Approval # _____   Date Entered _____ Initials _____

NAPM, P.O. Box 22160, Tempe, AZ 85285-2160 • 800/888-6276 or 480/752-6276, extension 401 • Fax 480/752-2299

OPTION I
Regular Membership

Regular Membership is when an individual chooses to join an Affiliated Association and National. Each Affiliated Association will set the annual dues for their local membership, which will include National dues.

Any individual that chooses this type of membership will receive discounts on both national and affiliate levels.

OPTION II
Direct National Membership

Direct National Membership is when an individual chooses to join the National level of NAPM only. The annual dues are $270.

This membership allows for discounts on the National level of products and services only.

OPTION III
Volume Discount Membership

With NAPM's new Volume Discount Membership, companies with 50 or more purchasing employees nationwide can save substantially on their membership dues. This category is available to corporations as well as governmental entities of every level and type.

The discount schedule is as follows:

Number of Members (nationwide)	Discount on Dues (without meals)
50-99	10%
100-249	20%
250 and over	30%

Volume Discount Membership is arranged through your company or government entity. Volume Discount members and all necessary information will be provided to NAPM headquarters by one individual from each company/entity. NAPM will invoice your company/entity for the correct amount of dues, and forward the affiliate portion to the affiliate. Any individual with Volume Discount Membership will receive the benefits of belonging to an affiliate and the National Association.

For more information contact NAPM at 800/888-6276 or 480/752-6276, extension 3111.

Principles and Standards of Purchasing Practice

LOYALTY TO YOUR COMPANY, JUSTICE TO THOSE WITH WHOM YOU DEAL, FAITH IN YOUR PROFESSION

From these principles are derived the NAPM Standards of Purchasing Practice.

1. Avoid the intent and appearance of unethical or com-promising practice in relationships, actions, and communications.

2. Demonstrate loyalty to the employer by diligently following the lawful instructions of the employer, using reasonable care, and only authority granted.

3. Refrain from any private business or professional activity that would create a conflict between personal interests and the interests of the employer.

4. Refrain from soliciting or accepting money, loans, credits, or prejudicial discounts, and the acceptance of gifts, entertainment, favors, or services from present or potential suppliers that might influence, or appear to influence, purchasing decisions.

5. Handle confidential or proprietary information belonging to employers or suppliers with due care and proper consideration of ethical and legal ramifications and governmental regulations.

6. Promote positive supplier relationships through courtesy and impartiality in all phases of the purchasing cycle.

7. Refrain from reciprocal agreements that restrain competition.

8. Know and obey the letter and spirit of laws governing the purchasing function and remain alert to the legal ramifications of purchasing decisions.

9. Encourage all segments of society to participate by demonstrating support

of small, disadvantaged, and minority-owned businesses.

10. Discourage purchasing's involvement in employer-sponsored programs of personal purchases that are not business related.

11. Enhance the proficiency and stature of the purchasing profession by acquiring and maintaining current technical knowledge and the highest standards of ethical behavior.

12. Conduct international purchasing in accordance with the laws, customs, and practices of foreign countries, consistent with United States laws, your organizational policies, and these Ethical Standards and Guidelines.

NAPM Antitrust Policy

It is the express policy and intention of NAPM to comply at all times with all existing laws, including the antitrust laws, and in furtherance of this policy, no activity or program will be sponsored or conducted by or within NAPM or any association affiliated with NAPM which in any matter whatsoever will represent or be deemed a violation of any existing law, including the antitrust laws. This statement of policy will be implemented by the publication of the "Principles for Antitrust Compliance," "Standards for NAPM Activities," "Standards for Membership and Professional Self-Regulation," and "Standards for Conduct & Use of Surveys" which are available to all members of the association upon request.

Dues, contributions, or gifts to this organization are not tax deductible charitable contributions for income tax purposes. Dues may, however, be deductible as a business expense.

Return to local affiliate association or:
NAPM
P.O. Box 22160
Tempe, AZ 85285-2160
Or fax application to 480/752-2299

STANDARD INDUSTRY CODES (SIC) — If you have responsibility for more than one industry, please use only the one three-digit code representing the major activity of the company, division, or plant for which you work. (Write the three-digit code on the reverse side of this form in the appropriate space.)

AGRICULTURE, FORESTRY, AND FISHERIES
- 010 Agricultural production - crops
- 020 Agricultural production - livestock
- 070 Agricultural services
- 080 Forestry
- 090 Fishing, hunting, trapping

MINING
- 100 Metal mining
- 120 Bituminous coal/lignite mining
- 130 Oil and gas extraction
- 140 Nonmetallic minerals, except fuels

CONTRACT CONSTRUCTION
- 150 General building contractors
- 160 Heavy construction contractors
- 170 Special trade contractors

MANUFACTURING
- 200 Food and kindred products
- 210 Tobacco manufacturers
- 220 Textile mill products
- 230 Apparel/other textile products
- 240 Lumber and wood products
- 250 Furniture and fixtures
- 260 Paper and allied products
- 270 Printing and publishing
- 280 Chemicals and allied products
- 290 Petroleum and coal products
- 300 Rubber and miscellaneous plastic products
- 310 Leather and leather products
- 320 Stone, clay, and glass products
- 330 Primary metal industries
- 340 Fabricated metal products
- 350 Machinery, except electrical

- 360 Electric/electronic equipment
- 370 Transportation equipment
- 380 Instruments and related products
- 390 Miscellaneous manufacturing industries

TRANSPORTATION, COMMUNICATION, AND UTILITY SERVICES
- 400 Railroad transportation
- 410 Local/interurban mass transit
- 420 Trucking and warehousing
- 430 U.S. Postal Service
- 440 Water transportation
- 450 Transportation by air
- 460 Pipelines, except natural gas
- 470 Transportation services
- 480 Communication
- 490 Electric, gas, and sanitary services

WHOLESALE AND RETAIL TRADE
- 500 Wholesale trade - durable goods
- 510 Wholesale trade - nondurable goods
- 520 Building materials/garden supplies
- 530 General merchandise stores
- 540 Food stores
- 550 Automotive dealers/service stations
- 560 Apparel and accessory stores
- 570 Furniture/home furnishings stores
- 580 Eating and drinking places
- 590 Miscellaneous retail

FINANCE, INSURANCE, AND REAL ESTATE
- 600 Banking
- 610 Credit agencies, except banks
- 620 Security commodity brokers/services
- 630 Insurance carriers

- 640 Insurance agents, brokers/services
- 650 Real estate
- 670 Holding/other investment offices

SERVICES
- 700 Hotel/other lodging places
- 720 Personal services
- 730 Business services
- 750 Auto repair, services/garages
- 760 Miscellaneous repair services
- 780 Motion pictures
- 790 Amusement/recreation services
- 800 Health services
- 810 Legal services
- 820 Educational services
- 830 Social services
- 840 Museums/botanical, zoological gardens
- 860 Membership organizations
- 870 Engineering/accounting/related services
- 880 Private households
- 890 Miscellaneous services

GOVERNMENT
- 910 Executive, legislative/general
- 920 Justice, public order, and safety
- 930 Finance, taxation, and monetary policy
- 940 Administration of human resources
- 950 Environmental quality/housing
- 960 Administration of economic programs
- 970 National security/international affairs

NONCLASSIFIABLE
- 999 Nonclassifiable establishments

FS

PH 51 8/99

INDEX